KIRK DC

MORE IS NEVER ENOUGH

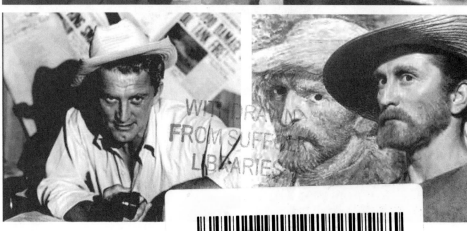

What is Blood Moon Productions?

"Blood Moon, in case you don't know, is a small publishing house on Staten Island that cranks out Hollywood gossip books, about two or three a year, usually of five-, six-, or 700-page length, chocked with stories and pictures about people who used to consume the imaginations of the American public, back when we actually had a public imagination. That is, when people were really interested in each other, rather than in Apple 'devices.' In other words, back when we had vices, not devices."

—The Huffington Post

Award-Winning Entertainment About
American Legends, Hollywood Icons, and the Ironies of Fame.

www.BloodMoonProductions.com

KIRK DOUGLAS
MORE IS NEVER ENOUGH

DARWIN PORTER & DANFORTH PRINCE

KIRK DOUGLAS

More Is Never Enough

Darwin Porter and Danforth Prince

ISBN 978-1-936003-61-7

Cover & Book Designs by Danforth Prince
Distributed worldwide through National Book Network
(www.NBNBooks.com)

PREVIOUS WORKS BY DARWIN PORTER
PRODUCED IN COLLABORATION WITH BLOOD MOON

BIOGRAPHIES

Playboy's Hugh Hefner, Empire of Skin
Carrie Fisher & Debbie Reynolds
Princess Leia & Unsinkable Tammy in Hell
Rock Hudson Erotic Fire
Lana Turner, Hearts & Diamonds Take All
Donald Trump, The Man Who Would Be King
James Dean, Tomorrow Never Comes
Bill and Hillary, So This Is That Thing Called Love
Peter O'Toole, Hellraiser, Sexual Outlaw, Irish Rebel
Love Triangle, Ronald Reagan, Jane Wyman, & Nancy Davis
Jacqueline Kennedy Onassis, A Life Beyond Her Wildest Dreams
Pink Triangle, The Feuds and Private Lives of Tennessee Williams, Gore Vidal,
Truman Capote, and Famous Members of their Entourages.
Those Glamorous Gabors, Bombshells from Budapest
Inside Linda Lovelace's Deep Throat,
Degradation, Porno Chic, and the Rise of Feminism
Elizabeth Taylor, There is Nothing Like a Dame
Marilyn at Rainbow's End, Sex, Lies, Murder, and the Great Cover-up
J. Edgar Hoover and Clyde Tolson
Investigating the Sexual Secrets of America's Most Famous Men and Women
Frank Sinatra, The Boudoir Singer. All the Gossip Unfit to Print
The Kennedys, All the Gossip Unfit to Print
The Secret Life of Humphrey Bogart (2003)
Humphrey Bogart, The Making of a Legend (2010)
Howard Hughes, Hell's Angel
Steve McQueen, King of Cool, Tales of a Lurid Life
Paul Newman, The Man Behind the Baby Blues
Merv Griffin, A Life in the Closet
Brando Unzipped
Katharine the Great, Hepburn, Secrets of a Lifetime Revealed
Jacko, His Rise and Fall, The Social and Sexual History of Michael Jackson
Damn You, Scarlett O'Hara,
The Private Lives of Vivien Leigh and Laurence Olivier
(co-authored with Roy Moseley)

FILM CRITICISM
Blood Moon's 2005 Guide to the Glitter Awards
Blood Moon's 2006 Guide to Film
Blood Moon's 2007 Guide to Film, and
50 Years of Queer Cinema, 500 of the Best GLBTQ Films Ever Made

NON-FICTION
Hollywood Babylon, It's Back!
Hollywood Babylon Strikes Again!
Staten Island's Historic Magnolia House
Volume One, Celebrity and the Ironies of Fame

NOVELS
Blood Moon,
Hollywood's Silent Closet,
Rhinestone Country,
Razzle Dazzle
Midnight in Savannah

OTHER PUBLICATIONS BY DARWIN PORTER
NOT DIRECTLY ASSOCIATED WITH BLOOD MOON

NOVELS

The Delinquent Heart
The Taste of Steak Tartare
Butterflies in Heat
Marika (a roman à clef based on the life of Marlene Dietrich)
Venus (a roman à clef based on the life of Anaïs Nin)
Bitter Orange
Sister Rose

CUISINE

Food For Love, Hussar Recipes from the Austro-Hungarian Empire,
with collaboration from the cabaret chanteuse, Greta Keller

Many Editions and Many Variations of *The Frommer Guides,*
The American Express Guides, and/or TWA Guides, et alia to:
Andalusia, Andorra, Anguilla, Aruba, Atlanta, Austria, the Azores, The
Bahamas, Barbados, the Bavarian Alps, Berlin, Bermuda, Bonaire and Cu-
raçao, Boston, the British Virgin Islands, Budapest, Bulgaria, California,
the Canary Islands, the Caribbean and its "Ports of Call," the Cayman Is-
lands, Ceuta, the Channel Islands (UK), Charleston (SC), Corsica, Costa
del Sol (Spain), Denmark, Dominica, the Dominican Republic, Edinburgh,
England, Estonia, Europe, "Europe by Rail," the Faroe Islands, Finland,
Florence, France, Frankfurt, the French Riviera, Geneva, Georgia (USA),
Germany, Gibraltar, Glasgow, Granada (Spain), Great Britain, Greenland,
Grenada (West Indies), Haiti, Hungary, Iceland, Ireland, Isle of Man, Italy,
Jamaica, Key West & the Florida Keys, Las Vegas, Liechtenstein, Lisbon,
London, Los Angeles, Madrid, Maine, Malta, Martinique & Guadeloupe,
Massachusetts, Melilla, Morocco, Munich, New England, New Orleans,
North Carolina, Norway, Paris, Poland, Portugal, Provence, Puerto Rico,
Romania, Rome, Salzburg, San Diego, San Francisco, San Marino, Sardinia,
Savannah, Scandinavia, Scotland, Seville, the Shetland Islands, Sicily, St.
Martin & Sint Maarten, St. Vincent & the Grenadines, South Carolina, Spain,
St. Kitts & Nevis, Sweden, Switzerland, the Turks & Caicos, the U.S.A., the
U.S. Virgin Islands, Venice, Vienna and the Danube, Wales, and Zurich.

BIOGRAPHIES

From Diaghilev to Balanchine, The Saga of Ballerina Tamara Geva
Lucille Lortel, The Queen of Off-Broadway
Greta Keller, Germany's Other Lili Marlene
Sophie Tucker, The Last of the Red Hot Mamas
Anne Bancroft, Where Have You Gone, Mrs. Robinson?
(co-authored with Stanley Mills Haggart)
Veronica Lake, The Peek-a-Boo Girl
Running Wild in Babylon, Confessions of a Hollywood Press Agent

HISTORIES

Thurlow Weed, Whig Kingpin
Chester A. Arthur, Gilded Age Coxcomb in the White House
Discover Old America, What's Left of It

A Word About Phraseologies:

Since we at Blood Moon weren't privy to long-ago conversations as they were unfolding, we have relied on the memories of our sources for the conversational tone and phrase-ologies of what we've recorded within the pages of this book.

This writing technique, as it applies to modern biography, has been defined as "conver-sational storytelling" by *The New York Times,* which labeled it as an acceptable literary de-vice for "engaging reading."

Some people have expressed displeasure in the fact that direct quotes and "as remem-bered" dialogue have become a standard—some would say "mandatory"—fixture in pop culture biographies today.

But Blood Moon is not alone in replicating "as remembered" dialogues from dead sources. Truman Capote and Norman Mailer were pioneers of direct quotes, and today, they appear in countless other memoirs, ranging from those of Eddie Fisher to those of the long-time mistress (Verita Thompson) of Humphrey Bogart.

Best wishes to all of you, with thanks for your interest in our work.

Danforth Prince, President,
Blood Moon Productions

CONTENTS

AND THE MOB. HOW HOLLYWOOD'S MOST RESPECTED DIRECTOR, ELIA KAZAN, SELECTED KIRK AS THE ACTOR WHO'D PORTRAY HIM IN AN AUTOBIOGRAPHICAL ART FILM THAT WAS LACERATED BY THE CRITICS. PLAYING TO THE ALT-RIGHT WITH JOHN WAYNE IN *THE WAR WAGON.*

Kirk Douglas in
20,000 Leagues Under the Sea

IN MEMORIAM
REST IN PEACE

THIS BOOK IS DEDICATED TO THE THOUSANDS OF
ONCE-YOUNG AND ONCE-BEAUTIFUL ENTERTAINERS
WHOSE DESIRABILITY, HEALTH, AND INCOMES FADED
WITH THE CHANGING LANDSCAPES OF AMERICA IN
THE 21ST CENTURY.

CHAPTER ONE

THE SON OF AN ILLITERATE RUSSIAN "RAGMAN,"
ISSUR DANIELOVITCH
SURVIVES POVERTY AND ANTI-SEMITISM
TO PURSUE THE AMERICAN DREAM

OLDER *SHIKSAS*, INCLUDING HIS TEACHERS, GO LOVE
CRAZY OVER THIS DASHINGLY HANDSOME TEENAGER,
INSTRUCTING HIM IN THE FACTS OF LIFE.

PART ROMANTIC HERO, PART DOSTOEVSKIAN ANTI-
HERO, ISSUR ASSUMES A WASP NAME AND
A NEW IDENTITY AS

KIRK DOUGLAS

In 1932, Kirk, aged 16, with his mother, Bryna.

The longest surviving male star from Golden Age Holly-wood, Kirk Douglas, once said, *"If you are born a complete nobody, and have dreams of becoming a somebody, know that it's going to be a rough, lonely, and rocky road, filled with potholes, before you get where you're going."*

"Be aware you might not get there, especially if you head to Hollywood by train, plane, car, or your trusty thumb stuck out on the highway."

"I was warned that Hollywood has the world's largest boulevard of broken dreams. I arrived in town planning to avoid that boulevard, regardless of how many detours I had to take."

"What happens to you on the way to the top is called life, with all its ups and downs, its pain and sorrow, but also its joy and happiness."

"I experienced it all, the deepest regrets, the greatest thrills, and, yes, stardom beyond my wildest dreams."

"Sometimes forbidden love knocked on my door, Lots and lots of beautiful women who wanted what I had to give them. In most cases, what appeared to be love in the forgiving moonlight never lasted when that sun in the morning brought a golden dawn to the Pacific Coast. I woke up, faced reality, hastily put on my clothes, and headed out the door back to home and hearth until my next adventure."

"My circumcised Jewish cock brought thrills to dozens of women. Mae West might have turned me down, but who needed that old drag queen when you had Lana Turner, Marlene Dietrich, Rita Hayworth, Linda Darnell, Ingrid Bergman — and the beat goes on."

***

The future movie star, Kirk Douglas, was born on December 9, 1916. He was originally named Issur Danielovitch, which would be a bit awkward on a movie marquee. His parents were Jewish refugees from Tsarist Russia, who had fled to America in 1910, settling in New Amsterdam, New York.

They were mired in poverty and speaking only Yiddish, but life was better than the brutality they had escaped from in Russia in a little town south of Moscow.

Jews were not only despised but killed in any of the frequent pogroms that swept across the countryside.

Little is known of their lives in the old country, as neither parent wanted to relive their ghastly time there, out of fear of giving their impressionable children nightmares.

Both Byrna ("Bertha") Sanglel and Herschel ("Harry") Danielovitch may have been born in the same year (1884), but records were not definite. One night in New Amsterdam, New York, Bertha related the most horrifying girlhood experience of her life to Kirk when he was eight years old. That horrible event had cast a shadow over her that would last forever.

Growing up in Russia, the daughter of Jewish farmers from Ukraine, she lived in constant fear of persecution. She'd heard that the first major pogrom had begun in 1821 in Odessa, but these anti-Semitic attacks had continued ever since. They were particularly devastating during a rampage that lasted from 1903 to 1908 when hundreds of Jews were slaughtered. The murderers were sometimes led by Russian Orthodox priests, echoing the rallying cry of "Kill the Jews!"

Jewish babies were torn from the arms of their mothers and slaughtered right in front of them by bloodthirsty mobs of hatemongers. Often,

The photo shows some of the bodies of the victims of the Belostok (Białystok) pogrom. It occurred between June 14–16, 1906 in a part of the Russian Empire now controlled by Poland. Between 81 and 88 people, mostly Jews, were killed by soldiers of the Imperial Russian Army and a group of thugs known as the Chernoe Znamia.

Although the violence began as a spontaneous outbreak of hatred, as it continued, it resembled a coordinated military action. Thuggish mobs and Tsarist soldiers broke into many Jewish homes and either killed people on the spot or dragged them outside to murder them The Białystok pogrom was one of a series of violent outbreaks against Jews in the Russian Empire between 1903 and 1908 in sites that included Kishinev, Odessa, and Kiev before sunset, bodies of the wounded or slaughtered were lined up in rows beside the cobble-covered streets.

The perpetrators were almost never arrested for their crimes. If they were, they received clemency by decree of the Tsar. The anti-Semitic squads knew they had the blessing of the Okhrana, the Tsarist Russian police.

The horse-riding Cossacks, in their elaborate military uniforms, often rode through the ghettos, menacing Jews. These belligerent soldiers were the most feared among the Russian Empire's military units, even more so than the hussars, dragoons, and lancers of the regular cavalry. For "sport," and after a night of heavy drinking in the dark, smoke-filled taverns, they would decide to ride through the ghetto and kill some Jews.

One windy night, Bertha was walking with her brother down a street heading home. Suddenly, five Cossacks on horseback appeared from around a corner. It was too late for the children to flee.

One of the mounted soldiers took the bayonet of his rifle and slashed it into the face of her screaming brother, splitting his head open into almost equal halves.

With jets of blood spurting from his head, he collapsed at his sister's feet. As she looked up, that same soldier took the butt of his rifle and crashed it into her head, causing her to collapse onto her dead brother's body.

She may have been out for an hour. When she revived, she screamed, as she was soaked in blood. For the rest of her life, that memory would haunt her nightmares, and she would never forget the image of the bloody pulp that had once been his beautiful, trusting face.

Blinded by the pain in her head, she staggered to her home to alert family members. Moaning in their agony, they arrived at the site to discover the remains of their offspring. The body was carried back to their house, where they cleaned it, dressed him, and buried him according to ancient Jewish tradition.

From that night forward,

Cossacks, members of the Imperial Russian Army who either perpetrated violence on the Jews directly, or who enabled, by looking the other way, the knife and club-wielding mobs who attacked and raped them.

4

Bertha vowed that she would one day find a way to flee to America, the land of freedom. Perhaps the streets were not made of gold, as legend had it, but at least she could lead what was left of her life without the fear of getting murdered. Her dream was to meet a good provider. That quality in a man was more important than falling in love, which she regarded as a foolish fantasy of impressionable schoolgirls, of which she was not one.

Such a man entered her life one day when she was shopping for turnips, potatoes, and cabbage, all that her family's meager budget provided.

He'd spotted her as he emerged from a local tavern. He stopped and looked at her like no man had ever appraised her before. In an impulsive move, he grabbed her bag of vegetables, squeezed her hand, and yanked her along as he raced down an alleyway and fled from the shouting vegetable vendor.

Three blocks later, he stopped in front of her home and handed her back her vegetables. "You look like a girl who does not have much money," he told her. "When you don't have cash, you have to reach out and take what you want."

"You mean, not pay for it?" she asked.

"That's exactly what I mean." He went on to tell her that he would visit her at four o'clock the following afternoon. "We'll go for a walk in the

On Easter Sunday In 1903, in Kishinev, a community of 110,000 people in the fertile region of the Russian Empire known as Bessarabia, 49 Jews were murdered, 700 houses were destroyed, and as many as 600 Jewish women were raped in a pogrom that replicated dozens of other mass murders occurring in other parts of Central Europe at around the time of the Herschel and Bryna's immigration to the U.S. .

The photo above shows some of the victims of the atrocities laid out before burial in a mass grave. Many scholars agree that every aspect of the Holocaust had been anticipated by the pogram in Kishinev park, and I will buy you some candy. Be ready for me because I don't like to wait for nobody."

***

Herschel Danielovitch had a brutal childhood. He suffered savage beatings from his drunken father, who struck him for the fun of it. By the time he was eight, he vowed to run away from him as soon as he was a bit older.

His father wanted him to become an apprentice to a tailor, but the boy had extremely large hands, which his father called "claws," comparing them to those on a Russian bear. Tailors were required to have a certain delicacy with their fingers, and Herschel had none.

Long before his encounter with Bertha, he took up with a tough street gang, who seemingly survived on whatever they could steal. By the age of ten, he had his first taste of vodka—and spat it out. But he didn't give up, trying it again and again until he became devoted to the bottle, an addiction that would continue for the rest of his life.

The street gang he hung out with beat up an older man in an alleyway one night and robbed him of all his money, which mounted to the equivalent of thirty U.S. dollars.

With that money, with a posse of his friends, he left their small town and headed north to Moscow. There were five of them and with that money they could not only eat well, but rent a prostitute for the night, too.

He remembered her as "over fifty, fat, and ugly," but she was willing to take on all five teenagers. Herschel would later explain "the facts of life" to his young son, Issur. "You put it in, pump up and down for about two minutes, then explode. It's a quick thrill, not a lot to it. Women are filthy animals, often diseased."

Herschel had spent many a winter without shoes, having to wrap his feet in burlap during the long Russian winters.

In 1881, Tsar Alexander III ruled Russia, imposing harsh conditions on Jews. Herschel's family during many a week had to get by on a small bag of potatoes.

An organ-grinder and rag-man—a collector of refuse—in Russia of the 1890s.

Jews were excluded from most walks of life, except one. They were subject to the draft, especially during the bloody conflicts of the Russo-Japanese War (1904-05).

In 1905, *The New York Evening Post* ran a story that claimed, "Russia, while denying her Jewish subjects all civil rights, does not object to sending them to Manchuria to stop Japanese bullets. For the Jew, however, military glory is denied. A Jewish soldier was not to become an officer."

Even when hostilities between Japan and Russia ceased, Jewish boys were still being drafted and often assigned to the front lines for the most dangerous of missions.

Herschel had no loyalty to his native land and had no intention of serving the Tsar.

He had continued to court Bertha, and there was talk of marriage. One night in 1908, he told her that he was going to flee to Belarus to escape the draft. There, he wanted to find work and save enough money to go to America.

She wanted to join him, but he told her she would have to earn enough money to pay her own fare. He would remain in touch with her from Belarus.

At that time, she had a 12-hour a day job in a bakery, and she vowed to flee to Belarus as soon as she could save enough money for her ship passage.

He kissed her goodbye until they'd meet again.

The troubled region of Belarus was not the most welcoming of places for a refugee from the Moscow area. Landlocked, it was bordered by Russia to the northeast, Ukraine to the south, Poland to the west, and Latvia and Lithuania to the northwest.

Herschel survived by taking "whatever filthy job I could." It appears that at times, he supported himself by robbing drunks.

It took two years for Bertha to earn the money for her own passage to America, and she wrote Herschel that she was ready to join him in Belarus' capital of Minsk. She found him there, living in a basement "with a lot of rats."

Together, they had saved the equivalent of a hundred dollars. The price of passage, in steerage, to the Port of New York was $37 per person.

Their harrowing tale of their journey to a port of departure for the New World included a walk on foot of some two hundred miles and would almost make a movie unto itself. They were able to join the exodus of the 100,000 Jews who fled from the Old World to the New World in 1910.

Steerage was a vile pit of crying babies, uncontrolled vomiting from those who suffered from sea sickness, almost no food, and the stench of feces and urine. The babble of languages spoken on board included Russian, Latvian, German, Polish, Lithuanian, and Yiddish.

Many men who later became entrepreneurial legends in the film industry also arrived in America as immigrants: William Fox, Lewis Selznick, the Warner Brothers, Adolphe Zukor, and Carl Laemmle.

Author Arthur Marx described the America that the immigrant faced during the first half of the 20th Century: "America was indeed the land of opportunity, especially if you were willing to work eighteen hours a day and had plenty of *chutzpah* and a little larceny in your soul to help you get over the rough spots."

Years later on Broadway, Herschel and Bertha's future son, Kirk Douglas, would attend a performance of the musical, *Fiddler on the Roof.* He enjoyed the play but viewed it as a sanitized version of the pogroms that often destroyed Jewish lives.

Russian immigrants at Ellis Island, circa 1906.

Fiddler on the Roof would emerge again on his 90th birthday, as his three sons—Michael, Joel, and Peter—performed a song-and-dance parody of one of the songs from the musical, borrowing titles from his movies.

Kirk cast a giant shadow through all Seven Days of May.
Out of the Past, *this* Juggler *played a great Doc Holliday.*
He crashed the Walls of Jericho, *'cause they were in his way.*
All women dreamed to be with him. All men wished they were gay.

***

Herschel and Bertha fit the description of "your tired and poor," from "the huddled masses" arriving for "processing" on Ellis Island in New York. Between 1892 and 1934, some 12 million immigrants, often with only the clothes on their backs, filed through this hellhole with all its stench. Gruff inspectors assigned shortened names to the new arrivals, since some were so illiterate they could not spell out their names in any alphabet or language.

Most of the new arrivals remained in New York City, settling into the Lower East Side of Manhattan. But Herschel and Bertha journeyed to Amsterdam, New York, near Schenectady, 210 miles north of Manhattan, to join his older brother, Daniel. Daniel had settled there after changing his last name to Demsky, abandoning the more awkward Danielovitch (son of Daniel).

Herschel himself followed suit and assumed the new name of "Harry Demsky," which was the name he'd pronounced to the rabbi who married him to Bertha after their arrival in America.

The little settlement of Amsterdam had been established by the Dutch in 1710. It had grown up on both sides of the Mohawk River. It grew and prospered, especially after the completion of the Erie Canal in 1825, beside which it was located. It reigned for a while as one of the leading manufacturing centers in America, especially known for its carpets, textiles, and pearl buttons.

As a newly married couple, Harry and Bertha set out to have a family, and a large one at that, although they hardly had enough to feed and clothe themselves.

Three daughters, Pesha, Kaleh, and Tamara, were born in 1910, 1912, and 1914, respectively. Issur (aka "Izzy,") the only boy in the family, the future Kirk Douglas, was born in 1916 when Europe was embroiled in World War I.

Bertha spun a legend about her son's birth, which she relayed to him when he was six years old. She said that one cold, snowy day in December, she became aware of a shimmering light in the yard. She rushed out to discover this beautiful gold box carved into patterns of fruits and flowers and suspended from heaven by silver strands.

Opening the box, she discovered a newly born baby boy bathed in a lavender glow and smiling up at her. She scooped up the infant and carried him into the kitchen. Looking back only once, she saw the golden box rising again into the sky toward heaven.

"My heart told me that you, my dear son, would grow up one day to become someone, someone really important, and you wouldn't be a failure like your father. For all I knew, you will one day be President of the United States. All things are possible in America."

More sisters were on the way: Twins Siffra and Hashka were born in 1918, followed by a final girl, Rachel, in 1924 when Bertha was forty years old. Apparently, or so it was reported, after that birth, she never had sex with Herschel (now known as "Harry") again.

As was the custom with many immigrants, the names of each of their offspring were Americanized. The sisters became Betty, Kay, Marion, Ida, Fritzi, and Ruth. Issur was renamed Isadore, a label he loathed. He detested his nickname, "Izzy," even more. "It rhymed with Dizzy, but for many years, I was known as Izzy Demsky."

"At least God could have given me a little brother," he said. "Can you imagine what it's like for a boy to grow up in a household with a horde of girls and my mother?"

To survive, Harry found a job. The "looms of Mohawk" became nationally famous, turning out more than twelve million square yards of carpet annually. Amsterdam was nicknamed "rug city."

On his second day in town, a Monday, he went to the employment office of the massive factory. He applied for a job, but was bluntly told, "It is the policy of our company not to employ Jews."

One of his reasons for escaping from Tsarist Russia was to avoid Jewish persecution. He was shocked to find such blatant anti-Semitism prevalent in America.

In desperation, he turned to an occupation known in Europe for centuries. Buying a wagon and a horse named "Bill," he set out to become the ragman of Amsterdam, perhaps the lowest profession in town.

Traditionally, in the old country, a "rag-and-bone" vendor collected unwanted household items and resold them for a small profit. In most cases, the ragman walked around with a bag slung over his shoulder. With Bill pulling his wagon, Herschel went from door to door, picking up discarded clothing, and pieces of scrap metal, such as zinc, copper, brass, and lead, plus lots of junk. He'd then resell the items at a small profit.

"For years, my family survived—make that 'barely survived'—on other people's junk," Kirk said. "One of earliest memories of my father was him going up and down the streets, calling out 'RAGS! RAGS!' I used to help him unload and separated the junk in our frontyard."

"I hate to admit it," the future Kirk Douglas claimed, "but my father was a *bulvan*. That's Yiddish for a boorish brute of a man, a loud-mouthed know-it-all."

Bertha had married Herschel with the hope that he'd be a good provider, but often there was not a morsel of food in the kitchen. He was a drunkard and always managed to find something to drink, even during Prohibition—perhaps a bottle of wine from the Italians, or grain alcohol from the Ukrainians.

He never ate with his family but preferred a small Polish restaurant five blocks away that provided a wholesome peasant dinner for thirty-five cents. When he filled up on that, his family back home sometimes survived on a box of cornflakes, if they were lucky.

A large and powerful man, Herschel got into a brawl once or twice a week. In his most daring feat, he took on seven men and clobbered all of them, a "victory" which landed him in court. The judge dismissed the charge, because he did not believe that one man could beat up seven burly opponents.

Izzy dreaded when his father finally came home at night. He never hit Bertha or his daughters, but "he managed to beat hell out of me at least three times a week, regardless of whether I had done something wrong or not."

In contrast, Izzy claimed that his mother "Let me get away with murder. I was her special child, as her only boy, delivered in that gold box. She would kiss me in front of the family, which angered Harry. He accused her of trying to turn me into 'a sissy boy.'"

Izzy learned early in life that being a Jew meant you had to be tough on the streets. He attended a Hebrew School about ten or so blocks from his shanty home. When school let out, he had to follow a circuitous route home to avoid any of several gangs, the most violent of which was the Lake Street Boys.

He always tried to evade the brutes, often a coven of Catholic Irish boys, but also a pack of Germans. Sometimes, he was not so lucky: Gang members hid in the bushes to ambush him. "Knock the hell out of that kike," he heard time and time again, along with the charge, "You killed Jesus Christ." On some occasions, he was hit in the head with a blunt object, causing concussions.

"They learned that from their fucking bigoted parents," Izzy said. "I came home bruised and beaten."

Bertha came to his aid, sometimes having to bandage him. She warned, "You've got to grow up to be strong. Study hard, work hard, everything is harder for a boy born a Jew."

"The saddest memory is growing up and watching my father leave the house," Izzy said. "Almost always, Bertha would plead with him, telling him there was no food in the house. Sometimes, she'd plead with him to give her a quarter, with which she could buy a few potatoes, perhaps to stew with a bone or two."

He invariably told her he had no money, although he managed to purchase food and those cheap Polish dinners for himself.

Antique view of Amsterdam, NY's main street, circa 1910. Although jobs were plentiful in its role as "carpet center of the Mohawk Valley," the local factories would not employ Jews.

***

11

Izzy became the breadwinner of the family when he was just eight years old. "Since we had no money to buy food, I stole something to put in our stomachs. I raided henhouses to harvest the warm eggs under the chickens. Nearly everyone in Amsterdam had a garden. At night, I would steal vegetables, uprooting potato plants or picking a cucumber from the vine. Italian families always had tomatoes. I'd wander into the nearby woods and pick berries. I'd steal fruit from street stands, especially luscious grapefruits and oranges. A lot of apples grew on trees nearby, and I picked them. My mother learned to cook apples in every known way."

There was one kosher butcher shop in town, and Izzy went there about once a week with very little money in his pocket. "I begged for bones, which Bertha could boil into a soup for us. No one seemed to want liver in those days, and he made the price very cheap, especially if it had reached its expiration date. We had a lot of liver back then. Mother would disguise the ripened flavor with a big onion fried with it."

A sad memory was the night the little barn in our backyard caught fire. "Bill was trapped in there, and the smell of burnt horseflesh assailed our nostrils. When the fire was put out, I saw his charred remains, a sight I'll never forget. It broke my heart."

As he was growing up, Izzy admitted that he was a cocky young boy. "I had to face a lot of oppression outside the house, and inside when my father came home. Often, I was providing something to put on the table, not him. He never thanked me for that. I hated being ordered around by him and suffering all those beatings. I had this maverick streak in me, a trait I would retain for the rest of my life."

"The only good memory I had of him was one night when he invited me to go to the saloon with him. He ordered a loganberry drink for me, and I felt like a man. It had a dark red taste, a sort of cross between a raspberry and a blackberry. I drank it with pride. That was the first time he actually showed me a little kindness."

Years later, Kirk Douglas recalled, "I hung out in many saloons around the world. I didn't need my father as a drinking buddy. By now I had my best friend, Burt (Lancaster) and 'The Duke' (John Wayne)."

Izzy worked forty menial jobs before joining the Navy in World War II. His father wasn't allowed to work in the carpet factory because he was a Jew, but that didn't stop his son from selling candy bars and soda drinks to the factory workers. Every day he hauled his little cart to the factory and peddled offerings. "Those were the good old days before vending machines were installed inside the factory. I made a little money. On most mornings, my sisters, Mother, and I had a box of cornflakes with milk for breakfast. On a slow day, those cornflakes and milk were our supper as well."

Even through all the hard times, he began putting a little money away every week, dreaming of having a stash to enroll in college one day. "I wasn't even in high school, and already, I was thinking of getting a college education. I lost my job as a pop and candy vendor and was willing to take any kind of job. Like my father, I was on the bottom rung of the ladder, but I didn't plan to spend my life there."

The best job he had was that of a paperboy, delivering bundles of newspapers and magazines to local stores and newsstands. _

He arose at five every morning, dressed hurriedly, and ran down to meet the train known as The 20th Century Limited. Called "The most famous train in the world," and originating in Manhattan, it often carried movie stars to the West Coast.

From 1902 to 1967, the streamlined train ran from New York City's Grand Central Terminal to LaSalle Street in Chicago. Passengers walked a crimson carpet rolled out in both New York and Chicago—hence the term "red carpet treatment" came into vogue.

The train did not actually stop in Amsterdam. Instead, as the train hurtled onward toward Chicago, a conductor tossed bundles of newspapers and magazines from the moving train onto the platform at Amsterdam. Izzy's job was to find and gather them up for distribution.

Years later, Kirk Douglas remembered looking in through the windows of that train as the black waiters served elegant breakfasts to the pampered passengers.

"You might describe my emotions at the time as 'California Dreaming.' I vowed back then, as poor as I was, that one day I would ride in the best compartment on that train, to the land of milk and honey, where you could wake up and walk out into your garden and pluck oranges off your trees for breakfast."

"It was a land of movie stars, palm trees, luxurious cars, elegant mansions, and beautiful women. Someday, in the days to come, it would be mine. I would stand every night looking at the Pacific Ocean as the golden sun disappeared into the Western sky to wake up the people who lived on the other side of the planet."

***

A turning point came when Izzy was twelve. He hitchhiked a ride to Schenectady but ran into trouble along the way. The driver who picked him up was a bit overweight and balding, and appeared to be in his mid-fifties.

13

As they drove along, the conversation became more and more personal. The driver asked him if he'd ever had sex with a girl. He also wanted to know if Izzy was able to experience an orgasm.

About two miles from Schenectady, the stranger's hands began to wander. Izzy demanded that he stop the car, and he got out, walking the rest of the way into town.

After exploring Main Street, he entered the Proctor's Theatre, a large movie house.

Ever since he'd performed in a play in grade school (he'd played the shoemaker in *The Shoemaker and the Elves*), he'd had this "crazy dream" of wanting to become a stage actor. If not that, then a movie star, although that seemed a bridge too far.

The picture he saw that afternoon was *The Mysterious Lady* (1928) starring Greta Garbo. Although at the time, Hollywood was in the early stages of converting to the Talkies, the movie was silent. He was mesmerized by the serene beauty of Garbo's face.

Directed by Fred Niblo, Garbo played Tania Fedorovna, a Russian spy charged with stealing military secrets from the Austrians.

Izzy found her film lover, Conrad Nagel, rather foppish and silly, and thought Garbo needed a more powerful leading man.

In her scenes, as he later remembered, her nipples were clearly visible. "I think this was the first time I was turned on by a woman's nipples. I was reaching puberty, and things were beginning to stir within my adolescent body. I never got a chance to meet the great Garbo, but, if I had, I would have told her that she was the first woman who ever turned me on."

After leaving the theater, he made a vow then and there: "I'm going to be an actor. I want to grow up and make love to beautiful women on the stage and on the screen. I want to walk into the dream factory where all things are possible."

Years later, he said, "Sometimes, boyish dreams do come true."

***

By the time he turned thirteen, the age of Bar Mitzvah for a Jewish boy, Izzy had saved $315 toward his college fund. When Harry learned of this stash, he asked to borrow it so he could buy pieces of scrap copper to sell at a good price. At the time, cop-

A fantasy that, for Kirk, later came true: a New York to Chicago ride (as a passenger) aboard the 20th Century Limited

14

per was selling on the open market for 25¢ a pound.

Reluctantly, Izzy turned over his hard-earned dough. His loan to his father could not have been extended at a worse time. Only two weeks later came the Wall Street crash of 1929, heralding a world-wide depression. In desperation, Harry was forced to dump his scrap copper on the market for 2¢ a pound. The loan from his son was never paid back.

Izzy's sisters were growing up, the oldest entering the job market and beginning to date seriously, with hopes of marriage around the corner. Their address on 46 Eagle Street was in the poorest and most undesirable part of town. Also, their house was increasingly dilapidated, and Izzy had once accidentally set it on fire. Although fire insurance had covered the cost, the burnt boards on one side of the house had never been replaced.

One of the sisters found a better house in a better neighborhood. The family was ready to move except for one dissenting voice: Harry himself. He stubbornly refused to go, and Bertha made plans to leave him, taking her growing children with her.

On moving day, after Bertha and her daughters had already left, Izzy remained behind to see his father. He was sitting alone at the kitchen table with a bottle of red wine, some herring, and a loaf of pumpernickel bread on which he was rubbing raw garlic cloves.

Herschel had no parting words for his only son. "A weird feeling came over me like I was looking at a stranger. I mean, his face looked familiar, yet I was aware that I had never really known him. The rest of our family, including myself, was starting out on a new life, but he seemed stuck in the past, refusing to budge. I wondered what was to become of him, but that was too much for me to think about on that big day. Without knowing what to say, I headed out the door, past all the junk in our frontyard—and didn't look back. I felt as if I had been circumcised once again, and a little more of my cock had been cut off."

In 1949, he discussed his origins with his new best friend, Burt Lancaster. "I created Kirk Douglas. But I had a little help from the chemicals in Bertha's ovaries and in Harry's nutsac."

***

When Izzy Demsky was fourteen years old, a remarkable woman came into his life. She was his English teacher, Mrs. Louise Livingston, the head of the English Department at Amsterdam's Wilbur H. Lynch High School. A widow, she had a son of her own, five years older than Izzy.

His relationship with Louise would stretch out for years to come. As he repeatedly told the story of his involvement with his teacher to Burt Lancaster and an array of other friends, he claimed, "The first time. What boy ever forgets that?"

Kirk always maintained that Louise reminded him of Deborah Kerr. Like the English actress herself, Louise was "the epitome of refinement, ladylike, a subtle beauty, restrained, poetic, understanding, forgiving, loving, and articulate."

"She should have been born in another time, notably the era of the romantic poets, Shelley, Keats, and Byron. She was a devotee of their poetry and would quote long verses from them word for word. She not only turned me onto poetry, but literature in general."

"Unlike my peasant parents, Louise was patrician, a member of the Daughters of the American Revolution. In a town where Gentiles did not socialize much with Jews, she was my champion, a voice of tolerance. My lowly station in life, the son of a ragman, didn't bother her in the least. She told me that I was remarkably good-looking, and that I had this inner glow that would serve me well if I pursued my stated goal of wanting to become an actor."

"She inspired me to read the classics, especially her favorite, Emily Brontë's *Wuthering Heights*. In some way, I think she identified with the heroine of that novel, and she often said I was like a young Heathcliff, wandering the Yorkshire Moors, although I found that comparison a bit farfetched."

"Even though it made me late for work, I often stayed behind to talk to her in class after the other kids piled out. We would just sit and talk and quote poetry to each other. I shared my hopes and desires with her. Sometimes, on weekends, we'd go for walks together. It was October and the leaves were turning and had begun to fall."

"October is my favorite time of the year," she told him. "There's something nostalgic about the season, a signal that another summer has come to an end, and that the cold winds of winter will soon be blowing in on us. It's a time of reflection, a time to fall in love."

He was stunned. "Did she mean us? I was just a street kid. She surely wasn't falling for a teenaged boy, who had just learned to jerk off only a few months ago. I knew zero about making love to a woman, only to my fist."

One night she asked him to take her to a movie matinee that began at 4PM. The Rialto was playing *Montana Moon* (1930), starring Joan Crawford in one of her first talkies. At the moment Crawford engaged in a lingering

16

kiss with Ricardo Cortez, Louise took his hand and placed it on her thigh. "I began to tremble with fright, not knowing if I was supposed to let my hand travel north to the forbidden zone. Her skin was smooth and creamy, and caused a stirring in me."

"So guess what? I just kept my hand in that position, and she took her own hand and pressed it down on mine. I was breathing heavily at this point."

Years later, Kirk would reflect on the first Joan Crawford movie he ever saw. "At the time, it would have been beyond my wildest dreams that one night I would actually plug Crawford herself."

"At St. Lawrence University, I was president of the student body and part-time janitor."

At the end of the film, Louise invited him back to her room at 34 Pearl Street where she lived on the top flor of a building occupied by other school teachers. She told him they had to be discreet so they wouldn't be spotted. "It was obvious to me that she was nervous about how young I was. If caught, she could lose her job. I sneaked up the steps when the coast was clear."

Once inside her bedroom, she took off her coat and invited him to do the same. The only light she turned on was a lamp in the corner with a dim bulb. As she sat down on her single bed, she patted the seat next to her, inviting him to join her. He was a bit reluctant, but soon came over and sat beside her.

"I wasn't ready to go all the way, remembering she was not only my teacher, but an older woman with an adult son."

"After a few more minutes on the bed, with her hands traveling over me, I bolted, grabbing my coat and fleeing out the door. What on earth did she want with an awkward schoolboy who had never seen a woman completely naked before, even though I lived in a house filled with seven females?"

"I lay awake for most of the night, feeling like a sissy, fleeing from the touch of a woman," he recalled. "I truly was convinced that she'd flunk me in English and never speak to me again. But the next day at school, she made no mention of the night before, or my panic,"

Three nights later, she invited him back into her bedroom, sneaking him in again. "We both knew that what we were contemplating was against the law, but that didn't stop us."

"She figured out a way of having sex with me without going all the way," he said. "She undid the buttons of my corduroy pants and reached in for my peter which was already hard. She went down on me. This I could do. In three minutes, I blasted off."

For the next week, this became a regular event between them. She kept fellating him until it was time to go forward. "She helped me out of my clothes until I was jaybird naked. Then she took off her own clothes, and she explored my body, every inch of it, and invited me to do the same with hers. I lingered over her breasts."

On looking back, it was not my greatest performance," he said. "I'm sure I wasn't the stud I played in *The Bad and the Beautiful,* making Lana Turner wild to have me. But I must have pleased her in some way, because she invited me for repeats throughout the rest of my school year. It's amazing we never did get exposed."

In 1956, he went to see Deborah Kerr emote with John Kerr (no relation) in *Tea and Sympathy,* a movie directed by Vincente Minnelli, the future director of Kirk himself. It was the tender story of a school teacher's wife who initiates a sensitive young boy into manhood with love and understanding.

In the role of Laura Reynolds, Deborah unbuttons the top of her blouse, just like Louise did for Kirk.

The movie sparked many memories in Kirk, and he sat through it three times before leaving the theater.

"As the weeks went on, I felt I became a competent lover for Louise, or at least I think I did."

"As Humphrey Bogart told Claude Rains in the final reel of *Casablanca,* 'It was the beginning of a beautiful friendship.'" That relationship lasted for decades to come, and they remained in touch through letters with long interruptions when he was away on location making movies.

"I never got around to seducing the real Deborah Kerr," Kirk said. "But my best buddy, Burt Lancaster, had the honor. He and Deborah did that iconic love-on-the-beach scene in *From Here to Eternity* (1953). Burt told me they continued their lovemaking but not on the beach—lucky bastard."

On looking back, he recalled, "I not only made repeated love to an older woman—my teacher, no less—but I did something even more terrifying for a Jewish boy. I ate bacon

Indelible early impressions: Kirk's first view of Joan Crawford.

18

and loved it. Guess what? The heavens didn't open up and Jehovah himself did not appear to condemn me to burn in hell's fire forever. So, as the years went by, I continued to eat all the bacon I wanted."

***

One of the highlights of his senior year was when he took a class trip to Albany on a bus with his fellow drama students. Their goal was to attend the performance of a touring troupe that starred Katharine Cornell, First Lady of Broadway, in *The Barretts of Wimpole Street.*

In a coincidence that occurs every now and then in a human life, one day, not so far into his future, Izzy would get to know Cornell herself and work with her on Broadway when he became "that darling boy" of Guthrie McClintic, her gay husband.

Even in high school, he continued to face anti-Semitic prejudice. He'd been attracted to a classmate, Ann Brown, one of the most beautiful girls in school. She had auburn hair and good figure.

He'd saved his money to attend the senior prom, and he mustered his courage and asked her to go with him.

She accepted, but on the afternoon of the prom, she came to him, telling him that she could not be his date. When he asked why, she was blunt: "My father found out you're a Jew and the son of a ragman. He won't allow me to associate with that type."

"I was stunned by the rejection, but I vowed right there and then I would get revenge on Gentiles. When I became rich and famous, I would date and screw only *shiksas* (non-Jewish girls) and maybe marry two or three."

Izzy was one of 325 students comprising the Class of 1934, receiving his high school diploma on June 27 at the Rialto Theater in the center of Amsterdam, that same theater where he'd made out with his English teacher.

The Rialto was still showing movies in the late 1940s and early 1950s, including titles in which Kirk by then was starring: *Champion, Out of the Past, Young Man with a Horn,* and *Along the Great Divide.*

His father didn't bother to attend his only son's graduation, but his proud mother and sisters did, watching in awe as he won awards for his acting, speech, and essay writing. He'd written "The Play's the Thing," in which he claimed that "Art can only be achieved by hunger."

"As God is my witness, I knew what hunger felt like. When I became rich and famous, I was going to order a juicy steak every night except when I preferred lobster."

Armed with his high school diploma, he entered the job market at the height of the Depression. The only thing he could find was a position as janitor at his Alma Mater, Amsterdam's Wilbur H. Lynch High School.

"It paid twenty bucks a week, and I was glad to get it, even though it meant cleaning toilets. The girls were cleaner animals than the boys. They seemed to do the most crapping."

"I worked hard and did a good job," he said. "But after a week, the school superintendent fired me, giving no reason."

Two years later, when he returned home from college, he headed to the cottage which Louise had rented after she'd moved from the boarding house. As he approached the door, he looked through the window and saw a man in his underwear in the living room. It was the guy who had hired me. Louise emerged from the bedroom in a bathrobe. Now he knew why the superintendent had fired him. It was out of jealousy. He must have learned about his affair with Louise.

"I learned my lesson well, and saw many examples in Hollywood, where actors got fired not always because they weren't doing a good job. Perhaps that superintendent, the ugly goat, was putting Louise into a position equivalent to the Hollywood casting couch, but I didn't have to do that. My talent saved me. I didn't have to go the casting couch route."

"For me, the one thing in my life I always knew, that was always constant, was that I wanted to be an actor. That in itself is an asset. I think half of the success in life comes from first finding out what you really want to do, and then going ahead and doing it. Of course, you need fierce determination, and you need to love your work. But let's be honest: You need a hell of a lot of luck—and I had that by the bushels."

***

Finding no work in Amsterdam, Izzy hitched three different rides before he reached the busy resort area of Lake George. Nicknamed "Queen of American Lakes," the long, oligotrophic lake lies at the southeast base of the Adirondacks near the northeastern corner of New York State.

In school, Izzy had read James Fenimore Cooper's *The Last of the Mohicans*, in which he referred to the lake as "Horican," in honor of the region's

Kirk as a high school cheerleader. The A is for "Amsterdam"

original Indian inhabitants. *[Its present name derives from King George II of England.]*

In 1791, Thomas Jefferson visited the area, writing that "Lake George is, without comparison, the most beautiful body of water I ever saw." It later provided inspiration for the painter, Georgia O'Keefe.

During its resort heyday, it became a fashionable retreat for millionaire families, including the Whitneys, the Rockefellers, and the Vanderbilts.

Having very little money, just enough to buy some food, he needed a place to stay for the night. After a park ranger threatened him with a gun when he knocked on the door of his log cabin, he fled into the forest, falling asleep under a tree. When he woke up early the next morning, he discovered a large and fresh pile of feces only three feet away. Had a grizzly bear visited him the night before?

After buying a 35¢ breakfast at a diner, he began the rounds once again, visiting hotels he had not stopped at the day before. By five o'clock, as the afternoon was coming to an end, he was about to give up when he spotted Orchard House. He'd heard it was restricted—"NO JEWS ALLOWED."

He introduced himself to the manager as "Don Dempsey," taking the last name from the fabled boxer, Jack Dempsey. He learned that an opening as a bellhop had become available since the young man who had held the job had to return to the Bronx to care for his stricken mother.

As a bellhop, Izzy soon learned that the hotel was overflowing with single women, either widows or those who had never found a husband. "They were all middle aged, not a beauty among them. Without sounding too immodest, they seemed to find me attractive. I had to make many a retreat when I found myself in their bedrooms with the door to the hall closed. These women were super aggressive—the most outrageous of them grabbed my goodies. Not only that, but a lot of the guys employed as waiters or working in the kitchen were homosexual. I was made many an offer, but it just wasn't my thing."

The owner of the hotel, Janet Wilson, "a bit on the pudgy side and wearing far too much makeup, had taken over the hotel after the death of her husband. She had flirted with me a lot that summer. Obviously, she didn't know I was a Jew. I was 'Don' to her."

She was always making anti-Semitic remarks. "To my knowledge," she told him, "I have never let a Jew into my hotel. I can smell them a mile away. I can't stand them. Some of then try to change their name to pass, but they don't fool me. No more Goldfish. No more Silverstein."

On his last day on the job, as the summer came to an end, she phoned him and invited him down a garden path that led to her cottage. "I have a surprise for you," she said.

Over drinks—in fact, several drinks—she continued her rant against Jews. "Another season and no Jews. I had to turn away at least six couples. The Nazis are firmly entrenched in Germany. Say what you will about Hitler, but he's on the right track eliminating Jews. The world would be a better place without these money-grubbing bastards."

As he later noted, "I found such hatred an aphrodisiac, producing an enormous erection."

He helped her out of her clothes, but retained his own, only pulling down his pants and underwear.

He thrust inside her and, as he was climaxing, he whispered in her ear. "That is a circumcised Jewish cock inside you. Do you think it will contaminate you? Maybe even make you die? I am a Jew. You are being fucked by a Jew."

There was no sound from her, and she looked as if she were about to faint.

"Needless to say, I did not get invited back next summer."

***

After graduation from high school, and to save money for college, Izzy got a job in the men's department of the M. Lurie Department Store. "I figured out how to beef up my college fund when I sold socks and underwear," he said. "I stole it. If I had a $5.95 sale, I would ring it at $4.95 and let a dollar bill cascade to the floor. I'd snatch it up later when no one was looking. That way, I saved $163 in nine months of employment, and the manager never caught on."

"At night, I continued to pursue my theatrical ambitions by joining the Amsterdam Little Theatre group. When *The Royal Family* was being cast, I tried out for the lead in this play which had opened on Broadway in 1927, the work of Edna Ferber and George S. Kaufman. My character of Tony Cavendish was clearly based on 'The Great Profile,' John Barrymore, himself."

When the play opened in London, it had starred Laurence Olivier in the role. Izzy had also gone to see the movie version which had featured Fredric March in the role that Izzy had assumed.

His mother did not want him to leave home, but his sisters urged him to go to St. Lawrence University in Canton, New York. Even though he did not have the money for tuition, Izzy felt he might be granted a working scholarship to pay it off. "At least I knew how to be a janitor."

"Two or three guys in this fraternity took a liking to me and invited me to their fraternity house for dinner with the idea of taking me on as a pledge. I waited for them to pick me up that evening, but they didn't show up."

The next day, one of the fraternity brothers told him why: "We thought you were Polish but found out you were a Jew. Our fraternity does not accept Jews."

"I was hungry most of the time, and still didn't have much to spend on food," Izzy said. "I came up with this plan. I'd go into the cafeteria and sit at one of the tables with some of the kids. I'd mooch stuff from their plate, which usually meant turnips or spinach. Bread was free at the counter, and I helped myself to the condiments, too. Mustard or ketchup makes a pretty good sandwich."

"I'd visit guys in the dormitory who often got care packages from home. I stocked up on their candy, fruits, and nuts. My luck ran out when the stern, gray-haired cafeteria manager learned what I was doing and ordered me out the door, never to set foot in the place again. She shouted at me and embarrassed me in front of the school. But many students were kind and slipped me things to eat."

The university was in Canton, a small town in New York State near the Canadian border, about 200 miles from Amsterdam. Its name had been inspired by the exotic, far-away port with the same name [but now called Guangzhou] in China. "I had to hitch five rides before I got there, the last in a pickup truck hauling horseshit for fertilizer."

"I arrived on campus smelling like shit but was ushered into the office of Dean Hewlitt. He took a sniff of me and eyed me skeptically. His first question was, 'How much money do you have?' He was not impressed with my purse but was impressed with my awards and my scholarship record. He granted me a student loan and enrolled me, although the fall courses had already started."

"I couldn't afford to live in a dormitory, so I got a job working for the two janitors, who let me sleep in their bleak quarters using a makeshift bed on the floor. In the afternoon, I did their dirty work, which meant latrine duty."

"Thus, I was launched on the road to a higher education—that's how it's done."

***

Every day he saw males walking around on campus, holding hands with their girls. They were big men on the campus in their white sweaters with the large letter "L" on their garments. These were the "Lettermen" who had earned the school initial by excelling in sports. "I decided I wanted a letter, too, but which sport would I be good at?"

For reasons not always clear to him, he chose wrestling, deciding he was going to work at the sport until he became a champion. "There were a lot of bruises on my way to glory," he recalled.

"On occasion, I got lucky in the romance department, especially with a gal called Elizabeth. She was quite buxom, and one moonlit night, we went for a swim by an old quarry when the weather warmed up. The water was still damn cold, and we huddled later in an old blanket on the side of a mountain. One thing led to another. We made love that night and slept until dawn, when we hurried back to campus. For some reason, I felt guilty."

"Along came Isabella Phelps, who sat in front of me in my German class," he said. "Believe it or not, her nickname was Izzy, same as mine. What a coincidence. At least we had that in common. She was a fine girl, and for the rest of my freshman year, she became my steady piece. Once, she brought up the possibility that we might get married after we completed the university, but I never pursued that. Marriage was the least of my goals."

"I also had a good friend on the faculty, a tall, thin man, a professor of economics. I won't give his name. He often invited me to his quarters where we listened to music and sometimes read poetry together. He was one hell of a cook. From his tiny kitchenette emerged one delectable meal after another. He learned my favorite dishes and prepared them for me any night I wasn't out with a girl."

"He didn't think much of my wardrobe, and bought me things I really needed, like a new suit of clothes or a pair of loafers. He even bought underwear for me. I remembered the first time he asked me to try on a pair to see if they fitted. He appraised my figure and complimented me on it, and he always attended my wrestling matches."

"Perhaps I should have gotten suspicious, but I was pretty naïve about some things in those days. When it came time for vacation, he invited me to go to Mexico with him—all expenses paid. I was overjoyed. I couldn't believe how nice he was to me. He was shaping up to be the father I had in name only."

"After a rough match wrestling, he would give me these great massages. I was not at all embarrassed to strip naked in front of him. He was the first person to make me aware that I had a body worth viewing."

"In the years to come, the whole world would see my physique on display."

Three weeks before the end of the school year, he invited me to drive south to his home state of Alabama, with a stopover first in Washington,

D.C., where we could visit all the monuments. After Alabama, we would head west into Texas and then cross the border into Mexico. I was over-joyed but told him I couldn't afford it. He promised to pay all my expenses and keep me well fed. What young freshman could turn down a chance like that? I was real lucky."

After Washington, they drove along the Gulf Coast. "I got to see the Mississippi River, and thought of Tom Sawyer and Huckleberry Finn."

After Texas, their goal was Mexico City, where the professor promised to take Izzy to a bullfight on Saturday afternoon. In Mexico City, the pro-fessor rented a modest hotel room with a double bed, which opened onto a balcony overlooking a plaza. "We got drunk on tequila and staggered back to the hotel. I passed out in bed with him. But at around three in the morning, I woke up with this odd sensation. He was going down on me."

In his memoirs, Kirk Douglas wrote that "I leaped out of bed. I didn't know how to handle the situation. Homosexuality was something new to me, some vague thing I had only heard about. Maybe I should have laughed and joked my way out of it, but I was incensed. And this poor, timid man became terribly upset. There was a pall over the rest of that trip."

Years later, Kirk would relate a different version of the trip to Burt Lan-caster and other close friends. "When I discovered what was going on with the professor down there, I was too far gone at that point—and I blasted off. But I made it clear to him that the previous night was not going to be repeated again, even though we shared a double bed."

Lancaster was far more graphic in describing to Kirk his own homo-sexual encounters as a young man when he'd also made gay porn.

After Mexico City, the professor drove him to the mountain town of Taxco, in Mexico's state of Guerrero, southwest of the nation's capital. Their first night in town, Izzy left the professor in his hotel room and wandered through the streets alone. There, he met Margaret Hayes, who was in her junior year at a college in San Diego. She invited him back to the hotel room which she shared with a female classmate.

"We did it," Izzy revealed. "It was my good luck that her roommate must have gotten lucky that night, too." She showed up for breakfast, hav-ing 'auditioned' a Mexican boy the previous night, or so she claimed. Frankly, I wasn't used to such liberated women as these California gals. Maybe it was all that sunshine that caused them to mature at an earlier age."

"When I returned to the professor's room at 10AM, he was pissed off at me," Izzy said. "He was damn jealous. He hardly spoke to me for the rest of the day. As we drove along that afternoon, I was lost in my thoughts.

I had heard from other actor wannabees at college that guys who go to Broadway or Hollywood have to get used to homosexual advances. The theater and movies attract guys who like guys in droves. At least that was what I'd heard. I decided then and there to brace myself for what was to come. That's what you get when you're born a good-looking mother-fucker like me."

"The first part of the trip through Mexico and back through the Middle West to New York State was not as enjoyable as the first part because of the tension between the professor and me. He continued to pay my bills and feed me well. I knew what he wanted, and in a way I felt sorry for him, but I could not bring myself to be his plaything."

"When we had to take a piss together at a gas station, I knew he was cruising me at the urinal, and I let him get a good look, but that was the extent of it. The trip must have been torture for him."

"When I returned to college that fall for my sophomore year, I stopped hanging out with the professor. Once or twice, I passed him in the hallway, and we merely nodded. I was polite but distant. After all, he'd been good to me."

There was a footnote to the professor story. At the end of his sophomore year, the professor invited a good-looking male classmate of Izzy's to go on a midsummer tour of Canada, just across the border. "I should have warned him," Izzy said. "But I didn't."

"When I saw my buddy that fall, I asked him how the trip had been through the wilds of Canada."

"It was terrific," the classmate responded. "The greatest adventure of my life, with all expenses paid. At night, all I had to do was lie back on my pillow and get the greatest blow job in the world. Is that guy talented!"

"Sometimes, I'd corner him during the day and demand a session," the classmate continued. "I was perpetually horny. You must try this specialty called 'around the world.' He discovered hot spots on my body I didn't know I had."

***

Izzy would be enrolled at St. Lawrence University from 1935 to 1939, graduating the year that Britain and France declared war on Nazi Germany, launching World War II. "I spent a lot of my time there, sweeping hallways and scrubbing stinky latrines," he said. "I don't romanticize my years at St. Lawrence. Much of it was hell, but I sharpened my survival skills. I'm against having a boy work his way through college. It's a waste of precious time that he could be studying or going out for sports—or perhaps just relaxing or dating. I had to scrounge for money and food. Many times, I went to bed without dinner unless the janitors brought me something left over from their dinner. I learned to make a sandwich out of almost anything—even pickle relish."

***

During his sophomore year, he tried out for the varsity wrestling team and won a place on it by defeating the only athlete on campus who had a wrestling scholarship. "He had the skill, but I had the fierce determination. I used every sinew, every muscle in my body to defeat him."

Izzy didn't make friends easily. An exception was Wally Thompson, the tallest man at St. Lawrence. "He was big and beefy, and he beat the hell out of a creep who called me 'a dirty Jew.' I was always grateful to Wally for standing up for me."

Izzy made another friend, a fellow student named Robert Irwin, who was five years older than the average senior at St. Lawrence. He was a talented sculptor and had a little studio off campus where he displayed his work to Izzy one afternoon. "He was kind to me, but I noted that he had this violent temper, which was never directed at me."

One day, Irwin asked Izzy if he'd pose nude for him, assuring him that he was not a homosexual.

Izzy agreed and posed for him on weekends. "Posing was a real rough job and very tiring, having to stand motionless, but in the end, he created a magnificent rendition of me. He even carved my circumcised cock."

One afternoon, Izzy went to Irwin's studio to hang out with him, only to discover that he was gone, as were his sculptures, including the nude of him. A month went by before F.B.I. agents showed up on campus searching for Irwin. Izzy compared the dragnet to the manhunt for the killer of the Lindbergh baby.

On Easter Sunday, 1937, in Manhattan, Irwin had strangled an artist's model and her mother, and their boarder had been stabbed through the heart with an ice pick.

Irwin was finally tracked down to where he was hiding out in a basement in Brooklyn. In court, it was determined that the sculptor was criminally insane, and he was sent to chains to the Dannemora (New York) State Hospital for Insane Convicts. [It was later renamed the Adirondack Correctional Treatment and Evaluation Center.]

Kirk Douglas recalled, "While I was preparing to play Vincent Van Gogh in Lust for Life, I used my memory of Bob to form my on-screen character. Both artists were insane. I never found out what happened to my sculpted nude. Maybe it's in somebody's collection today, and they don't know it's Kirk Douglas, the bigtime movie star."

***

After the end of Izzy's sophomore year, he found a summer job working in a factory in Rochester, New York, that manufactured steel drums and barrels. "It was dangerous work. Safety devices hardly existed back then. I think I was the only worker in the plant who had ten fingers. Everyone had lost at least one finger, often two or three."

"I lived in a cubbyhole with room enough for a single bed. It was a dismal life, and I didn't know if I'd survive the summer. And then I met Peggy."

"She had a bubbling personality and an infectious humor. She was only four feet and something. Most of her growth had gone into her tits. She would make the buxom blonde, Jayne Mansfield, look like Audrey Hepburn. She let me nestle in that ample bosom every night. After only our second date, those panties came off."

"I was a dinner guest at her home almost every night. Her mother was a great cook. For the first time in my life, I was able to reject third helpings after two overly generous ones. For lunch at the factory, Peggy would drive up in a Cadillac with the most ample lunch on the lot. My fellow workers wolf-whistled at her and teased me. It was out of jealousy."

"My co-workers never found out I was a Jew," Izzy said. "They were very crude, blue collar types, and they made racial slurs against Jews and 'niggers,' a term I would loathe for the rest of my life."

"The only worker I remember was a Canadian who'd migrated to Rochester. He was nicknamed 'Tattoo,' as much of his body was covered with them. Once, he invited me to go with him to the men's toilet. There, he pulled down his pants and showed me his ass. It had this tattoo of a cat chasing a rat into his asshole. That's the kind of classy guys I worked with."

At the end of August, Izzy was excited about facing his junior year in college, although he wondered how Peggy would figure into his life after his return to Canton. He'd been seeing her almost every night in Rochester. "She never said no when I asked for sex. Often, she was the one doing the asking. I was at my sexual peak in

Kirk with Wally Thompson. "He stood six feet four and beat up anybody who called me a dirty Jew."

those days, and I was always hot to trot back then."

"One night, we went for a long midnight walk and found a secluded spot to make love. When it was over and we were adjusting our clothing, she proposed marriage to me."

"But I can't!" he protested. "It's back to school for me, cleaning all those toilets and remembering the meals your mother fed me while I have a hot dog for supper if I'm lucky."

"It doesn't have to be that bleak," she said. "I've talked it over with my father. If you marry me, he'll get us a nice apartment until you complete your studies. He'll also give us fifty dollars a week for food and stuff. When summer comes, we'll go back to Rochester and live with them in their big house. He'll get you a good-paying summer job—no more dangerous steel mills!"

"But after college, I want to go to New York to become an actor," he said. "You can just imagine what a struggle that will be."

"It doesn't have to be," she said. "Father will get us an apartment in Greenwich Village. He'll support us. Don't view it as a handout. He considers it as an investment in your future, because he's convinced it'll be a golden one!"

"When you come home at night from drama school, or whatever, I'll have one of your favorite dishes prepared," she said. "Then we'll cuddle up. You know I can satisfy your 'raging bull' sexual demands."

"You certainly have proven that...and how!"

"Then what more can a young man ask?"

For the next few days, Izzy pondered that question for himself. It was a debate within himself as to who he wanted to be. He knew how very sexy Peggy was, but there was a problem. He didn't love her. "I didn't want to go through life without love, just being someone's kept boy," Izzy recalled.

One night, years later, he was discussing that decision with the gay author, Gore Vidal. Vidal had written a novel, *Judgment of Paris,* in which a young man faces a crossroads and must decide which road to take.

"It was with Peggy that I had to make my own Judgment of Paris," Kirk told Vidal. "I could take the high road living it up with Peggy on her father's dime—or else I could take the long, hard road of a struggling actor."

"In my heart, I thought I'd never make it as an actor unless I had hunger in my belly." Kirk said. "I also wanted to marry for love."

"On my final night, I told Peggy the bad news, and she burst into tears," he said. "I knew I was breaking her heart, but I had to go away listening to what my guts were telling me to do. It was a sad goodbye. I would always remember that summer with her. Many times in my future, particularly in those early days as an actor, I would regret my decision."

***

En route back to St. Lawrence for his junior year in college, Izzy stopped in his hometown of Amsterdam, a dismal detour from his trip. From there, he'd visit Schenectady for a reunion with his mother and sisters, who had moved there, occupying a modest home.

In Amsterdam, his father was still living alone at 46 Eagle Street in the house where Izzy had grown up. After disembarking from the train, he walked to the old homestead, finding the house looking more dilapidated than ever. At least a dozen cats were darting around, perhaps surviving by mutilating and feasting on the rats living in the basement.

He found his father sitting at the battered kitchen table, rubbing garlic over pumpernickel bread, doing exactly the same thing he'd done the last time he'd seen him. It was as if he'd never moved from this old wooden table that had never held enough food for a family of nine.

Harry had very little to say to him, other than "How's college?" After he finished off his bread, he rose from the table, telling his son, "You're a man now. Let's go bar hopping—on your dime from working the steel shifts."

And so they did.

"I never again would have so many boilermakers in one night, trying to keep up drink for drink with a seasoned pro like Pa. When it came to drinking, I was a total amateur, he a veteran of countless seedy taverns."

Harry introduced Izzy to every person he knew, referring to him as "the college man, champ wrestler of New York State."

Both men were intoxicated when Harry's friend, Stanley Rimkunas, volunteered to drive father and son to Schenectady.

At his mother's new home, Izzy staggered toward the front door as his father and Stanley drove off. Standing on the porch, Bertha shook her fist at her former husband for getting her son drunk. As a greeting to his mother after many months of absence, he threw up on her doorstep.

After a two-day stay, all was forgiven. "I told all the girls, especially Ma, farewell. It seemed that wedding bells for most of my siblings would soon be ringing."

The highlight of his junior year was his affair with an attractive teacher at his university. He was not in any of her Spanish classes but had met her in the cafeteria. She was 30-year-old Rita Garcia, who had migrated to New York from her native Puerto Rico. Her husband had bolted, running off with a younger woman in San Juan.

"I could now eat in that cafeteria where I was once kicked out for munching food," Kirk said. "I'd saved enough from the job at the steel mill."

Rita lived in a small cottage in back of a fraternity house. "I would sneak in there after dark where she always had a dinner prepared for me. Then we'd go to bed early to make endless love, and I'd depart before dawn. During my entire junior year, no one found out about our forbidden love. Teachers, or so I was told, were not to seduce their handsome, studly male students."

"Because of my wrestling acclaim, I was becoming a popular man on campus. Other girls tried to date me, and the campus beauty queen (what was her name?) succeeded. That was just heavy petting, no commando stuff. When I showered in the locker room, homosexuals always took the shower next to mine. I lathered up, putting on a good show for them. They soon got the message: They could look but not touch. It was a bit exciting, however, to be so admired as a hotsy wrestler."

"I hadn't abandoned my goal of becoming an actor," he said. "My first big break came in 1938 when I got the male lead in the St. Lawrence University production of *Death Takes a Holiday*. A play by Maxwell Anderson, Izzy had seen the 1934 movie starring Fredric March.

Death Takes a Holiday is a fantasy. Posing as Prince Sirk, "Death" comes to earth to see what it's like to be a mere mortal and to try to understand why humans want so desperately to cling to life. Along the way, the prince learns what it is to love.

"I was a hit," Kirk later recalled. "You might call it my first success in the theater." In 1998, its script would be the inspiration for Brad Pitt's *Meet Joe Black*.

***

That summer, through a connection he made, Izzy was hired as a "carnie" traveling around New York State in a caravan with other carnival performers. He got the job because of his skill as a wrestler.

"As a professional wrestler, I picked up new words like 'mark' and 'snozz.' On my first day on the job, I learned that the carnival's wrestling matches were fake, part of a rigged—and very secret—formula. The carnies use the word *kayfabe* to describe it, meaning 'keeping the secret from the ticket-buying public.'"

Roy Hingle, the carnival baker, claimed, "You're either in on the secret or else just a pigeon walking down the midway, enjoying the cotton candy and waiting to lose your rent money."

Years later, in 1956, Kirk would be reminded of Hingle when he went to see the hit Rodgers and Hammerstein stage musical, *Carousel*. Gordon MacRae was its star, interpreting the flashy, endearing, and macho character of Billy Bigelow, the rowdy carousel barker.

The star of Izzy's public wrestling match carnie shows was "Pinky" Plumadore, who was optimistically billed as "The Masked Marvel, the world's champion wrestler."

A burly, beefy hunk of man, he would appear and—after flexing onstage for a while—ask for a volunteer from the audience to come into the ring and engage in a match. Every night, Izzy would rise from the audience and volunteer, pretending to be an uninvolved "average Joe."

After changing into a pair of boxing trunks, he and Pinky would engage in a mock wrestling match that always looked authentic. "I sure ended up with a lot of bruises."

There was also a second act every night which cost the spectators extra. Billed as "A Fight to the Death," Izzy and the Masked Marvel became more intense during their round. At the end of their rounds, Izzy managed to escape Pinky's chokehold and emerge victorious. Izzy always received the loudest applause as the crowd rooted for him and not for the brute.

The carnival's other oddities and attractions included a Bearded Lady, a minstrel show, and a midget show. "The little people reminded me of those 'Munchkins' I'd recently seen in Judy Garland's *The Wizard of Oz* (1939).

For men only, there was a special late-night show that the carnival manager always feared might be shut down by the police. It featured "Super Stud," a Puerto Rican named Paco, who was celebrated for his 14-inch, very thick penis. After midnight, on stage, he would seduce three women, including one black performer. "I don't know how those ladies took him," Izzy said. "Of course, women gave birth to babies, so I guess they could handle Paco."

"Everybody seemed to be seducing everybody else," Izzy said. "The carnival was my first real introduction to life in the raw. You might call it a look behind the scenes at life among the depraved. Carnies always had a well-deserved reputation for immorality. All forms of sex were going on, and I mean *all!*"

He slept in a tent with three other performers, each of whom was a homosexual. "I had thought that homo men satisfied each other with blow jobs, but they also screw each other. They aggressively pursued me, but I kept them at bay."

For his own sex life, he'd met this gorgeous carnival dancer, Sadie Clarke, who was from Minnesota. "She was very sexy." In 1949, he'd gone

32

to see *Flamingo Road* in which Joan Crawford—at the beginning of the film—played a carnival dancer, wearing a flimsy black outfit, most of it see-through.

"Crawford, my future sex partner, reminded me of Sadie. She really could have taught a course in sex education, a graduate course, that is. What she could do with a feather was very erotic. She knew that there was no part of a man that should be ignored, from his armpits to his toes. That Sadie, what a gal! I would never meet her likes again."

"It's a wonder I had any energy left over for sex. The job was sixteen hours a day, seven days a week. Meals were included—hot dogs for lunch, a meat stew at night with lots of boiled potatoes. When not wrestling, I had to help out at the hot dog stand and got damn tired asking, 'Want fries with your dog?'"

He had another duty that involved "putting out fires," which meant rushing to meet any emergency. "There were quite a few of those that memorable summer."

When the carnival closed in any town, every member of the crew pitched in to shut it down, load it onto trucks, and head for the next town, where the routine began all over again.

"Some carnies survived this vagabond life—not me, buddy. A true carnie liked the easy sex, the constantly changing venues, the rootlessness, and the show-biz drama of it all. They were welcome to it."

The nomadic life was getting to me," Izzy said. "I decided to leave after six weeks, although that meant giving up those torrid nights with Sadie. The Fat Lady waddled after me to the very end, but never caught me. I avoided her clutches, fearing I would never be able to get it up for Fatso. After all, an erection is a mysterious thing. There's always the fear, each time one does, that it won't come back."

**

Through a drama teacher at St. Lawrence, Izzy got a job as a stagehand at a summer theater, the Tamarack Playhouse on Lake Pleasant in the Adirondacks.

The theater was the creation of a well-heeled actor, Malcolm Atterbury, the stepson of W.W. Atterbury, President of the Pennsylvania Railroad. Along with his wife, Ellen, he had funded the construction of the theater, which had opened as recently as 1938.

Both Malcolm and his wife booked plays in which they could co-star. The only name actor they had was Karl Malden, who would go on to greater glory on the stage and screen.

[There would be a footnote to the Malcolm Atterbury/Kirk Douglas story. In 1954, Kirk was filming Man Without a Star, *a Western released the following year.*

On the set, he met an extra, playing in an uncredited role as a rancher, Fancy Joe Toole. He almost did a double take. The actor was none other than Atterbury himself.

More than a decade later, on the set of Seven Days in May (1965), *Kirk met up with Atterbury once again. This time, he'd been cast as Horace, a White House physician.]*

As a stagehand that summer in Lake Pleasant, Izzy had to perform almost any task, including erecting sets, his main job. Occasionally, he was cast into a minor role, most often a walk-on. On some occasions, he had a line or two to deliver. In one scene, as he remembered it, he played a postman who arrived to announce, "I've got a letter for you."

"I became involved with the *ingénue,* who was a beautiful bitch," Izzy said. "She fell in love with me, but she was also shacked up with another stagehand who, like me, wanted to be an actor, but often ended up cleaning the latrines or picking up supplies in a pickup truck."

"She was a refugee from Baltimore with dreams of becoming a bigtime Broadway star," Izzy said. "She came on to me. All summer, anytime her beau was away, she cornered me and pressed sex. I came through for her, if I do say so myself. Obviously, I was giving her something her boy didn't deliver."

"I felt guilty for cheating and sorry for her beau," Izzy said. "One night, I told her of my feelings."

"Don't be a silly-dilly," she said. "We're both actors in the theater. Actors are artists who must function without guilt. Guilt is for the middle or lower classes. Ronald Reagan got it right: In his early days on the screen, he developed what he called '*leadinglady-itis.*' He fell in love with whichever girl he was making a picture with. The end of filming marked the end of the romance. It happens in the theater all the time. Get used to it."

That summer ended too soon. Shortly after Izzy's return to St. Lawrence, the autumn winds were blowing down from Canada.

***

During his senior year at St. Lawrence, Izzy was "The Big Man on Campus" (BMOC). Before the end of his junior year, in a surprise election, he had been elected president of the student body. "It was an amazing victory for me. Obviously, the Jew Boy, namely me, had a lot of non-Jewish admirers."

Sadly, he was informed on his first week back that many of the most generous members of the alumni were threatening to withhold contributions because the student body "had elected a Jew president."

The post, however, had many benefits. Izzy was assigned a double room with a private phone, and it cost him nothing. He could eat free in the cafeteria.

Ray Clarkson, the wrestling coach, welcomed him back and tried to get him to train for the American Olympic Wrestling Team. He was greatly disappointed when Izzy told him he didn't want to become a pro wrestler, but an actor. "Acting is a profession for faggots," Clarkson warned.

"I also got the lead in any school play in which I wished to star," Izzy claimed. "And I got my pick of campus beauties. To confess up, most of them didn't put out, and I settled for heavy petting. "The Spanish teacher, that hot piece of mine, had been fired, and I hoped it was not because of me."

"Frankly, I was not one of those gung-ho college boys. I planned, after graduation, to never set foot on campus again. I got tired of the school paper running editorials attacking me."

"At the university's 77th annual commencement on June 12, 1939, I introduced our guest speaker, Mayor Fiorello La Guardia of New York City. After the ceremony, he invited me to come and work for his administration that summer, but I didn't accept."

"As it turned out, decades later, I did return to St. Lawrence to accept an honorary degree."

In September of 1939, World War II was declared. After Germany invaded Poland, France and England declared war on the Nazis.

"Most of the boys in my class figured America would stay out of another foreign war in Europe, "Izzy said. "How wrong could a lot of smart-assed guys like us be? Soon, all of us would be sucked into the whirlpool of death and destruction. If Jews thought they had it rough in Tsarist Russia, it was nothing compared to what Hitler and Himmler had in store for them."

After graduation from St. Lawrence, Izzy headed back to the Tamarack Playhouse for another summer season. He did stagehand work, as before, but he also got more of a chance to appear in small dra-

The Tamarack Playhouse, where in 1940, a stagehand and summer intern, Izzy Demsky changed his name to Kirk Douglas.

matic roles. "Most of them were tried and true vehicles that had long been on Broadway, or even in movie adaptations. I hardly remembered them."

What he would remember forever is his decision to come up with a new WASP name. "I just couldn't see Izzy Danielovitch being a star on the Great White Way."

"I wanted something that started with a 'D,' since I was already using the name of Demsky. I got this book devoted to Leading Men in the movies and came across the name of Douglas Fairbanks, Sr., the former husband of Mary Pickford, America's Sweetheart during the silent era."

The first great action star, Fairbanks had interpreted the roles of both Robin Hood and Zorro onscreen.

Izzy finally decided to use Douglas as a surname. But what would be his first name? "A friend in the troupe suggested Kirk and I went for that. *Kirk Douglas.* What a great name. It didn't occur to me at the time that I would often be identified as 'of Scottish origin.'"

"I worked for a season at Tamarack with the future stage and screen actor, Karl Malden," the newly christened Kirk said. "He was the one who told me to change my name. Karl started out in the steel town of Gary, Indiana as Mladen Sekulovich."

"The first night I saw the name of Kirk Douglas printed in the *Tamarack Playbill,* I was thrilled. I vowed then and there that I would make that name known on all the continents of the world."

VIEW OF 52ND STREET IN NEW YORK CITY, CIRCA 1948

FROM THE GOTTLIEB COLLECTION AT WIKIMEDIA COMMONS

CHAPTER TWO

KIRK FALLS IN LOVE

SHE'S BRUNETTE, SHE'S BEAUTIFUL, SHE'S TALENTED,
& SHE'S "MISS NEW YORK,"
BUT SHE DUMPS HIM FOR JOHN F. KENNEDY

KIRK POSES NUDE

TO BUY SOME SECONDHAND CLOTHES

KATHARINE CORNELL

AMERICA'S THEN-MOST-FAMOUS STAGE ACTRESS
MENTORS KIRK'S BUDDING STAGE CAREER
UNTIL HER HUSBAND DEVELOPS A CRUSH AND
EXPECTS SEXUAL FAVORS FROM HIM

TALLULAH BANKHEAD

"OF COURSE, I HAD HIM, *DAH-LING*."

LAUREN BACALL

"I TOLD BOGIE WE NEVER DID IT"

"I was young and gorgeous, and everybody wanted a piece of me."

Before leaving the Tamarack Playhouse at Lake Pleasant, Kirk made arrangements to live at the nonprofit Greenwich Settlement House in Manhattan's Greenwich Village. He arrived at Grand Central Station on a train three days before his scheduled check-in agreement.

[Established in 1902 by social reformers spearheaded by Mary Kingsbury Simkhovitch, it helped recent immigrants adjust to their changed circumstances, and aided actors and artists in their battles to survive in the brutal housing markets of New York City. Eleanor Roosevelt was one of its supporters, and the doomed aviator, Amelia Earhart, had been a resident for two years beginning in 1927. For a period of his career, the abstract expressionist painter, Jackson Pollock (1912-1956), received free studio space for sweeping the ground floor.]

He'd decided not to visit his father *en route*—always a disappointment—in Amsterdam, or even his mother and sisters in Schenectady. "I wasn't up for that. Maybe I was selfish, but I'd become the errant son. Family ties weren't my chief focus. I was determined to become an actor."

"In Manhattan, I had to bury Izzy and let the Kirk Douglas *persona* take over. But I could never bury the harsh realities of my grim childhood growing up in Amsterdam. I thought of my mother living in constant despair, my father always drunk and violent. Every morning, as Izzy, I woke up frightened and feeling alone, although in a crowded household of six sisters."

"Years later, as a movie star, I often had to convey suffering on the screen. To do so, I summoned up those painful memories from my past."

"My life as Kirk Douglas truly began in Manhattan, although it was damn tough going at first. To me, New York is the most exciting place on Earth. I'd visit many countries and world capitals in my day, cities like London, Paris, and Rome, but nothing would ever equal New York—not even Hollywood."

He had to find some short-term shelter—and he did. For only a dollar a night, he became a three-day tenant at the Mills Hotel. Inhabited with hookers, drug addicts, and drunks, it had been the scene, within recent memory, of two brutal murders.

His room was no more than a converted broom closet—"Just enough space for an Army cot and my battered suitcase. But I didn't plan to spend much time there. In the wee hours of the morning, there would be a knock on my door from one of the hookers or from one of the homosexuals who wanted to suck me off, but I kept my door shut tight. I wasn't interested in the action so freely offered."

His first business involved seeing a lawyer, which he did the day after checking into the Mills. He'd saved fifty dollars, which was the price of getting his name officially changed to Kirk Douglas. No more Issur Danielovitch.

"My first three days in New York were a time of alienation and loneliness," he recalled. "I wasn't interested in the propositions I got on Times Square from both men and women. One middle-aged man in a business suit asked me how much I charged. My god, did I look like a male prostitute?"

"I was briefly flattered when one overly made-up aging hooker told me she usually charged but I could have it for free," he remembered. "No way!"

"It was refreshing to learn that many New Yorkers found me sexy. I knew that Karl Malden, no beauty prize winner, would have to rely solely on his talent to get ahead. As for me, Kirk Douglas, I felt I already had the two main attributes I'd need to make it as an actor: Good looks and talent. How could I lose?"

After a long and depressing three days, he was at last able to move into the safety and relative luxury of Greenwich House.

Kirk's bedroom was in an attic in one of the organization's nearby annexes—20 Jones Street—in a neighborhood filled with tenements, many of their tiny apartments peopled with starving artists.

After hanging up his meager possessions, he set out to explore Greenwich House itself. On its ground floor was a small theater for experimental plays. There was a modest gym where he could work out, and space for workshops devoted to pottery classes, dance lessons, and the arts.

On the second floor was a communal dining room offering breakfast and dinner. He'd have to let his stomach growl during lunch hour. At night, he filled up on Irish stew, which was served at least four times a week, with lots and lots of potatoes and cabbage.

He applied for a scholarship at the American Academy of Dramatic Arts, an

Greenwich House: This photo, snapped at about the same era that Kirk lived in one of its annexes, gives an idea of the many public services that Greenwich House offered to just-arrived "new Americans" and down-and-out artists trying to cope with the high cost of living in NYC.

organization founded in 1884 to train actors for the stage. He could not afford the annual fee of $500, and to his deep frustration, his scholarship application was rejected. But three days later, the board of directors at the Academy reversed their decision and granted him a scholarship. [*In 1940, during the course of Kirk's studies there, the Academy occupied space within Carnegie Hall on 57th Street and 7th Avenue.*]

His first term would be devoted to voice, makeup, dance, costuming, and pantomime. "I even took lessons in fencing, although I knew I'd never make it as a swashbuckler like my namesake, Douglas Fairbanks, Sr."

The school was next to the elegant Russian Tea Room, which attracted the Hollywood elite during their visits to Manhattan. Sometimes at night, he'd stand outside in the dark and watch the dinner guests arrive. One night, he saw Clark Gable come in with Carole Lombard; on another evening, it was the beautiful blonde actress, Constance Bennett.

"I felt like I was attending a Hollywood premiere," Kirk said. "So many stars and VIPs. I vowed that when I became rich and famous, I'd be parading inside to feast on caviar and to drink champagne. At the next table, I'd wave at Marlene Dietrich. Of course, in her case, I'd do more than wave."

***

Back in 1938, when he was still known as Izzy, he'd gone to see the Mickey Rooney movie, *Love Finds Andy Hardy.* "I could do the sequel, *Love Finds Kirk Douglas.* I was about to fall in love and have an affair with this lovely Irish lassie with sky-blue eyes and hair as black as Edgar Allan Poe's *Raven.*"

Her name was Peggy Diggins, and for a year, she'd held the title of Miss New York, making public appearances around the state. In 1939, she enrolled at the Academy. A few months later, she nabbed a role in a play written by the famous Broadway talent agent, Leland Hayward.

He signed her as a client and wired the aviator/producer/billionaire, Howard Hughes a a recommendation that he should cast her as a new star in his latest picture. Although she was evaluated as too tall for the part, and didn't get the role, she may have had an affair with Hughes. Soon, she was back at the Academy in New York.

Kirk met her when he was seated beside her in the basement theater at Carnegie Hall, watching a performance of *Tonight or Never.* Melvin Douglas had starred in an earlier version of it on Broadway in 1928, and in 1931, after it was adapted into a movie, he'd made his film debut in it opposite Gloria Swanson.

During intermission, Kirk chatted with Peggy in the lobby, finding her amusing and very likable. She responded to him, and he invited her for dinner at Greenwich House since he couldn't afford to take her to a restaurant.

She accepted and made an instant hit with the other diners, especially Dr. Simkovich, a Russian professor whose wife was the house manager.

During one of her early interchanges with him, she admitted to Kirk, perhaps with the belief that his parents had migrated from Scotland, "I have this thing for Scottish men, always wondering what's under the kilt."

"Did she really say that?" he asked himself, determining not to immediately tell her he was Jewish and spoil the illusion.

Over the course of their next four dates, she paid for their Broadway or movie tickets and for their dinners since she was making fairly good money as a model. According to

"I fell in love with Peggy Diggins, Miss New York, the first moment she walked into my life. Blame it on her Irish turned-up nose. But she dumped me and headed for Hollywood. Next thing I heard, she was dating Clark Gable."

Kirk, "I felt like a kept boy—that is, a kept boy who was falling madly in love with Peggy. She shared an apartment with a female roommate, who was always gone, perhaps sleeping over at her boyfriend's place."

"Peggy and I made love every night. She told me I was a great lover. My schoolteacher upstate must have taught me well."

Their romantic fantasy could not go on forever, and he knew it. Trouble arose when she told him that she had accepted an invitation from actor Burgess Meredith. He had invited her to a formal dinner dance, a charity event at the Waldorf Astoria priced at $50 a ticket.

"I could not afford to rent a tux, much less pay $50 for each ticket," Kirk said.

[Kirk was already familiar with the career of Burgess Meredith, who had starred in the 1935 Broadway revival of The Barretts of Wimpole Street *opposite Katharine Cornell. Kirk had gone to see it upstate, when it was on tour. More recently, he'd seen Meredith in his acclaimed 1939 interpretation of George Milton in* Of Mice and Men, *based on John Steinbeck's morality tale.*

Kirk had read that Meredith had been married twice and divorced twice, and that his first wife, Helen Derby, had committed suicide after the divorce.]

"Meredith was talented but short and ugly," Kirk said. "Other than talent, I didn't see what he had that I didn't have more of. The Ohio shitkicker would compete with me for another beautiful woman, Lauren Bacall. But I got my revenge. When I made *In Harm's Way* (1965), I was the star, with Meredith cast in a mere supporting role."

After the formal dance with Meredith, Peggy headed for Kirk's garret on Jones Street. There, she pulled off her gown and jumped into bed with him to make love. "She went for me instead of Meredith after all, and I felt like a real man," Kirk said. "Not only was the lovemaking the best ever, but I proposed marriage to her before the milkman arrived."

Within days, his short-lived happiness faded when Peggy told him she'd been offered a contract in Hollywood. Along with a dozen other actresses, she'd been selected as a "Baby Star" by the Motion Picture Publicists Association. *[Ironically, of those twelve candidates, the only one who ever evolved into a star was Joan Leslie, whose fame flickered out rather quickly.]*

Peggy bid Kirk goodbye and promised to write to him every day. Marriage would have to be postponed.

She never wrote one letter, but he followed her in the entertainment news. She was soon making a screen test with Clark Gable, still the King of Hollywood. Later, her picture appeared in the papers when she was dating John F. Kennedy, the son of the former U.S. ambassador to the Court of St. James's.

According to newspaper accounts, Peggy fell madly in love with the dashing young JFK. There were rumors of an impending marriage.

Kirk, however, didn't think that the

Burgess Meredith in 1936 riding a bike on the back lot of RKO during his filming of *Winterset*.

"Young, handsome, charismatic, and rich, JFK stole Peggy Diggins from me," Kirk said. "But he quickly dumped her. The future President and I would share many Hollywood beauties in common."

romance would last. Young Kennedy was known for starting fast with women and then dropping them. Young JFK was also quoted as saying one night in Palm Beach, "I'm not interested in women I've already seduced. When the conquest is over, I usually move on."

Indeed, soon after his brief encounter with Peggy in Hollywood, Kennedy was seen dating other women. The actor, Robert Stack, had introduced him to other beauties in the film colony.

"I was miserable, heartbroken," Kirk said. "She was heading for stardom. Even Louella Parsons predicted that in her column. She was to make her screen debut in *Honeymoon for Three,* a film eventually released in 1941."

The following summer, Kirk returned to the Tamarack Playhouse for another gig with summer stock. When he wasn't working, "I kept to myself. I sulked the time away and didn't want to date or make friends with my fellow actors. It was the summer of my discontent."

There was a footnote to his affair with Peggy: When she returned to New York that autumn, she phoned him at the Academy and invited him to her suite at the Waldorf Astoria. She told him that although she was back in New York, she was too busy giving interviews and posing for photos to see him that day. Instead, she told him to come by Saturday morning.

He arrived at 11AM and came up to her luxurious suite, where he found her in the previous night's makeup. She'd been escorted to the Stork Club by a handsome young actor named Robert Stack, who was unofficially known as "Jack Kennedy's pimp."

"She told me she had time just to have coffee with me," Kirk said.

"Room service will bring it, and you can drink it while I get dressed," she said. "I've got such a hectic schedule during my quickie visit."

At the door, she handed him one hundred dollars. At first, he refused, but since he was completely broke, "I took it, feeling real cheap. I left the hotel knowing our marriage was off, our love affair was over, and that I'd been paid off with a hundred-dollar bill. I vowed never to fall in love again."

"I followed her road to stardom in *Variety,*" Kirk said. "But like so many other hopefuls, that road turned into the Boulevard of Broken Dreams, an all-too-familiar pattern for thousands. She did, however, become part of the Navy Blues Sextet, billed as 'The Six Most Beautiful Girls in the World.' They toured military bases during the war."

Columnist Mark Hellinger cited his predictions about Tinseltown's best bets for super stardom: Rita Hayworth, Linda Darnell, Gene Tierney, Ann Rutherford, who had appeared in *Gone With the Wind,* and Peggy Diggins.

"Some of those ladies actually became love goddesses on the screen. I had affairs with three of them, Linda, Rita, and Gene, each of whom ended up tragically…as did Peggy herself."

One hot August day in 1957, he read in *Variety* that the former starlet, Peggy Diggins, had died in a car crash in Gulfstream, Florida. She was only thirty-five years old.

"Poor Peggy. Her dreams of super stardom never came true. She was my first love under my new name of Kirk Douglas. Sinatra nailed it when he sang of a love that disappeared with the summer wind."

***

Kirk's stay at Greenwich House eventually ended. Money was tighter than the tightest corset, so he had to find a place to live that was dirt cheap.

Not only that, but during his senior year at the Academy, he also had to find some kind of job to support himself. One of the aging actors who worked as a janitor at the Academy suggested he might become a male hustler, as he knew "many fine gentlemen who'd be interested and were willing to pay well. After all, Archibald Leach—later Cary Grant—got his start in New York that way," the janitor claimed.

"Sounds intriguing," Kirk said. "But I don't think I'm cut out for that."

Briefly, when he was near starvation, "practically existing on a quarter a day," he thought he might become some sort of gigolo. In a 1966 interview with *Redbook,* he admitted "I used to wear my shirt open showing off my manly physique when I prowled the streets of New York. I've always been a bit of an exhibitionist. In most of my movies, even though I'm getting older, I try to work in a striptease. One time, an older woman stopped me on Broadway and 42nd Street and told me I had great tits. I thought that was something a man told a woman."

"Back then, and for only a month or so, I considered becoming a poet instead of an actor. I wrote a poem a day until I had about thirty-five of them. Then I sat up one night reading them out loud. They were shit. They weren't even mediocre. I decided I'd better stick to acting. I was obviously no male version of Emily Dickinson."

At the Academy, he'd made a good friend in a young man named Bill Van Sleet. "He was a male model and was also the handsomest boy at the Academy, always perfectly dressed and well mannered. He told Kirk that in addition to periodic modeling jobs, and to support his sister in Greenwich Village, he worked as a waiter at Schrafft's, a restaurant at Broadway and 86th Street.

He said that two jobs for waiters had opened up, since a couple of male staff members had quit, deciding to take a Greyhound bus to Miami to start life anew with each other.

That afternoon, Van Sleet accompanied Kirk uptown to meet the restaurant's manager. "I must have made a good impression, because he hired me on the spot. I was to report to work the following day."

Schrafft's was a chain of moderately priced New York City restaurants that depended on "ladies who lunch" for much of their patronage. It also sold branded candy and ice cream, which made up a lot of its trade. Kirk called it "a creamed cauliflower and fried eggplant kind of place."

"I flirted with many of the overweight, late middle-aged women, for which I was tipped generously. How often do they find a good-looking kid, a devil like me, who'll flirt with them? Most of them hadn't received any male attention in more than thirty years."

With his first tip money, he rented a dingy little cubby hole on the Upper West Side for three dollars a week. It didn't have a window, and there was a foul-smelling toilet in the hallway. The communal showers were in the basement. "The other tenants who lived on my floor, a motley crew, wouldn't be receiving invitations to the Queen's garden party at Buckingham Palace."

At Schrafft's, he shared his waiter station with another aspirant actor, John

Schrafft's—one of a chain of restaurants that used to have 50 branches in New York City alone.

Two future stars, Kirk Douglas and John Forsythe (above), worked the same waiter station at Schrafft's, flirting with pudgy, middle-aged "ladies who lunch."

"These over-the-hill broads discovered how devastatingly handsome John and I were before Hollywood did."

Forsythe. "Some of the lady patrons considered John better looking than me, but I doubted that. I mean, he was okay, but didn't have my spark. He told me that his career choice was a toss-up between wanting to be a sports writer or an actor. I told him, 'Better stick to the sports page.'"

Years later in Hollywood, he and Kirk met at a party and laughed at their former gig at Schrafft's. By then, Forsythe had become a household name, thanks to his starring role in the hit TV series, *Dynasty* (1981-89).

"Bill (Van Sleet) and I always had plenty to eat at Shrafft's," Kirk said. "Many of the ladies who lunched there were dieting, and some of them ordered sandwiches which were cut in half. Often, they ate only half of the sandwich. Bill and I used to gobble down the other half on the way back to the kitchen."

Kirk later admitted, "I had my suspicions about Bill. He was dating this girl, but had never kissed her, or so he claimed. She was English, her parents in Bermuda."

[Ironically, at the time, Van Sleet was dating Diana Dill, who would become the first Mrs. Kirk Douglas.]

Van Sleet liked to hang out with Kirk after work. "We'd sit together and have a beer, and I couldn't help but notice that he'd gaze lovingly into my eyes. In spite of that girlfriend, I suspected he wanted to make it with me. I liked him, but I didn't think I had to put out because he got me that waiter's job."

Kirk told Van Sleet that he was having a hard time saving up enough money to buy some clothing for the winter. He needed a sweater, a suit, and an overcoat—"some underwear would also be nice."

His friend suggested that he join him in a modeling assignment, posing for a painting in the Greenwich Village studio of Peter Brooke, who was in his fifties. Brooke needed two handsome young men to pose nude for a Renaissance-style painting he was contemplating against a Tuscan background.

"Peter wants to depict us like a painted, doubled-up version of Michelangelo's *David*, standing side-by-side, gazing at each other while letting everything hang out."

"There's a problem," Kirk responded. "You may not know this, but I'm a Jew. That is, circumsized."

"No problem," Van Fleet said. "He can paint a foreskin on your prick, using mine for inspiration."

Kirk only reluctantly agreed, but the artist didn't exactly put him at ease. "Brooke reminded me of Franklin Pangborn in the movies. You remember him: That effete fussbudget—hands on his hips, a droopy puss, and a prissy look of disapproval."

"My bare-assed posing lasted an entire week, and it was embarrassing, with those two checking out my

jewels. Did I endure it for the sake of art? Like hell I did! I endured it for the seventy-five dollars I got at the end of the week—enough money to buy the second-hand clothes I needed at a thrift shop."

"What happened to Bill and me as those jaybirders in a Renaissance garden?" he asked. "That painting is probably hanging over the fireplace of some queen in Boston today."

***

Kirk's junior class at the Academy had been crowded, as it comprised about 175 young students, each with dreams of becoming a star on the stage or screen.

But by the beginning of his senior year, there had been a lot of elimination of students deemed to have no talent. Kirk emerged as one of only 78 hopefuls authorized to continue with their studies.

This time, as an upperclassman, he'd actually get to star in plays presented on the stage of the basement theater at Carnegie Hall. They'd each be directed by the formidable Charles Jehlinger, already a terrorizing legend among the city's drama students.

Gray-haired and rather withered-looking, Jehlinger was half deaf, and would permit no fakery on stage. He'd been the head drama coach at the Academy since 1923, and had taught acting, early in their respective careers, to Spencer Tracy, Katharine Hepburn, Hume Cronyn, Rosalind Russell, and Edward G. Robinson. In addition to Kirk, Jehlinger would move on to teach future generations of stars who included Grace Kelly, Jennifer Jones, Jason Robards, Anne Bancroft, and Robert Redford.

He was known for his quotes, which included "Don't think of acting: think of living."

"Life is the only true school of acting," he would say, and, "Human impulse is the only thing that counts—not stage directions."

"I was immediately intimidated by him when he turned those piercing eyes on me," Kirk said. "He stared back at the world through the thickest glasses known to mankind, but he seemed to miss nothing. Behind his back I called him 'Jelly.'"

The play in which he'd cast Kirk was called *Bachelor Barn* (aka *Housemaster*). First produced in London in 1936, it depicted the conflict at an English boarding school between a wise housemaster

Charles Jehlinger was the great dictator-director, labeling Kirk "a cheap stock actor."

and a puritanical younger headmaster.

Kirk played the lead, that of the older, more seasoned housemaster, his role inspired by Robert Donat's performance in *Goodbye, Mr. Chips. [Donat had won an Oscar for it in 1939, beating out Clark Gable for his portrayal of Rhett Butler in* Gone With the Wind.*]*

After endless rehearsals, Kirk was ready for the preview, a performance crafted specifically for Jehlinger's review. Nervous, he made his long-awaited entrance from the wings. But within a few seconds of his opening, the coach roared, 'GO BACK AND COME OUT AGAIN!'"

Kirk was ordered to stop and then to begin his opening lines again a total of seventeen times. None of his entrances pleased the master. Finally, with something akin to desperation, Jehlinger rushed down from the audience and onto the stage and bitterly lectured Kirk.

"His attack was vicious. He tried to tear me to shreds, not leaving any flesh on my bones. He told me I'd never make it as an actor, that I was wasting not only his time, but the time of everybody else in the cast. I was devastated."

Then he cancelled the rest of the preview.

"Embarrassed, I could not face my fellow actors," Kirk said. "I felt I had let them down. I knew then that I'd have to consider a new profession."

As he wandered dazed and shattered backstage, he spotted a beautiful young woman sitting on a trunk and sobbing.

"What in hell's the matter with you?" he asked. "I should be the one crying my eyes out."

"I'm crying for YOU!" she answered. "That god damn son of a bitch, that mean bastard. What gives him the right to treat you like that?"

He was immediately drawn to her and warmed by her sympathy. It was over apple pie and milk an hour or two later that he came to realize that she was Diana Dill—the would-be actress from the prominent Bermudian family who was dating his friend, Bill Van Sleet.

After leaving the Carnegie Coffee Shop, they went for a walk together in Central Park, where he cried openly. "I poured out my frustrations and all the sacrifices I'd made trying to become an actor."

The couple spent the rest of the day together. "Diana instilled in me that I could not let one attack on my acting destroy me. I had to go back and work even harder and face Jehlinger again. This time, I had to get into the character from the inside out."

"I faced Jelly again, and he seemed surprised. He didn't think I had the nerve to come back onstage again."

"'Perhaps you have the guts to be an actor after all,'" he told me. "For three days, he tore into me and my performance—and I took it, almost challenging him to blast all his fire and fury on me," Kirk said. "Of course, I lost my patience a few times. Once, I picked up a chair and almost threw it at him. But finally, I got through the play with not one damn interruption from Jelly Fart."

Right before graduation, Jehlinger told Kirk, "As an actor, you're crude but effective. You might even become an actor. A star? I doubt it. You're still young and inexperienced, with a lot of living to do. When you experience more of life, with all its heartbreak, humiliation, and pain, maybe you'll be seasoned enough to convey all those emotions on stage."

"I survived Jelly, and I survived the Academy, too. Years later in Hollywood, I met Edward G. Robinson, his former student. He told me he'd received far worse treatment from Jelly than I got."

"I have only one regret," Robinson said, "and that is that I didn't kill the son of a bitch. But I heard that he died in 1952. You're not supposed to speak ill of the dead. He's dead. Good!"

***

Kirk began to date Diana Dill on a very casual basis, simultaneously seeing a lot of other young women too. Most of them were wannabe actresses enrolled at the Academy, although a few were waitresses at Schrafft's. Diana referred to this coven of women circling around Kirk as "a mob."

He was hardly her steady date, as she was seeing two other boyfriends. Most of her interest centered on a man enrolled as a student at Yale, Dick Van Middlesworth from New Brunswick, New Jersey. Her other beau was Bill Van Sleet, Kirk's model friend from Schrafft's. She called them "The Two Vans."

Kirk became very jealous that Diana was seeing more of Van Sleet than him. One night he tried to break up her romance. "Don't you know that Bill is queer?" he asked.

"Just because he doesn't try to rape me when he takes me back to the door of the Three Arts Club where I'm living doesn't mean he's a homosexual."

Kirk is seen here having a drink with his future wife, Diana Dill. It was a case of opposites attracting. He was a "Ragman's Son," she the daughter of a prominent family in Bermuda.

In time, however, she would realize that Kirk was right about Van Sleet.

Since Kirk could not afford to take Diana to the theater or to restaurants, most of his outings with her were spent talking and walking, mostly through Central Park. He frequently spoke of his poverty as a child and his parents, both of them illiterate immigrants from Tsarist Russia.

She described her life in Bermuda, where her father was Attorney General. Her sister, Ruth, had married John Seward Johnson I, the heir to the Johnson & Johnson fortune. Kirk's nickname for her was "Miss-Everything-Is-Lovely Dill."

"She was the first aristocrat I'd ever known, I followed her around just to hear her talk."

Diana admitted to having a strong physical attraction to Kirk, but she prevented him from "going all the way. Night after night, he was persistent as hell, but I held him off."

She might have been concealing a fierce internal debate, but the night she decided to lose her virginity she turned to another virgin, Dick Van Middlesworth instead of Kirk. As the setting for her seduction, Van Middlesworth rented a room for $15 at the Lincoln Hotel.

"We were both virgins, and he was unskilled, but filled with an intense enthusiasm that knew no bounds." As she later recalled the experience, "It was damn painful."

Sometimes, but not often, Kirk and Diana discussed the war in Europe, wondering if England alone could stave off the Nazi onslaught after the fall of France in 1940. But the war seemed far away, and both of them had confidence that President Franklin D. Roosevelt would keep them out of foreign wars.

Kirk was still working as a waiter at Schrafft's, where he'd seen changes in the clientele since the war began in Europe. "Many wealthy European Jews became our customers. Often the women would arrive in mink coats and diamonds. Obviously, the richest of them had fled, but I wondered about the poor Jews who could not escape. What would happen to them?"

Several Broadway and Hollywood

Diana Dill admitted to having an affair with Errol Flynn—"He called me Dill Pickle"—before marrying Kirk.

"During our marriage, my husband seduced a string of love goddesses but managed to have two sons with me."

agents attended the Academy's plays in the basement theater at Carnegie Hall, looking for a potential star of tomorrow. Six agents wanted to sign the handsome, charismatic Bill Van Sleet. As one of them told Kirk, "Bill is movie star material. Women will swoon when they see him on the screen. As for you, I'm not so sure, perhaps summer stock for $25 a week."

As it turned out, the agents were wrong, as Van Sleet never appeared on Broadway or in a Hollywood film.

The only aspirant actress from Kirk's class who was offered a Hollywood contract was Diana herself. Kirk begged her to stay in New York and try for a break on Broadway, but "she was Hollywood bound with dreams of fame and fortune dancing in her head. I'd gone through this same routine with Peggy Diggins."

On her final night in New York, Diana paid for that same room at the Lincoln where she'd lost her virginity. This time, she surrendered to Kirk. "He was a delight. Sex with him wasn't painful at all...in fact, very enjoyable."

The next morning, he took her to Grand Central, where she boarded the Twentieth Century to Chicago where she would switch to the Super Chief, which would haul her the rest of the way to Los Angeles.

Kissing him goodbye on the platform, she promised, "We'll meet again."

Diana's departure did not mean that Kirk was to lead a lonely life in Manhattan. Months before, without her knowledge, he'd become secretly involved with a sixteen-year-old wannabe actress, the youngest enrolled at the Academy. Although he knew she was "jailbait," he was drawn to her and wanted to devote his spare time to her.

Born in New York, she'd been known there as Betty Joan Perske.

After her parents divorced, she changed her last name to Bacal with one "l," using the Romanian name of her mother. Later, as an usherette at the St. James Theater, and with modeling gigs on the side, she billed herself as Betty Bacall, adding that extra "l" to her name.

As the years passed, she evolved into one of the legendary names of Golden Age Hollywood: Lauren Bacall.

***

In Carnegie Hall's basement, Bacall had seen Kirk appear in a trio of plays, including as a fop in a Restoration Comedy. He became "my hero, this marvelous actor—blonde hair, blue eyes, cleft chin. I developed a wild crush on this dashing figure."

On their first date, they ordered fried rice, the cheapest item on the menu at a Chinese eatery in Greenwich Village, where he was living in a tiny room on Third Street.

"Things got so bad at one point I got myself arrested so that I could spend a night in jail—at least get a free meal. I avoided the showers because of stories I'd heard about guys getting raped. "

"This was my first romance," she recalled, "and I didn't know what to do. Was I supposed to let him kiss me at the end of the night? He did kiss me on our first date. Firm but not passionate. He wanted to date me again."

"Since neither of us could afford a restaurant, we often ate with my grandmother. She welcomed this nice Jewish boy who adored her cooking, even going for third helpings."

Bacall had such a crush on Kirk that she'd come into Schrafft's and nurse a cup of coffee for an hour, just looking at him. On most days, she couldn't afford to eat there. On occasion, he'd discreetly slip her a sandwich to conceal in her purse to eat later.

She mocked his long overcoat which virtually dragged the ground. Later, she persuaded her uncle to give him a better and shorter one that he no longer used.

Known to Kirk at the time, she was also dating Burgess Meredith, who had pursued Kirk's previous girlfriend, Peggy Diggins.

KIRK DOUGLAS & LOVELY LAUREN
THE FIRES OF YESTERYEAR

[The debate continues in Hollywood about which of her suitors took Lauren Bacall's virginity. There are three claimants: Kirk himself, Meredith, and Humphrey Bogart, Bacall's first husband.

Mart Martin, in his book on Hollywood seductions, in his sections on the "First Sexual Experience of the Stars," phrased it delicately:

Bacall "probably lost her virginity to her first husband Bogart, since she'd said, 'nice Jewish girls stayed virgins until they were married.' If she weren't a nice Jewish girl, then maybe first love Kirk Douglas was the lucky recipient."

In his memoirs, Kirk himself wrote, "How did I thank Betty for her generosity, the overcoat, the big meals? On a warm spring evening on a rooftop in Greenwich Village, I tried to seduce her unsuccessfully."

But that was not what he relayed to his male friends: "I was gentle with her, very loving. Before the morning came, I told her in a year or two I was going to marry her. At least I've found the one woman I wanted to spend the rest of my life with. Of course, she had to age two or three years."

Eventually, Bacall met Diana Dill at the Academy, and the two became friends. When Bacall stayed over one night at Diana's apartment, she discovered an 8" x 10" glossy portrait of Kirk on the end table of her sofa. During the course of the evening, Diana learned—while concealing her own involvement with him—that Bacall was dating Kirk. The next morning over breakfast, Diana gave Bacall some advice. She warned the teenager "Whatever you do, never marry an actor. They are not to be trusted, most unreliable. You'll end up getting hurt."

As a movie star, Bacall did not heed Diana's advice, going on to marry two actors: Humphrey Bogart and Jason Robards.

Diana didn't take her own advice either, and eventually wed Kirk Douglas herself.

At a Hollywood party, years after that, Bacall was dishing the dirt with Judy Garland and Lucille Ball. Each was telling the other "who was the first."

Ball named Johnny DeVita, a local hoodlum in Jamestown, New York, when she was fourteen. Garland cited Spencer Tracy, and Bacall put the blame on Kirk Douglas.

Bacall said it took place on the rooftop of a building in Greenwich Village, disputing Kirk's claim.

Howard Hawks, who directed Bacall in her first film, To Have and Have Not (1944) claimed that Bacall had cited Kirk as her "deflowerer."

Burgess Meredith left open the possibility that he was the one who "plucked the rose off the vine—that's 'plucked,' dear heart."

In a memoir, published in 1994, Meredith wrote: "God knows I was no dashing swain, but in a kind of mongrel way, I chased the foxes. My intention is to give a backward look at girls I adored like Betty Bacall before she met Bogie, and also—No! Enough is never enough, but it is all there is to say at the moment. Most of them, including Betty, are still alive as I write this."]

***

After graduation from the Academy, Kirk haunted the New York offices of Broadway talent agencies. Many were quite seedy-looking, with upholsteries long past their expiration dates. He was also an avid reader of *Actor's Cue,* which listed which upcoming plays were being cast.

At every office, he got nothing but rejections. "A couple of agents wanted to audition me all right, and one asked me to strip so that he could better see what parts I might be suited for. But I wasn't interested in that kind of audition."

"I learned early in life that an aspirant actor has to live with rejection. Even big movie stars get rejected time and again. Many roles I wanted to sink my teeth into went to Burt Lancaster, Charlton Heston, Richard Widmark—and most definitely, Robert Mitchum. Those guys just ripped the parts from my jaws."

Confronted with no work on Broadway, he signed for summer stock at the Nuangola Playhouse, which stood in a forest in the Poconos, near Scranton, Pennsylvania.

Although beginning as a stagehand, he was persistent, demanding and getting small parts. Before the end of the season, he was cast as the lead in five different plays. "They were coming at me so fast, with so much dialogue to learn, that I got confused about which lines belonged to which plays."

His meatiest role was in a play called *Broadway,* the 1926 work of the notoriously hated producer Jed Harris and playwright George Abbott. In 1929, Universal adapted it into its first talking picture.

"I liked the play and my role in it because I could use street slang in a hard-boiled realistic background," Kirk said. "I would later remember the play when I made another realistic New York drama, *Detective Story* (1951), one of my most famous movies."

By late September of that year, he was back at Schrafft's, waiting tables and gobbling down those half-eaten sandwiches. "For fifteen cents, at breakfast, I had a glass of OJ and a doughnut at Nedick's. On many occasions, I splurged on a coke at Walgreen's on Broadway at 44th Street, where out-of-work actors hung out—and there were plenty of those guys like me."

One day, he read that Katharine Cornell—hailed as the greatest stage actress on Broadway—in collaboration with her husband, Guthrie McClintic, were producing *Spring Again*, set for a Broadway opening in November 1941 at the Booth Theatre. He still remembered Cornell's magnificent performance in *The Barrett's of Wimpole Street*, which he'd seen when it had toured through New York State.

He went to Cornell's office at Radio City, where he was told by her assistant, Stanley Gilkey, to go to the Booth Theatre, where auditions were being held that very day.

With dreams that Cornell might pluck him out of the lineup as her new leading man, he arrived with hope but also with the fear of rejection. He immediately learned that although her husband, McClintic, would be directing it, Cornell would not be starring or even appearing in it.

That afternoon, McClintic was nowhere to be seen, having delegated the audition to his assistants. Kirk waited two hours before being called by the stage manager, who gave him lines associated with the character he might be playing: That of a telegram boy from Western Union. He was to sing his lines to the tune of "Yankee Doodle."

To his surprise, he got the part.

The next day, he met the two stars of the upcoming production, Grace George and C. Aubrey Smith. George was married to the famous theatrical producer, William Brady, who had been instrumental in launching the career of Humphrey Bogart.

A darling of theatrical critics, Miss George had gone from one triumph to another. They had included George Bernard Shaw's *Major Barbara, The School for Scandal,* and *Kind Lady.* "All I could do for her," Kirk later said ruefully, "was bring her a glass of coke before the curtain went up. She told me the drink made her 'high.'"

Born in 1863, C. Aubrey Smith was a distinguished English actor and—during his youth—a famous cricketer. He'd appeared in such films as *The Prisoner of Zenda* (1937) and had recently completed a secondary role in Alfred Hitchcock's *Rebecca* (1941) a film that had starred Laurence Olivier and Joan Fontaine.

When Kirk finally met McClintic, the director was most impressed with him. "He

Katharine Cornell in a TV production of *The Barretts of Wimpole Street* in 1956.

even made me his assistant stage manager and gave me more money," Kirk said. "He wanted me by his side all the time. I brought him his coffee. I lit his cigarettes. And I shared his daily lunch of a chocolate milkshake for him and one for me, too."

"Even though I was only a bit player, he gave me a private dressing room. He had my messenger boy outfit tailor made, and saw that it fitted real tight, feeling around my legs and butt a little too closely for comfort."

Kirk feared that McClintic was a homosexual and talked it over one afternoon with Smith. "Of course he is, and his wife, Miss Cornell, is a lesbian, engaged at the moment in a torrid affair with Tallulah Bankhead. You could advance your career by lying on McClintic's casting couch. I'm an old relic today, but when I was a young man, a studly cricketer, I was highly desired by homosexuals. I took advantage and launched myself in the English theater, which, as you know, is filled with stately homos such as Laurence Olivier and John Gielgud, among countless others."

"I'm not sure I'm cut out for the casting couch," Kirk protested.

"That's a choice every young man has to make for himself," Smith said. "Guthrie and Katharine have the ideal working relationship: a Lavender Marriage."

In his memoirs, in an abbreviated way, Kirk did at least refer to McClintic's homosexual interest in him. Alone with the director at his private home, he claimed that McClintic's "hands started to wander. Frightened, I bolted for the door."

Cast members during the run of *Spring Again* just assumed that Kirk was McClintic's "boy." It was common gossip. "I, for one, urged Kirk to give Guthrie what he wanted," Smith said. "I didn't see it as any great sacrifice on his part."

The scenic designer, Donald Oenslager, said, "It was obvious to all of us that Guthrie had the hots for young Kirk. When they went on the road with our play, Guthrie insisted that Kirk share his hotel rooms, and so he did in Massachusetts and Connecticut. Surely, something must have happened on those cold nights in New England. No one can be sure what happened, and Kirk, of course, to maintain his macho image, had to deny it."

In a "lavender marriage," Katharine Cornell and Guthrie McClintic in the library of their home at 23 Beekman Place, NYC, in 1940, about the time Kirk was working with them. An invitation to their home here was one of the most prized invitations in the NYC arts world at the time.

That Thanksgiving, shortly after the play opened, Kirk received a coveted invitation from Cornell to a lavish dinner at her elegant home at 23 Beekman Place. Its garden terrace opened onto a view of the East River. Photos of Cornell in her greatest roles lined the walls of a house filled with theatrical memorabilia.

She greeted Kirk and was overheard thanking him "for being so nice and helpful to my husband. He just adores you, talks about you all the time, and thinks you'll become one of the truly big stars on the stage, perhaps even having a Hollywood career."

The guest of honor that night was the formidable Tallulah Bankhead, the Southern belle from Alabama, who at the time was having a torrid affair with Cornell. A bisexual, her affairs were the most diverse of any stage or film actress. In Hollywood, they had ranged from screen Tarzan Johnny Weissmuller to "that divine Gary Cooper." In England, she'd seduced Sir Winston Churchill, and back on Broadway, John Barrymore. "I guess John and I had an affair, *dah-ling,*" she often said. "But we were so drunk it's hard to remember."

Although ferociously defending her self-image as a Southern lady, she was not averse to having affairs with African American entertainers, including singer Billie Holiday. If Churchill was an unusual conquest, so was Tallulah's affair with Hattie McDaniel, who had played Mammy in *Gone With the Wind.* According to Tallulah, "I lost the role of Scarlett O'Hara, but Mammy comforted me."

Although Kirk gave Tallulah almost no mention in his memoirs, she was far more gossipy, at least in private and after some drinks:

While she was touring in *Crazy October* in 1958, she described to its author, James Leo Herlihy, her version of what happened that evening with Kirk in the home of Katharine Cornell:

"*Dah-ling,* I was full of fish eggs (caviar) that dear Kit [i.e., *Katharine*] served, and tanked up on champagne. I followed this dashing boy, Kirk Douglas, into the bathroom. Since it was Thanksgiving, I fellated him."

As Herlihy related later, "Tallu, she admitted herself, was a grand Southern lady. She always said that she never let the

Tallulah Bankhead in *Lifeboat* (1944), by far her most famous movie. Famous, she was, for being witty, irreverent, outrageous, and fascinating..

truth get in the way of a good yarn."

"To my knowledge," Herlihy continued, "Kirk never admitted he had sex with either McClintic or Tallu. But it's been pretty well documented that she seduced Marlon Brando, James Dean, and Rock Hudson. And if she could seduce those gay or bi- guys, I don't see why she couldn't have conquered Kirk."

"If given half the chance," Herlihy continued, "I'd have gone after Kirk myself. As a consolation prize, I got Paul Newman, who wanted to play the Joe Buck character in my novel, *Midnight Cowboy*. Let's face it: Those Jewish guys, Douglas and Newman, are two of the sexiest men in films."

***

The December 7, 1941 Japanese attack on the U.S. Naval Fleet at Pearl Harbor sent shock waves through Kirk and millions of other Americans. Up to then, he hadn't given the war in Europe too much consideration, except for the horrifying reports reaching America's shores about the attempts by Hitler and Himmler to exterminate European Jews.

Now, war had come to America. There was a sudden fear of invasion, especially along its Pacific coasts. In the general confusion and consternation, many Californians began hastily evacuating their beach homes.

Kirk felt it was his patriotic duty to sign up for military service, preferably as a pilot in the U.S. Air Force. He'd have to put his acting career, such as it was, on hold.

At a recruiting station in Manhattan, as part of his application for entry into the Air Force, he was subjected to a battery of tests, both physical and psychological. He was twenty-five years old and was told by a recruiting officer, "You're a bit too old. We like to train much younger pilots."

He was shocked to learn that he'd flunked the psychological evaluation. "You seem too methodical. The Air Force needs young pilots who can make split-second decisions. Their own life, and those of fellow airmen, could depend on their ability to make accurate but quick decisions. You seem to like to mull things over."

After he was rejected, as he had been for roles on the stage, he turned to the recruiting officer and said, "You're losing a good man. Who knows? I might have become the first pilot to bomb Tokyo."

***

Feeling rejected and disappointed, Kirk turned his attention once again to making it as a stage actor. He learned that McClintic was casting a serious drama, Anton Chekhov's *The Three Sisters* with Katharine Cornell as the lead. She would be backed up by two distinguished actresses, Ruth Gordon and Judith Anderson. The minor roles were still being cast.

Ever since Kirk had finally turned down McClintic's sexual overtures, there had been tension between them. There were two roles for Russian soldiers, and Kirk—who reminded McClintic that he had Russian blood flowing through his veins—wanted to be cast as one of them.

McClintic seemed more distant from him than ever, but he eventually agreed to let Kirk play one of the soldiers.

The leading roles for three other male characters had already been cast with actors Alexander Knox, Dennis King, and Edmund Gwenn.

The plot revolved around the dismal story of the frustration and futility engulfing upperclass Russians before the revolution.

Kirk felt there was a lot he could learn about acting by watching this formidable array of talent during their rehearsals. He set about to ingratiate himself with all six of the leads.

Born in South Australia of English parents, Anderson was already a renowned stage star, and had been nominated for a Best Supporting Actress Oscar for her performance in *Rebecca* (1941).

Ruth Gordon was being courted at the time by the playwright, Garson Kanin, and Kirk admired her talent, especially her nasal voice and distinct personality. "She was very standoffish, with no time for a little unknown like me."

A Canadian, Alexander Knox had just appeared with great success in the Broadway production of *The Sea Wolf* (1941) and was just months away from filming his best-known movie, *Wilson* (1944).

An English actor, Dennis King, not only performed Shakespeare, but also starred in musicals, introducing such famous songs as "Rose-Marie" and "Indian Love Call."

Since Kirk had stopped being "cooperative," McClintic suddenly took the role of the more prominent Russian soldier from Kirk and awarded it to a more accommodating young man, whom Kirk found "effeminate."

Instead, Kirk was assigned the thankless role of a lesser soldier carrying a samovar and following veteran actor Gwenn across the stage. The Londoner is best remembered today for his iconic role of Kris Kringle in *Miracle on 34th Street* (1947). Gwenn cautioned him, "Just follow me onto the stage. No need to act like Julius Caesar invading Gaul."

Cornell, too, made it clear that she thought Kirk was overplaying the scene, telling him, "As a Russian peasant soldier, you're supposed to place the samovar on a table and leave. The way you're entering will make the audience feel you have something to say, which you do not."

"I was humiliated, but followed her advice until that day I, too, would have my shining hour on the stage."

Opening on December 21, 1942, at the Ethel Barrymore Theater, *The Three Sisters* ran for 122 performances.

"At the end, I decided to take off that peasant makeup and put my stage uniform into mothballs. I was going to join the military and put on a real uniform and go kill some Nazis or perhaps a few Japs. If the Air Force wouldn't take me, there was always the Navy."

The Japanese bombing of Pearl Harbor was a day that will live in infamy. For Kirk and the rest of the world, too, everything changed overnight.

CHAPTER THREE

ANCHORS AWEIGH!

KIRK JOINS THE NAVY

DYSFUNCTIONALLY PURSUING JAPANESE SUBMARINES IN THE PACIFIC

AS A BUNKMATE READS A COPY OF *LIFE* MAGAZINE.
KIRK LOOKS AT ITS COVER AND VOWS

"THAT'S THE GAL I'M GONNA MARRY"

AT WAR'S END, MAE WEST SAYS NO
BUT BROADWAY, ITS BABES, AND SOME OF ITS DIRECTORS SAY YES

On the left is Kirk as "Ensign Douglas" in 1943.

On the right much older, he appears as the movie version of the commander of the super high-tech aircraft carrier, *Nimitz*, in this sci-fi World War II film *The Final Countdown* (1980).

In the actual conflict, Kirk was made a Communication Officer in anti-submarine warfare. "War is such a stupid waste of time.Young people on a ship looking for other young people...and trying to blow them up."

At the Naval Recruiting Station in Manhattan, and in spite of his earlier rejection by the Air Force, Kirk once again tried to enlist for military service. After a battery of tests, both psychological and physical, he was given the bad news:

A doctor told him, "Your eyesight is borderline. According to your test results, you wouldn't be able to spot a Jap ship until it was about to collide with your vessel."

Kirk didn't give up. With a fierce determination, he began a series of eye exercises based on a book called *Sight Without Glasses*. Weeks later, he returned to the recruiting station, and this time he passed the eye exam—"but just barely," in the words of the examiner.

Two weeks later, he was crowded onto a train with dozens of other wannabe sailors, heading for South Bend, Indiana. "I hoped to become Ensign Douglas. I liked the sound of that and was proud to be serving my country in these times of peril."

South Bend, the cultural and economic hub of Northern Indiana, was the home of the University of Notre Dame. It was also known as the former manufacturing site of the long-gone Studebaker.

There, Kirk was enrolled in the U.S. Reserve Midshipman's School of Notre Dame, which flourished during World War II when the Navy took over parts of Notre Dame University as the number of civilians enrolled dwindled.

"We underwent one test after another, and I found them as hard as hell," Kirk said. "We were taught gunnery, seamanship, navigation…stuff like that. I found aircraft identification the hardest. We were told to identify a plane in only one-tenth of a second after its image was flashed on a screen."

"My fellow recruits—at least some of them—cheated on the exams. Someone was always slipping them the questions before the exams."

"I roomed with five other guys in cramped bunk beds. Most nights, they talked about pussy, although I suspected that two of my bunkmates had never seen one."

"At the end of the course, I became a communication director specializing in anti-submarine warfare. Nazi U-boats were a great menace, blowing up Allied vessels sailing to war-torn Britain with much-needed food and supplies. Our job was to find, track, and damage, or hopefully destroy, enemy submarines," Kirk said.

"To me, the whole concept of war was stupid. Old white men in London, Washington, Berlin, and Tokyo sent young men to die on land, sea, and air. These old guys were destroying the hope of tomorrow with their death machines. I didn't plan to become one of the casualties."

"After four months of study at South Bend, we were Midshipmen. Athletics kept us in shape and those infantry drills. We were given a carefully prescribed military wardrobe including what was called 'an athletic supporter'—read that as 'a jockstrap.'"

***

When Kirk read that Katharine Cornell was in Chicago performing in the road show version of *The Three Sisters,* he rode aboard an overcrowded wartime train during a weekend pass. He found a cheap hotel for only five dollars a night, although it had cost only a dollar before the outbreak of the war. Space was at a premium in Chicago, whose population had ballooned since the attack on Pearl Harbor.

After showering and getting dressed in his starched uniform, he walked thirty blocks to the Ambassador East Hotel, where he was told that Cornell was in residence. This landmark stood on Chicago's Gold Coast, having opened in 1926 as a companion to its sister, the Ambassador, across the street. The Pump Room had opened in 1938 and was a favorite place for drinking and dining when celebrities invaded Chicago.

Kirk headed for that "watering hole," figuring he could buy one drink and nurse it for an hour or two, perhaps getting to see Cornell make an entrance.

Proud to make his own entrance in his new uniform, he paraded into the room only to see Cornell and her party sitting at the first table. Spotting him, her eyes met his at the dawn of recognition. "Kirk Douglas!" she called to him. "Come and join us

The stage and its theatrics were radically different when Kirk was striving to join the ranks of its professional actors. This edition of LIFE magazine from November 19, 1951 displays a breathlessness and glamour that's gone with the wind. Each of the grandest stage divas of its era appear here, left to right, Lynn Fontanne, Katharine Cornell (Kirk's mentor and sometimes ally), and Helen Hayes.

for a drink!" Then she motioned for her waiter to bring a chair and to place it beside her, and beckoned Kirk to sit down.

After hearing about his having joined the Navy and after sharing a memory or two about his appearance in *The Three Sisters* production on Broadway, she discussed her own work in the war effort.

She had spearheaded fund-raising drives for the Red Cross. But her proudest achievement was helping to launch the Stage Door Canteen for servicemen in New York, most of whom were passing through. It was staffed in part by Broadway stars such as Katharine Hepburn and by Hollywood movie stars during their temporary visits to Manhattan.

Katharine Cornell, *grande dame* of the American Theater.

"Kit and I shared something in common," Kirk said. "We both liked beautiful women."

"Our boys in service get free food and drink and a chance to meet or dance with stars like Marlene Dietrich. Bette Davis and John Garfield have opened the Hollywood Canteen. One night, Helen Hayes and I washed dishes, and on another occasion, Lynn Fontanne and I served doughnuts and poured coffee for our men in uniform. I introduced you to Tallulah at my home, and she's a regular, except she constantly violates our rules about not taking some of the boys back home with her. I want to help in any way I can, and I see you do too by putting your acting career on hold while you serve in the Navy."

After about fifteen minutes, she dismissed him and wished him good luck. He had hoped that she'd invite him to dinner, since he was ravenously hungry, but she chose not to.

Before leaving, he asked her about her next project. "I might do *Antony & Cleopatra* on Broadway, but I'm not sure. At my country place, I'm becoming a farmer, with a cow, a horse, and some chickens—perhaps I'll get a couple of pigs. But that's only a diversion. The theater is in my blood, and I can't resist the call of 'Curtain going up!'"

After his reunion with the First Lady of the American Theater, Kirk walked back to his seedy hotel, stopping off for a hot dog. Along the way, he received an occasional proposition from hookers and homosexuals.

As he remembered it, he thought to himself, "I forgot to ask Miss Cornell if her husband was still in love with me."

64

***

Two weeks after returning to his base, Kirk noticed his bunkmate reading the current edition of *Life* magazine. He was astonished to see Diana Dill on the cover dressed in a checkered blouse and holding a parasol, looking like a fresh-face, rosy-cheeked country maiden.

"My God, I've dated that girl," Kirk announced in a loud voice.

"Sure you did," his bunkmate said. Another sailor on a nearby cot chimed in, "Yeah, and I've fathered a kid with her."

"Cut it out," Kirk protested. "That's the gal I'm gonna marry!"

Actually, he had not seen her in two years, ever since she left for Hollywood. That night, he wrote her a letter, asserting how much he'd missed her and expressing how the nights away from her filled him with loneliness. Since he didn't know her address in Hollywood, he sent it to *Life* magazine in New York, hoping that someone on the staff there would forward it to her.

A secretary at *Life* eventually sent the letter on to the John Robert Powers Agency, a Manhattan-based modeling agency, which had employed Diana after her failed attempt in Hollywood to become a movie star.

Diana Dill on cover of LIFE's wartime edition of May 3, 1943, presumably when everyone was dreaming of better days to come.

Naval Kirk, onboard his ship, brandishing a rifle with a movie-star smile.

[TIME FOR TRIVIA: *Established in 1923, the Powers Modeling Agency got involved in controversy after falsely claiming that John Wayne, Lucille Ball, and Marilyn Monroe had for a while done modeling gigs, as arranged by the agency. It had, however, once procured some modeling gigs for both Grace Kelly and Betty Ford, who eventually became First Lady.*

In 1943, the year Kirk wrote to her, the film version of a musical comedy, The Powers Girl, *starring Anne Shirley and Carole Landis, was about to be released.*]

Kirk's letter finally reached Diana, who answered it with a response she addressed to Kirk's lodgings in Indiana. "I'm modeling during the day, since my Hollywood career didn't pan out. Three nights a week, I empty bedpans at Bellevue, which attracts all the crazy lunatics in New York City. I'm anxious for our paths to cross again, as I have only the fondest memories of you."

[It would not be until 1999 before Kirk learned about Diana's experience in Hollywood. That was when she published a memoir, In the Wings. *In it, she described her affair with the dashing Errol Flynn, referring to him as "incredibly handsome, the most beautiful man I'd ever seen." In the same memoir, she also asserted that he had arranged an abortion for her.*

She had been set to play his younger sister in a Western, They Died with Their Boots On *(1941). This was the story of the flamboyant General George Armstrong Custer and his defeat by Indians at the Battle of Little Bighorn in the Montana Territory. At the last minute, the director, Raoul Walsh, wearing an eyepatch, cut her scene.*

She and Flynn became quite intimate, and he nicknamed her "Pickle" based on her last name, Dill. "Errol and I continued to make love in a hedonistic Eden, and I was becoming 'Californiated,'" she said.

But one night at the exclusive Chasen's restaurant, Flynn met a buxom blonde. Diana's last sighting of him was when he looked at her defiantly, burying his head in the blonde's bosom. Deeply offended, she fled from the restaurant.

With her career going nowhere, she flew back to New York to resume modeling. Trying to forget Flynn, she launched an affair with the super-rich Huntington Hartford, the A&P heir. "That man sold a lot of groceries," she said.]

In his letter to her, Kirk wrote, "As soon as I get another leave, I'm heading for Manhattan…and you!"

She wrote back, scribbling on a postcard, "I can't wait."

His leave came unexpectedly, and eagerly, he headed at once for Manhattan. After several attempts, he failed to reach Diana on the phone to alert her of his homecoming. As soon as he arrived at Grand Central Station, he put through another call to her without success, finally speaking to a secretary at her modeling agency. He was informed that Diana was visiting her family in Bermuda.

"The traitor!" he said, before slamming down the phone. For all Diana knew, he would soon be sailing off to war, perhaps dying in a deadly attack in some murky sea. Besides, he considered Bermuda as a dangerous location, lying out there somewhere in the Atlantic, vulnerable to an invasion by Nazi Germany.

After checking into the YMCA, he decided to follow the advice of Katharine Cornell and go to the Stage Door Canteen in the theater district. Operated by the American Theatre Wing, it offered servicemen like himself a night of dancing (maybe with a Broadway star), entertainment from a comedian or a big band, free food, and nonalcoholic drinks.

The Canteen was crowded with perhaps (his estimate) five hundred servicemen. He was stunned by the mixture of Allied nationals. In a 1943 article in *Theatre Arts,* the reporter claimed that on any given night, the Canteen was filled with British soldiers, airmen from the RAF, Chinese pilots, and "Negroes, Indians, Canadians, Australians, South Africans, Dutch soldiers, French sailors, and an occasional Russian."

He spotted Alfred Lunt, husband of Lynn Fontanne, carting off dirty dishes, and Gertrude Lawrence leading a conga line.

The Canadian American actor, Walter Pidgeon, approached him and introduced himself. "You don't need to tell me who you are, Mr. Pidgeon," Kirk said. "I saw you in *Mrs. Miniver* with Greer Garson." One of the smash hits of World War II, the 1942 film was a moving saga of how the British on their homefront maintained their spirit as the Nazis crept into their backyard.

When Pidgeon learned that Kirk was an actor, he invited him to come and stay with him. "I'll introduce you around," he said. "If you can act, you've surely got it made. You already look like a movie star."

They were interrupted by Katharine Hepburn, who had come over to greet Pidgeon. She didn't stay long, but told Kirk, "Be brave, be strong, keep your cleft chin up."

What happened later that night has long been the subject of speculation. Rumor has it that Pidgeon invited Kirk to spend the rest of his leave with him at his suite at the Walforf Astoria. Within two years, Pidgeon would be making *Week-End at the Waldorf* (1945) with Ginger Rogers and Lana Turner.

Kirk never mentioned that in his autobiography, and over the years, neither confirmed nor denied it. It would be years before Pidgeon would be "outed" as a homosexual. Revelations about his sex life were even published

Kirk could well have been (but wasn't) in this line-up of American military men during World War II waiting to get into New York's *Stage Door Canteen.*

The photo above was a scene from a movie of the same name released in 1943, and filled with cameos, walk-ons, speeches, and musical numbers from a wide array of stars, ranging from Katharine Hepburn to Helen Hayes, from Tallulah Bankhead to Harpo Marx.

in *The New York Times.*
Years later, when asked
about Kirk, Pidgeon had
a response: "He is such a
dear, dear chap, a charm-
ing young man who
lights up the screen in
any film in which he ap-
pears. I saw *Spartacus*
three times."

Kirk's days in Man-
hattan came to an end,
much to his regret, and he
had to return to Indiana.
Before that, he made the
obligatory trips upstate to
visit his father and
mother, still living in different towns. His father

Who's really checking into the Waldorf? In this photo from the iconic film, *Week-End at the Waldorf*, (left to right) Ginger Rogers, Walter Pidgeon, the Immortal Lana Turner, and Van Johnson.

Despite the heterosexual lust implied as one of the premises of the film, both of the male actors whose faces are visible in this publicity photo were gay,

was not at all proud to see him in his naval uniform, reminding him that he had fled Russia to avoid military service.

When, after a train ride, he arrived at his mother's house, she wept, telling him she had nightmares that whatever ship he'd be on would be attacked by Japanese submarines.

Soon after his return to the naval base in Indiana, he was informed that his unit would be shipping out to Miami for intensive training in anti-sub-marine warfare.

***

Even though World War II was raging, Miami struck Kirk as a play-ground, partly because of its large numbers of unattached young women.

During his first weekend pass, he hitched a southbound ride to Key West, convinced that he was living the good life. He wanted to continue onward to Havana, where he'd heard that "anything goes," but he didn't have time and feared wartime restrictions.

In the nation's southernmost city, he strolled along the main street, Duval, which was filled with sailors from the local naval base. He made Sloppy Joe's his hangout, since he'd heard it was the favorite of Ernest Hemingway.

As part of his hitchhiking trek back to Miami, he was picked up by a beautiful blonde driving a Cadillac. He briefly mentioned the pickup in his memoir, naming her as the recently divorced Gloria Travers, from Tacoma, Washington.

"She must have gotten a good settlement after her divorce," Kirk told another sailor, Jack Lloyd. "She took me to this elegant apartment in Miami and not only drained me, but was ready to roll the next morning, too."

"During my stay in Miami, I thought I had it made. For a while, at least, I forgot about Diana Dill. But in two weeks, I got a notice that I was to report for duty in New Orleans."

Faced with an upcoming two-week leave, he decided to dump Gloria. "I thought that within an hour of my departure, she'd bag another sailor. I phoned Diana in New York, and she wanted me to come up right away. Since I decided there was no future in being Gloria's kept boy, I returned to my home state."

**

In Manhattan, he retrieved Diana at the Barbizon Hotel for Women. "He was shorter than I had remembered him," she later wrote in her memoirs.

He was unaware that Diana had shuffled her social calendar to fit him in. Her most serious romance was with Norman Brooks, who had unrealistic dreams of becoming a poet. That affair was cooling and would end when he joined the U.S. Air Force.

At the time, Diana was also dating Richard Goddard, fifteen years her senior. "But he was a bit too humorless and stiff for me." Georges Gudefin, a dashing officer serving with the Free French, brought a dose of military glamour into her life, but he would soon be shipping off to North Africa. Somehow, she also managed to work in dates with two rival photographers, Sean O'Brien and Powell Brent.

Kirk immediately told her that for the remainder of his leave, he wanted to spend every day and night with her. He took her to Schrafft's for lunch, the same restaurant where he'd worked as a waiter. Several members of the staff remembered him, and the manager told him that he could have his old job back whenever he ended his tour of duty with the U.S. Navy.

After lunch, Diana and Kirk headed for Broadway, where he bought tickets to a frothy comedy, *Kiss and Tell*. Its star was a demure blonde, Joan Caulfield, who would be granted a film contract at Paramount to reprise her role on film.

There was a certain irony in Kirk's selection of that play. Following his discharge from the Navy, he took over the role in it that had previously been interpreted by Richard Widmark. *[Widmark would go on to a distinguished career in Hollywood, eventually co-starring in a movie with Kirk.]*

For dinner that night, Kirk had made reservations at the exclusive Penthouse Restaurant on Central Park South. Fearing he might not be able to afford it on an ensign's salary, Diana ordered the least expensive item on the menu.

After what he called "the best meal I've had in months," he grew serious and reached for her hand. "I want to let you in on a secret I've been carrying around. I plan to marry you."

"Aren't you rushing this just a bit?" she asked.

"A war's on. Everything is speeded up during a war. Let's tie the knot tomorrow."

"There's no need to be this impetuous," she answered. "If you want to rush into this just to get me to sleep with you, you can bed me any time you want, whether we're married or not."

"Sounds great, but I want to marry you, to stake my claim," he said.

As she confessed in her memoirs, "Sex that night was omnivorous. We couldn't stop fondling each other, yes, down there, too."

He would remember the next two weeks as "our pre-honeymoon. Nights were for love-making."

During the day, they went horseback riding. Although she was an experienced equestrienne, he got thrown from his saddle.

They also visited the Metropolitan Museum, rode the Staten Island Ferry, went ice skating, and strolled along Fifth Avenue. But mostly they went to the movies, seeing large-grossing box office hits of late 1942 and 1943: Betty Grable in *Coney Island;* James Cagney in *Johnny Come Lately;* and their alltime favorite, Humphrey Bogart and Ingrid Bergman in *Casablanca.*

Both of them feared that the war would separate them like it had the doomed lovers in *Casablanca.* "At least Bogie and Ingrid had Paris," he said. "Whatever happens, you and I will always have these past few days in New York."

On his final evening with her—"his wildest night of making love"— she woke up with him, sad and disappointed at his upcoming departure. As stated in her memoirs, they showered together, ate breakfast, and made love one final time before he packed.

They separated at Grand Central Station. He boarded a train for New Orleans, and she took one headed to Arizona for a modeling assignment.

***

When he reached New Orleans, Kirk, along with lots of other sailors, was hauled aboard a bus to the parish of Algiers, in the 15th Ward, lying on the west bank of the Mississippi.

Its association with the U.S. Navy dated from 1901, when a naval station opened here. It was hailed at the time as part of a grand scheme to make New Orleans a great naval port.

During World War II, Algiers became a repair yard for wounded ships and a training ground for "green" sailors. "Most of us had never even gotten into a rowboat before, but with the shortage of men, the military was having to take what it could get," Kirk said.

He missed Diana "something awful," and wrote her every day and spent most of his pay on phone calls to Arizona. Night after lonely night, he wandered the length of Newton Street, the heart of Algiers' black community and the site of seedy bars, Cajun restaurants, and jazz joints. "I ate a lot of gumbo."

His favorite hangout became the strangely named Greystone Voter's League, a bar known for its rhythm and blues. In time, it would become a venue for such fabled venues as B.B. King and Ray Charles.

After many a phone call and many a pleading letter, Diana finally agreed to marry Kirk. "I know you're a beautiful model, even appearing on the cover of *Life*. How about me casting you in a new role as a Navy wife who follows her man from port to port?"

Her family wanted her to postpone the marriage until after the war, at which time she might change her mind. "What made me finally agree to marry Kirk was that I missed my period," she later confessed.

To prepare for the arrival in New Orleans of his bride-to-be, Kirk rented an attic apartment in one of the landmark Pontalba Buildings.

[These red-brick buildings, standing on both sides of Jackson Square in New Orleans' French Quarter and lined with shops on their ground floors, dated from the 1840s. In his short story, Hidden Gardens, *novelist Truman Capote called them "the oldest, in some cases, most soberly elegant apartment houses in America."]*

In New Orleans, after another night of passion, Kirk introduced Diana to his best man (Frances Robinson) and a woman sculptor (Angela Gregory), who had agreed to be her maid of honor and the hostess at the reception that would follow the ceremony. A courtly Southern gentleman, Robinson had worked in the office of Katharine Cornell and Guthrie McClintic, where he met Kirk. Robinson arranged the music for Kirk's wedding. Years later, he was named assistant manager of the Metropolitan Opera in Manhattan.

The wedding, presided over by a Navy chaplain, transpired on November 2, 1943. Sailors in dress uniform raised their swords to form a kind of arbor under which Kirk and Diana walked toward the altar. The next day, they were married again in a Jewish ceremony by a rabbi, who asked them to sign a contract stating that their children would be reared and educated as Jews.

After leaving his quarters, Kirk turned to his new bride: "Don't worry. That contract is not enforceable. We'll raise our kids as we damn please. But if they're boys, I want them circumcised. After all, I'm a Jew."

The next day, as Kirk and Diana were walking through the French quarter, she spotted Richard Goddard, wearing a naval uniform and striding toward them.

She rushed into the arms of her former lover, giving him a big hug and a kiss on the mouth. Then she turned to introduce him to Kirk. "Dick, so glad to see you. I want you to meet my new husband. We were just married."

As she recalled years later, "It was one of the most embarrassing moments of my life. I could not remember his name."

"Hi," Kirk said, extending his hand. "I'm Douglas."

"Yeeesss...she stammered. Douglas." Adding to her embarrassment, she couldn't remember her new husband's first name, either.

"Kirk," he said. "Kirk Douglas. Diana is Mrs. Kirk Douglas."

After a brief chat, Goddard wandered off. "I'm sure," she said, "he was convinced that this sailor was a one-night stand."

***

The newlyweds were able to spend a romantic month getting to know each other and New Orleans, too. They learned to dine in out-of-the-way spots serving tasty Cajun and Creole dishes. "I developed a fondness for oysters," he said. "Makes me virile."

"Tell me about it," she said.

After their nights of love-making in the Pontalba Building, he'd ride the ferry across the Mississippi back to the Algiers Naval Station and report for duty. His fellow sailors were waiting for the commissioning of their patrol boat, PC-1139. It was being readied to sail down the Mississippi and across the Gulf of Mexico to Miami.

"There were about seventy-five young guys, of which I was the oldest," Kirk said. "None of them had had any experience at sea. Of the five officers, only the skipper had been at sea—and then only once. Talk about being green."

Once we sailed, I would be the Communication Officer and Officer of the Deck. Although I wasn't exactly sure what that meant, it sounded important. And, lest we forget, I'd be armed like I was in so many of those movies that lay in my future."

On the night before he set sail, he was "overzealous" in bed, explaining to Diana that this session in bed with her would have to last him until she joined him in Miami.

On the day his patrol boat left the dock, she stood beside the skipper's wife, waving at the crew and blowing kisses to Kirk.

What happened next, in her view, belonged in a Mack Sennett silent comedy.

Everything seemed to go wrong with the launch of PC-1139 as the crew rushed about hysterically. Their vessel crashed into a smaller boat with no one on board. They damaged it so badly, it began to sink.

Diana burst out laughing but shut up when she saw the stern glare of the skipper's wife.

"We finally got out of dock, but only after ripping the raft boat off another ship," Kirk said. "I was horribly embarrassed, humiliated, really. We were a laughing stock. But at long last, we were sailing down the Mississippi. It was peaceful. But then, to my horror, came a personal disaster. That queasy feeling developed into Grade A seasickness. I was the first man on board to be afflicted. In front of my fellow sailor boys, I vomited into a bucket on deck—all those oysters I'd had the night before."

***

As PC-1139 sailed around the tip of Florida, heading for the Port of Miami, Kirk was repeatedly seasick and had trouble holding down a meal. "At times, I felt I wanted to die and once or twice flirted with the idea of jumping overboard to become shark bait."

One afternoon, when the waters calmed down, he called a practice drill

This photo, snapped in the autumn of 1945, shows the PC-1139, rustbucket on which Kirk Douglas was stationed for four months from November of 1943 till February of 1944.

PC-1139 is anchored alongside an equivalent ship, PC-1243 at Chi Chi Jima, Bonin Islands north of Iwo Jima. Hastily begun in January of 1943 by the Defoe Shipbuilding Co. in Bay City, MIchigan, and launched in May of that same year, it was a rather small ship, with a displacement of 295 tns, a lenght of only 174 feet, a beam of 23 feet, and and draft of almost 11 feet. It was decommissioned in 1947, and its postwar fate is unknown, like he'd seen in war movies. He sounded the alarm for general quarters, and a madhouse ensued as the sailors darted about, trying to man their stations. It seemed that only the skipper had the authority to call a drill.

Skipper McCormach stormed onto the deck. "A dumb son of a bitch was one of his kinder words for me—that and 'cocksucker.'"

In early December, PC-1139 sailed into Miami, where Diana was waiting for him at the dock. She had ridden aboard a train from New Orleans and had managed to rent a small apartment on Miami Beach in a building where a number of married sailors lived with their wives.

"I set up housekeeping as best I could, although that was never one of my skills," she said. "Kirk had trouble getting his land legs back and staggered about a bit. Dinner was provided by the wife of a sailor downstairs. She was a good cook, and I paid her to prepare our meals at night."

The stopover was for two weeks, but one mishap after another delayed PC-1139's next launch for a full month. The first time it embarked from Miami, it scraped the side of a destroyer from the Soviet Union.

"My shipmates invited the Russians for a night of drinking," Kirk said. "They emptied the vodka bottles, as we went through a keg of beer."

After a few more delays, the ship sailed in mid-January, 1944. In retrospect the crew's time in Miami had seemed like a vacation—barbecues with the sailors and their wives in the backyard of their apartment house, frolicking on the beach, movies, love-making nightly.

"Kirk and I never put it into words, but there was the fear that once he sailed away, I would never see him again," Diana said.

PC-1139, by now fully equipped with radar, headed south into the open Atlantic toward Manzanillo Island and its port of Cristóbal, on the Atlantic side of the Panama Canal.

Meanwhile, Diana boarded a northbound train to New Jersey, where she'd live with her sister, Ruth.

When he wasn't vomiting over the railing, Kirk decoded messages, a job he found "particularly miserable."

One afternoon, two sailors—one a recent immigrant from Sicily, another an Irishman from Boston—got into a fight on deck. To stop them, Kirk drew his firearm and threatened to shoot them. The Sicilian stopped fighting, turned on Kirk, and dared him to fire.

"I learned a lesson for my future career in movies," Kirk said. "If I played a tough guy on screen and drew my gun, my character had to be prepared to use it."

"Strolling around Cristóbal was like a holiday," Kirk said. "A lot of beautiful WACs were running about ready to get plucked. I got me one, and we danced in this tavern to a Glenn Miller record I'd put on the jukebox."

"Her name was Mickey, like the famous movie star, Mickey Rooney. A buxom brunette, she was 23 years old, with a shapely figure. She came from Baton Rouge, Louisiana, where she told me her mother had once had an affair with the notorious governor, Huey Long. We did it back at her hotel."

"I wasn't concerned with adultery. It wasn't something I wanted to think about. In war, men in uniform avail themselves of sex wherever they find it, which was in every port. You didn't know if you would ever return to your wife or girlfriend, and the men understood that. You took pleasure whereever you found it. At sea, some of the straight sailors let the homosexual ones give them blow jobs. Let's face it: Men crave sex and are going to get it."

Almost every day, he wrote to Diana, and she replied with long, loving letters. In one of them, she described her visit to Schenectady, where she'd met his mother and sisters.

"Your mother was kind and gracious, but the sisters were a bit skeptical of this non-Jewish new member of the family. We drank blackberry wine at 11AM, which I figured must be some old Jewish custom. All of them send their love to you. When I left, your mother was in tears behind her rimless glasses."

*** .

Early the next morning, Kirk, with his libido serviced, sailed westward through the locks of the Panama Canal. His crew was granted a 24-hour leave in Ciudad de Panama (Panama City), that nation's largest city and capital.

It had a notorious reputation for its bordellos. Historically, it had been the starting point for Spanish expeditions setting out to conquer the Inca Empire. In 1671, the privateer, Henry Morgan, had burned Panama City to the ground.

During World War II, the United States built several military bases here, and the streets were filled with servicemen. Hundreds of young women, even girls, had poured into the city "to service the servicemen," as the expression went.

Kirk was eager to partake of the city's pleasures during his short stopover. Along with four members of his crew, who served directly under him, he headed for what he was told was "the hottest address in town," the Maison d'Amour. After crossing its threshold, he was greeted by Madame Rosita Carmen (an assumed name), a striking figure long past

75

her prime. Coiffed with magenta-colored hair and accessorized with green eye shadow and purple lipstick, she was one of the most distinctive-looking women in town. She employed twenty to thirty young hostesses during weekdays, increasing their number to as many as fifty on busy weekends.

She tried to cater to all tastes—brunettes, redheads, and blondes. Women came in all sizes, from short to tall, the age range varying from 15 to 23. Her motto, translated into English, was "Young men don't like to sleep with their grandmothers. Hence, no gal over 25 can work for me— that's just too old."

The working girls wore gaudily colored evening gowns with plunging *décolletages,* some so low as to show nipples. Madame Carmen had a strict house rule: No underwear. The servicemen were invited to reach up the gowns to feel the merchandise. "There's nothing wrong with a little foreplay," the madame claimed.

Kirk and his four buddies were invited to a private room upstairs where they were promised an exhibition. After they were comfortably seated, each of them positioned on separate cots, a Panamanian "Superman" entered with a 14-inch erection. He was followed by a shapely blonde and a redhead, obviously dyed. He then proceeded, without a lot of foreplay, to penetrate each of them as they cried out in pain, either faked or real. When he'd finished the show, five young women in varying skin tones, entered to seduce Kirk and his buddies.

He remembered his girl as knowing only two words of English: "*suckee*" and "*fuckee.*" She uttered those words just before her serpent-like tongue darted into his ear.

On the cots arranged side by side, each of the sailors began the sex act with the hostesses. As a specialty of the house, the madame sent in five beautiful Latino boys, one no more than ten years old. As the men plowed away, these youths massaged the "rosebuds" of each sailor with a tongue-lashing. The madame believed that caused each man to climax faster so that her girls could then move on to service other sailors waiting for them downstairs.

Years later, whenever one of them asked, "What did you do during the war?," Kirk relayed the details of his stopover in Panama City to such future co-stars as Johnny Cash and John Wayne

In his memoirs, he delivered a less graphic account: "Sex is a temporary cure for loneliness, a way to hang on to someone, to be close to someone, even for a short time. We were young in a frightening situation. Suddenly, we reached out to someone to cover up our fears."

***

As reluctant as he was to leave Panama City, Kirk, along with the skipper and the rest of the crew, headed for the Galapagos Islands, an isolated archipelago in the Pacific Ocean that belonged to Ecuador. He had first heard of the island chain in college when he had studied the theory of evolution and natural selection of Charles Darwin (1809-1882), the English naturalist. On the second voyage (1831-1836) of the *HMS Beagle*, Darwin had been stunned by the endemic species he'd discovered there.

The Navy had sent coded instructions that PC-1139 was to conduct mock anti-submarine activities with an actual U.S. sub. "In this war gaming, I had the worst eyesight of any man on board," Kirk said. "I was the last to spot a periscope emerging from the Pacific. I wouldn't have made a sighting until a gigantic Jap sub, like an enraged Moby Dick, had emerged twenty feet from our little PC-1139."

The crew was ordered to simulate an attack on an invading submarine before it could release deadly explosives.

"There was a real war going on, and here we were like actors appearing in a war movie, shades of my future as a movie star during the filming of *In Harm's Way*," Kirk recalled.

[That action/adventure war drama was released in 1965. Co-starring Kirk with John Wayne, its plot addressed the bombing of Pearl Harbor and its aftermath.]

"Speaking of stars, other actors, present and future, were also wearing military uniforms during the war effort. To name a few, they included Harry Belafonte, Ernest Borgnine, Jackie Cooper, Rock Hudson, Tony Curtis, Gene Kelly, Paul Newman, Jack Lemmon, and Robert Taylor. In some cases, these guys would be my co-stars in the films of tomorrow."

Their maneuvers off the coast of Ecuador ended when a coded message was sent from the Navy ordering PC-1139 to escort two other vessels—a cargo ship, *Cubits Gap,* and a floating dry dock—to Honolulu. Kirk's crew was then to head for the South Pacific on a search for Japanese subs.

It soon became apparent that Kirk's ship did not have enough fuel to make it to Hawaii, so the cargo ship had to tow it for part of the way. The crew aboard the cargo ship mocked Kirk's vessel, ridiculing it for their offer of "protection."

When it was determined that PC-1139 had traveled with them far enough, the skipper of the cargo ship ordered the towline to be disconnected, as his ship could make it for the rest of the journey without an "escort."

Kirk would always remember those days sailing through the Pacific as the most tranquil of his military career—that is, before disaster struck.

"Unlike the Atlantic, where I was constantly sick, the Pacific waters were smooth, sometimes with only a tropical breeze blowing. I was on deck from four to eight in the morning. The moon would break through the clouds, lighting up the phosphorescent whitecaps. When the moon disappeared behind clouds, there was inky blackness. It was a time of reflection."

He thought not just about Diana, but of other women he'd known intimately, too, including Peggy Diggins and his schoolteacher, Louise, who had taken the virginity of a fourteen-year-old boy. He reflected on Betty Bacall, wondering how she was handling the pitfalls of Hollywood. He planned, when he reached San Diego for refueling and a shore leave, to head north for a long, overdue visit with her.

Off duty, he would lie on his bunk in his skivvies, reading a paperback, *Tobacco Road*, or writing a letter to Diana. Quarters were cramped, and the only decorations were pinup pictures of Betty Grable and Rita Hayworth.

He feared that when he returned to Broadway, no more roles would be offered. With so many servicemen coming home, the race for jobs would no doubt be fierce, especially for actors. "The one thing I had going for me was my burning desire to succeed, and somehow, deep in my gut, I thought I'd make it."

On February 7, 1944, their idyllic sail ended abruptly. The sound of "ping*ping*, ping*ping*" signaled that an enemy sub was moving in on them. Rushing to their battle positions, the crew plotted their attack. Once the position of the enemy sub was fixed, the crew fired six explosive projectiles from its "mousetrap launcher."

The bombs would explode only on contact, and Kirk and the crew cheered when they heard a big explosion in the distance. His position during the attack was as the gunnery officer astern.

The skipper's voice came over the loudspeakers, ordering the crew to release a dye marker as they passed over the stricken sub, no doubt filled with dying young Japanese sailors.

Seconds after the order was issued, the PC-1139 was rocked with an eruption, sending Kirk and his fellow sailors sprawling onto the deck. He was hurled like a rocket against the side of the iron carrier for depth charges. He screamed in agony and his stomach felt like a sledgehammer had slammed into it. "My guts were rearranged," he recalled.

Doubling over in agony, he thought that a torpedo had hit the ship. Shouts from his men filled the air, and for the first few minutes, hysteria prevailed.

It soon became apparent that it had not been a Japanese torpedo that had hit them, wrecking their steering gear. Instead, in lieu of the dye marker the skipper had ordered, an inexperienced young sailor had released a Mark IX depth charge which had exploded at just 250 feet. Such a mistake came close to actually sinking their vessel.

Kirk could no longer fulfill his duties, as his stomach started to swell with bruises. Not only that, but one sailor from Oklahoma developed, from a blow he'd received, an instant case of acute appendicitis, thereby requiring immediate medical attention.

Orders came in for PC-1139 to reverse course and return to La Manzanilla, Mexico, which had medical facilities. The cargo ship sailed onward to Hawaii, free at last from its accident-prone escort.

South of Puerto Vallarta, La Manzanilla had about 2,000 inhabitants and a small medical center. Kirk suspected that the town sheltered more crocodiles, some of them twelve feet long, than humans.

En route, PC-1139 had been menaced not by Japanese aircraft, but by American planes. In the darkness, Kirk's vessel, on three separate occasions, was interpreted as a possible Japanese ship. He feared the drone of any airplane that zeroed in on them, ready to drop a bomb. He and his crew sent up frequent flares identifying PC-1139 as a U.S. vessel.

"One pilot coming toward us looked like he was ready to bomb us, only swerving at the last minute and sparing us," Kirk recalled.

Sailing into the Bay of Tenacatita, his ship docked at La Manzanilla. As he soon discovered, the bustling little port was peopled by dozens of *gringos norteamericano.* En route to the dock, they passed fishermen in small boats hauling in catches of sailfish, tuna, marlin, snapper, dorado, and "roosterfish."

After they'd docked, a broken-down ambulance hauled the stricken sailor to the small local hospital for an emergency operation. Kirk was examined too, but the doctor diagnosed him as without any internal injuries.

Walking about the town, and in spite of his pain, he had a ravenous appetite, purchasing tacos from the street *taquerios.* Later that evening, he became violently ill.

He scanned the horizon and its tall cliffs and could hear the "girly screeches" of yellow kiskadees and the prehistoric squawks of herons. A colony of black vultures gathered in packs, holding their wings out for an airing like ominous angels of death. "Are they waiting to have a go at me?" he asked a fellow sailor.

New orders came in for his ship to sail to San Diego. En route, he suffered severe stomach cramps and ran up a fever of 104 degrees. When the ship finally arrived in California, he was semi-conscious. With its dome light flashing, an ambulance rushed him to the Naval Medical Center [aka *the Balboa Hospital]* at San Diego. *[During the course of World War II, it received thousands of injured soldiers wounded in the Pacific.]*

A more thorough examination revealed that he did have internal injuries and might be confined for a long time. "I also found out that I had the world's worst case of amoebic dysentery."

His skipper visited him in the hospital, informing him that his crew had received orders to sail to the theater of war in the South Pacific. "We'll have to fight this man's war without you," he said. "Good luck."

"Good luck to you and all the guys," Kirk answered. It was increasingly obvious that his duty to the Navy was going to expire without any action.

***

While Kirk was away in the Pacific, his mail had piled up, mostly with love letters from Diana. Each of his sisters had written letters too, mostly expressing their concerns for his safety. Of course, he didn't expect letters from his mother, since she didn't know how to write. The same applied to his father.

One letter from Diana sent a shock wave through him when he learned that she was pregnant. It took two hours to reach her by phone in New Jersey, since switchboards during the war years were swamped with callers.

She told him about her new job at Squibb Chemical Company *[now known as Bristol-Myers Squibb Co., Inc.]*. It was testing this new antibiotic called Penicillin. It would reach the market before the Allied invasion of Normandy in 1944. It would be marketed with the claim "it cures gonorrhea in just four hours."

Before ringing off, Diana thanked him for the crocodile purse he'd sent her from La Manzanilla. Her final reassurances included the news that her pregnancy was proceeding smoothly, and both of them hoped that their first-born would be a son.

He assured her that "my sperm is so powerful it can only make boys." *[As it happened, all the known children that Kirk sired were males.]*

After many days, when it became clear that his medical treatments would have to continue for weeks at the naval hospital in San Diego, Diana quit her job in New Jersey and rode the train cross-country to be with him. In anticipation of her arrival, he rented a small apartment where they could set up temporary housekeeping.

He was able to check out of the hospital before her arrival. He received permission to live off-base, with the understanding that he'd report every day for medical tests and psychiatric counseling.

"I was on an extended vacation with Diana, paid for by the U.S. Navy," he said.

Days were spent mainly at the beach in front of the Hotel del Coronado, just across the bay from San Diego. After its opening in 1888, it was billed as the largest resort in the world. Over the years, it had hosted presidents, royalty, and movie stars such as Clark Gable and Errol Flynn. During the war, many Navy pilots from the nearby North Island Naval Air Station were assigned lodgings within the hotel as their living quarters.

Diana and Kirk often spent their nights at the Officers Club, where the attractive couple made many friends. Their plans involved settling in New Jersey as soon as his discharge came through.

One night she admitted to him that she was reluctant to introduce him to her family, since most of them had opposed the marriage. She revealed that her father was very anti-Semitic, and that he often made disparaging remarks about actors, considering many of them homosexuals. "He knows these two bigshot producers from Hollywood who often vacation in Bermuda," Diana said. "They told my father that in their early days, Gary Cooper, Clark Gable, and John Wayne had worn out quite a few casting couches."

She returned to New Jersey weeks before he did, because she wanted to have her baby on the East Coast, delivered by her personal physician.

After several more tests, Kirk's doctor at the Naval Hospital determined that his severe case of amoebic dysentery was likely to continue for many months. Around the time of the D-Day Landings in France (June of 1944), he was given an honorable discharge from the U.S. Navy, along with three months severance pay.

He phoned Diana with the news that he'd soon be flying to New York, where he wanted her to meet him.

With his lone suitcase, he rode the train north to Los Angeles, placing a phone call to Betty Bacall and inviting her to dinner at Frascati's Restaurant on Wilshire Boulevard. Thanks to news bulletins from the Warner Brothers Publicity Department, he learned that the girl he used to know as Betty was now being billed as Lauren Bacall.

It had been announced that she would soon be starring in *To Have and Have Not*. Eventually released in 1944, it was a film loosely based on an Ernest Hemingway novel. Her co-star would be Humphrey Bogart. Howard Hawks would direct them, with the understanding that Bacall was being groomed as a new Marlene Dietrich. In fact, Hawks ordered the studio's voice coaches to train her throaty voice into something even deeper.

To their dinner that night, Bacall had brought along the script of *To*

Have and Have Not, the texts and premises of which had been drastically altered by William Faulkner and Jules Furthman. With her "revised" screen voice, Bacall read her favorite lines to Kirk, the ones she'd deliver directly to Bogart on screen.

"You don't have to do anything or say anything. Maybe just whistle. You know how to whistle, don't you, Steve? You just put your lips together and blow."

After her (highly suggestive) recitation, Kirk predicted she'd be the film industry's new screen sensation.

The newly renamed Lauren Bacall appeared on the screen in *To Have and Have Not* with her future husband, Humphrey Bogart.

"She was one of my first loves and became my life-long friend," Kirk said.

Bacall was not happy about Hawk's choice for her leading man. "Bogie is old enough to be my grandfather. After all, he was born in the 19th Century. What sort of chemistry can I possibly have with gramps? My God, he was appearing in plays in New York way back in the 1920s."

She also devoted some of the dinner to discussion of his own prospects as an actor, urging him to stay in Hollywood and to try his luck as screen star. "All the big names like Clark Gable, Robert Taylor, and James Stewart will be returning from the war, but they're getting long in the tooth. The post-war era will need a whole new crop of young screen actors."

He told her, "I have my heart set on Broadway, and besides, Diana wants to live in the East. She didn't fare too well in Hollywood."

"I was surprised to hear that you'd gotten married," she said. "I still want you to think seriously about becoming a screen actor."

[When Kirk read in the paper that Lauren Bacall had married Humphrey Bogart on May 21, 1945 in Lucas, Ohio, he phoned her after her return to Los Angeles.

"You and Bogie must have found some chemistry after all," he said.

"I married him only when I decided you'd never get around to asking me and had gone off with another woman."

"You're kidding, of course," he said.

"Like hell I am!"

***

A visibly pregnant Diana was waiting on the platform of Manhattan's

Grand Central Station as Kirk's train rolled in. After extended hugs and kisses, and many questions about her pregnancy, it was time for her to drive him to his new, albeit temporary, home in New Brunswick, New Jersey.

Lying 27 miles southwest of Manhattan, the city stood on the southern bank of the Raritan River. It was home to both Rutgers University and Johnson & Johnson, the pharmaceutical giant famous for its baby powder.

Diana's sister, Ruth, had married John Seward Johnson I, heir to the Johnson & Johnson fortune. That company's sprawling factory stood on the opposite side of the river.

Diana had not told Kirk where they'd be living, wanting to surprise him. "She surprised me all right. Our new home would be a 60-room castle with turrets and a slate roof, a giant of a place, a fit abode for a dozen mad Frankensteins. It was owned by her father."

"Don't worry," she said. "We'll live only in the West Wing, which used to be the nursery."

She directed him down a dark, foreboding corridor, past bucolic 19th Century landscape paintings and portraits guarded by suits of armor standing guard. At the end of the corridor was a suite which they'd occupy for the next seven months.

Long denuded of its furnishings, their stately looking quarters had not been designed as a self-contained private apartment. The following day, they'd have to buy a mattress, a two-burner hot plate, and an old-fashioned ice box cooled with blocks of ice to keep their food from perishing.

That night, Ruth, Diana's sister, living at the time in the guest house, invited them for dinner, and he found her gracious and charming. He dreaded meeting her parents, however. They were expected to fly in soon from Bermuda.

After a week of settling in, Kirk, dashingly dressed in his Navy whites, headed off to Manhattan, where he planned to call on one casting office after another until he landed a job on stage. He thought the uniform might help him if a producer or director felt patriotic.

At night, he returned home to the spooky castle sometime after 2AM where, as expected, he found Diana asleep in bed. He wondered how safe she was all alone in such a menacing-looking place. Indeed, one night, about eight soldiers from nearby Camp Kilmer broke in and vandalized the drawing room. A portrait that Diana had posed for when she was thirteen had been slashed. Asleep in the building's far West Wing, she had not heard anyone breaking in.

Having had no luck in his rounds, he returned to Manhattan the next day and visited the offices of Katharine Cornell and Guthrie McClintic, learning that they had taken *The Barretts of Wimpole Street* to England to present it to Allied soldiers, many of whom would soon be crossing the Rhine as part of their invasion of Germany.

A secretary to McClintic remembered Kirk and arranged an appointment for him with Mae West, who was casting a play she was producing as a vehicle for herself and six musclemen. *[In the 1930s, her movies had grossed enough to save Paramount from bankruptcy. As such, she was still considered by investors as a viable, albeit faded, formula for show-biz success.]*

Kirk arrived for his audition at West's gaudily decorated apartment at 3PM. Everything was in white and gold. He joined a dozen or so other hopefuls, each of whom had a superb physique.

Fifteen minutes later, a young man, whom Kirk described as "mincing," ushered them into an adjoining room where he ordered each of the men to strip completely naked. Then he inspected each of their genitals, and handed out almost transparent G-strings, announcing that this would be what they'd be wearing onstage in the event they were hired. It was made clear that as a scantily clad phalanx of "worshippers," they'd carry Miss West, as she reclined in a chaise longue, onstage for the debut of her act.

Later, as part of the act, she'd very suggestively hand each of them a key to her bedroom, inviting them to "come up and see me sometime."

In his memoirs, Kirk gave only the most sanitized version of

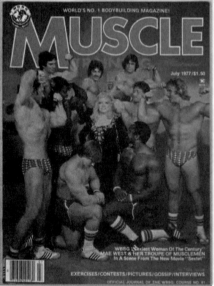

Although Mae West's "accessorization" of muscle men as part of her stagecraft was novel and innovative in the 1950s, by 1977, a widespread appreciation for its campy aspects had become part of the American mainstream.

In the lower of the two photos, Mae with a coven of bodybuilders is affectionately featured on the cover of the July, 1977 issue of *Muscle Training Magazine*.

The photo at the top shows Mae as a (perhaps) delusional vamp, also in 1977.

 *(caption, right margin)* ALLAN WARREN, FROM WIKIMEDIA COMMONS

his visit to the apartment of the self-styled, self-enchanted sex goddess. After a long delay, she emerged in a black *négligée* with plunging *décolletage*, wearing high heels so tall he wondered why she didn't topple over. At least the shoes gave her some height, as she was very short.

Each actor, including Kirk, lined up for her inspection. "She gave each of us a thorough exam, beginning at our feet and working her way north, spending at least two minutes on each man's package. And then she was gone."

A half-hour later, the 'mincer' entered and named the six candidates who had been cast. "I was not among them," Kirk said. "I guess I wasn't her type. I learned later that she liked only uncut men, and she could clearly see that I didn't fit that category. Also, I found out that she was a 'size queen,' preferring men such as Steve Cochran."

"At any rate, I was out on the pavement, wearing my Navy whites and pounding the theater district looking for work."

That secretary in the Cornell/McClintic office called Kirk the next day and asked him to return the following day for an appointment at 2PM. Richard Widmark, who had been playing an army lieutenant, was leaving the cast of the frothy comedy, *Kiss and Tell,* and she thought Kirk might be an ideal replacement. Ironically, Kirk and Diana were already familiar with the play, having seen it together when he'd stayed with her during one of his furloughs in New York.

Kiss and Tell had already been running at the Biltmore Theater for a year. Its plot centered on two teenaged girls who were boy-crazy, much to the horror of their trouble-making parents. One of its original stars, Joan Caulfield, had already moved on to Hollywood stardom, and had been replaced with her sister, Betty Caulfield.

The play had been produced by George Abbott and would run for 956 performances before closing in June of 1945 at war's end. A film adaptation, as configured by F. Hugh Herbert, would be released in October of that year starring Shirley Temple in the role of Corliss Archer.

After Kirk's audition, the director awarded him with the role about to be vacated by Widmark.

Kirk had dinner with Widmark a few

Depicted above is a poster for the 1945 movie that starred a post-adolescent Shirley Temple, and which was based on the Broadway Play in which Kirk Douglas had played a role.

nights later. A son of Sunrise, Minnesota, he was two years older than Kirk. Their dinner marked the debut of a long but competitive relationship. In the years to come, they'd often compete for the same roles. Eventually, they'd co-star in the same movie. Each envied the other.

Kirk was stunned when Widmark was nominated for an Oscar for his performance as the villainous sociopathic Tommy Udo in his screen debut, *Kiss of Death* (1947). In one iconic scene, with a demented giggle, Widmark sadistically pushes a wheelchair-bound Mildred Dunnock down a flight of stairs.

Like Kirk, he would carve out a career in gun-toting portrayals of cowboys, policemen, gangsters, and military men.

Richard Widmark with Marilyn Monroe in the film noir, *Don't Bother to Knock (1952).*

"Did Widmark get to Monroe before I did?" Kirk wanted to know.

***

One Sunday at New Brunswick, Diana introduced Kirk to her parents. He found her mother a birdlike, spry woman, much like Billie Burke on the screen. To his surprise, her father, Lt. Col. Thomas Melville Dill, was not as formidable or as hostile as his reputation had it. He and Kirk bonded, and "the Jewish question never came up," his son-in-law said.

However, at the end of the evening, after Kirk had retired to bed for the night, her father turned to Diana and said, "Actors are the parasites of society."

***

After dark, on the evening of September 24, 1944, Diana went into labor, and her sister Ruth drove her very fast to St. Peter's Hospital in New Brunswick. A patrol cop turned on his siren and chased their car to a stop at a red light. He pulled up alongside her window, demanding that she get out

When he was told why they were in such a hurry, he turned on his siren again and led her all the way to the hospital. There, Diana was rushed into the emergency room.

By midnight, she was screaming in agony. It was obvious that it would be a difficult childbirth. She cursed both the nurses and the doctors, directing most of her fury at Kirk for impregnating her. "Men have their fun, and women are left to bear the burden—it's all so unfair," she told the nurse.

In the delivery room, she was given a whiff of ether, as the doctors prepared to use forceps.

Michael Kirk Douglas, a future movie star, entered the world at 10:30AM on September 25. She'd wanted to call him Kirk Douglas, Jr., but his father objected, citing Jewish tradition which dictated that a child should not be named after a living person.

Kirk couldn't attend his son's birth, as he was scheduled to perform in a matinee of *Kiss and Tell* in Manhattan. A few minutes after the curtain went down, he hailed a taxi to Penn Station, where he boarded a train headed to New Brunswick, then jumped into another taxi to the hospital. There, he had time for only a brief visit with Diana and a quick look at his newborn before rushing back to Manhattan for the evening performance.

According to his wishes and Jewish tradition, he ordered that his infant son be circumcised.

Both Diana and Kirk felt that they'd availed themselves enough of Ruth's hospitality. When their infant son was only three weeks old, they moved to West 11th Street in Greenwich Village, near where Kirk had first lived when he came to Manhattan.

The rent was ninety dollars a month, an amount he could afford from the money he was being paid as an actor. He bought a pram for Michael for use during their strolls in Central Park.

He was doing well in *Kiss and Tell,* but he wanted to create a unique role for himself, not commandeer one that had previously been defined by another actor, in this case, Richard Widmark.

He heard that a play was being cast called *Star in the Window.* One of its writers was the soon-to-be-famous Sidney Sheldon.

Kirk attended an audition and met the co-author, a Hungarian, Laci Bus-fekete. He was given his lines and started to read. Within less than a minute, he was interrupted with, "That's enough. Thank you for coming."

He left the audition feeling rejected and depressed. He said, "Actors are often described as people who love rejection. That's not true. Every year, hundreds of young men and women come to Broadway or Hollywood hoping to make it big with their name up in lights. They never expected to meet with rejection but do. 'Too fat!' 'Too thin.' 'Too loud!' 'Too soft.' Most of them go home. I stayed."

The next day, he got a call from Sheldon. "The part is yours. The moment you walked in, we knew you were it, perfect to play the Russian soldier."

In the new role of Sergeant Steve, he played opposite Peggy Conklin. The play previewed in Washington, D.C., where a local critic evaluated Kirk as "a delight, always assured of himself and never missing a beat in his line of patter."

Assured that *Star in the Window* "shines bright," in the words of one early critic, the play headed to Broadway with a change in its title, having been renamed as *Alice in Arms*.

It opened on Broadway at the National Theater on January 31, 1945 and closed four days later after devastating reviews and very few ticket sales.

Kirk was in Sardi's when the first reviews trickled in. *The New York Times* defined it as "A plague on the house. The dialogue is so wooden it could splinter." Reviews in other newspapers were even worse. Sheldon went into hiding, and Kirk was out of a job once again.

***

On the streets of Manhattan one afternoon, Kirk ran into his old friend, actor Karl Malden, who had originally helped persuade him to change his name to Kirk Douglas. "Karl was very depressed, and who wouldn't be? He'd had sixteen flops in a row, or so he claimed. He'd been on the verge of moving back to Gary, Indiana, when a role was offered to him in a play called *Truckline Café*. He told Kirk that the male lead had not yet been cast, and he recommended that he try out for it.

"Maybe we'll get to work together," Malden said. "I've already signed as the second male lead."

The play by Maxwell Anderson was the first presentation of Playwrights Company, a theatrical partnership formed by Harold Clurman and his fast-rising director, Elia Kazan. The new company had grown out of the Group Theater's experiences in New York in the 1930s.

Kazan was already well-known in the theater world because of his recent film success with *A Tree Grows in Brooklyn* (1945), based on the bestselling novel by Betty Smith. Kazan had been designated as the producer of *Truckline Café*. Clurman would direct it.

The part that Kirk tried out for was Sage McRae, a psychologically disturbed veteran who had recently returned from World War II. He drowns his unfaithful wife in the Pacific before turning himself in. When Kazan first read the script, he told Clurman, "It's god damn dull," but he was finally persuaded to get involved.

Before auditioning, Kirk was introduced to his competition, a young actor from Nebraska named Marlon Brando. He auditioned first, reading passages set within a seedy café along the Pacific Coast Highway.

Kirk found Brando's reading a disaster. "He mumbles. I sat in the back and couldn't hear a word he said."

Suddenly, Kazan sprang up from his seat and headed for the exit, calling back to Clurman, "This guy might be your wife's fuck buddy, but he's no actor." *[Kazan was referring to Brando's acting coach, Stella Adler, a passionate advocate of Brando's talent, and probably a sex partner of his, too. Adler had told Clurman, her husband at the time, and only half in jest, "Unless you cast Marlon in the role, you won't get laid again.]*

With Kazan absent from the scene, Kirk auditioned next, aiming his dialogue directly at Clurman. At the end of his reading, Clurman pronounced his reading as brilliant. "I'll get back to you in a day or so, after I deal with that temperamental diva, Kazan."

Yet somehow in the days ahead, Clurman managed to convince Kazan that Brando would, after all, be perfect as the male lead. Malden was the first to call Kirk with the bad news.

Truckline Café became the first collaboration between Marlon Brando and Elia Kazan. Kazan would go on to make artistically acclaimed films that starred Brando, including *A Streetcar Named Desire, Viva Zapata!,* and *On the Waterfront.*

Truckline Café also marked the first collaboration between Marlon Brando and Karl Malden. Later, instances of other collaborations included *A Streetcar Named Desire, On the Waterfront,* and *One-Eyed Jacks.*

"Who was left out in the cold by this cozy coven?" Kirk asked. "Namely, me. Fuck 'em all!"

[Ironically, however, Kazan would eventually select Kirk from among all the actors in Hollywood, to star as the hero of his autobiographical film, The Arrangement *(1969).]*

***

When Sidney Sheldon emerged from his self-imposed "retreat from the world," following the failure of *Star in the Window,* he returned Kirk's four urgent phone calls. He hadn't answered his phone in days.

Kirk needed a job, and Sheldon had praised his performance in *Star in the Window.* The only vehicle he knew where Kirk

Rising Star, Marlon Brando, Kirk's competitor, in Truckline Cafe in 1946

might find a role was in *On the Town,* a new Broadway musical being directed by that show biz veteran, George Abbott.

"You were in the Navy," Sheldon said. "It's about three horny sailors who arrive for a short leave in New York City, where they go after a trio of girls."

"That sounds up my alley," Kirk told him.

"There might be a problem," Sheldon warned. "It requires singing and dancing."

Kirk did not hesitate: "I've been called a cross between Dick Powell and Fred Astaire."

He had greatly exaggerated his abilities, of course, but felt desperate in his search for a role. He contacted Abbott, who—based on Sheldon's recommendation—agreed to audition him.

Born in Forestville, New York, in 1887, George Abbott was already a legend in America's theater and film worlds by the time he was introduced to Kirk. He had first acted on the New York stage in 1913. His first great hit as a producer, aptly named *Broadway,* had wowed audiences way back in 1926.

When Abbott outlined what was needed for the role of Gaby, Kirk came close to panic. When he heard the names of the talent already associated with the show, he feared he could not compete. The music was by Leonard Bernstein, with book and lyrics by Betty Comden and Adolph Green. It was based on Jerome Robbins ballet, *Fancy Free.* Some of its songs, such as "New York, New York," would become classics. Its plot revolved around the adventures of three sailors who arrive in Manhattan during wartime, 1944, to pursue romance.

At the Adelphi Theater, Kirk was introduced to this array of Broadway talent, including the Swedish stage and film actress, Signe Hasso.

He didn't know he'd have to sing as part of his audition. Why hadn't he prepared something? Of course, he'd have to sing, he was, after all, auditioning for a musical. Spontaneously, he selected that old cornpone favorite, "I'm Red Hot Henry Brown/The Hottest Man in Town."

Amazingly, this assemblage of musical talent eventually offered him the role of Gaby. "We understood his limitations as a singer—of course we did," Abbott said. "But we didn't want a sailor right off his ship to suddenly sound like Bing Crosby. Kirk was a natural who would bring the right spirit to Gaby."

Kirk agonized and fretted obsessively over the show as it moved into rehearsals. Within a week, he developed what he called a psychosomatic illness, defining it as "history's worst case of laryngitis." The producers, who had scheduled its opening for December 29, 1944, held the role open

for him for ten days,

At the end of those ten days, when Abbott learned that Kirk was unable to utter a sound, he phoned Diana to tell her that he had replaced her husband with another actor.

"He was severely depressed and miserable for the next two weeks, filled with all that Russian gloom and doom straight out of a Dostoevsky novel," Diana said.

A week after the opening of *On the Town,* Kirk took Diana to see it. He even went backstage to congratulate the cast and its creators, paying special attention to John Battles, the actor who had replaced him.

"Kirk didn't say anything, but I knew he realized that Battles was far better in the part than he would have been," Diana said.

[On the Town was adapted into a Hollywood musical in 1949. "Gene Kelly took my part," Kirk said.

It would represent the third and final time that Kelly partnered with Frank Sinatra.]

Backstage at the Adelphi Theater, during the encounters described above, and as Diana was talking to George Abbott, Signe Hasso slipped Kirk her phone number.

Although Kirk never admitted it publicly, Leonard Bernstein claimed that Kirk and the Swedish actress had "a brief fling," as so often happens in the theater.

When Hasso was asked about it, she denied it.

In 1940, she'd signed with RKO in Hollywood, and the company billed her as "the next Garbo." But her career went nowhere at RKO, and she returned to the stage. She did go back to Hollywood to make two notable films, *The House on 92nd Street* in 1945 and *A Double Life* in 1947 in which she co-starred with Ronald Colman.

There's till some confusion about Kirk's allegedly romantic links to Hasso. Jerome Robbins said that she told him that "Kirk is one sexy boy. I've divorced my husband and I'm shopping around for another one."

HI SAILORS!

Publicity photo from the 1944 Broadway stage performance of *On the Town.* The actors depicted above include (*left to right*) Cris Alexander, John Battles (in the role assigned for a while to Kirk Douglas), and Adolphe Green.

"But he's taken," Robbins warned.

"Darling, no man is really taken," she answered. "The trouble with marriage is that women often marry the wrong man. But a husband can be dumped when a new and more exciting man enters a girl's life. The same thing is true if a man is married, and he is Mr. Right for her. There's such a thing called divorce that frees a man or woman from a failed marriage."

Mae West didn't want Kirk to come up and see her sometime, but the Swedish actress, Signe Hasso, was impressed with his manly charm.

***

Finding no work, Kirk took a chance and went back to meet with the director of *Kiss and Tell*, asking if he could have his old role back. As it turned out, the director was not pleased with Kirk's replacement, and agreed to re-hire him, providing he'd agree to stick around this time until the end of the play's run. *[It was a promise that Kirk would not keep.]*

Despite his somewhat tired re-involvement with *Kiss and Tell* and motivated by the burning desire to build a character and a role from scratch, he continued to show up at auditions for new plays.

The only opening he found was as a replacement for—once again—Richard Widmark in a controversial production of an avant-garde play called *Trio*.

Stepping into Widmark's shoes once again, he was cast as Ray MacKenzie, the boyfriend of a young girl who's being pursued by her lesbian schoolteacher. He had only three days to learn his lines and interpret the character.

His debut in the play became one of the most embarrassing onstage events of his life. During the third act's climax, he burst into the lesbian's apartment and catches his girlfriend amorously engaged with her. "I flung open the door as if announcing World War III, a raging dynamo. The audience laughed hysterically at me."

That night, in bed with Diana, he could not sleep, reliving his humiliation. "They made fun of me," he kept repeating.

For his performance the following night, he was far more subdued, walking slowly into the apartment and silently confronting his girlfriend and her teacher. This time, the audience made no sound, as if finding the scene spellbinding. His revised interpretation of the scene succeeded.

[Prior to Kirk's involvement in the play, Trio, *based on its lesbian theme, had*

run into trouble with the era's prevailing moral codes. Lee Shubert of the Cort Theatre had refused to book it. However, Elmer Rice, who held the lease on the Belasco Theatre, had allowed it to open in his theater on December 29, 1944.

Later, Paul Moss, New York City's License Commissioner, threatened Rice that if he didn't shut the play down, he wouldn't renew his theater license. Defiantly, Lee Sabinson, the play's producer, sued New York City for a million dollars in a widely publicized, very controversial benchmark in NYC's entertainment history.]

***

Kirk didn't wait around for the outcome of the legal dramas swirling around *Trio*. He moved on after successfully auditioning for a role in *The Wind is Ninety*, a drama with three acts scheduled for an opening at the Booth Theatre on June 21, 1945. It starred Wendell Corey, Blanche Yurka, and Bert Lytell.

Its writer, Ralph Nelson, would go on to greater fame as a movie director best known for *Lilies of the Field* (1963), for which Sidney Poitier won an Oscar as Best Actor. Nelson also directed Cary Grant in the comedy, *Father Goose* (1964), and *Charly* (1968), which brought Cliff Robertson a Best Actor Oscar.

In *The Wind is Ninety*, Kirk was cast as the ghost of an Unknown Soldier from World War I, who is guiding the (also dead) character of a World War II fighter pilot played by Wendell Corey. Because the characters of both Kirk and Corey were dead, they were supposed to be visible to the audience but not to the other actors.

Of the many actors Kirk worked with during the course of a decades-long career, he found Corey the most despicable. "He was a real snob and a shithead. Okay, so he was descended from Presidents John Adams and John Quincy Adams. He didn't have to call me 'a dirty little Jew' behind my back."

"In addition to being anti-Semitic, he tried to steal every scene from me, always upstaging me and trying to throw me off my mark. I hated working with him, and at one point, we almost came to blows. I told him he should go back to selling washing machines, his profession before he became an actor."

"I was amazed that he found success in Hollywood as a movie star," Kirk said. "He was not good-looking—far from it—and he had no charisma at all. Yet he appeared with some of Tinseltown's biggest stars—Monty Clift, Burt Lancaster, Barbara Stanwyck, Clark Gable, Robert Mitchum, Margaret Sullavan, Grace Kelly, Joan Crawford, James Stewart…even Elvis and Katharine Hepburn."

When the play opened, Corey got rave reviews, and Kirk was praised in *The New York Times*, the first time that had ever happened. The critic wrote, "Kirk Douglas is nothing short of superb."

That night, in bed with Diana, he complained in anger about the phraseology of the review. "Why did the fart have to add the word 'nothing?' Why couldn't he have just said 'Kirk Douglas is superb?'"

[In one of the ironies of Hollywood, Corey, an alcoholic and right-wing reactionary, died in November of 1968. His wife, Alice Wiley, phoned Kirk and asked him if he'd deliver the eulogy at his funeral.

He suggested that somebody else might be better. She seemed unaware of Kirk's longtime feud with her husband. "Finally, when she broke down and cried, I agreed to do it. Call it the greatest performance of my life as I gave a loving tribute to an actor I loathed.]

During the run of the *The Wind is Ninety*, Kirk bonded with two of the other actors: Blanche Yurka and Bert Lytell.

Born in 1887 in Minnesota, Yurka had made her Broadway debut in 1906. In time, she would play Queen Gertrude with John Barrymore in *Hamlet*. "I played his mother. He was forty-two at the time, and I was thirty-five."

Kirk had seen her in the film *A Tale of Two Cities* (1935), in which she had played the vengeful and bloodthirsty Madame Defarge.

Yurka advised Kirk never to marry an actress. "I was married to an actor, and he got jealous when my career soared and his didn't. Too much rivalry if you're both actors."

"It's too late," he answered. "I'm already married to an actress."

"Don't be surprised when it doesn't work out," she said.

He also befriended Lytell, who had been a popular star in silent films, having made his debut in 1917 in *The Lone Wolf*. His career as a film actor did not survive the debut of the Talkies.

"My heyday was in the mid-1920s, and today, I'm just holding on, taking whatever job I can get. The theater, my dear boy, has its ups and downs. Soon, I'll be doing uncredited walk-ons."

***

In his search for another role, Kirk met David Merrick. Their friendship began long before Merrick became a legend on Broadway as a Tony-winning and very prolific producer.

After an audition, he invited Kirk to join the cast of *A Raincheck for Joe*, with the understanding that he'd have to learn how to play the saxophone.

The romantic roundabouts of the plot involved the supernatural swapping by mistaken angels of the bodies of a boxer with a saxophone player, a police investigation of a mysterious murder, and a happy ending as the errant angels rectify their previous mistakes and the confused protagonists fall in love.

Kirk had seen the 1941 film adaptation of this play. It was entitled *Here Comes Mr. Jordan*, and it had starred Robert Montgomery, Evelyn Keyes (Kirk's future lover), and Claude Rains, cast into the role of a bumbling angel.

[Warren Beatty played the lead in the 1978 remake, whose title was changed to Heaven Can Wait.]

To prepare himself for the role of the saxophonist, Joe Pendleton, Kirk rehearsed the saxophone night and day for hours at a time. "I was driving Diana out of the house, not to mention my son."

A Raincheck for Joe was scheduled to open for tryouts in Detroit, but that never happened. Fast-changing events intruded to upset those plans.

Diana's father had died in Bermuda, and she flew there with their infant son, Michael. Her marriage to Kirk was not going well. He claimed, "We were wed before we really got to know each other."

She had more to object to than his saxophone rehearsals. She had learned that he had propositioned one of her best friends from college when she visited them in New York. "Not only that, but he put the make on my attractive niece when she, too, came for a visit. She was only seventeen. It made me wonder how faithful he was when he left the house. I had heard stories that he was playing around. We had several fights. I welcomed going away from him, not only to comfort mother after the loss of my father, but to talk about my marital problems with her."

"At least my marriage to Kirk had produced a wonderful son. But that was not enough. I also wanted a marriage based on mutual trust, and I didn't have that. I had a husband who tried to seduce any beautiful girl who came into his life."

Merrick eventually abandoned his plan to bring *A Raincheck for Joe* to Broadway, but Kirk didn't feel disappointed. Another, more intriguing, offer had arrived.

Unknown to him, Lauren Bacall and Humphrey Bogart had ridden aboard The Super Chief from Los Angeles to Chicago, and then continued aboard The Twentieth Century on to New

Hal Wallis "discovered" Kirk during a search-and-find for promising actors who might reasonably be transplanted from Broadway to Hollywood.

York. There, they'd had some conversations with the film producer Hal B. Wallis [aka "The Starmaker"].

When Wallis complained that there was a shortage of really good young actors in Hollywood, she suggested that he audition Kirk Douglas, whom she defined as "a really good actor—very dynamic."

On Broadway, Wallis attended a performance of *The Wind is Ninety* and departed from the theater deeply impressed with Kirk's talent. He remembered him as "lithe, barrel-chested, a six-footer with a mop of wavy blonde hair." [*Kirk must have appeared taller on stage, as he was always considered one of Hollywood's shorter leading men.*]

"He had a jauntiness about him," Wallis said. "A self-confident grace that commanded attention. He was everything that Bacall said he was."

Backstage, Wallis approached Kirk, finding him "bursting with energy and animal magnetism."

Before the night was over, he offered Kirk a chance at his first movie role. "You'll be starring with one of the best and most highly paid actresses in Hollywood, Barbara Stanwyck. You'll play her weakling of a husband in *The Strange Love of Martha Ivers* (1946)."

As Kirk recalled, he had second thoughts about abandoning his dream of a career on the stage and trading it for Hollywood stardom. He wandered the streets of New York. One older lady nodded to him as she passed him by.

It took a few seconds for him to realize that she was the widowed Eleanor Roosevelt who had nodded at him. Here she was, out walking by herself. No Secret Service. No more First Lady protocols. She seemed to be charting a new life for herself. "Maybe I could do the same, finding not only a new life, but new goals in Hollywood."

The next morning, he called Wallis. "Sign me up. I'm your new boy!"

"Believe it or not, it was David Merrick who walked me to Grand Central on my way out of town, advising me about Hollywood agents."

He boarded the Twentieth Century, which would pass through his hometown of Amsterdam, where his alcoholic, abusive father still lived. He remembered, as a little boy named Issur, how he would stand near the tracks as the elegant train glided by, dreaming of the day when he would be riding in it.

"That dream had come true," he said, as his hometown faded into the background.

Issur was now Kirk Douglas, moving into an unknown future.

CHAPTER FOUR

KIRK MAKES HIS SCREEN DEBUT

As the Henpecked, Alcoholic Husband of Barbara Stanwyck

Kirk's Mentorship with

RONALD REAGAN

Who Discusses a Malady they Share: "Leading-Lady-Itis"

BECOMING A HORNDOG

Kirk's Romantic Interludes with Hollywood's Female Greats:
Jane Greer, Linda Darnell & Several Others

Kirk Becomes an (Intensely Competitive) Friend of

BURT LANCASTER

"I started at the top for my screen debut with none other than Barbara Stanwyck, who a short time before was the highest-paid woman in America," Kirk said.

"In *The Strange Love of Martha Ivers*, I was a weakling and she was strong, but both of us were doomed to die."

Kirk always remembered the day he arrived aboard the
Super Chief in Los Angeles: "It must have been the hottest day of the year.
I felt I'd landed in the Sahara Desert. Here I was in a town built on the San
Andreas Fault. The trick was to pursue my dream while avoiding an earth-
quake. The pitfalls of Hollywood were known to me mainly through the
failure of my two loves, Peggy Diggins and Diana."

David Merrick had contacted the Famous Artists Agency, suggesting
they sign Kirk as one of their clients. Michael Pearman from that agency
was at the station to greet him. By taxi, he was taken to a rather seedy hotel
in downtown Los Angeles and escorted to his room. It was rather cramped,
with a window that opened onto a view of a nearby wall. "It's all that was
available," Pearman said. "With all these returning servicemen, it's impossible to rent a room anywhere."

Pearman had dinner with Kirk that night and filled him in on the Hollywood elite as it related to Famous Artists and to Kirk. Hal Wallis, it was
revealed, was eager to sign him.

Kirk was already familiar with two of the movies he'd produced, *The
Adventures of Robin Hood* (1938; it had made Errol Flynn a star), and
Casablanca (1942; one of Kirk's favorites).

As a member of Tinseltown's power elite, Wallis had even survived
Bette Davis, having produced two of her films: *Dark Victory* (1939) and *Now,
Voyager* (1942).

Back in New York, Wallis had
handed him a copy of the script of *The
Strange Love of Martha Ivers*, and Kirk
had avidly read it three times. He'd
been given the impression that he was
being considered for the role of that
film's male lead, Sam Masterson. But
during his westbound stopover in
Chicago, word had reached him that
Van Heflin—who had just returned
from military service in the Army Air
Corps—had been cast into that role,
instead. *[A deeply entrenched veteran
actor, Heflin had already won a best Supporting Actor Oscar for his portrayal of a
drunk in Johnny Eager (1942), opposite
Robert Taylor and Lana Turner.]*

Pearman told Kirk that although

he'd lost the male lead, he was still being strongly considered for the second male lead, the character of Walter O'Neil, Jr., weak-willed, alcoholic husband of the domineering Martha Ivers (Stanwyck). A woman of iron will, she's is the doyenne of the town, controlling the factory in Pennsylvania that employs most of the workers. She has used her power and influence to shoehorn her husband into a position as the town's attorney general, its chief law enforcer.

The film opens when Sam and Martha are early teenagers, planning to run away together. Her stern aunt, Mrs. Ivers, played by the sinister-looking Judith Anderson, learns about their plan and thwarts it.

A fight ensues when the domineering Mrs. Ivers starts beating Martha's kitten. After Martha strikes her, the older woman falls down the stairs, landing dead at the bottom.

Walter's father, who shrewdly and immediately appraises the situation, recognizes the possibility of defining Mrs. Iver's death as a murder rap against young Martha, and blackmailing her. To that effect, he downplay's Martha's role in the older woman's death. As such, young Martha—the heiress to the older woman's huge estate—becomes an ongoing meal ticket for him and his young son, Walter, Jr. Although it's very obvious that the young heiress doesn't love him, Walter, Jr. and Martha eventually get married,

Martha's real love remains Sam (Heflin).

Unplanned and unexpectedly, as an adult, Sam returns to his home town and re-enters Martha and Sam's life. A subplot revolves around his meeting Toni Marachek, a young woman who has just been released from jail.

The role of Marachek had just been awarded to Lizabeth Scott, an actress known for her "smoky" voice. In time, Scott would be hailed as "the most beautiful face of *film noir* in the 1940s and 50s."

The characters played by Scott and Heflin fall in love, even though Martha (Stanwyck) has intentions of taking up with Sam herself.

Heflin's motivation is un-

Van Heflin with Lizabeth Scott in *The Strange Love of Martha Ivers*.

"In the movie, I'm supposed to fall in love with jailbird Lizabeth Scott," Van Heflin said. "She was a sulky blonde with a husky voice, but I think she was hot for Stanwyck—not me."

clear: Has he returned to Iverstown with the intention of blackmailing Martha for the long-ago "murder" of her aunt and benefactor?

***

Kirk arose early on the morning of his screen test and reread the parts of the script that focused on Walter. Later, at Paramount Studios, he was ushered into a waiting room, where four other actors were also present and waiting to be tested. This shocked him, since Wallis had already promised him the part.

[*The other actors competing for the role included John Lund, Montgomery Clift, Richard Widmark, and Wendell Corey. Kirk already knew two of them, having replaced Widmark in two separate roles on the New York stage. Corey had remained his much-hated nemesis. He'd heard of Clift, who had earned good reviews for his 1942 stage interpretation of* The Skin of Our Teeth. *He'd been reviewed in it as "powerful, sensitive, and magnetic."*

Lund was a serious contender, having already starred with Olivia de Havilland in To Each His Own *(1946), for which she had won an Oscar.]*

Kirk was the first to be called by the director, Lewis Milestone. [*Milestone's parents, like those of Kirk himself, had been born in the old Russian Empire (now Moldova). Milestone's film, as financed by Howard Hughes,* Arabian Knights *(1928), had earned Milestone a Best Director Oscar at the first Academy Award ceremony. He'd also won an equivalent prize for his direction of Erich Maria Remarque's* All Quiet on the Western Front *(1930), which had made Lew Ayres a star.]*

Milestone was behind the camera filming Kirk from the moment he entered the room. and recorded on camera all five of his audition deliveries. Unaware that the camera had already been unrolling, Kirk pronounced at some point that he was ready for his take. In response, and enigmatically, Milestone told him, "You can go home now. I got what I wanted on the third take."

Back within his seedy hotel room, Kirk waited a week for a call from Paramount. When it came through, it was from Milestone himself. "You're our boy," he told him. "Or, put another way, you're Stanwyck's boy."

***

One of the first scenes Kirk filmed within *The Strange Love of Martha Ivers* was one of its most dramatic. In it, he and Stanwyck emoted on screen with the Austalian-born British actress, Judith Anderson. [*She had already*

100

been nominated for an Oscar as Best Supporting Actress for trying to drive Joan Fontaine to suicide in Alfred Hitchcock's Rebecca *(1940).]*

Stanwyck was popular with the crew. She often moved through their ranks, giving them hugs. They affectionately referred to her as "Missy."

"I was scared of her at first. She'd played opposite such leading men as Clark Gable, Henry Fonda, and Robert Taylor, her husband. I sensed that she was having trouble with Taylor. He had recently returned to Hollywood after service in the Navy."

Kirk chose a bad time to make his film debut: Hollywood was embroiled in a post-war labor dispute, and emotions were harsh, raw, and intense.

During the war years, the American Federation of Labor had promised not to have its members go on strike. However, in the immediate aftermath of Japan's surrender, Warner Brothers, 20th Century Fox, and Paramount were each being rocked with labor strikes and shutdowns.

By continuing to work during strikes, the actors and crew of *The Strange Love of Martha Ivers* were bitterly condemned by their colleagues as "scabs." Kirk could not leave the studio at the end of one of his work days, based on fears that whatever car he drove would be stopped, attacked, and turned over by angry picketers.

One day, four hundred organized protestors picketed the studio from a position just outside Paramount's main entrance, wielding clubs, chains, and knives. Two hundred police officers were summoned, and a battle ensued. The police used their nightsticks to club the strikers. Eighty people were injured.

"We were locked in at night, sleeping and showering in our dressing rooms," Kirk said. "It was a terrible time. All day, we could hear the angry shouts of plumbers, electricians, carpenters, blacksmiths, metal workers, and machinists. The smell of tear gas tainted the air, and Paramount's fire hoses were turned on the protesters."

Stanwyck was difficult on the set. At home, she was caught up in marital strife with her bisexual husband, war veteran Robert Taylor. Adding to her tension, she suspected that Scott was having an affair with Wallis, who was giving her extra footage

"To me," Kirk said, "there were three strong women in films—Bette Davis, Joan Crawford, and Barbara Stanwyck. And here I was in my first film—and she's cutting off my balls."

101

at the expense of Stanwyck's screen time.

When she learned that Scott's name would be listed immediately above the film's title, after hers and Heflin's, Stanwyck strenuously objected. In front of Kirk, she told Wallis, "I will only allow a recognized male or female star, not some unknown, to appear before the title." She lost that battle.

In *The Strange Love of Martha Ivers,* Stanwyck played a greedy, loathsome heiress. At the end of the picture, she and Kirk jointly commit suicide, and Heflin flees from Iverstown with Scott.

Stanwyck also got into a fight with Heflin. Cast as a professional gambler, he developed a way of upstaging her by rolling a coin over and over across his hand. "If you pull that trick on me again, I'll upstage you," she told him heatedly. "I'll raise my dress to fix my garter. That way, no one will look at you."

Happier times: Newlyweds Stanwyck and Robert Taylor after their elopement in 1939. By the time she worked with Kirk, their marriage was deeply unhappy but would linger on for years.

At first, she was indifferent to Kirk, who was nervous around her. "Frankly, after a few scenes with me, I won her over with my talent," he said. "We became good buddies."

According to Wallis, "I took a risk putting a powerhouse like Stanwyck opposite a newcomer like Kirk. She was very considerate with him and guided him along."

Finally, the film was wrapped. At around the same time, the strike came to an end.

After a preview of *Martha Ivers* Kirk lamented, "I feel I'll be typecast as a weakling, and I want to play tough guy roles. I found out I was turned down for some good parts, the directors telling Paramount that, 'Kirk Douglas is too weak for the role.' But at least I tried to make the weakling sympathetic."

In 1972, he told a reporter for *Films and Filming,* "If I play a weakling, I try to see where he is strong. If I play a strong character, I search for his weakness. An actor has to be damn careful that he's not typecast, which is often the case in Hollywood."

Film critic Tony Thomas wrote: "It was immediately apparent that Kirk Douglas, even though he may not have realized it himself, was a natural film actor. He had, and has, that strange and indefinable *something,* a presence like invisible phosphorescence. If matched with ability, it is the quality that enables an actor to become a star."

Moderately successful as a film, *The Strange Love of Martha Ivers* generated $3,250,000 at the box office. By 1974, the film had fallen into public domain, as its owners had failed to renew its copyright.

***

In a memoir in which he left out a number of spicy details, Kirk relayed the first time he was invited to a lavish Hollywood party. It overflowed with A-list celebrities from the movie colony who drank a cellar of champagne and feasted from a long table laden with giant shrimp and caviar. His agents at Famous Artists arranged his invitation as a way of introducing him to the Hollywood elite.

Since Diana was still in on the East Coast, the agency also arranged a date for him. Years later, he could not remember the name of the German starlet, only that she was blonde, blue-eyed, and beautiful, "a hottie who evoked that 1930s movie star, Jean Harlow."

When she saw his battered car, a 1937 Ford, she asked him to drive them in her car, instead, a more glamorous model crafted in 1946.

The party attracted about a hundred guests, many of whom Kirk recognized from the movies. He spotted Fred Astaire, Douglas Fairbanks, Jr., and Glenn Ford. The swashbuckler, Errol Flynn, somehow realized who he was and sidled up to him, whispering, "You know? I'll let you in on a secret, sport. I got your young bride before you did. I'm not known as 'in like Flynn' for no reason. Sorry, old chap."

"I wanted to punch the drunk, but I controlled my anger," Kirk said.

Flynn departed hurriedly, as Barbara Hutton, the Woolworth heiress, made a grand entrance and Flynn—known for having had an affair with her—rushed off to greet her.

Kirk was left wondering about Diana. Was she having affairs on the side like he was?

He was distracted with views at the party of Anne Baxter, Ginger Rogers, and Olivia de Havilland, but too shy to try to break into their gossipy circles.

He noticed that the German starlet seemed to know every male in the room, even though she'd been in Hollywood for only a few months. She must have made the rounds from bed to bed. Later, he spotted her in an animated conversation with a woman who turned out to be Frances Fonda, the wife of Henry Fonda. Fonda had met her—a young patrician widow— in England during his filming of *Wings of the Morning* (1937).

[When she was 42, Frances Ford Seymour Fonda (1908-1950), a Canadian-American socialite married at the time to Henry Fonda, made frontpage headlines across America by slashing her throat with a razor and miraculously surviving. Before that attempt on her life, she'd given birth to Jane Fonda, who became as famous a movie star as her dad.]

As the evening wore on, Kirk noticed the starlet talking not only with Frances, but with her husband, Henry, and also to his best friend, James Stewart. It seemed that Stewart had arrived at the party alone. Kirk was hoping that he would be invited to join this group in their conversation, but, even though he circled around it, he was not beckoned over.

Finally, during the final half hour of the party, when most of the other guests had already left, the Berliner returned to Kirk, beginning a conversation but soon after excusing herself for a visit to the women's room. Kirk waited for another thirty minutes, eventually asking a female member of the waitstaff to go check on her. The waitress returned to tell Kirk, "There's no one in there."

Then he asked the bartender if he'd seen the Fonda/Stewart party leave. The bartender told him, "They left through the back door with some blonde."

Angered and humiliated, he left the party and got into his date's car, which had been parked and still had its keys in the ignition. He drove it back to her apartment. There were no lights on. Since Stewart had arrived at the party alone, Kirk suspected that Frances had fixed him up with the German starlet.

He suddenly understood how the party game was played: His date had dumped him for a big-name star. Humiliated, he returned to his lodgings in his own battered old Ford.

He never heard from her ever again. But later, it became clear to Hollywood insiders that her frequent appearances spread-eagled on various of the studio system's casting couches never panned out for her.

He later described his first A-list gala on the West Coast as "my 'Welcome to Hollywood' party."

"Patience was needed on my part," he later said. "I knew that my day would come. When it did, I would be the man whose dates, after dumping their escorts, ran off with."

***

Diana, accompanied by her widowed mother and with Kirk's son, Michael, arrived at Union Station in Los Angeles and instantly found themselves homeless. Kirk, during his filming of *The Strange Love of Martha Ivers* on the Paramount lot, had been hiding behind locked gates as a means of avoiding violence from the striking union members outside.

During Diana's six-week sojourn in Bermuda, and despite the strenuous objections of her mother, she had spent almost every day with Sir Peter Gibbs, whom she described as "a lean and pink young man with a blonde mustache." Reportedly, both Diana and Gibbs found the other "enchanting."

"As a married woman, I should have said no," she wrote in her memoirs.

Diana, her mother, and baby Michael found temporary lodgings within the home of one of the agents at Famous Artists. A few nights later, newly aware of her presence in L.A., Kirk slipped off the Paramount lot in a studio limousine and came to their rescue. He had traded his apartment in Greenwich Village for a small unit on South Bedford. He drove his new family there. As Diana later said, and carefully observed by her mother, "We went to our bedroom with indecent haste."

Baby Michael was asleep as his father gazed down upon him after their long separation. At 4AM, Kirk beat a hasty retreat, heading back to Paramount before the early-morning return of the protesters.

When *The Strange Love of Martha Ivers* was wrapped, Kirk set up a rendezvous with his new agent, Charles Feldman, who had already taken a commission from Kirk's salary for his debut film.

For four days in a row, Kirk showed up on time for 4PM appointments, but on each of those days, he was turned away at 7PM when the office shut down. Finally, on the fifth day, Feldman agreed to see him, but only for ten minutes.

He was a well-known talent agent, one of the most famous in the film industry, although something of an enigma. He disdained publicity, and only his closest associates ever knew what he was up to. His first clients had been Joan Bennett and Charles Boyer, but soon, he'd signed such other stars as John Wayne and Marlene Dietrich. Greta Garbo was a friend, and so were Darryl Zanuck, Samuel Goldwyn, and Jack Warner.

Before the end of 1951, he'd take on Marilyn Monroe, both as a client and as her on-again, off-again lover.

After missing all those previous ap-

Uncooperative, unfriendly, and dismissive: Agent Charles Feldman. He believed in the casting couch—just ask Marilyn Monroe.

pointments with Kirk, Feldman finally had him ushered into his office a few minutes before closing time.

"We've got no film work for you at the moment," he barked. "You've been making a nuisance of yourself, showing up here every day trying to see me. When you become a name as big as John Wayne, then I'll see you!"

[Ironically, in just a few short years, Kirk would not have to wait to see Feldman. In 1950, Feldman produced a film starring Kirk: The Glass Menagerie *by Tennessee Williams.]*

With no money and no work in Hollywood, Kirk phoned his agent in New York, who was able to snag a role for him in a comedy/satire/farce called *Woman Bites Dog*. Leaving Diana and baby Michael behind, he flew to New York and began three weeks of rehearsals.

Diana had to surrender their apartment, and she and Michael lived in motel after motel until a small home, a Swiss-style chalet, became available on Vado Place in Laurel Canyon. Kirk had to put a down-payment on it before they could move in.

Woman Bites Dog went into rehearsals, during which Kirk worked smoothly with his leading lady, Elaine Stritch, an actress from Detroit who had made her Broadway debut in 1944. She was also a singer with a brassy, powerful voice.

She was fresh from an affair with Marlon Brando and spoke glowingly of his manly charms to Kirk. *[He had not completely forgiven Brando for "stealing" the lead role in* Truckline Café.*]*

Although quite young at the time, Stritch had already lost her innocence. She told Kirk that actors touring in plays often turned to each other at night when spouses or lovers weren't available. "It's an old tradition in the theater," she said.

"Makes sense to me," Kirk replied.

"With your wife in Hollywood, fucking God knows who, you might as well share my bed during the run of the play," she allegedly told him.

He gratefully accepted, but the convenience of nights together after days in rehearsal didn't last long. The producer fired her.

Mercedes McCambridge, a muscular (some said "very very butch") powerhouse of a woman, arrived to commandeer the just-vacated role. Orson Welles

Elaine Stritch as Mrs. Sally Adams in the 1952 Broadway version of *Call Me Madam.*

had called her "the world's greatest living radio actress."

"After working with Mercedes that first day, I realized she would not be a leading lady inviting me for a sleepover," he said. "She arrived with a beautiful brunette, and they seemed very much in love. Mercedes had recently divorced her husband. The girl was a *femme* as much as Mercedes was butch."

Woman Bites Dog opened at the Belasco Theatre on Broadway on April 17, 1946, closing three nights later after devastating reviews and very few ticket sales.

Hoping to get another picture deal, Kirk went back to Hollywood to set up housekeeping in a new home with his wife and infant son.

A week later, he met Ronald Reagan, whose marriage to the Oscar-winning actress, Jane Wyman, was grinding to an end. At the time, he was secretly dating a starlet soon to change her name to Marilyn Monroe.

After some male bonding, the new friends exchanged their views on love and marriage.

"My time with Diana in New Orleans was romantic bliss," Kirk said. "But now, I fear I'm not husband material. I need to devote all my attention to becoming a star, and not spend so much time every day fretting over how to put food on the table for a wife and son—and how to keep a roof over our heads. Besides, I don't think only one woman could satisfy me—maybe when I'm old and gray."

"During my marriage to Jane, I came down with *'leading-lady-itis,'* Reagan confessed. "That is, I fell in love with my leading lady, making love to her both on and off the screen. But when a picture is wrapped, we say goodbye, parting on friendly terms, maybe to work again one day, but for the moment at least, heading back to home and hearth. That's the way the game is played here in Hollywood."

"I'm going to follow your example, beginning with my next picture," Kirk said. "I just hope she's a looker."

***

Hal Wallis had no immediate picture for Kirk, so he lent him out to RKO to make *Out of the Past*, set for release in 1947.

At first, Kirk viewed it as just another B picture crime story, but over the decades, *Out of the Past* has become one

Jane Wyman married Ronald Reagan in 1940, the year of release of *Brother Rat and a Baby.*

of the greatest of all *film noirs*, especially celebrated for its haunting light patterns, the work of cinematographer Nicholas Musuraca.

Daniel Mainwaring wrote the screenplay based on his novel, *Build My Gallows High*. He then gave it to Humphrey Bogart, delivering it to his boat when he was onboard and about to set sail for Catalina. Out at sea, Bogie read the script and found the lead role similar to his part as detective Sam Spade in *The Maltese Falcon* (1941). In fact, Mainwaring later admitted that he'd been greatly influenced by *The Maltese Falcon*, which was hailed throughout Hollywood at the time as the gold standard for detective thrillers.

Bogie wanted the role but Warners rejected it, and RKO, then in the throes of being taken over by the aviator/producer Howard Hughes, bought it. He wanted to cast his favorite actor, Robert Mitchum, as the lead.

Warren B. Duff, a son of San Francisco, was named as its producer. He was known mainly for his screenwriting credits, including the 1938 *Angels with Dirty Faces*, starring James Cagney with Bogie in a supporting role.

A Parisian, Jacques Tourneur, was hired as its director, a somewhat odd choice since he was known mainly for low-budget horror movies which had included *Cat People* and *I Walked with a Zombie*, shot in 1942 and 1943, respectively.

Tourneur applauded the choice of Mitchum. A real-life tough guy with a prison record to prove it. he'd been nominated for a Best Supporting Actor Oscar for his role in *The Story of G.I. Joe* (1945). With droopy eyelids and laconic voice, he was, to some, "the epitome of cool."

Both the director and producer wanted "fresh new post-war screen faces" to round out the cast.

For the second male lead, they persuaded Wallis to temporarily free Kirk from his contract, thereby allowing him to work at RKO developing a role that was vastly different from the drunkard weakling he'd played in *The Strange Love of Martha Ivers*.

He set out to deliver an electrifying performance as Whit Sterling, a smooth-talking, deceptively even-tempered racketeer. "I was no Al Capone and movie *cliché* like those Edward G. Robinson and James Cagney roles of the 1930s. I wanted to play Wilt like a hood with charm, charisma, and refinement."

However, when he learned that Mitchum would be his leading man, he was not amused.

He'd only recently lost the lead in *Pursued* (1947) to Mitchum. Director Raoul Walsh screen-tested Kirk for the part and thought he was brilliant. When the footage was shown to the studio chief, Jack Warner, he told Wallis that he found Kirk's cleft chin "repulsive."

Robert Mitchum (good guy) and Kirk Douglas (bad guy) in *Out of the Past*.

Ironically, Mitchum, too, had a cleft chin, but Warner claimed that his was "acceptable."

Kirk was pacified when he learned that whereas he was making $25,000 for two and a half weeks' work, Mitchum was drawing only $10,500 for ten and a half week's work.

A minor role was played by Dickie Moore, the former child star who'd been cast as Mitchum's assistant at his gas station. In preparation for his role as a deaf mute, he studied sign language for a month.

Kirk (bad guy) with Jane Greer (bad girl) in *Out of the Past*

[Moore had a long career starring in 100 movies, notably the Our Gang *comedies, and he also appeared with Marlene Dietrich in* Blonde Venus *(1932). In 1988, he married Jane Powell, MGM's "songbird" of the 1950s, the union lasting until his death in 2015, at which time he was suffering from dementia.]*

Mitchum (good guy) with Jane Greer (bad girl) in *Out of the Past*

A former ballet dancer, Paul Valentine would play Joe Stefanos, Sterling's henchman. He was the husband of the famous stripper, Lili St. Cyr.

Out of the Past had three roles for women—one, a sweet thing; the others for *femmes fatales.* Virginia Huston, cast as Ann, was the love interest of Mitchum's character at the beginning of the film. She took her role seriously, "following him around like his pet poodle," according to Valentine.

The motivating force behind the film was the role of Kathie Moffat, which was awarded to the RKO starlet, Jane Greer, the girl with the "big Joan Crawford eyes."

Born in Washington, D.C., she began life as Betty Jane Greer. In 1940, at the age of 15, she suffered from facial palsy, which paralyzed the left side of her face. In time, she recovered, but her condition was said to have given her "a calm, quizzical gaze and an enigmatic expression." Capitalizing off that, RKO promoted her as "the woman with the Mona Lisa smile." She got rid of the Betty Jane name. "It's too sissy, too *ingénue*-ish, like Mary Lou or Mary Ann."

She became a beauty contest winner and professional model while still in her teens. When she joined the cast, she had achieved recognition in *They Won't Believe Me* (1947), playing a woman abandoned by the heel, Robert Young.

After reading the script, she referred to her role as "a part made in heaven."

Rhonda Fleming was cast as Meta Carson, the sultry but corrupt "secretary" to Eels (Kern Miles), who is blackmailing Sterling for his concealment from the IRS of the fortune he had amassed.

A hometown girl from Los Angeles, Fleming would morph into "The Queen of Technicolor," based on her fair complexion and flaming red hair.

She began working as a film actress while still attending Beverly Hills High School. Her agent was the notorious Henry Willson, known for discovering and launching the careers of the famous "pretty boys" of the 1950s. They included, among many others, Rock Hudson, Tab Hunter, and Robert Wagner. Fleming told Kirk, "When Alfred Hitchcock cast me in my first substantial role in the thriller, *Spellbound* (1945), he said I'd be portraying a nymphomaniac. I rushed home and looked it up in the dictionary. I was shocked."

Kirk might normally have fallen for Fleming had he not become enchanted with Greer instead. *[She would later work with Kirk in one of his most famous films,* Gunfight at the O.K. Corral *(1957), co-starring Burt Lancaster.]*

Part of *Out of the Past* is told in flashback, a familiar refrain in *film noir*. Mitchum, as Jeff Bailey (a former private eye from New York), is running a gas station in a small town in the Sierras. His assistant is "The Kid" (Dickie Moore), who is both deaf and mute. Jeff had moved there based on hopes that he'd escape from his past and settle down with his girlfriend, Ann (Virginia Huston).

Like a bed memory from "out of the past," Joe Stefanos (Paul Valentine) tracks Jeff (Mitchum) down and orders him to report to his former boss, Sterling (Kirk), who is living in a lodge beside Lake Tahoe. Mitchum is ordered to track down Kirk's former mistress, Kathie Moffat (Jane Greer), who, he says, stole $40,000 from him and shot four bullets at him, one of which actually hit and wounded him.

Jeff tracks Kathie, finding her in Acapulco, where he succumbs to her charms, as relayed in his awed screen dialogue: "And then I saw her coming out of the sun, and I knew why Sterling didn't care about that $40,000."

Kathie (Greer) seems to go for him, too, and they flee together, with the full realization that Sterling will be on their trail. In time, another of the gangster's henchmen, Fisher (as played by Steve Brodie) tracks the lovers to a remote cabin in the woods. After an altercation, Kathie fatally shoots him. Then she drives away, leaving Mitchum to bury his body.

Rhonda Fleming. "I was attracted to this fiery redhead," Kirk said. "Her green eyes and creamy skin were an added allure. But something told me to admire from afar."

Later, Jeff learns that Kathie, this genius of sensuality and treachery, is once again living with Sterling (Kirk), and has presumably told him about her romance and collaboration with Mitchum. Nevertheless, Kirk opts to hire Mitchum, despite his betrayal, for yet another job.

This time, the assignment involves dealing with Ken Miles (playing Leonard Eels), an accountant in San Francisco. He's been balancing Sterling's books and is blackmailing him with threats to reveal his larceny to the IRS.

The plot gets complicated, as Sterling (Kirk) and Kathie (Greer) seem to be plotting to frame Jeff (Mitchum) on a murder charge. The film evolves into a metaphor for a world of danger, corruption, and double crosses that can only end in disaster—and it does. The trio of principal stars each die at the end.

The debut of filming of *Out of the Past* was marked with dramas of its own. For transportation to the location, Mitchum chartered a four-passenger airplane at the Los Angeles airport, flying with some members of the crew to Bridgeport, California. A high-altitude hamlet in the Sierra Nevada, close to the Nevada border, it was (and is) noted for its reservoirs, streams, and forests. Although the small aircraft crashed upon landing. Mitchum escaped from the wreckage, hitched a ride into town, and joined Kirk and some of the crew at a local diner. Walking in and spotting Kirk, he immediately asked, "Got any gage? (i.e., marijuana)."

Because of bad weather, there were long delays in shooting. "Bob Mitchum occupied his time writing an ode to a farting horse," Kirk said. "He and I didn't really bond. We were rivals, after all. But we did talk a bit."

Noticing how dedicated Kirk was to his craft, Mitchum said, "Acting is the simplest of all professions. You show up on time, know your lines, hit your mark, and then wander off to get laid."

"I get drunk, follow pretty broads, make a fool of myself, and then stagger home to Dorothy." [Mitchum had married Dorothy Spence in 1940 and was still wed to her at the time of his death in 1997.]

In spite of his casual attitude, critic Roger Ebert hailed Mitchum as "the soul of film noir," and critics cited him as one of the finest actors of Hollywood's Golden Age.

During the shoot, Kirk grew tired of Tourneur's constant praise of Mitchum's acting and the citation of his "pantherlike movements, powerful silences, and expressive quiescence."

On several occasions, Kirk tried to upstage him and steal a scene. Once, he pulled a gold watch fob from his coat pocket and twirled it around like a propeller.

Behind his back, Mitchum referred to Kirk as "a pompous ass." Kirk told the director, "Bob is Hollywood's leading bullshit artist."

Twenty years after the filming of *Out of the Past*, Mitchum and Kirk would co-star in *The Way West*.

***

From the first moment Kirk met Jane Greer, his co-star in *Out of the Past*, he found her serene beauty and cool charm enchanting. The five-foot, five-inch actress with the dark brown hair and brown eyes had a deep-toned voice and perfectly chiseled features. "When she flashed that enigmatic smile at me, I was won over. Her loveliness was devastating. Whenever I could, I spent time with her."

After only three days of emoting for cameras with her, their relationship turned intimate.

In 1944, she had divorced Rudy Vallee, "The Vagabond King," after only a year of marriage. She was still being pursued by Howard Hughes, who had first discovered her when she'd posed for the June 1942 cover of *Life* magazine, modeling a uniform for the newly created Women's Auxiliary Corps.

"This sloe-eyed girl is quite a looker," the aviator/producer told his publicist and pimp, Johnny Meyer. "Get her for me. Put her under my personal contract."

Vallee also spotted her on that cover of *Life* and contacted her mother, telling her "Your daughter should be in pictures."

At the time, Vallee was as famous as the Beatles in the 1960s, and Hughes was one of the most widely publicized and richest men in America. Greer went for Hughes' offer.

Hughes stashed her in a house in Hollywood, with instructions to never leave it in case he decided to drop in. But after four months of isolation, she grew bored, unfulfilled, and restless, and began slipping out at nights for dates with Vallee. She married him in 1943. Hughes responded in fury. "I'll see that you never get cast in a movie."

Rudy Vallee...a disastrous marriage to Jane Greer.

"My marriage to Rudy was a disaster," she confessed to Kirk. "He was a pervert, insisting I dress up like a cheap whore. I had to wear a black *négligée*, black stockings, and black 'Joan Crawford fuck-me high heels'— yes, even in bed. He painted my face white and forced me to dye my hair black like Gale Sondergaard. He also demanded that I paddle him really hard—I mean, really, REALLY hard—before intercourse. He had other sexual interests outside our house: teenaged boys. Finally, I could take it no more and bolted."

Since Kirk was a married man, he and Greer had to slip around to out-of-the-way places where they were unlikely to be recognized. One night, they went for a swim at Malibu.

Howard Hughes...wanted to enslave her.

She told him it was the same spot where Hughes had once escorted her. "He was very depressed that night for reasons I didn't understand. At one point, he stripped off all his clothes and claimed that he was going to commit suicide by walking into the ocean and drowning. I tried to stop him, but he whirled around and knocked me down, causing my nose to bleed. Then he was gone."

She drove to the house of Johnny Meyer, Hughes' pimp and business assistant, for help. With two of Hughes' bodyguards, they searched the beach, but couldn't find a body.

"Johnny told me not to alert the papers, and three days later, Howard turned up with no explanation."

"You sure know how to pick 'em," Kirk said. "Vallee and Hughes—two weirdos, and now me, a happily married man."

"You must not be that happy, or else you wouldn't be cheating on your wife," she said.

"My trouble is that no one woman can sexually satisfy me—except present company, of course."

For a month, Kirk slipped around to see Greer, and Diana and he sustained a number of wrenching arguments. He returned later and later at night from the studio. Although she suspected that he was having an affair with one of his co-stars, she fingered the wrong actress, flame-haired Rhonda Fleming.

Before *Out of the Past* was wrapped, Greer approached him and told him she had to stop seeing him, but without explaining why.

On August 20, 1947, he read in *Variety* that Jane Greer had married Edward Lasker, a Los Angeles lawyer, a union that lasted until 1963.

Quite by chance, Kirk ran into her in 1952, when she was still under contract to MGM. She told him she was trying to get released from her contract. "Whenever there's a good role, MGM gives it either to Lana Turner or to Ava Gardner. There's no chance for another actress to develop stardom at MGM."

He never heard from her again until one night, at his home in 1984, he was watching an episode of the TV soap, *Falcon Crest,* and suddenly Greer appeared on the small screen. As he remembered it, "She was just as beautiful as ever, with those wonderful big eyes that could rival those of Joan Crawford."

***

Playwright Eugene O'Neill had written *Mourning Becomes Electra,* which was presented on Broadway at the Guild Theatre in the autumn of 1931, where it ran for 150 performances.

The play was a retelling of the Greek tragedy, *Oresteia,* by Aeschylus. The doomed and ancient characters were updated to a setting in Massa-

chusetts in 1865, at the end of America's Civil War. In its new version, it was still a saga of murder, adultery, incest, and revenge. Overlong and overwrought, the updated tragedy was divided into three parts: "Homecoming," "The Hunted," and "The Haunted."

Over the years, several screenwriters had tried to adapt O'Neill's play into a film, but the challenge proved too daunting. The goal involved condensing six hours of melodrama into a film of less than three hours. For its general release, it would be cut to a running time of 173 minutes.

Dudley Nichols, the screenwriter and director, assessed himself as the man who would succeed where others had failed. He was one of the most highly regarded screenwriters of the 1930s and 40s, having worked with such directors as John Ford, George Cukor, Howard Hawks, Fritz Lang, and Jean Renoir. Some of his greatest credits included *Bringing Up Baby* (1938), the slapstick comedy co-starring Katharine Hepburn and Cary Grant; the classic western *Stagecoach* (1939) with John Wayne; and Ernest Hemingway's *For Whom the Bell Tolls* (1943), with Gary Cooper and Ingrid Bergman. Nichols had previously been awarded an Oscar for *The Informer* (1935), starring Victor McLaglen.

He had recently directed Ros-

Mourning Becomes Electra: Is its setting in the Deep South appropriate to the nascent insanity of Greek tragedy? YES.

Above, Rosalind Russell in a moment of madness.

115

alind Russell in *Sister Kenny* (1946), the story of a nurse who discovered a treatment for infantile paralysis, only to receive years of opposition from the medical board.

She was not keen to star in *Mourning Becomes Electra,* feeling that the role of Lavinia Mannon was too florid and self-righteously angry, generating little sympathy. Actually, Russell wanted the mother role, and lobbied hard to get Oliva de Havilland cast into the role of her daughter. But ultimately, Nichols prevailed. Russell agreed to star as the daughter, and De Havilland was not hired.

[Both Sister Kenny *and* Mourning Becomes Electra *earned Russell back-to-back Oscar nominations for Best Actress, yet both of the films were miserable flops at the box office.]*

In this murky remake of the Greek tragedy, the distinguished Canadian actor, Raymond Massey, was cast as the doomed family patriarch, Ezra. Thanks in part to his commanding, stage-trained voice, he'd been recently Oscar-nominated for his performance in the title role of *Abe Lincoln in Illinois* (1940). He had also been praised for his performance as Joan Crawford's husband in her Oscar-nominated performance in the 1947 version of her film *Possessed. [Confusingly, Crawford had also performed in a movie in 1931 with the same name.]*

With Massey and Russell already cast, Nichols was able to secure financing, and a commitment that RKO would release the film in 1947.

He had seen Kirk perform in *The Strange Love of Martha Ivers,* and wanted him for the role of Peter Niles, a Yankee captain from the U.S. Artillery during the Civil War. Kirk (as Peter) falls in love with Lavinia, as portrayed by Russell.

"My part was colorless, and my affair with Lavinia was doomed—in fact, nearly all the characters were doomed. What a drag! Even while shooting it, I knew it would be a bomb at the box office."

Mourning Becomes Electra revolves around hatred and spite within the wealthy Mannon family. It unfolds after Ezra returns home from the Civil War for a reunion with his errant wife, Christine, played by the Greek actress, Katina Paxinou. *[Paxinou had made her American film debut in* For Whom the Bell Tolls *(1943), for which she won an Oscar as Best Supporting Actress.]*

Ezra (Massey) discovers that while he was away at war, his wife (Paxinou) has been conducting an affair with the sea captain, Adam Brant. *[That role was awarded to the British actor, Leo Genn. Genn was also a lawyer. After World War II, he had been one of the prosecutors at the trial of Nazi officers who had committed crimes against humanity at the Belsen concentration camp. During the filming of* Electra, *Genn was offered his next film role in* The Snake Pit

(1948), a film that eventually brought an Oscar nomination to Olivia de Havilland. Kirk was disappointed, having coveted the role himself, based on the challenge of working with De Havilland.]

Lavinia (Russell) detests her mother (Paxinou) for having committed adultery. Russell is also jealous because she has a sexual fixation on her father, something bordering on incestuous desire. As the plot thickens, Paxinou murders Massey.

Electra's second male lead, Russell's younger brother, Orin, was played by the distinguished (bisexual) British stage and film actor, Michael Redgrave. He was attracted to Kirk, finding him "dashing and charismatic."

"One night, he admitted to me that he was bisexual," Kirk said. "He was deeply troubled by it, saying that he sometimes cruised Victoria Station in London 'for some bloke for a night of degradation. These quick pick-ups leave me with a feeling of self-disgust.'"

Although there was no recollection that Redgrave ever directly propositioned Kirk, it became obvious to cast and crew that he wanted to.

[Redgrave became the father of two famous stars, Vanessa and Lynn.]

In *Electra*, conspiring as a husband-and-wife team, Russell and Redgrave murder Genn, their mother's lover. That act drives Paxinou to suicide.

No one ever said that the plot of *Electra* was uncomplicated. Consistent with its having been modeled on an ancient Greek tragedy, it carried an additional murky subplot: Redgrave's character also has a love interest, a

This RKO publicity still from *Mourning Becomes Electra* depicts one of the friendlier scenes from this Greek tragedy. From left to right are Nancy Coleman, Kirk, and Katina Paxinou.

woman portrayed by Hazel Niles, cast as Kirk's sister.

Niles was fresh from having performed as Anne Brontë in the movie *Devotion* (1946), a biopic devoted to the famous trio of literary sisters, the Brontës. In it, Ida Lupino was cast as Emily; Olivia de Havilland as Charlotte.

During the shoot, Kirk got to hang out with character actors he deeply admired: Henry Hull was cast as the groundskeeper for the Mannons. "I had first seen him in *Werewolf of London* in 1935," Kirk said. The Kentuckian had made many films, including *High Sierra* (1941) with Humphrey Bogart, and *Lifeboat* (1944) with Tallulah Bankhead.

A Bostonian, Thurston Hall, born in 1882, began working in silent films in 1915 and would be involved in the filming of an astonishing 250 movies before his death in 1958. Kirk was fascinated by his tales of working with Theda Bara in her vamp-costume melodramas. In time, he became typecast as a pompous and blustering authority figure. "Don't always expect a great role—just keep working at anything thrown your way," he advised Kirk.

"I sat through our long, unedited, early version of *Electra*," Kirk said. "I knew after watching it that it would do nothing for my movie career, except perhaps set it back."

Even though it flopped at the box office, *Mourning Becomes Electra* won critical praise, and both Russell and Redgrave received Oscar nominations for their performances.

Kirk did get an honorable mention for it in the *New York Daily News*. "The smiling, open face of Kirk Douglas as Lavinia's *fiancé* is an effective contrast to the dark complexities of the other characters until he, too, is altered by the tragedies."

Liberty magazine noted that even playwright Lillian Hellman [*author of The Little Foxes*] never thought up a family as unpleasant as the Mannons."

[*The most embarrassing moment in Russell's career occurred during the night of the Academy Awards presentations. So certain she was that she would win, she stood up before the winner was announced. Red faced and humiliated, she sat down as the name of Loretta Young—for her role in* The Farmer's Daughter (1947)— *was announced instead.*]

Years later, Kirk encountered Rosalind Russell at a party. "Michael Redgrave was so damn nervous all throughout the shoot," she remembered, "swallowing one pill after another. Dudley Nichols refused to change one line of the script because Eugene O'Neill was his idol. *Electra* was before its time. If released today, I think it would find an audience. Flops are part of life's menu, and I'm not a girl who misses any of the courses."

On Kirk's homefront, Diana wasn't pleased with her by-now exclusive role as a mother and housewife. The role she craved was that of a movie star.

After repeated attempts to speak to her Hollywood agent, he phoned back to tell her that John Ford had agreed to give her a screen test for a role in an upcoming movie, *My Darling Clementine* (1946). In many critical circles, it became known as one of the finest Westerns ever made. The major characters had already been cast with Linda Darnell as the female lead opposite Henry Fonda as Wyatt Earp and Victor Mature as Doc Holliday.

The title role of Clementine, Doc Holliday's former love interest from Boston, was still open. "The part was a schoolmarm type who gets into a fistfight with Darnell," Diana said.

Ford praised Diana's screen test, but the final decision lay in the hands of the studio chief, Darryl F. Zanuck. After two weeks, word reached her that Zanuck had rejected her "because of her crooked front teeth."

Producer Samuel E. Engel met with her in his office to transmit the bad news. She promised to arrange for a dentist to have her teeth fixed, but he said that it would be of no use. "Zanuck will find something else wrong with you."

"As for me, I find you look mighty fine—yes, mighty fine, indeed."

He suggested that he could get her a movie role, but that he expected some "cooperation" on her part. His intentions were all too clear. When he became sexually aggressive, she rejected him, telling him she didn't plan to launch a movie career "on my back."

[Ironically, in one of his future films, Kirk would also portray Doc Holliday, Gunfight at the O.K. Corral *(1957), co-starring with Burt Lancaster cast as Wyatt Earp.]*

Since Diana was still under contract to Fox, and would be until March, her agent called two weeks later to say that a supporting role had become available in *Forever Amber,* filming of which had begun

George Sanders (as a lord) and Linda Darnell (as a courtesan) in a publicity still from *Forever Amber* (1947)

in July of 1946. The first fifteen minutes of footage had been shot with Peggy Cummings, but Zanuck hadn't liked what he'd seen and had fired her.

The recasting of Amber immediately became one of the most hotly contested in Hollywood, the role eventually going to Linda Darnell.

As the most expensive movie that Fox had ever released, Zanuck had high hopes for *Forever Amber*, publicizing it as "Our answer to *Gone With the Wind*."

It was based on Kathleen Winsor's steamy bestseller about a London courtesan who rises to prominence in the court of Charles II.

Diana was assigned a small role, but two weeks later, during a routine medical checkup, her doctor told her she was pregnant. That night, she discussed her dilemma with Kirk, who told her it was fine with him if she wanted to terminate the pregnancy. He could drive her to a clinic in Mexico, where stars often went for an abortion.

After mulling it over, she decided that she wanted to keep the child.

At Fox, she entered into a conspiracy with the wardrobe mistress, Mary Croso, to keep her pregnancy a secret. For the first few months, they plotted to conceal her condition behind her frilly dress.

But seven months into her pregnancy, her condition had become obvious, and she was summoned for a meeting with Fox's director of casting. She was fired on the spot and told that Fox did not plan on renewing her contract.

In December of 1946, about a month before Diana give birth to her second child, Kirk had seemed unusually excited and animated when he announced that his friend, Elaine Stritch, had moved to Hollywood. Diana knew that she'd been his former co-star in *Woman Bites Dog*, a play from which she'd been fired.

Stritch had arrived in town with her parents, Mildred and George Stritch, an executive with the B.F. Goodrich Company. To celebrate their arrival, Kirk invited Stritch and her parents, along with the very pregnant Diana, to a dinner party at Don the Beachcomber. Diana decided that her suspicions about the possibility an ongoing affair were unfounded. Had it been true, she was certain that he would not have invited her to go along.

Diana later defined their evening as "one of the worst of my life." She sat in silence, wanting to pick up one of the drinks (being served in a coconut shell) and hurl it at her husband. "The two lovebirds gazed at each other with glowing eyes, hands and knees brushing together 'accidentally.'"

After dinner, with Stritch, her parents, and Diana in his car, Kirk dropped his wife off at their home, then continued with Stritch and her parents to their hotel a few miles away. He didn't return until 3AM, with the claim that his car had broken down. She didn't believe him. A fight ensued.

On January 23, 1947, labor pains set in, and Kirk broke speed limits racing his wife to the Cedars of Lebanon Hospital, running through every stoplight.

While Kirk was parking the car, she staggered into the emergency room just as her water broke.

In the waiting room an hour later, a nurse arrived to tell Kirk that he was the father of a baby boy. His parents had already agreed to name him Joel.

The birth of a son did little to improve Kirk's dismal marriage. He told his friends, "I'm very unhappy." He claimed that he and Diana had different temperaments, and he found it difficult to live in a compatible homelike environment with her. That's why he was not often at home.

"I think there was jealousy, the kind that actors have who are married," he said. "My career was getting launched, and hers seemed to be going nowhere." He also admitted, "I was having a number of affairs on the side. Hollywood has always been overpopulated with horny broads, and half of them were chasing after me. Over the years, I was especially fond of my leading ladies, but there were plenty of others, too. Let's face it: I like women. I was a bad, bad boy."

Diana was fully aware of this, and she and Kirk had many arguments about his constant womanizing. At one point she asked him "Do you have to fuck anything in a dress?"

According to Kirk, "By 1947, at least by 1948, I had come to realize that divorce was inevitable. The question was when. I knew she'd want custody of our sons, Michael and Joel, and that was okay with me."

***

Hal Wallis had seen Theodore Reeves' unsuccessful play with the bad title, *Beggars Are Coming to Town*. He saw in it a perfect vehicle for some of the young stars he had under contract: Kirk, Burt Lancaster, Lizabeth Scott, and Wendell Corey.

With a title change to *I Walk Alone*, it would be the third and final appearance of Lancaster with Scott, the dewy-eyed beautiful blonde. It would, however, be the first of seven that Lancaster would, in years to come, make as a co-star with Kirk.

Except for *I Walk Alone*, each of the future Lancaster/Douglas movies would have contain roles of equal importance for the two actors. In each of them, however, Kirk was billed after Lancaster.

Although Lancaster became Kirk's friend and confidant, they were also rivals and often got into bitter arguments, yet made up after a few days of pouting. On many occasions, they were considered for the same roles.

Columnist Sheilah Graham, the former lover of novelist F. Scott Fitzgerald, wrote a combined article about both Kirk and Lancaster, entitling it "The Terrible-Tempered Twins: Burt and Kirk."

Gossip columnist Sheilah Graham. "Frankly, I think Burt had the better physique."

She noted that both actors were excessively vain and always concerned with their appearances. Kirk had a habit of combing his hair with his hand all the time. Lancaster glided into a scene, but Kirk had to work himself into a lather before facing the camera. Both of them were excessively proud of their physiques, but when Kirk stood up, you saw that his legs were rather short."

"I noticed that both of them had a hard time controlling their tempers," she claimed. "At times, they took it out on the staff, who couldn't retaliate."

"Kirk was friendly to newspaper people, where Burt was almost always hostile," she said. "I asked Kirk why he was so cooperative with the press."

"I don't want to wake up some morning and hear someone say, 'Who is Kirk Douglas?' I recently heard a sixteen-year-old girl ask, 'Who is Greta Garbo?'"

In her article, Graham pondered why Wallis hired Kirk straight from Broadway, giving him a guaranteed $300 a week. "He was a total failure on the stage, but Wallis thought he might be ideal as Barbara Stanwyck's husband in *The Strange Love of Martha Ivers.*"

"Both Kirk and Burt had something in common, a trait that became more prominent as their star status rose," Graham said. "Each has a super ego, and each liked to tell a director how a picture be made."

***

Kirk had gone to see Lancaster's film debut in the 1946 *The Killers*, based on a short story by Ernest Hemingway. For the role of Lancaster's co-star, the producers cast Ava Gardner. "I was jealous" Kirk said. "Burt got to heat up the sheets with sultry Ava before I got my chance at her."

Wallis hired Robert Smith and John Bright to write the screenplay with

Byron Haskins directing. Haskins was known for his special effects, for which he had already earned three Oscar nominations.

According to Haskins, "After the first few days, I concluded I'd been working with a bisexual, a womanizing straight, a dyke, and a Jew-hater." *[He was referring, respectively to Lancaster, Kirk, Scott, and Corey.]*

Three of the stars—Lancaster, Scott, and Corey—had just filmed *Desert Fury* (1947), a film loaded with homosexual overtones.

I Walk Alone was a dark and shadowy *film noir* in which each of the characters was unsympathetic. In time, however, it became a classic of the post-war era.

The movie was one of the first pictures to show how crime had "evolved" since the Al Capone era. Some considered it an illustration of how gangsters had found a refuge within the top tiers of so-called respectable businesses. Kirk's role was particularly representative of that.

FILM NOIR: Burt Lancaster, Kirk Douglas in *I Walk Alone*.

After serving a fourteen-year prison term, Lancaster is set free and stumbles into this new world like a Rip Van Winkle who's been asleep for a long long time. The world had changed drastically since he'd last been out and about within it.

The relationship of Frankie Madison (Lancaster) and Noll ("Dink") Turner (Kirk) is established in a flashback aimed at their

Kirk Douglas, Lizabeth Scott, and Burt Lancaster

shared status as bootleggers during Prohibition. They're chased by police.

Noll (Kirk) flees when one of the cops is shot but promises to share his ill-gotten gains before he flees. Frankie (Lancaster) takes the rap, although it should have been equally shared.

After he's freed, Frankie heads for a swanky night club, the Regent, which Noll has created with their bootlegging profits. Frankie thinks he's entitled to his half share.

A friend from the 1930s, Dave (played by Corey) greets Frankie and—since he's fresh out of jail without a place to stay—escorts him to a hotel room. Frankie learns that Dave is now Noll's financial guru.

At first, Noll greets Frankie with open hospitality, treating him to a lavish dinner of *canard à l'orange* and vintage champagne. He even makes his mistress, Kay Lawrence (Lizabeth Scott) sexually available to his old pal. But Noll is a clever and icy thug, who does not want a partner, here to collect unpaid debts, muscling his way into his empire.

Wendell Corey in *Rear Window* (1954)

Noll plots Frankie's downfall. When Dave learns of his plan, Noll has Dave murdered, putting the blame on Frankie. Meanwhile, Kay has transferred her affections from Noll to Frankie.

Finally, justice catches up with Noll, who's gunned down by a policeman, allowing Kay and Frankie to pick up the pieces of their lives.

The director was unaware that Corey and Kirk "detested each other. An Arctic chill came over the set every time the two of them had a scene together," Haskin said.

"In my role, I was a real villain, cruel and heartless," Kirk said. "Did I mention avaricious, a real double-crosser who did not rule out murder? After the picture was wrapped, I knew I'd have to find more sympathetic roles—or else I'd be typecast, as Hollywood so often does with stars."

Lancaster and Scott would be the only stars billed above the title in *I Walk Alone.*

***

I Walk Alone was a hit at the box office, although Bosley Crowther, film critic at *The New York Times,* went negative. "It is notable that the slant of sympathy is very strong toward the mug (Burt Lancaster) who did the 'stretch' in prison as though he were some kind of martyr. He plays the role with all the blank-faced aplomb of Tarzan."

However, *Film Bulletin* stated that both Kirk and Lancaster delivered "superb performances."

The Hollywood Reporter asserted that "Kirk Douglas dominates every scene by the sheer force of his underplaying—a talent not much noted in the later stages of his career, but evident enough when seen in conjunction with the teeth-baring flamboyance of Lancaster."

During the shoot, Wallis had appeared on the set several times "to see how my children were faring with an untested director," he said. "It seemed that Kirk had two problems: He wanted to rewrite every scene in which he appeared, and, if it called for high drama, he overplayed it every time. Perhaps in time he could learn more control. Every time Burt wanted to show anger, he flashed his teeth like a mad dog."

Wallis later revealed that he had discovered Lancaster in a "bad play" in New York, *A Sound of Hunting*. "I saw talent there, but he seemed very reluctant to sign with me. He later told me he was suspicious of my approach because a lot of faggots were always coming up to him. I wasn't a faggot, God knows, but I was impressed with his good looks and those broad shoulders, as well as big, capable hands. I knew that women would really go for him on the screen."

***

In addition to Kirk and Burt Lancaster, Hal Wallis was betting on another handsome hunk for post-war stardom: Charlton Heston, an actor with a booming voice, no-nonsense countenance, and sculpted physique.

A former nude model, "Chuck was just the type of actor I was looking for, a real he-man, tall, rangy, and bony." He was described in *The New York Times* as "a tough hewn sort of chap who looks like a triple threat on a Midwestern college football team."

"I knew at once that Kirk, Burt, and Chuck could play the same roles," Wallis said. "If one were not available, I could always call on one of the other actors for the part. After all, the trio came from the same mold."

Heston wanted to play the lead in *Detective Story* (1951), but the role went to Kirk and became one of his most famous pictures. "For me, casting Kirk was a very tough shot— right between the eyes," Heston said.

"Oddly enough, I found that Lizabeth Scott was an ideal leading lady for all three

Kirk's competition for film roles: Charlton Heston, depicted here as *Ben-Hur* (1959).

125

of my beefcakes," Wallis said. "Liz was a pretty husky dame herself, if you get my drift. My boys would have to turn elsewhere to get laid."

"Two of the guys, Kirk and Chuck, starred in separate films with that flame-haired beauty, Susan Hayward," Wallis said. "I heard that both of them rehearsed their love scenes in her bedroom"

Kirk's deal with Wallis called on him to sign to one picture a year for a period of five years. After he starred in *I Walk Alone,* Wallis did attempt to sign him for a new personal contract for seven years.

That led to a violent argument in the producer's office, with Wallis threatening to drop him as a contract player if he didn't sign.

"Okay, kick me out on my ass if that's what you want," Kirk shouted at him.

Wallis did just that.

Years later, Wallis reflected on the volatile trio of actors he'd once signed. "Guys like Chuck, Kirk, and Burt were not willing to be owned lock, stock, and barrel by a studio, but wanted to chart their own careers. As they rose to stardom during the post-war era, the old studio system was breaking down. My studly trio wanted to work for more than just one producer or director, shuffling around between competing studios wherever they found a temporary niche—and so they did."

***

In 1960, Kirk was asked to name his least favorite films. *Mourning Becomes Electra* and *The Walls of Jericho* were at the top of the list of his least favorites. He claimed, "It is the curse of television that keeps bringing back these duds to embarrass me."

Many viewers went to see his 1948 *The Walls of Jericho* thinking it would be a Biblical epic. Actually, it was a soap opera set in 1908 in a small town, Jericho, on the plains of Kansas. Yet even though it had nothing to do with "swords and sandals," it was permeated with some of the same themes: Envy, hate, greed, love, scandal, ambitions, and murder. Kirk's role was minor, that of a supporting player to a trio of bigger name stars at the time: Cornel Wilde, Linda Darnell, and Anne Baxter.

It was one of Kirk's least favorite film projects. And in contrast to the implications of its name, it was not a "swords and sandals" epic. Instead, it was set in a small, gossipy town in Kansas.

Cast into the fourth lead of this 20th Century Fox film drama, Kirk faced a formidable roster of character actors as colleagues. Based on a novel by Paul. I. Wellman, and with a screenplay by Lamar Trotti and a running time of 111 minutes, it was directed by John M. Stahl.

Born in 1886 in Baku, Azerbaijan, Stahl was the son of a Jewish family who had fled from the Russian Empire, like Kirk's parents, and settled into New York. By 1914, Stahl was directing his first silent picture, and by 1924, he was part of the team that included Louis B. Mayer in founding MGM. Three years later, Stahl was one of the founding members of the Academy of Motion Pictures Arts and Sciences.

One of Stahl's most famous movies was the 1934 *Imitation of Life,* starring Claudette Colbert, which was nominated for a Best Picture Oscar. The following year, he made *Magnificent Obsession,* starring Irene Dunne and Robert Taylor. "That was the only movie I ever shot where the leading man was more beautiful than the leading lady," he recalled.

***

Of the supporting actors who played alongside Kirk in *The Walls of Jericho,* Cornel Wilde, a Hungarian, had begun his acting career in 1935, making his Broadway debut. A bisexual, he was the fencing teacher and off-stage lover of Laurence Olivier in the 1940 Broadway production of *Romeo and Juliet,* in which he played Tybalt.

In 1937, he'd toured with Tallulah Bankhead in a production of *Anthony and Cleopatra.* (She insisted that he perform for her on the casting couch as well as on the stage.) It was at this time that he met and married the actress Patricia Knight.

In 1951, Wilde would marry another actress, Jean Wallace, formerly wed to Franchot Tone, Joan Crawford's second husband. Wallace and Wilde starred in several films together.

On the set of *The Walls of Jericho,* Wilde had a reunion with Darnell, with whom he'd made the colossal flop, *Forever Amber,* in 1947.

Although Kirk didn't admit it, Stahl thought he was jealous of Wilde, who was highly athletic and often emphasized his physicality in his roles, as did Kirk himself

More competition for film roles: Cornel Wilde in *The Greatest Show on Earth* (1952)

in his own future films. A former member of the U.S. fencing team, Wilde was perfect as a swashbuckler, and was viewed as the new Errol Flynn of the screen, since the dashing star of the 1930s was aging. Wilde was also a good actor, having been nominated for a Best Actor Oscar in *A Song to Remember* in 1945. *[It was a film biography of Chopin co-starring Merle Oberon.]*

***

Kirk had long been a fan of Linda Darnell. A former child model, she was a daughter of Dallas, Texas, who rode to fame at Fox with co-starring roles in action films opposite the also-dashing Tyrone Power. Lying about her age, she became one of the few actresses who was a leading lady under the age of sixteen.

Life magazine had called Darnell "the most physically perfect girl in Hollywood."

[Kirk had read a 1944 edition of Look magazine which had named Hedy Lamarr, Ingrid Bergman, Gene Tierney, and Darnell as the "four most beautiful women in Hollywood." He made a bet with Lancaster that "I'll have every one of them."]

On the set, Anne Baxter was rather chilly toward Darnell. She had been set to star as Power's sweetheart in *The Mark of Zorro* (1940) but was dismissed in favor of Darnell. Baxter later got her revenge. Darnell had been signed as the female lead in *Swampy Water* (1941) but was dropped and Baxter replaced her.

In 1944, at the age of nineteen, Darnell had married the 42-year-old cameraman, a heavy drinker named Peverell Marley. He introduced her to alcohol, which later evolved into her addiction to the bottle.

Her unsatisfactory marriage was interrupted when the aviator, Howard Hughes, flew into her life. But their fling ended when he refused to marry her, so she returned to Marley and hung out with him until their divorce in 1952.

Bette Davis, Gary Merrill, and Anne Baxter in *All Aboout Eve 1950)*

The second female lead in *The Walls of Jericho* was Anne Baxter, a daughter of Indiana, and the granddaughter of famous architect Frank Lloyd Wright. Before *Jericho*, she had won a Best Supporting Oscar nod for her role in *The Razor's Edge* (1946), opposite

Left to right: John Hodiak, Ann Dvorak, Marjorie Rambeau

Tyrone Power.

Not long after making *Jericho*, she would be plunged into her greatest role as Eve Harrington in *All About Eve* (1950). Both she and her co-star, Bette Davis, would be nominated for Best Actress Oscars, perhaps canceling each other out and making way for Judy Holliday to win for *Born Yesterday*.

At the time Kirk met her, Baxter was still married to actor John Hodiak. Over lunch one day with Kirk, he found her very direct and outspoken. "My marriage to John is the longest winter of my life. Daily estrangement. But because of his reputation, he gets plenty on the side. His endowment has been compared to a very tall beer can."

In the fifth lead was a New Yorker, Ann Dvorak (pronounced *VOR-shack*, with a silent "D"). Born in 1911 to Anna Lehr, the silent film actress, Dvorak made her film debut in the silent film *Romana* (1916) in which she was credited as Baby Anna Lehr. Howard Hughes seduced her and groomed her for stardom. She became famous in such pre-Code films as *Scarface* 1932) with Paul Muni, or *Three on a Match* (also 1932) with Bette Davis and Joan Blondell.

Cornel Wilde, Linda Darnell, and Kirk Douglas in this publicity photo for *Walls of Jericho*

Baxter introduced Kirk to Marjorie Rambeau, another

supporting player in *Jericho*. A veteran stage and screen star born in 1889 in San Francisco, she had appeared in Baxter's film debut, *20 Mule Team,* in 1940, starring Wallace Beery, who had "put the make" on young Baxter.

Rambeau told Kirk fascinating stories of her life, especially when she and her mother lived in Nome, Alaska, singing and playing the banjo in saloons. "Mother made me dress as a boy, so that none of those drunks in those wild and woolly days would proposition me. As it turned out, I think I got more come-ons as a beautiful, porcelain-skinned boy than I would have as a small girl."

Rambeau was a leading lady on Broadway and had worked in silent pictures since 1917. One of her most memorable parts was the title role in *Tugboat Annie Sails Again* in 1940, again with Wallace Beery.

***

A son of South Carolina, Barton MacLane had appeared in many classic films, beginning in the 1930s. He had worked with such directors as Fritz Lang, Michael Curtiz, and John Huston, who cast him opposite Humphrey Bogart in *The Maltese Falcon* (1941).

In the plot of *The Walls of Jericho*, expect to encounter all the deadly sins. As the lead, Wilde was cast as Dave Connors, a lawyer in the dreary little Kansas town of Jericho. He's married to Dvorak in the role of Belle Connors who, to say the least, has a drinking problem.

He's actually in love with Julia Norman (Baxter), a fellow lawyer whom he loves but cannot marry.

Darnell, as Algeria Wedge, is the ambitious and conniving wife of the town's newspaper publisher, Tucker Wedge (Kirk). Tucker is Dave's best friend until his wife plots to destroy his political ambitions.

With three women after him, Dave has more than he can handle. The soap opera gets murky as tensions rise between Belle and Dave. She sues him for divorce and gets so angry, she shoots him. Belle (Dvorak) later claims that she was thrown into a jealous rage by the interference of Algeria (Darnell) into her already troubled marriage.

The movie ends with Julia (Baxter) going to the hospital, where Dave (Wilde) is recovering from the gun wound inflicted by his wife. The audience is left to assume that in time, he will divorce Dvorak and be free to marry Baxter.

The New York Times panned it. "For all the petty and major hates, jealousies, ambitions, with which it is supposed to seethe, *Jericho,* like Kansas, is generally flat.

As the hoodwinked husband, Kirk got only faint praise from *The New*

York Times, the critic calling him "competent."

***

Kirk later admitted that he was Cornel Wilde's best friend on screen, but Linda Darnell's best friend off screen. During the making of *The Walls of Jericho,* she and Kirk began a torrid affair.

She admitted to her best friend, tap-dancing Ann Miller, "I wasn't in love with my husband, and I really fell big for Kirk. He was something new for me—vital, handsome, dashing, and always exciting to be around. During the making of *Jericho,* I started coming home later and later. That led to many fights between my husband and me."

Throughout the course of these dramas, Darnell remained married to Peverell Marley, a close friend of Tyrone Power, her frequent co-star.

She told Kirk, "When I came to Hollywood, I was just a kid living on dreams. Everyone told me how beautiful I was, but I knew that would carry me only so far. I had to learn to act."

"Pev fell in love with my beauty, he never was in love with this timid, little insecure teenager he'd married. I knew nothing about men or what was expected in a wife, and he was not one to teach me. At times, I felt a wife had only one purpose and that was to lie under her husband at night until he got off, fell over in bed, and went to sleep"

As she told Miller, "Kirk was the only real lover I had known up to that point. I might have fallen for Ty, but I felt he was mostly attracted to men. During the pictures we made together, I met several male lovers of his."

Darnell admitted to having fallen very briefly in love with Howard Hughes. "He was strictly into the oral arts," she told Miller, who had already heard that from many of Hughes' other conquests, including both Ava Gardner and Lana Turner.

During the course of her affair with the bisexual Hughes, Darnell learned that he had also been Power's lover. When she confronted him with that as an accusation, Hughes admitted it. "You two dark-haired beauties always look good in private and on the screen in all the movies where you co-starred. Sexy, both of you, with lush contours. Regrettably, the censors won't let a camera reveal it, but Ty has a beautiful cock and you have beautiful

Darryl Zanuck in 1964.

"I make the bitches I hire at Fox put out."

131

breasts. Both of you have silky pubic hair in the exact same shade—you could be twins."

Darnell told Kirk and others that the greatest hardship she confronted as a star was having to deal with Darryl F. Zanuck, the head of Fox. "When I first went to work, he called me into his office one day and locked the door behind us," she confessed. "He talked to me for about ten minutes about my career, then called me over. Then he slid his chair back from his desk and exposed himself to me."

"How's that?" he asked. "A whopper in a town of whoppers."

"I told him how impressed I was, thanked him for the preview, and asked him to zip it up."

That was not the end of the story. As she told Miller, "After a few more attempts to seduce me, two weeks later, he forced me onto the couch, telling me that if I didn't cooperate, he'd ruin my career."

Simultaneous with her seduction by Zanuck, Darnell launched a heavy dating schedule in the early 1940s, beginning with teen idol Mickey Rooney, who was the box office champion in Hollywood. "He was so eager, he couldn't wait to get me home. He went at it right in the car."

Her fling with Rooney was followed by interludes with such stars as Kay Kyser, Eddie Albert, Jackie Cooper, and George Montgomery. Darnell even claimed that she'd had an affair with the German-speaking chicken farmer, Rudolph Sieber, the husband of Marlene Dietrich. "Marlene can have him. No wonder she turned elsewhere looking for romance."

As she told Miller, "Not every actor wanted to get into my pants. Dan Dailey was married but liked to wear my clothes. He was especially fond of my gowns and used to conduct midnight raids on the wardrobe department in an attempt to steal them."

"During the war years, I had all the good things that come with stardom, but I also experienced many of the bad things no woman ever wants." She also confessed that her husband, Pev, was more of a father figure than a lover.

"When Kirk came along," Darnell confessed to Miller, "He found me an easy conquest, even though he was married. I had learned by now that many married stars cheat on their spouses with other stars they might playing love scenes with."

When *Jericho* was wrapped, Darnell's affair with Kirk came to an abrupt end. She told him that she didn't want to see him anymore, at least not romantically. She and her husband had been unable to have children, and they were going to adopt a little girl whom she had already named Charlotte Mildred.

"What can I say?" Kirk asked. "It's been swell, really, really swell. Time for me to go for a long walk along the beach, gaze at the Pacific Ocean, and ask myself 'where do I go from here?'"

***

My Dear Secretary, distributed in 1948 by United Artists, was Kirk's first attempt to impersonate Cary Grant. "Scripts for light comedies came to Kirk Douglas and me only slightly soiled from the finger-prints of Grant after he'd rejected them," said Charlton Heston.

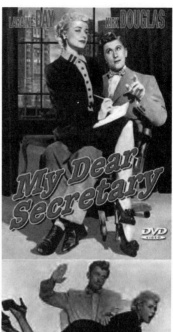

Such was the case when Charles Martin, the director and writer of *My Dear Secretary* sent the script over to Kirk. Not just Grant, but four other actors (Errol Flynn, Glenn Ford, Henry Fonda, and Peter Lawford) had already rejected it.

The script was old-fashioned and run-of-the-mill, the kind of plot that Grant and Rosalind Russell might have successfully handled in the late 1930s or '40s.

Kirk's role was that of a successful writer, Owen Waterbury, who is more of a playboy than a novelist. It seems he has a rotating door of beautiful secretaries he wants as mistresses. He's

Romantic foreplay? Laraine Day and Kirk Douglas.

hired many of them even when they didn't know how to type.

A serious wannabe novelist, Stephanie Gaylord, applies for the job because she is in awe of Owen's previous work. But soon after, she begins working for him, she becomes disillusioned. She finds him deeply in debt and unable to write the novel for which he has already been

Keenan Wynn, Laraine Day, and Kirk in *My Dear Secretary.*

legally contracted.

The supporting role of Ronnie Hastings provides the best comic relief, especially a scene when he, as Owen's best friend and enabler, tries to knead dough in the kitchen. He seems to be the only one in the cast able to cope with the egomaniacal Owen.

Publisher Charles Harris finds Owen's latest novel too ordinary, but secretly reads his secretary's novel and, with high hopes for its commercial appeal, releases it to the public. It goes on to win literary prizes and becomes a best seller, inspiring enormous jealousy from Owen. To complicate matters, Stephanie moves upstairs and hires a male secretary for herself.

But don't despair: Since this is a romantic comedy, not real life, Owen will redeem himself in Stephanie's eyes and they will live together happily ever after, or so we are left to believe.

As the female lead (Stephanie), Martin cast a lovely actress, Laraine Day, who was always pleasant but lacked the skill of a front-ranking actress. Columnist Sheilah Graham noted, "Kirk Douglas and Laraine Day have as much sexual chemistry as W.C. Fields and Mae West."

Kirk considered Day a fine lady but too puritanical for his taste. In New York, at Ebbets Field, home of the old Brooklyn Dodgers, she introduced him to her future husband, the baseball great, Leo Durocher. He persuaded the sports announcer to alert the stadium that Kirk Douglas was in the bleachers. Then he heard a chant in Brooklynese rising from the crowd, "KOIK, KOIK, KOIK!"

Day would soon marry Durocher and earn the title of "First Lady of Baseball."

Of all of Kirk's leading ladies, "Laraine was the purest," he said. "She didn't smoke, swear, or drink. She was such a strict Mormon she even shunned coffee or tea, although she did drink water."

She was a far-right Republican, and her political hero became Ronald Reagan, who had been cast as her leading man in *The Bad Man* (1941).

Later, she made a critical remark about Kirk that got back to him through grapevine gossip: "I worked with the real thing, Cary Grant, in *Mr. Lucky* in 1943, which was a hit. Kirk is merely the mock."

In *My Dear Secretary*, Kirk and Day faced a formidable array of scene-stealing supporting players, none more notable than Kennan Wynn as Ronnie, Owen's enabler. Kirk would appear with Wynn in a future film, too. The son of the fabled

Keenan Wynn...Van Johnson's lover.

vaudeville comedian, Ed Wynn, Keenan had a perfect comic timing, and would be a stock character actor in dozens of films beginning in 1934.

Over lunch with Kirk one day, Wynn told him a sad story. It was widely known in Hollywood that Keenan was the lover of Van Johnson, a leading man hailed as the guy every mother wanted her daughter to marry. Johnson, perpetually linked in the public imagination with June Allyson, were collectively hailed as "America's Sweethearts."

As a condition to Wynn's holding onto his contract at MGM, Louis B. Mayer demanded that he divorce his wife, Eve Lynn Abbott, whom he'd married in 1938, and allow her to marry Johnson as a means of concealing widely spread rumors about his homosexuality.

As the publisher *My Dear Secretary*, crooner Rudy Vallee was personally hostile to Kirk because he'd learned of his torrid affair with his former wife, Jane Greer.

In contrast to Vallee, Kirk found Irene Ryan very friendly. She played his maid, Mary. "This possum-skinning broad from El Paso was a hoot, a lotta fun, tough as nails," Kirk said. Ryan later became a household word when she played Granny in the hit TV series, *The Beverly Hillbillies* (1962-1971).

"Another Texas broad, the San Antonio cactus flower, Florence Bates, was cast as my landlady, Mrs. Reeves," Kirk said. "She may have grown up eating rattlesnake meat washed down with cactus juice, but she ended up playing *grande dames* on the screen. This powerhouse became the first woman lawyer in Texas but started acting at the age of 47. This full-figured belle often played a snob with a look of such disdain that it could melt steel."

"Londoner Alan Mowbray added a touch of distinction to the cast as Deveny," Kirk said. "He was often typecast as a stuffy butler, but he could also portray George Washington." One of his most famous roles was as the uptight husband of Vivien Leigh in *That Hamilton Woman* (1941). He soon discovers that she is carrying on with Laurence Olivier.

Like Ronald Reagan, Kirk liked to seduce his leading ladies, and he looked around, surveying the flock. With the understanding that Laraine Day was definitely off limits because of her association with Durocher, Gale Robbins, cast as Dawn O'Malley, seemed more available. Cast as a sexy blonde singer, actress, and model fond of wearing gowns with plunging décol-

Helen Walker with Tyrone Power in *Nightmare Alley* (1947)

letage, she had appeared on the covers of many magazines. As it happened, she was devotedly in love with her former high school sweetheart, Robert Olson, a member of the U.S. Air Force, whom she'd married in 1943.

For Kirk, that left the beautiful Helen Walker, cast as Elsie. She had just divorced Robert Blumofe, a studio attorney for Paramount.

Although she'd just made her most famous films, *Nightmare Alley* (1947), Kirk came into her life at one of her lowest points. She'd performed in that film opposite Tyrone Power, who had starred as a con artist, climbing to success through women drawn to his good looks.

Very briefly, Walker found comfort in Kirk's strong arms during a period when she lived in great fear that she had destroyed her career.

[In the final days of 1946, in her car en route to Hollywood from Palm Springs, she'd picked up three hitchhiking soldiers. Near Redlands, her car hit a divider and flipped over, killing one of the soldiers and seriously injuring the other two. The police charged her with drunk and reckless driving. Weeks later, one of the surviving soldiers filed a $150,000 lawsuit against her.]

After the picture they were making together was wrapped, Kirk dropped her. He didn't see her again but read in the newspapers that her home burned to the ground in 1960. "Some girls have all the luck," he said, meaning the opposite, of course. She died an alcoholic eight years later.

After sifting through the final cut of *My Dear Secretary*, Kirk said, "Time for me to move on. My talents lay somewhere else. I tried to play Cary Grant, but I wasn't Grant."

One critic claimed, "One of the troubles in casting a young Kirk Douglas is that he delivers the smooth, smug, and manipulative side of his character, but ends up obviously struggling and ultimately failing to make the humor work. The movie at times feels like a collection of actors, working in their own boxes, reciting lines and waiting for their cue."

***

Kirk's next picture, *A Letter to Three Wives*, had a long gestation period before its 1948 release by 20th Century Fox. It began as a short story, "One of Our Hearts" by John Klempner, in *Cosmopolitan*. He later ex-

Three Worried Wives: Which of their husbands, they wonder, has the wife-poacher run away with, and what's the meaning behind the letter?

panded it into a dull novel, *A Letter to Five Wives.*

Although there were many script problems to solve, film rights were acquired by 20th Century Fox in February of 1946. Zanuck wanted Ernst Lubitsch to direct it. But when producer Sol E. Siegel took over, he told Zanuck, "Ernst is past his prime. I want Joseph L. Mankiewicz."

"That arrogant son of a bitch," Zanuck said. "If he gets a hit with this, he'll be unlivable."

Siegel prevailed, and Mankiewicz came aboard, hiring Vera Caspary to adapt the screenplay. A hit screenplay that she'd already crafted had morphed into *Laura* (1944), starring Gene Tierney.

At one point, as actresses portraying the five wives, Zanuck wanted Tierney, Maureen O'Hara, Dorothy McGuire, Alice Faye, and Anne Baxter. The role of Baxter's onscreen husband was awarded to Tyrone Power, since, as a team, Baxter and Power had scored a previous hit with *The Razor's Edge.*

When the script ran too long, it was first cut to four wives, and then to three. At that point, the plot came into sharper focus. In essence, it was a portrait of married life in post-war suburban America, a comment on middle-class mores, money, sex, and class consciousness.

At last three actors and three actresses were assigned the roles of the husbands and wives. Jeanne Crain, as Deborah Bishop, is married to Brad Bishop (Jeffrey Lynn). Kirk Douglas, as George Phipps, is wed to Ann Sothern (Rita Phipps). Linda Darnell, as Lora May Hollingsworth, is married to Paul Douglas (Porter Hollingsworth).

At the debut of the drama, a messenger delivers three letters to three wives who are, as chaperones for a group of schoolchildren, about to embark on a riverboat cruise and picnic. That will place them out of phone contact until their return later in the late afternoon.

The three separate letters referenced in the film's title derive from the town's (unseen) *femme fatale*, Addie Ross. Each letter informs its recipient that the letter-writer is running away with one of their husbands, but not naming which one.

Kirk later said, "I got to play the male version of Addie Ross some time later when I made *The Bad and the Beautiful* with Lana Turner."

During their boat trip, the women have time to reflect on their husbands and the marital trouble that might compel them to leave. Histories of each of their marriages are skillfully relayed in flashback. The suspense builds.

When the wives return from their chaperoning gig, they each embark on a desperate search for their elusive husbands. Rita (Sothern) rushed into the arms of her on-screen husband (and off-screen lover), Kirk.

Deborah (Crain) returns home to be told that Brad (Lynn) won't be returning that night because of a delay in his itinerary. Feeling abandoned, she heads off to a dance at her country club. There, she encounters Porter Hollingsworth (as played by the gruff actor, Paul Douglas), who confesses to his wife, Lora May (Darnell) that he was the one planning to run off with Addie. He says, "But a man can change his mind, can't he?"

The voice of Addie Ross is heard once more, bidding everyone a good night.

The movie's producer, Sol C. Siegel, was instrumental in hiring Kirk. Otherwise, his role might have gone to Richard Widmark, his New York stage rival.

Siegel got his start in Hollywood working with John Wayne and Gene Autry.

After *Three Wives*, he would go one to greater triumphs, winning a Best Picture Oscar for *Three Coins in the Fountain* (1954). He also produced *Gentlemen Prefer Blondes* (1953) which solidified Marilyn Monroe's stardom. In the late 1950s, he became one of the chief executives at MGM.

As the never-seen-onscreen Addie Ross voiceover, Mankiewicz summoned Ida Lupino, who rejected the role. He then contacted Joan Crawford, who at first agreed to do it, but then for some reason backed off, having decided that her voice was "not quite right."

Mankiewicz then contacted Celeste Holm, who had the perfect voice for the role. She had recently won a Best Supporting Actress Oscar for her role in *Gentleman's Agreement* (1947), starring Gregory Peck. At first, she turned him down, but then Mankiewicz told her, "Crawford wants to do it, but I prefer you."

When Holm heard that Crawford wanted it, she said, "I'll do it!" As it happened, her soothing, yet provocative, voice was ideal as that of the husband-stealing temptress.

***

The plot of *Letter to Three Wives* incorporated "portraits" of three separate marriages.

Zanuck insisted that Crain and another Fox contract player, Jeffrey Lynn, play Mr. and Mrs. Brad Bishop. According to Mankiewicz, "Zanuck forced me to cast them. I wanted Maureen O'Hara and Richard Widmark."

Hailing from Barstow, California, Crain was Fox's "sweet young thing," a former beauty contest winner and model. Until then, her two most prominent roles had been *State Fair* and *Leave Her to Heaven*, both released in 1945. In the latter, she played the good sister of bitch Gene Tierney.

In *Three Wives*, Crain, as Deborah Bishop, is a shy, desperately insecure farm girl. As a WAVE in the Navy during World War II, she marries Brad, a handsome, upperclass bachelor (as portrayed by Jeffrey Lynn) who marries her, hauls her back to his hometown, and introduces her to his friends. At the party where she's presented to them, she appears in a mail order, most unstylish, gown.

The most lackluster of the movie's three husbands, Lynn was a stalwart son of Massachusetts who never developed any following and was always a second-tier star. Kirk said, "Poor Jeffrey never got over losing the role of Ashley Wilkes in *Gone With the Wind.*"

[In 1941, he and Ronald Reagan had appeared on the list of "The Top Ten Stars of Tomorrow," although in time, it became obvious that neither of them deserved to be designated as such.

However, Lynn did get to appear with Marilyn Monroe in Home Town Story *(1951), in which she was rumored to have given him a tumble. In another minor role, he appeared in* BUtterfield 8 *(1960), a film that brought Elizabeth Taylor, playing a highclass prostitute, an Oscar.]*

The second couple whose marriage was portrayed in the film were Mr. and Mrs. George Phipps (aka Ann Sothern and

PORTRAITS OF THREE POSTWAR AMERICAN MARRIAGES

Heir to privilege, Jeffrey Lynn with his deeply insecure, not-particularly-distinguished bride, Jeanne Crain.

Kirk, an idealistic professor of literature, with his distracted wife, lioness marketer, Ann Sothern.

Sexual obsession and loathing in the suburbs: Business mogul Paul Douglas with his tough, "fiscally interested" wife, Linda Darnell

139

Kirk). She is a highly paid writer of sappy soap operas, and he is an underpaid, sardonic, pipe-smoking teacher who knows his Shakespeare.

The differences that arise from their respective careers cause tension between them. The husband portrayed by Kirk is also said to have been involved with Addie. On his birthday, which Sothern forgets, she sends him a rare Brahms recording, delivered to his home, which absolutely thrills him.

In a memoir, Kirk wrote that "Ann and I rehearsed our husband-wife relationship offstage. I think Diana knew more than she let on."

The third couple, and the scene stealers of *Three Wives,* consisted of Mr. and Mrs. Porter Hollingsway, played by Paul Douglas in his film debut and Linda Darnell. [*She was fresh from her big flop,* Forever Amber, *and her brief fling offscreen with Kirk while making* The Walls of Jericho.]

As Lora May, Darnell is a sly minx born on the wrong side of the tracks. She morphs into a shameless gold-digger in pursuit of Douglas. He is the gruff and unpolished owner of a chain of department stores. The first time she visits his home, she discovers a photo of Addie on his piano. The filmscript rumors that he offered her frequent financial support, presumably for "favors."

[*As a joke, Mankiewicz placed on the piano a portrait not of Addie, but of Darnell's nemesis, director Otto Preminger, angled in a way that prevented movie audiences from seeing it.*]

As Darnell's rich husband, Paul Douglas in his film debut was a burly, dark-browed down-to-earth, no-nonsense type of guy, gruff and boorish as a spouse. "I'm no pretty boy like Monty Clift," he told Kirk. "I'm about to appear with him in a picture called *The Big Lift* (1950). You and Jeffrey are a hell of a lot better looking than I am in this movie we're making. But a film shouldn't be all pretty faces. Bogart and Paul Muni, and most definitely Edward G. Robinson, became big stars, and no one ever called them pretty boys!"

As back up for the three couples, Mankiewicz was very clever in selecting a strong supporting cast for the character roles.

The most unattractive role in *Letter to Three Wives* was played with her usual brilliance by Florence Bates, who had worked in Kirk's previous film. She plays Rita's boss, the castrating Mrs. Manleigh, with Hobart Cavanaugh cast as her henpecked husband.

Thelma Ritter played Sadie, the best friend of Connie Gilchrist, Lora Mae's mother. [*As a comic note, every time a train roars past the windows of their apartment, the whole kitchen shakes, rattles, and rolls. Ritter's character also works as a maid for Kirk and Sothern, proving that the town they occupy is very small, indeed. Instead of informing mealtime guests that "dinner is served," she shouts, "Soup's on!"]*

Barbara Lawrence was cast as "Babe" Finney, the younger sister of Lora Mae. She had a brief career, causing some to jokingly suggest that Hollywood should stage a Barbara Lawrence Festival, where maybe five fans might show up. Her big moment came in the 1955 *Oklahoma!* in which she got into a knockdown catfight with Gloria Grahame, cast as Ado Annie.

On the set of *Letter to Three Wives,* Kirk feared there might be some rivalry between Mankiewicz and himself over the affections of Darnell. Right after shooting began, she was disappearing for about two hours every day at noon into the director's dressing room.

Nonetheless, Mankiewicz got along smoothly with Kirk. Like Kirk, he was the son of emigrants, except his wife was from Germany, not Russia.

In *Three Wives,* he gave Darnell the best role of her life. The first time on the set, when she encountered Kirk, she shocked him. Although she looked as lovely as ever, with that porcelain skin and exquisite red lips, she had become more hardened. "From her mouth emerged a stream of profanity that would have made Frank Sinatra blush," Kirk said. "She blamed me for ending our affair, although she was the one who gave me my walking papers."

Kirk confided to Sothern that he was jealous of Mankiewicz. "He seems to mesmerize women—handsome, virile, dashing, and a great director."

"Except for the director part, you've got him beat…and more," Sothern assured him.

"What man couldn't love a woman who told him that?" he asked.

One afternoon, Mankiewicz bragged to Kirk, "I don't know what it is, but all my leading ladies fall head over heels in love with me."

Gene Tierney, who starred in *Dragonwyck* in 1946, reportedly had fallen madly in love with Mankiewicz during her recovery from her desertion by John F. Kennedy.

In another context, Judy Garland also was added to Mankiewicz's list of conquests. Garland was only twenty at the time and was thrashing through the anguish of moving from child star to adult roles.

Perhaps hearing of Darnell's affair with her husband, Mankiewicz's wife, the former Rosa Stradler, showed up on the set one day and was introduced to Kirk. He found his statuesque blonde beautiful and charming; she'd once been part of Max Reinhardt's Theater in Vienna. "Who needs Linda when he has Rosa at home?" Kirk asked.

Darnell later confided to Ann Miller, "No doubt about it, Joe is the love of my life." Unknown even to Hollywood insiders, her affair with the director would continue on and off for another six years.

[As Darnell's screen career burned out, she fell on hard times and increasingly turned to the bottle.

In a house fire in Glenview, Illinois, on April 10, 1965, Darnell was trapped in a blaze that swept through the apartment of her former secretary. She was rushed to Chicago's Cook County Hospital, where doctors found burns on 80% of her body. A man who claimed to be her fiancé identified her body. She died shortly after.]

At the 1949 Academy Award Oscar presentations, whereas Mankiewicz won two gold statuettes, one for Best Writing, another for Best Director, none of the stars of *Three Wives* was nominated. Three of them, however, were nominated for Oscars for their contributions to other pictures. They included Kirk for *Champion*, Celeste Holm for *Come to the Stable*, and Jeanne Craine for *Pinky*.

There was a postscript to *Three Wives*. Based on her visibility in that film, Darnell wanted to be cast in the title role of *Pinky*, a film eventually released in 1949. The role called for a black woman to pass as white. But the part went instead to Jeanne Crain, a role that earned her an Oscar nomination.

Mankiewicz went on to make his most celebrated movie, *All About Eve* (1950). Originally, Crain was given the title role of the scheming actress, Eve. But things quickly changed. Claudette Colbert, who had been contracted to play the lead as actress Margo Channing, injured her back and dropped out. *All About Eve* was recast with Bette Davis as Margo, with Anne Baxter *[who had lost out in appearing in* Three Wives*]*, replacing Crain in the role of Eve Harrington.

Mankiewicz talked to Kirk about appearing in *All About Eve* as Bette Davis' director and love interest. But at the last minute, Mankiewicz changed his mind and awarded the role to Gary Merrill, who became the fourth Mr. Bette Davis after the movie was released.

"Just as well," Kirk said. "Bette would surely have cut off my balls."

Mankiewicz liked Celeste Holm's voice in *Three Wives* so much, he awarded her the role of Karen, Margo Channning's best friend.

[In the 1955 Man Without a Star, *Kirk and Crain would co-star, and in 1970, Mankiewicz would cast Kirk as the lead in his cynical western,* There Was a Crooked Man.*]*

***

The brassy, hip-swinging sassy blonde of the 1940s, Ann Sothern, sashayed into Kirk's life on the set of *A Letter to Three Wives*. "The sexual chemistry between them exploded before my eyes," said director Joseph

Mankiewicz. "Fortunately, I had cast them as a man and wife in the film, so they conveniently used that excuse to retreat to her dressing room for rehearsals."

Kirk had been enchanted by Sothern's screen image after seeing two of the *Maisie* movies she'd spearheaded.

[In 1939, MGM had cast her as Maisie Ravier, a brash yet lovable Broadway showgirl, and the movie was such a big hit that it spawned nine sequels. Robert Young was her co-star. Always outspoken, she spread the word, "He's a lousy lay, if anyone's interested."

Louis B. Mayer at MGM had intended the role of Maisie for the platinum blonde bombshell, Jean Harlow, but the script was shelved after her untimely death in 1937.]

Day after day, Kirk got to know this fascinating creature. Born as Har-

WOMEN WE LOVE
Ann Sothern

riette Lake in North Dakota in 1909, she was about seven years older than Kirk. Both stars were still married at the time of their coupling, but each was contemplating a divorce, Sothern perhaps more seriously. In 1949 she divorced her husband, the actor, Robert Sterling. *[She had wed her husband in 1943. She'd been married before.]*

"It was one of those wartime marriages," she told Kirk. "Actually, we went through four years of trial separations and uneasy reconcilations that never lasted. We were okay in the sack, but it was over coffee at breakfast the next morning that we fought."

Lucille Ball, a publicity shot from the 1940s.

She admitted that both she and Sterling had taken advantage of the casting couch as a means of furthering their careers, causing Kirk to conclude that Sothern was not a good bet for keeping secrets.

She claimed that Cary Grant had seduced Sterling during the 1939 filming of *Only Angels Have Wings*, and that another bisexual, actor Robert Taylor, married to Barbara Stanwyck, had seduced him when they'd made *Johnny Eager* in 1941, co-starring Lana Turner. Sterling's next big film had been again with Lana in *Somewhere I'll Find You* in 1942. It had starred Clark Gable. Sothern had seduced Sterling when they were cast together as co-stars in *Ringside Maisie* in 1941.

Sothern fascinated Kirk with tales of her early days in Hollywood. As a redhead, she had started out as an extra in silents in 1927. She had spent most of the 1930s as the "Queen of the Bs" at either RKO or Columbia.

"In those days, you didn't need to be a good actor. All you needed was good looks and the benefit of a studio publicity machine grinding out wonderful lies about you. Actually, I never wanted to go into show business. I wanted to marry a rich man and eat coconut cake the rest of my life. My stage mother, a former concert soprano, had glitzy ideas for me. I thought I'd be a secretary."

No one knew Sothern intimately without soon meeting her best friend, Lucille Ball. "I'm the only person allowed to call her Lucille," she said. "A lot of people think she's tough, but that's just an act—she's soft inside."

"I'm a Hollywood princess—not a Hollywood queen," Sothern said. "But during those Maisie pictures, I used to get fan letters marked 'Maisie, Hollywood,' and the postman knew where to deliver them."

She set up a dinner for Kirk and Ball, with herself as hostess. Before she introduced them, she relayed some tantalizing details about her to Kirk.

Sothern and Ball had been best friends since their first meeting in 1933. Each of them had been cast as bathing beauties in a Darryl Zanuck melodrama, *Broadway Through a Keyhole*. "Zanuck with that 'whopper' of his, insisted on seducing both Lucille and me in the same bed."

Sothern asserted that she'd made her Broadway debut in 1931 in a musical, *America's Sweetheart*, with songs by Rodgers and Lorenz Hart.

Years later, "Lucille would learn that her future husband, Desi Arnaz, was regularly plowing his Cuban sausage into Hart as a means of advancing his career," Sothern said. "Both my husband and Lucille's husband revealed that not only do we gals have to lie on the casting couch, but that men have to do it too, if they feel that it's necessary to get ahead. Take Clark Gable, John Wayne, and Gary Cooper as prime examples of what I mean."

"Don't include me in that club," Kirk said. "I'm strictly a man for the ladies, although I've had plenty of offers from the other team."

"It's amazing that Lucille and I are still friends," Sothern said. "We might have been rivals. She always claimed that she got the roles I turned down. In 1942, I was cast as the lead in the film *DuBarry Was a Lady*, but at the last minute, the director rejected me and gave Lucille the role instead. I didn't return her calls for three months."

Based on Kirk's dinner with Ball, he found her amusing and fascinating, speaking with total candor about the realities of conducting business in the movie colony, especially if you're a woman.

She admitted that Arnaz was frequently gone from home, touring with a band. "Don't feel sorry for him. He gets plenty on the side. In some cases, three a night. He's insatiable."

Ball phoned Sothern the next morning and recommended Kirk as good husband material if he could divorce Diana. "Of course, right now, he has a few more oats to sow, I suspect. So you couldn't expect him to be faithful."

In another conversation with Kirk, Sothern claimed that while Arnaz was touring, "Lucille has launched two affairs with her leading men." She was referring to Franchot Tone, her co-star in *Her Husband's Affairs* and George Sanders in *Lured*, both films released in 1947. Sothern also claimed that Lucille had had affairs with big name actors who included Orson Welles, Henry Fonda, Robert Mitchum, and Milton Berle.

At the end of filming of *A Letter to Three Wives*, Kirk and Sothern delayed their return to their respective spouses for a few days. Kirk made the excuse to Diana that he had to meet with producer Gottfried Reinhardt about his proposal to co-star him in *The Great Sinner* (1949).

Reinhardt, who in the future would helm Kirk and Pier Angeli as trapeze artists in *The Story of Three Loves*, met with Kirk to talk over *The Great Sinner* (1949), the story of a compulsive gambler based on Dostoevsky's *The Gambler.*

He had lined up an impressive, top-rated cast, with Gregory Peck and Ava Gardner in the star roles. Kirk would have the third lead, appearing with such veterans as the great Ethel Barrymore and Walter Houston. Kirk turned it down, the role going to Melvyn Douglas.

When their weekend together was over, during his drive with Sothern back to Los Angeles, Kirk told her that as soon as he divorced Diana, she'd be the next Mrs. Kirk Douglas. At the time, she was in the throes of a divorce from Sterling.

Weeks later, with Ball, Sothern discussed a dilemma she'd suddenly confronted: "Kirk has stopped seeing me. I mean, all of a sudden, and without explanation."

"Dear one, I can tell you the reason: As you know, a cockroach can't walk across Hollywood Boulevard without me finding out. If I were a gossip columnist, I'd put Hedda Hopper and Louella Parsons out of business. It seems Rover Boy is commuting between the beds of Ava Gardner and Hedy Lamarr. It's called 'being a horndog.'"

Sothern looked shocked. "At least we have to compliment the guy's tastes. After all, Hedy and Ava are vying for the title of the world's most beautiful woman."

"As for that proposal of marriage he made to you, let's file it under 'what could have been,'" Ball said. "That's why Hollywood is called the Boulevard of Broken Dreams."

CHAPTER FIVE

AVA GARDNER

How Kirk Launched Their "Lusty Liaisons" (*His words*)
Their Affair Continuing On and Off for Years

CHAMPION

The Gritty Boxing Drama Which Rocketed Kirk to Stardom.
As a Fighter Without a Soul, He Becomes
Marilyn Maxwell's Offscreen Lover.

DIANA HEADS FOR THE DIVORCE COURT,

Winning Custody of Their Sons after Years of Kirk's Womanizing

KIRK IS IMPLICATED

in the Mysterious Disappearance of a Seductive Starlet

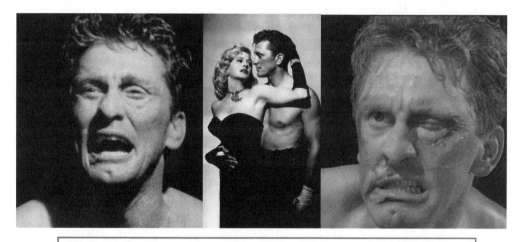

"Up until I was cast as Midge Kelly in *Champion,* I was a weak character on the screen. Now I had a chance to play an anti-hero, the first of such roles in which I would be cast. I was a college wrestler, but knew nothing about boxing. I went into training."

"To get the role, I had to perform a striptease for the producer and director, probably the only actor in Hollywood who had to do that to get a role, although actresses have to do it all the time. Oh, yes, Marilyn Maxwell was one of the fringe benefits of working on *Champion.*"

The "Lusty Liaison" between Kirk Douglas and the magnetic, sultry Ava Gardner began in 1947 when they appeared together in a radio program. They struck up a conversation after they went off the air, and she asked him to accompany her to Romanoff's.

There, Kirk saw Humphrey Bogart sitting alone at a table near the entrance. She introduced Kirk to Bogie, the star of his favorite movie, *Casablanca*. At first, he didn't say anything to Kirk, giving him a limp handshake.

His eyes remained on Ava. "How's our lil' old hillbilly doing tonight? Are you still eating possum and collards?"

"Don't knock hillbillies," she said. "I find that's what attracts 'em to me, *honey chile*," she said.

Bogie finally turned to address Kirk. "So you're the new kid on the block, come to Hollywood to retire us old farts."

"No one could replace you, Mr. Bogart," he answered. "You're my favorite."

"You probably use that line on Errol Flynn, Robert Taylor, and Clark Gable," Bogie said.

"I meant it sincerely, sir," Kirk said.

"Betty told me you're not to be trusted." He was referring, of course, to his wife, Lauren Bacall. "I'd better issue a warning to you right now. Let's get something straight. You're to stay away from my wife."

[Ava and Bogie would co-star in the upcoming The Barefoot Contessa *in 1954, directed by Joseph Mankiewicz, the same director who would soon be helming Kirk in* A Letter to Three Wives.*]*

After dinner, Ava invited Kirk back to her home "for a sleepover, baby boy."

He spent three days and nights with her without ever bothering to call home. Regrettably, that occurred at the time of a High Holiday for Jews, Yom Kippur. As a Jew, and celebrating a time-honored custom, it was a period for Kirk, theoretically, at least, to fast and be abstinent.

"I'd like to see any man keep up with Ava's constant demands for loving—morning, noon, and night—all on an empty stomach. My stomach was growling from starvation. It was painful watching Ava eat a juicy steak."

"I did my best, and I must have pleased her, because she invited me back for repeats. Not just in the next few days, but over the decades." Yom Kippur marked the beginning of his on-again, off-again affair with her.

"We'd even appear on the screen together. But I spent far more time discussing starring in movies with her that went to other actors."

"Her affair with my new best friend, Burt Lancaster, with whom she'd co-starred in *The Killers (1946)*, was over. So there was no jealous rivalry there to deal with. In fact, Burt became my *confidant* in all things related to Ava."

"That Southern minx, Scarlett O'Hara, had nothing on Ava," Kirk said. "To extend that *Gone With the Wind* reference, I was her Rhett Butler, not that weakling Ashley Wilkes. I never understood how a powerful, lusty broad like Scarlett could settle for that limp dishrag, Ashley."

Ava also had a best friend, Lana Turner, to whom Ava confessed, "When I went to bed with Kirk, I found that all the plumbing fitted perfectly. He was not too, too big, nor too small. After all, I didn't expect Frank Sinatra. Kirk likes to make love to a woman exploring all her hidden erotic zones. I don't know who his teacher was. He was a hell of a lot better than the two poor excuses I married—that little whoring runt, Mickey Rooney, and that arrogant son of a bitch, Artie Shaw. He'd married Lana, too."

In a few years, Kirk would be making love to Lana Turner on and off the screen in *The Bad and the Beautiful*. Lana and Ava had a long habit of sharing lovers.

From the moment Kirk met Ava, he was awed by her jaw-dropping beauty. "She was a Tarheel from North Carolina, and I was a Jew boy from upstate New York with illiterate Russian parents. But Ava and I clicked. Here I was in bed with this seductive temptress who nearly drove Frank Sinatra to the point of suicide. The woman Howard

Upper photo: Ava Gardner, as she appeared as a Hollywood cover girl in 1950. When Frank Sinatra saw the cover, he told friends, "I'm going to divorce Nancy and marry this Tarheel broad."

Lower photo: Kirk and Ava as they appeared and emoted together fourteen years later in the political thriller, *Seven Days in May* (1964).

149

Hughes begged to marry him rewarded him with a vase crashing into his head, causing a concussion."

It was Ava who had recommended Kirk to director Robert Slodmark and producer Gottfried Reinhardt to cast him as the third lead in *The Great Sinner*. Eventually released in 1949, It would star Gregory Peck.

That film's original vision had been to feature Deborah Kerr as Peck's leading lady, but Kerr was later—for a while at least—replaced by Lana Turner. Then, after Lana opted to extend

Ava Gardner with Burt Lancaster in *The Killers* (1946). She played Kitty, the seductive, double-dealing, two-faced *femme fatale* who had fatal affairs with just about every male she met.

one of her honeymoons in Europe, the role went to Ava. Lana, meanwhile, continued her honeymoon with her current husband, Bob Topping. "MGM often considered Lana and me for the same parts, as we were the two reigning glamour queens on the lot. But we never fought or backstabbed each other over roles, although I perhaps could have made *The Bad and the Beautiful* with Kirk. Alas, not to be."

In the months to come, a number of directors, actors, and actresses, and especially Kirk's agent, turned out to be a font of gossip about this new beauty in his life. Writer Kitty Kelley quoted a Hollywood insider, "Ava Gardner was sexually uninhibited, wild, all kind of goodies, and quick. She was gone and off with somebody else before you knew where you were."

She was said to take on lovers and discard them in the time it took to eat a sandwich. Her love affair with musician Mel Tormé lasted a couple of months. She made *The Hucksters* (1947) with Clark Gable. The King of Hollywood had been her screen idol as a girl, and she had no trouble replacing Tormé with him.

Both Lana and Ava enjoyed the charms of Turhan Bey. Of Turkish and Czech descent, he was a leading purveyor of exotic foreign roles on the screen. One night, the couple were on a double date with the English actor, David Niven and his girlfriend. Ava made off with Niven that night, leaving Bey at table with Niven's date, Peggy Maley, who was said to "have the most beautiful breasts in Hollywood," where the competition was stiff. *[Ava was also a contender, Rooney comparing her big brown nipples to the "dou-*

ble-long golden raisins of California."

"I didn't see much of Ava when she was co-starring with Robert Taylor in The Bribe (1949)," Kirk said. "Taylor's nights away from his wife, Barbara Stanwyck, were spent worshipping Ava's golden raisins."]

One night, Kirk dared ask Ava about her affair with "the ambassador's son," John F. Kennedy. She'd met him through their mutual friend, actor Robert Stack.

"I hardly remember it," she said. "He was one of those quick, in-and-out lovers. You got a pat on the ass, and he's on the phone talking to some jerk in Boston. The only thing I didn't like about Kennedy is that he stuck me with his big long-distance phone bill."

In the beginning of Kirk's affair with Ava, many of her nights were spent with actor Howard Duff, then 29 years old.

"I could hear Duff on the radio playing detective Sam Spade," Kirk said. "But Bogie was better in the movie."

"Burt (Lancaster) told me about this Duff guy when they had co-starred in *Brute Force* (1947). You know, my buddy Burt was bi, and he suggested to Ava a three-way with Duff. She was for it, but Duff said, 'definitely not—the whole idea is disgusting.'"

Duff fell hard for Ava, but she told him, "I don't believe in love. You can't trust it, and I should know."

Ava was appearing on and off the screen with Robert Walker in *One Touch of Venus* (1948). For the picture, she had to pose nude for the New York sculptor Joseph Nicolosi.

"The producers were a bit concerned about revealing her breasts and the pubic mound, the *mons veneris*," he said. "Miss Gardner gives the appearance of slenderness but possesses the roundness and fullness in the necessary places, which sets her apart from the emaciated female whose cadaverous outlines most American women seem determined to achieve."

***

As Kirk was mulling over the offer he'd received to appear with Gregory Peck and Ava Gardner in *The Great Sinner,* a second and most intriguing role was presented to him by Stanley Kramer, to appear in a film that, eventually, was also released in 1949.

It was *Champion.* It would be shot by Screen Plays Production and released by United Artists. The grim, gritty saga was of boxer Midge Kelly, who punches his way to the top, using and discarding anyone in his path, until he triumphs in the ring only to meet death in his locker room.

At first, Kramer thought of casting John Payne, a handsome star who had the physique of a boxer. He was available for $35,000.

Kramer thought about it before deciding on Kirk.

Kirk was vastly intrigued with the opportunity to portray an almost immoral character, albeit with a few good and strong qualities. He talked it over with his agent.

Charles Feldman told Kirk, "You'd be a crazy actor, a damn fool if you turn down *The Great Sinner*. It's going to be big, thanks to two of Hollywood's brightest stars, Ava and Gregory. Appearing with them might give you star status. They're also willing to pay you $40,000, the most you've ever been offered. Kramer wants to give you a paltry $15,000—and deferred payment at that. Besides, when I first met this Kramer guy, he was an errand boy around the studios."

To that, Kirk responded, "I was once a waiter in New York, serving rich desserts to fat ladies who lunch."

At the time, Kirk knew almost nothing about Kramer, other than what he'd read in an article about him in *Variety*. He had emerged intact from a tough neighborhood in Manhattan (Hell's Kitchen) known for its gangs. He also knew that Kramer's parents, like his own, were Jewish.

Kramer had set out to study law, but drifted instead to Hollywood, where he barely survived on odd jobs in the film industry, including moving furniture around on film sets. That eventually led to film cutting.

After service in World War II, Kramer returned to Hollywood, as did thousands of other ex-servicemen, and he could find no jobs. He decided to set up his own company, Screen Plays Production, on a shoestring. He now wanted to film *Champion*, which he told Kirk would become the greatest boxing film of all time.

Kirk was given a copy of the screen treatment by Carl Foreman, which he took home one weekend and read four times, sometimes saying the lines of the boxer, Midge, out loud.

Foreman was another unknown quantity to him. He had been born to working-class Jewish parents in Chicago and had broken into Hollywood by selling a screenplay to Monogram Pictures for the East Side Kids called *Bowery Blitzkrieg*. He was paid $25 for it. He had just recently written *So This Is New York* in 1948 for Kramer, starring Henry Morgan. It flopped at the box office.

Foreman had adapted the screenplay from a Ring Lardner short story. He was mainly a sports columnist, and his fiction had been praised by everyone from Virginia Woolf to Ernest Hemingway. Lardner was also said to have been the inspiration for the tragic character of Abe North in F. Scott Fitzgerald's last complete novel, *Tender Is the Night*.

Kirk also read the original Lardner story, and he noted a considerable difference in the character of Midge. The Lardner antihero was a boxer without a soul. Forman had added some soft touches to show that he was not a raging monster, but still, he would do almost anything—betray his women and his closest friends on his way to the top.

"After mulling it over, I decided to do it, and went to Kramer's office on Monday morning. He found the producer in conference with Foreman.

Both men assured him they were not homosexual when they asked him to remove his shirt. He did so and flexed his muscles.

"A boxer's legs are very important in the ring," Kramer said. "Your chest is perfect. Now would you take off your pants? I assume that you're wearing underwear."

"Assumption correct," Kirk said, taking off his pants and tossing them onto a nearby chair. Then he posed for inspection by both men, and each of them said he had the right body for the role.

Jokingly, Kirk said, "I hear many starlets get their start in show business by showing off their legs."

"That…and other things," Kramer responded. "Now you should begin your training as a boxer."

Before beginning training, Kirk arranged to see two boxing movies, mainly *Body and Soul* (1947) starring John Garfield. Some critics hailed it as "the first great film about boxing." Kirk was awed by the realism of the fight scenes, and he hoped he could replicate them in his own style.

He also arranged to

Character actor Paul Stewart (left) is depicted in a dressing room scene with Midge Kelly (Kirk), whom he manages, until the boxer betrays him.

see an early release of *The Set Up* (1949), starring Robert Ryan as a has-been boxer in his final match. After sitting through it, he decided that that role had little to do with Midge Kelly, who was on his way up, in contrast to the boxer portrayed by Ryan, who was on the verge of being thrown out the door.

Even before a single scene was put on film, Kirk began three weeks of intensive training as a boxer. He already knew how to skip rope as boxers do. He had learned that as a wrestler in college.

But for the technique of punching speed bags and hard bags, he turned to his trainer, "Mushy" Callahan, who had been the World Light Welterweight champ from 1926 to 1930.

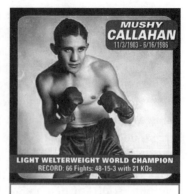

MUSHY CALLAHAN
11/3/1903 - 6/16/1986

LIGHT WELTERWEIGHT WORLD CHAMPION
RECORD: 66 Fights: 48-15-3 with 21 KOs

Boxing champ "Mushy" Callahan was hired to teach Kirk how to box.

"I didn't mean to, but I knocked him out three different times," Mushy said. "When I put on those gloves, I become a killer."

Born on Manhattan's East Side to a produce merchant, Mushy ended up playing extras in boxing films. After he finished with Kirk, he'd be working on *House of Strangers,* a crime drama starring Edward G. Robinson and released by 20th Century Fox.

As guided by Mushy, Kirk worked out the routines that Midge would execute in the ring. It involved moving forward toward his opponent, no matter how severe the blows. "Even when Midge gets his face smashed, I wanted to throw caution to the wind and get in the lucky blow that would carry me to victory no matter how battered, bloody, and bruised I was. In fact that would occur that very way at the end of *Champion*."

After a reasonable amount of training, Kirk was told that the director, Mark Robson, wanted to see him in a mock boxing match with Mushy, so that he could gauge how he moved about in the ring.

A Canadian from Montréal, Robson had begun his career in Hollywood as a film editor working on what has been hailed as "the greatest movie ever made," *Citizen Kane* (1941). As an assistant film editor, he'd survived many a ferocious battle with its star, Orson Welles.

Kirk and Robson worked smoothly together, and Kirk would follow his career for years. He took pleasure in Robson's successes, including *The Bridges at Toko-Ri* (1954). *[After that, Kirk overlooked Robson's directorial embarrassments, notably* Peyton Place *(1957) and Jacqueline Susann's* The Valley of the Dolls *(1967).]*

After watching their bout, Robson told Kirk he was impressed.

"Before Mushy, I had three left hands, but he's turned me into a passable fighter," Kirk said.

Over the years, Robson had nothing but praise for Kirk's film roles. He told the press, "I'm amazed at the diligence he applies to researching whatever role he is required to play, ranging from aerial gymnastics to juggling."

In a *Saturday Evening Post* story years later, Kirk cited *Champion* as the context for the diligence associated with learning skills associated with later films. "I'm willing to work long and hard to master a skill. Perhaps it's just another manifestation of my hamminess—a desire to create a sensation with an unexpected accomplishment, then throw it away by saying, 'It's really nothing.' But I honestly don't think that is it. It's not so much exhibitionism on my part, but a need to succeed at those games of 'let's pretend.' If I believe them hard enough, moviegoers might believe them, too."

"When *Champion* was released, and my body was on display, tons of fan mail poured in, mainly from horny women, but also from an army of homosexuals—we didn't call them gay back then."

He and Foreman had a serious talk that lasted five hours, going over the Midge character and *Champion's* intricate plot.

"I see Midge as a boxer who fights his way to the top by knocking out his opponents in the ring and backstabbing his friends, including the women who fall in love with him. In the end, he even double crosses Tommy Haley (Paul Stewart), who paved the road to Midge's fame in the ring."

Connie Kelly (Arthur Kennedy) is his crippled, faithful, and loyal brother throughout most of the film, at least until he can take it no more. In the opening, Midge and Connie (two badly named characters) hitchhike from Chicago to Los Angeles. From beside the road, they're picked up by a well-known boxer, Johnny Dunne (John Daheim). In the front seat with him is a beautiful but rather sullen, impatient, and dismissive blonde, Grace Diamond (Marilyn Maxwell).

The brothers thought they had an investment in a restaurant but found out they've been tricked. Desperate to survive, they take jobs at that seedy dive waiting tables and washing dishes. The restaurant is owned by Lew Bryce (Harry Shannon), who has a beautiful daughter Emma (Ruth

Roman). Midge pursues Emma and ends up an unwilling groom in a shotgun wedding engineered by her father.

He's not husband material and wants to go into the ring, and he does, winning a series of minor boxing matches, working himself up to face the champ, Johnny Dunne, the same man who had picked him up as a hitchhiker. Kirk "destroys" him in the ring and then goes after Diamond (Maxwell), the same (then skeptical and dismissive) blonde who had escorted Dunne when he'd picked up Kirk and his brother as hitchhikers.

With Dunne no longer a prominent (or winning) boxer, Maxwell

Ruth Roman (as Emma, Kirk's wife in *Champion*) whom he charmed, seduced, and abandoned early in the film.

sets her sights on Midge, warning him, "I'm expensive."

Midge wins the title and becomes a favorite with fans. As a sideline, he gets involved with a married woman, Palmer Harris, but her husband buys Midge off.

After a series of events, Dunne is ready to make a comeback, and Midge once again faces him in the ring.

The boxing match turns out as one of the most brutal ever filmed. Dunne constantly pounds Midge, repeatedly pummeling his fist into his face. Midge's manager wants to throw in the towel, since his boxer is seriously injured. But Midge summons some hidden reserve to deliver a knockout punch, even though (the audience learns later) he's bleeding, internally, from a cerebral hemorrhage.

Foreman told Kirk he wanted an ending that would be the most dramatic of any boxing movie ever filmed. Elated in the locker room, after the fight, and just before he collapses and dies, he smashes his

In *Champion*, Lola Albright played the spoiled and unfulfilled wife, Palmer Harris, of a cold and calculating boxing manager. When she falls madly in love with Kirk, her husband offers him a bigger percentage of the gate to leave his wife alone. When the boxer agrees, Palmer is distraught.

156

fists into the metal wall of his locker, crushing his once "killer hands" that, had he lived, would have finished his career as a boxer. In obvious agony, he holds his mangled hands up to his manager (and the audience) to inspect. It is his final act on earth.

***

Kirk's supporting players in *Champion* included a staggering roster of talent.

As his crippled brother, Connie, Arthur Kennedy had been born John Kennedy in Massachusetts, but had changed his name to avoid confusion with the Kennedy who became president. The year of *Champion's* release, he had won a Tony Award for Best Featured Actor in a Play for his performance in Arthur Miller's *Death of a Salesman*.

Kennedy had made his film debut as James Cagney's sibling in *City for Conquest* in 1940. He would soon be appearing opposite Kirk in Tennessee Williams' *The Glass Menagerie*.

Cast as Midge's manager, Tommy Haley, Paul Stewart had made his film debut in *Citizen Kane* and would later co-star with Kirk again in *The Bad and the Beautiful* and *The Juggler*.

Kirk knew that all three of his leading ladies were beautiful, and in the back of his mind, as he relayed to Kennedy, "I plan to knock 'em off one by one, beginning with Ruth Roman."

Born to a carnival barker in Massachusetts, the child of Lithuanian Jewish parents, Roman became a cigarette girl and a model before breaking into films.

Kirk was too aggressive in approaching her. "Since you play my love interest—later my wife—perhaps you should come to my dressing room for a rehearsal."

"Perhaps not," she answered.

"Ruth was a beauty, but all ice," he recalled.

"The year she worked with Kirk was pivotal in her career. She'd just completed *The Window* (1949) in which she was one of the killers who wants young Bobby Driscoll out of the way. She was about to co-star with Bette Davis in one of her worst movies, *Beyond the Forest* (1949), the film that ended her long and fabulous career at Warner Brothers.

"I watched Ruth's career over the years, and decided she was a survivor," Kirk said.

Arthur Kennedy as the Champ's supportive, long-suffering brother.

"After all, she even survived the sinking of the *Andrea Doria,* a disaster right up there with the *Titanic."* [*Registered in Italy, the Andrea Doria collided with another passenger liner, registered in Sweden, in a fog off the coast of Nantucket in 1956, Ruth Roman, on board with her three-year-old son, Richard, seemed to mimic in real life the role she'd played of a distraught mother in search of her child in* Three Secrets (1950). *Photos of Roman waiting on a pier in Manhattan for the return of her infant son (eventually, he was returned to her aboard one of the rescue vessels) created a tabloid frenzy that oddly evoked her earlier movie role.*]

After his turndown from Roman, Kirk cast a seductive eye toward another of his movie conquests, Lola Albright, cast as Palmer Harris.

The daughter of gospel music singers from Akron, Ohio, Albright was a sultry singer herself. While working as a photographer's model in Chicago, she was discovered by a talent scout and moved to Hollywood at the age of 23. Soon, she was appearing in two Judy Garland movies, *The Pirate* and *Easter Parade,* both released in 1948.

"Lola was in the throes of divorcing her first husband, Warren Dean, a Cleveland radio announcer, and it was obvious that she was shopping around for her next guy. I made a pass at her, and unlike Roman, that stuck-up bitch, Lola accepted. It turned out to be a two-night stand. I meant to carry on with her until the picture was wrapped, but along comes that blonde bombshell, Marilyn Maxwell, and I went bonkers."

[*In 1957, Albright sent Kirk her first album,* Lola Wants You, *with a note: "How have you been doing, handsome? Give me a call." She enclosed her private number.*

"*Lola wanted me on that album and in the flesh as well," Kirk said. "She was married to the famous actor, Jack Carson, but they would soon be heading for the divorce court. I was too involved at the time and for many reasons, turned down her tantalizing offer."*]

Shortly after the opening of *The Great Sinner,* Kirk went to see it. "Except for the beauty of Ava Gardner, it was a colossal bore. I knew I'd made the right decision to turn down the role of Armand de Glasse. It went to another movie star

Here's a scene from *The Great Sinner* (1949), the period romance that Kirk almost accepted a role in, had he not wisely opted instead to star in *Champion.* Melvyn Douglas took Kirk's role in the movie that co-starred Gregory Peck and Ava Gardner.

The Great Sinner was a box office flop, an ironic affirmation for Kirk's luck in opting for a winning script.

named Douglas—Melvin Douglas. *The Great Sinner* was a big flop at the box office, with MGM losing a million dollars. If I'd taken that role, my movie career might have ended in 1949."

In contrast, *Champion* was a big box office hit and shot Kirk into stardom. Made for a modest $600,000, it grossed millions at the box office, and *Rotten Tomatoes* estimated that 92 percent of its reviews were positive.

The *Hollywood Reporter* proclaimed, "Kirk Douglas, who had been edging himself rapidly up the stellar ladder, completes the climb with his performance in *Champion.*" *Look* magazine defined Kirk as "rousing in a role that makes him an important screen star overnight." *Variety* thought his boxing matches were "frighteningly realistic," and the *Los Angeles Times* claimed, "Douglas is quite irresistible, grinning and cocky."

Bosley Crowther of *The New York Times* had praise for *Champion*, though he thought it paled in comparison to John Garfield's *Body and Soul.* "Kirk Douglas, as an up-from-the-gutter kid, pushes himself into the prize ring and rises by stepping on heads. He does a good, aggressive job, with a slight inclination to be overly eager at times, which might amuse an old fight fan."

Film historian Ray Didinger claimed that "Kirk Douglas's image as a tough guy was established after the release of *Champion*....He saw it as a greater risk than the more lucrative offer to appear with Gregory Peck and Ava Gardner, but he felt *Champion* would be a greater opportunity. He took the part and absolutely nailed it."

Yet another historian, Frederick Romano, claimed that "The acting of Kirk Douglas is alarmingly authentic. Perhaps his best characteristic is his patented snarl and grimace. He leaves no doubt that he is a man on a mission."

Champion received eight Oscar nominations, including Best Actor for Kirk and a Best Supporting Actor nod to Kennedy. Both of them lost, Kirk to Broderick Crawford for *All the King's Men,* and Kennedy to Dean Jagger for *Twelve O'Clock High.*

One afternoon on the lot, after the release of *Champion,* Kirk encountered the gossip columnist, Hedda Hopper. From beneath her oversized hat, she frowned at him. "You know, Kirk Douglas, you've changed. The success of *Champion* has really gone to your head, you know. You're such an S.O.B. now."

"Not so, Hedda," he shot back. "You're wrong. Even before *Champion*, I was an S.O.B. You just never noticed before."

Her rival, columnist Sheilah Graham, had interviewed Kirk before, and she too saw him after the release of *Champion*. "He was wallowing in this new deferential attitude his fellow workers were showing him, part of the baggage that comes with stardom. It isn't always the star who changes with success, it's the people around him. They speak to him in more worshipping tones. As for Kirk, he not only believes everything good written about him, he adds more praise. His press agent and the publicity people tell him every day 'You're the greatest actor in the world. If Kirk had made *The Great Sinner* instead of *Champion,* he might be back jerking sodas at Schrafft's."

Graham also talked to his agent, Charles Feldman, who told her, "Kirk's a tough shit, but a shit with style. Don't quote me. I don't want to lose him as a client now that he's becoming a big star."

One night, Kirk, by himself, drove to a theater and gazed for one entire hour at its illuminated marquee that had spelled out with his name in lights—KIRK DOUGLAS IN CHAMPION.

"As the tears rolled down, I seemed to explode inside. 'Issur Danielovitch' I said to myself. 'You're a god damn movie star, and your new name is Kirk Douglas.'"

***

Long before Kirk began working with Marilyn Maxwell on the set of *Champion,* Frank Sinatra had already articulated her glories to many of the insiders of Hollywood. "She's a helluva broad," he frequently said. *[Sinatra had "heavily dated" her throughout much of the 1940s, a relationship which seriously threatened his marriage to his faithful, long-suffering wife, Nancy.]*

Maxwell had not confined her charms just to Sinatra. When she toured with Bob Hope on one of his USO tours, they became lovers, a relationship that continued after their return to Hollywood. Their affair became so open that Marilyn was sometimes referred to as "Mrs. Bob Hope."

Her most surprising affair was with Rock Hudson, and she was often cited as proof of his bisexuality. At first, she'd dismissed his gayness, writing it off as a "passing fad." But the fad stuck around. Although he proposed marriage to her, providing she'd let him have affairs with men on the side, she turned him town.

All her lovers found that she had not only beauty but loads of charm backed up with a zany humor and an infectious laugh. "She's the kind of gal you could have fun with, with no strings attached," Kirk told Stanley Kramer. "She was a good singer and dancer as well as an actress, and her career should have done better than it did."

"On some evenings I spent with her, away from Diana, we'd just listen to records when not going at it. She's a devotee of the Big Band era, and just adores Sinatra's songs. Even a little Doris Day. Coincidentally, my next picture would be with Day."

Since her affair with Sinatra was no secret, Maxwell often spoke about him to Kirk and others. Both she and Sinatra had begun their careers as band singers—in her case, she began singing with the Buddy Rogers Band when she was only sixteen.

She'd made her first film, *Stand By for Action,* in 1942, during which time she'd had an affair with the star of the picture, Robert Taylor.

Maxwell had also appeared on film with Judy Garland, who had introduced her to Sinatra. "Marilyn understood Frankie's restlessness," Garland said. "He told me he'd married too young and wasn't ready to settle down. He was always wandering the studio looking for the next beautiful starlet to seduce."

Maxwell confessed to Kirk, "I understand Frankie to his toenails. Nancy does not. He's impatient waiting around, as film making can be one long, dull process. I'm aware of the demands made on him by the press, reporters, photographers, and the endless publicity. Nancy just doesn't get it. She expects a horndog like him to return to home and hearth at night with the pasta sauce on the stove."

According to Kirk, "Marilyn had a lot of spunk, and I liked that in a woman. When I met her, she'd been divorced from actor John Conte and was heading into a second marriage to restaurateur Anders McIntyre. She told me she didn't love him but was marrying him for the security."

"Her future groom complained that she was spending too much time with me," Kirk said. "Her excuse was that she needed to rehearse a lot of difficult scenes with me for *Champion.* I was pulling that same line with Diana."

"Things were getting rougher at home with Diana. She knew what my 'rehearsing' with Marilyn meant. One night, I didn't show up to take her to a party. When I came in the door, I saw this note. In big red letters, she'd written, 'I've gone to the Cowans. You can go to hell!'"

"After *Champion* was released, Marilyn and I appeared on TV to promote it," Kirk said. "In those days, even though studios didn't want their stars appearing on the little black box, Marilyn and I performed one of the most dramatic scenes from *Champion.* It went over big. I vowed I might do television one

"Luck had nothing to do with my torrid affair with Marilyn Maxwell during the making of *Champion,*" Kirk claimed. "It was pure, unadulterated lust. Of course, I was moving in on territory also occupied by Bob Hope and Frank Sinatra."

day, as I saw it as the coming thing, a real threat to movies."

Two weeks after their TV appearance, Kirk phoned Marilyn for another date. She told him she could not see him anymore and put down the phone.

Later, he found out why. She'd taken up with Clark Gable, who had gotten her the role of "The Other Woman" in his latest movie, *Key to the City* (1950). In that comedy, Gable was cast opposite Loretta Young. While making *Call of the Wild*, with her in 1935, he'd made her pregnant. As a graceful way to handle the ostracism she and her newborn would probably have faced during that very different era, she disappeared for a few months from Hollywood and came back on the scene with an "adopted" daughter.

***

Stanley Kramer was so impressed with Kirk's performance in *Champion* that he seriously considered him for a role in his upcoming drama *The Men* (1950), a grim movie about paraplegic war veterans. Kramer and Carl Foreman, who had written *Champion*, would be working for the first time with the director Fred Zinnemann.

Kramer was the first to meet with Kirk, sharing his vision for *The Men*, conveying his goal of giving it the quality of an authentic documentary. The next day, he invited him to a rehabilitation ward in Los Angeles that housed veterans who'd been injured during the war.

Kirk was very sympathetic to the men, but never patronizing, and had many sincere and empathetic talks with them. One soldier he always remembered was Jack Purdue from Macon, Georgia.

When Purdue shook Kirk's hand, he held onto it for an extra long time, as if he hoped that some of Kirk's life force and raw masculinity might miraculously be conveyed to him.

"When I was a soldier in uniform, and on leave, all the gals went for me. I was blonde and handsome like you." Then Purdue sighed, as if sinking into despair. "I fear I'm not much good to a woman anymore."

"But I bet you'll carry on, find a new way of living, and maybe figure out how to hang in there." Then Kirk did an unusual thing, at least for him. He kissed the young man lightly on his forehead.

For at least three weeks, Kirk was set to be cast into the role of Ken Wilocheck, a real life former infantry lieutenant paralyzed from the waist down and sentenced to life in a wheelchair. A Nazi sniper's bullet had smashed into his spine during the closing days of World War II.

Kirk was given a copy of Foreman's script. He read it three times and decided that he'd be perfect in the role. He even plotted to get permission to confine himself to a wheelchair during the extended period he'd spend among the paraplegics in a Veterans' Administration facility, living and eating among them., sharing in whatever they did for amusement.

That Monday afternoon, he met with Zinnemann, conveying his own interpretation of the role. "I want to portray Ken as a young man whose body has betrayed him. Imagine me, Kirk Douglas, conqueror of beautiful women, playing a man who's impotent. "

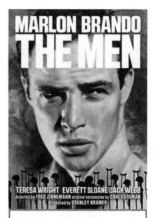

Corporate mendacity: The role Kirk thought he'd been given, until it was pulled out from under him by its producers. *The Men* became one of the early film role "plums" of Marlon Brando.

Unknown to Kirk, a new development had recently unfolded. Marlon Brando, who had made a sensation on Broadway as Stanley Kowalski in Tennessee Williams' *A Streetcar Named Desire,* had read the script and decided he wanted to make his film debut in *The Men.* "It's got 'Oscar' written all over it, and I'm your man," he told Kramer.

Kirk seemed to be the last player in the film's inner circle to learn of the new development. "I knew something was wrong when I walked in on that unholy trio of backstabbers," he said. "An actor can sense rejection five miles away. It smells that bad."

That fateful afternoon, Zinnemann, Kramer, and Foreman told him that all of them had united in their decision to give Brando the role, yet they held out a promise, telling him they were planning to make "the Western drama to beat out all other Westerns. Start thinking about playing a Western sheriff," Kramer told him.

"A Western for me? Kirk asked, a bit startled. "Me, a cowboy, a Russian Jew boy from New York State? Sounds great! A challenge—Just what I like."

"We've all but cast Grace Kelly as your leading lady," Kramer said. "She's anxious to meet you. I can set something up."

"Set it up!" he said. "Tell her that Kirk Douglas is ready, willing, and able to perform with her in more ways than one. Grace and I can go into rehearsals together long before filming begins. Besides, you guys will owe me one for turning me down in *The Men.* I would have been terrific."

He drove home that afternoon hating Brando. In New York, he'd been up against him during auditions for the play *Truckline Café.* "Those jerks went for the 'Mumbling Method,' not me. Brando will be my downfall,

Unless..." He paused as an idea struck him.

"I know they're going to film *A Streetcar Named Desire.* I saw Brando in it on Broadway. I know I can be a better Stanley Kowalski than him."

That night, he discussed his ambition with Diana. "For that role of the year, I'd do almost anything Tennessee Williams wants."

***

Kirk arrived in Hollywood when anti-Semitism was still rampant, at least in some quarters, even though some of the most important moguls in Hollywood were Jewish, notably Louis B. Mayer.

Kirk had already seen *Gentleman's Agreement,* the 1947 drama based on Laura Z. Hobson's best-selling novel with the same name.

The plot concerned a widowed journalist (played by Gregory Peck), who poses as a Jew to research an exposé of anti-Semitism in New York City and in Darien, Connecticut. It was nominated for eight Oscars and won for Best Picture, Best Supporting Actress (Celeste Holm), and Best Director (Elia Kazan), who in the future would become Kirk's director too.

A major star, John Garfield, took a small supporting role in it as Peck's longtime childhood friend who educates Peck in how a Jew deals with rebuffs and rejections. Dorothy McGuire, in one of her finest performances, would be nominated, because of it, for the Best Actress Oscar.

Kirk had been so moved by the film that he returned two more times to see it again. Ever since he'd grown up in Amsterdam, New York, he'd experienced anti-Jewish prejudice.

Of course, when he had arrived in Hollywood, no one seemed to know that he was a Jew. His appearance, his blonde hair, and a name like Kirk Douglas gave the impression that he was an American Gentile. "Most of my newly minted friends thought I was Scottish, in part because of my name. I should have worn a kilt."

Perhaps because so much of his time in Hollywood was spent pursuing beautiful women that he had not made—with the exception of Burt Lancaster—many male friends.

Then, Lex Barker entered his life. He was handsome, blonde, well-educated, and athletic, especially at tennis. He stood 6'4", with arguably the best physique in Hollywood. That made him ideal for his eventual casting as the tenth official Tarzan of the film industry.

A "babe magnet," Lex was married at the time to the redhead, Arlene Dahl, one of the most beautiful women in Hollywood. In 1951, he would divorce her and marry Lana Turner, Kirk's future co-star in *The Bad and the Beautiful* (1952).

At the beginning of their friendship, Kirk was unaware of Barker's prejudice. He'd seen him in *Cross-Fire* (1947). The first B film to receive an Oscar nomination as Best Picture, it had starred three actors named Robert (Young, Mitchum, and Ryan). Like *Gentleman's Agreement*, it dealt with the theme of anti-Semitism, a subject that was especially raw in the immediate wake of the Holocaust of World War II.

Kirk and Barker often dined together, spending the latter part of the evening—despite their respective marriages—"in pursuit of dames" (Kirk's words). "Lex was far more successful than I was. Girls literally dropped their panties when he walked in the door."

More competition in a Hollywood loaded with hot male actors: Lex Barker as Tarzan.

On three occasions, Lex invited Kirk to the Westwood Tennis Club, where they lunched together after a game. "Every time Lex stepped under the shower in the locker room, he gave all the members of the club penis envy," Kirk said.

One day during lunch, Barker told Kirk that he was proposing him for membership. "It's too bad we can't have a club here like we have back East. There are too many Jews in Hollywood, so we have to let a few in. The next thing we know, we may have to take in niggers, too."

"I understand your not wanting to play tennis with a dirty Jew," Kirk said. "But I've got to let you in on a secret. I'm a Jew. So I guess I'd better play tennis somewhere else."

That episode ended a budding friendship.

"Many times, I visited Palm Springs for the weekend, but I was blackballed from El Dorado Club," Kirk claimed. "Forgive my language, but its manager made its policy clear—'no kikes, no niggers.'"

"President Eisenhower joined the club after leaving office. And ex-President Gerald Ford, after being defeated by Jimmy Carter, became a member of the Thunderbird Club, the most violently anti-Semitic club in Palm Springs."

***

After flirting with two or three different titles, Stanley Kramer and scriptwriter Carl Foreman settled on *High Noon* as the best name for their controversial Western. Still in its planning stages, it was eventually released in 1952 by Stanley Kramer Productions and United Artists. With a running time of 85 minutes, it was made for a modest budget of $750,000, eventually generating sales of $12 million.

When Kirk learned that the director would be Fred Zinnemann, he was anything but pleased. This same director had helmed *The Men*, rejecting Kirk for the role and awarding it to Marlon Brando instead.

Zinnemann would eventually win four Academy Awards for his direction of movies that spanned a half-century. These movies included not only *High Noon* but such other hits as *From Here to Eternity* (1953) and *A Man for All Seasons* (1966). He directed and introduced a number of stars in their film debuts. In addition to Brando, they included Montgomery Clift, Meryl Streep, Julie Harris, and Pier Angeli, who evolved into one of the major loves of Kirk's life. He also guided many stars in roles that culminated in Oscar nominations: Frank Sinatra, Jane Fonda, and Gary Cooper.

Even though Kirk respected Zinnemann as a director, and even though he desperately wanted a role in his newly conceived upcoming *High Noon*, he feared a "double cross," confiding in his wife, Diana, "At the last minute he axed me in *The Men* for 'The Mumbler,'" a reference, of course, to Brando.

Finally, after many agonizing delays, Kirk was allowed to read Foreman's screen treatment for *High Noon*. He would focus on the role of its leading male character, Marshall Will Kane, newly married to Amy Fowler (Grace Kelly). The story centers around a town marshal torn between his sense of duty and his love for his new bride, who must face a gang of killers alone.

The movie went into pre-production at the time of the "Red Scare" sweeping across Hollywood. Senator Joseph McCarthy—Kirk called him "Tailgunner Joe"—had launched a probe (Kirk called it a "witch hunt") to ferret out communists in the film industry.

Carl Foreman was one of the chief suspects. While still polishing the script for *High Noon*, Foreman was summoned to appear before the House Committee on Un-American Activities. As televised, he confessed to the committee that he had been a member of the Communist Party a decade earlier when he was a young man. But he went on to assert that he had become disillusioned with the Communist Party, and especially with it leader, Josef Stalin, and eventually dropped out.

When Foreman refused to supply the names of other members of the Communist Party, he was defined as "an uncooperative witness" and blacklisted. Partly because of that, the script for *High Noon* was later interpreted as an allegory for McCarthyism. Foreman moved to England, where he continued to write filmscripts under pseudonyms that included "Derek

Frye."

The blacklisting had made a tremendous impact on Kirk, and he would later become known for defying it. "I didn't like to see half of Hollywood being terrorized by bullies. Some of the best actors in the business were losing their careers, notably Edward G. Robinson, Larry Parks, and John Garfield. Turncoats like Robert Taylor, Ronald Reagan, and Gary Cooper were far more cooperative. Those damn fools in Washington were seeing a commie behind and in front of every camera. Isn't America supposed to be the land of the free?"

Even though the cast for *High Noon* had not yet been made official, Kirk assumed that he was still the frontrunner for the role of its marshal.

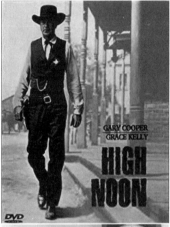

He was doubly assured of this when Kramer phoned to say that a dinner had been set up with his already selected leading lady, Grace Kelly. All that Kirk knew about her was what he'd read in *Variety*. A reporter had interviewed her when she first arrived in Hollywood for a supporting role in a Fox film, *Fourteen Hours* (1951).

Born into a wealthy Irish Catholic family from Philadelphia *[where her father, a three-time Olympic champion, was a wealthy brickmaker and building contractor]*, she eventually moved to New York, where she became a model and appeared on stage.

When Kirk went to pick her up in his car, he was dazzled by her serene beauty from the moment he spoke to her. En route to the restaurant, he was also impressed with her intelligence and white-gloved poise.

"She was a real blonde, not one of those bleached jobs like Marilyn Monroe and Jayne Mansfield," Kirk said. "She was crisp, ladylike, and just a bit aloof. I might have been put off by this icy blonde image, but for some reason, I found it sexy as hell. Her role in *High Noon* called for her to play a gentle Quaker wife. That would take some acting on her part. She was anything but—more of an Iron Butterfly."

Gary Cooper and Grace Kelly starred in *High Noon*, which was made during the height of the Hollywood blacklist, a time of political inquisition and personal betrayal.

Over dinner, Kelly surprised him by telling him that she'd seen his movies, and spoke knowingly about them, even telling him that she was eager for him to be her leading man.

When she talked about herself, she revealed a more human side and could be self-deprecating. "As a young girl, I was chubby, flat-chested, and myopic."

He learned that the two of them had something in common. They had each attended Manhattan's Academy of Dramatic Arts.

"I've already met with Zinnemann," she said. "I don't think he wants me in the role. He told Kramer that he found me very tense and even awkward."

"The last thing any man could say about you is that you're awkward. You could play the future Queen of England being crowned in Westminster Abbey."

She amused Kirk with her recently acquired insights into Hollywood. "The people here are holier-than-thou to the public, and unholier than the devil in reality."

At the end of their evening, after flirting with her throughout most of the dinner, he drove her back to her hotel. Although he made it obvious that he'd like to be invited to her room for a sleepover, she held him at bay.

She did kiss him on the mouth, however. "When you and I appear opposite each other in *High Noon*, there will be much more to come...so much more."

[In the immediate years that followed, Kirk watched from afar as Grace's career skyrocketed. Gossip spread rapidly about her, author Gore Vidal claiming, "Grace always seduces her leading men."

One of her former lovers in New York, Don Richardson, claimed, "She screws everybody she comes into contact with who is able to do something for her career. Agents, producers, directors, actors."

In time, her conquests in Hollywood became the stuff of legend: Clark Gable, Bing Crosby, Oleg Cassini, William Holden, Ray Milland, David Niven, James Stewart, Spencer Tracy, Cary Grant, and inevitably, Frank Sinatra.

"The only one missing from that list is yours truly," Kirk said. "I sure missed out on something. Who knows what would have happened if I'd gotten the lead in High Noon? *She might never have become the Princess of Monaco."]*

***

Unknown to Kirk at the time, he was near the bottom of the list of candidates for the male lead in *High Noon*. John Wayne was the first to have been offered the role of Marshal Will Kane. He rejected it, claiming that it was really an attack on Hollywood blacklisting, which he avidly supported. He told a reporter, "I'd lead the posse chasing the commie writer, Carl Foreman, out of Hollywood."

Next in line was Gregory Peck, who rejected the role because he considered it too similar to his recently made *The Gunfighter.* Months later, he said, "Turning down *High Noon* was the biggest career mistake of my life."

Three other actors—Monty Clift, Charlton Heston, and Brando himself—rejected it, too. That left only Kirk.

But just before Kirk signed for the role, Gary Cooper contacted Kramer, telling him he wanted the role and that he'd work for half his usual fee.

Kramer met with Cooper, finding him "old and tired. His career had peaked in the 1930s and '40s. Also, he was fifty years old, Grace twenty-one. He would photograph as her father, not her husband."

Then another development unfolded. Lettuce grower Bruce Church was willing to invest $200,000 in *High Noon,* but with the condition that Cooper would be cast as its male lead. "Need I remind you," he told Kramer, "that's a lotta lettuce?"

Cooper got the role, but he, too, felt a sense of awkwardness about having such a young bride. He suggested that Barbara Stanwyck might be more suitable. "I was born in 1901, Barbara in 1907. You could explain her marrying later in life, since her husband was fatally shot. That would make the plot more intriguing since she faced losing her second husband in a gunfight with the same killers who had shot her first husband."

After filming began, Cooper became enamored of Grace. As he confessed to Kramer in a comment that was later widely bruited around Hollywood, "She's like a cold fish until a man gets her pants down—and then she explodes."

"It was painful for me to turn down Kirk, since he'd done such a good job for me in *Champion,*" Kramer said. "But that was as a boxer. I couldn't quite see him as a Western hero."

[Ironically, as time went by, Kirk would become known and celebrated for his interpretation of Western heroes.]

High Noon received seven Academy Award nominations, with Cooper carrying off the big prize as Best Actor.

"That damn role belonged to me," Kirk lamented. "But I'd get even. In just a short time, I'd be screwing the love of Coop's life."

***

As their marriage ground to a dysfunctional end, Diana continued to live under the same roof as Kirk, but in a separate bedroom. The marital tension began to affect her adversely, and she needed a short vacation, imagining it as unfolding in Mexico where she'd "walk the beach, drink tequila, and read Schopenhauer."

Kirk was relieved that she'd be traveling with a well-known homosexual who often escorted unattached women to gala events in Hollywood. Incorrectly, Kirk assumed she'd be "safe" with him, but as it turned out "to my surprise and satisfaction," (Diana's words) "my escort suddenly decided to change his sexual orientation, if only briefly."

According to Kirk, "It's hard to tell exactly when love dies, as it did for me. My wife alone could not satisfy the raging needs I had within me at the time. I was still searching for the woman who could. Our marriage had gone south like Diana on her trip to Mexico."

"I went to see a psychiatrist, but, as it turned out, he was more fucked up than I was. On my own, I had to confront the ghosts of Issur and my awful childhood where, as an eight-year-old, I had to stroll the neighborhood stealing food for my mother and my six sisters."

"At times, I asked myself, particularly as I lay awake at three o'clock in the morning, what was wrong with fucking a lot of beautiful women? Back in the late 1940s and early '50s, Hollywood, in my prejudiced opinion, had some of the greatest love goddesses the world has ever known. To name a few, just imagine getting trapped in the boudoirs of Rita Hayworth, Ava Gardner, Lana Turner... Going after a beautiful woman, if truth be told, was thrilling for a night or two, a weekend, even a month, but it wasn't what I really needed. I wanted more, the perfect woman who would be all things to me. Every night, as I wandered the planet, I was in search of my own perfect woman, perhaps on some enchanted evening, as the song went, I would see her across a crowded room."

"Hollywood, of course, throws temptation at any young man, be he single or married. If he's a good-looking guy with a great body, he gets offers every day from horny females, both in personal encounters and in the form of letters. Beautiful girls even send you nude pictures of themselves in all forms of poses. If you're a known homosexual star, young men mail you pictures of themselves with erections."

"Most men, if red-blooded, can't resist such temptations. Sometimes, female members on my film crew sneak into my dressing room and lie in wait for me. I'm not knocking them, since I'm a very tolerant person, but homosexuals go after you in droves if you've got a good physique. Just ask Burt Lancaster. In time, Rock Hudson seduced more straight men than any other star in the history of Hollywood, or so I was told."

"Those gossipy old witches, Hedda Hopper and Louella Parsons, were like bloodhounds trailing Diana and me," he said. "I don't know which of them was worse. They were like vultures devouring the dead carcass of my failed marriage. At one point, Sheilah Graham wrote that our separation was only a publicity gimmick. I got her on the phone and called her a cunt. I know it's not right for a man to call a woman that, but I was seriously pissed off."

After Diana's return from Mexico, she and Kirk, in their living room, discussed the status of their marriage. Both agreed that it had failed, and neither of them held out any hope that it could be repaired. "We seemed to inhabit different worlds," she said.

She had long confronted him with charges of his womanizing, yet made no attempt to give him what he called "the Passion of Life."

He decided to move out of their house. "I left our lovely home, knowing I would no longer see my boys every day. I began the lonely life in a beautiful little guest house on top of Mulholland Drive, but I felt too isolated there and relocated into an apartment in Westwood Village, where I could more conveniently continue my sexual trysts with the *girl du jour.*"

As soon as she could, Diana, with Michael and Joel, relocated to Manhattan.

"Here I was, alone at last—no wife, no boys running through the house. But, in truth, I didn't spend a lot of time lamenting my state. I was now a bachelor-at-large, one with a roving eye, and it feasted on one woman after another. I found a way to fulfill my empty nights. I began a series of affairs with some of the most celebrated beauties on earth."

Inevitably, it came time for both he and Diana to hire divorce lawyers, and that launched an entirely new chapter in each of their troubled lives.

***

"After Joel was born in 1947, Diana and I, in time, came to realize that we were not right for each other, and we divorced amicably," Kirk wrote in his 2007 memoir, *Let's Face It: 90 Years of Living, Loving, and Learning.*

In her own memoir, *In the Wings,* Diana gave her philosophy of life at the time: "Be courageous, be compassionate, and for God's sake, have fun!"

"Even though I was divorcing him, I've always enjoyed Kirk's sense of humor," she said. "He could always make me laugh, which annoyed the hell out of me. But I think we both decided, too, we had to maintain a certain civility because of our two sons, Michael and Joel."

"Michael later said he was always grateful that we never did bad-mouth each other," Diana said. "Sometimes we probably wanted to, but we'd hold back. I think that after Kirk married Anne (Buydens), she made it easier, because she and I cooperated very much in terms of bedtime and what the kids could watch on TV—those kind of things."

In spite of her difficulties with Kirk, Diana still claimed that in her heart, "I still love this cocky young man who rose from the depths of poverty to establish himself in the firmament of great global stars in Golden Age Hollywood. In spite of my marital troubles with him, my mother still adored him."

When Kirk learned the name of the man who Diana had hired as her divorce lawyer, he called around to find that Arnold Crakower was the best divorce lawyer in New York.

He also learned that he was married to Kathleen Winsor, the author of the bestselling romantic potboiler, *Forever Amber*. It had been made into a movie starring Kirk's former girlfriend, Linda Darnell.

Winsor had hired Crakower when she was ready to divorce the big band leader Artie Shaw. In time, Shaw would have eight wives. *[Winsor was married to him from 1946 to '48. Others of his wives included Lana Turner (1939-'40), and Ava Gardner (1945-'46).]*

Ironically, Shaw came home one night and caught Ava reading *Forever Amber*. He jerked "such trash" from her hands and tossed it into their fireplace. But right after his divorce from Ava, he married Winsor.

After her bitter divorce from Shaw, Winsor married her divorce attorney, Crakower.

Since Shaw had experienced what Crakower could to do a celebrity in court, Kirk approached him one night at the Cocoanut Grove, suggesting they get together for a late lunch the following afternoon at the Brown Derby. The Big Band leader accepted.

He and Shaw had both been born into poverty-stricken Jewish families. Kirk had something else in common with him: He'd seduced Shaw's former wife, Ava.

Years later, in the 1950s, Kirk would also seduce another of Shaw's former wives, Lana Turner, and also his future wife, Evelyn Keyes. "We must have had the same taste in women," Kirk said.

He had met Shaw in New York when he'd attended the gala opening of Bop City, a new jazz venue on Broadway at 49th Street. Its celebrity-studded opening had attracted massive crowds, and the doormen had to turn away 5,000 fans.

The bill featured not only Shaw (top billing), but other artists who included Ella Fitzgerald.

Champion was playing at a movie theater down the street, and many fans had already seen it. Kirk claimed, "I got the most applause when I entered the auditorium. Flashbulbs were popping."

Other honored guests at the opening included Hazel Scott and her husband, the famous Congressman, Adam Clayton Powell. Before the night was over, Kirk got to chat with Harry Belafonte, musician Charlie Barnet, and Billie Holiday. Using Mae West's most famous line, she invited Kirk "to come up and see me sometime."

He also chatted with Milton Berle, who had cut the ribbon out front.

Mimicking the lingo of the night, Kirk said, "*Oop-bob-sh'bam!* What a night! Artie's wonderful music went over the heads of this unruly mob of gum-chewers wearing foppy 'bop-ties.'"

Back in Hollywood over lunch at the Brown Derby, Kirk talked first to Shaw, telling him that he had been assigned to portray the celebrated cornet player, Bix Beiderbecke, in his next picture, *Young Man With a Horn*, eventually released in 1950.

"Artie gave me a lot of tips about how to be convincing on the screen as a horn player and agreed to visit me at home to give me some more lessons about breathing and stuff."

When the subject of Crakower came up, Shaw's face became streaked with bitterness. "A rotgut son of a bitch. Before my bitter divorce from that greedy bitch Winsor ended, I was tempted to call Frankie (Sinatra) and have him send two of his gangster friends to wipe out Crakower."

Shaw's divorce from Winsor ignited a tabloid frenzy, as one revelation came out after another during the week-long proceedings.

Shaw poured out his anguish to Kirk. "She claimed I constantly beat her, and that on one occasion, after I knocked her down, that I plowed my foot into her face, sending her to the hospital. A TOTAL LIE. She also said that one night, I nearly choked her to death. She testified that I was just a gigolo, having married her to cash in on all the money she'd made from *Forever Amber*."

"Not only that, but she claimed that during our marriage, I'd had affairs with any number of other women—Marilyn Maxwell, Lena Horne, Judy Garland, Ann Miller, June Allyson, and Betty Hutton. She told the court I'd come home and flaunt a lipstick-coated handkerchief at her."

"With this Red Scare going on," Shaw said, "she also tried to destroy my career, claiming I was a registered member of the Communist Party and had tried to coerce her into joining. The tabloid headline read—'ARTIE TRIES TO TURN AMBER RED.'"

Of all of Shaw's eight wives, Winsor—as part of a deal spearheaded by Crakower—was the only one who received alimony. It amounted to about a million dollars.

As a defense in court against Crakower, Shaw recommended that Kirk hire Jerry Rosenthal, who had been his lawyer during his fight against the charges leveled by Winsor.

"I met Jerry the following day, but didn't really like him," Kirk said. "I thought he was a phony but that he had a lot of charm. He was bright and cagey, and I took him on."

Rosenthal told Kirk, "I not only handle divorces, but I'm also a father confessor, a high-finance wizard, a movie critic, and a conscience."

Virginia MacPherson, a United Press reporter, wrote that Rosenthal "was a handsome young man with about 20 clients since he'd passed the California bar in 1946. He is credited with applying psychology, reconciling parties, and juggling clients' finances. He is, in essence, a nursemaid for stars."

***

Diane sued Kirk for divorce in February of 1949, but it would not become final until January of 1951.

Kirk instructed Rosenthal to grant Diana "whatever she needs for herself and our sons—within reason, of course. I don't want to be left homeless."

Likewise, Diana did not want to destroy Kirk financially. "I felt he deserved the rewards of his recently acquired stardom, considering how hard he'd struggled and fought his way up every rung of the Hollywood ladder. I was mainly concerned with child support for our boys."

When Rosenthal and Crakower came together, their arguments weren't so much about Kirk and Diana. Instead, in some ways, they seemed to be re-fighting the Shaw/Winsor divorce. At one point, Rosenthal slugged Crakower, who fought back until Kirk intervened.

In court, California requires that a charge be levied against one of the spouses. Diana opted for mental cruelty.

Kirk and Diana even left the courthouse together, and both of them went back to the home he'd recently left. "We had some beers that night, and on CBS, ABC, and NBC, we watched news of our divorce," Kirk said. "We also agreed that our boys would be brought up outside any religion. I never insisted that they be raised as Jews."

Although Diana got custody of their sons, he was granted generous visitation rights. In the future, he would visit his kids at their new home on Central Park West in New York City.

At the time that Kirk divorced his mother, Michael was six years old, and seemed far more sensitive than his younger brother, Joel. "He suffered for years feeling abandoned by his dad," Diana said. "When I fought with Kirk about his serial adultery, and Michael heard us, he would burst into tears."

"My earliest memory is of dad and mother fighting," Michael said. "The only violence was in their raised voices. Those angry voices would clog my brain for years to come, and it disturbed me greatly."

"As I grew into a teenager, I saw more of dad on the screen making love to other women than I did of him in the flesh." Michael claimed. "I wanted to grow up to be just like him. Yet, in total contrast at times, I wanted to be the exact opposite of him."

In her memoirs, Diana wrote about beginning life anew at the age of 27: "Michael showed signs of deep anger since the divorce and from being a compatible, tractable child, had suddenly become very stubborn and rebellious. He challenged me at every turn. I took him to a child psychologist who observed him in play therapy, then lectured me gently to ease up on the discipline and give him loads of love until he feels secure."

In spite of kind words for each other, Kirk and Diana at some point in their lives did badmouth each other. Diana later wrote of Kirk "being drug-addicted and a sexually voracious bird of prey."

Decades later, Kirk threatened to boycott the marriage of Michael to actress Catherine Zeta-Jones if his ex-wife attended, calling Diana a "blabbermouth."

[After divorcing Kirk, Diana married producer Bill Darrid in 1956, and was still wed to him at the time of his death in 1992. Late in her life, in 2002, she wed Donald Webster, a U.S. Treasury Chief of Staff under Richard Nixon. She had met him at a party in Washington at the launch of her memoirs. She was still married to him at the time of her death in July of 2015, when she succumbed to breast cancer.]

***

Bix Beiderbecke, of German descent, was one of the most influential jazz soloists of the 1920s. He had taught himself to play the cornet largely by ear. In 1923, he'd formed the Wolverines, one of the best jazz ensembles of the era. His life was a tragedy, and he died at the age of 28, largely from alcoholism.

Novelist Dorothy Baker used Beiderbecke's life as an inspiration for her novel *Young Man With a Horn*. It was daring at the time, as one of the two characters was bisexual.

Warner Brothers acquired the film rights in 1945, but it sat on a shelf until the end of the 1940s since producer Jerry Wald could not find an actor suitable for the role of the horn player who, in the movie, was named Rick Martin.

After seeing Kirk in *Champion*, Wald concluded that the intensity he displayed as a boxer could be converted to the vitality needed for the musician.

As a musical advisor for the film, Wald hired Harry James, who had been famously married to Betty Grable, the box office star and pin-up girl of World War II. He worked with Kirk on and off for weeks, teaching him how to finger the valves and purse his lips. The music the audience heard during the film derived from James' own playing and "superimposed" (or dubbed) over Kirk's "merely the mock."

The New York Times later praised the music of James, claiming, "It flows wildly, searchingly, and forlornly from Rick Martin's (*aka* Kirk's, who was "dubbing" the music) beloved horn."

Jazz artist Bix Biederbecke, around 1923, with members of his band

The screenplay, only loosely based on Beiderbecke's life, was the work of both Carl Foreman before he fled to England, and Edmund H. North. After finishing the script, North would work on the 1951 sci-fi classic, *The Day the Earth Stood Still*. Before teaming with Foreman, he'd worked on the screenplay for Joan Crawford's 1949 classic, *Flamingo Road*.

In historical defiance of the bleak circumstances of Beiderbecke's early death, Wald demanded that his scriptwriters develop a happy ending. His exact, perhaps sappy, demand was to depict "rise, fall, and redemption."

He defined his decision to cast a celebrity musician, Hoagy Carmichael, into the film as "divine inspiration." In real life, this talented pianist and songwriter was a friend of Beiderbecke. And in the movie, he would be configured as a friend of Rick Martin (aka Kirk), and also as the narrator.

Wald hired the Hungarian director, Michael Curtiz, the director of *Casablanca,* to helm *Young Man With a Horn.*

He selected Lauren Bacall and Doris Day as the film's leading ladies. [*He had previously helmed Doris onscreen for her first movie role, and he'd already made stars out of both Errol Flynn and Olivia de Havilland.*]

In *Young Man With a Horn*, Rick, as an orphan, sees a trumpet in the window of a pawn shop. He works hard at odd jobs and saves enough to buy it. After many long struggles, and stints in seedy dives and honky-tonks, he lands a gig with a big band.

There, he meets a beautiful blonde singer, Jo Jordan (Doris Day). She falls in love with him, but makes a mistake and brings a friend, Amy North (Bacall) to hear Rick play. Rich, neurotic, and complicated, she pursues Kirk and eventually marries him. From the start, the relationship is doomed.

Although she seems to be more lesbian than straight, her lesbianism is only implied, as the Production Code of the time would not allow any depiction of homosexuality on the screen. Rick's marriage to North almost dooms him, as he sinks into alcoholism. He's rescued by Jordan, who rises to become a successful singer.

The lesbian theme would appear again in Baker's next novel, *Trio*, which opened as a play on Broadway until a group of Protestant clergymen forced the city to shut it down.

One day during Kirk's filming of *Young Man With a Horn*, Joan Crawford came onto the set. At the time, she was on the studio lot preparing for her upcoming role in *The Damned Don't Cry* (1950). Reacting to her presence as a superstar on his set, Wald invited Crawford to lunch. After spotting Kirk, Crawford suggested that Wald include him, too, with the justification, "I might use him as my leading man in one of my upcoming pictures."

During lunch, Crawford was most flirtatious with him, and, according to Wald, Kirk flirted right back. She always liked to be the first to seduce the new kid on the block, but she had been tardy in getting around to Kirk.

Before leaving the studio that day, she took down Kirk's phone number and promised to call him.

Kirk hadn't seen Bacall in several years, even though she'd been instrumental in setting up his fateful link to Hal B. Wallis. Neither had Bacall gone out of her way to include him in her life, fearing that Bogie would be jealous because of her early affair as a teenager with Kirk in Manhattan.

"It was great being back with Betty again," Kirk said. "We hung out together talking about old times. I admit I flirted outrageously with her. The old flame had not died. We even talked about what our lives would have been like had we married in New York. In not so subtle a fashion, I found ways to remind her that I was much younger than her husband, too."

One afternoon when Bacall and Kirk were not scheduled to appear on the set, she invited him to lunch at the Westwood Golf Course, where Bogie was a member. "I nailed her on that," Kirk said. "'Why would you let your husband join a club that didn't allow Jews,' I asked her. If the manager finds out we're both Jews, he'll kick us out on our asses.' Betty didn't have an answer for that."

Bacall later confided to both Judy Garland and Frank Sinatra, "Kirk stirred up old feelings I had as a girl when I had this powerful crush on him. I was tempted to renew our intimacy, if only to get back at Bogie. He was sailing almost every weekend on his boat to Catalina and taking along his hairdresser and mistress, Verita Thompson."

***

The novel that had inspired the script for *Young Man With a Horn* was more *avant-garde,* racially, than the movie that it inspired. According to Kirk, "I had read Dorothy Baker's novel in which my other leading lady was a black girl," Kirk said. "But this was 1950 and interracial romance was strictly forbidden on the screen, and in some states it was outlawed. So instead of a black girl, I got a freckle-faced blonde, Doris Day."

"She became my alltime least favorite leading lady," he said. "She was the remotest performer with whom I've ever worked. That cheerful, smiling *persona* is merely a mask to hide her much darker side. I mean, we didn't feud or anything, but we were cold and indifferent to each other. She was supposed to be in love with me on the screen, but I think she held me in contempt. She told Curtiz that I was the most self-centered actor she'd ever met."

She later wrote that working on *Young Man With a Horn* was "totally joyless."

Some critics found her performance rather wooden, except when she sang her most memorable number, "With a Song in My Heart."

"Making the movie with Douglas was a very frustrating experience," Day said. "It carried me back to my early days singing with a band, and the dialogue brought back painful memories I had tried to forget. As the cornet player, he opened a dark chapter in my life during my first marriage to the sulking Al Jorden. His ghost still haunted me. It was an abusive union, and I had to use makeup to cover bruises from his frequent beatings. Even the old songs I sang brought back the nightmare that was my life in those dreadful days." She'd married Jorden in 1941, divorcing him in 1943.

Harry James, the film's musical consultant, phoned Doris's manager during the shooting of *Young Man With a Horn*. He was blunt: "What do you think is my chance to nail Doris?"

"Zero odds," the manager responded. Yet despite the anguish their associa-

Young Man with a Horn, Kirk with one of his least favorite colleagues, Doris Day.

178

tion caused her, Columbia Record's ten-inch studio LP featuring Day and James hit the top spot on *Billboard's* popular album chart.

Day was not the only star disappointed in the final cut of *Young Man With a Horn.* "The film was nowhere near as good as it should have been," she said "and Curtiz didn't have to call all of us actors 'bums.'"

Kirk echoed Bacall's sentiments, claiming, "The picture did not turn out to be the movie it could have been. Betty and I were perfect in our roles. So were all the other performers—that is, all except one…Miss Doris Day."

Lux Radio Theater broadcast a sixty-minute radio adaptation of the movie in March of 1952, with Kirk reprising his film role.

***

During the shooting of *Young Man With a Horn,* Kirk was offered the lead in six other pictures, all of which he rejected, referring to the scripts as "crap."

Stanley Kramer offered him the lead in *The Four Poster,* but he rejected it. During one of their phone conversations, Kirk told him, "My first reaction is that I wouldn't be suitable for the role, but, after reading all those other lousy screen treatments, I'm beginning to think I'd be the last to know what role I'm suited for."

***

The disappearance of the beautiful starlet, Jean Spangler, is listed as one of the fifteen most famous unsolved murders or disappearances in Hollywood.

Even today, Kirk's name is still linked to Spangler's unsolved disappearance. It was depicted on a televised episode of *Mysteries and Scandals* in 2001. Megan Abbott's 2007 *noir* novel, *The Song Is You,* centers on the case.

The story begins when director Michael Curtiz, on a long weekend in Palm Springs, spotted Spangler in a bathing suit at a resort. That night, he seduced her, and the next week, he cast her in an uncredited role in Kirk's (then-newest) picture, *Young Man With a Horn.*

He told Kirk, "This hot little beauty is

As old friends reunited, Kirk posed for publicity pictures with Lauren Bacall on the set of *Young Man With a Horn* years after their first meeting and love affair as an impoverished actor and model in New York City.

headed for bigtime stardom. I'm never wrong about these things."

A native of Seattle, Spangler had moved to Hollywood, where she worked as both a model and a dancer at the Earl Carroll Theatre and later at Florentine Gardens.

In 1942, she'd married manufacturer Dexter Benner. Two years later, the couple produced a daughter, Christine. In 1946, they divorced.

Reportedly, Kirk was stunned when he heard a bulletin broadcast over the radio about Spangler's mysterious disappearance. At the time, or so he said, he was having an off-the-record tryst with the movie star, Evelyn Keyes. In reference to Spangler, Kirk also said to the police, "I don't even remember who she was."

He phoned Ted D. McCord, the cinematographer on *Young Man With a Horn*. He reminded Kirk that he'd recently shot a scene with Spangler and that he had flirted with her. "You even asked her out on a date that night." He said he'd also warned Kirk that "the dame is trouble, a real starfucker."

When confronted with her disappearance by the police, Kirk said that in an attempt to break the date they'd

TV ACTRESS FEARED VICTIM OF SEX FIEND

SEARCH INTENSIFIED—Police continued their search yesterday for a man named "Kirk" and a "Dr. Scott," names found in Jean Spangler's purse, picked up in Griffith Park. The missing actress is shown in studio, dressed for part in a film.

Kirk Douglas Questioned in Girl Mystery

HOLLYWOOD, Oct. 13—(AP)—

"... was a detective who Brown that I didn't remember girl or the name until a called it was she who an extra in a scene with picture 'Young Man Horn,'" Douglas said.

"Then I recalled that a tall girl in a green d that I talked and -kid her a bit on the set, a done with many othe around on a day of shoot

previously arranged, he had phoned her mother, Florence, and asked to speak to Spangler. When her mother told him that she wasn't there, he asked the mother to inform her daughter that "something has come up, and I can't make our date."

According to Kirk's police testimony, that was the last contact (or lack thereof) that he ever had with the victim.

Here's how events unfolded on the night of October 7, 1949, when she faded from view: Spangler was living at the time in Los Angeles, on Colgate Avenue in the La Brea residential complex. The apartment she occupied belonged to her mother, and it was shared by Spangler's five-year-old daughter, her brother Edward, and her sister-in-law, Sophie.

Shortly before leaving the apartment, never to return, Spangler told Sophie that she was meeting with Benner, her ex-husband, to see why he was so far behind in his child support payments. Benner would later establish that he'd been somewhere else that night. Florence, Spangler's mother, was visiting relatives at the time in Louisville, Kentucky.

Two days after she was reported missing, the police came across her purse at the Fern Dell entrance to Griffith Park, about five and a half miles from her apartment. Her purse was discovered with one strap broken, as if it had been jerked from her arm. Robbery was ruled out because its contents, including valuables, were still inside the purse. The police chief of Los Angeles ordered sixty of his men to search every inch of the park, but they found no body.

Sophie told police that Spangler was three months pregnant, with a fetus presumably planted there by Kirk.

The secret that Spangler shared with Sophie was that she was planning to submit to an abortion, which was illegal at the time. Inside her purse was a note which read: "Kirk, Can't wait any longer. Going to see Dr. Scott. It will work best this way while mother is away." The note appeared to be unfinished.

When the morning newspaper arrived Palm Springs, Kirk was horrified by a headline that had been planted above his picture: FILM STAR ENTERS SPANGLER INQUIRY. The text that followed read:

> *"Actor Kirk Douglas entered the investigation of the disappearance of the actress, Jean Spangler. The statuesque showgirl's mother returned from Kentucky and expressed grave concerns over her daughter's safety."*

With all that publicity, including news about it broadcast over the radio, Kirk was summoned to the Beverly Hills Homicide Bureau for questioning. There, he was besieged by reporters and photographers.

With Thad Brown, chief of the homicide squad, Kirk established an alibi, speaking of his tryst with Evelyn Keyes in Palm Springs on the night of Spangler's disappearance.

Some reporters speculated that although Kirk might not have been directly responsible for Spangler's disappearance, he might have hired it done. Revelations about a married film star impregnating and then murdering a starlet might have destroyed his fast-evolving film career.

Kirk was not the only suspect in the Spangler affair. At the Florentine Gardens, Spangler had met David Ogul, a henchman for gangster

Mickey Cohen. Two days after Spangler's disappearance, Ogul himself dropped out of sight.

Then, Spangler's mother, Florence, contradicted Kirk's testimony. Whereas Kirk stated that his relationship with her was only superficial and that he'd call her home only once to cancel a date, her mother relayed a different story, claiming, "Douglas phoned on several occasions, and he often came by our apartment building to pick her up, always parking outside, never coming in. Since we were on the ground floor with the window open, all he had to do was blow his horn. My daughter constantly spoke of Kirk."

Kirk Douglas maintained, "It must have been another man named Kirk."

Then another friend of Spangler appeared: David Breskkin, of Laguna Beach. He came to the police station with two male friends. All three of them maintained that Kirk Douglas had accompanied Spangler to a swimming pool party they had recently hosted. "All of us had seen *Champion*, so we knew who he was."

Another movie star, Robert Cummings, also knew Spangler. He claimed that she had told him that she was having an affair with Kirk, and that she had asserted, "It's not serious. He's already married. But I'm having the time of my life."

Later, Kirk thanked Brown for investigating the case and for clearing his name. He reported that Brown had concluded that Spangler was a "psychopathic liar and that I was not involved with her in any way except for that brief scene we'd done on camera."

Today, the Jane Spangler case remains one of the best-known unsolved mysteries of Hollywood. No one knows for sure what happened to Spangler on that long-ago night in October of 1949.

***

In the early 1950s, Kirk was about to begin the most glamorous and seductive period of his life. "The glamour queens of Hollywood just couldn't seem to get enough of this Jew boy," he said. "My phone kept ringing all night. These hot-to-trot goddesses wouldn't let me alone."

"All the old matinee idols like Gable and Flynn were saggy-jowled and overweight, with wrinkled faces. I was still young, hot, and rarin' to go. I was the Sultan in a harem!"

CHAPTER SIX

HOLLYWOOD'S LEADING HORNDOG
Between Marriages, Kirk Earns His Merit Badge

"THE JEWISH STALLION"
Invades the Boudoirs of Joan Crawford, Barbara Stanwyck, Hedy Lamarr, Evelyn Keyes, Rita Hayworth, Marilyn Monroe, Pier Angeli, & Gene Tierney

THE GLASS MENAGERIE
Kirk Plays "The Gentleman Caller" opposite Jane Wyman In Tennessee Williams' Southern Tragedy

In a tense scene from Tennessee Williams' *The Glass Menagerie,* Kirk (left) looks on as Arthur Kennedy (lower right) comforts Jane Wyman, his sister in the movie. Standing beside Kirk, Gertrude Lawrence surveys the scene with a look of anguish.

Before Lawrence was cast, Tallulah Bankhead called Kirk, telling him she was going to be screen-tested for the role of Amanda. On the final day of the test, she showed up drunk and lost out.

183

When Kirk reached the century mark of his life in 2016, a celebration of his birthday was featured in newspapers across the country. The *New York Post*, in "Second Coming" headlines, announced "Kirk's Century of Conquests: Legendary Hollywood Horndog Turns 100."

His rampant promiscuity had already been bruited through the media. In 1971, he appeared on *The Dick Cavett Show*, ostensibly to promote his latest Western, *A Gunfight*. But his TV host didn't seem interested in that.

"I was ambushed," Kirk recalled. "ABC had compiled film clips of some of the Hollywood goddesses I'd made love to. Even so, it was only a partial list. There was a lot the fuckers didn't know about."

The celebrity quotient and numbers of beautiful women Kirk had been intimate with seemed staggering: Lauren Bacall (she was still denying it, and so was he), Ann Sothern, Marlene Dietrich, Gene Tierney ("I like women with an overbite"), Ingrid Bergman, Lana Turner, Marilyn Maxwell, Susan Hayward, Patricia Neal, Ava Gardner, Linda Darnell, Evelyn Keyes, Joan Crawford, Hedy Lamarr, Faye Dunaway, and Pier Angeli.

Director Alfred Hitchcock once said, "It's very hard for an onscreen romance not to carry over into an actor's private life." Of course, in Kirk's case, an actress did not necessarily have to appear with him on the screen for him to become sexually involved."

According to Kirk, "I'm a son of a bitch, plain and simple, a real S.O.B. As I look back, I realized I was attracted, except for my beloved second wife, to neurotic women."

In his autobiography, *The Ragman's Son*, Kirk admitted that he had frequently cheated on his first wife, Diana Dill, and also on his second wife, Anne Buydens, but much less so.

"That doesn't mean that I don't love Anne dearly. Although I was happy in my marriage, I on occasion messed around a bit. My reputation as 'The Hollywood Horndog' was well-deserved."

Although he started seducing older women at the age of fourteen, he really earned his Don Juan diploma beginning in 1950, before his second marriage. "Some of the most beautiful women in the world came and went from my bedroom," he boasted. "In nearly every case, they left wonderful memories. I had to leave out several affairs from my memoirs. Either the women were still alive and didn't want to be outed, or else they were married at the time and didn't want their husbands to find out."

"Once, around ten o'clock at night, the phone rang. I picked up the receiver to hear a most seductive voice with a foreign accent, perhaps German."

"Is this Mr. Kirk Douglas?" the voice asked. "I'm Hedy Lamarr."

***

Before Hedy came into Kirk's life, he had dreamed about her ever since he'd seen her both on the screen and in *Look* magazine. It had named her one of the four most beautiful women in the world. He'd read of her exploits and heard the latest from the gossip mavens. The centerpiece of multiple scandals, this lovely Austrian brunette somehow managed to retain an aura of mystery. Like Kirk, her parents were Jewish. She had won her first beauty contest when she was twelve.

There had already been many prominent men in her life. The list was long and included a husband she later described as a whip-wielding sadist. Others included Spencer Tracy, Clark Gable, John Garfield, Howard Hughes, Errol Flynn, director Otto Preminger, David Niven—even John F. Kennedy.

Mart Martin, a chronicler of star seductions, wrote: "Lamarr's conquests included the father of her best childhood friend; a female roommate at a Swiss boarding school; several studio wardrobe women; several starlets at MGM; an impotent Texan; and various and sundry other men and women."

Tap-dancing Ann Miller wrote, "People like Hedy Lamarr do our industry a disservice by publicizing their sexual conquests."

The most outrageous rumors about her, widely distributed but never confirmed, was that her first husband, Fritz Mendl, an Austrian munitions manufacturer, pimped her out to his two best customers, Hitler and Mussolini.

On the phone that long-ago night, Hedy asked Kirk if she could visit him the following night to discuss appearing with her in the picture she was about to make, *Lady Without a Passport*.

[Hedy had just completed her most successful box office hit, Samson and Delilah *(1949), co-starring with Victor Mature in Cecil B. DeMille's epic. In a move that surprised most of Hollywood, before awarding it*

Hedy Lamarr had a question for Kirk before she seduced him: "Do you think a woman can be too beautiful?"

185

to Hedy, he had offered the role of Delilah to the zany and sometimes manic-depressive Betty Hutton.

At the time, Hedy was probably the most notorious A-list actress in Hollywood. She had been artfully nude, running through a forest in her first movie Ecstase (Ekstase *in German*), shot in 1933 when she was eighteen. It had been banned in Germany and America, but copies of it were secretly and frequently shown around Hollywood.]

At the time of her dalliance with Kirk, Hedy was between husbands, having divorced actor John Loder in 1947. She was not yet married to Ted Stauffer, a nightclub owner and former bandleader whom she would marry in 1951.

She was late arriving at Kirk's home, but he embraced her warmly and even kissed her lightly on the lips as a greeting.

She spent part of their evening amusing him with stories of working with DeMille and her co-star, Victor Mature. "As Samson, he had bigger tits than mine."

She finally handed him the script for *Lady Without a Passport*. In it, she had already been cast as Marianne Lorress, a penniless Austrian refugee from the Buchenwald concentration camp. She is in Havana, trying to gain entry into the United States. The male lead, Pete Karczag *[the role she was proposing for Kirk]*, is a U.S. immigration officer statiioned in Havana, where he falls in love with her.

She told Kirk that she made the mistake of her life when she turned down the female lead opposite Humphrey Bogart in *Casablanca* (1942). "It went to that Swedish peasant, that Nordic Witch, Ingrid Bergman. I also rejected the female lead in *Gaslight* (1944), which went to her, too."

At one point, she reached into her purse and produced an admiring letter from a fan, one David Garner from Tacoma, Washington, and read it to Kirk out loud: "You are the most spectacular creature since God created Eve. You rank up there with Helen of Troy, no doubt you were her in a previous life. In the Middle Ages, you were the beautiful Agnes Sorel."

"No wonder DeMille cast me as that temptress, Delilah," Hedy said.

According to many witnesses, Lamarr was a bit of an egomaniac. She

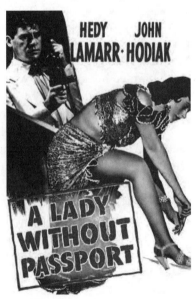

spent a good part of her first hour with Kirk talking about previous screen roles and praising her own beauty. Finally, she turned to him and said, "I'm tired of talking about myself. What do *you* think of me?"

"I'd rather show you than tell you," he answered, guiding her up from the sofa and escorting her into his bedroom.

He later recalled the event. "In *Ecstasy*, Hedy had to fake an orgasm. With me, she had multiple orgasms. I'd never seen that before in any woman. It was only later that I learned that around Hollywood, she was known as the 'Queen of Orgasms.' She was most unusual in that regard."

Lamarr was the only movie star who actually described, in print, in her memoirs, her affinity for multiple orgasms. "I hear men have orgasms while watching me on the screen, or else masturbate under their coats during my love scenes," she said to him.

The next morning, Kirk read the script to *Lady Without a Passport* and didn't like it. "It evokes *Casablanca* but seems like routine fare."

Eventually released in 1950, its male lead was eventually assigned to John Hodiak, who was married during its filming to Anne Baxter, with whom Kirk had worked on that financial flop, *The Walls of Jericho*, back in 1948.

He phoned Hedy, telling her that he could not appear in her film, as he was considering staring in Tennessee Williams' *The Glass Menagerie* instead. "But that doesn't mean that you and I can't be friends. How about tonight?"

"I'll be there," she said. For the next three nights, she showed up for love-making with Kirk. On the fourth night, she invited him to a party at the home of Errol Flynn, with whom she was also conducting an affair. Kirk may not have known at this time that this swashbuckling film star had seduced his first wife.

They drove together up the road to Flynn's hilltop house on Mulholland Drive. As they got out of the car, Kirk held Hedy's hand, looking down upon the lights of Los Angeles.

Inside, a party was in full swing. Flynn greeted them, kissing them both on the lips, as was often his custom.

Hedy had warned Kirk that some of the bathrooms in Flynn's home had full-length mirrors with "looksee" glass. "You can't see anything except your own reflection, but Errol and his voyeur friends can look in at you from behind, seeing and judging whatever you're doing in the bathroom."

Dinner was one that neither Hedy nor Kirk would ever forget.

Flynn liked to pull stunts and practical jokes on his female guests. Once, he put a snake in the dressing room of his frequent co-star, Olivia de

Havilland. For Hedy that night, he devised something sexier. In collusion with his actor friend, Bruce Cabot, he had hired "Freddie" as one of the waiters that night. He went on to pull similar stunts on other actresses who included Joan Collins.

According to Hollywood legend, there had been three different "Freddies," one in the 1930s, another in the 1940s. The third, in the 1950s, was now waiting for Hedy.

Each of them had a penis that extended for more than a foot. When not impersonating waiters at upscale dinner parties, they "played for pay" with men or women, perhaps with the host himself.

Freddie would induce an erection before serving salad from a bowl with a hole in its side. He would then serve the salad to a guest, usually a female, his erection "plugging the hole" in the side of the bowl. In theory, at least, as a woman lifted salad greens from the bowl, the sight of Freddie's erection would elicit a scream.

But for Hedy's arrival with Kirk, Flynn had planned a different set of logistics. This time, Freddie's mammoth organ was arranged atop a silver tray and artfully surrounded with upscale hors d'oeuvres—quail eggs, caviar, smoked salmon, slices of *carpaccio*, and prawns.

Hedy (no stranger to formal dinner parties) became rather aggressive, stabbing into the *hors d'oeuvres* with the serving utensils. Howling in pain, Freddie dropped the tray and retreated into a nearby bathroom for emergency first aid that was administered by Flynn's sometimes lover, matinee idol Tyrone Power.

[Power, it was said, was interested in shooting a "blue movie" of Freddie performing autofellatio. It was Power, that night, who volunteered to take Freddie home for additional first aid, at least until he was ready to model for photos and have sex with his "nurse."]

Before the end of the evening, Flynn staged a ballet he had choreographed, as interpreted by about a dozen mostly female entertainers, each of them nude. His guests, most of them

Errol Flynn with Bette Davis in *The Private Lies of Elizabeth and Essex* (1939)

188

drunk, applauded loudly.

As Kirk was getting ready to leave with Hedy, Flynn whispered to him, "Say, sport, I have a great idea. Why don't you select one of the ballet dancers, maybe even two, and you and Hedy can come to my bedroom for an orgy. You'll love it."

He bowed out, but Flynn extended another, roughly similar, invitation for the following night. "This time, it'll be just the two of us."

"Sounds like fun," Kirk said, "but I'm fully booked."

"I understand," Flynn said. "Some way, somehow, I'm determined to have you, if only for a night. I always get my man…or woman, as the case may be. You have a better chance of getting laid if you swing both ways. Good night, sport." He then gave Hedy a long, passionate kiss, and they were gone.

This was Kirk's last night of passion with Hedy. He tried to contact her several times in the future, but she was always busy.

[Today, Hedy is known as "The Mother of the Cellphone." Her reputation as an inventor stems from before and during World War II. She learned, perhaps from her first husband, the Austrian munitions merchant, that radio signals controlling the speed and direction of torpedoes could easily be jammed and sent off-course. Responding to that, and in collaboration with her friend, the music composer George Antheil, she synchronized a miniaturized player-piano mechanism with a radio transmitter. Adept at switching frequencies at random intervals, it became the foundation of a new system of military defense.

She patented her invention, sent it to the U.S. Navy, and later took credit for "helping win World War II," even though her much-improved anti-missile system was not used until the Cuban missile crisis.

In 2014, fourteen years after her death, she was posthumously inducted into the National Inventors Hall of Fame.]

***

After the release of *Champion* (1949), Kirk was bombarded with fan mail, mostly from women, young or old, and gay admirers who had been turned on by the physique he displayed as a boxer. His mail included an occasional attack, but his ego was strong enough to let him toss them aside.

The message he paid the most attention to was a telegram from Joan Crawford. It said, "You're brilliant, a champ with charisma I haven't seen since Gable. I predict bigtime stardom for you."

In response, also in a telegram, he lauded her, too: "I fell in love with you in *Forsaking All Others*. You were never lovelier."

"Thank you," She answered, again by telegram. "Most people praise me for *Mildred Pierce."*

"*Flamingo Road* is my favorite. Perhaps I'm being indiscreet. I've had fantasies about you for years."

Finally, abandoning the telegram format, she phoned him and invited him to her house.

When he arrived at her immaculately maintained house the next evening, Crawford greeted him in her foyer with a light kiss on his lips. As with all her dates, she had carefully mapped out their evening, informing him that she'd made reservations at Ciro's.

"Right then and there, I decided to assert my manhood,"

Kirk recalled. "No, we're going to Don the Beachcomber's." She looked shocked because I don't think she was used to being countermanded. But she gave in to me. Don the Beachcomber's it was."

"Our dinner there was interrupted several times by autograph seekers. I must say, being the grand lady she was, Crawford had mastered entrances and exits, most dramatic, with me tagging along as her puppy dog."

"Since she was already a Hollywood legend, and because fans were beginning to know who I was, the 'hot lines' to Hedda and Louella were buzzing before the night was over. I'm sure that by morning, those two gossipy old bitches would have us ready to announce our marriage."

"Even before we left the restaurant, I realized that Crawford was the equal of not only my strong-willed mother, with her sense of survival, but all six of my sisters, too."

As Kirk related, Crawford was so hot for him that after he drove her home from the restaurant, she invited him inside and then attacked him in her foyer, taking off her clothes and urging him out of his pants. He later referred to sex with her, there in the foyer, as "professional and clinical, rather impersonal."

Professional it was, as she'd had a lot of experience. She'd made two porn films in the 1920s, *Velvet Lips* and *The Casting Couch.* In the latter 1920s, she was known for wearing out casting couches, later commenting about it wryly with "It sure beats hell out of the cold, hard floor."

Joan's rival, Bette Davis, said, "Joan screwed every male star at MGM,

190

except Lassie." In addition to four husbands *[They included Douglas Fair-banks Jr. and Franchot Tone]* her off-screen lovers starred Cary Grant, Clark Gable, Tyrone Power, John Garfield, Spencer Tracy, and Rock Hudson.

When she'd made *Reunion in France* (1942) with John Wayne, she'd given him a bad review: "Get the Duke out of the saddle, and you've got nothing."

In the middle of the sex act, she paid Kirk a strange compliment: "You're real clean. I liked it when you shaved your armpits to make *Champion.*"

"I always had light hair under my arms, and I never shaved them," he said.

"During intercourse over the years, I received many compliments, but never one like this. I discovered that one of the ways Crawford got off was by licking a man's armpits during intercourse."

As they were putting on their clothes in the foyer, she gave him another strange compliment: "We sure went to heaven," she said, which was her reference to screwing. Then she said, using a term that was still unfamiliar: "I like the attention you paid to my ninny pies," which he figured out meant her breasts.

Although Crawford had praise for Kirk, none was forthcoming from him. "She blew away my early fantasies of her," he said. "That and her foul breath."

As part of a tour, she led him upstairs and into the bedroom of her two adopted children, Christina and Christopher. "Both of them were strapped to their beds, and she looked to me for approval, but I found nothing to compliment her about."

He later wrote, "I got out fast."

Crawford is never mentioned again in his memoirs, although during the many decades that followed, they often showed up at the same galas, parties, and award presentations.

Scandalous stories associated with another of his visits to her home eventually became bruited throughout Hollywood, even though some insiders have dismissed them as merely gossip and innuendo. Kirk, however, was candid about relaying them to his friends.

After not hearing from Kirk for three weeks, Crawford phoned again, concealing a plan to seduce him again. Whereas before, she'd used flattery and her status as a glamourous icon as a lure, this time she held out a different kind of bait, suggesting that he might be her co-star in an upcoming film, *This Woman Is Dangerous,* set for a release in 1952.

Kirk showed up at her house to discuss it. He sat in her all-white living room as she pitched her ideas about the role he would play. Crawford would establish her character as a female crime boss, the mistress of a cold-blooded killer. When it's established that she's on the verge of going blind, she turns for help to a doctor, Ben Halleck, who might restore her sight. Crawford fans can almost predict the plot from this point onward: She falls in love with the doctor.

[That role ultimately went to the Warner's star, Dennis Morgan.]

Without reading the script, Kirk perceived the project as a woman's picture, with the doctor cornered into a lackluster secondary role. There, on the spot, he suggested that he might be better cast as the killer, but she rejected that idea.

After discussing the movie and his possible involvement in it for about an hour, the doorbell rang, and Crawford went to answer it, since the maid had been dismissed until the following morning.

It was Barbara Stanwyck.

` Kirk later told Michael Curtiz, who had helmed Crawford in *Mildred Pierce* (1945), "Stanwyck had been rather cold to me when we shot *Martha Ivers,* but on that night, she was warm and gracious, really quite charming, even kissing me on the lips."

After seating herself as part of a trio that also included Kirk and Crawford, she spent a good part of the evening discussing her upcoming divorce from Robert Taylor.

[Perhaps unknown to Stanwyck, Crawford had had an affair with Taylor when they had co-starred in The Gorgeous Hussy *(1936). Hedda Hopper, with sarcasm in her voice, in public, had asked Crawford, "Who was the Gorgeous Hussy, you or Bob?"]*

"Bob has never been faithful. Joan told me he had this torrid affair with her third husband, Phillip Terry. I heard reports that he was screwing starlets when he made *Quo Vadis* (1951). He may have plugged his co-star, little Miss Deborah Kerr. I'm divorcing Bob because that's what he wants. I would prefer to continue our lavender marriage. Being married is a good front for us, but he wants out. I intend to make him pay—and pay dearly."

[Stanwyck was true to her word. For the rest of his life, until his death in 1969, he had to mail her a large monthly alimony check.]

For additional insights and confirmation of these events, one must turn to Crawford's maid of three years. When she was fired for not showing enough diligence in her housekeeping, the maid tried, unsuccessfully, to peddle her account of the events to the tabloids and scandal magazines.

No editor dared print her claims, but word traveled quickly along the Hollywood grapevine about this *ménage à trois* scandal. The former maid asserted that when she reported to work, as planned, on the morning after Kirk and Stanwyck's arrival, Stanwyck was "just leaving" and didn't even speak to her.

Then, at around 8:30AM, Crawford and Kirk came down in bathrobes, followed by the children. The maid recognized the bathrobe Kirk was wearing as having belonged to Crawford's former husband, Phillip Terry.

"I later discovered that the guest bedroom had not been used, but the one in Miss Crawford's boudoir certainly had been. It was obvious to me that Miss Stanwyck, Miss Crawford, and Mr. Douglas had shared the same bed that night. Miss Stanwyck had already visited Miss Crawford on many nights for sleepovers. I'm not that dumb. I knew what was going on. Mr. Douglas struck me as a horndog. Don't tell me that when he went to bed with those two hussies, he didn't come on like gangbusters."

***

After her birth in Port Arthur, Texas, Evelyn Keyes moved to Georgia, where she grew up. Even as an eight-year-old, she dreamed of a career in show business. When she was eighteen, she became a chorus girl. In Hollywood, she was put under contract by Cecil B. DeMille, and appeared in a number of "B" movies such as *Sudden Money* in 1938.

The following year, she was cast into the role

Scarlett O'Hara (center) and her sisters. *Left to right,* Ann Rutherford, Vivien Leigh, and Evelyn Keyes.

193

for which she is best remembered today: Scarlett O'Hara's younger sister in *Gone With the Wind* (1939).

Before filming of that epic began, she discovered that she was pregnant. Since she desperately wanted the role, she had an abortion. Sadly, the procedure went badly, leading to complications and her inability to conceive other children.

At the time, she was married to Barton Bainbridge, but he committed suicide in 1940. Later, she married two famous screen directors, Charles Vidor (1944-45) and John Huston (1946-1950).

When her marriage to Huston ended, and as a free agent once again, she began to date. One of the first men to take her out

Evelyn Keyes

was the gay actor, Farley Granger. "At the time, he was trying to decide if he liked men or women," Keyes later claimed. "He was having an occasional affair with a female, notably Shelley Winters."

He invited her to a gala one night hosted by Charles Feldman, Kirk's agent. Feldman had taken over the Crescendo Nightclub on the Hollywood Strip for a big, star-studded private event.

Keyes was seated next to Kirk who, as his date, had brought Rhonda Fleming, the "Queen of Technicolor," noted for her flaming red hair and porcelain skin.

Kirk was so courtly to Rhonda," Keyes said. "He was constantly gazing lovingly into her eyes, and she seemed to be returning his adoration. I thought they were in love, or at least having an affair, although I could not be sure."

Keyes had just seen Kirk in *Champion*, where "I fell in love with his physique in the boxing ring. I was struck by his male beauty—that shock of hair, that dimple, that strong jaw."

"I decided to take a chance," she said. "My opportunity arose when Rhonda went to powder her nose, and I slipped Kirk my phone number. I was coming down from my divorce from John (Huston) and I was seven years from marrying the bandleader, Artie Shaw. Kirk took my number, looked at it, smiled with appreciation—and that was that. Both of us circulated for the rest of the night."

"Even though Farley was my date, he spent a lot of the evening making goo-goo eyes at Tony Curtis. John Wayne came up to introduce himself to me, as if I didn't know who in hell he was. I deliberately offended this right-winger by claiming I was a communist. He drifted away and was replaced with Huston. I said to him, "Aren't you that old coot I once married?"

"One and the same. Better than ever, still drawing the babes to me," he answered. "The younger the better."

Although Kirk had paid almost no attention to Keyes at the party, he phoned her the next morning. "How about it, doll?" he asked. She thought that line might have come from a boy in high school.

Then he said something that surprised her: "I have this hunch that you and I need each other desperately, as we're trying to get over our divorces."

Thus began one of Kirk's best affairs, lasting a total of four months. According to Keyes, "He was having a lot of mental problems, and I was, too. We spent many a night counseling each other. Sometimes he'd pace the floor, ranting, 'I'm just a ragman's son, cock in hand.'"

That cock wasn't always in his hand," she said. "I should know. He kept me busy."

At the time of her affair with Kirk, Keyes was under contract to Harry Cohn, the much-hated mogul who ran Columbia.

Producer Budd Schulberg referred to Cohn as "the meanest man I know, an unreconstructed dinosaur."

Hedda Hopper asserted, "Cohn was the man you stand in line to hate."

Director Elia Kazan weighed in with "He liked to be the biggest bug in the manure pile."

Cohn had installed a secret passageway leading from his office to the dressing rooms of his starlets under contract. "I give the bitches work, and they give me their cunts. After all, Hollywood is about cunts and horses."

His more high-profile affairs starred Marlene Dietrich and Lucille Ball. He was one of the first producers to demand "casting couch rights" from Marilyn Monroe.

The lone holdout who didn't succumb to him was Keyes herself. "The dirty little man disgusts me," she told her fellow contract players.

Two weeks into her affair with Kirk, he came at her request to Columbia Studios, but was barred at the gate. The guard informed him that Cohn had ordered that he could not come onto the lot. "But I just got a damn invitation to his home for his New Year's Eve party. What's going on here?"

Two days later, Keyes wanted to have lunch with Kirk again, but this time, she met him at Columbia's entrance. From there, he escorted her across the street to a public eatery.

After their lunch, when she returned to Columbia's entrance with Kirk, the guard still barred him and told Keyes that Cohn wanted to see her in his office at once.

There, Cohn began to quiz her in the most personal of terms: "I hear you're dating that bum, Kirk Douglas. Do you lay down for him?"

"With that gorgeous body of his, I'd be a fool not to," she answered.

"Do you go down on him?" Cohn demanded.

"Of course I do. I go down on any man I date."

"A big cock?" he asked.

"It's parlor sized." Then she stormed out of his office, knowing that her days at Columbia were numbered.

One weekend, Kirk invited Keyes to go with him for a weekend in Palm Springs, but she was busy and could not make it. Details of what transpired that weekend remained unclear to her until much later.

"Obviously, as I finally heard, Kirk met the girl of his dreams at the Racquet Club there, a mating ground of off-the-record assignations. It was 'goodbye Evelyn, great knowing you, kid.'"

Months later, as the preface to another vacation, Kirk flew alone to Acapulco without making a hotel reservation, arriving during one of its busiest weeks. There were no vacancies, at least not at any of the hotels where he wanted to stay.

Quite by chance, he ran into the producer, Mike Todd, who, coincidentally, was shacked up with Evelyn Keyes. Kirk told Todd about his room problem, and the producer invited him "to join Evelyn and me at our villa. I understand you used to be her boyfriend."

"True, but I've forgotten about that now."

"Good, then you're welcome."

At the villa, he found Evelyn warm and inviting, the perfect hostess. "Mike seemed to adore her as I had once."

When Todd went to tell his Mexican manservant to mix some drinks for them, Keyes turned to Kirk. "What happened? One day you just disappeared without a trace."

"You know me, the tumbling tumbleweed who just keeps rolling along."

"Well, with you out of my life, I've met the man I desperately love," she said.

The next day, Kirk went waterskiing with Keyes. Mike remained at the villa, always on the phone. After skiing, she returned to the villa to be with him while Kirk opted to do some exploring on his own.

He went to the ruins of an ancient temple which Mayans had used to sacrifice virgins. "I was alone in the ruins—that is, until I spotted this gorgeous girl who looked like a dead ringer for the daughter of Dolores del Rio, assuming she ever had a daughter. We hit it off immediately. The decaying sculptures in the temple seemed devoted to the worship of male genitalia. For the next hour, this beauty was a 'worshipper.'"

Two weeks later, when Keyes and Todd moved out of their rented villa, Kirk wanted to repay them and invited the loving couple to spend a few days with him at his home in Los Angeles. He was somewhat surprised when they accepted.

On Monday, after a friendly weekend together, Todd had to fly to Las Vegas on business.

"He seemed to trust me, and I appreciated that," Kirk said. "I was alone in my house with my former mistress. We were relaxed around each other, at least most of the time. Then that old sexual tension returned. At around 11PM I headed to my bedroom, trying to conceal my raging hard-on, and she retreated to the guest room. I lay awake in bed, thinking thoughts I didn't want. I got up and locked the door to my bedroom. It was not that I was locking her out. I was locking myself in. After all, I was not a shit."

He genuinely liked both Keyes and Todd. Their affair ended long before Todd met Elizabeth Taylor.

Keyes later wrote two memoirs.

She told friends, "I lost Kirk. I lost John. I lost Mike. And I lost so many others, even Artie Shaw. I'll probably end up a fag hag."

When she was in her 70s, Keyes became the best friend of Tab Hunter and his husband. "I adored Evelyn," Hunter wrote in a memoir. "She was full of piss and vinegar."

***

After his divorce from Diana, Kirk lived through a period where he drifted from one boudoir to another, night after night. Now that he'd become a star, the possibilities seemed endless. Some of his fellow entertainers—Errol Flynn, Sammy Davis, Jr., Frank Sinatra, and Eddie Fisher—had made their promiscuities famous, almost defiantly bedding a different woman every night.

During that period, whose length Kirk estimated at about two months, most of the women who passed through were soon forgotten. He never found even one from whom he requested a repeat performance. During some seductions, he never even bothered to ask the name of his partner.

By his own admission, each night seemed to grow less satisfying than the one that preceded it. For a time, he tried masturbation. "I developed a romance with my hand, which in some cases was more satisfying than some of the partners I'd had. Even so, it wasn't enough, although it helped me develop a relationship with myself."

Although his life was about to change, he grew more and more depressed. "I was searching for love in all the wrong places. Then one day I met *Gilda*, the love goddess of the world. She was luscious. She came to me. I didn't have to chase her. She was Rita Hayworth."

Rita Hayworth with Glenn Ford in *Gilda* (1946)

He had first became enamored of Rita during her reign as one of the most popular pinup girls of World War II, competing with Betty Grable, whose left leg had been voted as the loveliest in the world. Runners-up were Lana Turner, Dorothy Lamour, and Hedy Lamarr.

"I always found my life amazing. Just think, little Issur got to bed three of those goddesses, except for Grable and Lamour. I guess you can't have everything."

"It wasn't the pinup of Rita that made me fall in love with her," he said. "It was the night I saw *Gilda*, that 1946 *film noir* she made with Glenn Ford, her lover on and off the screen. I was mesmerized by her beautiful hair and figure as she elegantly danced that striptease number with a glove while dressed in a low-cut black satin gown. Her 'Put the Blame on Mame' number excited my sexual fantasy. I practically came in my pants. From then on, Rita, to millions of horny guys, became the ultimate *femme fatale*."

Rita was introduced to sex when she was just a young girl. Born Margarita Carmen Cansino in Brooklyn to a Spanish Flamenco dancer, Eduardo Cansino, and an Irish-American Ziegfeld Girl, Volga Haworth. Rita later changed her name to "Hayworth," adding a "Y" to her mother's maiden name.

As she grew older, Rita became her father's dancing partner. At night, he abused her and forced her into an incestuous relationship.

From her father's arms, she'd migrated into an ill-fated marriage (1937-1943) to a con man, Edward C. Judson. As a means of launching her (money-making) career in films, he pimped her to a number of producers and directors.

Surprisingly, she refused to go to bed with Harry Cohn, her boss at Columbia. She later said, "He became obsessed with me, perhaps because he couldn't have me. He did what he could to get even by degrading and humiliating me. He even put a hidden microphone in my dressing room."

Other high-profile affairs were with Tony Martin, Victor Mature, Robert Mitchum, Tyrone Power, Gilbert Roland, and with Kirk's agent, Charles Feldman. Another of her trysts was with Howard Hughes. The only bad review she got was a churlish comment from Peter Lawford, who told Kirk, "She's the worst lay in the world. She was always drunk, and she never stopped eating, even during intercourse."

Eventually, Rita told Kirk, "I'm a good, gentle person attracted to men who are bastards and abusive to women."

He assured her that she would encounter only love from him.

Rita's second marriage (1943-48) was to Orson Welles before he became obese. They produced a daughter, Rebecca.

Her marriage to Prince Aly Khan on the French Riviera in 1949 became the most publicized in the world. He was hailed as "the greatest lover of our times, and was also known as "Casanova, a sybarite, gentleman jockey, auto racer, hunter, pilot, horse breeder, soldier, and Muslim religious leader.

Like all her other marriages, this one was a royal disaster. As Barbara Leaming, the biographer, put it, "Aly seemed happiest with Rita not when she was herself, but when, in a fit of temper, she enacted his fantasy of the fiery *Gilda*."

Rita's romance with Kirk became public knowledge when a photographer at Ciro's sneaked up on them and snapped their picture for the tabloids. "They looked like lovebirds," the *paparazzo* said.

The affair generated a lot more press than it might have, since it was her first date in the wake of her split from Prince Aly Khan.

One night at a Hollywood party, Welles told Kirk, "Rita's life has been filled with pain. I regret I was the cause of much of it. But there were so many other guilty men."

He also told Kirk, "In spite of all those screen roles of the 1940s, I think that in the long run of time, Rita will remain famous for two things: lending her name to the drink 'the margarita,' and the fact that her sexy image was pasted onto the first atomic bomb detonated at Bikini Atoll."

Unlike Lawford, Kirk, from the moment of their first encounter, found Rita "vivacious, desirable, and ever so sexy. She always had this come-hither look in her eyes, even over morning coffee. I liked the way her auburn hair cascaded over her creamy shoulders. Even those part-time dykes, Joan Crawford and Marlene Dietrich, went for her."

One of Kirk's alltime favorite scenes in a film was the "Put the Blame on Mame" number that Rita had performed in *Gilda*. "When she learned how much I got off on it, one night in my living room, with music, she reprised it for me, privately, stripping down and going where the movie camera didn't dare go. Suddenly, like a vision of beauty, she appeared before me in her Juel Parks lingerie, and even that cascaded to the floor. I think I attacked her aggressively that night, since I couldn't wait to get her to the bedroom."

"Of course, as a lover, I couldn't compete with her third husband, Prince Aly Khan, the son of the Aga Khan, and Vice President of the U.N. General Assembly representing Pakistan. [*Rita was married to him from 1949 to 1953. Together, they produced a daughter, Princess Yasmin.*]

Kirk was told that the womanizing prince was a master of the ancient art of *Imsak*, i.e., the indefinite postponement of ejaculation (*coitus reservatus*). As a young man, the prince had been sent to Cairo to practice the technique in that city's bordellos.

In spite of Rita's beauty, he found her a sad, lonely creature—"Gorgeous as hell but depressed and desolate at times. She was about the most insecure lover I've ever had. I tried to reassure her, telling her that she was beloved around the world."

To that, she'd respond, "That's only because of my looks. A woman loses her beauty and allure if she lives long enough. What will I do then?"

After a few weeks, Kirk decided to walk out on her. "I fled from the love nest. There were needs deep within her I could not satisfy. I wondered if any man could. She was so bruised early in life, I feared that she'd never recover. She had never found the security she sought. I was afraid she'd eventually pull me down into her well of despair, and I wasn't ready for that. I had a lotta living to do. I felt like a cad, but I bolted."

[*For years after his breakup with Rita, Kirk maintained the fondest, yet sad, memories of her. "I often thought of what might have been. Maybe both of us could have fought off our demons together."*

Around 1960, she began to suffer the first stages of Alzheimer's Disease, which wasn't diagnosed until 1980. It was a slow, agonizing decline, but she continued to make films until 1972, when she appeared in The Wrath of God *and then faded from the screen forever.*

She died in 1987, at the age of 68. Fans across the world, including Kirk, mourned her passing.]

***

"You'd think my affair with Rita might have sworn me off love goddesses for a while, but it didn't," Kirk said. "I had the studio get me in touch with another emerging love goddess. A whole new breed of actresses was emerging on the scene in the 1950s to replace those screen sirens who had dominated the 1940s. I wanted to sample what Marilyn Monroe was like. I had a studio executive hold out the possibility that I wanted her to play opposite me in my upcoming movie, *Ace in the Hole."*

"I thought the only woman who could make better love than Rita Hayworth was this sexy, emerging blonde starlet, Marilyn Monroe."

When Kirk learned that his agent, Charles Feldman, was "shacking up" with her, he phoned him. "You don't mind me trying out Marilyn, the honeypot?" he asked.

Marilyn arriving at Ciro's Restaurant in 1953 at a party honoring Louella Parsons.

"Not at all. Marilyn sleeps around."

"Tell her I'm considering her for the slutty waitress in that script you sent over, *Ace in the Hole."*

"Gotcha!"

Two hours later, Feldman called back. "She's excited to meet you. She promised to drive over to see you at eight o'clock tonight."

Marilyn had not yet morphed into a superstar at the time she was involved with Kirk. Having already placed three bottles of champagne on ice, he'd been waiting impatiently for her arrival, and was rather angry when she didn't arrive until 10:30PM. "But when I saw her in this tight-fitting white dress, two sizes too small for her, all was forgiven."

Almost every day, he'd heard something about this new starlet on the horizon. Many men, including Ronald Reagan, between wives at the time, had already seduced her.

She was alleged to have said, "When I become a star, that means I've sucked my last cock—unless I want to."

Elia Kazan, Kirk's future director, later said, "Marilyn was just a simple, decent-hearted kid that Hollywood eventually brought down, legs apart."

The director, Nunnally Johnson, alerted Kirk. "Copulation, I'm certain, is an uncomplicated way of saying 'Thank you.' To Rock Hudson and Marilyn, sex is no more than eating a sandwich."

Marilyn's encounters with Kirk, brief though they were, transpired during one of the most troubled periods of her existence. Her mentor, protector, and agent, Johnny Hyde, had died at the age of 51 in December of 1950.

"Johnny came into my life about the time I was fearing I'd become a waitress in a diner for life."

"There were some weeks after I landed in this town that I nearly starved to death," she said. "You might even call me a streetwalker, although, unlike the other prostitutes, I never took money and picked up men on the side streets off Sunset Boulevard. I settled for a good meal. Depending on the time of day, I negotiated for a big breakfast, lunch, or dinner.

"Then along comes Johnny to save me. He became my guiding light. He persuaded John Huston to give me a supporting role in *The Asphalt Jungle* (1950), and he got Joseph Mankiewicz to see a rough cut of it, which led to my role in *All About Eve* (also 1950) with Bette Davis and Anne Baxter."

"I felt so horrible when I heard about Johnny's death in Palm Springs," she said. "He'd invited me to join him, and I turned him down. Indirectly, I might have caused his death. His doctor told him that having all this sex with me was damaging his already weakened heart."

She shared a bizarre story with Kirk that made him shudder. "To say farewell to the man who had done so much for me, I slipped into his house late at night where his body was in a casket. I spent the rest of the night on top of his body. But I slipped out in the pre-dawn before anyone in his family woke up and discovered me."

Marilyn went on to tell Kirk that she was excited by the possibility that he might be her co-star. She had found his performances in *A Letter to Three Wives* and *Champion* "thrilling. You know, if our sexual chemistry comes across on the screen, we might become as fabulous a team as Clark Gable and Lana Turner. She's my ideal."

Finally, Kirk discussed the possible role he had in mind for her. The film would be released by Paramount and directed by Billy Wilder. *[If she'd gotten the part, Wilder would have entered her life long before he directed her in that alltime hit comedy,* Some Like It Hot.*]*

Her role in *Ace In the Hole* would be that of Lorraine, a shallow, slutty, manipulative wench who runs a diner and is married to a man trapped underground in a cave nearby. Preoccupied with trying to escape from this dull little settlement in New Mexico, she's unconcerned about her husband and the agonizing death he's inevitably facing.

"I could do that," Marilyn chimed in. "In fact, that's how I might have ended up if Johnny hadn't come along."

After the second bottle of champagne, Marilyn stood up on wobbly high heels and began to strip down before him, evoking memories of Rita Hayworth.

"Marilyn was no Rita, who was far more sensual," Kirk said. "Marilyn had a great body and firm breasts. But then she said something that shocked me.

"Forgive my nigger ass. I know it's too big."

"I couldn't believe that she said that. I told her she was perfect, ass included."

The next day he phoned Feldman to report the details of the night before. "Frankly, I found sex with Marilyn dull, truly boring."

"You're the first man I ever heard say that about her," Feldman said. "She usually gets raves."

"The passion wasn't there for me," Kirk said. "To be blunt, there was also a problem with her hygiene. I think her idea of getting ready to go out was to skip a bath and spray on more Chanel No. 5."

"I should have warned you," Feldman said. "Before we go at it, I take her into the bathroom where we strip down and take a shower together. All that lathering up makes me really hot. It's very erotic."

"Now you tell me," Kirk said.

Even if he didn't like Marilyn in bed, he still recommended her for *Ace in the Hole* to Billy Wilder, who rejected her, preferring Jan Sterling instead.

***

Although Marilyn was "aced" from *Ace in the Hole*, but in 1960, the idea of teaming her with Kirk emerged again.

She and Gregory Peck were set to co-star in *The Billionaire* for a 1960 release, as directed by George Cukor. It was a romantic comedy about a billionaire who falls for a showgirl and disguises himself as a dancer to win her. She had made it clear that she did not go for men of wealth.

There were many "kinks" in the original script, and she and Cukor agreed to bring in Arthur Miller, her playwright husband, as a script doctor.

After Miller had finished his rewrites, and the revised script was forwarded to Peck, he wanted to bail out, telling Fox he'd return the $100,000 advance. He complained that Miller had cut down his part while enlarging Marilyn's.

Consequently, Cukor was forced to negotiate with some of the leading actors of Hollywood about filling in for Peck. But one by one, rejections came in from Charlton Heston, Peter Lawford, James Stewart, Cary Grant, Rock Hudson, and Tony Curtis.

[Curtis and Marilyn were not particularly good friends. He had been one of her early lovers when she'd first arrived in Hollywood. He'd just finished working with her on Some Like It Hot *(1959) for Billy Wilder, and he'd been frequently enraged when she either showed up late or didn't appear at all. He had famously said, "Kissing her was like kissing Hitler."]*

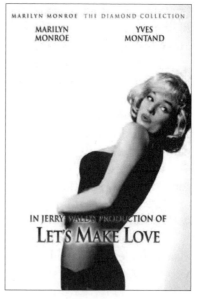

Cukor didn't let Kirk know that he was the last on the list of actors considered to co-star with Marilyn. But eventually, it was agreed that he'd be part of a working lunch at the Fox commissary with Cukor and Marilyn.

"It was obvious during our reunion that Marilyn was still pissed off at me for not getting her cast in *Ace in the Hole*," Kirk said. "Now, she was a bigger star than me, and she made sure that day that I knew it."

After that lunchtime meeting, Cukor never called Kirk back, not wanting to tell him that Marilyn had nixed him as her leading man.

Arthur Miller had seen the French entertainer, Yves Montand, perform in a one-man show in New York, and recommended him to Cukor, who eventually hired him. The first time Marilyn met him, she told Cukor, "I find him very, very sexy." The next day she reported to him. "I think Yves invented French kissing…and other things."

Even though Montand was married at the time to the French actress, Simone Signoret, he embarked on a torrid affair with Marilyn.

The title of the musical they were making was changed to *Let's Make Love,* which they did every night.

In 1960, during the first week of the release of *Let's Make Love,* Kirk went to see it. He later claimed, "I didn't miss much not getting the role in this turkey. Montand was welcome to the part, and Marilyn was lackluster."

In 1988, Kirk gave almost no details about his involvement with Marilyn, other than writing: "The public insists on believing the fantasies of Hollywood stars. Marilyn Monroe on the screen was the sexiest woman in the world. In real life, she was *blah,* and always late."

***

Novelist Ayn Rand, born in Russia in 1905 and a graduate of the University of Leningrad, emigrated to the United States in 1926. In 1943, she published her most famous novel, *The Fountainhead,* the saga of a fictitious architect based loosely on Frank Lloyd Wright. It became a bestseller and was acquired by Warners which eventually turned it into a 1949 release. Originally, it was slated as a vehicle for Humphrey Bogart and Barbara Stanwyck.

There was also a strong woman's role in it, that of Dominique Franco in this objectivistic potboiler about sex, greed, corporate corruption, and the ultimate triumph of the individual over the masses.

The first time Dominique lays eyes on the protagonist, she wonders "what he looks like naked." The romantic hero is a stern intellectual, who believes that "the world is perishing from an orgy of self-sacrificing."

Gary Cooper was urged by his wife, Rocky, to take the role, even though, in his cinematic past, he'd been known for his portrayal of self-effacing heroes. There was a fear that his devoted fans would not accept him as such an arrogant, abusive character.

For his role, he demanded $275,000. Bogie had dropped out weeks before.

Many actresses in Hollywood coveted the strong role of Dominique. Even without Bogie, Barbara Stanwyck stubbornly wanted the female lead, hoping she'd be greenlighted.

Rand announced to the press that she'd sent the script to Greta Garbo, her choice. For about a week, Garbo considered a return to the screen, which she'd abdicated at the beginning of the 1940s. She finally rejected it, saying, "I will not play love scenes with Gary Cooper."

Patricia Neal with Gary Cooper...a May-to-December romance.

205

Then other actresses ferociously competed for the role, including rivals Joan Crawford and Bette Davis. Also under serious consideration were Ida Lupino, Lauren Bacall, and Eleanor Parker.

Finally cast was a relative newcomer to Hollywood, a beauty from Kentucky, Patricia Neal. Things had moved fast for her since her debut in movies. She'd made her screen debut as Ronald Reagan's love interest in *John Loves Mary*, a film released the same year (1949) as the more meaty and more famous *The Fountainhead*.

Neal was a quarter of a century younger than Cooper, appearing on the screen with a wide, flat face, a voluptuous figure, and a husky and sultry yet soothing voice. She would go on to greater roles, including an appearance in *Hud* (1963) for which she won a Best Actress Oscar starring opposite Paul Newman.

While shooting *The Fountainhead,* she fell in love with her co-star, and Cooper returned her devotion. When Rocky found out, she exploded in jealous fury, calling Neal "a redneck from Kentucky who eats cornbread and blackeyed peas."

Kirk had seen her love scenes with Reagan, and he called her for a date. She had admired his screen image ever since she'd seen *A Letter to Three Wives*. She accepted his invitation and asked him to accompany her to the premiere of *The Fountainhead* at Warners Beverly Theatre.

[According to many witnesses, because of implications associated with her lover's status as a married man, Neal could not be seen in public with him. She therefore restricted their rendezvous to private encounters, usually intimate dinners which she cooked for him herself. Only on two occasions did they break their own rule and make a rare appearance in public, where they were photographed together.]

Kirk made the ideal escort, courtly and charming. At the time, he was unaware of her affair with Cooper, one of his film favorites.

As he sat next to her through the premier of the movie she had been a part of, Kirk could sense Neal's frustration. The audience seemed to shift back and forth, impatiently. Kirk said, "It was too intellectual for that crowd."

Ominously, in the lobby, members of the audience seemed to ignore Kirk and Neal as they emerged, subdued, from the darkened theater. Only one person came over to greet them, and that was Virginia Mayo, soon to be Kirk's co-star. She took Neal's hand, saying, in a bitchy, catty voice, "My, weren't you bad!"

Following the premiere, Kirk escorted Patricia to Ciro's, where Jack Warner was tossing a gala party for the cast and other Hollywood luminaries. At one point, Cooper came over to join Kirk and Neal at table, where they were on their second bottle of champagne.

"We chatted," Kirk said, "with Neal doing much of the talking. Coop was polite with me, but very reserved and had almost nothing to say to me. After all, I, along with other post-war actors, were taking over roles that in days of yore might have gone to Clark Gable or him. Later, I found out why. He was god damn jealous."

After the party, Kirk drove Neal home, where he suggested that he'd like to come in for a nightcap. She later wrote, "I found him sexy and attractive, but my heart at that point belonged to Gary, whom I had to slip around and see in private, even having dinners at home with him before making love."

After that, Kirk became Neal's frequent escort whenever she had to make a public appearance and needed a man on her arm. Gossip columns were filled with rumors of their torrid affair. One night after returning to her apartment from Ciro's, he sat with her on the sofa, perhaps thinking that his chance had come. He reached for her and held her in his arms, passionately kissing her.

As he was guiding her to the bedroom, she broke away at the last minute. "I can't go through with this. I'm in love with Coop, and we're in the middle of a love affair. We're very much in love, and he plans to leave Rocky and marry me."

Once again, he settled for a good night kiss.

About twenty minutes after his departure, her doorbell rang. It was Cooper, who had been parked outside. "I saw that bastard, Kirk Douglas, trying to make love to you. I was standing outside your living room window looking in, spying on you two lovebirds."

Suddenly, he slapped her really hard. She was startled, but he immediately apologized. "I was jealous out of my mind. I'll never do that again. Please forgive me."

Even during some of the weeks that followed, Kirk continued to see her for a while, settling for some "heavy petting" after checking the street to see that Cooper wasn't parked across the road.

"Patricia still held out on me, although on some nights, I came very close to conquest," he recalled. "But I guess I couldn't compete with a legendary seducer known as 'The Montana Mule.'"

[*Among Cooper's legions of conquests were such stars as Tallulah Bankhead, Ingrid Bergman, Claudette Colbert, Marlene Dietrich, Lupe Velez, Merle Oberon, even Mae West, Howard Hughes, and Cary Grant. Clara Bow had told a reporter, "Coop's hung like a horse and can go all night." Cecil Beaton, the noted photographer and costume designer, claimed that the bisexual director Edmund Goulding "worshipped Cooper twice a day, once in the morning, and again in mid-afternoon.*

That is, when I wasn't choking on that thing myself. Not bad for an offspring of a mother who wanted a girl so much she dressed her son in skirts until he had to go to school."]

According to Kirk, "In time, my schoolboy adoration for Patricia faded, and I turned elsewhere for love-making. But our friendship endured, and we would co-star in a movie together. Not only that, but I found her the perfect *confidante* to discuss my troubled love life."

One night, she told him that years before, Cooper had tried to maneuver the studio into assigning him, not Kirk, the musician's role in *Young Man With a Horn*, opposite Lauren Bacall and Doris Day.

"That ol' cowpoke," he said. "He not only steals my girl, namely you, but almost took that part away from me."

One rainy Monday night, Neal phoned Kirk, asking him to come over. Driving there through a storm, he arrived at her apartment to find her distraught. She confessed to having aborted Cooper's child, at his request. "The doctor held up the longest needle in the world. I closed my eyes and thought I would die. I can still hear the sound of scraping ringing in my ears."

That night, he slept in her bed, cuddling her, occasionally hearing her weeping. He left the next morning, assuring her, "I will always be there for you." He hired a nurse to look after her until she recuperated.

"From that night our friendship was cemented. I liked being able to discuss my own love affairs and troubles with her. On one occasion, I met her for dinner and told her I'd fallen in love."

"Do I know her?" she asked.

"I'm in love with the elusive *Laura* herself."

Neal, who had seen all the great films of the 1940s, knew at once who he meant. It was a reference to actress Gene Tierney, who had immortalized herself with her portrayal of the mysterious protagonist of Otto Preminger's mystery/romance released in 1944.

***

"When I first met the beautiful Gene Tierney, I think I fell in love with her overbite before I fell in love with the rest of the woman," Kirk recalled years later. "I adored her. My first wife, Diana, had an overbite. So does my second wife (Anne Buydens)."

Before he met Tierney, he had already fallen in love with her screen image. In addition to *Laura*, one of his other favorite films was *Leave Her to Heaven* (1945), for which she'd won a Best Actress Oscar for her portrayal of the narcissistic, jealous *femme fatale*.

208

Tierney had been born in Brooklyn, but Kirk found her "the most unlikely person to come from that borough. She was more of a Connecticut girl, where she later lived."

In Hollywood in 1939, under contract from Columbia, she met the aviator/producer Howard Hughes, who set out to seduce her. Fox signed her as a contract player in 1940 and cast her into the controversial *Tobacco Road* (1941).

At the beginning of Kirk's affair with her in the early 1950s, she was in the final throes of her divorce from Oleg Cassini, as Kirk was from Diana Dill.

In June of 1943, pregnant with Daria, the first of her two daughters, Tierney was greeting fans and signing autographs. One contaminated fan of her got up from her sick bed to request her autograph. That fan, infected at the time with rubella (German measles), passed the illness on to Tierney who contracted the disease at one of the most vulnerable times of her pregnancy. Horribly affected by rubella, Tierney's daughter was born physically and mentally disabled, partially blind, and deaf. Much of her life would be spent in an institution.

The incident was later used as the motivation for Agatha Christie's novel, *The Mirror Crack'd from Side to Side*. Published in the U.K. in 1962, it was adapted into a movie in 1980 starring Elizabeth Taylor and Rock Hudson.

Although Kirk left out many of the juicier details about his affair with Tierney, he admitted in his memoirs to her touches of kinkiness, at least as regards one of her favorite preferences.

"She kept her second-floor window open on the nights I was scheduled for visits. She kept a ladder outside, and she wanted me to climb it, invade her bedroom, strip off all her clothes and mine—and madly rape her. She told me she'd wear a garment she wanted to get rid of so that I could rip and tear it off her body. Talk about bodice ripping! For her, these nighttime attacks were an aphrodisiac. 'It puts me in the mood for sex,' she claimed."

"Our romance was going hot and heavy one

Gene Tierney in *Tobacco Road* (1941). Both John F. Kennedy and Kirk turned down her proposals of marriage.

209

night when the subject of marriage came up," he said. He told her he never planned to marry again after the failure of his union with Diana. "That institution is just not for me, because I have a cheating heart. I really don't know if Gene thought seriously about marrying me after her divorce came through from Cassini," he said, "and my divorce became final from Diana. After hearing that I would not marry her, she got pissed off and ordered me out of her bedroom. She didn't want me to go out the front door, but descend via the ladder to the ground."

"Oddly enough, our friendship continued long after I quit raping her. Later, she explained why she'd been so angry when I refused to marry her."

In 1946, after his return from World War II, former Navy Lieutenant John F. Kennedy, visited the set of *Dragonwyck*. At the time, Tierney was separated from her husband, Oleg Cassini. She fell for him, finding him "devastatingly attractive and charming." A months-long torrid affair followed until she began dropping hints of marriage.

Based on his political ambitions, JFK told her he could not marry her because she was not a Catholic. And he planned to be President one day, which meant that he had to find the right spouse.

[Ironically, Cassini, Tierney's ex, would become the favorite designer of Jacqueline Bouvier Kennedy when she was First Lady. "It could have been me," Tierney lamented to Kirk.]

"It seemed that Gene had a hard time getting men to marry her," Kirk said. "After we broke up, she began an affair with Prince Aly Khan, who was negotiating a divorce from Rita Hayworth. He'd met Gene during her filming of *A Personal Affair* in 1952 in Europe. His father, Aga Khan III, put an end to their romance."

***

As the years passed, although Kirk's friendship with Tierney continued, he'd go for months, even years, without any mutual contact. He was sorry to hear that her health had deteriorated, and that she struggled for years with manic depression. She lost out on a lot of potential roles because of that, including one of the female leads in *Mogambo* (1953), the role going instead to Grace Kelly.

Eventually, Tierney was confined to the Institute of Living, a residential psychiatric facility in Hartford, Connecticut, where she underwent electric shock treatments. Once, when she tried to escape, two interns tracked her down and hauled her back, kicking and screaming.

Years later, freed from that facility, she campaigned aggressively against electric shock therapies, asserting, "It destroyed part of my brain."

In 1960, she married a Texas oil baron, W. Howard Lee, who had once been married to another of the world's most beautiful women, Hedy Lamarr. They lived together until her death in 1981.

"For the first time in her life, I felt she had married a man who could bring some stability to her life," Kirk said. "She had a rough time after his death. I always regarded her with affection. I mourned her death in 1992 at the age of seventy, only thirteen days before her birthday. The life of a glamorous movie star is not always a fairy tale."

***

A new saga in the very dysfunctional life of the Winfield family began when Charles Feldman and Jerry Wald, as producers, set out to bring *The Glass Menagerie* to the screen. They envisioned it as a 1950 release directed by Irving Rapper.

Casting was a major issue. Tennessee rarely got his wish when it came to the stars who'd perform in the screen adaptations of his plays. Originally, he'd wanted Teresa Wright for the role of Laura. "Her sad eyes and the aching vulnerability in her voice would make her ideal as Laura," he told Feldman.

But by the time Tennessee reached Hollywood, he had changed his mind, telling Feldman, "Only Judy Garland can capture the poignancy of Laura."

The producer had his own ideas. "I'm pitching the role of Amanda to Ethel Barrymore and the part of Laura to Jeanne Crain."

Over the next few weeks, Feldman ran into roadblocks and kept calling Tennessee to announce changes in his vision for the cast. In the first of these, he announced, "I think Gene Tierney should play Laura, with Montgomery Clift in the role of The Gentleman Caller." Tennessee at least liked the idea of Clift.

[Tierney found a certain irony

211

at being considered for the character of Laura, which, as previously mentioned, was also the title of her most famous movie, released in 1944 to great acclaim.]

Two days later, Feldman called again with another change: "How about Marlon Brando as The Gentleman Caller, and Tallulah Bankhead as Amanda?"

"As much as I adore Tallulah, don't you think she's a bit strong to play a gentle Southern belle?" Tennessee asked.

Before Feldman called again, he'd spoken to Brando. "Marlon said he'll never work with Tallulah again unless the Earth is attacked by Martians."

[In 1947, Tallulah and Brando had starred together, with frequent outbursts of spleen, rage and fury, in Jean Cocteau's play, The Eagle Has Two Heads.]

Since Tallulah and Bette Davis often vied for the same roles, it was inevitable that she, too, wanted to play Amanda.

Rapper was Davis' friend and supporter, having directed her in *Now, Voyager* (1952), *The Corn in Green* (1945), and *Deception* (1946). He would helm her again in *Another Man's Poison* (1952) with her husband, Gary Merrill.

Feldman hated the idea of hiring Davis, and nixed the idea, claiming that Davis was so temperamental that she'd hold up production, drive the rest of the staff crazy, and run up costs.

A week later, Feldman called Tennessee again: "I've come up with the best idea of all— Miriam Hopkins, that Savannah Magnolia, as Amanda, with Ralph Meeker as the Gentleman Caller. He's less than lovable to work with, but brazenly masculine and appropriate for the role."

As it turned out, none of these actors was cast. Jack Warner made the ultimate decision about the four actors who'd appear in the film version of *The Glass Menagerie*: Jane Wyman as Laura, Gertrude Lawrence as the mother from hell, Kirk Douglas as the Gentleman Caller, and Arthur Kennedy as the deeply frustrated brother.

Tennessee based Kennedy's role of Tom—a frustrated man who worked in a warehouse by day and writes poetry at night—on himself. Tom has been uncomfortably positioned as "the man" of the Winfield house, since his father, a telephone repairman, as quoted from a famous line in the play, "fell in love with long distance" and had bolted to sites unknown and had never been heard from again.

The character of Laura was inspired by Tennessee's tragically disabled sister.

And the coveted role of the sexually hysterical and disastrously domineering Amanda Winfield was drawn from the playwright's own mother.

The setting was steamy St. Louis, where Amanda urges her son to bring home a possible suitor for his crippled sister, Laura (Wyman). Tom

(Kennedy) selects Jim (Kirk), not knowing that Laura has had a crush on him since high school. No one in the family is aware that Jim is already engaged.

In the autumn of 1949, Wyman flew to Los Angeles aboard a flight from London. Still recovering from her divorce from Ronald Reagan, she had recently made *Stage Fright* (1950) for Alfred Hitchcock.

She claimed, "Hitch and I had our difficulties. I wanted to look more beautiful, but he insisted that I play the role as Little Brown Wren. The glamour puss, as always, was my co-star, Marlene Dietrich. She was pissed off about having to take second billing."

Waiting for Wyman at Warner Brothers was the screen adaptation of Tennessee's beautiful "memory play," *The Glass Menagerie*, which had—to huge acclaim—starred Laurette Taylor on Broadway.

Tennessee had fashioned a screenplay with a lot of work and rewriting by Peter Berneis, a screenwriter and minor actor from Berlin. Tennessee was not impressed with his alterations.

Kirk had accepted his role in *Glass Menagerie* with the understanding that it was kinder, softer, and gentler than what he'd portrayed in *Champion*. He later regretted having taken the role.

Over lunch with Kirk in Warner's commissary, Wyman said, "Here I go again, playing another handicapped person." She already owned an Oscar for her portrayal of a deaf mute in *Johnny Belinda* (1948). In *Glass Menagerie*, she would play the crippled and emotionally fragile character of Laura. The title of the play (and the movie adapted from it) derived from her prized collection of small, fragile, glass animals, one of which was a unicorn.

Although it had been pre-

Kirk with Jane Wyman in the film version of Tennessee Williams' *The Glass Menagerie*.

arranged that the film would be distributed by Warner Brothers, there were rumblings from Louis B. Mayer at MGM. He had telephoned the well-known literary agent, Audrey Wood, claiming that he owned the film rights to *The Glass Menagerie* because Tennessee, during his brief gig as a salaried scriptwriter at MGM (a gig he hated), "wrote the play on our dime. By giving this to Warner's, he's biting the hand that fed the little faggot. I'm finding it harder and harder to cast Greer Garson. But she'd be great as Amanda. I also resent Williams' criticism of my judgment at MGM."

[*Tennessee had told the press that he had been dropped by MGM "in retaliation for my unwillingness to undertake another stupid assignment after I fucked up on* Marriage Is a Private Affair *for Lana Turner."*]

Mayer's threat of a lawsuit did not materialize, and eventually, to his humiliation, he lived to see his own daughter, Irene Mayer Selznick, produce Tennessee's second film, a screen adaptation of *A Streetcar Named Desire*, for Warner Brothers, not MGM.

Tennessee had doubts about Gertrude Lawrence playing Amanda. He knew her as a singer, dancer, and musical comedy performer. *The Glass Menagerie* would be Lawrence's only film in which she worked at an American studio with an otherwise all-American cast.

Since, contractually, Feldman had the power of casting, Tennessee relented from his opposition to Lawrence. Nevertheless, he threw in a dig, "Is Lawrence bringing Daphne du Maurier to Hollywood with her?"

[*Both Tennessee and Feldman knew that Lawrence and the world-famed novelist were lesbian lovers. When Tennessee actually met Lawrence, he was provocative: "In London, Noël Coward told me that he lost his virginity to you when he was just thirteen years old. According to Noël, the two of you did it on a train."*

"That story is absolutely true," she answered. "I fear I scared off the boy from women for life."]

Tennessee had also feared that Wyman, aged 36, was too old for the part, but the co-producer, Jerry Wald, assured him she'd be terrific. "Jane, of course, isn't fresh anymore. But she studies a character for weeks and throws herself into the part."

Visiting the set, Tennessee eventually met with Wyman, later defining her as "a strong, cold, and determined bitch."

Steel Magnolia mother (Gertrude Lawrence) with her tormented son (Arthur Kennedy) in the film version of *The Glass Menagerie*

After the film was wrapped, Kirk stopped by Wyman's dressing room to say goodbye.

She seemed in good spirits, telling him, "After all these handicapped roles, I'm playing in *Three Guys Named Mike,* and I'm being pursued by three handsome beaux: Van Johnson, Barry Sullivan, and Howard Keel."

"Good," Kirk said. "Only one of those guys is a homosexual."

During his screening of the film's final cut, Tennessee sat with his Sicilian-American lover, Frank Merlo, and with Marlon Brando. When the "The End" flashed across the screen, Tennessee rose angrily to his feet and stormed out. He later referred to the film as "a travesty," and to the casting of Gertrude Lawrence as "a dismal failure." He had little to say about Kirk's performance.

Tennessee also attacked the script produced by his co-writer.

"Peter Berneis added a ridiculous scene that distorted my play but gave Kirk Douglas more footage in which he could yak."

[The scene Tennessee was referring to had been added to depict Jim's attempt to instill more confidence in Laura.]

Kirk portrayed his character, in the words of one critic, as "hardy, loquacious, a garrulous gossip of self-confidence."

Kirk himself was not pleased his performance and had very little to say about it in his memoirs.

***

When it was released in 1950, the filmed version of *The Glass Menagerie* did not do well at the box office. Even Kirk expressed his disappointment. "Unfortunately, the movie was not well directed," he said, "and Gertrude Lawrence's vanity had to be appeased. She insisted on a flashback, where she was young and glamorous, so no one would think she was the old lady that she actually was. The elements didn't mesh; the movie just didn't come off."

Bosley Crowther of *The New York Times,* claimed, "Gertrude Lawrence's Amanda is a farcically exaggerated shrew with the zeal of a burlesque comedienne...Her Southern accent has an occasional Cockney strain."

Richard Griffith of *Saturday Review* disagreed: "Not since Garbo has there been anything like the naked eloquence of Amanda's face with its amazing play of thought and emotion."

Tennessee himself asserted, "I detested the film. As I predicted, Lawrence was a dismal error in casting. The film version was a dishonest adaptation of my play. I would soon get used to that in Hollywood's other attempts to film one of my dramas."

215

Tennessee would also be disappointed with other filmed versions too, notably a 1966 TV premiere of *The Glass Menagerie*, starring Shirley Booth as Amanda, with Pat Hingle and Hal Holbrook as the two male leads. He retained his low opinion, even after actress Barbara Loden as Laura won raves for her "transcendent performance," and some reviewers called the film "one of the greatest broadcasts in the history of television." Booth was nominated for an Emmy.

Regardless of those accolades, a disheartened Tennessee said, "Whatever it was, it was not my play."

Although reluctant at first to dive into the role of Amanda, Katharine Hepburn agreed to portray her in a 1973 version for television. Her cast colleagues included Sam Waterson, Joana Miles, and Michael Moriarty. The teleplay marked Hepburn's first appearance in a made-for TV movie.

Hepburn feared her sharp New England accent was wrong for that "Steel Magnolia" she was playing. She was right. Many critics noted how Hepburn's Southern drawl came and went. She also infuriated Tennessee by rewriting much of Amanda's dialogue "to make it right for me."

He forgave Hepburn when she told him that his character of Amanda "was the most tenderly observed, the most accessible woman you've ever created."

For yet another film, Paul Newman directed his wife, Joanne Woodward, in a 1987 film version of *The Glass Menagerie*. Woodward joined the long list of actresses who had attempted the role of Amanda. In his critique of that rendering, Desson Howe (known after 2003 as Desson Thompson), in the *Washington Post* criticized the acting and found much of the dialogue "time consuming, inflated, dated, and theatrical. The film's few good moments happen when mouths are firmly shut. Woodward is a disappointment, speaking in a low, squeaky voice—a kind of laryngitic falsetto. Newman emphasizes the artificiality of the theater and distances you from the play."

The critic for *Variety* found it "a reverent record of the Williams play that one watches with a kind of distant dreaminess rather than an intense emotional involvement. There are brilliant performances well defined by Newman's direction."

In Tennessee's ultimate summation, he said, "Nothing ever equaled that night of March 31, 1945, when Laurette Taylor as Amanda came out and cast a glow over the theater."

***

Driving home from work, Kirk was relieved that *The Glass Menagerie* was in the can, yet dreaded its reception from both the press and the public.

Both Jane Wyman and Gertrude Lawrence had told him that they fully expected to be nominated for an Oscar; each planned to compete against the other.

[FOOTNOTE: The Glass Menagerie *had the misfortune to be released in 1950, the same year that some of the best pictures in the history of Hollywood came out, too—notably Bette Davis in* All About Eve *and Gloria Swanson in* Sunset Blvd. *Each of those actresses gave the finest performance of their lives. Judy Holliday, also in the best role of her life in* Born Yesterday *won, and Eleanor Parker, Kirk's future co-star, had also been cast that year in her finest role,* Caged.

Jack Warner thought that Kirk might have a chance that year as Best Supporting Actor, since he wasn't really the star of Menagerie. *His leading competitors for the prize included George Sanders for his role in* All About Eve; *and Erich Von Stroheim for* Sunset Blvd.

Despite Kirk's backing by the studio and by Jack Warner, personally, the campaign to even get him nominated failed. Sanders walked off with the gold, and All About Eve *won Best Picture, but* The Glass Menagerie *wasn't even nominated.]*

As he was stuck in Los Angeles traffic, mulling over his Oscar prospects that day, Kirk almost didn't stop in time for the brake lights in the car ahead that suddenly flashed orange. The two-door blue sedan in front of him had slammed on its brakes, and he had almost piled into it.

Suddenly, the sedan's passenger door opened, and a young girl in a suede jacket rushed out to greet him.

He recognized her at once as the child star Natalie Wood, whom he'd seen in *Miracle on 34th Street* (1947), starring Maureen O'Hara, John Payne, and Edmund Gwenn as Kris Kringle.

"Mr. Douglas, will you sign my jacket?" She thrust a pen at him.

"Glad to," he said.

At this point, her mother, Maria, had exited the car from behind the wheel and rushed to the driver's side of Kirk's car to greet him too.

By this time, the traffic light had changed, and the cars behind them were blowing their horns.

"Kirk, I'm Maria. This is my daughter, Natalie Wood. Don't you think she's beautiful? She's talented, too. Perhaps you can

Natalie Wood as Maria in *West Side Story* (1961)

217

use her in one of your pictures."

"Sounds like a great idea," he said, anxious for them to get back into their car.

Before she left, Natalie delivered a passionate kiss on his lips, as least as passionate as a twelve-year-old girl can manage.

As Kirk later reported to his friend, Burt Lancaster, "I somehow think that Natalie Wood lies in my future, but not until she blossoms. The bulb has not opened yet."

When Kirk went to see her emote opposite James Dean in *Rebel Without a Cause* (1955), he saw that she was on her way to womanhood. In 1958, he sensed that his time with Natalie had come. That afternoon, Lancaster had phoned to say that Natalie would be starring with them in the upcoming *The Devil's Disciple.*

"Oh, and yeah, Lancaster added. We'll also be working with Laurence Olivier."

British stage stars Vivien Leigh with her husband, Laurence Olivier, before many film fans knew anything about Scarlett O'Hara or Heathcliff.

CHAPTER SEVEN

KIRK'S PALM BEACH HEIRESS

AND THE ROLES THAT
ERROL FLYNN, JFK, &
THE DUKE & DUCHESS OF WINDSOR
PLAYED IN HIS LIFE

ACE IN THE HOLE & DETECTIVE STORY
HOW TWO OF HOLLYWOOD'S TOP DIRECTORS STEERED & DI-
RECTED HOLLYWOOD'S NEWEST MALE STAR

SHIRLEY TEMPLE
(LITTLE MISS LOLLIPOP)
PLEADS WITH KIRK TO SAVE HER CAREER

WEDDING BELLS SOON?—Screen actor Kirk Douglas and socialite Irene Wrightsman McEvoy sup at New York's Stork Club during a visit in the east. It has been rumored that the two may soon wed.

Irene Wrightsman McEvoy, the unhappy daughter of one of Texas' most talked-about oil-men, was so famous that when she appeared with Kirk Douglas at New York City's Stork Club in the early 1950s, this promotional photo was replicated on the society pages of newspapers as far away as Louisiana.

Kirk drove alone to Palm Springs for a three-day vacation. There, at the Racquet Club, he had a morning chat with Clark Gable. Later, he had lunch with Lew and Edie Wasserman.

Kirk was fully aware of the power of Lew Wasserman in Hollywood. He represented clients who ranged from Bette Davis to an actor she called "Little Ronnie Reagan."

In time, Lew would become Kirk's own agent and preside over the "ultimate" Hollywood talent agency for movie stars, MCA. He was instrumental in getting Reagan elected as President of the Screen Actors Guild, which ultimately put him on the road that led to the White House.

Arriving late to join them for lunch was a beauty who stunned Kirk. She was Irene Wrightsman, one of the two daughters of Charles Bierer Wrightsman, an American oil executive and art patron. He virtually presided over Palm Beach society.

In Kirk's memoirs, he gave Irene the most glowing report—at least from a physical point of view—of all the many goddesses he had known.

"Irene was one of the most beautiful girls I've ever seen," he wrote. "Black hair framing creamy white skin, dark eyes, and a dark red lipstick. Her ankles and wrists were tiny, her bosom slightly overdeveloped for her small frame. In a word, stunning."

As it turned out, she was in Palm Springs with her lover, the fashion designer, Oleg Cassini. The playboy was the ex-husband of Gene Tierney, one of Kirk's recent sexual conquests.

As the luncheon progressed, Irene, in full view of the Wassermans, flirted outrageously with Kirk. Before the end of the luncheon, it was obvious to all that she was prepared to dump Cassini and spend the next three days in Kirk's suite.

As she left the table with him, Irene told Edie, "Tell Oleg I had to return suddenly to Los Angeles because my mother has become desperately ill."

[A decade later, Cassini had either forgiven or else forgotten about Kirk making off with Irene. When he opened his exclusive "Le Club" in Manhattan, he sent Kirk an invitation, and he flew in for the occasion.

"This little Jew boy found himself in high-falutin' company," Kirk said, sitting at a table enjoying caviar and champagne with Ray Stark, Stavros Niarchos, Aristotle Onassis, and Gianni Agnelli.

Two weeks after his departure from Palm Springs, Kirk encountered Edie at a party, and she told him what had happened to the suddenly abandoned Cassini.

"Oleg met two of the most beautiful blonde twin guys I've ever seen. Both were studying fashion design and had rented a private villa nearby. Right in front of me, they invited Oleg for a swim, and he disappeared for two days with these

gorgeous creatures. I don't think Oleg is a homosexual, but from what I'm told, he doesn't mind being 'serviced' from time to time—you know, for variety's sake."]

Three days after Kirk returned to Hollywood, Irene phoned and invited him to dinner to meet her mother, the former Irene Stafford.

At the dinner, catered by servants, the mother drank more than she ate. She had divorced Charles Wrightsman, Irene's wealthy father, and the mansion where the dinner took place was part of her financial settlement.

At around 10:30PM, she bid everyone good night and retired for the night. Her daughter invited Kirk into the library, a cozy setting with a blazing fireplace and walls lined with books.

After locking the door, she very slowly began to remove her clothing in front of Kirk, who sat in an armchair by the fireplace.

Then she lay down on the thick carpet and invited Kirk to disrobe. He felt awkward seducing her under the same roof as her mother, but his libido won out.

Five minutes later, Irene's mother began pounding on the library door. "I know you're in there. Open up! I'll put a stop to what's going on in my house!"

Kirk looked close up and into Irene's face, trying to figure out what to do.

She dug her fingernails into the skin of his naked back. "Fuck Mother! Better yet, fuck me!"

Within a few days, Irene packed a suitcase and moved with Kirk into his modest digs on Vado Place, in the Hollywood Hills, where, to his surprise, she turned out to be a superb cook. "I thought a rich girl like you always let the servants cook."

"It's a hobby of mine," she answered, "but I let the servants wash up after me."

Her move to Vado Place marked the beginning of a two-year, rather tumultuous relationship.

Before Kirk and Irene had settled in together, word reached him from Paramount that director Billy Wilder was ready to begin shooting his next picture, *Ace in the Hole*. He was to fly to Albuquerque, New Mexico for work on a film scheduled for a release in 1951.

Wilder had just completed one of his two most celebrated films, *Sunset Blvd* (1950), starring William Holden and Gloria Swanson. His second most famous film, *Some Like It Hot* (1959), starring Marilyn Monroe and Tony Curtis, lay in Wilder's future.

Irene didn't want a separation of three months at the very beginning of their love affair, so he invited her to go to New Mexico with him.

***

Ace in the Hole (1951), a Paramount release, marked a milestone in the career of Billy Wilder, who had escaped from Hitler's Nazi Germany. For the first time, he was producer, director, and writer. The film also remains, even today, one of Kirk's alltime greatest screen performances.

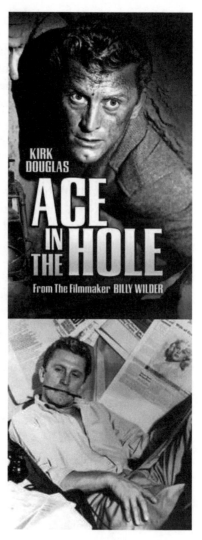

This rather cynical drama was also the first film that Wilder made after breaking with his long-time partner, Charles Brackett. In addition to working together on *Sunset Blvd.*, they'd collaborated on *Lost Weekend* (1945), the grim story of an alcoholic (as portrayed by Ray Milland, who won an Oscar for it) and his descent into ruin and despair. A supremely pertinent subject at the time, it also won an Oscar as Best Picture of the Year.

"Other than *Champion*, this was my biggest challenge to date," Kirk said. "I played a down-on-his luck reporter, Charles Tatum. I'm sleazy but enterprising, and on the trail of a hot story to put me back on top again. Wilder told me to play it cynical, unethical, and unscrupulous, without any redeeming value."

In both his writing and directing, Wilder gave *Ace in the Hole* a sheen of *cinéma verité*. The plot begins when the editor of a small newspaper sends Kirk, as Tatum, and his sidekick, a photographer (as portrayed by Robert Arthur) to cover a rattlesnake roundup in the arid scrublands of New Mexico.

They stop for gas at a dusty, isolated, and windswept souvenir shop with a gas station and a ratty-looking diner. They learn that the owner of the station, Leo Minos (Richard Benedict), has been trapped nearby within an otherwise abandoned Indian mine beneath the "Mountain of the Seven Vultures."

The bored and shallow wife of the endangered man is Lorraine Minosa, as played by Jan Sterling. A waitress in her husband's diner, she doesn't seem to be in mourning. Actually, she's planning to pack her bags and flee from this bleak and lonely outpost as soon as she reasonably can. She's looking for bright lights, romance, and big-city glamour.

Tatum (Kirk) realized that his media spin on an incident like this could land him on the frontpages of national newspapers again. Motivated by raw ambition and a lack of scruples, he turns to other locals who might be corrupted, including the local sheriff Gus Kretzer (as played by Ray Teal); and the local engineer who's been charged with the rescue operation. Tatum manipulates both of them into prolonging the rescue—which could have been concluded in twelve hours—into an international, flashbulb-popping drama that's strung out for six agonizing days.

The publicity he generates transforms the arid landscapes around the diner into a carnival that attracts bus tours and caravans from as far away as Los Angeles. Vendors move in to exploit the atmosphere with food stands, souvenir stalls, and live music—an ironic commentary on the misguided values of American commercialism and media sensationalism.

Residents of nearby Gallup, New Mexico, were hired as extras for 75¢ a day and brought onto the set in ten-hour shifts. If they arrived by car and agreed to let it be used as part of the scenery, three extra dollars per day were added to the owner's paycheck.

Now in sexual and emotional collusion with Lorraine, Tatum behaves in ways depicted as obsessive and sadistic. He coaches her in her portrayal of a grieving and hysterical wife. He demands that she pose for photographers in church and appear suicidal for reporters.

In responding to that, she informs Tatum, "I don't go to church much. Kneeling bags my nylons."

According to moral standards in movie-making of that era, an unrepentant villain like Tatum cannot go unpunished. With reluctance, Wilder, as the scriptwriter, has Lorraine plunge a knife into his stomach. He'd have preferred a more cynical ending where Tatum returns to New York in journalistic triumph as a media hero.

[In one of the film's early monologues, Tatum recalls how much he misses New York, comparing it to backwater Gallup. "There's no pastrami here! No garlic pickles! No Madison Square Garden! No

A morality tale about sleazy journalism. Kirk with Robert Arthur.

223

Yogi Berra!"

In prepping that dialogue, Kirk asked Wilder "What in hell is a Yogi Berra?" His director was surprised that Kirk didn't know who the star of the New York Yankees was.]

***

During the filming of *Ace in the Hole,* Kirk bonded with his fellow actors.

Jan Sterling had recently married Kirk's friend, actor Paul Douglas, who had co-starred with him in *A Letter to Three Wives.* "Because Paul is a friend of mine, Jan is one leading lady I'm not going to screw," he told Wilder.

According to Sterling, "Whenever a director wants a flashy whore in a *film noir* or a blonde bimbo in a saucy comedy, I get a call. I guess they're trying to tell me that I come across like a tramp."

Over lunch one afternoon, she told Kirk a bit of theatrical lore that involved one of his future co-stars, Laurence Olivier.

Before Sterling had married Paul Douglas, she'd been wed (1941-1947) to the Canadian actor, Jack Merivale.

In years to come, Merivale would be linked to a far more celebrated actress, Vivien Leigh. He became her lover after her divorce from Laurence Olivier. According to reports from various sources, the bisexual Olivier had seduced Merivale before Vivien ever got a chance at him.

Playing Kirk's journalistic assistant and photographer in *Ace in the Hole,* Robert Arthur was a very minor actor who appeared in a few roles during the 1940s and '50s, beginning with an uncredited part in *Mildred Pierce* (1945), the film that brought Joan Crawford an Oscar. The boyish-looking actor tended to portray teenagers and young adults throughout the course of his early career.

In the mid-1940s, Arthur had sustained a sexual fling with another then-struggling bisexual actor, Rock Hudson. About a year after the filming of *Ace in the Hole,* Arthur encountered Rock at a Hollywood party.

At the party, Arthur confided to Rock that he had developed a powerful but unre-

Jan Sterling playing a shallow, slutty waitress—the role Marilyn Monroe wanted and never forgave Kirk for not supporting her campaign to get it.

quited crush on Kirk Douglas during filming in the New Mexico scrublands.

[In his later years, as a Log Cabin Republican, Arthur campaigned aggressively for gay rights on behalf of senior citizens. His last appearance on the screen was with Ronald Reagan and Nancy Davis in Hellcats of the Navy *(1957).]*

***

During the filming of *Ace in the Hole* (also released as *The Big Carnival*), Wilder talked to Kirk about an upcoming film he was writing and planning to direct. The lead role was that of Sefton, an American "hero-heel" being interred in a prisoner of war camp in Nazi Germany.

Wilder told Kirk he'd be great playing the role of Sefton and gave him the draft of its screenplay. Kirk read it that night. Finding "too many loopholes in it," he returned it, telling Wilder, "It's not for me."

Later, he claimed, "That was the career mistake of my life."

In 1953, William Holden, who had portrayed that film's main character, won an Oscar as Best Actor for his role of Sefton, a cynical, easy-to-dislike sergeant who wasn't trusted by the other British and American detainees planning to escape. The name of the film was *Stalag 17*.

As the winner, Holden beat out one of the most impressive lineups of male stars in the history of the Academy: Marlon Brando for *Julius Caesar*; Richard Burton for *The Robe*; and Burt Lancaster and Montgomery Clift, who vied with each other based on their roles in *From Here to Eternity*.

***

Critics came down hard on *Ace in the Hole*, and audiences preferred other films in vogue at the time. Competition was stiff in a year when world-class films proliferated. They included Marlon Brando and Vivien Leigh in *A Streetcar Named Desire*; Humphrey Bogart and Katharine Hepburn in *The African Queen*; and Elizabeth Taylor and Montgomery Clift in *A Place in the Sun*. The Best Picture that year was Gene Kelly's *An American in Paris*. Ironically, Kirk's own *Detective Story*, released the same year, also emerged as a box office hit, thereby lessening the commercial success of *Ace in the Hole*.

William Holden, the Oscar-winning star of *Stalag 17*, the World War II prisoner-of-war film that Kirk, to his huge regret, rejected.

Bosley Crowther of *The New York Times* called *Ace in the Hole* "a dramatic grotesque." The *Hollywood Reporter* rather preachily reviewed it as "a brazen, uncalled-for slap in the face of the Free Press."

When Kirk read those reviews, he said, "I guess Billy Wilder and I hit too close to home."

More than fifty years after its release, *Ace in the Hole* has become a cult classic and a favorite of the critics, appearing in most polls as one of the 500 best films of all time.

Roger Ebert in the *Chicago Sun-Times* wrote, "Kirk Douglas' focus on energy is almost scary. There is nothing dated about his performance. It's as 'right now' as a sharpened knife. Kirk could freeze blood when he wanted to in his most savage role."

The *Village Voice* called the movie "so acidly *au courant* it stings."

Director George Stevens had Kirk's role in *Ace in the Hole* in mind when, in 1991, he presented him with the American Film Institute's Life Achievement Award. "No other leading actor was ever more ready to tap the dark, desperate side of the soul and thus to reveal the complexity of human nature."

***

On location in New Mexico during the filming of *Ace in the Hole,* Kirk received a call in his dressing room/trailer from Errol Flynn. He and his new mistress, the actress/singer/dancer Patrice Wymore were in the nearby town of Gallup, shooting a very routine western, *Rocky Mountain* (1950).

Kirk was surprised that the former swashbuckler already knew his mistress, Irene Wrightsman, very very well. Kirk accepted Flynn's invitation to dinner, although Irene warned him that he'd be stuck with the tab. "Errol never picks up a check."

[Irene was right. After all the champagne, and he'd ordered only the most expensive items on the menu, the tab came to $325, including the $50 tip Errol added for the waiter. He handed it over to Kirk to pay.]

Kirk hadn't seen Flynn since his evening with Hedy Lamarr at his party on Mulholland Drive. Apparently, it had been years since Irene and Flynn had spent any significant time together. "They hugged and kissed like lovers," Kirk said. He planned to interrogate her later.

He was introduced to Wymore, Flynn's co-star in *Rocky Mountain*, finding her "a bit icy but graceful." After a lifetime of dissipation, by this point in the early 1950s, Flynn was looking worse for wear.

He spoke with disdain about the film he was making. In it, he played a Confederate officer trying to persuade a coven of outlaws to join his militia with the intention of bringing California and the American Southwest under the control of the rebel Confederacy.

It became obvious to both Kirk and Irene that Flynn and Wymore had fallen in love. As an expert dancer, Wymore had performed brilliantly with Gene Nelson in her first movie, *Tea for Two* (1950). One critic had hailed them as "the new Fred Astaire and Ginger Rogers."

"I fell in love with Patrice here," Flynn said, "because she reminds me of my mother, Marelle."

"How very flattering," Wymore said, taking her index finger and pushing it into his chest.

Flynn dominated the conversation, filling it with stories from his early days growing into manhood on the other side of the world. He'd been born in Tasmania in 1909. He claimed that his forebears were among the ill-fated crew of the *H.M.S. Bounty*.

[Ironically, his first movie appearance was in In the Wake of the Bounty *(1933), a pseudo-documentary in which he portrayed Fletcher Christian.]*

"My introduction to sex led to a thrashing," he confessed, "when my mother caught me masturbating, but that didn't seem to stop me. As a pupil in Sydney at the Northshore Grammar School, I performed my first striptease on the playground for eight little schoolgirls who had never seen a penis. Later, with five other boys, I was the star of our daily circle jerk."

"At one point, I ran away from home and got a job in Queensland *[Northeast Australia]* castrating lambs. In those days, you stuck your face into the genitals of a young male sheep and bit off his testicles."

"I was such an adventurer…I set out to discover the whorehouses of the world, from Calcutta to Ethiopia, even landing in the more refined bordellos of the French Riviera."

As dinner progressed, Wymore and Irene excused themselves to powder their noses. It was then that Flynn confessed his problem. "Patrice and I are discussing wedded bliss. But only two weeks ago, I proposed marriage to Princess Irene Ghika of Romania. I asked her to marry me, even though she has not yet mastered the culinary sexual arts."

"If she marries me, Patrice

Two views of Patrice Wymore: *left*, a publicity photo from *Rocky Mountain* (1950) with Errol Flynn and *right*, a promotional photo from Warner Brothers.

knows the kind of man I am. A leopard can't change his spots. If she wants to chance it and marry me, she's aware of what a gamble that would be. She can cook Indian curry, she can dance, she can sing, and she has both dignity and beauty. She's also short-sighted and wears glasses. What more can a man ask?"

When the women returned from the ladies' room, the channels through which his own Irene had met Flynn were made clear: She had been married (from 1942 to 1944) to the notorious Australia-born playboy, Freddy McEvoy, "the world's greatest bobsledder" and Flynn's closest friend.

McEvoy was known for marrying heiresses. Irene was only eighteen at the time. It was obvious to Kirk that McEvoy wanted to attach himself to the fortune of Irene's father, Charles Bierer Wrightsman.

Kirk knew that both McEvoy and Flynn were in the ranks of "the greatest cocksmen of Hollywood." Flynn confessed that McEvoy and he had gotten into some recent trouble after checking into the Hotel Nautilus in Miami. "Freddy and I shared our suite with this seventeen-year-old girl we picked up on the beach. She wanted to take on both of us. She spent the night in our bed and was still asleep when we checked out the next morning for a flight to Los Angeles. But as we were hailing a taxi out front, a doorman summoned us back inside. We learned that a maid had discovered the girl dead in our bed. We were detained in Miami for several days. There was a police investigation and an inquest. An autopsy later revealed that the kid had died of a heart attack."

Flynn's tablemates at dinner that night listened politely, but no one expressed any reaction.

Months later, Kirk ran into Patrice and Flynn at a party in Los Angeles, having heard they'd gotten married in Monte Carlo, with McEvoy as his best man.

"There was a hitch," Flynn said. "Just as we were exchanging vows, a frog [i.e. , Frenchman] arrived with a writ charging me with the rape of a sixteen-year-old girl from Provence."

"Were you guilty?" Kirk asked.

"Yes, but passing some francs to the girl's father got the matter settled. Charges were dropped and the wedding continued a few hours later."

"Since our marriage, Errol and I have been just like two kids having fun," Patrice said. "Okay, he's forty-one, and I'm only twenty-four, but we both

Playboys about to "work'" a society wedding: Errol Flynn *(left)* and Freddy McEvoy.

228

feel like we're sixteen, laughing at the same jokes and making love. Our friends think we're nuts. But what the hell—it's all a delightful game. But don't make a mistake in what you're thinking. Both of us are madly in love."

"Good luck to you, kids," Kirk said. "You'll need it."

At that point, Edie Wasserman, the party's hostess, approached their corner of the room. "Kirk darling, Joan Fontaine has arrived, and she wants to talk to you about her sister, Olivia."

[Of course, she was referring to Oliva de Havilland, Flynn's former co-star.]

***

After his grueling performance in *Ace in the Hole,* Kirk, in need of some R&R, flew with Irene for a vacation at the Palm Beach estate of her father, Charles Wrightsman, the former oil executive.

"I knew he was one of the richest men in the country," Kirk said, "but what I didn't know was that he had sadistic streaks of cruelty. Irene told me that when she and her sister, Charlene, were growing up, he ruled them with an iron fist."

"If they did everything he said, and as they grew into womanhood, he would award them with diamonds and Balenciaga gowns. But whenever they crossed him, the gravy train of goodies came to an abrupt end."

Wrightsman was waiting for them at the Miami airport. From there, with his co-pilot, he flew with them aboard his private plane for the short hop onward to Palm Beach.

Kirk noticed that Irene, in the presence of her father, became extremely agitated. By the time they landed, she had fallen ill, suffering from what she called "the worst migraine of my life." The moment they got to her father's estate, she went to her bedroom and collapsed. Her needs were tended by an elderly woman from Stuttgart, Germany, a family retainer who had cared for Charlene and Irene since their childhoods.

Charles told Kirk that he wanted to give him a tour of his art collection, but that it would have to wait until the next day because it was time to get dressed for a cocktail party he was hosting. The Duke and Duchess of Windsor were vacationing in Palm Beach, and he'd invited them as the guests of honor.

Kirk admitted in his memoirs that he was "very much interested" in an encounter with the Duke and Duchess of Windsor. However, in those memoirs, he also noted that he was exhausted, and that, because he wanted to be on hand in case Irene needed him, he opted not to attend the cocktail party.

That was not the case. His curiosity won out, and he did attend the party to meet the Duke and Duchess.

Wrightsman responded "The party is in the parlor, and you might be summoned, if needed." He went on to say, "And Irene's beloved nanny is in charge. She has nursed my daughter through all her previous illnesses, both mental and physical, and she'll handle any problem that she encounters."

***

It is not known why Kirk wrote in his memoirs that he did not attend the Wrightsman's cocktail party. The handsome Austrian actor, Helmut Dantine, remembered having a long conversation with Kirk that afternoon as they were waiting for the arrival of the Duke and Duchess.

Kirk was aware that in 1947, Dantine had married Charlene Wrightsman, Irene's younger sister. *[The marriage lasted until 1950.]*

Out on the patio, the actor confessed to Kirk, "My marriage is all but over. She's divorcing me and wants custody of our son. Charles broke up our marriage. He seems jealous of me. He accused me of marrying Charlene for her money. He'll do the same with you—you just wait and see. He wants to possess his daughters, control their lives. I'm flying out of Palm Beach in the morning."

"You don't think Charles thinks I'm after Irene's money?" Kirk asked.

"I don't know," Dantine answered. I read a feature story about you in the Palm Beach newspaper. Charles will never accept you into his family. For him, you belong to the wrong religion."

"I see," Kirk said.

[Kirk had seen Dantine onscreen, especially in two of his most famous movies, the first as a frightened Nazi pilot in a confrontation with a terrified Mrs. Miniver *(1942), portrayed by Greer Garson, after his plane crashes on English soil.*

Of course, Kirk, like everybody else in Hollywood, had already seen Humphrey Bogart and Ingrid Bergman emote in Casablanca *(1942). In it, the character portrayed by Dantine had tried gambling as a desperate means of obtaining money to pay for a visa so that he and his wife could escape from Morocco.*

As a teenager, Dantine had been involved in an anti-Nazi movement in Vienna. But when he was nineteen, as part of the Anschluss, the Germans "annexed" Austria and threw him in jail. "I spent three months in a Third Reich concentration camp until my parents bought me out. I fled to California."

"A talent scout from Warner Brothers spotted me when I was broke and needed a break," Dantine told Kirk. "I learned that in America, there was something known as the casting couch."

230

"There sure is," Kirk said, "but I've never had to perform on it."

"You're lucky," Dantine said. "The agent who put me there got me a contract at Warners, and I found myself starring with Ronald Reagan in International Squadron *in 1941. Then I played with Errol Flynn and Reagan in* Desperate Journey *(1942). The agent made it clear that if I wanted to work at Warners and get cast in any of his films, I'd have to 'put out,' as you Americans say."*

"Did you?" Kirk asked.

"I did, time and time again. And I'm not proud of it."

As long as Dantine kept delivering, the roles kept coming. In Edge of Darkness *(1946), he was cast as a Nazi officer battling Flynn. "When some of the fan mail it generated was addressed to me, Jack Warner told me he had more than a 'Hollywood Hitlerite' on his hands. Guess what? He cast me as a Nazi running loose in Canada and fighting Flynn again in* Northern Pursuit *(1943).*

"After the war," Dantine continued, "I took over Marlon Brando's stage role in the Broadway play by Jean Cocteau, The Eagle Has Two Heads, *with Tallulah Bankhead. She insisted that I visit her dressing room nightly after the curtain went down, which it did for only 29 more performances."*

"I've been there and done that with Tallulah myself," Kirk said.]

At that point, the butler arrived to announce that the Duke and Duchess had arrived, and that they were in the foyer, waiting to greet the other guests. Both actors moved forward. Jokingly, Kirk asked Dantine, "Do you know how to curtsy."

***

At the Wrightsman's cocktail party, Kirk was introduced to the Duke and Duchess of Windsor. He found both of them professionally polite, with forced, insincere smiles.

Without being too obvious about it, he closely observed them as the party progressed. The cream of Palm Beach society—about fifty guests equally divided among men and women, with an average age of about fifty—were on site to pay their respects to this exiled royal pair and to gape.

Shortly before eight o'clock, the large living room was cleared. Only ten people, including Kirk, the Wrightsman's house guest, had been invited to the intimate private dinner that followed the (larger) cocktail party.

Helmut Dantine in *Mrs. Miniver* (1942)...portraying a Nazi menace.

Irene remained ill and in bed upstairs, unwilling to see anyone except for her childhood nanny who attended to her every need.

At the dinner table, Kirk continued to discreetly scrutinize the Royals. When the salad was served, the Duke picked up a leaf of lettuce with his finger and began to nibble on it. Wallis slapped his hand, instructing him to use a knife and fork. Like a dutiful schoolboy, he obeyed her.

[As the golden-haired Prince of Wales, idolized as a bachelor by millions, Edward, then the Prince of Wales, had met Wallis after her second divorce. Although she was hardly a dazzling beauty, he was said to have fallen under her spell. She evoked a well-dressed mannequin, aloof and rather snobbish.

When King George V died in 1936, the Prince of Wales (renamed Edward VIII in the immediate aftermath of George V's death) had ascended to the British throne. Emotionally, he was deeply involved with Wallis Warfield Smith, a twice-divorced American citizen.

In time, Wallis filed for her second divorce. Strident conflicts were immediately voiced by Parliament and, among others, Winston Churchill. As king, Edward was Head of the Church of England, and Heads of the Church of England did not marry divorced women.

The powerbrokers around him urged (some same, demanded) that he drop Wallis, but he refused. On December 11, 1936, now demoted from King of England to "merely" the Duke of Windsor, he married Wallis in a small, private ceremony in France.

The press and millions of readers would follow the couple with fascination for the remainder of their long, widely gossiped-about lives. In the late 1930s, Churchill feared—with ample justification—that the Duke and his Duchess maintained Nazi sympathies. Consequently, the Duke was banished from the U.K. and installed as governor of The Bahamas, then an isolated and very remote backwater of the British Empire.]

As dinner at Wainwright's home progressed, Kirk found it hard to believe that the Duchess loved her Duke. If anything, she seemed to hold him in contempt. Midway through the dinner, after she'd scolded him for the second time, he was publicly reduced to tears.

Ulick Alexander, a British Army officer and courtier, attempted to explain their dynamic: "The Duke of Windsor thrives on the sexual perversion of self-abasement,

Posh, gossipy, eccentric, bitter, and notorious: the Duke and Duchess of Windsor in 1950.

232

not that unusual an oddity. It is clear to me and to those around His Majesty that the Duchess frightens him. That is not as bad as it sounds. He seems to take some enjoyment out of his fright, the way we might do while watching a horror movie."

Philip Ziegler, the distinguished British biographer and historian, questioned if the Duchess ever loved her husband, or whether she was merely exploiting him.

Over coffee and after-dinner drinks, the Duke expounded on world affairs: "If I had been allowed to marry Wallis, making her my Queen, the world would be a far different place than it is today. For one thing, England would never have entered World War II. I could have made a deal with Hitler whereby England remained neutral, like Sweden. Unlike Churchill, I would have allowed Hitler to concentrate his military machine on Stalin's Red Army. They'd have delivered a fatal and final blow. Hitler would have crushed communism, and we would not be facing the dangers that Western Democracies do today from the Soviet menace."

After a while, the Duchess tired of what she called the Duke's "prattle" and inserted her own opinion: "Enough of England and what might have been. I hate that country. I will go to my grave regretting and denouncing what it did to Edward and me. It cast us out, made us exiles."

[When Kirk returned to California and relayed to his friends what the Duchess had said, they were skeptical. However, in January of 1963, in an article for Mc-Call's, the Duchess was equally outspoken when she went public with her discontent. "My husband has been punished—like a small boy who gets a spanking every day of his life for some transgression. The Monarchy's lack of dignity toward us is unforgivable. I resent them for it. A government-manufactured curtain of asbestos protects the Commonwealth from dangerous us. During the war, Churchill made Edward the Governor of The Bahamas, putting us out of harm's way. In that remote place, he figured we'd stay out of trouble and not embarrass the monarchy."]

***

After dinner, Charles wanted to show off his fabulous art collection, one of the most impressive personal assemblages of art in America.

He was especially proud of Vermeer's *Portrait of a Young Woman* and Gerard David's *Virgin and Child with Four Angels*. In time, he would donate part of his collection to the Metropolitan Museum of Art in Manhattan, works by Tiepolo, Rubens, Georges de La Tour, Giovanni Battista, and El Greco.

He would also furnish eight Wrightsman rooms at that museum with 18th-Century French furnishings and decorations, and a trio of galleries for the display of *objets-d'art*.

"For a little Jew boy named Issur, I was moving in the top echelon of rich Americans," Kirk said, "and dating his daughter, who was still upstairs, sick in bed."

***

The following night, Kirk attended, alone and without Irene, a party in Palm Beach to honor the strikingly handsome Stanley Mortimer. He was married at the time to Babe Cushing (later Mrs. William Paley), the most stylishly dressed woman in America.

Alone at the party, he fell prey to Suzan Ellison Temple, a rich widow in her eighties, who from time to time, had more than a few cocktails. Known as the most relentless and indiscreet gossip in Palm Beach, she was said to know every dark secret in town—"but only about those that mattered, not the riff-raff."

Temple was violently anti-Semitic. She had once proposed to the town council that a sign be posted at Palm Beach's city limits: NO JEWS ALLOWED.

Kirk decided not to "out" himself as Issur, but instead to listen to what she had to reveal about Irene.

She had plenty to tattle, including a raft of stories dating from when Irene was married to Freddy McEvoy during the war, when she was "the surrogate wife," according to Mrs. Temple, of Errol Flynn. "They were a love triangle," she claimed. "Poor Irene had to take on both of them, and she was only a teenager at the time. Errol likes them young. They also hosted the most notorious parties in Hollywood."

"I have known Charles Wrightsman since he first arrived in Palm Beach," Temple said. "Those two girls of his are emotionally disturbed—Irene is a real mental case. Charlene is a bit more level-headed than her sister, but she's no temple—*my last name!*—of mental health, either. One night, she stabbed one of her lovers, a golf pro, but he survived. Charles paid him to keep quiet. There's more!" she said.

"When they were just little girls, Charles would strip them down and sadistically paddle their bare butts. From what I heard, that got him excited. In time, as his daughters matured, he forced himself on both of them."

"Mrs. Temple," Kirk said, "you've given me an earful, but I've got to go to digest all this new information. I disliked Charles on sight. Now I hate him if what you say is true."

"It's as true as a verse in the Bible," she answered.

Before he left, he asked her, jokingly, "Are you related to Shirley Temple?"

"I'm not, but I know a lot about that brat. Louise Brooks—you know, the former movie star—called Shirley a 'tough little slut.' Darryl F. Zanuck used to summon Little Miss Lollipop into his office every afternoon and feed her his 'Great Big Lollipop' that he's always exposing to starlets at Fox."

"Dear Lady, please excuse me—that's all for me tonight."

Escaping from the gossipy old bird, he left the party. She reminded him of Billie Burke in a role she played so well, that of a "chirping birdie."

If he thought he'd escaped from scandals and gossip associated with Shirley Temple, he was wrong. After his return to Los Angeles, he'd not only get involved with her personally, but with her ex-husband, John Agar, too. [*They'd star together in an upcoming film, an oddity for Kirk, a western.*]

Two days later, still in Palm Beach, Kirk ran into gossipy Mrs. Temple again. "Have you heard the latest? Last night, the Duke attended this elegant dance where they brought in musicians, part of a dance band they imported from New York. The Duke asked them to play show tunes from *Annie Get Your Gun* and *South Pacific,* and he sang the most popular numbers from both musicals. It was a disaster. That's not all...Later, he danced the Charleston with one of the handsome waiters. I think His Majesty is coming unglued."

[*As the years passed, Kirk heard rumor after rumor about the Duke and his Duchess. Disillusionment had set in like a cancer, but they still showed up at parties and as long-term houseguests of the socially ambitious and very wealthy, keeping up appearances and, according to some, freeloading.*

At a party in Hollywood, Kirk encountered Noël Coward, who indiscreetly confided, "The Duke is a closeted homosexual. At this event one night at the Ritz in London, he propositioned me."

In 2012, the private sex lives of the Duke and Duchess received their closest scrutiny. The leading Hollywood pimp, Scotty Bowers, published his memoirs: Full Service: Adventures in Hollywood and the Sex Lives of the Stars.

As a Marine returning to Hollywood after World War II, he operated a gasoline station near Paramount Studios that evolved into the centerpiece of a network for the pimping of young veterans. Their patrons included both the gays of Hollywood, many of them closeted movie stars, and lonely and/or horny women.

Handsome, well-built, and well-hung, Scotty had been lured into the scene when a customer at the gas tank propositioned him and took him home. It was Walter Pidgeon, the actor who had scored such a big hit as the romantic lead in Mrs. Miniver (1942) *with Greer Garson.*

From then on, Scotty made the rounds. As business flourished, he rounded]

up more and more out-of-work men, some of them actors and many of them veter-
ans from the war effort. He also began supplying comely looking girls to straight
men who included Desi Arnaz.

Scotty's memoir earned both a review from The New York Times *and a spe-*
cial profile of Scotty in its Sunday Styles section. Some of his more shocking claims
included supplying a total of 150 girls to the lesbian actress, Katharine Hepburn.
Scotty exposed her relationship with Spencer Tracy as platonic, and Scotty himself
admitted to frequently "servicing Spence."

Not only that, but he spent a weekend at the home of one of his rich male
friends. At the same party appeared J. Edgar Hoover and one of his studly G-
men from the F.B.I. For dinner, Hoover appeared in drag.

Perhaps Scotty's most startling revelations centered on the Duke and Duchess
of Windsor. Scotty rented himself out to the Duke—"He was a good cocksucker"—
and he supplied beautiful young girls to the Duchess. He was also allowed to call
the former king "Eddy."

When Kirk heard this, he said, "So that's the lowdown on what was billed as
'The Romance of the Century.' If that were true, then the Century is in grave trou-
ble."]

***

In his memoirs, Kirk claimed that he first spotted John F. Kennedy at
the Hollywood home of the prominent agent, Charles K. Feldman. "I knew
him as the son of the former ambassador, Joseph Kennedy, and as the Senator from Massachusetts," Kirk said. "He was talking in the far corner with
some beautiful starlets and would soon disappear upstairs to one of Feldman's guest bedrooms, or so I was told."

Feldman astonished Kirk by telling him, "You've just seen the future
President of the United States."

Kirk's encounters with JFK were more elaborate, personal, and scandalous than what he revealed in his memoirs. There were encounters as
early as 1950, back in Palm Beach, at the Wrightsman's mansion. As Irene
remained ill and in confinement in her bedroom upstairs, Charles Wrightsman, Kirk's host, had invited the young politician, JFK, over for a swim
and a game of tennis. Kennedy was in town for a short vacation and staying at the nearby Kennedy compound.

"Jack will be bringing along his boy, Lem Billings, his slave, actually,"
Charles said.

Kirk was stunned by the statement, not really understanding its implications.

Within about an hour, JFK arrived with Lem, each wearing swimming

236

trunks and T-shirts. Still relatively young, JFK vigorously shook Kirk's hand, flashing a smile. Whereas Kirk found him handsome and charismatic, Lem was diffident, shy, and not nearly as attractive.

On that balmy, Sunday afternoon in Palm Beach, Kirk and Charles played some games of tennis against "Jack and Lem"—and lost. After the game and before lunch, they decided to go for a swim. Very casual about nudity, as indeed were most of the Kennedy family, including Rose, JFK pulled off his swimming trunks and jumped into the pool. Dropping his own trunks, Kirk dived in, too, followed by Lem, who modestly retained his trunks. Charles remained anchored on a chaise longue nearby, skeptically observing and evaluating his guests.

Later, lying side by side in the nude, each on a chaise longue, Kirk and JFK chatted pleasantly. It was the beginning of a long association that would continue through his White House days. Lem waited on JFK, fetching his sunglasses and a few minutes later, bringing him coffee. Then he went into the dressing room and emerged with some lotion which he rubbed on JFK's back. Charles did not join in any of this, but remained several feet apart, observing the two nude men. Finally, he got up and headed for his mansion, after announcing that lunch would be served in half an hour.

In the locker room, Lem helped JFK, who had complained of a back ache, get dressed, even putting on his socks.

The conversation at lunch included speculation about whether Harry S Truman would seek the Democratic nomination for President again in 1952. Irene remained in her room.

Soon after, a lobster salad was served. JFK and Lem departed, heading back to the Kennedy compound.

That night, Charles invited Kirk for a pre-dinner drink on one of his terraces, asserting that he had something to discuss with him.

He was very blunt and went straight to the point. "I've got to warn you about Irene. She might not have told you, but she's been in and out of mental institutions. She'll go for months and seem relatively okay, and then, all of a sudden, she'll go over a cliff into deep despair. At such times, she's likely to become violent. Old Joe Kennedy dropped in on me one day, and I told him about Irene being mentally ill. He suggested I should subject her to a lobotomy like the one he had performed on a daughter of his own. Ever since, I've been thinking about it, considering it as an option for Irene."

"But I'm not aware of Irene being mentally ill," Kirk said. "At times, she becomes irrational, but insanity? That's overstating it."

"I felt I had to warn you in case you're considering marrying my daughter," Charles said. "And I want to make something perfectly clear: Marriage between you two is out of the question."

"There's another problem," Charles said. "I don't want you to think I'm queer or something, checking out a guy's dick, but I couldn't help but notice that you're circumcised. I thought that with a name like Kirk Douglas, you might have Scottish ancestors. Forgive me for asking, but are you a Jew?"

"Yes I am, and I'm proud of my heritage," Kirk said. "My name, Kirk, is for the marquees. My birth name is Issur Danielovitch."

"You must understand. I have a position to uphold as the Dean of Palm Beach society. If my daughter married a Jew, I'd be ostracized. Don't get me wrong: I have nothing against Jews, although I find them greedy and crooked in business. If you married Irene and had children, I'd be the grandfather of Jew kids—and that's utterly unthinkable."

"Rest assured, C.B.," Kirk said, knowing that only his best friends referred to him as C.B. "This little Jew boy is not going to marry your daughter. Maybe one of these days you'll wish I had." The he stood up, announcing, "I'll not be at dinner tonight. Tomorrow, I'm flying back to Hollywood. Thank you for your gracious hospitality."

"Is Irene going back with you?" he asked.

"That's up to her," Kirk said. Then he turned and headed back into the house to pack his luggage for an early departure. He phoned Irene's room. She told him that not only was she well enough to return with him to Los Angeles, but that she was looking forward to it.

***

[Over the years, Kirk gradually learned just who Lemoyne Billings was. Born in Pennsylvania and adored by the Kennedy family (who called him "Lem"), he was a particular favorite of the family matriarch, Rose, and of Jack's younger brother, Robert. The exception to this was Old Joe Kennedy himself, who complained whenever he visited "You're surely not bringing that queer here again?"

"Yes, I am," JFK always replied, in a rare defiance of his domineering father.

It was said that JFK and Lem "bonded for life" when they first met at the Choate School for Boys in Connecticut. JFK was "sweet sixteen," Lem

JFK and Lem Billings in Palm Beach in 1940

238

seventeen, a year ahead of JFK in school. They bonded to such a degree that Lem elected to remain a year behind in school so that he could room with "my new friend Jack."

That summer, the two young men toured Europe together, sleeping in the same bed wherever they traveled. Lem always joked about Jack being "oversexed."

After Jack married Jacqueline Bouvier, she told her sister, Lee Radziwill, "From the beginning of my marriage to Jack, I knew that also meant accepting Lem. He was always hanging around like a puppy dog, begging for a crumb from his master's table."

In a surprisingly candid confession, Lem once admitted to Jacqueline, "the only man I've ever loved, totally and completely, is John Fitzgerald Kennedy."]

***

After the glitz and glamour of Palm Beach, Kirk was eager to return to work. Irene, since leaving her father behind in Florida, had a miraculous recovery from whatever it was that had bothered her in Palm Beach and became her fun-loving self again.

Although exhausted from the cross-country flight, she demanded that he make love to her the moment they returned home. "You've been neglecting me," she said.

"You forget," he said. "Your sick room was off-limits during my stay at your father's house."

The script of his next picture arrived from Warner's the next day. *Along the Great Divide*, eventually released in 1951, would be a grim Western that involved a hazardous trek across Death Valley.

Although Kirk did not know how to ride a horse or shoot a gun, it would be his first cowboy picture, a genre in which he would excel in the years to come.

A Warner Brothers picture, *Along the Great Divide* was set to be produced by Anthony Veiler and directed by Raoul Walsh. So far, Kirk was the only actor cast. The female lead was still uncertain, but names floating about included Rhonda Fleming, Anne Baxter, and Coleen Gray.

Kirk was anxious to know which actress would be cast as Ann Keith, the daughter of the cattle rustler who's about to be hanged. As a means of finding out, he phoned Walsh.

"I haven't decided yet," Walsh said. "The role could be played by any actress under 30 in Hollywood. Any suggestions?"

"Anne Baxter," Kirk said. "She was in *The Walls of Jericho* with me and was great in *All About Eve.*"

"She'd be okay, but after her success as Eve Harrington, she's probably loaded down with offers."

The script had been written by Walter Doniger, the saga of a marshal, Ken Merrick, the role already assigned to Kirk. With his two deputies, he rescues a cattle rustler from a lynch mob led by a local cattle baron convinced that the aging rustler killed his son.

Doniger was a New Yorker who became known in for his direction of early episodes of the TV Westerns *Cheyenne* (1955-1963) and *Maverick* (1957-1962), and in the 1960s, many episodes of the soap opera series, *Peyton Place.*

Walsh had told Kirk that he'd sent the script to John Agar in hopes that he'd play one of Kirk's deputies. Walsh had liked his screen presence when he'd appeared with this then-wife, Shirley Temple, in *Fort Apache* (1948), the John Ford Western with John Wayne. Walsh informed Kirk that Temple and Agar were heading for the divorce courts.

Kirk was not immediately impressed with the script for *Along the Great Divide.*

The morning after he read it, he received a phone call from Shirley Temple. From 1935 to 1938 *[i.e., between the ages of 7 and 10]* she'd been the biggest box office attraction in the world. But by the early 1950s, she was at a crucial point in her career, trying to cross the bridge from child star to a young adult actress. Whereas Natalie Wood would successfully transition herself into new cinematic venues, another child star, Margaret O'Brien, would not. Kirk had already met Temple, and their brief encounter had not unfolded in a way he'd liked.

[In her memoir, Child Star, *Temple wrote about her awkward introduction to Kirk, even though she left out all the spicy details.*

She was at Ciro's with John Agar, her husband at the time, and he excused himself to go to the men's room.

Seizing the opportunity, Kirk approached her table and invited her to dance. She accepted. Together, they circled the edges of the dance floor, saying nothing. He held her so close she had a hard time breathing. When the music stopped, he whispered in her ear what he wanted.

"The only time I had heard such graphic language was in a Westlake bathroom," she wrote.

"What?" she blurted.

"Tipping his handsome head back, he displayed his cleft chin and toothy, confident

Along the Great Divide, Kirk Douglas, and John Agar...once known as "Mr. Shirley Temple."

240

smile. He repeated his request."

"Wow! She exclaimed.

Her memoirs left the reader dangling, unclear about many of the subtleties of their exchange. She retreated back to her table. Agar, by now, had returned from the men's room. He had been followed by three of his gay fans who had stood beside him at the urinal to see his display.]

When Kirk later met with his director, Walsh, he told him what he'd whispered into Temple's ear.

"I told her that as a boy, I'd seen her in Bright Eyes *(1934), where, at the age of five, she'd sung 'On the Good Ship Lollipop.' I revealed to her that I'd gotten a hard-on in the theater as I watched her sing, and that I wanted to stick my dick into her pouty little mouth."]*

When Kirk met with Temple the following afternoon, he was surprised to discover that she'd become a chain smoker, so unlike her image in her movies. He kept lighting her cigarettes as she talked about her career dilemmas and her divorce from Agar. "My fans have deserted me. They've never forgiven me for growing up."

"Because of my stocky body as a child, rumors, particularly abroad, spread that I was an adult dwarf playing a little girl on the screen," she lamented.

She told him that her former studio boss, Darryl F. Zanuck, told her that she should go to Europe for a few years, gain some maturity, and return to Hollywood with a name change as a calculated scheme for a "comeback" as an adult.

Her last film role had flopped. She'd also been rejected when she'd auditioned in 1950 for a production of *Peter Pan* on Broadway.

"Instead of throwing in the rag, I want to have one more chance, playing that daughter who treks across the desert with her father and falls in love with you,"

Kirk told her that he had no objection to her appearing in the part, but warned her that he was not in charge of casting. "All I can do is pass along your interest to Walsh, and to recommend you."

The next day, during a conversation with Kirk, Walsh

Two Views of Virginia Mayo from *Along the Great Divide*, not Kirk's favorite leading lady.

241

looked astonished at the idea of including Shirley Temple in his Western.

"You must be kidding. What's in it for you? I bet you're fucking Little Miss Lollipop. I've already cast Virginia Mayo. She's cross-eyed, but we can shoot around that."

***

Young adult movie star wannabe: Shirley Temple. She wants Kirk to co-star her.

Although he'd had reservations about the *Across the Great Divide*, Kirk felt he'd be in good, capable hands with two film veterans like Walsh and the producer, Anthony Veiller.

A New Yorker, Veiller was better known as a screenwriter than a producer. Between 1934 and 1964, he would write 41 screenplays and be twice nominated for a Best Screenplay Oscar. The first was for *Stage Door* (1937), starring Katharine Hepburn and Ginger Rogers; the second for *The Killers* (1946). It had introduced Kirk's friend and future co-star, Burt Lancaster, who emoted onscreen with Ava Gardner. Kirk would work again with Veiller, who would write the screenplay for *The List of Adrian Messenger* (1963).

Walsh was one of the most important and influential directors in Hollywood, having worked with such legendary stars as John Wayne in *The Big Trail* (1930), *High Sierra* (1941) with Humphrey Bogart, and with James Cagney in *White Heat* (1949). He would also make three of Clark Gable's last movies. He had also been an actor, appearing as John Wilkes Booth in D.W. Griffith's *The Birth of a Nation* (1915).

Walsh wore a patch over his eye. He spread the myth about himself that it had been pecked out by a buzzard in Arizona when he'd had a role as an actor in the flick *In Old Arizona (1928)*, the first major "Talkie Western." Actually, that was fiction.

Instead, as a motorist, a jackrabbit had crashed through his windshield, a fragment of jagged glass cutting deep into his eye, blinding him for life.

Kirk needed this survivor of many a Western to teach him how to ride a horse and fire a six-gun.

The day Kirk lunched with him, Walsh was like no Manhattanite he'd ever known. Before his migration to Hollywood, he'd been a sailor, a bronco buster, and a prizefighter. In silents, he'd directed *The Thief of Bagdad* (1924), with Douglas Fairbanks, Sr.; and *What Price Glory* (1926) with Victor McLaglen. He was both director and co-star in *Sadie Thompson* (1928) in which Gloria Swanson was cast as a prostitute.

Walsh told him that most of *Along the Great Divide* would be shot on location near Lone Pine, California, in the High Sierra. In addition to that, long, high-drama segments would be filmed in driest spot with the most extreme temperatures in America, the Mojave Desert.

As filming progressed, Kirk liked Walsh less and less.

"I detested him and despised working with him," Kirk said. "He was a mean, crusty old buzzard, a one-eyed monster. He told me that John Wayne would have been better cast than me, and that Humphrey Bogart could have played it better, too. Just what every actor wants to hear!"

"He really liked violence. Once, he got excited to the point of orgasm while watching a dangerous stunt in which a stuntman, a kid from Colorado, almost got killed. The horses were abused during the shoot. I love horses and hated to see them mistreated. Just like Walsh mistreated me. What a bastard!"

***

Kirk met Agar for lunch after he'd been cast as his deputy, Billy Shear. He was at the end of his marriage to Temple. It had been an ill-suited union characterized by egomania, wrong-minded expectations, possessiveness, alcoholism and, on his part, adultery.

Kirk had seen Agar in two pictures with John Wayne, *She Wore a Yellow Ribbon* (1949) and *The Sands of Iwo Jima,* released the same year. The latter had brought Wayne an Oscar nomination.

"Agar had a drinking problem, and he was often drunk on location, as his life seemingly was coming unglued," Kirk said. "But I got along with him—but not with Miss Mayo. She and I didn't fare as well."

Mayo, the quintessential, voluptuous blonde, was at the peak of her career. She'd been defined in one feature article as "a pinup painting come to life." The Sultan of Morocco had declared her as "tangible evidence of the existence of God."

Walsh and Mayo had recently completed another Western, *Colorado* (1949), with Joel McCrae as her leading man.

Mayo told Darwin Porter, at her home in Thousand Oaks, California, shortly before her death in 2005, "I liked working with Burt (Lancaster) in *The Flame and the Arrow* (1950). He was real friendly, great body, flashy smile. He also tried to feel me up

Director Raoul Walsh was "detested" by Kirk.

243

every chance he got."

"I didn't care for Kirk Douglas at all," she said. "Very pushy, full of himself, always fighting with Raoul over every scene, delaying production."

[Kirk's opinion of Mayo? "Rather dumb, an icy blonde of little talent. Burt was welcome to her.]

At first, Kirk had a warm response to Walter Brennan, who played Pop Keith, the cattle rustler he rescues from a lynch mob and the father of the character portrayed by Mayo.

He regarded Brennan as one of the finest character actors in Hollywood, having been nominated for three Oscars in a row: *Come and Get It* (1936), *Kentucky* (1938), and *The Westerner* (1940), the latter with Gary Cooper, in which Brennan had played his sidekick. In fact, Brennan had made a career of playing sidekicks to other actors, as he had for Humphrey Bogart in *To Have and Have Not* (1944).

Kirk and Brennan, however, never became friends, because Kirk was turned off by his Alt-Right politics and his status as a self-avowed racist. "All these Lefties, all of them troublemakers, are getting all these niggers stirred up. Frankly, I think these spooks should be rounded up and shipped back to Africa where they belong."

The other supporting roles in *Great Divide* were played by some of the most durable and time-tested actors in Hollywood. Cast as Kirk's second deputy, Ray Teal had recently appeared with him as the corrupt sheriff in *Ace in the Hole*. In time, he would appear in a staggering 250 films and 90 TV dramas. His longest-running gig being that of Sheriff Roy Coffee on NBC's hit series, *Bonanza* (1960-1972). In time, he also starred in three of Marlon Brando's films, *The Men* (1950), *The Wild One* (1953), and *One-Eyed Jacks* (1961).

Morris Ankrum was cast as the vindictive Ned Roden, the cattle baron who wants to hang Brennan for allegedly killing his son. Like Teal, he would become a veteran of 270 films, usually cast as military men or other authority figures such as scientist, banker, judge, even a psychiatrist. He also became popular in those Hopalong Cassidy films, and once played Jefferson Davis resigning from the U.S. Senate to lead the Confederate South.

Merrick (Kirk) insists on escorting Pop Keith (Brennan), under arrest, to Santa Loma for trial. During their trek across the vast desert, the Roden gang, vowing vengeance, are hot on their trail.

As the plot unfolds, it's ultimately determined that Brennan is innocent, and he follows Mayo and Kirk into the sunset. They've fallen in love, but strictly on the screen.

Variety defined *Along the Great Divide* as one of "The Top Box Office Hits of 1951."

***

Flying into New York, Kirk, after checking into a suite at the Plaza Hotel, went directly to the Manhattan's 16th Police Precinct, joking to the sergeant he met there, "I've come to turn myself in."

He had a better excuse than that. In his next movie, *Detective Story* (released in 1951), he had to play a ruthless character, Lt. James McLeod. As part of the preparation for his role, he wanted to observe the drama of a Manhattan police precinct during the course of a busy week. After a brief confab, and with the permission of New York City's Police Commissioner, Kirk won approval "to hang out with you boys."

The Commissioner had already seen *Detective Story* as a play on Broadway. Ralph Bellamy had starred in it as the aggressive detective, the role eventually shouldered by Kirk in the film adaptation.

Kirk was looking forward to working with director William Wyler, but also dreading it. His reputation as "Forty-Take Wyler" had preceded him, as he was known for the relentless pursuit of perfection. Henry Fonda had informed Kirk that on the set of *Jezebel* (1938), Wyler had ordered fifty takes for a brief scene, going on and on until Fonda delivered what Wyler was seeking.

[Kirk was surprised when Wyler selected him as the lead for Detective Story, *because Wyler had recently rejected him as the lead of his previous film,* Carrie *(1952). Wyler had wanted Cary Grant, who had turned it down. Then, Wyler had considered, and rejected, Kirk, Gary Cooper, James Stewart, and Spencer Tracy, but in Wyler's view, none of them had the suave sophistication that* Carrie *needed. Eventually, Wyler awarded the role to Sir Laurence Olivier.]*

Like the NYC Police Commissioner, Wyler, too, had seen *Detective Story* on Broadway. In addition to Bellamy, its key players had included Maureen Stapleton and Meg Munday as the detective's (i.e., Kirk's) wife. Wyler wanted only four members of the play's cast to reprise their roles in the film adaptation. They included character actors Joseph Wiseman, Michael Strong, Horace McMahon, and, in her film debut, Lee Grant.

Wyler then announced that Paramount had hired Dashiell Hammett to adapt the Broadway play to the screen. But after the passage of three weeks, Hammett had not produced a single page of script. Wyler fired him and replaced him with his brother, Robert Wyler, who brought in Philip Yordan as his co-author.

Wyler also arranged for the production of a short, one-week run of the theatrical version of *Detective Story* onstage at the Sombrero Theater in Phoenix, Arizona, presumably as a test run for the cast before the start of filming. On opening night, Kirk's throat went dry, and for a moment or two, he couldn't utter a word. But he recovered in time to get on with the drama.

Kirk had high hopes for the film, especially since Wyler—one of the most bankable directors in Hollywood—was at the helm. Wyler had been born in a bilingual frontier of the German Empire, now Alsace-Lorraine in eastern France.

In the 1940s, Wyler had helmed two of that decade's biggest hits, *Mrs. Miniver* (1942) with Greer Garson and Walter Pidgeon; and *The Best Years of Our Lives* (1946). Starring Fredric March and Myrna Loy, it evolved into the highest-grossing film of the '40s and brought Wyler an Oscar as Best Director.

Over the course of his career, Wyler had guided many actors to Oscar wins, notably Bette Davis for her performance in *Jezebel* (1938), and Olivia de Havilland for her role in *The Heiress* (1949). Olivier credited Wyler with teaching him how to act on a big screen during his direction of *Wuthering Heights* (1939), for which he too received an Oscar nomination.

Wyler would make cinematic history by directing more than thirty-six actors and actresses to Oscar nominations, a record. Of these, fourteen actually won, also a record.

After about a week of working with Wyler, Kirk complained, "I'm excited by the challenge of portraying a character who is right to a fault, but a man who pre-judges others and destroys himself." He also interpreted the detective's relationship with his wife as too weak, and set about to depict a softer, gentler side of the otherwise very tough and abrasive Detective McLeod.

At first, Kirk claimed, "Wyler is wrapped in an impenetrable shell. Maybe Bette Davis could crack through to him using sex, but I can't go that route."

Kirk with Eleanor Parker...wife with a past.

As filming progressed, however, he concluded that Wyler was "a very warm, human person with a sense of humor like a kid who throws bags of water from a sec-

246

ond-floor window on the hapless passersby on the street."

Detective McLeod would evolve into one of Kirk's most unsympathetic film portrayals, an easily enraged cop who dealt with criminals by busting their faces in. Critic Manny Farber defined McLeod as "a one-man army against crime, an authoritarian sadist."

The psychology behind his hatred of crime stemmed, the script reveals, from his crooked father and his mistreatment of his son.

Yet despite McLeod's shortcomings, he displays love and tenderness for his gentle, understanding wife, Mary. That is, until he uncovers a notorious chapter in her past.

Red-haired Eleanor Parker was one of the finest film actresses of her day. This "cat-eyed" and talented beauty stood out so vividly in *Detective Story* that she was nominated for a Best Actress Oscar, though she lost to Vivien Leigh for *A Streetcar Named Desire*.

[Parker had recently been nominated for a Best Actress Oscar for her prison drama, Caged *(1950), but lost to Judy Holliday for* Born Yesterday.

One of Parker's best roles was that of the disabled opera singer, Marjorie Lawrence, in Interrupted Melody *(1955), opposite Glenn Ford. Her performance brought her another Best Actress nomination. Today, she is mostly remembered for her interpretation of the Baroness in* The Sound of Music *(1965).]*

Wyler had hired one of the best supporting casts—perhaps the best—of any film released in 1951. In the third lead, William Bendix played veteran police detective Lou Brody, tough on the outside, tender inside. He seems to have sympathy for the myriad characters with ruined lives who pass through the station house.

[A Manhattanite, Bendix was usually cast into blue-collar roles, except when he played the title role in The Babe Ruth Story *(1948), considered the worst sports biopic ever made. He became accustomed to playing "second fiddle" to bigger stars such as James Cagney, Alan Ladd, and Bing Crosby. For the general public, he became best known for his role as the male lead in the TV sitcom,* The Life of Riley *(1953-1958)]*

McLeod's chief concern, and the object of his most zealous hatred, is Karl Schneider (played by George Macready), an abortionist who, the audience learns, is responsible for the death of many young women. *[The Production Code did not allow the word "abortion" to ever be mentioned in the film, forcing its screenwriters to suggest the procedure without actually naming it.]*

As part of the plot, McLeod learns that his wife, before knowing him, had a "carnal romp" with a

William Wyler..."Stars win Oscars in my films."

247

gangster and subsequently, an abortion. The news seems to drive him crazy. He confronts Mary with her past shame, something she has concealed from him.

George Mcready, Gladys George, William Bendix...each a character study in *Detective Story*.

His illusions shattered, and devastated by the revelations about his wife, McLeod's world seems to have been turned upside down.

As McLeod, onscreen, Kirk hated Schneider, the abortionist (aka Macready), but bonded with him in real life and away from the camera. One of Kirk's all-time favorite movies had been *Gilda* (1946), starring Rita Hayworth and Glenn Ford in a deadly triangle with the character played by Macready.

He told Kirk, "A lot of the public didn't get it that Glenn and I were playing homosexuals."

Macready specialized in polished villains and had a big scar on his cheek, the result of a car accident where he'd been thrown through the windshield. He and Kirk would meet again six years later when they co-starred together in *Paths of Glory* (1957).

In the most sympathetic roles in the film, Cathy O'Donnell and Craig Hill portrayed sweethearts. He'd been arrested for embezzling $400 to take his girlfriend to the Stork Club.

Wyler was kind to O'Donnell, since she was his sister-in-law, having married his brother, Robert, who had crafted her role in his screenplay.

[O'Donnell had won acclaim with her portrayal of the loyal sweetheart of a disabled Navy veteran, Homer Parrish, in the World War II drama, The Best Years of Our Lives *(1946). The anguished character of Homer was movingly interpreted by Harold Russell, a true-life double amputee.]*

Opposite her in *Detective Story* was Craig Hill, an exceedingly handsome actor who hoped that this role would launch him into the big time. He was widely sought out by members of Hollywood's gay colony, most visibly by Rock Hudson.

Veteran actor Horace McMahon played Lt. Monaghan, the precinct captain who tolerates McLeod's excess force because he knows he's an honest cop.

Gladys George, cast as Miss Hatch and a specialist in portraying floozies, told Kirk, "If you want to get laid, come to my dressing room any time. I'm ready, willing, and able, and still able to show a guy a good time in spite of how time marches on."

[In her glory days, she had starred as Madame Du Barry, the mistress of John Barrymore in Marie Antoinette *(1938). Kirk had also seen her as Dana Andrew's blowsy stepmother in Wyler's* The Best Years of Our Lives.*]*

Following her proposition of Kirk, he asked her, "To take you up on your offer, do I need to make an appointment?"

"Not at all, baby. Any time, any place."

Yanked from Broadway, actor Joseph Wiseman was cast as a villain, Charles Gennini. His character was described as "a demented, homicidal burglar, a degenerate fourth offender with feline depravity."

As the Brooklyn-born shoplifter, Lee Grant wrote about her role in *Detective Story* in her memoir, *I Said Yes to Everything.* In the movie, she steals a purse from Saks Fifth Avenue and is arrested. Even though she was only twenty at the time, makeup aged her for the role.

She was so effective that she was nominated for a Best Supporting Actress Oscar, losing to Kim Hunter for her portrayal of Stella in *A Streetcar Named Desire.*

Grant's career came to a sudden halt when she refused to testify against her husband, Playwright Arnold Manoff, before the House Un-American Activities Committee. For the next twelve years, she was blacklisted, but bounced back with TV appearances in *Peyton Place* (1965-66). She was also cast in *Valley of the Dolls* (1967); *In the Heat of the Night* (also 1967), and *Shampoo* (1975), where she played Warren Beatty's older lover. For that, she won an Oscar as Best Supporting Actress.

Grant also knew Kirk's actor son, Michael. In her memoir, she recalled "Every A-list actor and director hung out at Brenda Vacarro and Michael Douglas' house in Benedict Canyon. You got stoned just opening the door back in the 1970s."

As for Michael's father, she called Kirk, "A big, big star. Gorgeous. Intense. Amazing."

Most film directors of Broadway plays like to open up the screen to broader camera vistas, including outdoor scenes. Not Wyler. Except for one scene in a police wagon, he confined his grim drama to the interior of a police precinct.

To avoid monotony, Wyler wisely hired

Craig Hill and Cathy O'Donnell...young lovers in jeopardy.

249

photographer Lee Garmes, who won praise for his "fluid, restless lensing that keeps images flowing."

[Garmes had previously worked with Josef von Sternberg on Morocco *(1930), which had starred Marlene Dietrich and Gary Cooper. As phrased by critic Walter Mitchell, in* Morocco, *Garmes had created "rippling shadows providing a northern light to shine on the face of this German* femme fatale.*"]*

At the climax of *Detective Story,* McLeod steps directly into an oncoming bullet fired by a desperate gangster who's trying to escape from the precinct. As he lies dying, he cites lines from the Catholic Act of Contrition. *[O my God, I am heartily sorry for having offended Thee, and I detest all my sins because of Thy just punishments, but most of all because they offend Thee, my God…]*

On a rushed schedule, it took only five weeks to shoot this gritty police drama.

Bosley Crowther of *The New York Times* called it "a brisk, absorbing drama with a fine, responsive cast. The film, however, is more skillful than profound, just a melodramatic *tour de force."*

Variety cited Kirk for "bringing a spark of compassion to the role of the ruthless detective that makes the finale closer to tragedy than melodrama."

***

Before the end of the shoot, Kirk had retired early and was awakened one night by frantic pounding on the door to his suite.

Sleepily, he headed toward the door, thinking it was room service bringing an item that had not been included with his earlier order.

In the dim light of the hallway, he confronted Ava Gardner.

Without an invitation, she rushed inside and bolted the door behind her. Her face in panic, she turned to him and said: "It's Frankie. He's got a gun."

Frank Sinatra and Ava Gardner on their wedding day in 1951. Their marriage became famous for its turbulence.

CHAPTER EIGHT

HOLLYWOOD'S HORNDOG INVADES THE BOUDOIRS OF

LANA TURNER, AVA GARDNER, MARLENE DIETRICH, & GLORIA GRAHAME

KIRK'S AFFAIRS WITH A FAUX INDIAN PRINCESS AND A CELEBRATED SOCIALITE END IN

SUICIDES

KIRK PUTS THE "BAD" INTO

THE BAD AND THE BEAUTIFUL

OFFSCREEN DRAMA FROM ITS FEMALE LEADS

Before Kirk Douglas co-starred with the luscious Lana Turner in *The Bad and the Beautiful*, her reputation had preceded her. He looked forward to appearing as her co-star.

"She was not even an actress...only a trollop," said Gloria Swanson. "She was the type of woman a guy would risk five years in jail for rape," Robert Taylor said of her allure.

"She was amoral," Louis B. Mayer proclaimed. "If she saw a stagehand in tight pants and a muscular build, she'd invite him to her dressing room."

Awakened from inside his lodgings in New York City, at the Hampshire House on Central Park South, Kirk got up from his bed to see who was pounding on his door. Surely a room service waiter wouldn't be that rude. Dressed in his jockey shorts, he opened the door, but only a crack.

There, in the dim light of the hallway stood a frantic-looking Ava Gardner, who had just announced that Frank Sinatra was chasing her with a gun, no doubt his .38. "He's after me," she said with hushed desperation. Then, without permission, she pushed past Kirk and stormed inside.

"Oh, Kirk, Kirk, I'm so afraid. You'll protect me, won't you?"

"Sure I will. Now settle down. You're safe here."

She looked around "Got something to drink?"

"Bourbon. You southern gals drink bourbon, don't you?"

"We sure do, *honey chile.*"

Kirk had heard that both Ava and Sinatra were staying within the same building, in lodgings owned by Mannie Sachs.

After he managed to calm her down, he learned what had gone wrong. Sinatra had thrown a jealous fit.

"He's threatened to kill me. He claims I've been screwing—get this, will you?—Robert Taylor and Robert Mitchum, and that I've resumed my affair with Clark Gable."

"Has he learned about us?" Kirk asked. "I don't want him to come gunning for me."

"Your name didn't come up," she said. "What set Frankie off was when he heard me phoning Howard Hughes," she said. "He still has the hots for me, mainly because he knows, no matter how rich he is, that I'll never commit to him. He called to tell me that his spies had learned that Frankie is back to diddling that blonde bitch, Marilyn Maxwell, when she isn't screwing around with Bob Hope."

"I'm not surprised," Ava continued. "I went way the hell out to Fort Lee, New Jersey to hear Frankie perform at Bill Miller's Riviera Club. Blondie was in the audience and it was obvious that Frankie was directing all his love songs to her—and not to me. I got pissed off, stormed out, and took a taxi back to Manhattan."

[Both Ava and Sinatra took separate flights back into Los Angeles, where they made up after he promised not to see Maxwell again, a vow he would not keep. Their truce did not last long. Not only did he hear Ava talking on the phone to Hughes, but one of his spies told him that she was seen leaving Hughes' home after midnight.

He was in Palm Springs at the time, but broke speed limits getting back to Hollywood where he'd gone on a drunken rage, attacking Ava.

Before rushing out the door, he'd told her, "When I find the son of a bitch (i.e., Hughes), I'm putting a bullet right between the fucker's eyes. When I get back, I'll blast your face in, too. The beautiful Ava Gardner will look like the Creature from the Black Lagoon."

She related to Kirk that Sinatra had been coming unglued for weeks. She told the story of what happened three nights before when she was dining at Frascati's in Los Angeles with her friends, Lana Turner (Sinatra's former girlfriend) and the singer Lena Horne.

"Lena has forgiven me for taking away that role she wanted, that of the mulatto in Show Boat," Ava said. "She would have been terrific in it, but Louis B. Mayer didn't want to cast a black woman."

"Our crazy Sinatra stormed into the restaurant, spotted us, and started shouting, 'LESBIANS! LESBIANS! LESBIANS!' Everyone stared at us in disbelief. Then he stormed out, yelling 'Both of them are dykes—a blonde and a black pussy—all in a night's work for Miss Ava.'"

Later, we had one of our most violent fights," she claimed. "Frankie and I are great in the sack. It's only when I head to the bidet that the fights begin."]

"I'm at the peak of my career, and that time in the life of an actress can go by so fast," Ava lamented. "But instead of concentrating on another acting gig, I've been dealing with that maniac. I turned down *Carrie* in which I, a *lil' ol'* Southern gal, would have co-starred with Laurence Olivier."

"I came close to getting Larry's part myself," Kirk said. "If I had, you and I'd have been the co-stars in *Carrie*."

He finally reached for her. "Come to bed," he said. "Both of us could use some cuddling."

"Ava didn't resist," he recalled. "She turned herself over to me. I didn't play roughhouse. She got enough of that from Sinatra. I was loving and gentle, responsive to her needs. I needed to repair her wounds, and I was there for her."

"Before she left, I told her I would always be there for her. At around 10AM, she called Sinatra, finding that he had sobered up and settled down, begging for her to return."

"I told Frankie that I spent the night with my sister," Ava said to Kirk. "I don't think he believes me, but he'll accept it for the moment. We make up, we fight, we make up…and so it goes. After a few more months of this, we'll both be burning on a very low flame."

Later, he related the details of that episode with Ava to Burt Lancaster, who'd had an affair with her during their making of the *film noir, The Killers* (1946).

"Sooner or later, one of them will kill the other," Kirk said to Lancaster. "Their love affair is just too violent. But I promised her that I'd be there for her next crisis," Kirk said. "In some ways, Ava and I, although from totally different backgrounds, are kindred spirits. North Carolina sure turns out some remarkable women…and some stunning beauties, too," he said.

When Kirk wrote his memoirs, he included an account of the panicked, late-night door-pounding by Ava that we described above. But perhaps fearing reprisals from Sinatra, he conveniently omitted the intimacies with her that followed. In his book, he described a brief chat, a kiss on her cheek, and a parting a few minutes after her arrival. Considering Sinatra's temper and passion for reprisals, that was perhaps the safest option.

Other exchanges with Ava loomed in his future.

***

As Frank Sinatra and Ava Gardner remained locked in their doomed relationship, Kirk found himself in a troubled affair with a very troubled young woman, too: Irene Wrightsman. Beauty masked her fragile inner core and a psyche that frequently hinted might either explode or break down at any minute.

In Palm Beach, her multi-millionaire father, Charles Wrightsman, had insisted that she was mentally ill. At the time, Kirk more or less dismissed that allegation, suspecting that Wrightsman's intention involved "scaring me off."

But after living with her for a while, he came to believe that her father's assessment was accurate.

Kirk was often absent from their Hollywood apartment and sometimes didn't return until late. Irene seemed starved for companionship and, as such, had taken up with a young woman, Dolores Johns, offspring of a prominent family in Sacramento. As he soon discovered, John's father sent her $4,000 a month for her maintenance and upkeep. Based on the monetary standards of the early 1950s, that was a lot of money. In contrast, Charles Wrightsman sent Irene only $600 a month.

Dolores, born and bred in California, became a regular at Kirk's apartment. Nearly every late afternoon, she was there when he returned from his workday. When she wasn't shopping, Johns showed Irene the attractions of Los Angeles. Once, they even migrated as far south as Tijuana for the bullfights. Kirk was either too busy or else didn't want to go on these excursions.

In the beginning, he was pleased that Dolores took over the care, feeding, and amusement of Irene. "I was very erotically charged by Irene but didn't really want to hang out with her. We had little in common, and our interests didn't match. What she most talked about with Dolores was Hol-

254

lywood gossip."

"They told me that Cary Grant had been arrested in the men's toilet of a department store, and that it had been hushed up. They said that Audie Murphy, the most decorated American soldier of World War II, was a closeted homosexual. And I was told that Fred Astaire and Grant's boyfriend, Randolph Scott, had had a torrid affair during their filming of *Follow the Fleet* (1936).

"I also heard that Joan Crawford and Barbara Stanwyck were lovers. And that Tallulah Bankhead was having an affair with Hattie McDaniel, a.k.a 'Mammy' in *Gone With the Wind* (1939). Of course, knowing Tallulah, that 'rumor' might have been true."

"All this focus on lesbianism made me suspicious of Dolores and Irene," Kirk said. "When I was away, were they, too, having an affair?"

One night after Dolores, Kirk, and Irene returned from dinner at Don the Beachcomber's, Irene revealed some intimate details about her early life for the first time. She'd been drinking heavily that night, and often interrupted her confessions with racking sobs. Kirk believed what she said.

Irene asserted that when she was fourteen, during her enrollment at an exclusive boarding school, she had attacked her roommate with a knife after accusing her of stealing a gold necklace from Tiffany's. Later, the missing jewelry turned up.

"I was hauled away by this cop. Enraged, I began fighting with him. I had long, sharp nails, and I raked the side of his face so badly, making him bleed. He's probably scarred for life. Then, my bastard of a father had me committed to a mental institution in Miami," she said, "where I lived like a frightened, caged animal. For eight months, they wouldn't let me out of that hellhole, enduring violence and humiliation beyond my wildest dreams. It was there that I began to truly loathe my father. My hatred lives on today."

"Once, when I felt I could not survive there for another day, I turned over the dining table where I was eating with seven other girls. I was carried out, kicking and screaming, and confined to a padded cell. The worst was yet to come."

Irene burst into tears before unleashing her most upsetting revelation: She said that during her confinement in the asylum, she was repeatedly raped by the male orderlies, and had to endure lesbian sex from a burly, heavyset matron. "I couldn't fight them off, they held me down. My life was living hell. I felt like Olivia de Havilland in *The Snake Pit* (1948)…only worse."

After her release, Irene claimed, "I was much worse when I got out than when I went in. So much for mental rehabilitation."

She remained a prisoner even after her return to her father's luxurious mansion in Palm Beach. "I'd been back for only three days before my father came into my bedroom after everyone else was asleep. Just like those orderlies at the asylum, he forced himself on me...night after night, often making me bleed. He never apologized, viewing the blood as affirmation of his manhood. He told me that my mother had complained that he was too big."

"I think he was also forcing himself onto my little sister, Charlene. She was very withdrawn, and the two of us never confided in each other. She lived in her own special world, never inviting visitors inside."

"When I told my mother what Charles was doing to me, she slapped my face and said I was lying. "You're a very sick girl, and if you continue to spread these hideous accusations, I'll see that you're hauled in a straitjacket back to the asylum."

"Family dinners were an agony," Irene continued. "If one of us did something that pissed off my father, he'd pick up his dinner plate and smash it in our face."

"One night because of some infraction—I don't remember what it was—he beat me so severely I had to be rushed to the hospital. My father told the doctor that I'd fallen down the stairs."

"When I could take it no more, I ran away from home. With just the clothes on my back and with absolutely no money, I began hitchhiking on the southbound side of the highway until a middle-aged, rather heavyset man picked me up in his battered truck. When he found out I was hungry, we stopped at this seedy little dive in Tavernier, where he had a turtle steak and I had a sandwich and a banana split."

"Then we drove all the way to Big Pine Key, where we turned onto an unpaved road that opened onto a view of the water. It was a real Keys backwater—no one else lived there. His home was a dilapidated trailer that looked pre-war, very tiny."

"At first, he was kind and solicitous, suggesting that I take a shower, since I was hot and dirty from the road. When I came out of this little cubicle, he was waiting with a dirty towel. I knew what was in store for me, and I submitted. What use would it have been to resist? He might have killed me."

"That night, after he fell asleep, I slipped out of the trailer and ran back to the Overseas Highway and headed south toward Key West. As I was walking along, alone in the night, a squad car from the Monroe County Sheriff's Office stopped me. Two patrolmen ordered me into their car. They got me to admit that I was Charles Wrightsman's daughter and that I lived in Palm Beach. For a bed that night, I slept in an unlocked jail cell."

"My father arrived the next day to take me home. He was boiling over in anger, but artfully concealing it from the sheriff. He played the role of a concerned father very well. We spent the next few hours driving up the Keys in total silence. When we got home, he ordered me to my bedroom."

"There I stayed, locked in, for fifteen days and nights. He had a servant bring me my meals. I wasn't in a padded cell, but it evoked one. When he let me out, he told me that my boarding school had refused to take me back—and no other school wanted me. He hired a private tutor."

"The story was as painful for Dolores and me to hear as it was for Irene to tell it," Kirk said. "She retreated to her bedroom, and Dolores asked me if she could stay over, since I had an early appointment."

"I hate to tell you this, but Irene has often talked to me about committing suicide," Dolores said. "I think I should be here for her in the morning when she wakes up."

***

Dolores was not only there the following day, but in the days that followed, too. When Kirk returned to the apartment at the end of his work day, Dolores was already there, bringing Irene the vodka tonics she requested.

He became suspicious, thinking that Dolores might be involved in a lesbian relationship with Irene. He'd been in Hollywood long enough to know that such liaisons were far more common than the public knew.

"This may sound a bit crazy," Kirk told his agent, Charles Feldman, "but I can't get enough of Irene sexually. I am not in love with her, never have been, but I'm erotically charged by her. We have long bouts of passionate lovemaking."

Having heard her "confession" in front of Dolores, Kirk had nothing but sympathy for her. "I had been born a poor Jew, she a rich Gentile living in the lap of luxury. But her life seemed more like hell than mine."

As the weeks passed, her drinking increased. "By five in the afternoon, she was usually zonked. I never said anything. I figured that the alcohol buried long-suppressed memories, though fearing it might lead to her self-destruction."

Late one Saturday afternoon, he returned to the apartment at around 6PM. Near the entrance, he heard voices coming from the living room. At first, he figured that Irene was having a conversation with Dolores.

But it was a man's voice he'd heard. Walking into the living room, he came face to face with Sydney Chaplin, who was sitting on the sofa beside Irene.

Sydney Chaplin in the Broadway stage version of *Funny Girl* in 1964 with Barbra Streisand, for which he won a Tony Award.

Kirk was not at all surprised to find Sydney *[the good-looking second-born son of Charlie Chaplin and Lita Grey, his co-star in* The Gold Rush *(1925)]* there. He and Irene had dined with him on several occasions, and Kirk often played tennis with him.

Irene seemed to like Sydney very much. Even if she'd been morbid all day, she always blossomed in his presence. "At least he can do something I can't," Kirk said. "Cheer up my moribund girlfriend."

"Personally, I always felt a little bit sorry for Sydney," Kirk said. "Imagine having the Little Tramp for a father, one of the most famous men on earth. There was no way that a son could escape the long shadow of Charlie Chaplin. Perhaps Sydney could have gone into another field. So what did he do? He became an actor. But I suspect that his film career will go nowhere."

After some greetings, Sydney, Irene, and Kirk decided to have dinner together at Chasen's that night, with the understanding that Sydney would rendezvous with his date, Shelley Winters, before dinner at the bar. Kirk was informed that he'd have to pick up the tab, since Charlie Chaplin had restricted his son to an allowance of $300 a month.

"I'll have some money coming in soon," Sydney told Kirk. "Dad has given me a role in his new movie, *Limelight* (1952)."

Kirk had met Winters before. At parties, she was always urging him to get her cast as his leading lady in one of his films. "I'm sure you saw me in *A Place in the Sun* (1951). I was better than Elizabeth Taylor, who just stood there looking beautiful, and Monty Clift, who went through the movie looking glazed."

"That's what I like about you," Kirk said. "An actress must believe in her talent."

Winters then revealed that she was set to star opposite Frank Sinatra in *Meet Danny Wilson* (1952). During its filming, the press would report that Sinatra referred to her as a "bowlegged bitch of a Brooklyn blonde."

She'd retaliate, labeling him as "a skinny, no-talent, stupid Hoboken bastard."

Shortly after their greeting, Winters whispered to Kirk, "Keep my dating Sydney under your hat. I'm having an affair with your buddy, Burt

Lancaster, and he'd be furious if he knew I'd been fucking Sydney."

Winter's reputation as a seducer of Hollywood studs is already deeply embedded in Hollywood lore. Over the years, she'd be sexually linked to William Holden, Sean Connery, Marlon Brando, Clark Gable, Ronald Colman, Robert De Niro, Errol Flynn, Howard Hughes, and John ("my biggest thrill") Ireland, among many others who included messenger boys, studio grips, and waiters picked up randomly.

Kirk didn't interpret Shelley's romance with Sydney as anything more than a casual fling. "I'd heard that Sydney, like me, was going through one starlet after another, just like his father did during his heyday."

Shelley Winters in *A Double Life* (1947).

During dinner, Sydney excused himself for a visit to the men's toilet. While he was away, Winters told everyone that Lita Grey, Sydney's mother, had been quoted as saying that her husband [*i.e., Sydney's father, Charlie*] could have as many as six orgasms a night. "I feel cheated," Winters quipped. "The most that Sydney can go is three rounds."

"You poor, deprived lady," Kirk said, mockingly.

"Syd is always on the lookout for his next seduction," Winters said. "You'd better keep a beauty here like Irene under lock and key."

"Oh, shut up!" Irene said, a bit too defensively for Kirk's taste. He wondered if she, too, were having an affair with Sydney.

***

To Kirk, the next three weeks seemed unbearable. He and Irene weren't getting along and picking petty arguments over minor incidents like not lowering the toilet seat or the lack of orange juice in the refrigerator.

On three separate occasions, Irene had demanded that he marry her, and each time, he'd refused. She had exploded into violent fits. At one point, she went into the kitchen and started throwing and breaking porcelain.

Kirk finally decided that he'd had enough and maneuvered her into an apartment of her own, even pre-paying the rent. That ended badly: After ten days of separation, she called him at 3AM to say that she'd swallowed a bottle of sleeping pills. The police and an ambulance were summoned. Doctors rescued her in time by pumping out her stomach.

When she was released from the hospital, she begged him to take her back into his apartment, and he reluctantly agreed. "There was the sex thing," he told Burt Lancaster when he explained to him why he'd allowed her to return.

The following week, he returned home early in the day and found Sydney there, dressed in his tennis clothes. "Irene is a better tennis partner than you, old boy," Sydney said. "You've been replaced on the court."

"Just so I'm not replaced somewhere else," Kirk said, his bedroom humor all too obvious.

Irene wasn't the only crisis unfolding in his life at that time. He wanted out of his Warner's contract. He'd done all right in *Young Man With a Horn*, but both *The Glass Menagerie* and *Along the Great Divide* had been box office disappointments. He was also very disappointed at his new assignment, a not-particularly-promising picture entitled *The Big Trees*, scheduled for a release in 1952. *[He felt that after the success of* Champion, *he'd evolved into a "hot property" in Hollywood, and that his agent should screen out unimportant, or lesser, scripts.]*

Kirk's agent since 1946, when he'd first arrived in Hollywood, had been Charles K. Feldman, a tough, flamboyant operator with far too many clients to devote all of his attention to Kirk's career.

"I felt that the time had come for me to put a firecracker into the assholes of my agents," Kirk said.

[Ray Stark, later a producer, represented him at Famous Artists Corporation. Stark was often the target of Kirk's complaints. Stark defended himself to Feldman, saying that he'd already sent any number of good scripts to Douglas, adding, "My God, he even turned down Stalag 17."*]*

Some of Kirk's letters to Feldman survived the passage of the decades. In one of them, he wrote: "Maybe I'm a difficult client, and that is entirely possible, as some people at your agency seem to think. Perhaps I'm too demanding. What is wrong, however, for wanting quality roles? A times, I think I'll have to go out and find them myself."

"And that is exactly what I'm going to do."

Consequently, he met with Feldman and asked him to go to Warners and tell the brass there that he'd do a picture for nothing if they'd release him from his contract.

"You must be kidding," Feldman said.

"Like hell I am. DO IT!" Kirk said.

Within a week, Warners had accepted his offer, probably because executives believed that Kirk was no longer the "bankable star" they'd thought.

As soon as he heard the news, he determined to start shopping around for some memorable roles. "I want a script that has 'Oscar' with my name on it."

***

Before Kirk went north to Oregon to film for *The Big Trees,* Irene made a surprise announcement. Her younger sister, Charlene Wrightsman, was coming for dinner with her new beau. He had proposed marriage to her.

"Who's the lucky victim?" he asked.

"It's someone you know, but if I tell you, it won't be a surprise."

"Bring him on," Kirk said.

That night into Kirk's apartment walked Charlene on the arm of Igor Cassini (aka Cholly Knickerbocker), author of a popular gossip column for the Hearst newspaper chain.

"Here is my husband-to-be," she announced. "Soon, I'll be Mrs. Alexandrovich Loiewski-Cassini."

Kirk had met Igor briefly in Palm Beach, and items about him often ran in his gossip column. In social circles, Igor was also known as the brother of the fabled designer, Oleg Cassini, with whom Kirk had competed for the affections not only of Irene but, for a brief moment, Gene Tierney, too.

The dinner, cooked by Irene, was relatively uneventful, until "Igor put on his Cholly hat" (Kirk's words). "When are you going to marry Irene and make an honest woman of her?" he asked.

Charlene chimed in, "We could make it a double wedding at the Russian Orthodox Church in Manhattan!"

"Just think of the publicity," Igor said, his eyes lighting up. "It could be massive. I'll break the news in my column."

Cholly Knickerbocker, the pseudonym for Igor Cassini, wrote a syndicated gossip column that was devoured by the self-designated "smart set" he catered to. Depicted above is the banner for one of his columns. Whether on any particular day it was lurid or gossipy or poignant, one thing was certain: EVERYBODY read it.

Kirk grew silent, as he had no intention of marrying Irene.

The conversation inevitably turned to Igor's brother, Oleg Cassini, the King of American Fashion. "Oleg and I, growing up as brothers, were the most bitter of rivals and the dearest of friends."

[After receiving news of the upcoming marriage of his brother, Igor, to Charlene Wrightsman, Oleg told the press, "My brother, through his column, is a real power in New York, Newport, Palm Beach, or wherever the rich gather to divert themselves."

Years later, Oleg would also reveal, "Igor's equanimity was most apparent in his relations with his former wives. I once saw him at '21' in Manhattan having lunch with three of them, a neat trick for a man to pull off after he's divorced the entire trio."]

When Charlene retreated to the kitchen to help Irene prepare dessert, Igor became confessional: "I'm always falling in love. But now, I'm trying to convince myself that I'm in love with Charlene. Of course, I'm attracted to Charles Wrightsman's dough and his social connections in Manhattan and Palm Beach. But here I go again. 'Another mistake,' I'm telling myself. My first marriage in 1940 was to Austine Byrne McDonnell, the Hearst writer known as 'American Journalism's Most Magnificent Doll.' She was screen-tested for the role of Melanie in *Gone With the Wind,* the part going to Olivia de Havilland instead. After I dumped her, she married William Randolph Hearst, Jr."

"My second marriage was to Elizabeth Darrah Water, the fashion designer. We have a daughter, Marina."

"Now, it's my third attempt. I'm no fool. I know this one, like the others, won't last. Like her sister, Charlene is unstable. Don't mention this, but you'd be a fool to marry Irene. Her own father told me he might have to have both sisters committed to an asylum. When I first met her, Charlene was a shy, bashful, fat little girl, sulking around C.B.'s mansion in Palm Beach. She later told me she'd had a crush on me since the first day she saw me."

"Poor, dear Charlene. As you know, she married that bisexual actor, Helmut Dantine, whose career seems to be going nowhere unless you cast him in one of your pictures. He illegally cashed all of Charlene's bonds. Until I talked him out of it, Charles was plotting to have him arrested."

"Her father wanted her to marry Peter Salm, the Austrian-American heir to the Standard Oil fortune, but she went for me, instead. She claims I'm a better lover than Peter."

Kirk sat impatiently listening. He later recalled, "Poor Issur is getting a baptism into what high society thought about love, money, and marriage."

Igor continued: "When Wainwright divorced Irene's mother and married his second wife, Jayne, she decided to redecorate their Palm Beach House, which was filled with 18th-Century French antiques. Instead of putting them into storage, she gave a lot of them to Charlene to decorate our home."

"So if you opt to marry Irene," Igor said, "I have an idea about how you, even though you're a Jew, can advance yourself in Beverly Hills society. Wainwright has lots of art and antiques in storage. Buy a mansion in Beverly Hills, fill it with his antiques and paintings, and throw some chic parties. I'll promote them, and you, in my column.

"But as you pointed out, I'm a Jew," Kirk said.

"If you've got enough power and prestige in Hollywood, you can get away with being a Jew. Of course, in Newport or in Palm Beach, that would be a lot less likely. I must caution you, however: Getting money out of Wainwright is tough. He gives Charlene only $6,000 a year. Yet he'll pay $75,000 for a chair authenticated by the Louvre. Jayne's poodle sleeps on a couch once reserved for the pet dog of Marie Antoinette."

"Since I'm a gossip columnist, I have to tell you a zinger. Charlene once had an affair with her neighbor in Palm Beach, Senator John F. Kennedy. She told me he was a horrible lover—only two minutes in the saddle and with an Irish cock that's not all that impressive."

"Old Joe Kennedy and I get along great," Igor said. "I'm more or less his *protégé*. He's advising me how to make money from my limited funds. In return, I supply him with beautiful girls. When we're out with one of his recent conquests, I pass her off as my *puta*."

"We call that a beard," Kirk said.

Kirk had heard enough and was relieved when Charlene and Igor said good night. He didn't attend their wedding but continued to run into Igor at parties.

In 1962, at the home of Lou Wasserman, Igor, still married to Charlene, chatted with Kirk. "The world is my oyster. I'm making $200,000 a year, and my marriage is sorta okay. Like Irene, Charlene is one mixed-up girl. My social life is glorious. Even President Kennedy invites me to play golf with him, and I hang out with Allen Dulles [*Head of the CIA*]."

"As you know, Oleg is Jacqueline's official designer, and the First lady calls me her favorite columnist."

Then he leaned over to whisper something into Kirk's ear. "I'm telling you this in the strictest confidence. Jacqueline and Oleg are having a secret affair. She calls it a revenge fuck to get back at Jack for fucking Marilyn Monroe and a hundred other girls."

Little did either man know at the time the tragedies awaited both Charlene and Irene.

Two days after entertaining Igor Cassini and his wife, Charlene, Kirk kissed Irene goodbye and flew to San Francisco. There, he rented a car, and, wanting to be alone, he drove north to Humboldt County in Northern California for the location shooting of *The Big Trees* (1952). It was the last picture he'd make as a contract player for Warner Brothers.

Its plot originated with Peter B. Kyne whose novel, *Valley of the Giants*, was set against the backdrop of the California Redwoods. His novel had already been adapted into three separate movies, the first of which was directed by James Cruze in 1919. *[It was thought to have been lost to history until it resurfaced in a film archive in Russia in 2010.]*

Kyne's novel was adapted into yet another film in 1927, as directed by Charles Brabin; and then again in 1938, when Warners dusted it off and reshot it in Technicolor as *Valley of the Giants*. The blonde stud, Wayne Morris, was its male lead, supported by Claire Trevor, Charles Bickford, Alan Hale, Sr., and Donald Crisp.

To save money on the fourth manifestation of this increasingly tired plot, Warners ordered its director to use background footage from the 1938 version and recycle it into Kirk's 1952 remake.

Although he wasn't excited by this property from the days of World War I, Kirk welcomed the opportunity for solitude as he drove north and mulled over his ongoing obsession with Irene. Maybe a new movie would take his mind off her.

Screenwriters for this newest remake had tried to update the plot, but not enough to please Kirk. He'd been cast as Jim Fallon, a greedy timber baron seeking to decimate the Sequoia Forest. His character is slick and unscrupulous—he's a confidence trickster—"and I hate the part," he said.

His timber cutters and sawmill crews deeply offend a devout nearby community of Quakers, who view the ancient redwoods as living symbols of God's majesty.

He dined that night with his producer, Louis F. Edelman, and with his director, Felix Feist. Kirk was not impressed with the credentials of either. Privately, he complained, "Both Louis and Felix have 'B' pictures written across their foreheads."

Edelman's claim to fame was that from 1935 and 1952, he'd produced 39 films. His biggest hits being *You Were Never Lovelier*

(1942), starring Fred Astaire and Rita Hayworth; and the gangster classic, *White Heat* (1949), with James Cagney and Virginia Mayo.

As for Felix, in 1936, he had directed Judy Garland and Deanna Durbin in a short film, *Every Sunday,* which Kirk defined as "No big deal."

Felix was getting ready to helm Nancy Davis (she had recently married Ronald Reagan) in that laughable sci-fi tale, *Donovan's Brain* (1953). Nancy would have to wait until the 1980s to take over running the Free World.

Kirk's unscrupulous character of the timber baron, Jim Fallon, confronts a Quaker community led by Elder Bixby (Charles Meredith). To complicate matters, he falls in love with the man's daughter, Alicia, the leading lady who brings him to redemption. Her character—that of the "good girl"—was interpreted by Eve Miller. In contrast, the flamboyant saloon and dance hall showgirl was played by Patrice Wymore.

Kirk bonded with other cast members, including Alan Hale, Jr., the son of a very famous father, his namesake, Alan Hale, Sr. Alan, Jr. had appeared with James Cagney in *The West Point Story* (1950), and he was on the verge of co-starring with Audie Murphy in *Destry* (1954). Hale Jr. was big and burly like his father. Ironically, the name of the character he played in *The Last Big Trees* was "Tiny."

The always reliable character actor, Edgar Buchanan, was cast as "Yukon Burns," Jim's (i.e., Kirk's) right-hand man, a grizzled old ex-Alaskan.

Kirk was also introduced to his leading lady, Eve Miller, a beautiful young woman who had grown up in nearby San Francisco. Familiar with the terrain in which they were shooting, she volunteered—when they got some time off—to drive him to some of the beauty spots in the area.

He invited her to lunch, during which he apologized for his unfamiliarity with her film career. *[She'd been appearing in movies since the end of World War II.]*

"Actually, there's little that was memorable," she said. "I had an uncredited role in *Beyond the Forest* (1949), the film that finished Bette Davis' career at Warners."

Before coming north, Kirk had received a call from actress/director/producer Ida Lupino, who more or less claimed to have discovered Eve. She assured Kirk, "She's very talented, a lovely girl, and I think that the two of you will make a fine couple on the screen. I used my influence to get her cast opposite you."

The Big Trees, Kirk with Eve Miller...a sexual invitation.

"You sound like you're in love with her," Kirk said.

"No, but I predict that you will be before the end of the shoot."

Over lunch, Eve told him that during World War II, "I was Rosie the Riveter, working as a welder in a shipyard in San Francisco. But after a few months, I entered show business, dancing in the *Folies Bergère* in Francisco—a place that tried to imitate the original in Paris."

"I'm sorry I missed that," he said.

"If you'd like to see what I showed—actually more than I showed—at the *Folies*, you can visit my room at eight o'clock tonight."

He was taken aback only slightly by her sexual invitation. As a handsome movie star, he was by now used to all kinds of sexual propositions, even though he was from time to time surprised by how bold some women could be.

Enigmatically, he didn't immediately accept. "At eight o'clock, let's see what happens."

He hadn't made up his mind to begin an affair with Eve. But then a call came in from Igor Cassini, who told him that his wife, Charlene, had recently visited her sister Irene at Kirk's apartment.

"Irene was drunk, really crazy. There was a damn orgy going on there. Since you went away, she seems to have become unglued. We didn't stay too long, and, as we left, we saw Irene heading to your bedroom with two guys, one of them black. Charlene found out that Irene is also hanging out a lot with Sydney Chaplin."

Kirk revealed to Igor Cassini that "Irene was driving me crazy. She seemed desperate, going out of her mind. I wanted to separate myself from her, but I also wanted to be with her. I was mixed up, miserable, wanting to break up, yet wanting her at the same time. Now that I had learned what she'd been up to in my absence, I decided to pay a visit to Eve after all."

Exactly at eight o'clock, Eve greeted Kirk in her hotel room wearing a sheer black *négligée*. "She was a highly desirable woman," he admitted to Felix the next day. "We fucked the night away."

"Please, save some of that emoting for the camera," the director quipped.

Kirk was under no particular mandate to be faithful to Irene, particularly now that he knew she was carrying on with other men, and perhaps—on occasion—with other females, too. He'd always suspected Dolores and her. As he told Felix, "For the last few nights, Eve and I have been going at it like gangbusters."

Then she told him that she'd fallen in love with him.

"Let's take it easy," he cautioned.

"No," she said. "You're a doll, and I'm going full speed after you."

At work and on the set, Kirk bonded with Patrice Wymore, whom he'd met in New Mexico before her marriage to Errol Flynn. She chatted pleasantly with him and asked on two different occasions to get together with him in the evening, but he kept putting her off. He didn't want her to know about his romance with Eve.

Late one afternoon, and in an impulsive move, he called Irene. "I was still obsessed with her, so much so that I finally asked her to marry me. I had already worked it out with the staff at Warners. They had agreed to arrange transportation for her to visit me on location."

As it happened, Eve overheard Kirk on the phone with Irene, discussing marriage.

Kirk in a tense moment with Eve Miller in *The Big Trees*. "She wasn't supposed to fall in love with me."

"Eve went ballistic," Kirk said. "I thought we'd just been having a little fling, but she took it like a big love affair. She threw a fit, threatening to kill me and herself, too. But I didn't take the threat seriously."

"As it turned out, my reunion with Irene—whose emotional condition had deteriorated— was disastrous. Going to bed with her was like going to bed with a department store mannequin. I was making love to a zombie. I knew it was over with her. I suggested that she return to Los Angeles, and she went willingly.

Eve returned to Kirk's bed the following night, having forgiven him for his transgression. Over the next few days, she finished all of her scenes with him, and—though free to return to her apartment in Los Angeles, she refused to leave until Warners insisted that she show up for the filming of *The Story of Will Rogers* (1952), starring Will Rogers, Jr. and Jane Wyman, Kirk's former co-star. The famous director, Michael Curtiz, had cast Eve into that film.

After a tearful goodbye, Eve demanded that Kirk drop Irene and hook up with her after his return to Los Angeles. When she saw that he hesitated, she threatened once again to commit suicide if he deserted her.

He didn't believe her.

With Eve out of the picture, Patrice Wymore moved in on him in her place. She was emotionally disturbed. "I'm very, very upset. I need to talk to someone, and you're the only one I can confide in."

He promised to visit her that evening in her hotel room.

When he got there, he realized that she'd been crying. He took her in his arms and hugged her close. "It's Errol," she said. "As you know, we've only recently been married, and trouble has already set in. Our former screen swashbuckler in in bad shape, physically, a real 4F. He's convinced that his lifespan will be short, and he says he's going to live it to the hilt until the very end. Ever since his last meeting with Jack Warner, he's been going crazy. Jack reminded him that his films weren't making money, and that the studio was thinking about dropping him. Then Errol called Jack a 'wily son of a bitch,' and before storming out of his office, he yelled back, 'And I'll live to piss on your grave.'"

"I don't know where he is now," Wymore continued, "or who he's with. Right from the beginning, it became obvious that he would not be faithful to me. I hear rumors, but I don't believe them. I hear that he even sleeps with young men, boys in some cases."

She turned to Kirk. "Oh, please, hold me in your arms. I need comforting tonight."

The next morning, after Felix evaluated the sky and weather conditions as perfect for the scene and camera work he had in mind, he phoned Wymore in her hotel room. He was moderately surprised when Kirk picked up the phone instead of Wymore, who was in the shower at the time. Kirk promised to pass Felix's message about being needed on the set along to her.

Felix told Hale, "Eve just left. So has Kirk's girlfriend, Irene. That Kirk wasted no time. I mean, no time at all. I found out that he spent the night with Patrice Wymore Flynn. What a horndog. How I envy him!"

***

The Big Trees flopped at the box office, *The New York Times* describing it as "a stormy and sometimes silly saga, not terribly far removed from the Warners *Valley of the Giants*. Its plot and emoting seem to be as old as the giant redwoods with which they are concerned."

Warners had so little regard for Kirk's latest film that when it came time to renew its copyright, they allowed it to fall into the public domain.

[POSTSCRIPT: There were follow-up developments to the Kirk/Eve Miller affair. After their separate returns to Los Angeles, he received three letters from her, each threatening suicide if he didn't take her back.

At first, he ignored them. He later learned that people who make suicide threats often carry through.

He read in Variety *that Eve had a minor role in the feel-good baseball biopic,* The Winning Team *(1952), starring Ronald Reagan and Doris Day, with whom*

Kirk had previously starred in Young Man With a Horn. *Subsequently, Kirk phoned Doris for an update, and explained his involvement with Eve and his concern about those suicide notes.*

"You're off the hook, Romeo," Doris said. "She's gone bonkers over Ronnie. I'd been dating him, and he asked me to marry him. But then along came Miss Nancy Davis, who got herself pregnant. She's getting him instead, something that has Eve threatening suicide again. I'll keep you updated with any new developments."

Kirk didn't hear back from her. However, about five weeks later, he received another suicide threat from Eve. This time, he called Virginia Mayo, with whom he'd recently appeared in Along the Great Divide. *She was now the co-star of Ronald Reagan's newest picture,* She's Working Her Way Through College *(1952).*

Mayo reported: "Eve is hopelessly chasing after Reagan, trying to break up Nancy and him. She doesn't have a chance. She's threatening suicide, but Nancy has our boy locked up."

During the next few years, Kirk didn't hear from Eve again until July 21, 1955 when he read a news item in Variety. *Eve had become involved with a minor actor, Glaze Lohman. After a bruising fight, he'd stormed out. Left alone in the kitchen, she stabbed herself in the abdomen. Somehow, the police were alerted and broke in, finding her bleeding on the floor. Rushed to the hospital, she underwent four hours of surgery and survived.*

The next time Kirk heard about her was once again in Variety. *Only nine days after celebrating her 50th birthday—a bad time for a former ingénue—she committed suicide in Van Nuys and was buried at Forest Lawn.*

A police officer who found her body scooped up the suicide notes she'd left behind. They'd been recently written and were addressed to Glaze Lohman, to Ronald Reagan, and to Kirk himself.

"Her last movie role was in The Big Bluff *(1955)," Kirk said. "At long last, Eve was no longer bluffing.]*

***

Arriving after midnight on a flight back to Los Angeles after his filming of *The Big Trees*, Kirk went directly to his apartment. He didn't know if Irene would be there or not. She'd left a note addressed to the maid saying that she'd be spending the weekend at the apartment Kirk had rented for her, and for which he was still paying the rent.

Most of her clothing and many of her possessions were still at that address. Hailing a cab, he rode to the apartment for which he still possessed a key.

He unlocked the door and looked into the darkened living room. If she were sleeping, he didn't want to awaken her. He tiptoed to the bedroom, thinking that she was asleep or away for the evening. The door was open. When he stepped inside, he stumbled over a chair near her vanity table.

"Who's there!" she called out, thinking that it might be a break-in. She switched on the lamp beside her bed and stared into his startled face. The sleepy body next to hers raised up in bed.

It was Sydney Chaplin.

All three of them stared at each other, no one uttering a word. After one last look, Kirk left, never to return.

For the next few days, Irene tried to reach him, but he wasn't available. He had checked into a bungalow at the Beverly Hills Hotel, using an assumed name and instructing the staff there that he didn't want any visitors. They were used to such requests.

Years would pass before he saw Irene for a final time.

***

In 1962, Kirk flew to New York. A decade had passed since he had caught Irene in bed with Sydney Chaplin. Having wed Anne Buydens in 1954, Kirk was now a married man.

Somehow, he'd heard that Irene was also in Manhattan, staying in her father's very deluxe suite at the Hotel Pierre. Since Kirk had seen her last, he'd received only sketchy details about what had happened to her.

Apparently, there had been two marriages, the latter of the two, allegedly, to an Italian count, who lived with her for a while in Switzerland. As her dependence on alcohol and, later, drugs, deepened, both of her marriages had failed...or so he had heard.

He opted to phone her at the Pierre, and to invite her to a play at a Broadway theater. But when he put through a call to her at her hotel, he was told that "Miss Wrightsman is not accepting calls." He left his phone number and message for her with the telephone operator.

A few hours later, she returned his call, her voice a bit shaky. She agreed to meet him at 7PM in the lobby. For some reason, she didn't want him to come to her suite.

He arrived on time and phoned her from the lobby. This time, the operator connected him to her suite. A man's voice answered and seemed rather hostile but passed his call along to her. She picked up the receiver.

When she descended to greet him, he was shocked by her appearance, likening it to that of a cadaver. Those years of drug abuse had taken their toll. She looked at least twenty years older than she actually was.

She sat with him in the lobby of The Pierre, chatting, although neither of them discussed their marriages.

After a few minutes, a bellhop summoned her to pick up the house phone. From some distance away, Kirk heard her angry voice. When she returned, she told him that a problem had arisen, and that she'd have to cancel their date. "Anyway," she said, "I think you said you were taking me to a play by Tennessee Williams? Or was it Arthur Miller? Frankly, I've had enough drama in my life without seeing more of it on a stage."

With that, she gave him a light kiss on the cheek. "Before our world turned cold, there were some good times."

"There sure were," he answered. "Let's remember what might have been."

"I shall," she said. Her parting words before she hastily departed, probably to deal with that man in her suite, alarmed him: "Goodbye, Kirk. I'm going to die."

That was the last time he ever saw her.

[The final chapters of the former Mrs. Charles Wrightsman and her two daughters, Charlene and Irene, were written in 1963 and 1965.

In the early winter of 1963, Mrs. Wrightsman committed suicide.

A few months later, on April 8 of that same year, Charlene and her 14-year-old daughter, Marina Cassini, watched the 35th Academy Awards presentation on television. Then Marina went to bed in her own room. She would never see her mother alive again.

During the night, Charlene swallowed the contents of a bottle of sleeping pills. The next morning, she was found dead by her maid.

Igor Cassini, Marina's father, later told Kirk what had happened: "After her body was removed, I found pills everywhere, in the pockets of her clothing, under her pillow, even in her shoes. Charlene followed her mother's example—suicide by overdose. But Irene, or so I'm told, is still alive."

Two years later, in 1965, Kirk heard that Irene, at the age of forty, had also committed suicide. He was not informed of the exact circumstances of her death, but suspected that she, too, had overdosed on sleeping pills.

The saga of Charles Wrightsman would continue until May of 1986 when the Associated Press carried the news that he had died at the age of ninety. He was praised as a benefactor for his massive contribution of paintings and rare antiques to the Metropolitan Museum in Manhattan.

Kirk later wrote: "Two beautiful girls and their mother commit suicide, directly or indirectly, and he lives to be ninety. What is God doing? How is God running the shop?"]

***

Freed from the "bondage" of his contract with Warner Brothers, Kirk was eager to accept film offers. One that particularly intrigued him came from Howard Hawks' Winchester Pictures for a movie called *The Big Sky*, a film eventually released in 1952. Hawks would both produce and direct it.

He had long admired Hawks, who had helmed some of his favorite movies. Critic Leonard Matlin defined him as "the greatest American director who is not a household name."

Born in Goshen, Indiana, Hawks seemed a master of almost any genre: Comedies, gangster movies, *film noir*, dramas, Westerns, even science fiction. At the time of these negotiations with Kirk, he'd just completed *The Thing from Another World* (1951).

More than a decade before, Hawks had directed Gary Cooper in *Sergeant York* (1941), for which he was nominated for the Best Director Oscar. He didn't win, but Cooper beat out Orson Welles in *Citizen Kane* to become Best Actor.

Kirk had really been impressed with how Hawks had made a star of his friend, Lauren Bacall, thanks to having cast her opposite her future husband Humphrey Bogart in *To Have and Have Not* (1944). His portrayal of strong, tough-talking female characters came to be defined as "the Hawksian woman."

Kirk wished he'd played either of the two leading men in Hawks' 1948 Western/action/romance, *Red River*, starring John Wayne and Montgomery Clift.

The moment the script arrived for *The Big Sky*, Kirk dropped whatever he was doing and read the screenplay twice. Its plot was based on a popular novel of the same title by A.B. Guthrie, Jr.

Kirk was delighted that the screenplay was by the respected screenwriter, Dudley Nichols. He had hit Hollywood in 1929, working with such directors as George Cukor and Fritz Lang. Some of Nichols' greatest screenplays included *Stagecoach* (1939), with John Wayne, and *For Whom the Bell Tolls* (1943), with Gary Cooper and Ingrid Bergman.

The Big Sky was billed as a Western yet was more thoughtful than many other films of that genre. Set in the 1830s, it was the saga of two rugged frontiersmen, Jim Deakins and Boone Caudill. They set out on a perilous journey to explore the vast, uncharted wilderness of the Northwest Territories.

Even on the first reading, Kirk was convinced that the role of Deakins was tailor-made for him. He would play a lusty, bumptious, boisterous frontiersman who enjoyed drinking and brawling. He meets up with a traveling companion, Boone, and they set out on a life-changing adventure.

Kirk's agent, Charles Feldman, had told him that many of Hawks' films, notably *Red River*, involved "a love story between two men," and that *The Big Sky* was not an exception.

Hostile at first, Boone and Deakins soon became bonded-at-the-hip companions as they pass through hostile Crow Indian country to reach territory controlled by the friendly Blackfoot Indians, with whom they could trade furs.

Historically, the Blackfoot Indians were nomadic fishermen and hunters of bison. They ranged across the vast landscapes and rivers of the Northern Great Plans of the American West.

Of course, because of the Hollywood Production Code, a woman has to play a vital role in any story about bonding among men. In this case, she was an Indian princess with the unlikely name of "Teal Eye." Soon, Boone, Deakins, and Teal Eye are involved in a love triangle.

Before they embark on their journey, Deakins and Boone are joined by Boone's Uncle Jeb Calloway and with "Frenchy" Jourdonnais, the owner of the *Mandan*, a sailing barge capable of traveling up the Missouri River into territory occupied by the Blackfoots.

Naturally, there's trouble along the way. Rival traders almost sabotage their trip. The worst of them is a killer named "Streak," who captures Teal Eye and tries to burn Frenchy's boat.

Having agreed to star in Hawks' newest movie, Kirk was introduced to the cast.

His co-star was Dewey Martin, cast as Boone, an exceedingly handsome, well-built actor from Katemcy, Texas. He was a war hero who'd gravitated to Hollywood, hoping to parlay his handsome face and studly body into a career.

Kirk with Dewey Martin. Gay audiences interpreted Dewey's gazing at Kirk as "the look of love."

He first found work in an uncredited role in *Knock on Any Door* (1949), starring Humphrey Bogart and John Derek. Hawks had just completed *The Thing*, in which he'd give Dewey a role. By 1955, he'd again be cast with Bogie in *The Desperate Hours*.

Elizabeth Threatt had been a fashion model before Hawks interpreted her as ideal for the Indian princess. *[All of her dialogue in the film was uttered in some approximation of a Native American dialect.]* She had dreams of becoming a film star, but that didn't happen. She left acting and the film industry after her performance in *The Big Sky* and faded into a footnote in Hollywood history.

A native of Gravelly, Arkansas, Arthur Hunnicutt was typecast in his usual role, that of a stoic, grizzled denizen of America's rural heartlands. He'd just completed *The Red Badge of Courage* (1951) with Audie Murphy.

Hunnicutt told Kirk, "I got my start on Broadway by working for seventeen months in the basement of the Algonquin Hotel in the damn laundry. To judge by the condition of the sheets I laundered, there must have been a lot of fucking going on, especially when Miss Tallulah Bankhead was in residence."

The Big Sky was shot on location in remote locations in and around the Grand Teton National Park in northwestern Wyoming. The cast was assigned tents with wood floors. As the star, Kirk got his own tent, which was subdivided into two separate "rooms."

At one point during the filming, Kirk and his agent, Ray Stark, took advantage of the wilderness setting for some bonding with their respective sons, Michael and Peter, fishing with them on the Snake River, and driving into Yellowstone for a view of Old Faithful.

"I was sorry to see my kids go," Kirk said. "I wish we'd bonded more."

On location, although Hawks more or less kept to himself at the end of most work days, Kirk tried to bond with the other actors, eventually developing a friendship with his co-star, Dewey Martin.

Dewey was a former hero of World War II. When quizzed, he revealed some of his experiences during the war. He joined the U.S. Navy in 1940, a year before the Japanese attack on Pearl Harbor. In the Pacific, he'd piloted a Grumman F6F Hellcat, which he had to ditch into the ocean when his aircraft carrier was damaged. He'd also fought in the Battle of the Bulge, where Nazi soldiers staged their last major offensive against the West.

In the closing months of the war, in 1945, Dewey was captured by the Japanese. "It was the strangest experience. On several occasions, they paraded me naked in front of them at night, jabbering about my dick—at least, that was where they were looking. I felt like some prized bull. One night, two of the Japs dressed in drag and became flirtatious with me, or at least pretended to be. The whole god damn experience was just so fucking bizarre."

On location, Kirk also bonded with Elizabeth Threatt. Based to some degree on her genetic lineage (she was half Cherokee), she'd been cast as the Blackfoot Princess, Teal Eye. "One Sunday afternoon, when we had the day off, we went skinny-dipping in the river. Later, we lay totally nude, enjoying each other and the hot Wyoming sun on the river bank. She turned and smiled, looking into my eyes."

"I thought that was a prelude to sex, and in some way it was. In her South Carolina drawl, she asked me to beat her with my belt. The pants I wore that day had a thick black leather belt with studs. I thought she was just kidding around, but the look in her eyes told me what I didn't want to hear."

"She was a masochist, a first for me. She really wanted me to beat her. I held off until she begged for it. I struck her harder. My stomach recoiled at the idea, until I saw that she was getting off, masturbating and screaming, 'harder, harder, harder.' She had her climax."

When I finished the job, I left that day with a new concept of self: Beneath my smiling, polite surface lurked a sadist." *[Kirk revealed these details in his memoir,* The Ragman's Son.*]*

According to Kirk, "Unlike most of my pictures, I didn't fall in love with my leading lady. In this case, my leading man was falling for me. Hawks seemed aware of that, and it made this movie about male bonding more effective."

Years later, chronicles of gay cinema would include stills from *The Big Sky* with Dewey gazing lovingly at Kirk. "That was about all that the Production Code allowed back then, since even the word 'homosexuality' was forbidden on the screen," Kirk said.

"As shooting progressed, Dewey asked if he could share my tent, since he detested his own, citing a number of problems," Kirk said. "I had wanted Michael to share my bed, hoping for some father-son bonding. That didn't happen, but Dewey crawled into bed with me. Nothing happened, not at first, and I thought no more about it. but as the days went by, he moved closer and closer into my orbit, hugging me and even seeing that I had clean underwear. At first, I thought he was kind of rehearsing for the buddy-buddy role he was playing. But—and I don't want to go into any graphic

Elizabeth Threatt got nude with Kirk.

275

description—he got too familiar one night, and I had to ask him to move out the next day."

"His feelings were hurt, and he confessed that he was in love with me," Kirk said, "but his heartbreak didn't last very long. After I bumped him, he began sharing the tent of Jim Davis, an older actor who was very handsome, too. Hawks had cast him as the villain of our movie, a killer named Streak."

"I KNEW Jim was straight, or at least I thought so. But out here in this wilderness, a man sometimes needs more than his trusty hand at night. He and Dewey had a brief fling that lasted until the end of shooting. Then Jim returned to home and hearth. I find that sometimes happens when straight actors go on location."

***

Born in what is now Ukraine, Steven Geray plays "Frenchy," the riverboat captain in *The Big Sky*. He takes Boone and Deakins up the danger-filled Missouri River. Along the way, he picks up the Indian princess, who has escaped from her captors. She quickly attracts the romantic attentions of both Boone and Deakins.

On a stage in Budapest before World War II, Geray became widely known for his hilarious impersonations of Benito Mussolini and Adolf Hitler. For that, he was beaten up by fascists. "As you Americans say," Geray told Kirk, "I had to get out of Dodge City...and fast!"

In 1941, he arrived in Hollywood with ten dollars in his trousers. But he was a true survivor and ended up acting in some of the most famous films of the 1940s and 50s. These included *Gilda* (1946) with Rita Hayworth; *In a Lonely Place* (1950) with Humphrey Bogart; *Call Me Madam* (1953) with Ethel Merman; and *To Catch a Thief* (1955) with Cary Grant and Grace Kelly.

"To amuse us at night, Geray would do those impersonations of the dictators," Kirk said. "No wonder he had to escape to the West."

In the movie's final scenes, Teal Eye decides that it's Boone (Dewey) she wants. Dewey says "goodbye forever" to Kirk, then goes off to live with the Indian princess amid the Blackfoots.

Male bonding, real or simulated, in *The Big Sky*. Dewey Martin (left) with Kirk.

Although many critics considered *The Big Sky* a bit long and drawn-out, it was favorably reviewed for the most part, except for the inevitable brickbats. Some criticism was leveled at Hawks for peripheral scenes that included mock barroom brawls and some corny theatrics.

The musical score for *The Big Sky* always got raves, having been created by the Russian-born composer, Dimitri Tiomkin, who had fled to America after escaping the Russian revolution. Ironically, this Russian *émigré* became known throughout the film industry for his composition of music for Westerns, none better than the theme song ("Do Not

Hungarian dissident Steven Geray

Forsake Me, Oh My Darlin") of Gary Cooper's *High Noon*. Tiomkin also wrote the musical score for the film version of Edna Ferber's *Giant* (1956), starring Elizabeth Taylor and Rock Hudson; and the musical score for Kirk's upcoming film with John Wayne, *The War Wagon* (1967).

Russell Harlan would be nominated for an Oscar for Best Cinematography (Black and White) and hailed for his scenic vistas of the Northwest.

Variety noted, "The performance of Kirk Douglas as the frontiersman is one of his best, a sincere characterization, equally impressive whether the scene is drama, comedy, or action." Cited was a scene in a seedy tavern where a drunken Kirk sings "Whisky Leave Me Alone."

Critic Joseph McBride rather uncharitably commented on "Douglas' constant earl-splitting smile, baring an expanse of teeth that Burt Lancaster could never have managed. It makes a spectator wonder how he avoids giving his mouth muscles a Charley Horse."

The Saturday Review said, "*The Big Sky* represents a step forward for Hollywood. It's replete with Indians, buffalo, and Western scenery, but it's more than your typical Western. It becomes almost the first true Hollywood attempt to equate, with some honesty, the events with the geography."

***

After the location shoot, Kirk never saw Dewey Martin again. He was surprised when, in 1956, news of his marriage to the sexy and sultry Peggy Lee was aired. Beautiful and blonde, with a platinum cool and inimitable whisper, she had always been one of Kirk's favorite singers. Dubbed "the Queen," she was the female equivalent of Frank Sinatra and Bing Crosby.

Over the years, Kirk had encountered her on several occasions, but never spending any time alone with her.

At a private party at Ciro's, he met her once again when she appeared before him in a shimmering white gown. "How's the marriage to Dewey coming?" he asked.

"Dewey is a disaster, always sulking and moody. He's extremely jealous, throws fits and insults my friends, including Frankie Sinatra, who slugged him one night. I'm divorcing the bastard. I should never have married him in the first place. I suspect he doesn't even like girls. I saw the movie you guys did. In some scenes he looked like he'd fallen in love with you."

"Maybe he was in love with me," Kirk said. "I'm very lovable. You should try me out sometime."

She looked him up and down. "Perhaps I'll take you up on that offer some rainy night, big boy."

At the party, their mating game came to an abrupt end when Duke Ellington tapped her on the shoulder.

***

After his return from Wyoming, Kirk learned that Howard Hawks wanted him for one final scene he needed for the continuity of his editing. It was to be shot at the studio. An artificial lake had been simulated atop a sound stage.

"When I arrived on the set, I told Hawks that I had caught a dreadful cold in Wyoming, and that a scene with me in the lake might make me really ill."

"You'll be fine, my boy," he responded. "Let's be a trouper about this."

"With great reluctance, Kirk complied, immersing himself, fully clothed, in the water. Time and time again, he was called to reshoot the scene. Between takes, a prop man handed him a wool blanket to wrap around his soggy body.

"By the end of the day, I was coughing violently, getting sicker and sicker. That Hawks is a sadist. I ended up in a hospital for three weeks with terminal pneumonia. When I was finally released from the hospital, the only person who seemed to care was Billy Wilder."

"I read in the papers that you were in the

Peggy Lee...an invitation to love.

278

hospital with pneumonia," Wilder said, "and that now you're at home recovering. I had lunch today with Marlene Dietrich, who just finished a publicity tour for *Rancho Notorious* (1952), a picture she detests. She wants to nurse you back to health. For some reason, she gets off on being a caretaker. Can I send her over?"

"Marlene Dietrich!" he said. "THE Marlene Dietrich, *femme fatale* of the 20th Century? Send her over right away! I can't wait!"

A few hours later, Marlene, in *"hausfrau* drag" (Kirk's words), arrived with a bag of groceries and a suitcase of clothing and body aids.

Kirk had met her before, at a commissary lunch that Wilder had hosted for the two of them. During the course of that lunch, Wilder had insisted that as a screen team, the two of them would be "dynamite."

In his memoir, Kirk wrote that "Marlene was a most unusual person. She seemed to love you more if you weren't well. When you were strong and healthy, she loved you less."

Kirk was being discreet. Beginning when she appeared as his cook, bottlewasher, and nurse, he launched a friendly affair (*une amitié amoureuse,* as the French say) with her that would stretch over decades. Details about the nature of their relationship were revealed to this book's senior author, Darwin Porter, in part by her *confidante,* the Austrian chanteuse, Greta Keller. Also, bits and pieces of their affair have been pieced together based on what he said to friends over the years.

Kirk had been enchanted by Dietrich for decades. Her appearance in *Destry Rides Again* (1939) had particularly thrilled him. She had co-starred in it with James Stewart. During its filming, they had an affair that led to an abortion.

In 1949, twenty years after the release of Dietrich's German-made film, *The Blue Angel* (1929), Kirk made it a point to finally see her classic interpretation of Lola Lola, the tarty, top-hatted, ambisexual cabaret entertainer. When it was presented in West Hollywood, he attended a screening within a revival theater whose audience consisted mostly of gay men.

A decade later, Kirk had made it a point to see the 1959 remake of *The Blue Angel,* this one starring Mai Britt and Curt Jurgens. Kirk's conclusion? "There is only one Marlene Dietrich and probably there will

Marlene Dietrich in *Rancho Notorious* (1952)...sex without gender preference.

279

never be another like her."

Kirk did admit that he'd had "affectionate sex" with Marlene. His use of that term in his memoirs was because, according to Greta Keller, they did not have vaginal (conventional) intercourse, as she preferred fellatio. She told him, "You men always want to put your things in—that's all that most of you really want. With fellatio, you can control the action…with the other, you can't."

"But the man should always be in control during sex," he claimed.

"Not always, dear boy," she answered. "You do it my way—or no way."

Of course, he submitted to her wishes. "You're on."

Prior to Kirk, Dietrich's list of lovers had become legendary: Maurice Chevalier, Colette, Edith Piaf, Gary Cooper, Joe DiMaggio, Orson Welles, Frank Sinatra. She'd even been intimate with Generals George Patton and James Gavin. As she jokingly remarked, "I inspired them to win World War II."

Marlene expressed only praise for Billy Wilder, the man who'd brought her together with Kirk. "He is a master builder who knows his tools and uses them expertly to frame out the structure on which he hangs the garlands of his wit and wisdom," Marlene said. "You may not know this, but Billy offered me the role of Norma Desmond in *Sunset Blvd.* He had conceived the character as one of those foreign women who became screen vamps in the 1920s but didn't have good enough voices to make Talkies. Think Pola Negri."

According to Kirk, "I never understood the German word *Zeitgeist* until she explained it to me. It means 'the spirit of the age, the feeling and aura of a historical era."

"Marlene fed me well, a fabulous cook, and she makes the world's greatest omelette," Kirk said. "Her own eating habits are strange. She doesn't have anything in her stomach until she drinks a glass of champagne at three in the afternoon. She prepares a feast to eat at midnight, her only food all day. How she can drift off to sleep after consuming such a large banquet, I'll never know."

"Sometimes, she doesn't sleep," he said. "I once caught her up at two in the morning, sitting by the open window in my bedroom, just staring up at the stars like a little girl."

In the late 1950s, Kirk met with Wilder again and talked about Marlene during the period when the director was thinking once again about co-starring them together in a movie.

"I've been intimate with a lot of Hollywood goddesses," Kirk confessed. "But Marlene is a different kind of love goddess in that she has feminine allure subtly mixed into a brew of masculine aggression—it's a turn-on for me, even though she is uniquely androgynous."

After he recovered from his pneumonia, and Marlene moved out, he lunched with Wilder, partly to report on the healing experience he'd had during time in her care.

"If I had to invent the ideal woman, it would be Marlene," Wilder said. "Because she's promiscuous, some fools call her a whore. I'm sure you saw our film, *A Foreign Affair* (1948), in which she played a prostitute trying to survive in postwar Berlin. The most interesting woman character in any picture is a whore. Every man in love is a sex pervert at heart."

"Of the many things I admire about her is that she can have sex without consideration of gender," Wilder said. She once told me, and I agree, that in Europe, it doesn't matter so much if you're male or female. Her exact words were, 'You can love anyone you find attractive.'"

Kirk admitted that part of his attraction for her involved her being German—in fact, that she was the most famous German woman on the planet. "I'm a Jew, and we know what Hitler thought about Jews…or did to Jews. But Marlene is one German who is not a Nazi and, most important, has no prejudice against Jews. A Gentile or a Jewish man, such as myself…that doesn't matter to her."

She had told Kirk, "I respect Jewish heritage. I will not try to explain the mystic tie I have with these people. It is stronger than blood. It binds me to them…and to you."

"She has a calculated cool about her public *persona,*" Kirk said. "In private, she's a woman of complicated desires, with a fierce passion about life, which is always burning in her heart. To the world, she is enigmatic. Even though I know her, she's still a mystery to me. My God, she had the balls to defy Hitler and Goebbels, who wanted to make her the Queen of UFA. To those psychos, she was the epitome of a Teutonic goddess."

[Universum-Film Aktiengesellschaft (UFA) was founded in 1917 and produced films until the end of World War II, during which time it functioned as a propaganda tool for the Nazis.]

"During the war, defiantly supportive of the American war effort, she got right down in the muddy trenches with American soldiers to give them an open-mouthed kiss. What a woman! They don't make 'em like her anymore."

***

In part because of his familiarity with the quirks of one of his era's most visible "love goddesses" (Marlene Dietrich), Kirk seemed well-equipped for his role opposite another major-league love goddess, Lana Turner. MGM was about to link them in their latest blockbuster *noir* film about Hollywood, *The Bad and the Beautiful* (1952). "It seems that I have this thing for blondes."

Its director, Vincente Minnelli, having recently emerged from his divorce from Judy Garland, had cast Kirk in the role of a ruthless Hollywood director, Jonathan Shields. He'd play another anti-hero, a venue he'd previously defined in *Champion, Ace in the Hole,* and *Detective Story.*

Meeting Minnelli at MGM, Kirk jokingly said, "There may be some confusion about the title. Lana, of course, represents the beautiful, me the bad. But some of my most loyal fans consider me bad and beautiful too."

"So do I, handsome," Minnelli said, flirtatiously. "Why don't you come up and see me sometime?"

"That's not an original line," Kirk said with a smile. Impulsively, he then startled Minnelli by kissing him lightly on his lipstick-painted mouth.

He had long known that the talented director of musicals was gay, later saying, "Vincente was the only director I ever worked with who appeared on the set wearing lipstick. At least he was straight once—long enough to produce Liza Minnelli."

At the time, Minnelli was at the peak of his career, having won an Oscar nod for *An American in Paris* (1951) starring Gene Kelly, with whom he'd fallen in love.

On his first day on the set, Kirk lunched with Lana Turner. At the end of their meal, he predicted, "This is the beginning of a beautiful friendship," borrowing the line from Humphrey Bogart in *Casablanca.*

"There was a desperation about Lana, and she turned to me for assurance," he said. "She hoped we'd have a real sexual chemistry on the screen...and perhaps off, although I was guessing at that point."

"I'm afraid that my career will nosedive if I'm in another flop," she said. "The movie I just finished, *The Merry Widow* (1952), did all right. But now, I want to show I can excel in a modern melodrama without all those lavish costumes that make me look like some god damn mannequin." Then she predicted that their script, a proposed Hollywood-on-Hollywood genre, might bring them acclaim.

Its origin dated back to 1949 when it was published in the *Ladies' Home Journal* as a short story, *Of Good and Evil*, by George Bradshaw. It was later expanded and renamed *Memorial to a Bad Man* and later lengthened and retitled as *A Tribute to a Bad Man*.

Bradshaw had based his story's lead character (producer Jonathan Shields) on the notorious Broadway mogul, Jed Harris, "the Terror of the Great White Way." But when its conversion into a film was assigned to producer John Houseman, he wanted to change the venue from Broadway to Hollywood.

[Houseman's motivation? He didn't want to make another movie about Broadway because of the recent success of All About Eve *(1950), in which its co-stars, Bette Davis and Anne Baxter, had each been cast as Broadway stars, generating performances that earned Oscar nominations for each of them. Wisely, with the intention of not appearing "derivative," he preferred to transpose the story's theme into the more "modern" venue of the film industry.]*

When Lana was signed, with the provision that she would receive top billing, Dore Schary, the new head honcho at MGM, wanted the film's title changed to reflect Lana's public notoriety. The revised title was *The Bad and the Beautiful*. At first, Houseman objected, calling it, "dreadful, loathsome, cheap and vulgar," but after the picture became a hit, he said, "It was one of the greatest titles ever devised."

Whereas both Minnelli and Houseman were desperately eager to bring the script to the screen, MGM's studio chief, Dore Schary *[he had replaced Louis B. Mayer]*, needed to be convinced. He felt that even at best, the picture would be a "B," and consequently allocated it a modest budget of a million dollars. Contractually, he approved of Lana's services for only four weeks of shooting, because he wanted to cast her as a follow up in another Technicolor musical, *Latin Lovers*, alongside her current lover, Fernando Lamas, typecast.

Lana, however, loudly emphasized that her portrayal of Georgia might be the equal of her interpretation of Cora in *The Postman Always Rings Twice* (1946). "I didn't get the Oscar for that, but here's a second chance for me," she told Minnelli.

Minnelli, at the time, was somewhat depressed, coming down from his divorce from Garland. "Many of my friends wondered why I wanted to make such an anti-Hollywood movie," he said. "I told them I didn't see Kirk's role as that of an unregenerate heel—first, because we find out that he has a weakness, which makes him human; and second, because he's as tough on himself as he is on everyone else, which makes him honest. That's the complex, wonderful thing about human beings—whether they're in Hollywood or in the automobile business or in neckties."

The theme song for *The Bad and the Beautiful* was penned by David

Raksin, and it became a jazz standard. A decade later, that same theme was recycled into the musical score of another Kirk movie, *Two Weeks in Another Town.*

In a nutshell, the plot of *The Bad and the Beautiful* centered around Shields and how he used and abused his star, Georgia; his writer, James Lee Bartlow; and his director, Fred Amiel.

Minnelli originally offered the role of Shields to Clark Gable, hoping for another Gable/Turner co-starring package. But the aging King of Hollywood, whose box office allure was slipping, turned it down. Minnelli then presented it to Spencer Tracy, Lana's former co-star, who rejected it. But Kirk, when it was offered to him, accepted immediately. ("I can be ruthless.")

When Lana first heard a layout of the plot, and learned about her character, Georgia Lorrison, she said, "I play a soggy mess, the daughter of a world-famous actor, who is sinking into oblivion, until I'm rescued by an unscrupulous producer, Kirk, who propels me into stardom. I make the

Two views of Lana, an actress desperately trapped in a crazed-with-ambition love affair with her director, as portrayed by Kirk, in *The Bad and the Beautiful.*

big mistake of falling in love with him, the story of my life. I believe in Georgia. Besides, she's a better character than those in the other turkeys presented to me."

Minnelli told Lana that her character was clearly based on the alcoholic Diana Barrymore (1921-1960), daughter of "The Great Profile," John Barrymore. But the buzz in Hollywood suggested that Georgia might be based on any number of stars, former and present. At one point, Jennifer Jones insisted that the character of Georgia Lorrison had been based on her, and that the character of Jonathan Shields had clearly been inspired by her husband, David O. Selznick. Many scenes taken from his own life, she said, had been inserted into the script.

[Selznick, the widely disliked producer of Gone With the Wind, *was not the*

only inspiration for Kirk's character of Shields. Val Lewton, the Russian-American producer and screenwriter, also came to mind. He'd become notorious at RKO for his low-budget horror films, and infamous for his cost-cutting techniques and the abuse of his low-paid actors. His biggest hits had been Cat People (1942), The Curse of the Cat People (1944), and The Body Snatcher (1945), based on a short story by Robert Louis Stevenson.]

In *The Bad and the Beautiful*, Shields and his director, Fred Amiel, are depicted making a low-budget quickie employing "cat people."

A New Yorker, Barry Sullivan having just completed *Payment on Demand* (1951) with Bette Davis, was cast as Amiel. Sullivan had cropped up in films with Lana before, notably in *A Life of Her Own* (1950), *Mr. Imperium* (1951), and later, *Another Time, Another Place* (1958).

In spite of Sullivan's relatively average looks, he would in time co-star with some of Hollywood's other leading ladies, notably Loretta Young, Esther Williams, Jane Wyman, Joan Crawford, and Oliva de Havilland.

A Canadian actor, Walter Pidgeon, was cast as the unflappably genteel producer, trying to diplomatically, and for profit, reunite Shields with the actress and creative team he betrayed.

Charles Schnee was assigned, as a scriptwriter, to adapt Bradshaw's short story about a brouhaha on Broadway into an explosive, gut-wrenching creative crisis in Hollywood.

Schnee had once been a partner in New York's experimental Mercury Theatre, working alongside both Houseman and Orson Welles. His former screen-writing credits had included *Red River* (1948), a hit Western starring John Wayne and Montgomery Clift. In an attempt to guide Shnee in the development of Lana's character, Minnelli instructed him to incorporate some of the (hysterical and overwrought) characteristics of his ex-wife, Judy Garland.

Dick Powell's role as the writer was said to have been inspired by Paul Elliot Green, an academic turned screen writer whose main credit had been *Cabin in the Cotton* (1932), starring a very young Bette Davis *["I'd kiss ya, but I've just washed my hair."]*

Leo G. Carroll played director Henry Whitfield, modeling his character on Alfred Hitchcock, with whom he'd worked in several pictures, including *Rebecca* (1940) with Joan Fontaine and Laurence Olivier.

As secondary players, Minnelli lined up some superlative talent. They included some big name stars whose careers were in decline..

A sultry blonde, Gloria Grahame, played Rosemary Bartlow, Powell's wife. Her character was defined by one critic as "a Southern belle with calculated *cutesy-poo* mannerisms." She betrays her husband in the movie and runs off with the fading Mexican matinee idol, Victor ("Gaucho") Ribera, as portrayed by Gilbert Roland. Together, they escape from Los Angeles in a plane that crashes and kills them both.

Other luscious females cast into secondary roles included Elaine Stewart as Lila and Vanessa Brown as Kay Amiel, the wife of the character portrayed by Sullivan. Stewart plays a ruthlessly ambitious starlet who engineers a fling with Shields. With measurements of 34-25-36, she later appeared in Hugh Hefner's *Playboy*.

Born in Vienna, Jennifer Brown and her Jewish family had fled to Paris to escape persecution from the Nazis after their takeover of Austria in 1938. Thanks partly to her IQ of 165, she'd already been a star on the radio series, *Quiz Kids*.

In a pivotal scene at the end of the movie, Barry Sullivan (left), Lana, and Dick Powell eavesdrop on a phone conversation that producer Walter Pidgeon is having with Jonathan Shields (Kirk).

Although Shields has betrayed each of them in separate ways, it is sort of obvious that they are going to agree to be sucked into his whirlpool again—and work on his latest film.

On the set, Kirk had a reunion with Paul Stewart, cast as Syd Murphy. He and Kirk had worked together on *Champion*. "We did pretty well with that one, and my gut tells me you've got a hit with *The Bad and the Beautiful* too." Stewart said.

"Incidentally, I've talked with Stanley Kramer. He's already cast me in a film, *The Juggler,* to be shot in Israel. He wants you for the lead—or at least he's considering you."

"That's the first I've heard of it," Kirk said. "There could be a problem, though. The only thing I know how to juggle is my balls."

Kirk had a strange encounter on the set with the once very famous Francis X. Bushman, who had been assigned to a small role. Throughout most of the 1910s and 1920s, during the film industry's silent era and long before Clark Gable, Bushman had been hailed as "The King of Hollywood."

[Kirk quickly surmised, on seeing him, that that had happened a long long time ago. During his heyday, Bushman received so much fan mail that he hired a young woman as his secretary. She was none other than Louella Parsons.]

Bushman had been a big star at MGM until he angered Louis B. Mayer by making him wait two minutes. "I was banished for twenty-five years," he told Kirk. As they were chatting, an aging grip called out to him, "Welcome back, Francis!"

Kirk had seen Bushman in *Ben-Hur,* the most lavish spectacle of the 1920s, when it was re-released in a revival theater. Bushman had portrayed the malevolent character of Messala. Ben-Hur had been portrayed by Ramon Novarro, a gay actor who was notoriously bludgeoned to death in his apartment (in 1968) by two male prostitues. There was a certain irony here: When *Ben-Hur* was reprised for a re-release in 1959, Kirk would be offered (and would refuse) Bushman's role of Messala.

Paul Stewart..."You don't have to have a pretty face to succeed in movies."

In his capacity as author of the short story that had inspired it, Bradshaw had wanted to write the screenplay for *The Bad and the Beautiful* too, but Minnelli had turned him down. He was hired, however, to produce a fifty-page scenario of his original story with amplifications. Minnelli hoped to cull from the scenario some additional material to add to the screenplay already in production by Charles Schnee.

Bradshaw was gay, as was his closest friend, the TV producer, Rogers Brackett, who at the time had a live-in lover, the then-unknown James Dean. Brackett had been supporting him and procuring minor jobs for him in TV. Before that, Dean had been a street hustler. Although Bradshaw did not like Dean personally, feeling that he was exploiting Brackett, he ultimately relented to his friend's plea, "Please write in a small part for Jimmy."

Bradshaw followed through and created a pivotal role for Dean.

It was inserted into one of the key moments in the film: After a triumphant win at the Oscars, Lana's character of Georgia Lorrison arrives, uninvited and unannounced at the mansion of Jonathan Shields. There, to her horror, she encounters his new lover. According to Bradshaw's early vision of the scene, as tailor-made for James Dean, it is not a sultry female brunette who emerges from his bedroom at the top of the stairs, as was depicted in the film's final cut.

Instead, the interloper was obviously a gay male: James Dean, provocatively undressed, wearing only a snug pair of white boxer shorts.

Francis X. Bushman, as he'd appeared in the silent version of *Ben-Hur* in 1925.

Bradshaw invited Kirk to his apartment for a presentation of the then-scenario of the movie, as he had composed it to that point. He justified the homoerotic aspect of Dean's brief insertion into the script as follows: "To pull off Lana's later hysterical breakdown in the moving car, I felt that the script needed something more startling than just a beautiful, seductive tart at the top of the stairs. A producer who's fucking a starlet… that's nothing but a big, boring *cliché*. Come on…it's about time we started defying the Production Code. Let's face it: It's 1951, not 1934."

James Dean in *Giant* (1956).

He lost the chance to be cast as the lover of the character portrayed by Kirk in *The Bad and the Beautiful*.

Kirk said, "I'd like to play such a scene. It might get a lot of press and beef up box-office. But will the Production Code allow it? I think not!"

He was right. The character was reformatted into a sultry (female) brunette, Elaine Stewart, who emoted provocatively from her position at the top of the stairs.

Kirk hardly thought about Dean after his role in *The Bad and the Beautiful* was eliminated and a woman shoehorned into place instead. Little did he know that Dean would become a competing figure in one of his most disastrous—perhaps the most disastrous—of his love affairs.

***

Lana was eager to begin working with Kirk, telling Minnelli, "I think we'd make a dynamic duo on the screen, perhaps generate as much body heat as John Garfield and I did in *Postman.*" She'd been impressed with Kirk ever since she'd seen him opposite Barbara Stanwyck in *The Strange Love of Martha Ivers* (1946).

After about a week of shooting, the gossip maven, Hedda Hopper, arrived on the set, interrupting a conversation between Kirk and Lana. "I hear you kids may have a poten-

Elaine Stewart, insulting Lana, invading her space, and pushing her to the brink of madness in *The Bad and the Beautiful* (1952)

tial hit on your hands."

Then she turned to Kirk. "But I still think you're a son of a bitch."

"I've always been a son of a bitch," he answered. "But what about Lana here? Who is she?"

"Drop the 'son of'…and you've nailed her," Hopper said, before turning her back on the stars of the picture and walking away.

***

Lana always appears on those lists of Kirk's seductions, despite denials from each of them that they never had an affair during the filming of *The Bad and the Beautiful.*

In his memoir, Kirk wrote, "I was ready for it," meaning a seduction of Lana. "But she was going with Fernando Lamas, who was terribly jealous. He was always around. Nothing happened."

Again, he was being discreet. Lana told a different story to Minnelli, Ava Gardner, and Walter Pidgeon, all of whom knew her well.

Kirk admitted that he liked Lana…liked her "a whole lot. The only thing I didn't like was that MGM was giving her star billing over me."

Lamas certainly wasn't hanging around the set as Kirk claimed. For verification, one could ask Dolores del Rio, Arlene Dahl, or Esther Williams. Lamas had once told the press, "I got into movies to meet broads, and I'm a great Latin lover. Evita Perón, the co-dictator of my native land, Argentina, can vouch for that."

Rumors became so rampant in Hollywood about their alleged affair that Lana placed a call to Louella Parsons, who had suggested, in print, many times that Lana tended to seduce her leading men. "I never see Kirk after we close down the set for the day. Yet items keep appearing in the press about us having an affair. I'm in love with Fernando Lamas, and no other man means a thing to me."

Kirk continued to deny an affair with Lana. Were they telling the truth? After all, she regularly denied affairs with Clark Gable, Robert Taylor, and many others. Witnesses on the set, including Minnelli and such observers as co-star Dick Powell, claimed that she did have an affair with Kirk. "What Lana told Parsons was true: *i.e.,* that she never saw Kirk after working hours," Minnelli said. "But what about those long visits to her dressing room with its pink satin sheets, when they weren't needed on the set by me? Esther Williams always seemed to have that empty glass against the wall of Lana's dressing room, listening. She said they did have an affair, but one far more subdued than the rowdy sex with Lamas."

***

The most artfully histrionic sequence in *The Bad and the Beautiful* occurs when Lana, as the rejected Georgia Lorrison, becomes hysterical while fleeing in her car after being confronted with the infidelities of Kirk's character, Jonathan Shields.

She has begged Shields for time alone with him (just the two of them), but Elaine Stewart, as the ambitious starlet, has just appeared at the top of his stairwell, and Kirk as Shields has just kicked her (Lana, as Georgia), out of his house. What emerged on celluloid became one of the most iconic scenes in motion picture history.

In preparation for its filming, Minnelli had wrapped every other scene in the picture, with the exception of Lana's near-fatal flight from Shields' house. During the scene, she's screaming, thrashing, and sobbing hysterically behind the wheel of a moving car. Minnelli allowed her three weeks off before he was ready to bring her back to the studio for the filming of that complicated scene.

By then, Kirk had moved on to other projects, shooting *The Story of Three Loves* (1953); and Sullivan had departed for the filming of *Jeopardy* (also 1953) with Barbara Stanwyck.

***

MGM didn't mind sounding a bit sleazy in its advertising of The Bad and the Beautiful. Included among its headlines was: *NO HOLDS BARRED IN THIS STORY OF A BLONDE WHO WANTED TO GO PLACES …AND A BIG SHOT WHO GOT HER THERE THE HARD WAY!*

After its release, producer David O. Selznick was seen sneaking into a movie house in Pacific Palisades. He was debating whether he should sue Metro-Goldwyn-Mayer for libel for the movie script's parallels to the character portrayed by Kirk. As Selznick sat through it, he did indeed recognize himself in the character of Jonathon Shields, including his habit of kicking off his shoes.

John Houseman had also suffered working for Selznick, and in some respects, Selznick interpreted it as Houseman's revenge. "For John, it's payback time."

David Thomson, Selznick's biographer, wrote, "He huffed and puffed, not sure whether to be flattered or offended by Kirk's portrayal. After thinking it over for several days, he decided not to sue MGM."

One critic defined *The Bad and the Beautiful* as "The most exacting detailed study of the dream factory ever presented in the movies from the grand homes of the stars to the funeral of Shields' father, where he pays mourners to show up."

At 5'9", Kirk wanted to cover up his shortness, so he wore lifts. In some scenes, that distorted his walking, and in some long shots, you can even spot the lifts.

***

Kirk did admit to having a one-night stand with Gloria Grahame. "It's not the sexy way I'm looking at you, it's the thought behind my look," she told him.

"Tell me more," he urged.

"The reason I look sexy on the screen is that I think about getting screwed as I play a role."

He had found Grahame intriguing ever since she'd been embroiled in a Hollywood scandal with her then-husband, director Nicholas Ray, and with his thirteen-year-old son, Tony.

The teenager came to visit his father one day and found Grahame—his new stepmother whom he'd never met before—home alone. His father was still at the studio.

Within a few hours of their first encounter, Tony was in bed fornicating with her. At that spectacularly embarrassing moment, Ray walked in and caught them in the act.

He kicked his son out of the house and divorced Grahame.

When the boy came of age, she married him.

When Kirk asked her about the scandal, she was frank: "I've had a lot of big-name stars, including Robert Mitchum. My sister is married to Bob's brother. Of all my conquests, thirteen-year-old Tony beat hell out of them all."

After that, Kirk always viewed Grahame with a certain fascination.

Later, Kris Kristofferson said, "Grahame is sexy in a strange way. Like a woman begging you to wallop her in the mouth 'cause she'd just love it."

Gloria Grahame. Kirk wanted to know, "Am I better sex than your thirteen-year-old stepson?"

After *The Bad and the Beautiful,* Cecil B. DeMille cast Grahame in *The Greatest Show on Earth,* which was voted Best Picture of 1952. In reference to her, the director said, "Gloria has the manners of a schoolgirl, but the eyes of a sorceress."

***

Kirk received almost universal praise for his performance as Jonathan Shields. *["I'm going to ram the name of Shields down their throats," was a line in the film that he passionately and memorably delivered.]*

Newsweek claimed that his performance was "close to perfection, a role calculated to make almost any Hollywood actor wince while he works. Douglas blends *chutzpah* and wracking self-disgust."

Critic Tony Thomas wrote, "The role was a *tour de force* for Kirk Douglas. One of

Albert Johnson in *Film Quarterly* said it best:

"*Lana Turner emerges from the mansion in white ermine and drives away. Her sobs soon build to hysteria, and lights of cars send flashes across the windows as she reaches a moment of unbearable frenzy. She releases the steering wheel entirely, and screams in emotional agony. Her foot presses the brake. One hears only her screams, the honking of passing auto-horns, and, suddenly, it's raining.*"

"*The car bumps along uncontrollably for a second, then comes to a standstill. Turner falls over the wheel, still sobbing uncontrollably as the sequence fades. It is superb theater, one of the great moments of human despair shown in cinematic terms and a prime example of the coordination of actress, director, and cameraman which can create a perfect moment of dramatic poetry upon the screen.*"

the meatiest ever handed to a Hollywood actor—not only a subtle, dramatic vehicle, but an opportunity to reveal the character of the kind of film producer the actors know but do not love. The casting is almost beyond questioning."

Bosley Crowther of *The New York Times* weighed in with: "Kirk Douglas is best as the producer—a glib, restless, unrelenting gent whose energies and resources are matched only by his perfidy and gall. Granted that the producer is an extreme and eccentric type, he is nonetheless realistic and reflective of many legends of 'genius.'"

Crowther of *The New York Times* continued with a denunciation of Kirk's co-star: "Lana Turner is an actress playing an actress and neither one is real. A howling act in a wildly racing auto—pure punk—is the top of her speed."

Many other reviewers disagreed, claiming that Lana's car scene was one of the most exciting sequences in a picture in a decade. Author Jeanine Basinger wrote: "None of the sex symbols who have been touted as actresses—not Rita Hayworth or Ava Gardner or Elizabeth Taylor or Marilyn Monroe—have ever given such a fine performance as Lana did in *The Bad and the Beautiful.*"

The *Los Angeles Times* wrote: "The film is *What Makes Sammy Run?* and has the bitter flavor of *Sunset Blvd.* and *All About Eve* and, like the latter, is told in flashbacks by Shields' victims."

***

The night before the Academy Award nominees were announced, Lana threw a party to celebrate *The Bad and the Beautiful.* She staunchly believed that it, along with her performance within it, would be nominated for Oscars. "I've waited a long time for this," she told Kirk and others. But after the nominees were announced, and she was not included among them, she sank into despair. The other nominees included Lana's friend, Susan Hayward, for *With a Song in My Heart,* as well as Joan Crawford for *Sudden Fear,* Bette Davis for *The Star,* and Julie Harris for *The Member of the Wedding.* Shirley Booth would ultimately walk off with the Oscar for her role in *Come Back, Little Sheba.*

Kirk had seen Lana before the nominations were announced. Whereas he'd been nominated as Best Actor for his performance in *The Bad and the Beautiful,* he lost the award to Gary Cooper for *High Noon.* The other nominees included Marlon Brando for *Viva Zapata!;* Alec Guinness for *The Lavender Hill Mob;* and José Ferrer for his stunning portrayal of Toulouse-Lautrec in *Moulin Rouge.*

The cast and crew of *The Bad and the Beautiful* had high hopes that it would be nominated for Best Picture of the Year, but it wasn't. That year's Best Picture was awarded to Cecil B. DeMille's *The Greatest Show on Earth,* starring Betty Hutton, Cornel Wilde, James Stewart, Dorothy Lamour, and Gloria Grahame. Grahame did win the Best Supporting Actress Oscar, not for the circus picture, but for the character she portrayed in *The Bad and the Beautiful.*

The picture did, however, win a number of minor Oscars: Robert Surtees for Black and White Cinematography; Helen Rose for Best Black and White Costume Design; Charles Schnee for Best Adapted Screenplay; and Cedric Gibbons, Edward Carfagno, Edwin B. Willis, and Keogh Gleason for Art Direction and Set Decorations.

Lana complained to Kirk, "We might at least have been nominated, but Dore Schary was against us from the beginning. He doesn't think much of me as an actress, and he did absolutely nothing to sell our picture to the Academy, whereas other studios were wildly promoting their selections. It's not fair!"

"You should have won that Oscar," she went on. "It's Schary's fault, that bastard, and his message pictures. Regrettably, roles like my Georgia Lorrison and your Jonathan Shields come along as rarely as a true, everlasting love."

In a 1972 interview in *Films and Filming*, Kirk said, "Minnelli did a wonderful job, since it's very difficult to make a film about filmmaking. Somehow, you'd think it would be easy for filmmakers to do that, but most of the attempts seem false, and I thought *The Bad and the Beautiful* was an exception: a pretty honest movie."

***

When Kirk was presented with his next role, he was unaware that he would fall for the girl on the flying trapeze.

Pier Angeli with Kirk Douglas in *The Story of Three Loves* (1953).

CHAPTER NINE

PIER ANGELI,
HOLLYWOOD'S PERPETUAL *INGÉNUE*

SWINGING HIGH ON A FLYING TRAPEZE, KIRK FALLS IN LOVE.
SHE'S UNCLEAR, EVASIVE, AND ROMANTICALLY UNFOCUSED
KIRK LATER DEFINES THEIR ENGAGEMENT AS "A BIG MISTAKE"

THE JUGGLER

KIRK'S INVASION OF ISRAEL: FOR THE FIRST TIME, HE'S CAST AS A JEW

ULYSSES

KIRK, LIKE THE MYTHICAL HERO OF THE ODYSSEY,
WANDERS THROUGH EUROPE AS A TAX EXILE

ANNE BUYDENS

TORN BETWEEN TWO LOVERS, KIRK MEETS THE WOMAN HE'LL EVENTUALLY
MARRY. (SHE'S HANDLING PUBLICITY FOR *ULYSSES*.)

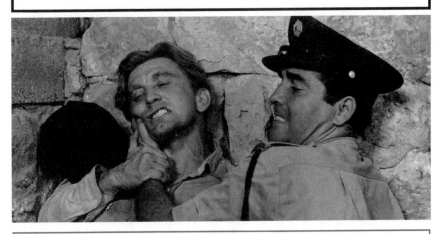

As reviewed by Michael Atkinson, "*The Juggler*...is a modest movie fairly oozing with a strange and unique confluence of historical markers. It was the first Hollywood film shot in the newly minted nation of Israel....It confronts a relocated concentration camp survivor (Kirk) unable to overcome his war-borne fears and neuroses."

Kirk defined his involvement in the film as one of the key elements that helped him get a grip on his self-identity as a Jew.

The director, Sidney Franklin, born in San Francisco in 1893, had helmed his first movie in 1916 and worked with many legends from the film industry's silent era. They had included Mary Pickford in *The Hoodlum* (1919); and Greta Garbo in *Wild Orchids* (1929). Later, he'd directed, Louise Rainer and Paul Muni in *The Good Earth* (1937). Long associated with the successful adaptation of novels and stage plays into high-grossing Hollywood films, and eager to work with some of the emerging stars of the 1950s, Franklin was deeply impressed with Kirk's potential as a screen actor.

Over lunch with him, Franklin pitched a romantic trilogy entitled *The Story of Three Loves,* an anthology of three loosely interconnected love stories, two of them doomed, one of which would succeed. Their sub-sections were entitled *The Jealous Lover, Mademoiselle,* and *Equilibrium.* The last of these would star Kirk as a guilt-ridden trapeze artist named Pierre Narval. With an all-star cast, with one of the most impressive lineups of talent for any movie released in 1953, the film would be distributed by Metro-Goldwyn-Mayer.

According to the story line of *Equilibrium,* Narval was at a low point in his career. As a means of increasing ticket sales, he had experimented with increasingly dangerous aerial techniques, one of which had led to the death, two years before, of his partner. Disgraced in the aftermath of his accidental death, no other trapeze artist would work with him.

Kirk was intrigued with the idea of being the man on the high-flying trapeze. He'd read in *Variety* that Ricardo Montalban, the Mexican actor, had already been assigned the role, but that it wasn't going well for him.

Before signing, Kirk visited Montalban, who had been rehearsing the role for weeks. "I just can't seem to make it," he confessed, "and I've already told Franklin that the part isn't right for me. To hell with it—the role is yours. Here's just a word of advice: Don't break your neck."

After he signed, Kirk was given a copy of the complete script, the work of six different writers. The stories within the trilogy begin aboard a cruise ship as each of three protagonists—a ballet choreographer, a governess, and a trapeze artist—recollect the nuances of their previous love affairs.

Berlin-born Gottfried Reinhardt, son of the fabled Austrian theater director Max Reinhardt, would direct two of the segments (*The Jealous Lover* and *The Trapeze Artist*) within the trilogy. After fleeing from Nazi Germany, and as a newcomer to Hollywood, he had worked as an assistant to Ernst Lubitsch and had helmed Greta Garbo in her final film, *Two-Faced Woman* (1941). In 1961, he'd direct Kirk again in *Town Without Pity.*

In *The Jealous Lover,* James Mason was cast as Charles Coutray, a ballet composer and impresario who's enamored of a ballerina, Paula Woodward (Moira Shearer). Her ferociously protective guardian, Aunt Lydia (Agnes Moorehead), tries to prevent her from performing, arguing that her weak heart might lead to a fatal stroke. (It does.)

Kirk bonded with Mason and would soon work with him, co-starring in an adventure story for Walt Disney.

A British actor from Yorkshire, Mason had been the top box office attraction in the U.K. during the closing months of World War II. He was known for his "languid but impassioned" vocal talent and for his brooding anti-heroes in melodramas that had included *The Wicked Lady* (1945). He

Three Loves: Vignette #1:
"THE JEALOUS LOVER," a ballet drama pitting James Mason against the Scottish ballerina Moira Shearer.

Three Loves: Vignette #2:
"MADEMOISELLE" When a witch grants the wish of a horny eleven-year-old to transform himself into an adult man, he emerges as Farley Granger in the photo above on the lower right

The object of his affection? She's French, she's his former governess, and she's portrayed by Leslie Caron, who became world-famous five years later for her performance in the title role of *Gigi* (1958).

would soon be assigned a role that Kirk envied, playing opposite Judy Garland in *A Star Is Born* (1955).

The celebrated international ballerina, Moira Shearer, born in Scotland, had first achieved fame in *The Red Shoes* (1948) as Victoria Page. That was followed in 1951 by *The Tales of Hoffman*.

Although Agnes Moorehead attained her greatest fame as Endora, a witch, in the hit TV series, *Bewitched* (1964-1972), she was a distinguished actress known for her chilly portrayals of haughty, arrogant characters. In 1937, she'd joined Orson Welles' Mercury Theater. He later cast her in *Citizen Kane* (1941), one of the best films ever made.

The trilogy's second episode, *Mademoiselle*, featured Ethel Barrymore, the First Lady of the American Theater, playing a witch, Mrs. Hazel Pennicott. The role of the beautiful French governess, "Mademoiselle," starred the Parisian actress and dancer, Leslie Caron. She had just achieved renown with Gene Kelly in *An American in Paris* (1951). In time, she'd be one of the few dancers who performed not only with Kelly, but with Fred Astaire, Mikhail Baryshnikov, and Rudolf Nureyev.

The whimsical plot of *Mademoiselle* centered around the wish that Ethel Barrymore granted to a bored eleven-year-old, Tommy, as played by Ricky Nelson. She grants his unusual request: He wants to be transformed, now, into a man. She instructs him to wrap a ribbon around his finger and to say her name at 8PM. PRESTO! He becomes Thomas Clayton Campbell, a handsome young man, Farley Granger, who'll remain in that incarnation, but only until midnight. During those precious hours, he falls in love with his governess (Caron), whom he has intensely disliked until that magic moment.

The authors of this book confess that they are diehard fans of Zsa Zsa Gabor, the "Bombshell from Budapest" whose life was reviewed in a 2013 biography from Blood Moon Productions.

She appears in Vignette #2 ("Mademoiselle") as part of a two-minute cameo, flirting (unsucessfully) at a bar with Farley Granger, who plays his scene less skillfully than she plays hers.

The always-fascinating Zsa Zsa Gabor, the Bombshell from Budapest, appears in a brief scene with Granger as a flirtatious and desirable woman at a bar.

Vincente Minnelli, who had just helmed Kirk in *The Bad and the Beautiful*, directed *Mademoiselle*.

In the segment that most intrigued Kirk (*The Trapeze Artist*), a nineteen-year-old Italian actress, Pier Angeli, was cast into the role of Nina Burkhardt. Early in the episode, Kirk rescues her after her attempted suicide. (He hauls her, half-dead, out of the Seine in Paris.) Her husband has been murdered by the Nazis, and she is morose and guilt-ridden.

As she seems to have no fear about dying, he asks her to join him in his death-defying gig as a trapeze artist. When she agrees, he begins training her on the high wire, although his friends predict that his latest obsession will kill her, too.

Richard Anderson had the segment's third lead as Marcel, a friend of Nina. Anderson would later appear in one of Kirk's best-known dramas, the anti-war *Paths of Glory* (1957).

In his early conceptualizations of *The Trapeze Artist*, Reinhardt had envisioned its stars to merely stand on a high-wire platform wearing tight-fitting leotards. It was understood that the dangerous aerial stunts would be executed by professional circus performers who eventually included a high-wire acrobat named Harold Voise.

Voise, however, soon learned that Kirk wanted to perform some of his own stunts. "He was one fast learner," Voise said, "like nothing I'd ever seen before. He even learned to do the tricky bird's nest, which had him swinging by his calves, body arched up, and crossing over to another acrobat, who would 'catch' him. He also learned how to make a 'crossover' from one catcher to another."

As Kirk described in a memoir, "I swung back, turning around in midair, catching the bar that was hurled to me, and then swinging back to the platform."

As for his female co-star,

Three Loves: Vignette #3

"THE TRAPEZE ARTIST" Survivors of wartime tragedies reconcile their respective anguish in high-wire circus acts whose dangers bring them back to a respect for art, romance, and life itself.

Depicted above are its stars, Pier Angeli and Kirk Douglas.

Colliers magazine had gushed: "In Pier Angeli, a nineteen-year-old Italian girl, Hollywood has found an actress who eludes the town's traditional classifications and whose unvarnished beauty have already caused her to be called 'The New Garbo.'"

What impressed Kirk was how quickly Pier, too, learned to perform high above the ground. "She was frail-looking with her lovely face and dark eyes, a true Renaissance Madonna, but she had guts," he said. "I fell in love with her as she was swinging on the trapeze. Before the end of the picture, I was engaged to her."

Athletically gifted, Kirk even did most of his own stunts.

On the final day of rehearsal for their new high-altitude gig, their boss insists that their climax be particularly spectacular and death-defying, a "Leap of Death," without a safety net, in front of a live audience. They succeed, but then Narval decides that as a couple united in love, they'll quit the circus and walk away to a happy future together. Back aboard that cruise ship, Narval is joined by Nina, who by now has fallen in love with him.

In reference to *Trapeze Artist*, critic Dennis Schwartz wrote, "This glossy art film bombed at the box office, even though it was a decent middle-brow piece, with fine acting and lots of star power, best represented by Kirk Douglas."

Sanderson Beck wrote, "The movie is about love and romance, but even more than that, it's about artistry and its appreciation, whether it be music and dance or poetry or death-defying performance."

The sets, as devised by Cedric Gibbons, the leading scenic designer in Hollywood, would be Oscar-nominated.

***

[*"My role in* Three Loves *came before the Burt Lancaster 1956* Trapeze," Kirk wrote. "I went to the set during the shoot. Burt had been a circus acrobat and gymnast, so he didn't have to go through all the training that a neophyte like me had to do. Why was I there? I'll tell you if you must know. I wanted to make sure he wasn't padding his crotch to make himself look bigger than me.}*

***

Kirk was not alone in his pursuit of Pier Angeli. He faced competition from Vic Damone, a popular singer of the 1950s. Columnist Dorothy Kilgallen wrote that Damone "haunted the set" where *The Story of Three Loves* was being filmed. On three separate occasions, Damone and Pier were seen dancing together at the Mocambo.

Even in his postwar stint in the U.S. Army, while stationed in Munich, Damone had dated Angeli during her filming of *The Devil Makes Three* (1952) with Gene Kelly.

Only two weeks later, Kilgallen reported that Kirk had been spotted at Jack's on the Beach, "feeding fish" to Pier.

As Kirk and Pier increased the frequency of their dating, MGM publicists took advantage of their off-screen romance to promote their latest film. Pictures of them as trapeze acrobats in tight-fitting costumes ran in newspapers throughout the country.

As their courtship intensified, Pier invited him home to meet her formidable mother, Enrica Pierangeli, who seemed hysterically intent on safeguarding the virginity of her daughters. *[Pier's twin sister had changed her name to Marisa Pavan. Like her sister, Pavan had signed a studio contract at the age of nineteen.]*

When Kirk arrived at the family's home, Enrica was still in the kitchen and did not immediately appear. Pier invited him into the garden, where he spotted Pavan, strolling arm in arm with the Italian film director, Vittorio de Sica. "If anything, Marisa was even lovelier than Pier," Kirk remembered.

As it later turned out, although Enrica did not object to her daughters dating older men, de Sica was not Pavan's lover, but a trusted family friend from Italy. He had introduced Pier to the movie-going public through her debut in the film he'd directed, *Domani è troppo tardi* in 1950.

To some degree, Kirk was already aware of de Sica's career as a neorealist film director, having seen *The Bicycle Thief* (1947). In time, Turner Classic Movies would cite it as one of the fifteen most influential movies in cinematic his-

In the mid-1950s, Kirk began aggressively networking with European film directors, one of whom was Vittorio de Sica.

He's depicted above with Sophia Loren in this publicity still from *Pane, Amore e (Scandal in Sorrento;* 1955).

301

tory.

At the time, Kirk was on the verge of spending eighteen months outside the U.S. as a bona fide "tax exile," part of tax-avoidance scheme that was both in vogue and legal at the time. During drinks with de Sica, he told him about his plan, and then said, "Right now, based on U.S. tax laws and how I might benefit from them, I'm searching for scripts in movies that will be shot overseas—especially in Europe."

De Sica promised to introduce him to two director/producers, each a friend of his, Dino de Laurentiis and Carlo Ponti. "I heard they're planning to adapt Homer's *Odyssey* into a film. Perhaps they'll cast you into the lead if you don't mind doing a striptease in one of those skimpy costumes."

During dinner, Enrica was exceedingly polite to Kirk. She beamed at his lavish praise of her Italian cooking, and her "beautiful, elegant daughters." Yet when he left, she was highly critical of him, telling Pier, "He's far too old for you. You'll still be a young girl when he's a grandfather."

[Kirk was sixteen years older than Pier.]

"You'll need to find a God-fearing Catholic boy to marry and give you good Catholic children, not this Jew." Enrica scolded. "That is the will of God."

***

Since Marisa Pavan and Pier Angeli were twins and under roughly equivalent film contracts, Kirk wondered if they'd compete for the same roles, and perhaps for the same men. "If you could go for one, you might also fall under the other's spell," he said.

Actually, his prediction came true during the filming of Tennessee Williams' *The Rose Tattoo* (1956), co-starring Burt Lancaster and Anna Magnani.

The role of the daughter had first been assigned to Pier, but she suddenly became unavailable because of another film commitment. Pavan was called in to replace her and performed so well that she received an Oscar nomination for Best Supporting Actress.

When Vic Damone realized that Pier and Kirk were getting serious and had informally become engaged, he turned his romantic intentions away from Pier and toward Marisa Pavan instead.

[The Damone/Pavan romance lasted only until the dashing French actor, Jean-Pierre Aumont, entered her life. He fell for her and they were married in 1956. In marked contrast to Pier and her many tragic affairs, Pavan and Aumont produced two sons and remained married until his death in 2001.

Pavan's last role on the big screen was in a secondary role Solomon and

Sheba (1959). The epic would be largely forgotten today were it not for the sudden death of its matinee idol star, Tyrone Power. During one of its dueling scenes, he suffered a fatal heart attack. Yul Brynner was called in to replace him, co-starring with Gina Lollobrigida.

Pier was long dead when Kirk re-entered Pavan's life. They'd been cast as Alex and Celia Vandervoort in a four-part TV series (1976) The Moneychangers, *based on Alex Hailey's bestselling novel.]*

***

By now, Kirk had advanced deep into business negotiations with film producers De Laurentiis and Ponti, who seemed willing to include him as the star in at least eighteen months of film projects in Israel, France, and Italy—sufficient to qualify him as a U.S. "tax exile" as defined by the IRS at the time.

He'd begin his offshore residency with a short sojourn in Rome. En route, from California, he organized a stopover in New York City for a reunion with his sons, Michael and Joel. They were being reared by his divorced wife, Diana Dill, in a modest Manhattan apartment on 86th Street.

Perhaps feeling guilty for the neglect of his sons, he met with a realtor to discuss the purchase of a five-story brownstone that was on the market for $90,000. He believed that in a few years, when his boys came of age, the property would be worth "a cool million, perhaps a lot more." From all predictions, the value of Manhattan real estate—if it were in the right neighborhood—would soar.

His aim involved putting the deed in the name of his sons. But when he proposed that, Diana strenuously objected, demanding that the building be listed in her name instead.

"But what if you marry again, and your new husband runs into financial trouble? He might sell the property, and my boys would be out on the street."

After a long argument, she held to her demand. That gift to his sons never materialized. Later, the property sold for three million dollars.

In disappointment, he returned to his suite at the Sherry-Netherland.

He read in Dorothy Kilgallen's column that Marlene Dietrich was in town, staying at the Waldorf Astoria. He called her.

She seemed delighted to hear from him. "I have several places I want to go, and I need a handsome beau on my arm."

With regrets, he told her that he'd booked a flight to Italy and that it was scheduled for departure later that day.

In response, she said she'd be over to see him off, and that they'd have

303

a conversation to catch up on old times in a limousine, in which she'd ride with him to Idlewild airport and then, after leaving him at the airport, she'd use to return to Manhattan.

Within the hour, clad in a beautifully tailored, olive-colored pants suit with a pink scarf, she entered his suite at the Sherry-Netherland. He took her in his arms to kiss her. He'd have advanced further than that were it not for a phone call from the driver announcing that his limo had arrived.

En route to Idlewild, and in the back seat of the car, "we made cuddly love," he later confessed. Actually, Marlene asked him to remove his jacket to cover her head as she demonstrated her time-tested oral skills in the moving car. When he had climaxed and it was over, she pronounced, "Now that's a proper send-off for my lover boy."

[As has been widely printed in many sources, Dietrich had performed fellatio on many a soldier (or general) in the back seat of a Jeep or Army vehicle when she entertained the American troops in World War II.

As reported by biographer Mart Martin, "Dietrich preferred fellatio, as she felt it allowed her to control the situation. According to her husband, Rudy Sieber, she met George Bernard Shaw only once. As was her custom on meeting and talking with someone with whom she was impressed, Dietrich knelt at his feet, unbuttoned his fly, and removed his penis. "Of course, I had to do it before we could talk," she said.]

As he exited from the car and headed into the airport to check in for his flight, leaving her behind for her own return to her hotel, both of them agreed, as very understanding friends, to meet again whenever their schedules coincided.

Within less than an hour, Kirk Douglas, aged thirty-five, was airborne on his inaugural flight to Europe, the first of many more to come. He had scheduled a reunion with Pier, his informally designated bride-to-be, for the first evening of his arrival in Rome. "She'd be on her native soil and could show me Rome. I was excited like a kid. The adventures in store for me could only be imagined."

***

At Rome's Fiumicino Airport, as he stepped on European soil for the first time with the intention of continuing on in a few days to begin a film project in Israel, Kirk remained filled with a sense of joy and excitement. If all the deals he'd pre-arranged worked out, he'd be shooting a trio of movies in locations that included Israel, France, and Italy. His eighteen-month status as an American "tax exile" had begun.

He eagerly anticipated a reunion with Pier, hopefully without her dreadful mother in the background.

Outside of customs, two young Italians, representatives from the De Laurentiis-Ponti film company, were waiting to greet him. They informed him that both of their bosses were eager for him, a bigtime American movie star, to play the lead—beginning in a few months—in their upcoming production based on Homer's *Odyssey*.

He was asked if he spoke Italian, and he assured each of the men that he did. Fortunately, they kept the conversation in English, since he spoke only a few words of Italian. He planned to learn it before the beginning of filming. Perhaps Pier would teach him.

The representatives had booked a suite for him at the very upscale Excelsior Hotel—a favorite of visiting movie stars. A distinguishing characteristic involved its location astride the Via Veneto, where hundreds of good-looking denizens of "Hollywood on the Tiber" paraded every night, patronizing the avenue's stylish cafés and gossiping outrageously. Rome was vibrant and alive, and Kirk wanted to check it out.

Anthony Quinn, Kirk's future co-star in *Ulysses,* had fond memories of the Via Veneto. He recalled that on any night you might encounter Ingrid Bergman, William Holden, Gene Kelly, Errol Flynn, Anna Magnani, Audrey Hepburn, Gary Cooper, Gregory Peck, Jennifer Jones, "and our upcoming leading lady in *Ulysses,* Silvana Mangano."

According to Quinn, "As Kirk paraded along, he was the most successful, overwhelming everyone with his infectious enthusiasm. He and I, one night, played a game of one-upmanship as a gauge of how well our star power measured up. With the understanding that a big star would receive all kinds of offers during the course of just strolling along, directors and producers were all over the place every night. We decided to walk from the Excelsior to the Porta Pinciana and back. Kirk topped me with nineteen movie offers. That was two more than I got."

On his first night in town, Kirk tried to connect by phone to Pier. First, he called her apartment where she lived with her mother, Enrica. An aging male voice came on the line, speaking almost no English at all. From what Kirk understood, Pier and her mother were in Venice, staying at the Gritti Palace. He wasn't able to speak to her until the following morning, when she called him.

She immediately apologized for not meeting him in Rome, claiming that her sister and mother had insisted that she accompany them to Venice.

He told her that he'd join her there at once, despite her preference for wanting to postpone their reunion until after he shot *The Juggler* in Israel.

He responded, "I'm coming anyway. I want to see you. No excuses."

Planes departed every hour from Rome for Venice, and he caught one of the next flights. But when he arrived at the Gritti, he found that Enrica was very much in control. She would not let him see Pier alone and unescorted. "All I got was a kiss on the cheek. At that point, I had never even fucked her," he recalled.

He opted to return immediately to Rome and to delay the glories of Venice till another day. Pier whispered to him that things would be different when he returned from Israel.

[Months later, Kirk learned that Pier and her domineering mother had had a showdown. The power balance in their relationship had shifted since Pier became the family's breadwinner. Rebelling and screaming back at her mamma mia, she said to her, "I'll do what I god damn please, and I'll have any man I want, including Kirk Douglas."

He also learned that Pier, by now a darling of the paparazzi, had been dating other men. She had recently flown to London and into the suite of Dean Martin. Two weeks later, she was photographed hand in hand on Rome's Via Veneto with Clark Gable. Then, during time in New York, she dated Oleg Cassini, who took her to nightspots that included the Stork Club.

"That Oleg fucker," Kirk said when he heard about it. "First Gene Tierney, then Irene Wrightsman, now Pier. We're competing again."

Eventually, word leaked out that Pier was having an affair with a tall, dark, and very handsome actor, Carlos Thompson. Descended from German and Swiss parents, he had carved out a career for himself in Spanish-language films shot in Argentina.]

Pier eventually wrote to tell Kirk that she was back, once again, in Rome, and that she'd be waiting there for him after his return from Israel. In the meanwhile, she had a role in *The Flame and the Flesh*. Released in 1954, it starred Lana Turner and "that heartthrob," Carlos Thompson.

Disillusioned by the frustrating status of his dysfunctional engagement, Kirk told Stanley Kramer, "My sweet and virginal Pier is beginning to seem like used goods."

***

Stanley Kramer's *The Juggler*, eventually distributed in 1953 through Columbia Pictures, was the first American film ever shot on location in the recently founded and fast-emerging nation of Israel. Both Kramer and Kirk were hoping to repeat the success of the previous hit they'd made together, *Champion*.

In the autumn of 1952, after a two-hour flight from Rome, Kirk visited Israel for the first time. He was immediately caught up in the "intoxication" and growing pains of a nation being born, rising, it seemed, from the ashes of the Holocaust.

Israel had emerged victorious after its 1948-49 War of Independence. Thousands upon thousands of Jews, both Ashkenazi and Sephardic, were arriving daily, even though the country wasn't ready to receive them. There were major shortages of food, housing, schools, and hospitals.

In Jerusalem, Kirk checked into Israel's most upscale hotel, the King David. "I was shocked to discover that there was not a single deli in the entire country. And the locals didn't even know what a hot pastrami on rye was."

Kramer had hired the controversial Edward Dmytryk to direct. He'd received a Best Director Oscar nomination for his stark, controversial 1947 thriller about anti-Semitism, *Crossfire*. It had starred three "Roberts": Mitchum, Ryan, and Young.

The year he released that film, he was called before the House Un-American Activities Committee, at which he refused to testify. With that, he became a member of the "Hollywood Ten" who were sent to prison for refusing to give evidence against other left-wing sympathizers in the entertainment industry. RKO fired him.

Terrified of the repercussions, Dmytryk acquiesced and agreed to testify, outing directors and actors, correctly or incorrectly, as communist sympathizers, thereby destroying their careers. As a reward for his "cooperation," he was allowed to continue working in Hollywood. After *The Juggler*, he helmed one of the greatest critical and financial successes of 1954, *The Caine Mutiny*, starring Humphrey Bogart and Van Johnson.

A New Yorker, Michael Blankfort, wrote *The Juggler's* screenplay, based on his own novel. *[Blankfort harbored a controversial and embarrassing secret from his recent literary past. In 1950, he'd been a "front" for his friend, the black-listed writer Albert Maltz. Regrettably, when one of Maltz's screenplays* (Broken Arrow; 1950) *was nominated for an Oscar as Best Screenplay of the Year, Blankfort claimed credit for writing it, ignoring any link to Maltz.]*

In Israel, in preparation for his upcoming performance, Kirk practiced throwing and catching balls in the air with a retired professional juggler, David Gould. "I had the same dedication to juggling that I did to learn the art of the trapeze," Kirk said. "David called me a fast learner."

Kirk had been cast as Hans Muller, a bitter, neurotic, and

emotionally disturbed survivor of the Nazi concentration camp where his wife and children were gassed.

According to the script, Muller had arrived by ship at the port of Haifa in 1949, mentally deranged and haunted by his past. He panics and attacks an Israeli policeman who questions him. Imagining him as a Nazi stormtrooper, he knocks him out, then perceives that he has killed him.

As a "just off the boat" immigrant, he goes on the run, a mentally fragile refugee on the lam in a strange new world. On his trail is Karni, an Israeli detective (played by Paul Stewart) who wants to help him more than he wants to imprison him.

[Stewart and Kirk had been friends even before they got to Israel, having appeared together in both Champion *and in* The Bad and the Beautiful.*]*

Sleeping in the countryside, Hans (Kirk) encounters a homeless orphan, as portrayed by Joey Walsh, whom he befriends and enlists as his guide. They bond, like father and son, and Kirk teaches the boy how to juggle. *[The script establishes that before the war, Hans had been a circus and vaudeville performer.]*

When the boy is injured in a minefield, Hans takes him to a hospital at a nearby *kibbutz*. There, he meets Ya'El (Milly Vitale), a widow whose soldier husband was killed in Israel's War of Independence. They bond and fall in love.

Eventually Detective Karni (Stewart) catches up with him and informs him that the policeman he attacked was knocked unconscious but wasn't killed.

"This was my first time playing a Jew on screen," Kirk said, "and I wanted to do a good job, not only for my career, but for my people."

Filming was arduous, physically difficult, and exhausting. As *Variety* reported, "Kirk Douglas has been working as hard as any actor ever did. Be it running up alleys that start at about 70 degrees, 20 and 30 takes, and climbing Israel's mountains, making personal appearances where 5,000 to 6,000 fans almost tear his clothes off, he manages to keep a cheery and excited attitude towards his work and his people."

Kirk's love interest in *The Juggler*, Milly Vitale, was beautiful, Italian, and born in Rome. She had already appeared in a number of Italian postwar films, and in Holly-

Kirk nurturing Joey Walsh, a homeless orphan, in *The Juggler*.

308

wood, she'd worked with actors who included Bob Hope. Although she eventually got cast in the 1956 epic, Tolstoy's *War and Peace,* her career never reached the heights of Gina Lollobrigida's or Sophia Loren's.

Kirk soon became aware that Dmytryck and Vitale were engaged in an affair, prompting him to turn elsewhere for lovemaking. "Another leading lady eluded my clutches," he lamented.

He found Israel filled with beautiful girls, and, for the most part, each of them was direct. "If they wanted a man, they didn't beat round the bush, but made their desires clear. They'd come right up to you and say, 'I want you to make love to me.' Of course, some ambitious starlets in Hollywood do the same thing."

Once, at the beginning of four days when he wasn't needed for filming, he stopped off at a bar for a drink. Standing beside him was Leah Rubin, an eighteen-year-old Israeli soldier with a gun in her holster. As they chatted, he learned that, like himself, she was at the beginning of a furlough from her duties. Before their drinks were finished, she asked him to drive with her in a Jeep to Eilat, a military port and beach resort, on the Red Sea, at the southernmost tip of Israel. There, they sunbathed, went

"Milly Vitale and I were lovers only on the screen," Kirk said. "At night, she went off with the director."

In reference to Kirk's performance in *The Juggler,* critic Michael Atkinson wrote: "He chafes, he spits bile, he's a human dynamo perpetually on the verge of a meltdown.

"Waching Douglas act in his prime can be harrowing...he's so in your face you can taste the sweat and feel his body heat and fear his possible instability...laying bare so much painful hostility that it made Method actors seem positively dainty. There's never been anyone like him."

scuba diving, and made love.

When their time together ended, Kirk kissed her goodbye. "There was no promise to meet again, no mushy stuff. It was just an interlude…and now it was over."

During filming in the days that followed, Kirk migrated with the other actors and crew to northern Israeli outposts near the Lebanese border: Shavei Tzion and Nahariya. Each had been established in 1938 by German Jews fleeing from the Nazis and expanded with Sephardic Jews from North Africa in the years that followed. Each of the settlements, at various points in its history, had been or was eventually subjected to rocket attacks from across the border.

As one of the world's most famous Jews, Kirk was invited for an audience with David Ben-Gurion. Born in Poland, he'd been the first Prime Minister and First Defense Minister of Israel, filling both those positions from 1948-1953 and again from 1955-1963. [*He was also famous for sustaining morale with pithy quotes that included: "Anyone who doesn't believe in miracles is not a realist. In Israel, in order to be a realist you must believe in miracles."*]

In advance of their encounter, two security guards retrieved Kirk from his lodgings and drove him to the rather bleak office of the major founder of the State of Israel. *Time* magazine later defined him as one of the 100 most important figures of the 20th Century.

Ben-Gurion thanked him for his role in bringing the first American film crew to Israel, and suggested to Kirk, "You should be a Jew first, a Hollywood star second."

He then invited Kirk to emigrate to Israel, expressing hope that he'd establish a movie studio with the goal of depicting "our fight for survival against almost impossible odds." On the spot, Ben-Gurion devised a cinematic pitch wherein "a young Israeli soldier falls in love with a beautiful girl, also an Israeli soldier, and how together they unite in a fight against terrorists."

Kirk didn't commit. "Great idea! I'll think about it."

"Now run along," Ben-Gurion said. "I've got a country to run."

During whatever free time he could muster, Kirk toured the attractions of Israel, deciding that it wasn't Canaan, a land of milk and honey, but an arid, barren land fighting hard to accommodate Jews from around the world, many of them fleeing from atrocities.

Kirk was also invited to meet Moshe Dayan, Israel's most famous general. Noteworthy for the black patch over his left eye, he'd been Commander of the Jewish Front during the 1948 Arab-Israeli War. Later, he was named Chief of Staff of Israel's Defense Forces. He would also become the fighting symbol of the State of Israel during 1967's "Six-Day War" against

Egypt.

On three separate occasions, Dayan, accompanied by his first wife, Ruth, visited Kirk on location during his filming of *The Juggler*.

[In 1971, after 36 years of marriage, Ruth would divorce him, citing his numerous extramarital affairs. In the wake of her divorce, she wrote an autobiography, Or Did I Dream the Dream? *in which she devoted a chapter to "Moshe's bad taste in women."]*

Once, the Dayans invited Kirk to dinner at their home. He had initially evaluated their home as somewhat modest, yet it was "filled with priceless antiques." During its construction, as workers were laying its foundations, they'd unearthed antiquities which Dayan had acquired from them.

At their home, Kirk was introduced to Ya'El, their daughter, still in her early teens. She'd later become a novelist. Kirk gave her a dime. "If you ever make it to Hollywood, and you're at least seventeen, use that dime to give me a call."

Years later, after she'd reached the age of seventeen, Ya'El flew to Hollywood. Kirk was the first person she phoned.

"Remember me?" she asked. "I'm here."

Kirk never revealed what happened next when they actually came together, other than exclaiming, "She had grown up...and how!"

***

Although praised for the acting of Kirk and Stewart, *The Juggler* performed badly at the box office. Critic Dennis Schwartz found "the storytelling as dry as the desert. The psychological bent main character never comes across as someone I feel sympathetic to—which should have been given to any survivor of Auschwitz. Kirk tried hard to be moving, but all that emotional *angst* expressed by him as he sticks out his jaw and juggles his sentimental lines never touched any of my sensitive areas."

A few days before the end of filming, Dmytryk's wife, the actress Jean Porter, flew in to join her husband on the set. Dmytryk immediately retreated with her into a trailer, where he remained with her for three hours.

Kirk had warmly greeted her. She'd been born in Cisco, Texas, in 1922, where she was voted "most beautiful baby in Eastland County." She'd begun appearing in movies in 1936. By 1941, she'd evolved into a minor actress at MGM. She never made the bigtime, but co-starred with Mickey Rooney, Esther Williams, Abbott & Costello, and Red Skelton.

Kirk had seen only one of her movies, *Till the Edge of Time* (1946), starring Robert Mitchum and Guy Madison. Its director had been Edward Dmytryk, who fell for Porter during the movie-making process.

[Porter retired from the screen in 1961 and lived a very long life, dying in January of 2018. Married to Dmytryk in 1948, she remained wed to him until his death in 1999.]

Vitale was immediately discarded as Dmytryk's mistress, much to her dismay. Kirk offered whatever comfort he could. Then he walked off the set of *The Juggler*, calling his director, Dmytryck, "a fink."

When its producer, Kramer, saw the final cut, he said, "Kirk is full of *chutzpah* and class."

On the plane to Rome, whereas the director was near the front, cuddling with his beautiful wife, Kirk sat in the rear of the plane, in a seat beside Vitale, who was quietly sobbing on his shoulder.

He tried to explain to her that male stars or directors often made love to their leading lady during a shoot and then abandoned the liaison after the film was wrapped. "These romances go the way of the summer winds."

"I had my own problems to deal with," he said. "Just where in hell was Pier Angeli?"

***

Back in Rome, Kirk uneasily settled into the Excelsior Hotel, immediately calling Pier at the apartment she shared with her mother. The same old man answered the phone, this time informing him, "Pier no here."

It took some time, but Kirk finally learned that she was in Sardinia, the birthplace of both Pier and her twin sister, Marisa Pavan.

For an hour he tried, in vain, to reach her, leaving messages. At six o'clock that evening, a call came in from Cagliari, Sardinia's capital, and the town in which the twins had been born.

Kirk was a bit harsh with her, chastising her for not being in Rome to greet him. "What in hell are you doing in Sardinia, wherever in hell that is?"

Her only explanation was that she and her mother, Enrica, had to take care of some family business. She promised to return to him before he had to migrate onward to Paris. In the background, it sounded like she was attending a party. He heard a man's voice calling for her in Italian.

Stunned by her indifference, he attended a meeting that night with Dino De Laurentiis and Carlo Ponti to discuss pre-production issues associated with their upcoming film, *Ulysses* (1954), in which he'd been assigned the lead.

As promised, Pier eventually returned to Rome, but with only a few hours to spare before his flight to Paris. She was also due in Hollywood to star in her next movie, *The Silver Chalice* (1954), with Virginia Mayo and

Paul Newman in his film debut.

Kirk had only a two-hour visit with Pier at her apartment, sitting in the living room across from her mother. Apparently, Enrica was back in control of her daughter after she'd broken free and dated a lot of men ranging from Dean Martin to Clark Gable. Vic Damone also remained a fixture in her life.

As it turned out, both Kirk and Pier were on the same plane, along with *Mamma Mia*, with the understanding that he'd disembark at the airport in Paris, and that she and her mother would continue onward, without a change of equipment, to New York and Los Angeles.

Aboard the plane, Kirk sat in a seat beside Pier, with Enrica immediately across the aisle. The weather was so bad that the plane couldn't land at Orly in Paris but had to continue to Limerick in Ireland instead.

"We spent the rest of the night in the airport lounge, at a table with Enrica, drinking Irish coffee. When dawn came, the weather cleared. I kissed Pier lightly on the lips before meeting Enrica's disapproving look. They left for New York and I flew to Paris to begin shooting *Act of Love*."

"Pier's last words to me were, 'We'll meet again.'"

"I sure as hell hope so, since we're engaged," he answered.

***

While shooting in Paris, Kirk heard all the latest gossip about Pier in Hollywood.

Virginia Mayo, the star of *The Silver Chalice*, had appeared with Kirk in *Along the Great Divide*. From France, he placed three calls to her to check up on Pier in California. Mayo was very frank with him.

"Paul (Newman) at first referred to Pier as 'virginal' and described her 'refreshing innocence.' But from what I heard, she wasn't all that virginal. She told me that Marlon Brando had 'deflowered' her on a grassy knoll across from the Roman Colosseum when Vittorio de Sica was trying to get them to co-star in a movie together."

In Paris, Kirk also heard that Brando had been escorting her around, after a long interval, and visited, yet again, her home. Brando had told a reporter, "Pier is my ideal of womanhood."

[Brando was known for dating, and seducing, foreign girls, preferably brunette and petite, a description that fit Pier.]

Another reporter interviewed Enrica, who told him, "Marlon is like the adorable son I never had. He is filled with love and compassion for my family, unlike another bigtime movie star who shall go nameless."

"I guess she meant me," Kirk said after hearing that. "Marlon sure

313

knows how to win over a *mamma mia.* Let's face facts: Enrica's main objection to me is that I'm a Jew."

***

Kirk's next movie, to be shot in France, began as a novel, *The Girl on the Via Flaminia,* by Alfred Hayes. A Jewish writer born in London, he had emigrated with his parents to New York when he was three. Kirk was familiar with the work of Hayes because he'd received an Academy Award nomination for *Teresa* (1951), the role that had introduced Pier Angeli to American audiences.

The Girl on the Via Flaminia was a bittersweet love story about a star-crossed affair between a lonely World War II G.I. and a beautiful orphan girl who is homeless, penniless, and lacking identity papers. It had been set in Rome, in December 1944, six months after its liberation from the Fascists by Allied troops. The bordello trades are flourishing as sex-starved American soldiers line up for their chance at overworked prostitutes.

Kirk felt that the setting for the film adaptation of Hayes' novel should have remained in Rome, but the film adaptation's director, Anatole Litvak, wanted it moved to Paris, claiming that he had a greater affinity for that city. Litvak, a veteran (and strong-willed) producer and director, was certainly the boss. For a script, he had turned to Irwin Shaw, one of the most popular American novelists of the postwar era.

[Born to Russian-Jewish immigrant parents, Shaw, in time, would sell 14 million copies of his novels, one of his most popular being The Young Lions. *Originally published in 1948 and praised by the* Washington Post *as one of the four epic American war novels that emerged in the immediate post-war era, it was adapted into a film with the same name. Released in 1958, and subject to shock and outrage when its filming required the replication of historic events where actors impersonated Nazis, in uniform, on the streets of Paris, it co-starred Marlon Brando and Montgomery Clift.]*

Both English and French-language versions of Kirk's newest film would be produced and respectively entitled *Act of Love* and *Un acte d'amour.* The English-language version would be released by United Artists in 1953.

Visiting Paris for the first time, Kirk checked into the deluxe Hotel Raphael, the home away from home for such film stars as Eliza-

beth Taylor and Gregory Peck.

Kirk was eager to explore Paris, and he set out to discover it on his own. At first, he did all the tourist things, such as visiting the Louvre to pay homage to the *Mona Lisa*, and later, to scale the Eiffel Tower and parade down the Champs-Elysées.

He wanted a more in-depth look, hoping to follow in the footsteps of Ernest Hemingway, Gertrude Stein, F. Scott Fitzgerald, and Picasso. He patronized the Left Bank cafés they'd known, including Le Dôme and La Rotonde, wondering if he might spot Jean-Paul Sartre.

On his first evening, he strolled along the moonlit Seine, passing a series of lovers, including two male couples. The permissiveness of the tableau made him wonder who was seducing Pier in other parts of the world.

In the postwar era in Paris, Kirk encountered a number of American expatriates drawn to the City of Light. Some of them were patronizing such tourist traps as Maxim's or the Folies-Bergère. But others, some of them refugees from Greenwich Village, were seeking what Hemingway had called "Super Sodom and Grander Gomorrah."

Although she'd made her pronouncement in the 1920s, Kirk agreed with Gertrude Stein that "Paris is the 20th Century."

He wandered endlessly along the riverside quays, down hidden little streets with ancient shops and tiny little bistros, passing vendors, street markets, and even ragpickers like his father. Such evocative settings had provided inspiration for poets from Apollinaire to Villon.

On his fourth day in Paris, it was time to report to work for a meeting with Litvak, the Soviet-born Lithuanian filmmaker who could write, direct, and produce films in various countries and languages. He'd already directed many big stars in memorable roles, including Olivia de Havilland in *The Snake Pit* (1948). *[It earned her an Oscar nomination.]*

Litvak's greatest achievement had been the filming of documentaries during World War II. One of the best of these, *Why We Fight,* earned him commendations from the governments of France, Britain, and the United States. Even the Soviet dictator, Josef Stalin, praised his work.

After watching another of Litvak's films, *Decision Before Dawn* (1951), General Douglas MacArthur asserted that it should be designated as Best Picture of the Year.

Soon, Kirk was calling Litvak "Tola."

"Perhaps his greatest mistake was in marrying Miriam Hopkins," Kirk said, "although he didn't last long wedded to that Georgia gal. She handles every role with the subtlety of a wrestler, and castrates her leading men, or so I've heard."

Kirk asked Litvak if, after he'd completed the English-language version of their film, he could reprise his performance for the French-language version, even though he did not speak the language. Litvak had tentatively promised the role to Jean Gabin.

Litvak said he'd decide in two months, with the understanding that Kirk would have to appear in a screen test, reprising, in French, his English-language performance.

Kirk immediately embarked on the daunting task of learning to understand and speak French, hiring Madame LaFeuille as his teacher. He studied and practiced with her day after day and many nights, too.

"I think she was falling in love with me, as we were practically living together. She was amazed at how quickly I had picked up the language, enough to pass the screen test."

Although The Raphael was one of the finest hotels in Paris, Kirk wanted an apartment of his own. Post-war apartments were hard to come by, but he found one in the nearby suburb of Boulogne-Billancourt at 31 bd. d'Auteuil, near the Bois de Boulogne. He'd go there for walks, sometimes wearing his character's soldier's uniform, after a day of filming. He received many solicitations from strolling prostitutes and from an occasional gay male. "I turned all of them down," he said.

Litvak wasn't convinced. "On two occasions, I phoned his apartment, once late at night. What sounded like a young French girl answered the phone."

As Kirk later confessed, "When I wasn't taking lessons from Madame LaFeuille, I learned the language of love in my boudoir with various mademoiselles."

***

Act of Love opens as an Army veteran, Robert Teller (Kirk), visits Villefranche on France's Côte d'Azur in the early 1950s. In a flashback, he relives his experience there as an American soldier in the weeks that followed the liberation of Paris in 1944. He meets and falls in love with Lise Gudayeu (Dany Robin), a beautiful French orphan with no money or identity papers. She's hiding out from the police.

He befriends her, passing her off as his wife, and eventually, they fall in love. A dragnet lands her in jail. Kirk rescues her.

He asks for permission to marry her from his commanding officer, Captain Henderson (George Matthews), who opposes the marriage, asserting that too many young American soldiers are entering into these ill-fated marriages with local women looking for a meal ticket. He announces his intention of transferring Kirk, but he deserts and is later caught and arrested.

"Dany Robin was a beautiful French actress who escaped my clutches," Kirk confessed. "She later co-starred opposite Peter Sellers in *Waltz of the Toreadors* (1962). She had recently married a fellow actor, Georges Marchal, so I didn't want to disturb her marital bliss."

[David Shipman, a critic for The Guardian, *defined her as one of the first post-war French ingénues—very pretty, fragile, chic but elfin, shy but assured and with an ardent naivety which so well reflected the country's then optimistic view of itself."*

Tragically, in 1995, Robin and her second husband, Michael Sullivan, were burned to death when a fire swept through and destroyed their apartment in Paris.]

Kirk's co-star in *Act of Love* was the French actress Dany Robin. Their ill-fated World War II romance ends with her suicide.

In real life, she was burned to death when a fire swept through her apartment in Paris.

Robert Strauss was cast as a gruff American Army sergeant, Johnny Blackwood, who tries to help Kirk get a marriage permit. *[The same year that he appeared with Kirk in* Act of Love, *Strauss also filmed* Stalag 17 *alongside William Holden, whose role Kirk had unwisely rejected. Strauss played "Animal" Kuzawa, a performance which later earned him a nomination for Best Supporting Actor of the Year.]*

In the film, wrenched back to "the present" (i.e. Villefranche in the early 1950s), Kirk, now an Army veteran during peacetime, encounters his former commander, Captain Henderson and his wife.

Henderson is smugly convinced that he saved his former underling from a disastrous marriage. "I bet you haven't seen the girl since the war," Henderson says to Kirk.

"You're right," Robert (Kirk) replies. "They pulled her body out of the river shortly after I was transferred."

[Matthews, as Henderson, was perfect in his portrayal of a domineering (and in this case, misguided) all-American military officer who destroys Kirk's true love. He often played hardened military types and had the face for it: a pug nose, a jutting lower lip, foreboding eyebrows, and a tall, burly physique.]

Ironically, Sydney Chaplin had also nabbed a role, a minor one, in *Act of Love*. He hadn't encountered Kirk since he'd been caught in a compromising position with Irene Wrightsman long ago and far away in Los Angeles. They chatted only briefly, making no mention of Irene.

On the set, Kirk hardly noticed a young, blonde, French girl. Cast in the film as "Mimi," she was bundled in a heavy overcoat. Later, when she reappeared in his life as Brigitte Bardot, Kirk would take notice.

Act of Love seems better appreciated by film aficionados today than at the time of its release. Litvak himself confessed, "It didn't work out as well as I thought it would, some of which was my own fault."

Kirk had been fully aware that he was a decade older than the role he'd been assigned to play.

In France after World War II, Kirk encounters his former Army commander (George Mathews) and his wife, who are tourists.

During the war, Mathews' character had blocked Kirk's marriage to the young French girl he loved, which led to her suicide.

Nonetheless, he imbued it with youth and vigor. *The Hollywood Reporter* wrote: "The performances of the cast are constantly moving. Kirk Douglas punches over his role with a fierce intensity skillfully softened by tenderness."

***

In the midst of his frustration and despair over Pier Angeli, Kirk met Anne Buydens, a surprising choice as a future mate. When they were introduced, it was almost inconceivable that he'd be with her in 2019, at the time of this writing.

She was born in Hannover, Germany, in 1919 to wealthy parents, Sigfried and Paula Michelle Marx. Her father was the rich owner of a chain of textile stores.

When Anne was a teenager, she moved with her parents to Belgium, where their marriage unraveled. Her parents moved on to other loves, especially her mother, who had a rotating list of beaux.

Anne was sent to boarding school in Switzerland, where she became adept at languages that included Italian, French, and English, in addition to her native German.

After schooling, she moved to Paris, where she remained throughout the course of World War II and its Nazi occupation. She worked for a film company there (Sonor Pictures), inserting German subtitles into the context of French- and foreign-language films.

Unaware of the exact nature of Anne's work, her maid defined her as a spy and reported her to the Gestapo. After intense interrogation, she was set free.

Even as a young woman, Anne had a high sense of fashion. Still working for Sonor Pictures at the end of the war, she was asked by her company to assist with the production of an upcoming NBC program called *Paris Cavalcade of Fashion*. As its producer, she played a major role in introducing Christian Dior's "New Look" that would soon sweep across America.

Her director was Robert Capa, the noted photographer.

[A crisis exploded shortly before the fashion défilé that formed the core of the TV special. Capa was nowhere to be found. When Capa didn't respond to frantic phone calls, Anne jumped into a taxi and headed for his hotel. There she found him in bed with Pamela Churchill, the daughter-in-law of Sir Winston.

Deserting his mistress, Capa ran with Anne, half-clothed, dressing himself in the taxi, and made it to the fashion preview on time.

Later, after two name changes and many reincarnations, Pamela Churchill Hayward Harriman was appointed as the U.S. Ambassador to France by then-President Bill Clinton. She died of a heart attack sustained in the swimming pool of the health club at the Ritz Hotel in Paris in 1997.]

In time, Anne became skilled as a publicist, and was hired by director John Huston to help navigate him through the shooting of *Moulin Rouge* (1952). It starred José Ferrer as the 19th-century painter, Toulouse-Lautrec, his growth stunted because of a childhood accident.

Anne had been friends with Anatole Litvak, who was currently helming Kirk in *Act of Love*. Litvak phoned her, asking if she'd take over as publicist for Kirk's latest film. She rejected the offer as she had limited knowledge of his film career.

[Years later, she recalled that in her initial dialogues with Litvak, she'd mentioned that during one of her transatlantic crossings, Kirk's movie, The Big Trees, was shown to passengers onboard. "Many of them laughed," she said. "That movie was just terrible."]

In Paris, Litvak asked again if she would at least meet with Kirk, and she agreed.

At the studio, the still photographer, Chim Seymour, ushered her in to present her to Kirk, referring to his dressing room as "the lion's den." She had read in the French press that Kirk's nickname was "Le Brute Chéri."

She recalled their first meeting, claiming, "He was the most forceful, energetic, and demanding man I'd ever met. He was brash, a take-charge kind of man, rather intimidating. He looked like he'd be a horror to an employee."

In contrast, he found her poised, elegant, and impeccably dressed in a navy blue suit with a white collar that framed her subtle beauty.

He outlined the position to her before she decided against it. "I don't think I'm suited for the job," she said. When she rose to leave, he said, "*Au revoir.*"

Even though she'd rejected the job, Kirk couldn't erase her from his mind. When an invitation came in from Claude Terrail, who operated Tour d'Argent, a spectacular and very exclusive restaurant in Paris, he phoned her. "We'll have a great meal and we'll get to see the back side of Nôtre Dame lit up at night."

She begged off, claiming that she was tired and would merely whip up an omelette for a light supper—and then off to bed.

As he put down the receiver, he spoke out loud. "Fuck her! To hell with her!"

Yet he still didn't want to give up on her, for reasons he didn't fully understand at the time. On his third call to her, she accepted a revised version of the job he'd initially offered. He had decided to quit putting the make on her and get to know her. As she gradually opened up to him, he didn't like what he was hearing.

During the war, and desiring a Belgian passport, she had entered a marriage of convenience and had become Anne Laure Buydens. The couple no longer lived together, and she was now the mistress of a much older man, Ramon Babbas, the CEO of Parfumerie Patou.

After a few days, and rather slowly, she and Kirk began to date. For most of his conquests, he liked to seduce the woman of his choice after their first night out. Not so with Anne. He had to settle for a light kiss, similar to what he was getting from Pier Angeli, to whom he was still nominally engaged, despite their long separations.

Anne agreed to go with him to the Cirque d'Hiver, the City of Light's then-current manifestation of a venue he knew very well, the circus. Spotting Kirk as he entered, one of its directors privately asked "if he would participate." Dressed in a tuxedo, Kirk wondered what he'd be called upon to do—surely not get into white tights and perform on a trapeze as he'd done in *The Story of Three Loves?*

Leaving Anne alone in the audience, he went behind the scenes for a consultation with management. Then, after the elephants had performed, Kirk came out, still clad in his tux. With fanfare, the announcer introduced him as the crowd went wild with applause. "My job," Kirk said, "was to scoop up big piles of shit. I'd worked with animal shit before when I was Issur growing up in New York State."

Back in his apartment, he made love to Anne for the first time. He later told Litvak, "This young woman has the potential to make me forget all about Little Miss Stuck-up, Pier Angeli. I think, if given half the chance, I could fall in love with Anne."

In the days ahead, she concealed from him the gossip column reports about Pier dating (many) other men. Vic Damone had remained "a constant" in her life.

Since he had rented a rather large apartment, he felt that the time had come for him to invite his sons, accompanied by his ex-wife, Diana Dill, for a three-week holiday in Paris. Both of his sons were recovering from chicken pox.

His invitation was accepted, and Kirk, along with Anne, was waiting at Orly Airport when the trio from New York came through the gate.

He introduced Anne as "my assistant," but Diane suspected that she was far more than that.

That night, Diane was assigned sleeping quarters in his apartment building's attic, in a maid's room not directly connected to, the much larger apartment downstairs. Meanwhile, Michael and Joel slept in the main apartment, in the bedroom next to Kirk's. Anne, meanwhile, retreated to her own apartment in another part of Paris.

After a fretful night of coughing, Diane awakened the next morning having broken out with chicken pox herself. When Anne arrived, she became aware of Diane's condition and phoned a doctor.

During Diane's recovery, Anne took care of Kirk's ex-wife, making chicken soup and bringing other foods for her. The two women became friends...well, sort of.

When Diane recovered, Kirk invited her and his sons for a walk in the nearby Bois de Boulogne. As Kirk remembered, "Mike took my hand and placed it in Diane's. He looked up at us and said, 'Now we're a family again.'"

Diane later said, "I have no such memory."

Back within his apartment, Kirk and Diane got into a fierce argument. He accused her of "not giving my great success as a movie star more credence." Anne tried to make peace between them.

Soon, the vacation was over, and Diane, with Michael and Joel, flew back to New York.

Waiting for them at Idlewild was Bill Darrid, her future husband.

[Diane and Darrid would live together until his death in 1992. After that, in 2002, she would marry for the third time, this time to actor Donald Webster at the Devonshire Parish Church in Bermuda. The marriage would last until her death in July of 2015.]

***

As part of a career promotion, Anne Buydens was designated as "Mistress of Protocol" for the Sixth International Film Festival at Cannes, an event scheduled from April 15-29, 1953.

The origins of the Festival dated from 1932, but it was shut down during the Nazi occupation of France in World War II. The present Festival de Cannes was re-established in 1946. In the early 1950s, rampant with showbiz scandals and high-profile celebrities, it attracted a lot of tourism and press attention.

In advance of the 1953 Festival at which Anne was involved, Kirk flew to the Côte d'Azur with her, checking into a suite of his own at the Carlton. *[In contrast, she was installed in accommodations of her own, next door at the Hotel Miramar.]* "Anne's knowledge of the major languages of Europe sure paid off," Kirk said. "She switched from one tongue to another with amazing dexterity."

During the day, Kirk spent his time in a bathing suit on the beach, studying the array of bikini-clad beauties who paraded before him as he tried to memorize the script of his upcoming film, *Ulysses*. Many of them went topless, having descended on Cannes with hopes of getting noticed by a director or a major-league player in the film industry.

During most of his early trips to the beach, Kirk had not been recognized, perhaps because of the beard he was growing for *Ulysses*.

But word soon got out, and he was mobbed by young women, some no more than fourteen years old. Nearly all of them were clad in the briefest of bikinis, a style of beachwear for the most part forbidden on the beaches of America. Some of the girls begged for him to autograph their almost nude bodies, often directly on their breasts.

As he later said, "I never felt so masculine, such a macho man as I did back then. My male ego had never been as reinforced. Had I wanted to, I could have had two or three affairs a day. The mademoiselles handed me an array of phone numbers, even though most of them didn't speak English."

One Saturday afternoon, a voice stood out from the rest, calling to him, *"Keerk! Keerk!"*

Breaking through the coven of fans, a seventeen-year-old blonde emerged in a skimpy, chartreuse bikini. As he remembered her, she had "a long, graceful neck, succulent red lips, shapely legs, and blossoming breasts which were on ample display except for a string which served as the top for her bikini."

As it turned out, she was Brigitte Bardot. She had met him during her brief appearance in his recent film, *Act of Love*. The character she'd played had worn a heavy coat. Although he hadn't appreciated her then, he certainly did now.

To escape from the mob, he retreated with her to the rear room of a sidewalk café. It was nearly empty since most of the other customers had congregated at tables outdoors.

"We chatted pleasantly, as she spoke some English," Kirk said. "She told me her dream of becoming a movie star."

"I want to be the Parisian version of Marilyn Monroe," Brigitte said.

He was fascinated by her. "More than fascinated," he later confided to Dino De Laurentiis. "I got a hard-on just talking to her."

He was disturbed to learn that about a year before, she had married the French director, Roger Vadim. Even so, a wedding ring hardly curtailed her flirting.

Brigitte Bardot, who gave new meaning to "Vive la France!" in *And God Created Woman* (1956)

She had started out training as a ballerina and was later a dancer and teen model. "At ballet school, they called me 'Bichette (i.e., "Little Doe),'" she said.

"Bardot was somewhat precocious," Kirk later told De Laurentiis. "She seemed to be rebelling against both her parents and Vadim. She was like a childwoman—one foot in maturity, the other back in the nursery."

"She told me that she hoped I would one day make her a star in

The first time Kirk met Bardot, she was in a skimpy bikini. On their second meeting, on the beach, she wore a simple summer dress.

Instead, it was he who showed off his body in swimming trunks, and the beard he'd grown in preparation for his portrayal of *Ulysses*.

323

Hollywood. I fear I made promises I would never keep, although telling her that I saw an opening, since Betty Grable and Lana Turner had devolved into pinups salvaged from the 1940s, and Marilyn Monroe was spiraling out of control. I told her 'You might have a chance, with my help, of course, to become the new sex symbol of America.'"

"It is my most cherished dream," she replied.

A roaming photographer snapped a picture of Kirk with Brigitte. Copies of it, formatted as a postcard, later became tourist souvenirs.

Kirk is listed in many sources as one of the early admirers of France's most iconic "sex kitten." A few years later, Vadim cast her in *And God Created Woman* (1957), the film that morphed her into a mega-celebrity and international sex symbol.

Neither Brigitte nor Kirk ever admitted to an affair, although the staff at the Carlton leaked to "those voracious scandalmongers" (Kirk's reference to the press) that she was seen coming and going from his suite almost every afternoon until the end of that year's Festival.

Vadim stated that he knew that his wife had adulterous affairs during their marriage. He could hardly complain. In Vadim's future lay such beauties as Jane Fonda ("sweet, sensuous, and full of laughter"), and Catherine Deneuve ("slender, her figure that of a shy and discreetly perverse adolescent straight out of a novel by Colette").

In years to come, Kirk and Brigitte remained friends through future spouses and lovers. The last time he heard from her was when she sent him that photograph of the two of them snapped together at Cannes in 1953.

On it, she wrote, "My dear Kirk, were we not so nice and young and beautiful? Love, Brigitte."

***

During 1953's Film Festival at Cannes, as Kirk was still romantically linked to Pier, "wherever in hell she was," and spending significant time with Bardot, Anne Buydens was enmeshed in imbroglios of her own. On their third evening in Cannes, when she was invited to spend it with Kirk, she announced that she'd already committed to a date with her former boyfriend, Joe Drown, the owner of the ultra-chic Bel Air Hotel in Los Angeles. He was flying to Cannes that afternoon from Paris, and she'd accepted a dinner invitation.

According to Kirk, "Even though my own love life was not above reproach, I was seriously pissed off."

He didn't remain idle. In a memoir, he recalled a brief fling with "a

324

beautiful blonde French girl." Again, he was being discreet. Barbara Lang was blonde and beautiful, but not French. She had emerged from Pasadena, California in 1928, the daughter of the silent screen star, Maureen Knight. She was in Cannes hoping to be discovered. A fashion model and nightclub singer, she wanted to become "like Marilyn Monroe on the screen."

When she'd met Kirk on the beach, the attraction was mutual and immediate. On an impulse, he asked her to drive with him to St.-Tropez. There, they checked into what later became La Yaca, a quintessentially Provençal hotel whose accommodations were scattered among four historic houses, one of which had been occupied by Colette in 1927.

Barbara Lang in 1958...a starlet who wanted to become "another Marilyn Monroe."

"Kirk and I hardly ever left the room," Lang said. "I admit I had an ulterior motive. I wanted him to cast me in his next picture. Regrettably, that didn't happen. He drove me back to Cannes, and I saw him two more times at Hollywood parties. Our relationship went nowhere. To him, I was just another pickup on the beach."

[Today, Barbara Lang doesn't even merit a paragraph in the history of Hollywood, becoming one of dozens of those "Fifties Blondes" who emerged in the era of "sexbombs, sirens, bad girls, and teen queens" of the Eisenhower era.

She signed on as an MGM starlet in 1956, and a year later turned down a role in Elvis Presley's Jailhouse Rock *(1957), although she didn't turn down Elvis. She also appeared briefly in* Party Girl *(1958), co-starring Robert Taylor and Cyd Charisse.*

The following year, after divorcing her first husband, she attempted suicide by overdosing on sleeping pills.

After two more failed marriages, she landed as a regular on the TV soap opera, All My Children *(1973).*

The last time she saw Kirk was at a party at the home of producer Ray Stark. "Kirk no longer remembered who I was."

Descending into alcoholism, Lang died in July of 1982, lonely and forgotten.]

***

The producers of *Ulysses,* Carlo Ponti and Dino De Laurentiis, met Kirk and Anne in Cannes to discuss their upcoming epic and the logistics of its

325

filming in Italy. Before the end of dinner, Anne had been hired as Publicity Director for the film. That delighted Kirk, because they would not have to be separated.

Then Ponti graciously offered the use of his villa, nestled in the hills above Amalfi, to Anne and Kirk so they could have a romantic holiday together in Italy before the debut of filming.

"It was like a pre-honeymoon," Kirk said. "Anne and I got to know each other and make passionate love every day. We'd go rowing, and I'd sing romantic love songs to her in Italian. Our favorite was '*Come bella far l'amore quando è sera* ('How Beautiful It Is to Make Love in the Evening.') Of course, I was no Mario Lanza."

Together, they visited the Isle of Capri and boated through the Blue Grotto. Kirk had a special request: He wanted to see the cliff in Capri that the Emperor Tiberius had made infamous. Nine-year-old boys were imported to his palace there from Rome as "ingredients" for one of the Emperor's horrifying fetishes. After sodomizing a boy, he'd order his guards to throw him over the cliff onto the jagged rocks below.

During the final weekend of their stay within his villa near Amalfi, Ponti arrived with his wife, Giuliana Fiastri, whom he'd married right after World War II. They spent most of their time there battling through domestic squabbles about Ponti's recent affairs with actresses Mai Britt and Sophia Lazzaro. [*Lazzaro was a buxom Neapolitan beauty whose name Ponti changed to Sophia Loren before casting her in* Anna *(1951).*

Ponti would marry Loren in 1957, but—because of confusion associated with the legal status of his first marriage, and with the approval of Loren, and fearing that he might be charged with bigamy and with Loren facing the charge of "concubinage"—he had his union with Loren annulled in 1962.

Eventually, Ponti and Loren, motivated by the fact that divorce was legal in France at the time, became citizens of France. They were married again in 1966, their union lasting until his death in 2007.]

On their final day at the Ponti's villa, Anne turned to Kirk and said, "You make me so happy."

In response, he reminded her that he was still engaged to Pier Angeli.

Back in Rome, it was humiliating for Anne when Kirk took her to Bulgari, the Tiffany's of Rome, to buy an engagement ring for Pier.

"Kirk never hid his feelings about Pier, misplaced as I thought they were," Anne said. "She was the fantasy woman of his dreams, innocent, malleable, and adorably provocative. I certainly couldn't compete on that level. But I hoped he would finally see her as the manipulative child-woman she was."

"Anne was not like a typical wife in America," Kirk said. "She was sophisticated about men, like many other European women, knowing that jackals like us will stray from time to time."

"He never tried to hide his dalliances from me," Anne said, "even after our marriage. I came to accept his infidelity as part of the deal. As a European, I understood it was unrealistic to expect fidelity in a marriage. In Paris, I had known Charles de Gaulle's driver—she was also his mistress—and many more like her. In more recent years, François Mitterand's mistress and their children came to his funeral at the invitation of his wife. Only the Americans find that outrageous."

What was Kirk's reaction to Anne's measured response?

"I'm a sonofabitch, plain and simple. I'm probably the most disliked actor in Hollywood, and I feel good about that...because it's me...that's who I am. I was born aggressive, as a boy, stealing other people's chickens and chopping off their heads so that I could put something on the table for my mother and sisters. So I was born aggressive, which means that I'll probably die aggressive, cursing my nurse."

***

When the Film Festival at Cannes ended, Kirk and Anne traveled together to Italy, where shooting was to begin on *Ulysses*, its screenplay inspired by Homer's ancient *Odyssey*.

They arrived, midway through May, at the scenic fishing village of Porto Ercole, whose name translates as "Port Hercules." Set on the western coast of Tuscany, the town was the site of the summer residence of the Dutch Royal Family.

On his own, Kirk set out on foot to explore the town. He visited the local church where Caravaggio, the emotionally unstable baroque painter and master of strong contrasts in light (*chiaroscuro*), had died.

A converted fisherman's cottage, facing directly onto the sea, had been set aside for them, and, with Anne, Kirk turned it into a cozy love nest. Every morning, they journeyed by launch to a location ten miles offshore for scenes that were shot aboard a replica of an ancient Greek ship.

At the end of every work day, Kirk would jump from the top of that ship's highest mast into the blue, salty waters. Then, in yet another display of his swashbuckling abilities, he'd swim for about a mile and half before climbing aboard the motor launch and returning to Porto Ercole.

Until he got involved with *Ulysses*, he had never heard of its director, Mario Camerini, who had helmed Italian-language films since 1923. Camerini had risen to prominence in the 1930s, mostly for Italian comedies starring Vittorio de Sica. "I rarely could understand what he wanted, so I played Ulysses my way," Kirk said.

[Coincidentally, and through no fault of his own, many people Kirk knew, both men and women, and including Camerini, committed suicide.

In February of 1981, at the age of 85, in the lakeside resort of Gardone Riviera, Camerini jumped from the fifth-floor balcony of the San Giovanni Hospital, where he was being treated for advanced prostate cancer.]

Shortly after his arrival, Kirk met his co-stars at a party hosted by Dino De Laurentiis and his beautiful Italian wife, Silvana Mangano. She'd been cast in *Ulysses* as both Penelope and Circe.

In 1946, at the first beauty pageant staged after the war, Silvana had won the title of Miss Rome and begun a torrid affair with Marcello Mastroianni.

Later, she was discovered by De Laurentiis, who married her in 1949. That was the year she achieved international acclaim in *Bitter Rice* opposite Vittorio Gassman.

Lux Film produced *Ulysses* and, as such, were—technically speaking—the employers of both Ponti and De Laurentiis. Kirk had never seen *Bitter Rice (Riso Amaro),* so a screening was set up for

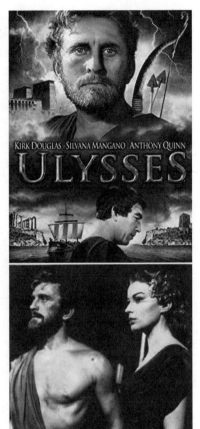

Ulysses (Kirk) with Penelope (Silvia Mangano) and Circe (also Silvia Mangano).

him. He was astonished to learn that its plot included "abortion, crime, illicit sex, a gruesome murder, suicide, nudity, and a realistic childbirth scene. In America, the Catholic Legion of Decency had classified it as a 'C,' meaning condemned."

In future films, Silvana would be directed by some of the biggest names in Italy: Pier Paolo Pasolini, Vittorio de Sica, and Luchino Visconti.

Born in Tripoli, Libya—then a colony of Italy—Rosanna Podesta had moved to Rome after World War II. At the time she'd met Kirk, she had just married the movie producer, Marco Vicario. She had been cast in *Ulysses* as Nausicca.

Like Silvana, she, too, would achieve international fame. In 1956, she interpreted the title role in *Helen of Troy.* A voice coach helped her learn her

328

English-language lines by rote. In that film, a young Brigitte Bardot appeared alongside her.

Rosanna would receive additional "exposure" when she posed, half-naked, for Hugh Hefner's *Playboy* in March of 1966.

Anthony Quinn was cast in *Ulysses* as Kirk's rival, Antinous, who is trying to coerce Penelope into marriage with the claim that because Ulysses has been missing for ten years (since the end of the Trojan War), he's never coming back.

Kirk and Quinn became friendly competitors both on and off the screen. "We had this game of one-upmanship to see which of us could deflower the most beautiful girls. We'd both been intimate with Evelyn Keyes."

In reference to Quinn, Keyes had told the press, "There is simply too much of Tony—yes, down there, too."

Quinn had already been famously quoted as saying: "My aim is to impregnate every woman in the world."

"That goal was too ambitious," Kirk said. "Yet during the filming of *Ulysses,* he seemed to be working his way through the ladies of the cast and crew at the rate of two or three a day."

Formerly married to Katherine DeMille, the daughter of the famous director, Cecil B. DeMille, Quinn sometimes seduced from the A-list: Carole Lombard, Rita Hayworth, Maureen O'Hara, Ingrid Bergman—and yes, George Cukor.

Quinn had nothing but contempt for his role—that of an unscrupulous nobleman—in *Ulysses.* "Kirk and I made a lousy attempt to replicate Homer's epic. This was my first Italian film, and it was a mess of a picture. But it introduced me to the glory of Italy and its women. At the time, I had no idea of the place that the ancient fortress of Cicero occupied in the hearts of the Italians. I walked through the script. Seeing it again, years later, I wished that I could play it over again and get it right."

[Quinn and Kirk would soon move on to greater glories together in Lust for Life *(1956).]*

Seven writers were hired to adapt Homer's epic to the screen. One of them was Irwin Shaw, who had crafted the script for Kirk's *Act of Love.* Another acclaimed member of their oft-changing ranks was Ben Hecht, who in 1927 had

Leader of the pack eager to usurp the power of Ulysses: Anthony Quinn.

won the first Academy Award for Best Story of the Year for *Underworld.*

In a memo to Ponti, Kirk wrote, "I am sorry you guys tossed aside much of the contribution that Hecht made to the script. He's the best in the business, and we should have incorporated all of his scenes. We need more pantomime, less talky-talky."

Kirk bonded with Hecht from the moment he met him. He said that at the age of sixteen, he'd run away from home to Chicago. "When I got there, I haunted the streets, whorehouses, police stations, courtrooms, theater stages, jails, slums, madhouses, fires, murders, riots, banquet halls, and bookshops."

The fantasy film saga of *Ulysses* focused on the Greek hero's attempts, over the course of a decade, to return home after the Trojan War. His wife and Queen, Penelope, has been patiently waiting, fending off overeager suitors.

En route, Ulysses meanders through an epic anthology of heroic adventures. They include a murderous confrontation with the one-eyed Cyclops. *[With his comrades, Ulysses escapes by getting the Cyclops drunk, then thrusting a battering ram through his single hideous eye.]*

Our hero also survives the temptations of the Sirens by plugging the ears of his men as they navigate through treacherous waters near their lair yet lashing himself to his ship's mast so that he can listen to, but not be killed by, their seductive songs.

Other Ulyssean adventures include surviving a sexual encounter with the Sorceress—Circe, a role interpreted by Silvana—who temporarily transforms his entire crew into pigs; and a romance with a princess (played by Rosanna Podesta) who nurses him back to health after he's washed up onto a beach at Phaeacia.

A Bard with many adventures to talk and sing about, Ulysses, at last, returns to Penelope, evicts her suitors from his palace, and lives happily ever after as a celebrated hero and role model to other Greeks and the cultures that admired them.

To promote his film, Dino De Laurentiis asked his wife, Silvana Mangano, to fly with Kirk to the Venice Film Festival. They made a spectacular entrance in a gondola draped with flowers and navigated by three singing gondoliers. In the press reports generated bv the event, paparazzi referred to them as "The Beard and the Beautiful."

Anne accompanied them. With Kirk, who was a guest of honor, she attended a screening of his *The Bad and the Beautiful.*

The critic for *TV Guide* interpreted *Ulysses* as "a soap opera, but one that is a tasteful and surprisingly literate work. Kirk Douglas gives a restrained and thoughtful performance, way above the run of those 'sword-

and-sandals' epics."

[Kirk's Ulysses *is credited as the prototype for a series of costume dramas filmed in Italy between 1958 and 1965. Designated as "peplum" films, their name derived from the tunics (peplums) worn by the actors. The American bodybuilder Steve Reeves perpetuated the genre with his interpretation of the title role of Hercules in 1957. Nineteen Hercules sequels would follow.]*

***

In Porto Ercole, preoccupied with the filming of *Ulysses,* and with the belief that she was off filming somewhere in South America, Kirk had not heard from Pier.

But one afternoon, he returned, alone, to his rented cottage. In its living room, he noticed something that hadn't been there before: An enlarged and framed publicity photo of Pier on one of the tables. She had inscribed it with, "Kirk, I've been watching you."

He confirmed with the chambermaid that Pier had persuaded a young Italian man to drive her to Porto Ercole, but just for a few hours. When she didn't find Kirk, she opted not to wait, explaining that she had an appointment at 8PM that same day, in Rome.

When Kirk was finally able to tear himself away from Porto Ercole for an excursion to Rome with Anne, she was long gone—he knew not where. On a newsstand near the Spanish Steps, he spotted a likeness of her on the cover of *Paris-Match.* He didn't buy it, but stood staring at it for a moment, realizing, "I'm still in love with her."

He tried to put her out of his mind and to enjoy the wonders of the Eternal City. To an increasing degree, his links to Pier seemed pointless and hopeless, and he began weighing the advantages of a marriage to Anne, instead. Whereas he doubted that he'd ever be exclusively faithful to her, she, on the other hand, still maintained her own romantic attachments, particularly to Ramon Babbas.

In Rome, Carlo Ponti had arranged for Kirk to stay at a lively villa on the ancient Via Appia Antica, over which Roman soldiers had, for centuries, trod off to war. With its flower gardens and scenic terraces, it also had a pool where he could swim in the nude.

A staff of three servants was on hand to take care of him and the villa. Although she still rented a room at the Hotel de Ville, Anne was a frequent "sleepover."

He learned that Pier was in London, finishing scenes in the Lana Turner movie, *The Flame and the Flesh.* In that film, Pier, along with Carlos Thompson, were Lana's second-tier co-stars.

Kirk had arrived in Rome during the peak of its "Hollywood-on-the-Tiber" paparazzi-fueled glamour, and as such, members of the California film colony often made it a point to visit him in his villa.

For years, because he was less and less willing to commit himself to any individual studio, Kirk had dreamed of establishing a movie production company of his own. Nevertheless, his agent, Charles Feldman, showed up at his lodgings in Rome with a freshly drafted contract that would commit him to a three-picture deal with 20th Century Fox. Its terms had already been approved by Darryl F. Zanuck.

The first part of the contract would assign him a role in *The Robe*. Eventually released in 1953, it was the saga of a Roman Centurion who presides over the crucifixion of Christ. It was understood that Victor Mature had already nabbed one of its key roles; that Kirk's part would be smaller than Mature's; and that by far the most visible role would be filled by Richard Burton.

After reading the script, Kirk rejected it. The role he'd been offered eventually went to Michael Rennie. As accurately observed by Kirk, "*The Robe* is gonna be Burton's show."

The Robe—the first picture ever formatted in CinemaScope— became a big hit and led to an Oscar nomination for Burton. Its female lead, incidentally, had been Jean Simmons, who would become Kirk's co-star in *Spartacus*.

***

Ray Stark had been Kirk's agent when he'd worked for the Famous Artists Agency. Now, he was fast-rising as one of the richest and most prolific independent producers in postwar Hollywood. His heyday would come in the 1960s and beyond when he produced the massively acclaimed *West Side Story* (1961). Back in the 1950s, he was still pitching projects to Kirk.

In Rome, he presented Kirk with a tempting offer for him to play the male lead in Walt Disney's *20,000 Leagues Under the Sea*. Eventually released in 1954, it was to be shot in CinemaScope and based on the popular novel by Jules Verne.

Kirk once boasted to Stark, "I changed the course of world history." Although that sounded outrageous, It had some basis, albeit remote, with reality.

Stark had approached Kirk and proposed that he host a weekly TV series sponsored by General Electric. An audio version of the series had already been featured as a weekly radio broadcast, attracting Cary Grant,

Judy Garland, William Holden, and Jane Wyman, who had used it as a forum for dramatic readings of skits, mysteries, and plays.

Beginning in February of 1953, the radio series morphed into a hit TV series, the General Electric Theater, thriving until 1962 as a prime-time staple within the then-relatively-limited roster of network broadcasting.

Once a week, as hosted by a "Master of Ceremonies" (a platform being offered to Kirk), G.E. would present a 30-minute drama. *[The deal stipulated that he'd have the option of appearing as an actor in as many of the episodes as he wanted. Over the years, the celebrities who appeared in televised episodes of the G.E. Theater read like a Who's Who of the entertainment industry: Fred Astaire. Nancy Davis Reagan, James Stewart, and Gene Tierney.]*

Television rescued Ronald Reagan's faltering screen career.

Kirk didn't want to obligate himself to such a commitment, so he phoned Ronald Reagan. Broke and at a low point of his career at the time. Reagan jumped at the chance.

In time, the General Electric Theater made Reagan rich, and its brass, all of them staunch Republicans, became the force behind persuading him to switch his allegiance from the Democratic to the Republican Party. Later, as General Electric's most visible and most televised spokesman, Reagan visited 135 GE facilities, greeted a quarter of a million people, and delivered endless "feel-good" speeches.

"The Great Communicator" later credited these engagements for his skill as a public speaker. Those skills later helped propel him to the U.S. presidency in 1980.

"Ronnie will owe me one for that," Kirk said.

***

Suddenly, seemingly coming out of nowhere and without any advance warning, Pier showed up at Kirk's rented villa in Rome. After a few awkward moments, and after some recriminations from Kirk, she won him over, particularly after leading the way into his bedroom. His reservations and resentments were set aside after she nibbled his ear and whispered, "You are the only man for me."

Pier toured through the glories of Rome with him, strolling hand in hand down the Via Veneto as the paparazzi snapped their cameras. They dined together in small, secret *trattorie*, enjoyed the Colosseum and the Spanish Steps, and wandered through the Vatican Museums and St. Peter's.

His relationship with Anne was put on hold, and she remained at the Hotel de Ville.

"It was like falling in love all over again," Kirk said at the end of Pier's visit.

He always maintained that he never had sex with Pier. But freed of Enrica, she spent the nights in his bedroom at Villa Gioia—at least, that's what the servants leaked to the Roman press after Kirk's checkout.

Eventually, Pier had to leave. Before her departure, he agreed to join her in London on her 21st birthday, June 19, 1953.

As it turned out, he could not attend her birthday celebration. On her actual birthday, she went out on the town with her dashingly handsome leading man from *The Flame and the Flesh*, Carlos Thompson. As she remembered it, "I wore the tightest dress I'd ever worn and the highest heels."

Instead, Kirk flew into London the following day and checked into the Dorchester. For her birthday dinner, he invited her to the Caprice. Prince Charles was also dining there that night.

He ordered a bottle of champagne and presented her with the engagement ring that he and Anne had bought for her at Bulgari's in Rome. She accepted his proposal.

On his final night in London, Pier slept over in his suite at the Dorchester.

In the six months that followed, with long distances separating them, both Kirk and Pier maintained busy but entirely separate schedules. Another rendezvous, (as odd as that sounded to all their friends and to everyone who was watching) wasn't scheduled until New Year's Eve in Paris.

The suspicion that Pier was wiser, more mature, and perhaps more manipulative than she appeared arose when she told a reporter from the *London Mail*, probably in reference to Kirk, "In Europe, we're expected to marry men, but in America, the men are likely to be little boys."

Back in Rome, increasingly aware that there were serious dysfunctions associated

Kirk with Pier Angeli in *The Story of Three Loves*. Their on-screen romance wasn't as turbulent as their private life together.

with the girl of his dreams, Kirk resumed his relationship with Anne. She was discreet enough not to pressure him about Pier, or even to mention her.

***

In his capacity as a tax exile from the United States, Kirk enjoyed his time in Rome during its "Hollywood-on-the-Tiber" phase. That meant that he could reconnect with "my old gang from the West Coast" stationed in Rome at the time. He ate pasta at the Taverna Flavia with Frank Sinatra and drank martinis with Elizabeth Taylor in the bar at the Excelsior.

In fact, one night at the Excelsior when Kirk was doing exactly that, Gina Lollobrigida, provocatively clad in a dress with plunging décolletage, made a spectacular entrance. The paparazzi defined the simultaneous appearance of Taylor and Lollobrigida in low-cut gowns as "the Battle of the Bosom."

When Mike Todd flew into Rome, he didn't keep it a secret. He was there to promote Todd-AO, a new technology for the widescreen, 70-mm format he'd developed in association with the American Optical Company for movie projectors. Informally, he described the format as "Cinerama out of a single hole."

He immediately phoned Kirk to invite him to a dinner party. "Just imagine *Ulysses* projected onto a wide, curved screen with multi-channel sound!"

The party was in honor of Todd's mistress, Evelyn Keyes, who had, for a while been Kirk's mistress too. He had last seen Todd and Keyes back in Acapulco when Todd had invited him to come live with them in their villa there

In spite of his having walked out on her, Kirk and Keyes had remained friends. "But, as he admitted to Todd, "Our passion has *Gone With the Wind.*" Of course, he was referencing the film in which she had portrayed Scarlett O'Hara's younger sister.

The elegant dinner party was hosted by Alfredo alla Scrofa within a 400-year-old building on the Via della Scrofa, a street that bore his ancient family's name. Within recent memory, it had entertained everyone from Mussolini to Ava Gardner. In time, Arthur Miller and Marilyn Monroe would show up, there, too.

During the cocktails that preceded dinner, although Kirk tried to catch up on news from Hollywood, Todd became irritated and began chastising Keyes loudly and within earshot of everyone, who froze as they listened to his denunciations.

335

"You actresses don't want a real man. You, like all the others, just need a faggot hairdresser following you around. Take your contemporaries—Lana, Ava, and Rita…" Then he stopped to point out Ingrid Bergman, chatting in a faraway corner with two Italian producers. "All of you, including Ingrid, could have found happiness with a man if you weren't so god damn self-enchanted."

When the producers broke from Bergman, Kirk headed in her direction. She had been on *Look* magazine's poll of the world's most beautiful women, and whereas he'd already "conquered" some of the film industry's other legendary beauties, she had remained elusive.

She greeted him warmly, and they exchanged compliments on their respective screen performances. "I fell in love with you when I saw you in *Casablanca,*" he said.

She returned his compliment, telling him that her favorite male character was his portrayal of Jonathan Shields in *The Bad and the Beautiful*.

As he was putting the make on her, Todd called her away to introduce her to some of his other guests.

Before dinner was served, Kirk asked Todd if he could be seated next to Bergman.

Todd's answer was "No. The host reserves that honor for himself as I'm pitching a film deal to her."

Instead, Kirk found himself seated between the journalist, Martha Gelhorn, the ex-wife of Ernest Hemingway, and Irene Selznick. "Before the dinner was over, Martha put the make on me, and Irene told me she should produce a film in which I could star."

At the end of the evening, he decided that his seduction of the elusive Bergman, the second-most famous actress to emerge from Sweden (after Garbo), would have to wait for another day. Eventually, Kirk and Bergman would interact as co-stars in the same film.

"Little Issur Danielovitch is determined to get her yet."

Ingrid Bergman with Bogart in her most famous romantic fantasy, playing Ilsa in *Casablanca* (1942).

As time went by, Rick and Ilsa would always have Paris.

CHAPTER TEN

KIRK DUMPS PIER ANGELI

Dismissing Their Affair as a "Silly Fantasy"

20,000 LEAGUES UNDER THE SEA

Doing It for Disney: Kirk Plays a Lusty Mariner

WEDDING BELL BLUES

After Committing Herself to Kirk,
Anne Suffers a Physical Attack from Her Jilted Lover

"I DEDICATED IT TO MOTHER"

Kirk Launches His Own Independent Film Production Company

This promotional photo, released during the filming of Disney's *20,000 Leagues Under the Sea,* shows Kirk in an animated discussion with Walt Disney himself. Nothing could have cemented the growing perception that Kirk was near his peak as a star whose image could sell not only movies but theme parks, souvenirs, sheet music, and memorabilia.

Kirk's romance with Anne Buydens continued without heating up, since—although they were almost never in the same city together—he maintained a fantasy about Pier as the love of his life. Often, he didn't even know what continent she was on.

Anne and Kirk flew to Brussels because he wanted to visit the sites where she grew up. During their time there, they dined with her former husband, Albert Buydens, and his new girlfriend.

"It was very sophisticated, very friendly, very European," Kirk said. "Their marriage had been one of convenience...not a real marriage."

"After we left the restaurant that night, Albert's girlfriend gave me a light kiss on the lips, Albert kissed Anne's cheek, promising that he'd be her friend for life."

From Belgium, Anne flew to her base in Paris, and Kirk winged his way to Munich, where he spent three days recording for the American Armed Forces Network.

When he returned to Paris, he made several failed attempts to reach Pier. "It wasn't a question of where she was, but who she was with—perhaps it was with Dean Martin. At least, they could speak Italian during love-making. I didn't think much would come of that. One night a drunken Dean told me, 'I just hop on, plug the hole, turn over, and go to sleep. In the morning, after a quick pat on the ass, I'm out the door.'"

It was December 9, 1953, his birthday, and Kirk was all alone when a telegram arrived. It was from Diane Dill, the mother of his two sons, notifying him of the hospital in Albany, New York, where his father was dying. She suggested he fly back to America at once.

"Some birthday," he lamented.

He put off thinking about it for the moment, at least, because he'd received an invitation from his director, Anatole Litvak, for a business conference at his rented home. Although he didn't really want to attend, he headed there anyway.

When he arrived at its front door, he was surprised that no lights were on. He rang the doorbell anyway. It was immediately flung open by Litvak, who ushered him into the darkened house.

All of a sudden, the lights went on. To his amazement, the room was full of beautiful women. The first he recognized was the actress, Leslie Calvet, with whom he'd had a previous fling. To his shock, he studied the faces of the other young women, each of whom he recognized from one or another of his one-night stands.

Only Anne could have set that up. He had already confessed most of these short, meaningless affairs to her, but he hadn't mentioned a few of the others. "How did she do it?" he asked Litvak. "Clever girl."

When he turned around, he saw her emerging from Litvak's kitchen with a birthday cake, candles blazing. "Speak of the devil."

As he recalled, "It was the strangest birthday of my life, one I'll remember to my dying day. At least all the gals in the room knew what I carry around in my pants—and how Kirk Douglas makes love."

Only the night before, he'd informed Anne that he was still in love with Pier, and that he planned to spend New Year's Eve with her.

"I knew then that I had to end our affair," Anne said. "It was too heartbreaking for me. I rounded up these girls as an act of revenge. He'd already told me about most of them, the others I found out on my own. I have my ways."

"At the end of the party, I kissed Kirk goodbye, telling him that I would not be in Paris when he was with Pier. I refused to tell him where I was going and warned my maid that I'd fire her if she revealed my whereabouts. It was time to remove myself from the presence of one Mr. Douglas. Elvis would call him a hound dog. But horndog might be more apt."

***

With the intention of honoring his dying father, Kirk flew to New York City, and transferred immediately onto a connecting flight to Albany. He was fully aware that his father, Herbert Danielovitch, might be dead by the time he reached the hospital.

A nurse escorted him to his father's room, where he was asleep. Kirk stood over the bed, looking at him. As a boy, his father had seemed so big and strong but now he looked shriveled. Kirk quietly moved a chair to a position beside the bed and remained there. Exhausted from the transatlantic flight, he drifted off as if in a reverie, thinking about this sick man beside him whose life was quickly ebbing.

Instead of feeling sorry for his father, Kirk felt sorry for himself. He'd wanted a loving, supporting father, "but Issur never got that." Even after Kirk became an internationally famous movie star—a triumph that provided his father with a monthly allowance, put a roof over his head, food on the table, and all forms of medical care—he had never congratulated him on his success.

Although it was a time of dying, and a time to forgive, he couldn't find a place in his heart to absolve his father for his many failures.

"He was always wanting something from me, giving nothing—not even a pat on the head. I would have settled for that. But Nothing! Nothing!"

When Kirk opened his eyes, his father was staring at him like some long-lost figure who had miraculously re-entered his life. In a very weak voice, the dying man said, "Stay with me."

"I might have," Kirk later recalled to Anne, "if he'd only said 'son,' which he did not."

"As if a force took over my body, I performed one cruel final act," Kirk said. "I told him, 'I can't stay. I have sons of my own waiting for me. I made a vow I'll never ignore my sons the way you ignored me as a boy. A boy needs his father.'"

"I looked at him for a final time," Kirk said. "Such a sad, pathetic figure, having lived a life useful only to himself. After a final glance, I left. One dreadful chapter, that of Issur, ended that day. He would no longer be part of the life of Kirk Douglas."

Kirk with his father, Herschel ("Harry") Danielovitch. Even in death, no father-son reconciliation.

Growing up in a house filled with women. Kirk with his six adult sisters.

***

During his flight from Albany back to New York City, Kirk tried not to think about his father. Instead, he concerned himself with sons Michael and Joel, with whom he would spend Christmas. He'd been away for so long, he wondered if they'd even recognize him.

He'd already bought a truckload of presents for them, and hoped they were the right ones. Boys of their age changed interests so fast.

After landing, he transferred at once to the Manhattan apartment of his ex-wife, Diana Dill. She'd informed him in advance that she'd be away for the day, perhaps deliberately, thereby allowing him uninterrupted time with his sons.

And that he did, taking them for a walk in Central Park, visiting the zoo, and buying them lunch with chocolate sundaes.

Later that day, the presents he'd arranged were delivered and placed around the tree, with the understanding that they'd be opened on Christmas Day, after his return to Paris. When Diana returned to her apartment later that day, she was friendly but reserved, sublimating herself for the benefit of his dialogues with his sons. He discussed their plans and their schooling, urging them to consider attending college one day in California.

Joel was more open and receptive to him than Michael was. Apparently, his older son still hadn't forgiven him for leaving Diana. He also seemed to have been indoctrinated by Diana about his illustrious (maternal) ancestors and the major roles they had played in the history of Bermuda.

In the living room was a photo of the Bermuda-built barque, *Sir George F. Seymour,* in which Diana's forbear had raced from Bermuda to Ireland in thirteen days in March of 1858.

"The way my boy talked, I felt he might become a sea captain. I warned them, regardless of what profession they chose, to stay out of the movie business. It was too wicked an industry for two nice boys like them. I fear that neither of them listened."

***

From New York, Kirk flew back to Paris. He was looking forward to spending New Year's Eve with Pier Angeli—or was he? As he later recalled, "Some buzz was gong off in my brain, questioning my real feelings toward this girl to whom I was still engaged."

He later wrote—although some sources disagree—that he never had sex with Pier. Pier herself told one of her best friends, Debbie Reynolds, that she and Kirk had had intercourse several times.

Since Pier would be in Paris without *mamma mia,* intimacies with her could transpire without her maternal chaperone. But that raised a perplexing issue: Did the idea of sex with her still appeal to him? Their previous bouts in bed had not been all that satisfying, as she just lay there with her head on the pillow, showing little if any response to his lovemaking. It was almost as if she were enduring it only for his pleasure—and not her own. Perhaps Enrica had indoctrinated her with the belief that sex was something to be endured as a means of producing children.

In Paris, Pier was staying at the swanky Hotel George V, whose lobby was always filled with the most expensive hookers in Paris.

Thinking that she might want him to arrive early (they hadn't seen each other in months), he phoned her there. They'd made plans to celebrate the New Year at a dinner/dance at La Tour d'Argent.

She put him off, telling him that she had to get her hair done and pick up a gown that had needed tailoring. "You want me to look great tonight, don't you?"

"That doesn't matter so much to me," he said. "I'd rather you invite me over to fuck you."

"You American boys can be so crude."

When his taxi arrived at the George V, Pier was waiting for him in the lobby. He approached to kiss her, but she turned her cheek, claiming, "I don't want to spoil my makeup."

A festive aura, live music, and lots of elegant food waited for them at Tour d'Argent, which had prepared for the arrival of the cream of Parisian society. At table beside a window, Pier sat with Kirk, watching the nuances of the richly illuminated back side of Paris' medieval cathedral, Nôtre-Dame.

After midnight, he invited her to stroll along the foggy banks of the Seine, the world's most romantic river. Lit by lamps, dozens of Parisians and a scattering of tourists had the same idea. There was a lot of love-making, the stand-up variety.

"I would always remember that night," Kirk said. "It was cold, and the wind was blowing. Something was wrong and had been wrong all night. She was distant, and my feelings were churned up. I thought of Anne, wondering where she was. I expected to be invited back to share Pier's suite for the next three nights, but did I really want to go, after putting it off for so long?"

In front of her hotel, he paused on the sidewalk without entering the lobby. She looked puzzled, as if wanting to ask why he'd stopped. She had not yet extended an invitation.

"Is something wrong?" she asked.

"You've been elusive all night," he said. "I feel I don't know you anymore. We've been engaged, but most of the time, I never even knew what continent you were on, much less who you were with.

"Are you accusing me?" she asked, not concealing the anger in her voice.

"I don't think our engagement is going to work out," he said. "Mind returning my ring?"

She removed and returned his engagement ring, which he dropped into his pocket. Tears filled her eyes. "Will I see you tomorrow? Perhaps you'll feel different then."

"No," he replied. *"Domani à troppo tardi."* *[That had been the name of her first movie,* Tomorrow Is Too Late *(1950)].*

She turned and walked inside the lobby, as he headed to the nearby Champs-Elysées. He didn't mind the night wind. His obsession with her was over.

"The whole relationship was just a silly fantasy of an adorable, giggly little girl who was just playing games with men."

***

In the first pre-dawn hours of the first day of 1954, Kirk sat alone in his hotel suite, wondering if he'd made the right decision about letting Pier go. He finally concluded that she had never been his in the first place.

At 7AM, he phoned Anne's apartment, knowing that at least the maid would answer.

She told Kirk, "Miss Buydens said that she'll fire me if I tell you where she's hiding."

"I had to use all my macho charm, but I finally got the maid to tell me that Anne had retreated to a small hotel in St.-Paul-de-Vence, in the hills above Nice."

He put through a call. Anne picked up the receiver. In his most enticing voice, he told her, "It's all over between Pier and me—the engagement, everything. I miss you something terrible. I love you. Come back to me. I'll be waiting for you at the train station in Paris, where I'll take you in my arms and never let you go."

"I don't want my heart broken again," she said.

"I'll mend your heart, not break it," he said.

As promised, he was waiting at the railway station in Paris to meet her. He took her in his arms and kissed her passionately. "I can't face the New Year—or any year in the future—without you at my side, preferably in my arms."

Kirk had already accepted the lead role in another movie, *20,000 Leagues Under the Sea,* but shooting would not begin for a month. He invited her to accompany him to the ski resort of Klosters in the Graubünden (Grisons) region of eastern Switzerland, even though he did not know how to ski.

Anne with Kirk in Klosters...a pre-marital honeymoon.

They traveled there as part of what they defined as a pre-honeymoon, joining friends who included the director, Anatole Litvak; the novelist, Irwin Shaw; and the *Life* magazine photographer, Robert Capa.

With a passionate intensity, as was his style, Kirk hired the best ski instructor at Klosters and set out to ski the slopes, eventually graduating to the more dangerous ones. Before the end of the month, he'd entered the slalom race, competing against experienced skiers, and came in second.

Finally, word reached him that Disney was ready to begin shooting *20,000 Leagues Under the Sea* in The Bahamas. He and Anne returned to Paris, where she resumed her work. After only a single night there, she rode in a taxi with him to the airport to see him off.

As he was kissing her goodbye, an attendant from Air France approached him. "Mr. Douglas, Pier Angeli is waiting in the First Class Lounge and wishes to see you."

He looked at Anne before responding to the messenger: "Tell her, please, that Mr. Douglas is not receiving visitors today." Then he kissed Anne goodbye and headed to his plane after promising her that "we'll meet again…and soon."

Anne was later quoted as saying, "I want to understand him, and finally decided he's dragged

— LES VOYAGES EXTRAORDINAIRES —

— J. HETZEL, ÉDITEUR —

The lower photo displays the frontispiece from the first edition of *Vingt mille lieues sous les mers*, by the French adventurer and author, Jules Verne, as published in 1871 in Paris by J. Hetzel.

The upper photo displays Kirk amid the visual effects Disney labored to perfect during the filming of *20,000 Leagues Under the Sea*. Then innovative, they concealed the underwater rigging that maneuvered the *Nautilus* through fogs and hurricane-force winds.

this way and that with raw emotions. He's insecure and plagued with self-doubt, no doubt a holdover from his brutal childhood. He needs to be reassured all the time. In essence, he's still a big child, Issur grown up, at least in body."

***

In 1870, the French novelist, Jules Verne, published *20,000 Leagues Under the Sea,* a fantasy adventure set on a submersible ship that could travel to the bottom of the ocean to discover sea monsters and denizens of the deep.

Over the course of many years, Hollywood would adapt it into several different films showcasing actors who included Lionel Barrymore and Thomas Mitchell, who's remembered today for his portrayal of Scarlett O'Hara's father in *Gone With the Wind.* The Verne novel's first celluloid adaptation was made as a silent film in 1916. A "postmodern" version was released in 1997 as a made-for-TV miniseries.

During its pre-production phase, Kirk had met with Walt Disney himself at a meeting that established the fee he'd receive. After Kirk voiced the lowest figure he'd accept, Walt looked surprised, then asked, "Is that for just *20,000 Leagues Under the Sea,* or is that for six pictures?"

"The tightwad finally agreed," Kirk said. "Actually, he wasn't a tightwad, shelling out a budget of at least five million to make the picture."

As director, Disney selected Richard Fleischer, who was Jewish, like Kirk. *[Fleischer was surprised when he heard that he'd been selected by Disney as the film's director: His father, Max, had been one of Walt Disney's chief rivals. Fleischer was a director with whom Kirk worked smoothly. He later hired him to direct his movie,* The Vikings.*]*

After reading Earl Fenton's screenplay, Kirk complained to Disney, "There are no women in this film. I'm hot to play the lusty sailor, so I want the movie to open with a scene of me in port with a beautiful girl on each arm. I like to be depicted as a dashing ladies' man, a real tough guy."

Disney thought that Kirk was making a good point and agreed to shoot it that way.

Instead of cartoon characters, Disney wanted to craft a live action/adventure in Technicolor, and the first science fiction film to be shot in CinemaScope. From the beginning, he wanted Kirk as Ned Land, a cocky and roguish harpoonist. He is supported by the evil Captain Nemo, as played

345

by James Mason.

Kirk had appeared on celluloid in *The Story of Three Loves,* alongside Mason before, albeit within different sub-sections. Before the debut of shooting, the two actors battled over star billing, with Kirk prevailing. *[Gregory Peck had also lobbied for the role of Captain Nemo, but Disney preferred Mason.]*

The other two male leads, Paul Lukas as "the Professor," Pierre Aronnax, and Peter Lorre as Conseil, had each been born in what had been the Austro-Hungarian Empire. In the film, Lukas played a naturalist, with Lorre cast as his assistant.

[Charles Boyer had originally been offered the role of the professor, but he had to reject it because of another film commitment.]

Kirk had long admired Lukas in his screen roles, notably when he'd won the Oscar for Watch on the Rhine (1943), in which he'd starred opposite Bette Davis.

Kirk had also admired the work of Lorre in Casablanca, *but also in films with Sydney Greenstreet. "Poor Peter," Kirk said. "His gallbladder horror, with all that pain, was relieved by morphine. He had become an addict."*

Despite the inclusion of these internationally acclaimed actors, the real star of the movie was its art direction and special effects, which would win Academy Awards for 1954.]

In a nutshell, the plot of *20,000 Leagues Under the Sea* involved an investigation into the mystery of various ship sinkings. During their moments of greatest peril, survivors had reported a sea monster, something that resembled a giant whale with a long horn that it used to ram and sink

RECYCLING A SHOW-BIZ HIT AS A THEME PARK ATTRACTION: The sets that Disney crafted for *20,000 Leagues* were so avant-garde that the company's planners opted to reincarnate them in the Tomorrowland subdivision of Disneyland in Anaheim where they remained as profit-generating exhibits from 1955 till 1966.

Later, variations of these sets were installed in the Magic Kingdom Park at Walt Disney World near Orlando, where, from 1971 till their removal in 1991, they were among the most popular destinations at the Park.

their vessels.

With the understanding that Captain Nemo controlled the most advanced technology of his era (the 19ᵗʰ Century), he had designed his underwater vessel to resemble an equivalent monster.

Known as the *Nautilus,* the submarine has a hideously long tail, electric eyes, a snout that doubles as a battering ram, and metallic ridges along its spine. Its length measures two hundred feet, and the actors housed inside it make it clear that it's the scientific "*ne plus ultra*" of its era.

The film's most dramatic moment has Kirk battling a giant squid during a fierce storm at sea.

Location shooting would be in The Bahamas and Jamaica. Kirk wrote frequent letters to Anne in Europe, describing his undying love and how much he missed her. In her absence, he found

Disney even commissioned a rousing "sea chanty" for Kirk to sing, a catchy tune entitled "A Whale of a Tale."

It was recycled as a jukebox ditty and as sheet music for resale later.

"amusements" wherever he went, confessing to and describing some of them in his memoirs.

One night, as he was gambling at a casino in Nassau, he spotted a very good-looking young woman. "She looked like Claire Trevor, but had a 'peek-a-boo' Veronica Lake haircut, and smoked a cigarette just like Bette Davis."

He pictured himself as Bogie as he approached her. No introduction was needed, as he simply whispered, "I'll meet you in the parking lot in ten minutes."

He drove her to his hotel. "I was Bogie all night long. She was insatiable."

***

In Jamaica, he was booked into lodgings at Round Hill, the posh and socially connected resort near Montego Bay. During the day, scenes of him fleeing from "cannibals" were filmed. Later, presented as entertainment for hotel guests, a group of "copper-colored girls (his words) were dancing and singing Calypso. I hate to think how young they were. I didn't want to end up in jail. But my hormones were working overtime."

The staff reported that a parade of young girls was seen coming and going from his bungalow during his stay at Round Hill.

When location shooting ended for *20,000 Leagues Under the Sea*, Kirk returned to Hollywood for filming of scenes within the Disney Studios. Anne was still working in Europe.

One afternoon, gossipy Hedda Hopper appeared, unannounced and malevolent, on the set. To her, Kirk said, "The wandering gypsy, namely me, is footsore from being footloose in Europe. I'm happy to be home again. We're making a great film for Walt, but I had to shave off my beard. A beard is great because it gives a man a hiding place."

On the Disney lot, a giant water tank had been installed for the filming of additional scenes. Mason came very close to drowning in it until a member of the crew, trained as a lifeguard, had rescued him. When the incident was described to Walt Disney, he said, "Thank god I have insurance."

When Kirk bid his final goodbye to Mason, the British actor said, "There have always been ups and downs in my life, though the downs do seem to have been more frequent than the ups."

At the premiere, when a reporter asked Kirk what he thought of *20,000 Leagues Under the Sea*, he said, "It's a Whale of a Tale," words from a chantey his character had sung in the movie.

The Disney film morphed into one of Kirk's biggest hits, generating some $30 million at the box office.

Critics for the most part responded favorably. Bosley Crowther, in *The New York Times*, wrote, "It's as fabulous and fantastic as any of Disney's cartoons. It should prove a sensation, at least with kids." Another critic, Steve Biodroski, hailed it as "one of the greatest science fiction films ever made."

***

[POSTSCRIPT: *After* 20,000 Leagues Under the Sea *opened to big box office, a surprise invitation came in from Walt Disney. Michael and Joel were in town at the time, visiting their father, and Disney invited Kirk and his sons over to his property.*

"Uncle Walt" rightly assumed that Kirk and his boys would be interested in his private collection of toy trains, the largest and finest in the world, and so extensive that it required the constant maintenance of a full-time engineer. Michael and Joel spent a few hours riding them over bridges and through tunnels. "My boys were delighted," Kirk said, "and so was I."

About a month later, he was made aware of a home-style video of himself, with

Michael and Joel, being aired as part of an episode within Disney's hour-long weekly TV show. Most of the episode promoted 20,000 Leagues Under the Sea, *but a final segment showed the Douglas family, father and sons, riding the toy trains across Walt Disney's property.*

Furious at this invasion of his family's privacy, and since Disney had never asked his permission, Kirk felt exploited. His family had been configured as unpaid participants in what was tantamount to a commercial for Disney.

He fired off a letter to "Uncle Walt," and a few days later, he received a hand-delivered letter of apology from Disney himself.

Thinking that the matter was settled, he put it out of his mind until two months later, when the same episode was aired yet again on Disney's TV show. Kirk immediately called his business manager and lawyer, Sam Norton, who advised him to sue. "I think you can clean up on this one," Norton predicted.

Kirk filed suit, asking the courts to grant him $450,000 for invasion of privacy. The case dragged through the legal system from 1954 to 1959, when Anne persuaded him to drop it, fearing negative publicity. "Walt is a beloved figure. Suing him could harm your standing in this town."

Finally, he had his attorney drop the charges, claiming, "Let's face it. Suing Walt is like suing God."

***

Kirk flew into Los Angeles and moved into a small tract house at 1609 San Ysidro Drive. A few doors down lived Danny Kaye, who, three days later, invited him over for lunch.

As they sat beside the pool, Kaye suggested that Kirk take a swim before lunch. "I didn't bring my trunks," Kirk told him.

"They're not needed here."

Standing up, Kirk said, "Whatever you say, good buddy." Then he stripped naked and swam three laps.

Later, after he returned home, he admired the decorating touches that Frances Stark, the wife of producer Ray Stark, had applied to his new home. Yet it still needed more paintings and art objects. Instructing Anne to pick up some art in Europe, he sent her a check for $7,000, knowing how good her taste was.

He was eager for her return to the States. He had learned that she'd be working to publicized Marlene Dietrich's next picture, and he worried that Marlene might discuss their sexual history with his new girlfriend.

Kirk's first house guests were Mike Todd and his mistress, Evelyn Keyes, Kirk's former mistress. This was yet another of several house party sleepovers he'd already shared with them in Mexico and Europe.

After a few days of congenial hanging out, Todd flew to Las Vegas for business, leaving Kirk alone in his house with Keyes.

After dinner on their first night alone together, Kirk retreated to his bedroom, locking the door behind him. He later speculated, "Was I locking her out or was I locking myself in?"

After Todd's return from Vegas, Kirk observed "From the sounds coming from my guest room, he made up for lost time away from her (Kirk's words)."

Suddenly they were gone, and Kirk felt lonely.

He hosted a small dinner for Ray and Frances Stark as a thank you for her decorating. She asked if she could bring a guest, and he said he'd be delighted.

"I won't tell you who she is, but if you've ever gone to the movies, you'll know at once."

Over dinner, Merle Oberon was the epitome of grace, charm, elegance, and beauty. She had always been an enigma to Kirk. Obsessively mysterious, she had told many lies about her origins and background. One of them was a myth she had perpetuated for decades about having been born in Tasmania.

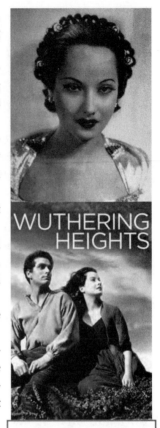

Two views of Merle Oberon. Lower photo: with Laurence Olivier in one of the most famous romantic dramas of Hollywood's Golden Age.

She was actually the product of an illicit relationship between a 12-year-old Indian girl in Bombay (British India) and a much older English Army officer.

Kirk had been attracted to Oberon since she'd appeared in *Wuthering Heights* (1939), the wildly romantic tale of tormented love in which she'd co-starred opposite Laurence Olivier as Heathcliff.

Earlier in her career, she'd been known as "Queenie" O'Brian before her first husband, the producer/director Alexander Korda, changed it to Merle Oberon.

[Coincidentally, in 1987, Kirk would co-star in an ABC-TV miniseries called Queenie, based loosely on Oberon's life.]

Over dinner, she flirted openly with him, and he flirted right back. Frances later referred to their sexual dynamic as "The Mating Game."

Oberon was known around both London and Los Angeles as a

nymphomaniac. The photographer, Cecil Beaton, said, "Merle is as promiscuous as a man enjoying a quickie behind the door."

She specialized in seducing movie stars. She had been noted for musing, sometimes in the middle of the sex act, something akin to, "I can't believe I'm fucking James Cagney..." or perhaps, David Niven, with whom she'd fallen madly in love, or Errol Flynn, George Brent, Maurice Chevalier, Gary Cooper, or Eddie Fisher, Rex Harrison, Darryl F. Zanuck, or Prince Philip behind the back of Queen Elizabeth.

Vivien Leigh said, "Merle had both Rhett Butler and Ashley Wilkes," Scarlett O'Hara was referring, of course, to the male stars of *Gone With the Wind* (1939). Even Senator Ted Kennedy tried to get in on the army marching in and out of Oberon's boudoir.

After the Starks left Kirk's house after his dinner party that night, Oberon remained behind. She and Kirk didn't go to bed right away but talked a bit. She told him that she did not like sensitive, neurotic men like Montgomery Clift, preferring instead the less complicated, athletic, and virile type as represented by him.

She spoke briefly of her life, asserting that she missed the adventure and excitement of the British Empire as it had existed before World War II. "I'm a devotee of Colonial Britain."

"Money is terribly important to me," she said. "I'm trying to collect a lot of it while I'm still young and beautiful. That way, when I've move on in years, I'll be able to afford a much younger man. The more beautiful he is, the better."

[She achieved her goal, marrying a man 25 years her junior, Robert Wolders in 1975.]

"Don't you think it's time we hit the hay?" Kirk asked.

"What a colorful American expression!" she answered. "One that reflects one's rural background. I must warn you, I like to explore every inch of the male body, leaving no part of a man unattended. Many American men don't know what their zones of passion are until their bodies are thoroughly explored. I am anxious to see your breasts. Men salivate over a woman's breasts. But from what I'm told American women ignore the breasts on their men. I can often arouse sensitivities in men who never had parts of their body thoroughly appreciated before."

Kirk stood up, took her hand, and suggested, "Let's not talk about it—let's do it."

After a weekend of love, "including a few tricks that Merle learned in a Bombay bordello" (Kirk's appraisal), she went home. Two nights later, she phoned for another rendezvous.

He turned her down. "I'd satisfied my curiosity about this older woman and wanted to move on to my next conquest. It was awkward for me to reject such a fabled beauty, but I didn't want to become another stud horse in her stable."

**

It was midnight and Kirk, for a change, was alone in his bed. Suddenly, he was awakened by the incessant ringing of his doorbell. Who in hell could be calling on him at this hour? For certain, he was not going to throw open the door.

Putting on a robe, he stood behind his locked front door and called out, "Who's there?" Had some deranged fan, a stalker, found out his home address?

"It's Pier," came that unmistakable voice. "Let me in! I've got to see you!"

"Go away!" he shouted through the door. "It's over! All over!"

She didn't answer, but he heard her sobbing. From what he knew of her, she didn't take rejection lightly.

Then, when she pounded again on his door, he turned and walked away, retreating to his bedroom, where he turned on some late night music to drown out her final pleadings.

[Before he died in a car crash in 1955, James Dean launched an affair with Pier Angeli. From the beginning, he was realistic about her: "Our affair was fire and ice," he said. "Before I came along, and in spite of that angelic face, Pier had already screwed half of Hollywood."

The singer, Vic Damone, was still involved with Pier at the time of her liaison with Dean, and when Dean departed from her life, in 1954, Pier wed Damone. Four disastrous years of marriage followed. Damone was a wife beater, among other deficiencies.

In 1962, she married the Italian composer, Armando Trovajoli, no great beauty who was sometimes mistaken for her father. By 1969, they had separated, ending her married life.

Two years later, at the age of 39, she was found dead, having committed suicide by a barbiturate overdose at her home in Beverly Hills.]

**

A few days later, Anne Buydens flew into the Los Angeles airport, dressed like a fashion model posing for a Christian Dior catalogue. She wore a stylish hat with a black veil.

"Traveling incognito?" Kirk said to her as he rushed to embrace her.

352

He lifted her veil to discover four patches of raw, burnt skin, each beginning to crust over into scabs.

"What happened?" he asked.

"I'll explain later," she promised.

For appearances sake, she had booked herself into the Bel Air Hotel. He kissed her again after she promised to show up at his new home at 7PM to spend the night in his arms.

No sooner had she settled into her room at the Bel Air that she received a phone call from its manager, the hotel heir, Nicky Hilton. He promised that all her expenses at the hotel would be picked up if she'd grant him "visitation rights." She politely rejected his offer.

Anne Buydens, modeling a dress by Christian Dior during his "The New Look" era.

Later that night, after her arrival at Kirk's new home—soon to be her home, too—he delayed bedding her until he'd taken her on a tour. Both of them agreed that all that the house needed was some art on the otherwise bare white walls, and she agreed to help him select some.

Then she explained why her face was scarred. She'd taken a ship from France to the Port of New York because she was desperately in need of some relaxation.

In Manhattan, she'd checked into the Sherry Netherland Hotel. There, she received a phone call from her longtime lover, Ramon Babbas. He had flown to New York from Paris and, like her, was also staying at the Sherry Netherland. He invited her to dinner, and she had accepted, planning to use the evening to break off their affair.

After their meal, she returned with him to his suite so that they could talk privately. She knew that if she broke up with him in the dining room, since he had a violent temper, he might create a scene.

He'd been drinking heavily, and he was also smoking a cigarette when she delivered the news that she was on her way to Los Angeles to marry Kirk Douglas.

"I forbid you to see that conceited bastard ever again."

When she refused to acquiesce, he'd stabbed his lit cigarette into her face in four painful jabs. Then he ran to the open window fronting the street, eighteen floors below. Drunkenly, he maneuvered himself outside onto the ledge. She rushed to yank and tug at his dead weight body, managing to maneuver him back inside, where he collapsed onto the floor.

She immediately called his New York office for help and advice. Its manager arrived with a doctor, who administered aid to her face and to remain on site until his boss calmed down and sobered up.

Early the next morning, she boarded a flight to Los Angeles to follow through on the plan to marry Kirk.

On May 29, 1954, they flew together to Las Vegas to get married, applying for a marriage license at the license bureau, a venue that was famously open for business twenty-three hours a day.

Anne Buydens, on the beach at Cannes in the mid-1950s.

The Justice of the Peace who performed the ceremony evoked a Texas cowpoke, with boots, a large silver belt buckle, and a western-style shirt. "Honest John" Lytell spoke with a Southern drawl that stretched from Dallas to San Antonio.

They mutually agreed to define their previous vacation in Klosters as their honeymoon. She had to return to Paris to conclude her business affairs. There, she encountered difficulties in getting documents she needed from the American Embassy. She also had to endure a "too intimate" inspection from a gynecologist.

While she was away in France, Kirk, still in Los Angeles, reported every workday to the back lot of 20th Century Fox for the filming of his newest movie, *The Racers*.

***

In Los Angeles, one of the first business meetings Kirk attended after his extended time abroad was one that had been scheduled with Darryl Zanuck at 20th Century Fox. At the time, the studio chief was one of the most powerful and abrasive in Hollywood.

Although Kirk did not admire or even like the man, he respected his cinematic genius. In person, he was short, arrogant, ruthless, and cocky, a caricature of a cigar-smoking movie mogul. According to many accounts, he bedded between one and three Fox starlets every day, shutting down the studio for his afternoon "fuck break."

Zanuck was competitive and not very businesslike during Kirk's first five minutes in his office. "Had any hot pieces of ass lately?" Zanuck asked Kirk. "I hear you're a real horndog."

"I get by," Kirk said, modestly, not wanting to stimulate competition with the tycoon, whose reputation included abusive seductions of hundreds of starlets.

Kirk himself had had carnal knowledge of some of them: Marilyn Monroe, Linda Darnell, Gene Tierney, and—more recently for Kirk—Merle Oberon. Ava Gardner, another actress whose charms had been bestowed on both men, once

Bella Darvi with Kirk in *The Racers* (1955).

Kirk's love affair with Darryl F. Zanuck's mistress was confined only to the screen.

discussed Zanuck with Kirk: "The only thing bigger than his cigar is his cock, which he likes to unzip and show. A long time ago, when he pulled it out for Little Miss Muppet, Shirley Temple, the brat ran screaming from the room."

Sitting across from Zanuck, Kirk was reminded of a comment made by Marlon Brando. "Zanuck bears a striking resemblance to Bugs Bunny. When he enters a room, his front teeth precede him by three seconds."

In ways that would almost certainly get him drummed out of the industry today, in the more sexually abusive 1950s, Zanuck got away with promoting himself as Hollywood's #1 Stud. "A gal ain't been fucked until I've ridden her. All the starlets at Fox tell me I'm the best. I can also go all day and night."

"That sure has me beat," Kirk said. "After three rounds, I'm finished."

"I always bring the new bitch I've hired at Fox into my office and lock the door," Zanuck said. "Then I unzip in front of her and jerk off to get her excited. When I've done that, I mount her like a bull."

"That's all very enticing," Kirk said, "but I'm sure you didn't summon me here today to discuss your exploits, even though I'm impressed."

"I want you to sign a three-picture deal with Fox, beginning with a movie called *The Racers*. You'll play the lead—a racecar driver."

Kirk turned down the offer, explaining that he'd soon be forming a production company of his own. He was intrigued, however, with the idea of playing a racecar driver, so he signed for that as a part of a single-picture deal. The role, he believed, might challenge him.

"For your co-star, I'm casting this hot little foreign number. She's my new mistress and I've changed her name to Bella Darvi. What gives my affair with her an extra flavor is that she's bisexual. I always get off watching two women have sex. After I watch them for a while, I grab one of them and send her to heaven. You should try it sometime."

"Indeed, I will," Kirk said. "Just hearing about it gets me all hot and bothered." He tried to disguise the sarcasm in his voice.

***

Although Kirk did not like Zanuck, he applauded his choice of director for *The Racers* (1955). Henry Hathaway was a virtual legend when he helmed Kirk in his latest movie. He'd been cast as an Italian bus driver with a burning ambition to win the Grand Prix de Napoli in his garage-built car, competing against the most expensive race cars in Europe. The fast action picture contained some of the best all-time footage of car racing.

Since his stint as a child actor at the age of ten in silent pictures, Hathaway had gone on to helm Gary Cooper in seven films. One had been *The Lives of a Bengal Lancer* (1935). He was also known for directing westerns with John Wayne and Randolph Scott. In time, he would direct the Duke in *True Grit* (1969), a film that brought Wayne a Best Actor Oscar.

Hathaway had directed "The Blonde of the 1930s," Mae West, in *Go West, Young Man* (1936) and also "The Blonde of the 1950s," Marilyn Monroe, in her first starring role, *Niagara* (1953).

Kirk had to control his temper around the equally temperamental Hathaway. "He was a workhorse," Kirk said, "demanding endless takes until he felt I got it right. He made it clear that he didn't want any suggestions from some actor. He was very competent in action scenes, however."

Behind his back, Kirk with a certain contempt, referred to Hathaway as "The Marquis." [*Hathaway's grandfather, a Belgian diplomat named the Marquis Henri Léopold de Fiennes, had settled in San Francisco after his failed attempt to acquire the Sandwich Islands (now Hawaii) for the Kingdom of Belgium.*]

The producer of *The Racers* was Julian Blaustein, best remembered today as the force behind the cult sci-fi movie, *The Day the Earth Stood Still* (1951). He had awarded Marilyn Monroe a key role in *Don't Bother to Knock* (1952), in which she appeared opposite Richard Widmark and Anne Bancroft.

Blaustein had just finished making *Désirée* (1954), in which Marlon Brando played a solemn Napoléon Bonaparte.

The script for *The Racers* by Charles Kaufmann was based on the life story of the champion race car driver, Rudolf Caracciola.

Its plot involves a driver (Kirk) who meets a ballet dancer (Bella Darvi) when her poodle runs loose and causes him to crash his car to avoid killing her pet. They fall in love.

Hathaway told Kirk that Darvi was needed "for window dressing," and because Zanuck wanted a showcase for his mistress. "Besides, we're making her a high fashion *dévotée* because we want to work in some fashion shows and some scenic shots of Paris and Rome. That way, we'll attract some women who don't want to see a movie that focuses just on some damn cars racing around a track."

Gilbert Roland, cast as "The Devil May Care" Dell-Oro, was "the Knight of the Speedways." He had worked with Kirk on *The Bad and the Beautiful,* in which he'd played the Latin lover of the adulterous Gloria Grahame.

The other veteran driver was played by Cesar Romero. Katy Jurado, was perfectly cast as his wife, Maria. Lee J. Cobb, the racing team manager, is seen chomping on his cigar and bellowing orders like a drill sergeant. The minor Austrian actor, Charles Goldner played Kirk's mechanic and companion, Piero. He'd gotten his start in British films in the 1940s. He had recently appeared in *The Master of Ballantree* (1953), starring Errol Flynn.

Bronx-born to a Jewish family, Cobb was a brilliant character actor best remembered for *On the Waterfront* (1954) starring Marlon Brando. Cobb was usually portrayed characters who were arrogant, intimidating, and abrasive—sometimes judges or cops.

In 1951, Cobb was accused of having been a member of the Communist Party. After being summoned to testify before the House Un-American Activities Committee, he refused to "out" other members, thereby condemning himself to banishment from any future film made in Hollywood. Repenting, he reappeared before the committee in 1953 and revealed as Communists the names of twenty industry players.

When Kirk asked him why he'd done that, Cobbs said, "I was desperate. I had no money, a family to support, I hated myself for doing that, but I felt my main loyalty was to my family Life doesn't always give you easy

Talented, sultry Latinos: Katy Jurado and Cesar Romero in *The Racers*. They both preferred studly men as their bedtime companions.

357

choices."

Of Cuban and Spanish heritage, Cesar Romero was known as a "gay blade" around Hollywood. As a lifelong bachelor, aging actresses often configured him as their (platonic) escorts to gala events: Joan Crawford, Barbara Stanwyck, Ann Sheridan, Ginger Rogers, Jane Wyman, Lucille Ball, and Linda Darnell.

Hathaway later revealed that "Caesar came on to Kirk, but Kirk didn't bat for his team."

As Maria Chávez, Jurado delivered her usual brilliant performance. She had been a major movie star in Mexican movies during its "Golden Age heyday" (1940 to the early 1960s). She'd was often cast as a villainous *femme fatale.* In 1952, she had one of her most high-profile roles, appearing with Gary Cooper and Grace Kelly in *High Noon.*

When she first met Kirk, she'd been nominated for a Best Supporting Actress Oscar for her performance in *Broken Lance* (1954) opposite Spencer Tracy.

It was common gossip in Hollywood that the sultry Latina often seduced some of Tinseltown's leading men, including not only Gary Cooper, but John Wayne, Gilbert Roland, Anthony Quinn, and Burt Lancaster.

Marlon Brando told Kirk, "Katy has enigmatic eyes, black as hell, pointing at you like fiery arrows."

In reciprocation, Jurado said, "Marlon and I are true friends of the soul."

It was Hathaway who claimed that on several occasions, Kirk visited Jurado's dressing room. "She usually got her man. Kirk stayed in her love nest a long time. Of course, they could have been playing poker."

For the most part, *The Racers* met with hostile reviews and lost a million dollars at the box office. Critic Spender James described its "banal story and questionable characterizations. Some of the lines are laughable as when a dying Gilbert Roland tells Kirk Douglas, 'Gino, my crankcase is leaking,' as he clutches his crushed chest."

Philip Scheuer of the *Los Angeles Times* was kinder: "Once again, Kirk Douglas is playing the heel he was in *Champion.* It is his achievement that, though the taut wires that bind him to us snap one by one, one or two are still holding fast at the finish, and we are able to rejoice in his discovery that he retains some decent instincts."

***

It took only one scene with Zanuck's mistress, Bella Darvi, for Kirk to conclude that she could not act. He complained about it to Hathaway, who answered, "What choice do we have? Zanuck insists on her as your co-star. She probably has talents that go beyond acting."

Behind her back, Kirk referred to her as "Bella Donna," and made comparisons of her looks (but not her talent) to the French actress and dancer, Leslie Caron.

In 1928, Bajla Wegier (Darvi's birth name) had been born the daughter of a Jewish baker and his wife in Sosnowiec, Poland.

After the Nazi takeover, she and her three brothers were shipped off to concentration camps. Darvi ending up in Auschwitz. She was released midway through the war, in 1943.

Reportedly, she emerged looking healthy and well fed. That led to speculation that during her stay in Auschwitz, she'd been kept in an apartment for sex with Nazi officers.

By 1950, she'd married a successful businessman, Alban Cavalade, apparently for his money. Two years later, she divorced him, received a hefty settlement, and headed to Cannes with a stylish wardrobe. Her goal involved meeting a producer who would morph her into a movie star with the casting couch part of the plan.

In Cannes, she won over not only Zanuck but his wife, Virginia. She so ingratiated herself into their circle that Virginia invited her to live with them in Hollywood.

That led to all sorts of gossip and speculation, since Zanuck was rather open about his affair. There were even rumors of a *ménage à trois,* and it became widely known that Darvi was bisexual.

During the second week of shooting *The Racers,* Virginia showed up to see how Darvi was emoting. To Kirk's surprise, he found her candid about her husband's affair, which by now, was any-thing but secret.

"Darryl doesn't have the temperament to be a respectable husband," Virginia told Kirk. "He's Tarzan of the Apes. I know that to hold onto him, I must allow him to enter the jungle, thumping his chest and swinging from the trees."

When Kirk saw the first rushes of his scenes with Darvi, he went to Zanuck and complained, "There is just no chemistry between us. Is it too late to replace her?"

"It's your job to make an explosion between you two on screen. That's why I hired you. The gal makes me feel seventeen in bed

Bella Darvi told Kirk, "If you're bisexual, you double your chances."

with her. Her greatest acting occurs in the boudoir, where she's Eleanora Duse, Sarah Bernhardt, even Greta Garbo."

Kirk invited Darvi to lunch one day, hoping to understand her better. She shared her "philosophy" of life over chicken salad.

"It doesn't matter who you sleep with. Americans make such a fuss over that. Love, whatever in hell that is, doesn't matter either. Only one thing matters, and that is money. I'd do almost anything for money. You see, I'm addicted to gambling. Darryl and I often go to Las Vegas, where he covers my losses."

Then she looked at Kirk and asked, "Would you do that for me?"

"Hell, no!"

"Then you won't be enjoying my charms."

Since Zanuck could have any starlet he wanted on the Fox lot, Kirk wondered, "Why Darvi?"

One of Zanuck's friends, Henry Fine, tried to explain it to Kirk. "Whenever you come near Darvi, you can just feel the heat emerging. She's one of the sexiest females I've ever encountered, a great ball of shimmering fire."

"But she doesn't light my fire," Kirk said.

Zanuck's previous onscreen gamble with Darvi had only recently failed. He'd cast her in *The Egyptian* (1954), alongside Marlon Brando. After only a week on the Fox lot, Brando had bolted, telling the press, "I can't stand Bella Darvi."

Zanuck threatened a lawsuit, but immediately replaced Brando with Edmund Purdom.

Critics attacked Darvi's performance in *The Egyptian,* calling her "a high-priced harlot who comes across as a five-cent piece."

[For the role of Nefer, the seductive Babylonian courtesan in that film, Zanuck passed over Marilyn Monroe, who had wanted the part.]

In many ways, Zanuck was gambling on Darvi to light up the screen in *The Racers.* But after he sat through it, he realized that that wasn't going to happen.

After the film's failure, Darvi returned to France and appeared in a few lackluster foreign films. She put on weight and continued to gamble with money she didn't have. She turned to Zanuck to help pay off her gambling debts, and although their affair was over, he continued to help her financially until 1970.

Darvi suffered from severe bouts of depression as her debts mounted and made two separate suicide attempts.

Finally, in September of 1971 from inside the small efficiency apartment she was occupying at the time in Monaco, she turned on the gas for the final time and committed suicide.

Here, a mystery emerges. She gassed herself to death, but her body wasn't found until nine days later when one of her neighbors objected to the stench from her apartment. But if she'd died with the gas on, who turned it off? That led to speculation that she had been murdered, but nothing was ever proven.

Back in Hollywood, when Kirk heard the news, he said, "It's so very sad. Another of several actresses I've known who couldn't go on living till the end of their natural lives. Another suicide! For Darvi, Hollywood Boulevard was an avenue of broken dreams."

Claire Trevor in *Man Without a Star* playing a good girl with a bad reputation.

***

Aaron Rosenberg, a self-styled "Jew from Brooklyn," met with Kirk to tell him that he'd signed King Vidor as director of his next picture, Universal's *Man Without a Star,* a Technicolor Western scheduled for release in 1955. Its title conveys its theme: If a man doesn't have a star to keep him steadfast, he's doomed to wander aimlessly.

At first, Kirk objected to working with Vidor, expressing his belief that this son of Galveston, Texas, born back in the wild days of 1894, had seen his day—albeit after an amazing run of hit movies.

"My god, maybe you don't know this, but Vidor has been signed to direct *War and Peace* (1956) with Audrey Hepburn and

Kirk, a free spirit who hates barbed wire, with Jeanne Crain in *Man Without a Star*

Henry Fonda," Rosenberg said. "I wouldn't call that washed up."

Kirk was finally won over because Vidor had directed some of his favorite movies, including the World War I classic, *The Big Parade* (1925), starring John Gilbert. Kirk had seen it in a revival house. Vidor had also turned out *Stella Dallas* (1937), starring Barbara Stanwyck; *Duel in the Sun* (1946) with Gregory Peck and Jennifer Jones; and, most recently, *The Glenn Miller Story* (1954) with James Stewart. During the course of his career, Vidor had been nominated as Best Director five times.

[Less conclusive, Vidor also had also directed his share of disasters. He had helmed Beyond the Forest *(1949), the film that became famous for ending Bette Davis' long career at Warner Brothers.]*

The script for *Man Without a Star* had been written by Borden Chase and D.D. Beauchamp.

Vidor assembled a superb cast that included Jeanne Crain and Claire Trevor as the female leads. Supporting players included the veteran actor, Jay C. Flippen, Richard Boone, and William Campbell, with whom Kirk, as the male lead, would conduct a "bromance."

As Dempsey Rae, Kirk plays a wandering, easygoing cowpoke, free and footloose, a whiskey-slugging "man's man" who arrives in a small Wyoming cattle town with his sidekick, played by Campbell. Kirk is teaching him how to be a cowboy.

Soon, Kirk's rough-and-tumble charm captures the imaginations of the two leading ladies, Trevor as a saloon hostess with a heart of gold, and Crain as a cattle baroness.

[Whereas Trevor had played kind-hearted women of ill repute before, Crain, noted for playing "sweet young things," had been deliberately cast against the image she'd been cultivating. According to Kirk, "Just another working actress still pissed off that she'd lost the role of a lifetime, that of Eve Harrington in the 1950 All About Eve, *that had brought Anne Baxter a nomination for Best Actress."*

As the villain, Boone was always reliable and ideal for a Western. Whereas his father was a descendant of the frontiersman, Daniel Boone, his mother, like Kirk's, was a Russian Jew. *[Boone is well-remembered by a certain generation for his key role in the hit TV series* Have Gun—Will Travel *(1957-1963).]*

Macho and self-reliant, Boone had been an oil rigger, a bartender in a rowdy Texas saloon, and a U.S. Navy tail gunner for torpedo bombers in World War II. He had recently starred with Richard Burton in *The Robe* (1953) as the Roman Centurion assigned to crucify Christ. In time, he would appear in four movies with John Wayne. He'd co-star again with Kirk in Elia Kazan's *The Arrangement* (1969).

In *Man Without a Star,* opposite Kirk, Boone played a gunfighter hired by Crain to run roughshod over smaller ranchers.

Kirk as a cowpoke in a jam in *Man Without a Star*

An actor from New Jersey, William

362

Campbell, was assigned a minor role as one of Kirk's sidekicks. Although he'd portrayed a co-pilot in the airplane disaster adventure, *The High and the Mighty* (1954), his greater fame derived from his 1952 marriage to Judith Exner. She would become the notorious simultaneous mistress of both John F. Kennedy and the Chicago-based mobster, Sam Giancana.

Richard Boone..."I can lick any man in sight."

In *Man Without a Star*, expect range wars, barbed wire boundary clashes, a sexual stew, stampedes, barroom brawls, horse chases, gun twirling, and a theme song by Frankie Laine.

Kirk performs a gun-twirling stunt and picks the banjo while singing the saucy tune, "And the Moon Grew Brighter and Brighter."

Throughout the film, it's made clear that the character he plays hates barbed wire. His theme song should perhaps have been, "Don't Fence Me In."

Kirk and Vidor had their own slugfests during the shoot. His director later said, "Kirk is a tireless worker and a first-rate performer. But he's real aggressive and will stand up to you and fight you in almost every scene, always suggesting what he thinks is a better alternative to your own painstakingly worked-out plan. He's something else to put up with. Here's some advice to his future directors: Put on your boxing gloves, like the ones he wore in *Champion*."

Man Without a Star did well at the box office, and for the most part, was favorably received. *The Hollywood Reporter* called it "a personal *tour de force* of lusty, outdoor comedy."

[Actually, it was too full of blood and drama to be defined as a comedy at all. A "horse opera" might have been more appropriate as a defining term]

Kirk had signed with Universal a profit-sharing arrangement, but he was disappointed with the final bookkeeping, calling it "creative accounting."

***

As an international star, Kirk solicited certain roles—and didn't get them. Likewise, he was presented with major star parts, but, for various reasons, rejected them. Up until then, one of his "worst judgments" (his words) involved turning down the lead in *Stalag 17*, a role that later brought a Best Actor Oscar to William Holden.

Holden ended up as the third lead in a movie in which Kirk wanted the star part. Working with producer Ray Stark as early as 1951, Kirk tried to acquire the rights to the Clifford Odets play, *The Country Girl.* Its plot focuses on an alcoholic actor given his last chance to resurrect his fading career.

Kirk wanted to present it first as a play, as he had with *Detective Story,* and then produce it as a film. Although he lost the rights to produce it on Broadway, he still lobbied to play the lead when Paramount acquired it with the intention of mounting it as a movie. His interest was aroused even more when he learned that Grace Kelly had been offered the lead in the movie version. He visited her on two different occasions to discuss his chance of being cast as her co-star, with Holden in a secondary male role.

Word got out and there were rumors of a brief affair, although that was never confirmed.

Before she became Princess of Monaco, Kelly was known for seducing her leading men, ranging from Gary Cooper to Ray Milland, from Clark Gable to James Stewart.

Paramount ended up casting Bing Crosby, and the script was rewritten to define the character he played as that of a singer instead of an actor.

Kirk also lost the lead in *Pal Joey* to another singer, Frank Sinatra. Harry Cohn at Columbia acquired the film rights and ordered that it be adapted into a musical. He wrote to Kirk that, with the change in the plot, the role would no longer be suitable for him. He held out the possibility of working with him in the future.

When *Pal Joey* was released in 1957, Sinatra was teamed with Rita Hayworth, with whom Kirk had had a previous affair, and with Kim Novak, his future co-star in *Strangers When We Meet.*

Sometimes it was Kirk who did the rejecting. William Wyler tried to persuade him to accept the second lead (the role of Messala) in MGM's 1959 remake of *Ben-Hur.*

Wyler had already offered that film's leading role, that of Ben-Hur himself, to Rock Hudson, but his studio refused to let him move (albeit temporarily) to MGM. Wyler then assigned that role to Charlton Heston.

Kirk was insulted that Wyler didn't offer him the role of Ben-Hur from the very beginning. "I would have been your best choice," he told Wyler. "I'm sorry you didn't see that. You can take the 'sloppy seconds' role of Messala—and shove it."

The role of Messala went instead to Stephen Boyd.

One role that Kirk coveted was that of Henry Higgins in the 1964 movie version of *My Fair Lady.* The rights to the musical had been acquired by Warner Brothers for an unprecedented $5 million. Audrey Hepburn had already been cast as Eliza Doolittle.

"I could never understand why Lerner and Loewe chose Rex Harrison over me. I can sing a hell of a lot better than that prissy Brit. My romancing of Audrey would also be far more believable. Harrison came off more like her uncle. Hell, I would even have lain on George Cukor's casting couch—just kidding, fellows." He was speaking to the press at the time.

Even the very famous director David Lean once got in touch with Kirk, asking him to play the role of the reporter/narrator David Lowell Thomas in *Lawrence of Arabia* (1962), even though it was a minor part.

At first, Kirk thought that Lean was offering him the lead, and he became rather miffed when he learned that the key role of T.E. Lawrence had gone to Peter O'Toole after Marlon Brando had rejected it.

The lesser role intrigued Kirk, but he then proceeded to make demands that Lean considered "outrageous. He didn't want to star in our film… He wanted a coronation."

Kirk not only wanted second billing after O'Toole, he demanded to be paid the same amount as the lead. "I had to turn Kirk down," Lean said. "Not only was the salary demand absurd, but I had already promised second billing to Alec Guinness. Arthur Kennedy, Kirk's co-star in *Champion* and *The Glass Menagerie*, played the reporter."

There were some leading roles that Kirk coveted but didn't get. They included the male leads of both *Ben-Hur* (assigned to Charlton Heston) and *My Fair Lady* (assigned to Rex Harrison)

Kirk had to turn down a role he was eager to play because of earlier commitments. Producer Harold Prince contacted him to play Tevye, an overworked Jewish milkman with five daughters, in the Broadway production of *Fiddler on the Roof* (1965).

In a memo to Kirk, he said, "Word has reached me that you sing fine and have a strong vocal power, I think you'd be marvelous in the part."

"Regrets," Kirk said later. "I've had a few."

Kirk was inspired b y his close friend, Burt Lancaster, to form his own independent production company. The big studios, such as Warners and MGM, had fallen from the lofty pedestals they'd occupied in the wake of the Supreme Court's antitrust ruling of 1947. New regulations dictated that studios could not exhibit their own movies. Before that, studios had their own theaters for exclusive distribution of their films. After that ruling came down, Fox, RKO, et al, no longer dominated movie production as a vertically integrated oligopoly.

The field was clear for independents to launch their own film production companies. Other actors hoping to become movie producers included Frank Sinatra, Rita Hayworth, Henry Fonda, Robert Mitchum, Joan Crawford, and Cornel Wilde, although most of them did not succeed.

The idea of stars controlling production of their films was not new. Back in the 1920s, the leading players of that era formed United Artists, presided over by Mary Pickford, Charlie Chaplin, Douglas Fairbanks, Sr., and director D.W. Griffith.

Movies, too, were changing. The old Production Code was under challenge, particularly with the imports from Europe where directors and stars were more daring.

"A new wave was hitting our shores, with a trend to co-production deals, and I wanted to ride the crest of that wave," Kirk said.

In an interview he gave in 1960, he looked back on his early years as an actor in the late 1940s and 50s. "It's intensely lonely being an actor, god damn lonely. You work like a Trojan, you strive, you suffer, and one day you find you've arrived. But don't expect a dream factory like you thought it would be. You're now buffeted from every side. You face a lot of shit: Bad business deals, crooked lawyers out to bankrupt you, disastrous experiences, on-location deaths, egomaniacal directors, self-enchanted co-stars, and utterly ridiculous situations of all kinds."

"If you're a good-looking guy like me, every starlet wants you to plug her and half the men are after you if you're touted as a sex symbol."

"For my career, I wanted to be more in charge, to do it my way, to select my own roles—and not be under some slave management contract."

"Sometimes, a star feels he has less to contribute than the writer and director," Kirk said. As head of a production company, an actor can get in at the inception of a film, searching for the scripts worthy of going before the camera and getting involved in all the creative aspects of filmmaking. A lot of us are going to fail. Here's hoping it won't be me."

In 1955, he launched his own production company, Bryna Productions, named after his mother.

Sam Norton, his business manager, said he'd save a fortune in taxes. According to Kirk, whereas income he defined as personal was being taxed in those days at an astonishing 92%, income defined as corporate income was taxed at the lesser rate of 52%.

Of course, an independent company needed a big-name star to generate box office. "and Bryna needed me," Kirk said. "Here I am, ready, willing, and rarin' to go."

"Going independent was a big gamble," he said. "You might even lose your jockey shorts. I'm not much of a gambler, but what the hell! Issur is on the march!"

***

To launch Bryna Productions, Kirk selected an unusual Western, *The Indian Fighter*. Released in 1955, it was the saga of a frontier scout leading a wagon train through hostile Indian country, who unwittingly gets involved with the daughter of a Sioux chief.

For the script, he hired one of the best screenwriters in the business, Ben Hecht, who co-authored it with Frank Davis.

Kirk chose the property because he was drawn to the lead character, Johnny Hawks. Since he was in great physical shape, he could "show off" in front of the camera, Indian wrestling and pony riding, 1870s style.

He was once known for the number of Indians he'd killed, but after the Civil War he'd made peace with the tribe. "I like the part because in the role of Johnny Hawks, I'm fairly bursting with testosterone. I'm a work-for-a-price rogue; I get to ogle a beautiful Indian maiden taking a bath, and I'm vigorous, brimming with *machismo*. In this role, I can make John Wayne and Jimmy Stewart look like virginal maidens."

As producer, he hired William Schorr, the former associate producer for two of his recent movies, *Ace in the Hole* and *Ulysses*.

After much consideration and several meetings, he tapped André DeToth to direct, confident that he would keep the plot moving "at a breakneck speed."

A Hungarian, DeToth had, among other achievements, two claims to fame. He had directed the first 3D film, *House of Wax* (1953), despite being unable to see in 3D himself. From 1944 to 1952, he'd been married to Veronica Lake, the famous peek-a-boo girl of World War II films, known for her long strand of blonde hair that fell across her right eye. In 1950, he'd received an Oscar nomination for his screenwriting on *The Gunfighter* starring Gregory Peck.

[Years later, Kirk would encounter DeToth in Hollywood, where he told him of a horrendous or-

deal he had suffered. During his scouting for film locations after the Yom Kippur War, he'd been kidnapped by militant Arabs, who pistol-whipped him and vengefully interrogated him. "They had a knife and were going to castrate me, thinking I was Moshe Dayan, the Israeli commander, because of the patch over my eye from a childhood injury. When they stripped me, they found that my cock still had foreskin, and they decided that I therefore was not a Jew. You might say that my foreskin saved my life. In your case, you'd better not get kidnapped by Arabs during any of your shoots in the Middle East."]

Manhood and colonization in the Old West: Three views of Kirk in *The Indian Hunter.*

Kirk personally selected every actor to play every part, even the minor ones. He decided on Walter Matthau as Wes Todd, the villain; and his ex-wife, Diana Dill, as the attractive, husband-hungry widow with an adolescent son, as played by Michael Winkelman.

If Diana Dill thought that she and Kirk might reconcile and reunite, she was wrong. In a memoir, she painted an unflattering portrait of Kirk on location. He was understandably nervous about launching the first film produced by his new business entity.

"He dealt with his insecurity by taking it out on cast and crew," Diana charged. "He was quite officious in every department. He even gave line readings to actors in all the key roles. He tried that with me, and I objected, telling him, 'We'll both appear on screen sounding just like Kirk Douglas.'"

"At the last minute, he would change camera shots that had been painstakingly worked out by DeToth. He came down hard on Matthau, the most talented actor in the cast," Diana said. "He came to me and asked me to intercede, but I had to tell him, 'I'm just a hired hand like yourself. Let's hold out and endure. It'll only be a month out of our lives.'"

"When I saw the final cut, it was a disappointment to me," she said. "I never got a handle on my role as the wagon train widow. One of

Kirk with his ex-wife, Diana Dill, whom he included in the cast of *The Indian Fighter* as part of an actor's dynamic that everyone in Hollywood found remarkable.

my hardest scenes was having to drive a six-horse team at breakneck speed. I sure wasn't a budding Dale Evans. I case you don't remember, she was known as the 'Queen of the Cowgirls' and married to that thing, Roy Rogers."

Matthau, as the villain, traded whiskey to the Indians for their gold. He's aided by his companion in crime, Chivington (Lon Chaney, Jr.). At the end, Hawks has no problem turning Todd over to the Indians, who subject him to the speeding tip of a burning arrow as the fulfillment of their brand of justice.

[Walter Matthau is most often remembered as Oscar Madison in the hit TV series The Odd Couple *(1970-1975). Like Kirk, he had humble origins, his father a Ukrainian Jewish peddler. The year he co-starred with Kirk, he had also appeared with his best friend, Burt Lancaster, in* The Kentuckian *(1955). In time, he'd co-star with Kirk again in* Lonely Are the Brave *(1962).*

A reporter once asked Matthau who his favorite co-star had been. "Jack Lemmon," he answered. "Anybody but Kirk Douglas."]

Walter Abel was cast as the U.S. Army Captain Trask. In the history of the movies, he'd known better days, his highlight in 1935 when he'd starred as D'Artagnan in *The Three Musketeers.*"

Milwaukee native Eduard Franz played Chief Red Cloud. He told Kirk, "I was King Ahab in that Biblical epic, *Sins of*

Walter Matthau as the evil villain in *The Indian Fighter.*

Jezebel (1953); and Chief Broken Hand in *White Feather* (1955). Now I'm playing another Indian Chief, and I'm slated to play Jethro in Cecil B. DeMille's *The Ten Commandments* (1956) when this is over. What's strange is that I'm the least likely Indian or Old Testament prophet you'll ever meet."

Franz also revealed that before he started making

Two views of Eduard Franz. "Some idiot decided I could play an Indian."

movies, he'd tried to eke out a living as a chicken farmer in Texas. "In either business, I've had to put up with a whole lot of shit."

The hardest role to cast was that of "the sexy Indian girl," Onahti, the daughter of Chief Red Cloud (Franz). "The young women who showed up to audition looked like some Los Angeles college girl with a feather in her hair."

Anne Buydens, married and pregnant with Kirk's child, had recently leafed through a copy of *Vogue,* and spotted a photo of an Italian fashion model, Elsa Martinelli, depicted emerging, dripping wet, from a pool. She was attired in a man's shirt. It clung to her body, emphasizing her voluptuous figure. When Anne showed the layout to Kirk, he said, "That's our Pocahontas." Then he paused. "But can she act?"

He had to get in touch with her, and he'd read in the article that she was dating, of all people, Oleg Cassini.

"We must have the same taste in women," Kirk said. "Gene Tierney, Irene Wrightsman, and now Elsa Martinelli."

Cassini reluctantly provided Elsa's contact information, and Kirk called her.

At first she didn't believe that he was "Keeerk Doooogalas." *[She had a strong Italian accent, and her English was skimpy.]* She asked him to prove that he was Kirk Douglas by singing "A Whale of a Tale," from *20,000 Leagues Under the Sea.* When he'd finished, she was convinced.

She was flown to the West Coast, where she met with Kirk. As she admitted later to DeToth, "I find him very masculine, very powerful as a man, definitely my physical type." Of course, she expressed that in Italian, which DeToth understood, although he didn't speak it fluently.

"We don't need a specific language, because we speak in the language of love," she said.

Although Martinelli was un-married at the time, Kirk wasn't, and DeToth reminded her that their boss had a pregnant wife waiting for him in Los Angeles.

"All Italian men cheat on their wives, so I assume that American men do the same?" she said. "I'm crazy for this *Keeeeerka.*"

Kirk with the Italian actress and model, Elsa Martinelli, cast as an Indian maiden in *The Indian Fighter*

They showed their affection for each other when DeToth filmed them frolicking together in a river near Bend, Oregon—an unusual romantic pairing for Westerns of that era, a cowboy with an Indian princess.

[In the case of Kirk, it was yet another affliction of "Leading Lady-it is," and part of an affair that lasted only until the end of filming.

In the years to come, Elsa divided her time between the U.S. and Europe, appearing in both English (a language she eventually learned) and French or Italian.

When she got a small role in The V.I.P.'s *(1963) with Richard Burton and Elizabeth Taylor, Burton slipped away from his violet-eyed wife for a fling with her. He resumed their liaison again during their appearance together in* Candy *(1968). "This time, I had both Burton and his co-star, Marlon Brando," she confessed to a reporter in Rome. "I am not ashamed."]*

Over lunch one day, Kirk had a reunion with Ray Teal and shared memories of their co-starring gig in *Along the Great Divide*. According to Teal, "I was actually a saxophone player in Michigan, but directors always put me in Westerns."

Cast into the role of Briggs, Elisha Cook, Jr., was a familiar screen face, even to movie-goers who didn't know his name. He specialized in roles calling for cowardly villains and neurotics and is still remembered for appearing with Humphrey Bogart as Sam Spade in *The Maltese Falcon* (1941).

He told Kirk, "If Bryna needs a fall guy, I'm it. No one's better at playing a weakling, a sadistic loser, a hoodlum, or someone who gets murdered—either shot, strangled, or poisoned."

One night in Oregon, Kirk dined with Lon Chaney, Jr. and Alan Hale, Jr., both of whom had minor roles in *The Indian Fighter*. Kirk had first seen Chaney in *The Wolf Man* (1941), in which he'd been adept at portraying a monster.

"Lon liked to keep the whiskey flowing, and was a mean drunk, getting into some bloody fights in the local taverns," Kirk said.

"Alan was more affable, somewhat like the character of "the Skipper" he'd play in the hit TV series *Gilligan's Island.*" [*Hale, Jr., had previously worked with Kirk on* The Big Trees.]

"I was very frank with them that night," Kirk said. "Both of them were the sons of actors far more famous than they were."

"It must be hard for both of you going into the movie business in which your dads had earned much fame, especially Lon Chaney, Sr. Doesn't it bother you, knowing you can never measure up to your fathers?"

"It's a living," Hale said. Chaney ignored the question. Kirk expressed his fear that his sons, Joel and Michael, would one day also enter the movie business. "If they do, they'll never make it on their own, certainly not attaining my fame. I think both of them will go through life being known as the sons of Kirk Douglas."

He decided to invite Michael and Joel to a vacation in Oregon for a reunion with both of their parents. That left Anne pregnant and alone in Los Angeles to celebrate her first wedding anniversary.

Before their arrival, Diana had complained to him about the difficulty of rearing such strong-willed boys. She had discovered that Joel was dyslexic and having difficulties in school.

She was also worried that Michael was joining a leather jacket and motorcycle gang, members of which wore boots, Elvis-style pompadours, and "duck's ass" hairdos.

Kirk demanded that DeToth cast his sons in a scene in his movie. He wrote the scene himself. In it, they're depicted in a lookout tower, screaming "The Indians are coming! The Indians are coming!"

Their scene ended up on the cutting room floor. For their screen debuts, each of them, especially young Michael, would have to wait for another day.

In one scene, Kirk insisted on performing his own stunt. In it, his horse takes a fall. He was directed to lean back in the saddle before yanking the horse's head around to the side, an action which would "instruct" the animal to begin a "controlled fall" onto its side.

Instead, he leaned forward as the horse swung its head to the side, the full force of its swing hitting Kirk directly in the face. Screaming in pain, he realized that he'd broken his nose.

The Indian Fighter generated good box office, grossing some two and a half million dollars Released by United Artists, it was praised for Kirk's acting and its wide scenic vistas of Oregon.

CHAPTER ELEVEN

LUST FOR LIFE

KIRK'S PORTRAIT OF VAN GOGH

THE VIKINGS

BLOOD-THIRSTY AND NORDIC, KIRK INVADES, GOUGES, PUNCHES, AND
MURDERS. INGRID BERGMAN SAYS "NO" TO A ROLE IN THIS NORSE
OPERA, BUT "YES" TO AN APPEARANCE IN KIRK'S BOUDOIR

ROYAL ROMANCES

WITH THE PRINCESS OF AFGHANISTAN AND THE QUEEN OF IRAN

MORE WESTERNS

GUNFIGHT AT THE O.K. CORRAL & LAST TRAIN FROM GUN HILL

A TOP SECRET AFFAIR

OR AT LEAST SOME DYSFUNCTIONAL DRAMA WITH SUSAN HAYWARD

PATHS TO GLORY

ONE OF THE GREATEST "WAR TO END ALL WARS" MOVIES EVER MADE

As the Viking, Einar, Kirk Douglas lured fans wanting gore and violence.

In *The Vikings*, as a ferocious Norse warrior, he indulges in bloody hand-to-hand fighting as he tries to conquer England.

Variety **announced, perhaps prematurely,** that Bryna Production would produce *Lust for Life,* the tragic story of Vincent Van Gogh, as directed by Jean Negulesco.

The Romanian-born director was also a painter. "He did a portrait of me," Kirk said, "later adding a beard and a straw hat. We both decided I looked exactly like Vincent Van Gogh."

The next day, lawyers for MGM threatened to sue, claiming that their studio had long ago purchased the screen rights for the novel that Irving Stone had written in 1934.

In 1946, they had gone into pre-production, starring Spencer Tracy, but the deal fell through.

Through his lawyer, Kirk eventually hammered out a deal with MGM, agreeing to star in the movie, not to produce it. As part of the negotiation, Kirk made a proposal they rejected: He would star in MGM's film without charging a fee, if they'd give him a Van Gogh painting in lieu of a salary. He informed the press, perhaps as part of an early marketing ploy, "I can play Van Gogh, but I can't afford to own him."

As for Negulesco, although he never got to direct a biopic of Vincent Van Gogh, that same year, he helmed *How to Marry a Millionaire,* a block-buster hit starring Marilyn Monroe, Lauren Bacall, and Betty Grable.

Norman Corwin was hired to adapt Stone's novel for the screen. He had written a highly successful film, *The Blue Veil,* a 1951 melodrama star-ring Jane Wyman. The former Mrs. Ronald Reagan received an Oscar nod for Best Actress.

Lust for Life, eventually released in 1956, reunited the trio who had turned out the highly successful *The Bad and the Beautiful.* Once again, John House-man was designated as producer. He told the press, "It must have been hell living with Kirk during the shoot. He steeped himself in the tormented life of Van Gogh. All in all, he was a pain in the ass to have around—all an-guish, suicidal, the guy was taking it far too seriously."

Vincente Minnelli was his director once again, proclaiming, "No other actor was even considered for the part. Kirk is blessed with tireless energy, a

willingness to try anything, and a complete disregard for his own looks."

Kirk read Irving Stone's novel, *Lust for Life,* three times. Born in the Netherlands in 1853, Van Gogh was a Post-Impressionistic painter who became one of the most influential figures in the art of the Western world. During the final two years of his life, in a fit of madness, he created 860 oil paintings, of which *The Potato Eaters* and *Sunflowers* are the most celebrated.

Stone, among other sagas, also wrote *The Agony and the Ecstasy,* based on the life of Michelangelo. Originally, seventeen publishers had rejected *Lust for Life.* When it was finally published, it became a bestseller.

Anthony Quinn signed to play Van Gogh's fast friend and erstwhile rival, Paul Gauguin. *[Quinn had recently co-starred with Kirk in* Ulysses.*]*

"Minnelli just loved everything I did," Kirk said. "He thought I was perfect in every scene, almost unheard of. It was obvious to cast and crew that he was in love with me. I played his attraction for me to my advantage but didn't put out for him."

"Both Minnelli and I knew that Van Gogh had been a latent homosexual, perhaps having the hots for Gauguin," Kirk said. "But Houseman told us that the brass at MGM wouldn't go for depicting that."

"The director even consulted me about casting the supporting players, especially the role of my brother, Theo, who supported Van Gogh throughout his life," Kirk said.

A Scottish actor, James Donald, who would soon co-star with Kirk in

Their resemblance was eerie and uncanny. Left photo is a self-portrait by Van Gogh; right photo is of Kirk.

The Vikings, was tapped.

Although it was an essentially a man's film, two actresses were hired. One of them was Jeanette Sterke, cast into the role of Kay, Van Gogh's cousin who rejected him as a suitor because he was poor. Sterke had emigrated to England to escape from the Nazis.

The other female role, that of Christine, a prostitute, went to Pamela Brown. That same

Kirk (left) as Van Gogh, Anthony Quinn (right) as Paul Gauguin. The brass at MGM objected to depicting Van Gogh's homosexual lust for his fellow artist.

year, she co-starred with Laurence Olivier in *Richard III.* In time, she'd bring both Cleopatra and Eleanor of Aquitaine to the screen, too.

The always-reliable Everett Sloane, cast as Dr. Gachet, comes to the aid of the doomed Van Gogh and is empathetic to the agonies of the art world. Ironically, Sloane had himself portrayed Van Gogh in 1950, in a Philco-Goodyear TV production, *The Life of Vincent Van Gogh.*

[Like so many actors Kirk worked with, Sloane—fearing he was going blind—committed suicide with a barbiturate overdose in August of 1965.]

Born in 1891 in Chicago, Madge Kennedy was cast as Anna Cornelia Van Gogh. She had first appeared on Broadway in 1912. On the set, she gave Kirk some enigmatic advice: "I have discovered that one of the best ways to act is to make your mind as vacant as possible."

"To me, Madge represented the vagaries of show business," Kirk said. He was referring to how this once distinguished actress ended up playing Aunt Martha on TV's *Leave It to Beaver* (1957-63), and later as an uncredited secretary in Marilyn Monroe's *Let's Make Love* (1963).

During the shoot, Quinn outrageously held to the fantasy that the ghost of Gauguin was haunting the set. At one point he called a halt to filming when he was painting a woman. Minnelli indulged him in his fantasy, especially after Quinn told him that the spirit of Gauguin had appeared to him, telling him that he was not holding his paintbrush correctly.

The director, George Cukor, was called in to helm a scene one day when Minnelli was not available. After Cukor left, Quinn told Kirk that when he was a young actor, trying to break into show-biz, Cukor had invited him to his home where he "plied me with liquor and showed me girlie magazines to give me an erection. He promised to make me a big star if I'd let him give me a blow-job. I was drunk enough and young enough to believe him. The next night, I was seduced by Mae West. This was my welcome to Hollywood."

Cukor did cast Quinn in *Wild Is the Wind* (1957), in which he played opposite Anna Magnani. He was a lusty, domineering Italian immigrant whose wife is carrying on with his adopted son. The role got Quinn an Oscar nomination.

In his memoir, *One Man Tango*, Quinn delivered a highly sanitized version of his encounters with Cukor and Miss West.

Much of *Lust for Life* was filmed on location in France, Holland, and Belgium at the actual historical sites frequented by Van Gogh. In Arles, Kirk slept in the bedroom where Van Gogh had died.

"When we shot in the little town of Auvers-sur-Oise, some of the older residents actually thought that Van Gogh had returned," Kirk said. "By then, my hair had been cut in the style of Van Gogh, my beard dyed a reddish tint."

Minnelli tried to be as authentic to historic aesthetics as possible. At one point, he ordered his crew to spray paint a field yellow to more closely evoke a Van Gogh landscape.

The artist, Robert Parker, re-created ersatz canvases that gave the illusion of having been painted by Van Gogh. In addition to that, some 200 of the master's actual paintings from private collections were added to the context of the film, too.

Cedric Gibbons, the most famous art director in Hollywood (and the man credited with the design of the Oscar statuette), was in charge of the sets. He had previously worked on the sets for Kirk's *The Bad and the Beautiful*

Van Gogh suffered from depression, anxiety, delusions, and psychotic episodes. He is often cited as a "case study" for the juxtaposition of mental instability and creative genius. In time, he would cut off part of his left ear and spend time in a psychiatric hospital in St.-Rémy de Provence, where scenes from *Lust for Life* were shot. His mental state had deteriorated greatly by 1890, when he committed suicide by shooting himself in the chest with a revolver, dying two days later at the age of 37.

Although his paintings are worth millions today, Van Gogh sold only one of the 1,600 he created. His celebrated painting, *Sunflowers*, from 1887, sold for $40 million in 1986, the highest price for any painting at that point in time. A year later, *Irises* broke that record, going for $50 million.

At the wrap of *Lust for Life*, and to prepare for Kirk's next picture, his beard had to be removed. For publicity purposes, Kirk shaved off his dyed red beard in front of millions of viewers watching *The Perry Como Show.*

He claimed that in the weeks following the completion of his film, he developed a nervous habit of feeling his ear to confirm that it was still there.

Kirk attended a private screening of *Lust for Life,* where he talked to John Wayne, his future friend and co-star. After the film was shown, the Duke drove with Kirk to the home of Merle Oberon for a private party. Behind the wheel, Wayne asked Kirk, "Have you humped our hostess yet?"

"Been there, done that," Kirk answered.

"You know, kid, I'm god damn disappointed in you," Wayne said. "Playing a fucking pantywaist. It's obvious even to a fool that Van Gogh was in love with his brother, Theo. Me and you should stick to macho roles like you played in *Champion.* There aren't many of us left. Gary Cooper is still hanging around. Of the new stars, Aldo Ray is macho. But the 1950s has brought us a string of nelly queens: Tony Perkins, Rock Hudson, Tab Hunter, Troy Donahue."

Writing in *The New York Times,* Bosley Crowther praised Minnelli for relying "upon color and the richness and character it gives to images to carry their tortured theme. The cold grayness of a mining district, the reds of a Paris café, the greens of a Provençal village, or the golden yellows of a field of ripening grain—these are the stimuli that give us a sensory knowledge of the surroundings that weigh upon Van Gogh and reflect the contrasting umbers and purples of that fated man."

Harrison's Reports claimed, "Kirk Douglas does outstanding work as Van Gogh." The *Washington Post* cited Kirk for delivering "a performance of powerful sensitivity."

However, *Variety* called the film "slow moving and unexciting." The *Monthly Film Bulletin* wrote, "Kirk Douglas' performance remains essentially an American study in neuroticism."

Most critics claimed that the infamous ear-slashing scene was handled with impeccable taste by Minnelli.

Of his own performance, Kirk said, "I played the tormented genius whose devotion to his art consumes, engulfs, and finally leads to his self-destruction."

Lust for Life lost more than two million dollars after it was released.

***

[FOOTNOTE: *During Kirk's filming of* Lust for Life, *"a blessed event," as childbirth is often called, occurred. On November 23, 1955, at the Cedars of Lebanon Hospital, Peter Vincent Douglas, Kirk's third son, was born to Anne and him.*

Kirk had wanted a girl but got Peter instead. "My seed is so powerful it will only produce boys," he said. "I bet no one can figure out how I made Vincent his middle name."

"I just hope that my latest boy does not enter the motion picture business."

Kirk's wish was not granted. Years from the day he said that, his third son launched Vincent Pictures.

***

Soon after the release of Lust for Life, *Kirk attracted a distinguished but unexpected fan: the painter, Marc Chagall (1887-1985), the last of the early European modernists.*

Born in present-day Belarus, Chagall was a Russian-French artist of Jewish descent. Enclosed with a personal letter to Kirk was Chagall's autobiography, Ma Vie.

Kirk with his infant son, Peter Douglas. His middle name was Vincent.

"I want you to bring the life of Marc Chagall to the screen," he wrote. "I've had a far more interesting life than Van Gogh. Pablo (Picasso) himself said I am the only painter left who understands what color really is. Fuck those Sunflowers."

Kirk already had met Chagall when he was vacationing at the exclusive Hotel du Cap on the French Riviera at Antibes. He came across him one afternoon after he spotted him painting under an umbrella on the beach. Chagall later invited him to his villa up in the hills, where he showed him his latest paintings.

"It was a sad day when I had to inform this remarkable artist—and a Jew at that—that I could not bring him to the screen. I didn't want to impersonate another world-class painter back-to-back, but had I done so, I'd have preferred to be Michelangelo for a screen adaptation of The Agony and the Ecstasy.

That didn't happen. That movie was released in 1965, but with Charlton Heston cast as Michelangelo.]

***

Producer Hal B. Wallis had long been a devotee of Westerns, having made *Dodge City* (1939) and *Virginia City* (1940) with Errol Flynn, and *Oklahoma Kid* (1939) with James Cagney and Humphrey Bogart.

Wallis had gone to see John Ford's *My Darling Clementine* (1946), starring Henry Fonda as Wyatt Earp and Victor Mature as Doc Holliday. "That was a good movie but loaded with romantic fluff. I want to make a movie about Holliday and Earp that sticks close to the truth and that focuses mainly on their *Gunfight at the O.K. Corral.*"

Burt Lancaster had two more pictures to make for him, and Wallis thought he'd be ideal in the role of Wyatt Earp. But Lancaster wasn't at all interested until he'd heard that Wallis had secured the film rights for the Broadway hit, *The Rainmaker.* He promised Wallis that he'd play Earp if he'd give him the role of Starbuck in *The Rainmaker* opposite Katharine Hepburn. A deal was struck.

Wallis knew that the role of the dying gunslinger, Doc Holliday, would be more difficult to cast. Whatever actor was assigned to the role would have to portray a consumptive in the terminal stages of tuberculosis. That meant that he'd have to do a lot of coughing throughout every stage of the film.

Lauren Bacall had privately told him that her husband, Humphrey Bogart, was slowly dying of cancer. Wallis knew that it was risky, but he thought Bogie would be perfect in his last movie role, looking ravaged as the script dictated. But Bogie turned it down.

Wallis then considered three very different actors, Richard Widmark, Jack Palance, and Van Heflin, none of whom got very excited about the role. Wallis then focused on Kirk, with whom he'd been angry ever since he'd rejected a long-term contract with him. Yet a call to Kirk elicited yet another negative response. "I don't want to make another Western so soon after releasing *The Indian Fighter.*"

A few days later, Lancaster phoned Kirk: "Good buddy, I want to work with you again for Hal. I'm going to play Wyatt Earp in *Gunfight at the O.K. Corral,* and I want you to co-star with me as Doc Holliday." It took about an hour on the phone and a drunken night with Lancaster before Kirk greenlighted his participation.

It was during the making of *Gunflight at the O.K. Corral* that "Burt & Kirk" became highly competitive friends. Each of them could play the same roles and characters. Because of the strong bond they'd crafted, Wallis began calling them "The Bobsey Twins." Lancaster and Kirk had first worked together on the set of *I Walk Alone.*

For the screenplay of *Gunfight at the O.K. Corral*, Wallis hired Leon Uris, the son of a Polish-born immigrant, who became a paperhanger shortly after his immigration to Baltimore. Uris had shown an early talent for writing, and at the age of six, he wrote an operetta inspired by the death of his beloved dog. Amazing for a man who became a world-famous novelist, Uris failed English class three times.

Kirk Douglas as Doc Holliday and Burt Lancaster as Wyatt Earp in *Gunfight at the O.K. Corral*

When Kirk met him, he was in the early stages of writing his best-known work, *Exodus*. Published in 1958, it traced the history of Palestine from the late 19th Century through to the founding of the State of Israel.

Uris had a reputation for fleshing out the bare bones of history into some highly imaginative fiction. Wallis wanted him to stick as closely as possible to the facts associated with Earp and Holliday, though admitting that he needed to "sanitize" them a bit.

The two gunfighters were hardly heroic. Holliday was a drunk and a racist, hating blacks and Indians. Although a lawman, Earp ran a brothel on the side, and accepted "protection money" and bribes from casino operators. The actual gunfight lasted only thirty bloody seconds, but Wallis wanted it depicted as a long, drawn-out battle between the forces of good and evil. Historians of the Old West, after the film was released, pointed out sixteen major factual errors.

Tucson, Arizona, was used as one of the backdrops during filming. "I wanted my film to have that burnt-out, brown look of a Remington painting, of which I own several," Wallis said. "My cameraman, Charles Lang, got my vision and really came through for me."

Originally, Wallis offered Barbara Stanwyck the role of Laura Benbow, a glamorous gambling lady. Stanwyck rejected the role, finding it "very secondary—it's really a love story between two gunfighters."

Had Stanwyck accepted, it would have united her once again with Kirk for the first time since *The Strange Love of Martha Ivers*.

Kirk set about researching the life of Doc Holliday with the same intensity he'd investigated the life of Van Gogh, He discovered that he was a careful dresser who slept every morning till midday. Then he'd eat a two-pound buffalo steak washed down with at least a pint of whiskey.

Kirk was delighted to learn that he was getting twice the salary of Lancaster, who got top billing. Lancaster was still bound by the relatively modest terms of his contract with Wallis.

As his director, Wallis hired John Sturges [*no relation to Preston Sturges*], because he'd been impressed with the way he'd handled *Bad Day at Black Rock* (1955) with Spencer Tracy. He was nominated for a Best Director Oscar for that movie.

Believed to be Wyatt Earp (left) and Doc Holliday.

"Although John was from Illinois, he could have been a Western hero himself. He had a powerful build and was very tall," Wallis said. "I figured that he was man enough to stand up to those two temperamental divas, Kirk and Burt, who always tried to direct their own movies."

[*Coincidentally, Sturges, a decade later, would direct* Hour of the Gun, *in which he cast James Garner as Wyatt Earp and Jason Robards as Doc Holliday.*]

"I liked John Sturges's work so much I hired him again to direct Kirk and Tony Quinn in *Last Train from Gun Hill*," Wallis said.

After consideration of several actresses for the role of The Gambling Lady, Wallis gave it to Rhonda Fleming, then known as "The Queen of Technicolor" because of her fiery red hair.

She was at home in the Western genre, having already appeared in *Tennessee's Partner* 1955), with Ronald Reagan. There were rumors, never confirmed, of an off-screen affair with him. At the time, Reagan was in the early stages of his marriage to the MGM starlet, Nancy Davis, who kept a close rein on her formerly errant husband.

Kirk and Fleming got along well as friends, not as lovers. This was one leading lady who would elude him, as she would Lancaster.

Fleming told Kirk she'd been discovered at the age of sixteen when enrolled in Beverly Hills High. "At first, I thought that Henry Willson [*the talent scout who approached her*] was a child molester, but I soon learned he went for the boys, namely Rock Hudson, Tab Hunter, and Guy Madison. Throw in Rory Calhoun, too."

Both Fleming and Kirk had known each other since they'd co-starred with Robert Mitchum in *Out of the Past*, "way back" in 1947.

Fleming told Kirk that Alfred Hitchcock had offered her the role of a nymphomaniac in *Spellbound* (1945) alongside Gregory Peck and Ingrid Bergman. "I rushed home and looked up that word in the dictionary—and was I shocked!"

***

Gunfight at the O.K. Corral depicted an actual event that took place on October 26, 1881 in Tombstone, Arizona. A lawman (Wyatt Earp) and an outlaw (the terminally ill Doc Holliday) forge an unlikely alliance that leads to a gunfight against the Clayton Boys, a motley gang of cattle thieves and thugs.

Sturges (as director) and Wallis (as producer) compiled a list of some of the best supporting actors ever appearing in a Western.

Empathetic, attractive actresses: Rhonda Fleming and Jo Van Fleet in *Gunfight at the O.K. Corral*

The fourth lead, a saloon girl of low morals, went to the immensely talented Jo Van Fleet, who played Kate Fisher. She's involved in an affair with Doc Holliday. Elia Kazan had previously cast her in *East of Eden* (1955), for which she'd won a Best Supporting Actress Oscar as the embittered mother, now the madam of a brothel, of the character played by James Dean. Before *O.K. Corral*, she'd filmed *The King and Four Queens* (1956), starring Clark Gable.

At one point during filming, Kirk asked Lancaster to watch him film a scene with Van Fleet. "She's a real Method actress, and in this scene, I'm supposed to hit her hard. We've done eight takes, and she keeps accusing me of holding back. 'Harder, harder next time,' she said. I want you to watch me get it right."

During the next take, as witnessed by both Sturges and Lancaster, Kirk struck her as hard as he could, knocking her out. Then he turned to them and said, "When a gal tells me to go harder, I take her at her word. S&M-ers in the audience will really dig that scene."

"Ease up, man," Sturges protested. "Do you think you're making *Champion?*" He'd already called a doctor to attend to Van Fleet.

Lyle Bettger, cast as the leader of the Clayton gang, always seemed menacing on the screen. His best-known performance was as the wrathfully jealous elephant handler in the

Jo Van Fleet manhandled and (in real life) injured during her staged struggle with Kirk.

Oscar-winning Cecil B DeMille epic, *The Greatest Show on Earth* (1952).

As Johnny Ringo, John Ireland gets romantically involved with Doc Holliday's girlfriend, Kate. In a confrontation with him (Kirk), he throws a glassful of liquor in his face and challenges him to a shoot-out, but Kirk refuses.

[Coincidentally, Ireland had also starred in My Darling Clementine *(1946) with Henry Fonda, Linda Darnell, and Victor Mature. One of its scenes had depicted its own version of the gunfight at the O.K. Corral.]*

During the second week of filming, Kirk and Sturges were talking about Ireland and his almost legendary reputation in Hollywood. "I don't want you to think I go around checking out men's peckers, but a while ago, I took a piss with Ireland," Kirk said. "Those rumors spread by women are true. That dick of his stretches from Tucson to Phoenix."

In Hollywood, Ireland's star conquests had included everyone from the gay actor, Montgomery Clift, his co-star in *Red River* (1948), to Joan Crawford, with whom he'd appeared in *Queen Bee* (1955).

Other star seductions included a sixteen-year-old Tuesday Weld, Shelley Winters, Sue Lyon *(star of* Lolita in 1962), and a blonde named Barbara Payton, who later became a prostitute. He also seduced Natalie Wood, who told friends, "John Ireland has four times more dick than Elvis."

Jack Elam, cast in *O.K. Corral* as Tom McLowery, "gave me the creeps every time I saw him," Kirk said. "He had this hideous squint and was always the villain in a number of Westerns. That ugly squint derived from when he was a Boy Scot, when one of the kids stuck a pencil in his left eye, blinding him. I'd seen the guy in *High Noon* with Gary Cooper, where he played the town drunk."

O.K. Corral was shot in Arizona, Elam's home state.

John Hudson was cast as Virgil Earp, Wyatt Earp's brother. "I got to hang out with Burt and Kirk, two real pros. For a change of pace, I appeared with Elvis Presley in *G.I. Blues* (1960). I'd have done better had not my twin brother (William, also an actor) gone after parts meant for me."

Kirk found himself working once again with the menacing character actor, Ted de Corsia, who had played Captain Farragut in *20,000 Leagues Under the Sea*. This time, he was cast as "Shanghai" Pierce, a bully who rides into Tombstone to threaten the townspeople at their local dance.

The gang members wound Charlie Bassett (Earl Holliman), but Earp and Holliday scatter their ranks and fend them off. Billy, their youngest member, was portrayed by Dennis Hopper. *[Ironically, Hopper had grown up in Dodge City, the cattle town in Kansas where the historical figure of Wyatt Earp had once been sheriff. Hopper and Holliman had each recently appeared in* Giant *(1956), the Texas epic that had starred Elizabeth Taylor, James Dean, and Rock*

Hudson. Hopper had also appeared with James Dean in Rebel Without a Cause *(1955).]*

During Hopper's involvement in the filming of *O.K. Corral,* he was still young and naïve. Some members of the crew played a practical joke on him, convincing him that the local sheriff was after him for impregnating an underaged local girl.

They kept him out of sight in an isolated hideaway for three days, bringing him food and drink. Finally, Hopper wised up and came out of hiding. "You bastards, there is no sheriff on my ass."

Dennis Hopper with Burt Lancaster in *Gunfight at the O.K. Corral.*

Another rising young actor, Martin Milner, was cast as Jimmy Earp. This son of Detroit would go on to greater glory when he starred in the hit TV series *Route 66* (1960-64).

As Sheriff Cotton Wilson, Frank Faylen was a show biz veteran, born to parents who lived and worked on a showboat. They brought him out on stage, showing him off to audiences, when he was less than a year old.

He is still seen every year at Christmas on television across the country, as he played the friendly taxi driver in the classic movie, *It's a Wonderful Life* (1946), starring James Stewart. He was also in *Funny Girl* (1968) with Barbra Streisand.

Off screen, Lancaster would play a dual role in Kirk's life, both as his best friend and as his major rival. DeForest Kelley, the actor cast as Morgan Earp, yet another of Wyatt's brothers, said: "Burt and Kirk may have been good buddies, but they competed on camera for the best angles, fighting for that Cecil B. DeMille closeup that Norma Desmond wanted in *Sunset Blvd.* (1950). Their rivalry reminded me of Dean Martin and Jerry Lewis early in their careers."

Sometimes, Lancaster enjoyed teasing and taunting Kirk. Once, they were standing side by side, outdoors, after having shot a scene together. Lancaster had removed his shirt, displaying his splendid physique.

Four local girls approached and "tongue-wagged" at him, requesting his autograph and ignoring Kirk.

Lancaster turned to them and said, "Ladies, this is Kirk Douglas standing beside me. Why not ask for his autograph, too? Perhaps you don't recognize him because he's not wearing his built-up lifts."

It seems improbable, but it was reported that in reaction to that cutting jibe, Kirk wept.

***

During filming, Kirk and Lancaster did not seduce their leading ladies, as was their recurring custom. Instead, they spent all their free time together, staying in one or another of their bedrooms, talking until two or three o'clock in the morning, even if they had an early call the next morning on the set.

One morning, Wallis confronted Kirk when he arrived late and sleepy-eyed. "What are you guys doing until the early hours of the morning? All of Hollywood knows that Burt is bisexual. Are you guys fucking? Has he converted you to his team?"

"I didn't even know he was bi-," Kirk said. "We're just good buddies. As the biggest screen goddesses in Hollywood know, I'm a man for the ladies."

Later, Kirk credited the huge success of *O.K. Corral* to the strong bond that had flourished at the time between its male stars, as portrayed through the characters of Wyatt Earp and Doc Holliday.

"Burt and I will go down in film history as all those manly love relationships between two actors. I'm thinking of Spencer Tracy with Clark Gable and Paul Newman with Robert Redford."

The New York Times noted it, too. "Lancaster looks like a man who has nothing better than the electric chair when he has to leave Holliday to ride off to join the heroine, in this case, the beautiful, flame-haired Rhonda Fleming."

Most critics hailed *O.K. Corral* as a return to the old gambling, boozing, shoot-em-up Westerns of yesteryear. *Life* claimed, "*Gunfight at the O.K. Corral* has everything." *Variety* praised "the inspired casting of Burt Lancaster with Kirk Douglas."

Of course, there were a few brickbats, one coming from the *Washington Post*, which found the movie "blood thirsty, empty-headed, and good fun of its sort." The *Monthly Film Bulletin* defined it as "overlong and overwrought."

It became a smash hit, receiving two Oscar nominations, one for film editing, the other for sound recording.

Many critics found the Frankie Laine theme song for *O.K. Corral* too evocative of the music that played within Gary Cooper's *High Noon* (1952). *O.K. Corral's* theme had been written by Dmitri Tiomkin, who had also crafted the music for Kirk's *The Big Sky*.

Kirk and Lancaster didn't receive any Oscar nominations for *O.K. Cor-*

ral, but each was nominated for the Best Actor prize at the Laurel Awards, with Lancaster winning.

Today, *Gunfight at the O.K. Corral* is considered one of the top 100 Best Westerns of all Time, or so claimed the Western Writers of America, presenters of the annual Spur Awards.

***

For tax purposes, Sam Norton, Kirk's lawyer and business manager, informed him that Bryna Production would have to make some low-budget films in which he would not appear. Kirk wasn't excited by the idea, fearing that this extra burden would distract from the pursuit of his own career, but he agreed to it as a tax-saving device. "Bring on the scripts," he told Norton.

The first he read was *Spring Reunion.* Released in 1957, its plot centered on a fifteen-year reunion of the Carson High School Class of 1941. It was the story of Maggie Brewster, once voted the most popular girl in her class, during her reunion with Fred Davis, voted most likely to succeed. Life hasn't worked out the way they had dreamed. The theme revolved around, "can they rekindle an old flame?"

Betty Hutton met with Kirk and agreed to play the lead, which was a sort of comeback picture for her, as she had not been seen on the screen since 1952. Earlier in that decade, she had replaced Judy Garland in *Annie Get Your Gun* (1950) and had starred in Cecil B. DeMille's *The Greatest Show on Earth*, a circus drama (1952), voted Best Picture of the Year.

As Hutton later claimed, "I didn't know that *Spring Reunion* would be my *adieu* to the screen, after all my box office triumphs in the 1940s and early 1950s. But it was. It was a dreadful picture—a big bomb at the box office. My co-star, Dana Andrews, showed up drunk every day."

Jean Hagen was cast as its third lead.

[Hagen had been sensational as the

Purple prose for an unsuccessful movie from Bryna Production—so awful, it ended Betty Hutton's career.

silent screen star with the squeaky voice in Singin' in the Rain (1952) *In it, she had based her interpretation on the historical figure of Laura La Plante, who had been hailed decades earlier as the most beautiful girl of the silent screen. Ironically, La Plante herself was cast as one of the players in* Spring Reunion. *It would mark her final appearance on the screen.]*

In his evaluation of the film, one critic wrote, "This movie is a real stinkeroo. The plot is so old, you expect to see mold growing on it."

For Bryna's next low-budget release, after the spectacular failure of *Spring Reunion*, Kirk plotted the casting of Eleanor Parker in *Lizzie.* She had played his wife in *Detective Story* (1951). It had won her a Best Actress nomination.

Directed by Hugo Haas, *Lizzie* was also released in 1957. It's the story of a woman with three distinct personalities. Its script had been adapted from the 1954 novel, *The Bird's Nest,* by Shirley Jackson. Its film version introduced one of the most popular pop songs of its era, "It's Not for Me to Say," sung by Johnny Mathis.

Kirk cast Richard Boone—his co-star in *Man Without a Star*— as Parker's psychiatrist.

Joan Blondell, a big star in the 1930s and '40s, was cast as Parker's aunt. "I was reduced to playing a drunken slut," Blondell said. She's seen in a horse blanket bathroom drinking a lot of bourbon.

After the author (Jackson) of the novel on which the film had been based saw the film's final cut, she wrote a sarcastic memo to Kirk: "Better luck next time. I am not impressed. Suggest you retitle it as *Abbott & Costello Meet a Multiple Personality.*"

Lizzie (1957) bombed at the box office. According to Kirk, "Joanne Woodward made *The Three Faces of Eve* (also 1957), also with a theme of multiple personalities, and made off with a Best Actress Oscar."

After two financial losses, Kirk believed that his third Bryna Production film *The Careless Years* (1957) might make some money. The story of frustrated young love,

Eleanor Parker's *Lizzie* bombed at the box office. But Joanne Woodward in a film with the same plot walked off with an Oscar.

it starred Dean Stockwell, a former child star of the '40s, and a new discovery, Natalie Trundy, who was only sixteen when she appeared in Bryna's film. The couple want to get married. During the course of the film, they confront their parents' objections.

After its release, a critic noted that Stockwell looked like the Second Coming of James Dean, and that Trundy evoked the younger sister of Doris Day. Boswell Crowther of *The New York Times* wrote, "The pace is slow, the writing uninspired, and the approach to the issue is *naïve* and repetitious." Another critic defined its poor boy/rich girl theme as a "little Ozzie-and-Harriett artifact."

Before the year ended, Kirk greenlighted one more independent film entitled *Ride Out for Revenge*. It was clearly understood that for tax reasons associated with Bryna Production, he would not appear as its star.

A Western, it was defined as "a black-and-white Civil Rights oater." One of its themes dealt with the plight of the American Indian. It would star Rory Calhoun, Gloria Grahame, Lloyd Bridges, and Joanna Gilbert.

Kirk already knew Grahame from the cast of *The Bad and the Beautiful.* As he told his director, Bernard Girard, "I knew her in the sense that David knew Bathsheba."

The male lead was assigned to Rory Calhoun, famous for his casting couch links to the notorious talent agent Henry Willson. Calhoun had already appeared in two films with Marilyn Monroe, *How to Marry a Millionaire* (1953) and *River of No Return* (1954). Cast as Marshal Tate, Calhoun oozes a stoic *machismo* and lusts for "Pretty Willow," the daughter of an Indian chief named "Yellow Wolf" (Frank DeKova). Meanwhile, Grahame as Amy Porter—a widow who has recently lost both her spouse and her father in an Indian massacre—lusts after Calhoun.

Lloyd Bridges was uncharacteristically cast into one of his alltime most despicable roles, that of Captain George, a greedy, racist, and cowardly "jerk face" of a cavalry officer.

Chief Little Wolf was played by the handsome actor Vince Edwards, who would go on to greater glory as TV's *Ben Casey* (1961-66). It was during his filming of *Ride Out for Revenge* that Edwards posed for a full-frontal nude that became a collector's item among America's gay men.

Edwards later told Kirk, "I knew that I was terribly miscast, but I carried on as a brave Indian brave."

The reviews of *Ride Out for Revenge* were rather critical, and it opened to half-empty theaters.

Kirk was exasperated with the wrong (i.e., profitless) direction in which Bryna was moving. He informed his tax advisors, "From now on, I'm going to star in every Bryna film we turn out, regardless of the tax consequences."

With a minor exception or two, he kept that promise.

***

The then-famous novelist, John P. Marquand, had emerged as a respected and highly commercial writer. In 1938, he'd won a Pulitzer Prize for *The Late George Apley,* and in 1951, he'd written a hot-selling patriotic romance, *Melville Goodwin, USA,* about publicists trying to cover up an adulterous affair between a heroic, charismatic, and married U.S. general and the rich and glamorous media duenna charged with describing him to her millions of readers.

At the time—although its innuendos were too daring for the movies to touch—Warners bought its film rights and ordered scriptwriters Roland Kibbee and Allan Scott to "clean it up." *[They made many changes. The credits for the movie that evolved stated that the film was based on "characters" from Marquand's novel, rather than from the plot it described. Also, in the movie adaptation, the general is described as a bachelor, not as married and adulterous.]*

H.C. Potter was hired to direct the film that evolved from all this, and which was not associated in any way with Bryna Production. With the approval of its producer, Martin Rackin, Potter invited Humphrey Bogart and his wife, Lauren Bacall, to star in it. Bogie would portray the much-decorated two-star general, Melville Goodwin (aka "Iron Pants"), and Bacall would play Dottie Peal, a wealthy newspaper publisher modeled on Clare Booth Luce, then one of the most famous and influential women in America.

Although Bogie and Bacall accepted the roles, early in the filmmaking

Susan Hayward and Kirk Douglas are having the time of their lives in the hit of their lives!
'Top Secret Affair'

'Ironpants' Goodwin —toughest young general in the U.S. Army!

Cutest cutie that ever did her duty —gives 'Ironpants,' a new wrinkle on love!

Presented by Warner Bros.

process, during one of his wardrobe fittings, Bogie collapsed—he was suffering from cancer at the time—and had to be rushed to a hospital. Then Bacall announced that she had to drop out, too, so that she could stay at home and care for Bogart.

Rackin then cast his favorite actress, Susan Hayward, as the female lead, and offered the general's role to Kirk Douglas. It represented a rare opportunity for him to star in a romantic comedy.

According to the novel's film adaptation (entitled *Top Secret Affair* and released in 1957), Dottie is vehemently opposed to Iron Pants' appointment as Chairman of America's Joint Atomic International Commission, preferring that a close friend of her powerful father get the post instead. With charm and duplicity, she invites the general to her estate on Long Island with the intention of embarrassing and entrapping him. With this goal in mind, she installs hidden microphones and hires a photographer.

Her plan backfires *[AH! THE '50s!]* when she falls in love with him. When he uncovers her plot to entrap him, he walks out.

She plots revenge at his Senate Confirmation Hearing. Expect love to triumph in the end.

Warners hired four leading character actors as supporting players.

Paul Stewart was cast as Phil Bentley, the socialite's cynical assistant. *[Stewart had previously appeared with Kirk in Champion.]*

Roland Winters was cast as the autocratic and dim-witted Senator Burdick. *[Winters was widely known for six separate portrayals of Charlie Chan during the late 1940s.]*

Jim Backus, as Colonel Homer W. Gooch, portrayed Kirk's eccentric press agent. *[Backus provided the voiceovers for Mr. Magoo, the nearsighted cartoon character. Later, he was widely applauded for his portrayal of Thurston Howell III in the TV series* Gilligan's Island *(1964-1992).]*

Susan Hayward, preparing a drink or two, in *Top Secret Affair*

John Cromwell was cast as General Daniel Grimshaw, Kirk's commanding officer. Cromwell had recently been removed from the Hollywood blacklist, as defined by the U.S. House of Representative's Un-American Activities Committee. Before his appearance on that list, he had developed a distinguished career as both an actor and director, helming stars who included Bette Davis and Gary Cooper.

Susan Hayward, the granite-hard and very tough actress from Brooklyn, was already an A-list star in the league of Barbara Stanwyck, but sexier and better-looking. She'd already been nominated for five Best Actress Oscars, finally winning the gold in 1958 for her portrayal of Death Row inmate Barbara Graham in *I Want to Live*.

"All the guys, including Kirk Douglas himself, were trying to get into Susan's drawers," said Roland Winters. "She rejected all of us, and Kirk was seriously pissed off, since he'd had great success in bedding most of his leading ladies already—well, some of them…"

Before *Top Secret Affair*, Susan had been known for her *haute* seductions of two future presidents, Ronald Reagan and John F. Kennedy. Other flings occurred with Howard Hughes and Oleg Cassini. During her breakup with actor Jess Barker in 1954, she'd attempted suicide.

Just prior to her involvement in *Top Secret Affair*, she'd fallen in love with Floyd Eaton Chalkley, a rancher, businessman, and former Federal agent from Georgia. She'd made plans to marry him and move to Georgia. During filming, he stayed at the Beverly Wilshire Hotel and sent a bouquet of yellow roses, her favorite, to the set every day.

[For reasons known only to himself, Kirk, in his memoirs, never mentioned either Top Secret Affair *or the major-league actress who had starred in it with him, despite her status as the most high-profile actress with whom he'd ever worked. Famously egomaniacal, insecure, and high-maintenance, Hayward might*

have conflicted with him about issues related to ego.

Kirk might also have resented her friendship with the film's producer, Rackin, who had affectionately nicknamed her "Hooligan," and referred to her as "my buddy-buddy." Kirk suspected that Rackin was collaborating with the film's director "to throw the picture Susan's way in all our scenes together."]

Hayward later said, *Top Secret Affair* was a good picture, but no one came to see it."

Bosley Crowther in *The New York Times,* said, "The writers and director…tried to blow up a light romantic pastime out of characters that don't hold air. And because they are constantly deflating, the whole thing tends to wheeze. Kirk Douglas and Susan Hayward play the top roles with bruising aggressiveness, and Paul Stewart, Michael Fox and Jim Backus sigh and suffer as assorted underlings. But they can't get this operation soaring. *Melville Goodwin, U. S. A.,* is a bore."

***

When movie buffs gather for discussions about the great films associated with World War I, they're likely to immediately recommend *All Quiet on the Western Front* (1930) and Kirk Douglas' *Paths of Glory* (1958).

The first of these had earned a Best Director Academy Award for Lewis Milestone; a Best Picture Oscar for its all-round excellence; and had morphed its anguished hero, Lew Ayres, into a major-league star for his haunting portrayal of a young German infantryman, based on a novel by Erich Maria Remarque.

The title of the second of those two iconic films about "The Great War" derived from an excerpt from Thomas Gray's elegy from 1751:

> *The boast of heraldry, the pomp of pow'r*
> *And all that beauty, all that wealth e'er gave*
> *Awaits alike th'inevitable hour*
> *The paths of glory lead but to the grave.*

Paths of Glory (1958), a Harris-Kubrick Production, was a shattering indictment of the insanity of war. Its plot revolves around a French general's demand that his trench-weary soldiers attack a heavily fortified German outpost known as "anthill."

The French warriors have little chance of taking the hill, so the order, in essence, is a death sentence configured as a suicide mission.

When the few remaining survivors retreat back to their trenches, they face court martial and execution for their "cowardice."

As a warning from the military administration directly to their rank-and-file, only three of the "disobedients" are selected to stand trial.

They are defended in military court by Colonel Dax (Kirk), who's fully aware that a guilty verdict has already been determined, and that the victims, in the name of military honor, will be shot by a military firing squad. What makes the executions doubly horrible is that one of the miscreants, Private Pierre Arnaud (Joe Turkel) was so badly injured after starting a prison fight the night before his death that he must be carried to his execution on a stretcher, then tied into place, vertically and in agony, so that he can be shot.

Still in his late twenties, a brilliant young director, Stanley Kubrick, had teamed with a producer, James B. Harris, to form Harris-Kubrick Productions. As partners, they had acquired the film rights to a novel, *Paths of Glory,* penned by Humphrey Cobb. As a Canadian soldier, he had served in World War II, fighting at the Battle of Amiens in northern France. His *Paths of Glory* had been based on a true incident.

[Humphrey Cobb was also a screenwriter, having crafted the scripts for, among others, Humphrey Bogart's film, San Quentin *(1937). He is not to be confused with the Kentucky humorist, Irvin S. Cobb (not related), who wrote a non-fiction account of World War I which was also entitled* Paths of Glory.*]*

After acquiring the film rights, Kubrick contracted for a writer named Jim Thompson to craft a film treatment (which he rejected) of Humphrey Cobb's novel. Then he turned to the Southern novelist and screenwriter, Calder Willingham, a native of Georgia known today as "the father of modern black comedy." Willingham was part of that coven of respected novelists who arose after World War II and whose ranks included Norman Mailer, Gore Vidal, Truman Capote, and James Jones.

Harris and Kubrick shopped Willingham's script from studio to studio, facing one rejection after another, always hoping to convince an A-list movie star to endorse its merits and to agree to appear in it. To that end, they tried to sign Richard Burton, James Mason, and Gregory Peck, but none of them was interested or available. *[Of course, Kubrick and Mason would, years later, work together on* Lolita *(1962) in which Mason portrayed a pedophile.]*

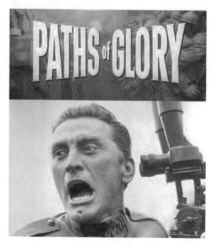

Finally, Kubrick sent the script to Kirk, who agreed not only to star in it, but to arrange its financing and filming as part of a distribution deal through United Artists. He warned Kubrick, "*Paths of Glory* will be a labor of love. Don't expect it to be a money-maker."

Hearing that, Kubrick was disappointed because his struggling new company needed cash. He had worked on the script himself, and even ended up with a happy ending.

Cast as Private Arnaud, Joe Turkel was so badly injured, he had to be carried on a stretcher to face the firing squad.

When Kirk read the revised script, he denounced Kubrick as a "stupid son of a bitch," demanding that he return to the original, more nihilistic version, which he did without protest. As originally inspired by Cobb, the script was a chilling portrait of military arrogance, ego-driven stupidity, and injustice.

Consulting with Kirk, Kubrick cast the secondary roles, too. Ralph Meeker was assigned the second lead of Colonel Philippe Paris, an officer who is accused of cowardice in the face of the enemy. Usually Meeker had played muscular, sullen, macho types, as he did on Broadway in *Mister Roberts* (1948), and in William Inge's *Picnic* (1953).

[When the theatrical version of Picnic, *in which Meeker had starred, was adapted into a Hollywood movie, Meeker rejected the equivalent film role, that part eventually going to William Holder.*

Kirk was somewhat jealous of Meeker, having been told that he had seduced Pier Angeli before he did. Meeker had starred with Angeli in MGM's Teresa *in 1951.]*

Veteran actor Adolph Menjou, cast as the self-cen-

Kirk called *Paths of Glory* "one of my shining hours on the screen. Every major studio turned it down, but I went for it."

tered and haughty French general Geôrges Broulard, was at the twilight of a brilliant career, during which he'd appeared with some of his era's greatest cinematic stars, including Rudolph Valentino, Janet Gaynor, Fredric March, Gary Cooper, Marlene Dietrich, Spencer Tracy, Katharine Hepburn, and Barbara Stanwyck.

Kirk thought Menjou perfect for the role, although he detested his politics. He had cooperated with the House Un-American Activities Committee, outing communists or former communists in the film industry during the witch hunts of Joseph McCarthy.

Cast as the arrogant, perhaps insane General Paul Mireau, George Macready returned to work with Kirk again after their experience together on *Detective Story*. Nearing the end of his film career, Macready would make two more films with Kirk before fading from the movie scene.

During the early stages of filming, Kirk complained of how Macready's part had been scripted. "He was a major French general, so he couldn't be that much of an idiot. Work on his lines. While you're at it, I need major script work on Colonel Dax (my part) too. Right now, my character is just 'Noble Joe,' lacking in depth and dimension. Come back to me with a better characterization. I don't want to have to do it myself."

Getting fifth billing, Wayne Morris had been a sort of name star in the late 1930s at Warner Brothers, starring alongside some of the bigger names in its stable; Bette Davis, Edward G. Robinson; Humphrey Bogart; even fast-rising Ronald Reagan. Morris had been a U.S. Navy pilot during World War II and resented the role he'd been assigned, that of the weakling, Lieutenant Roget. But since his career was in decline, he accepted it. He would die soon, expiring in September of 1959 at the age of forty-five of a coronary occlusion.

Richard Anderson was cast as Major Saint-Auban, the prosecuting attorney, remorselessly and relentlessly demanding that the death penalty be imposed on the three unlucky soldiers. He had previously worked with Kirk and Pier Angeli on *The Story of Three Loves*.

Appearing almost as a philosophic afterthought during the final few minutes of *Paths of Glory* was Christiane Harlan, a German *bierhalle* wench who's dragged out in front of the war-weary (enemy) French soldiers and forced to sing a wavering rendition of "The Faithful Hussar."

Kubrick became so enamored of Christiane that he divorced his wife the following year and married her. On this, his third marital attempt, the director got it right. Their marriage lasted until his death in 1999.

In the filming of her vocal rendition during the final moments of *Paths of Glory*, Kirk learned a bitter anecdote: Harlan was a descendant of the Nazi filmmaker Veit Harlan. At the request of Joseph Goebbels, he had been instrumental in the compilation of the most virulently anti-Semitic propaganda movie in cinematic history, *Jud Süss* (*Suss the Jew*; 1940).

In reference to Christiane, Kirk later wrote, "I hope her ancestor was gnashing his teeth somewhere in hell that his 'pure' blood was mingling with 'Jud' Kubrick's." *[Kubrick had been born to Jewish parents in the Bronx.]*

Although *Paths of Glory* was set in France, Kirk opted to film it near Munich, shooting most of the film's interiors at Bavaria's *Geiselgasteig* Studios. They had been heavily bombed in Allied air raids during World War II. Other, more formal, interior shots were filmed in a suburb of Munich at Schleissheim Castle, the baroque summer residence of the Bavarian rulers of the House of Wittelsbach.

When Kirk could take time off, he visited the nearby site of the Nazi Concentration Camp at Dachau. "It was a sad, heartbreaking sight for me. None of the locals admitted to me that they knew that stinking smoke coming from Dachau meant burning Jewish bodies."

Paths of Glory launched Kubrick on his own road to glory. Directorship of *Dr. Strangelove* (1964) lay in his future.

When asked about Kubrick, Kirk delivered a harsh appraisal: "He has an ego that knows no bounds. At times, it's out of control, wanting to take credit for everything. Time and time again, he goes way overboard. In essence, he's a talented shit."

Nevertheless, Kirk hired Kubrick again to direct his most acclaimed film, *Spartacus* (1960).

At the end of *Paths of Glory*, Kirk delivered one of his most memorable screen lines: "There are times when I am ashamed to be a member of the human race."

Box office was poor, but most of the reviews were favorable. *Saturday Review* hailed it as "so searing in its intensity, it will probably take its place in years to come as one of the screen's most extraordinary achievements."

Bosley Crowther of *The New York Times* wrote: "The close, hard eye of Mr. Kubrick's sullen camera bores directly into the minds of the scheming men and into the hearts of the frightened soldiers who have to accept orders to die."

Because of its negative portrayal of the French military,

Christiane Harlan sings "Ein treuer Husar" ("The Faithful Hussar") in the final scene of Stanley Kubrick's *Paths of Glory* (1957)

Paths of Glory was banned from French movie theaters, although secret copies for private screenings were smuggled in and displayed. Unwilling to antagonize its neighbor, Switzerland also issued a ban against the film. Belgium, however, allowed the film to be shown, although issuing an on-screen warning that the saga represented "only an isolated case and did not reflect upon the gallantry of French soldiers." The U.S. military also banned it from screenings on its military bases in Europe.

In an interview with film critic Roger Ebert in 1960, Kirk said, *"Paths of Glory* was the summit of my acting career. Oscar should have had my name on it. It is a picture that will still be good years from now. I don't have to wait fifty years to know that. It has an economy of expression that is almost brutal. There is no nostalgia, only nightmare."

***

The Vikings, released in 1958, became one of Kirk's most ambitious action-adventure films—and one of the most dramatic. Funneling its production through his own company, Bryna, he set out to re-create the sadistic blood-thirsts of the Vikings during their attacks on "the three kingdoms of Britannia."

First, Kirk had to secure the rights and to have the theme shaped into a screenplay. Then he had to scout film locations and supervise the construction of replicas of Viking ships, some of them seventy-five feet long.

Kirk had recently read a novel, *The Viking,* by Edwin Marshall, and thought, "It would make a hell of a movie." Marshall's works had reached the screen before, as when his novel, *Benjamin Blake,* was adapted into a film, *Son of Fury* (1942), star-ring Tyrone Power. Marshall's most recent film adaptation, *Yankee Pasha* (1954), had starred Jeff Chandler and Mamie Van Doren.

When he wasn't writing novels, Marshall was a big game hunter, roaming across the landscapes of India and Africa.

Kirk had been impressed with the scriptwriting of Calder Willingham for *Paths of Glory,* so he hired him to

Cast as Eric (Tony Curtis, left) and Einar (Kirk), the two men are half-brothers, but unaware of it. They become enemies and fight, during which Kirk, as Einar, loses one eye.

adapt Marshall's novel to the screen. Willingham, a native of Georgia, was an odd choice. He was known for potboilers in a Deep South setting. He would later work on such films as Marlon Brando's *One-Eyed Jacks* (1960), and *The Graduate* (1967), starring Dustin Hoffman and Anne Bancroft.

To take on such a mammoth project, Kirk, as the (uncredited) Executive Producer, hired Jerry Bresler as its detail-fixated producer. Kirk been impressed with Bresler's organizational skill when he'd produced *Spring Reunion* with Betty Hutton and *Lizzie* with Eleanor Parker, both released in 1957 for Bryna Production. Despite the fact that both of those had flopped, Kirk nonetheless decided that Bresler was the man for the nuts and bolts of this "Norse Opera." *[Two Gidget films lay in Bresler's B-picture future.]*

Since epic scenery would play such a vital role in *The Vikings*, Kirk hired one of the best cinematographers in the business: Jack Cardiff

[The son of English music hall entertainers. Cardiff flourished as both a cinematographer and director, working with, among many others, Alfred Hitchcock and John Huston. He was at home photographing movie icons: Katherine Hepburn, Sophia Loren, Audrey Hepburn, Humphrey Bogart, Marlene Dietrich, and even Arnold Schwarzenegger.

Cardiff died in East Anglia, England, in 2009, and in the following year, a documentary was released devoted to his half-century in the business. Kirk was interviewed for the film along with such figures as Lauren Bacall, Martin Scorsese, and Charlton Heston.

Shown at the Cannes Film Festival, the documentary was entitled Cameraman: The Life and Work of Jack Cardiff.]

Kirk preferred to cast *The Vikings* himself, assigning himself the lead of Einar, a ferocious and relentlessly macho Viking warrior. There were three other leading roles, too, including the female lead, his leading lady, Morgana, a Welsh princess. Before casting the other male roles, he wanted to "nail down" the female lead, as he suggestively expressed it.

For years, Kirk had wanted to co-star with Ingrid Bergman, and he saw an opportunity to cast the Swedish star in *The Vikings*, a Nordic

Viking Einar (Kirk) is shown masked (top photo) and unmasked (lower photo) and ready to rumble.

epic that might intrigue her.

[He'd been captivated by Bergman's image ever since Look magazine had named her, along with Gene Tierney and Hedy Lamarr, as the world's most beautiful women, and since he'd already seduced Lamarr and Tierney, she remained a challenge. He read a recent statement from her first husband, Petter Lindstrom, who had told the press, "Ingrid told me she couldn't work in a film unless she was in love either with her director or her leading man."]

He'd met Bergman on separate occasions, at parties, once at the home of Mike Todd. He opted to set up a private meeting with her in Rome.

Bergman's tender and demure screen image of the 1940s didn't match her private life. One of her directors, Alfred Hitchcock, once said, publicly and ungallantly, "She'd do it with a doorknob."

[She had, indeed, already seduced many of her leading men, including Leslie Howard in Intermezzo (1939). During the filming of Dr. Jekyll and Mr. Hyde (1941), she was sexually intimate with both its director (Victor Fleming) and her co-star, Spencer Tracy. The following year, Humphrey Bogart fell for her both on and off the screen in Casablanca.

When it came to seductions of her leading men, 1945 was her busiest year in the boudoir: Bing Crosby in The Bells of St. Mary's, Gregory Peck in Spellbound, and Gary Cooper in Saratoga Trunk.

When she'd had an affair with the Italian director, Roberto Rossellini, in the late 1940s, the violent backlash of public opinion temporarily derailed her American film career. After a six-year exile outside the U.S., she was justly rewarded with a Best Actress Oscar for her role in Anastasia (1956). The character she'd played had claimed to be the youngest (and last surviving) daughter of the assassinated Russian Czar Nicholas II.]

Before arriving on her doorstep, Kirk had sent her the Willingham script, and, after reading it, she agreed to see him.

The details of that meeting have never been made public, either by Bergman or by Kirk. What is on the record is that she found the role of the Princess Morgana "too bland, too weak, not a real star part." After her huge success and comeback Oscar, she wanted a much stronger female role.

Bergman, however, was not gone from his life forever. When he was assembling a cast for *Spartacus* (1960), he once again got in touch with her, offering her the role of the slave girl, Varinia. Bergman rejected that, too, objecting to the script as "too bloody."

Details of their brief afternoon fling might never have been known were it not for Anthony Quinn who he co-starred with Bergman several years later in *The Visit* (1964).

Eventually, he and Kirk began gossiping about Bergman. Both men admitted to brief affairs with her, Quinn complaining that "she wouldn't do all the things a whore would," and Kirk saying that he planned not to write about it in any future memoir.

Late in her life, during an interview with a reporter in Stockholm, Bergman chose not to mention any involvement with Kirk, except for a passing reference: "A brief interlude, nothing less, nothing more."

***

Kirk finally decided on the husband-and-wife team of Tony Curtis and Janet Leigh as co-stars in *The Vikings*. Curtis would be Eric, a slave but royalty, and Janet would be Princess Morgana, the Welsh princess with whom both Einar (Kirk) and Eric (Curtis) fall in love. Unknown to the men during their murderous battles, they are half-brothers.

Kirk had not been impressed with many of Curtis' early films, which had included swashbucklers, westerns, and light comedies. He'd gone to see *Houdini* (1953), in which Curtis had starred with Leigh, and Kirk decided that both of them were talented.

What really stood out for him was when Curtis co-starred opposite Kirk's friend, Burt Lancaster, in *Sweet Smell of Success* (1957). The following year, Curtis would be nominated for an Oscar for the character he portrayed in *The Defiant Ones* (1958). Curtis had played a bigoted white escaped convict chained to a black man, Sidney Poitier.

Before Curtis signed for the role, Kirk assured him that *The Vikings* was not going to be another of those "sword-and-sandals" movies. What most tempted Curtis was Kirk's promise that both he and Leigh would walk away "with a cool million."

Upper Photo: Curtis (bastard son of a Viking King) has fallen in love with Janet Leigh (a Welsh Princess) .

Lower photo: Kirk, when it comes to Leigh and everything else, seems to have fewer scruples than those of his half-brother.

401

"Kirk and I became friends," Curtis said, "even though he is a control freak. It's either his way or the highway. He is a perfectionist and a real tightwad."

Later, Curtis recalled, "While making this film, often in harsh weather conditions in Norway, where it seems to rain all day, I talked about my marital problems with him, treating him like my uncle. My marriage was crumbling but still had a way to go. I was screwing women on the side, just like Kirk. Each of us was biting at the leash every chance we got to bed a beautiful woman. We're both devotees of adultery. I had another reason for relating to Uncle Kirk: He suffered moods as black as mine."

Kirk had always been attracted to Janet Leigh's beauty but was not enthralled by her acting abilities. He hired her before her iconic appearance in Alfred Hitchcock's *Psycho* (1960).

But Orson Welles, who had agreed to narrate *The Vikings*, highly praised Leigh's acting, and eventually persuaded Kirk to the contrary. Welles revealed that he'd cast Leigh in *Touch of Evil*, a *film noir* that was released the same year as *The Vikings* (1958). She would co-star in it not only with Welles, but with Charlton Heston and Marlene Dietrich too.

"Among the stars in *The Vikings*, I was the only Dane," Janet Leigh said. *[Some of her ancestors had come from Denmark. Leigh had been discovered by Norma Shearer, who had reigned as Queen of MGM in the 1930s.]*

As the gruff, rough Ragnar, Kirk's father, the raucous leader of the ferocious Viking clansmen, Ernest Borgnine was ideal, even though he was born in 1917, Kirk in 1916. Heavy makeup did a lot to age him appropriately.

"Borgnine was not a beauty prize winner," Kirk said. "He had this gap-toothed Cheshire cat grin." During the months he was filming with Kirk, he was married to Katy Jurado, the Mexican actress with him Kirk had starred in *The Racers* three years earlier.

After divorcing Jurado in 1964, Borgnine married Ethel Merman. "Our marriage ended on our wedding night." In her memoirs, Merman left a page blank when it came to reporting details associated with their very brief and utterly disastrous marriage.

Kirk had first recognized Borgnine's talent when he played Fatso in *From Here to Eternity* (1953), the character who beat up Frank Sinatra. Before working with Kirk, Borgnine had also won a Best Actor Oscar for *Marty* (1955), in which he'd played a warm-hearted butcher looking for love.

Another key role was assigned to the Scottish actor, James Donald, who had played Theo Van Gogh, brother of the artist in *Lust for Life*. Kirk liked the way he'd handled that role, and cast him in *The Vikings* as Egbert, a nobleman of Northumbria.

Alexander Knox was cast as the kindly Father Godwin. He offers comfort when Princess Morgana confesses to him that she is pregnant after her rape by Ragnar.

Knox's most notable moment on the screen had been his portrayal of President Woodrow Wilson in *Wilson* (1944), for which he won an Oscar nomination.

Cast as Ragnar, Ernest Borgnine is thrown to his death in a pit of hungry, devouring wolves.

He was never officially blacklisted during the McCarthy witch hunt, but his liberal views had hurt his career. Kirk was glad to work with this champion of First Amendment rights.

Weather conditions in Norway were harsh, and Kirk remembered standing with Curtis under a tarp for more than a month, waiting for the never-ending rain to stop. As the film's chief financial backer, he was greatly distressed when production ran way behind schedule. Hundreds of extras stood around getting paid but not able to do anything. The tension reached a boiling point when, on top of everything else, the crew wanted their salaries raised.

Every day before the beginning of filming, Kirk had to be fitted with a painful contact lens, a prop that conveyed the impression that he'd had his eye gouged out.

One of the most dramatic scenes in the movie is when Ragnar is captured and sentenced to die by being tossed into a pit filled with ravenous wolves. Eric (that is, Curtis) cuts his prisoner bonds and gives him a sword so that he can die an honorable Viking's death. Ragnar, with the sword, jumps into the pit, laughing madly on his way to Valhalla, hacking away at "wolf-demons" until the only sounds the audience hears is their ripping apart of his flesh.

In one scene, Eric (Curtis) insults Einar (Kirk) and they battle. When Einar "wins," Curtis is tied up and tossed into a slop-pool to be eaten by giant crabs. Eerily, and with touches of Runic mysticism and intervention from the Norse God, Odin, he escapes.

Both of the half-brothers, Eric and Einar, are in love with the buxom and very blonde Princess Morgana as portrayed by Janet Leigh. A climactic battle scene is choreographed on the vertigo-inducing ramparts of a castle. At one point, Einar is about to plunge his sword into his brother but hesitates. Eric (Curtis) uses the delay to fatally stab his brother (Kirk), then grants him a fiery Viking funeral, sending him off to paradise in Valhalla. His body is engulfed in flames aboard a ship sailing off into the mist.

Bosley Crowther, writing in *The New York Times,* said, "There isn't much doubt that Kirk Douglas plays the Number One Boozer and Bruiser on the Norsemen team. He set out to make the godarnest wide-screen and color action film that's physically possible within the confines of ancient castles, grotesque rowboats, and bushy beards, and, by George, he looks as if he's got it. The plot and story at times are as tangled as some of the beards."

The Daily Express reviewed it too, writing, "*The Vikings* is, in fact, a blood-thirsty fandango of smash, kick, gouge, and punch, which would be lamentable to watch were it not for one thing: It is played throughout with a tongue-in-cheek sense of serio-comedy that makes you laugh out loud in moments when you might be shuddering with horror. It is rough, riotous, and wholly enjoyable."

In his capacity as owner of Bryna Production, the tax-avoiding business entity that had produced *The Vikings,* Kirk took no salary but earned sixty percent of the film's profits. As such, he took home two million dollars.

***

After the location shooting in Norway, Kirk flew to a film studio near Munich for filming of *The Vikings'* interior shots. He checked into the city's most opulent hotel, the Vier Jahreszeiten. At the time, one of its wings was being rebuilt after its destruction by an Allied bomb in 1945.

He was there on the night of the 1956 Academy Awards presentations in Hollywood. He had been nominated for the Best Actor Oscar based on his portrayal of Vincent Van Gogh. According to reports, he was favored to win, in part because two of the other competitors had appeared within the same film. *[i.e.,nominations for the late James Dean and Rock Hudson had each derived from appearances in the epic film* Giant, *and therefore, to some degree, split the vote cast by fans of that particular movie.]*

Yul Brynner had also been nominated (for his role in *The King and I*), and so had Laurence Olivier (for his performance in the title role of *Richard III*).

The lobby of the Vier Jahreszeiten was filled with reporters and photographers waiting for a statement from Kirk about the outcome of the Oscar jury's decision. *[For the actual event back in California, Burt Lancaster had been commissioned to deliver an acceptance speech for him in the event that he won.]*

After dinner, Kirk had retired to his suite, exhausted. If he won, he'd be summoned to the lobby for interviews.

Shortly after midnight, a phone call was put through to his room. The voice on the other end "was very soft, very seductive, beautifully accented, very feminine, and most cuddly."

After talking a bit, and against his better judgment, he invited this mystery woman to room 502. Clad only in his pajama bottoms, he opened the door and confronted a stylishly dressed young woman he later described as "beautiful, ravishing, slightly Eurasian looking."

She identified herself as Princess Safia-Tarzi of Afghanistan. According to Kirk, "At that time, I didn't even know where the hell Afghanistan was. She came into my room, which became the place she rested her head for the next three nights…not that she got much rest. Nor did I. She was straight from *Arabian Nights*. Someone must have taught her all the secret techniques of how to satisfy a Sheik in olden days. But I won't go into that."

Before she departed after "days and nights of lust," he'd learned a lot about her and her country, which fascinated him. He wanted to go there one day.

Kirk's visitor was the mysterious daughter of King Amanullah and his consort, Queen Soraya

[Amānullāh Khān dysfunctionally ruled Afghanistan from 1919 to 1929, presiding over that nation's murky, confusing, and fragmented distancing from Britain during what's known as the Third Anglo-Afghan War. His hopes of modernizing the region based on European models was thwarted by inbred local customs and accusations of collaboration with colonial profiteers. In 1929, he abdicated

Two views of Safia-Tarzi of Afghanistan.

On the left, in 1968 , she is seen against a backdrop of Afghan horseriders for a press and publicity shot loosely associated with *Vogue* and with efforts to promote tourism and industry. She's modeling one of her own designs.

On the right, she appears in 1969 within her studio/boutique in Kabul.

and fled into exile, first to British India and then to Italy and Switzerland, where he died in 1960.

He was replaced by "The Bandit King," the tribal guerilla fighter and petty thief, Habibullah Kalakani, who was himself deposed and executed with his brothers and aides nine months after seizing power.

Amanullah's consort, Soraya Tarzi, (aka Queen Soraya), was born in 1899 and educated in the then-relatively sophisticated Syria, then part of the Ottoman Empire. She became celebrated in liberal circles throughout the Middle East and fêted during diplomatic visits to England, Germany, and India as a diplomatic helpmate to her husband and a strong advocate of women's rights. Evaluated today as one of the most influential women of her era, she was almost universally condemned by the local mullahs. The second of three wives of the Amanullah, she was "replaced," as his consort, and, at the invitation of the Italian government, spent the final years of her life in exile in Rome, dying there in 1968.]

According to Kirk, "When she stood at my door, Safia didn't look anything like my concept of a woman from the Middle East. There was no veil. She wore a chic black gown with *décolletage* and high heels with a diamond-and-ruby necklace she said was three hundred years old."

Safia told him, "My mother and father, the King and Queen of Afghanistan, practiced monogamy, something unheard of at the time. My mother urged girls to get an education. I was sent to Istanbul to study. My parents toured Europe, dressing like modern monarchs. When their photos, snapped in diplomatic settings, were shown in Kabul, they caused outrage—so much that they had to abandon the throne."

Kirk stayed in his room with Safia for the remainder of the evening, regretting his Oscar ceremony loss that night to Yul Brynner. Whereas Kirk was not acknowledged for his performance as Van Gogh, his "teammate," Anthony Quinn, won the award for Best Supporting Actor for his eight-minute appearance as Paul Gauguin in *Lust for Life*.

"There is no justice," Kirk said. "I went through the agonies of the damned. I even cut off my ear—and Quinn gets an Oscar...You figure it out."

[Norman Corwin also won an Oscar for Lust for Life's *screenplay, and Cedric Gibbons also got one for his art direction of that film.*]

"Yul Brynner and that damn bald head of his beat my ass," Kirk said. "Yet all was not lost that night. I got the consolation prize in the shapely form of Princess Safia."

After their three-night stand, she disappeared, the cosmopolitan by-product of colliding cultures and conflicting worlds. He doubted that he'd ever see her again. But years later, at the home of Gregory Peck in Hollywood, "He introduced me to Safia. We were most cordial, pretending we had never met before," Kirk said. "I was with Anne at the time, and it was the discreet thing to do."

[*Safia-Tarzi eventually evolved into a fashion designer whose works appeared on the pages of* Vogue. *In Kabul, during a lull in its hostilities, she opened a boutique whose widely publicized merchandise, photographed on models posed in front of ancient Afghan ruins and at local bazaars, included avant-garde re-interpretations of goatskin coats. A mysterious, under-reported figure, and the sophisticated symbol of an unpopular "colonial" regime, she evolved—perhaps unwillingly— into a Europeanized symbol for the emerging role of women in Afghan society. Eventually, the Taliban forced many of the women of Afghanistan back into the Middle Ages.*

Safia-Tarzi, something of an adventuress whose rare appearances in international media sometimes backfired with ominous repercussions, died a few years later when the hot-air balloon she'd raced in across the English Channel exploded and crashed near Paris.]

***

After his completion of *The Vikings* in Munich, Kirk flew to Paris for a reunion with Anne and their new son, Peter. Pumped with the belief that he had a box office hit on his hands, he planned to go on an art-buying binge through Paris' Left Bank art galleries.

There, motivated by the advice of savvy investors, he became enamored with the works of Maurice de Vlaminck (1876-1958). Kirk's buying binge occurred just before that artist's death in October of 1958, after which the value of his canvases increased considerably in value.

[*In league with Henri Matisse and André Derain, Vlaminck had been a leader of the art movement known as Fauvism. Flourishing from 1904 to 1908, it was known for its intense colors and a radical departure from the lines and representations of the natural world. Its name derived from "Les Fauves" (Wild Beasts), originally assigned by an art critic as an insult. Something of a firebrand at the time, Vlaminck had attacked both Picasso and Cubism in general, accusing them of "dragging French painting into wretched dead ends."*

To some degree, Kirk appreciated Vlaminck for his endorsement of Van Gogh. "I love him more than I do my own father."]

Kirk acquired several of his paintings, bargaining their prices down in some cases, from $20,000 to $10,000. With the intention of using them to decorate the walls of his home in L.A, he wrote to Anne, "Izzy, the collector of rags, bones, bottles, and now artwork, is on his way."

***

At his hotel in Paris (George V), an urgent message was waiting from Jerry Bresler, who had accompanied him to "The City of Light." *[Bresler had helped Kirk produce* The Vikings.*]*

Bresler told him that Soraya Esfandiary-Bakhtiary, the (divorced and exiled) former Queen of Iran wanted to renew their acquaintance that evening at her "usual" hangout, the bar at the very posh Plaza

Queen Soraya was regally photographed after her marriage to the ill-fated Shah of Iran in 1951.

Athenée Hotel on the Avenue Montaigne in the city's 8th Arrondissement.

[In one of history's most lavish weddings, Soraya had married the Shah of Iran in 1951. In 1958, in one of the most gossip-permeated breakups in the Middle East, he divorced her, ostensibly for her failure to produce an heir.

In the aftermath of that divorce, the Shah married Farah Diba (later, after her coronation, known as Shahbanu Farah Pahlavi). She produced two sons and two daughters, and remained as his wife and official consort until the collapse of his government in 1979 and his death a year later. Soraya, in the meanwhile, in exile and living mostly in Paris, received a large annual stipend and some of the honors associated with her former role as a queen.]

Bresler summarized the situation succinctly: "Soraya needs a new gig. She's been demoted, and she wants to become a movie star. That's what she wants to discuss with you—after all, you own a movie production company. Seems like the little Jew boy, Issur, is hanging out with royalty from the Middle East. I guess that's one of the perks that comes with being a bigtime movie star."

Kirk had once harbored a crush on Soraya, based on the many magazine covers she had graced with her regal beauty. Once, at his temporary rented lodgings at a villa in Rome, he had invited her to attend a cocktail party he was hosting there.

Soraya had arrived that evening in Rome with her German-born mother, Eva Karl, who proceeded to get intoxicated. Accompanying them were two very handsome, blonde-haired German security guards. "Were they her lovers?" he wondered.

In Rome, he had found Soraya very attractive, though missing that "special quality" he looked for in a woman. Their rendezvous lasted for only about an hour before she departed with her entourage. As he reflected, "It would have been better leaving my dream of her alone without trying to convert it into reality."

He had not seen her since the party he had hosted in Rome. In Paris, he entered the bar at the Plaza Athénée [*where by now and in years to come she was something of a regular fixture, much to the horror of the conser-*

As a wealthy royal exile and film star wannabe, Soraya made headlines across Europe.

vative mullahs back in Iran]. This time, he found her more aggressive. Those years on the Peacock Throne of Iran had changed her. Over drinks, she discussed her desire to be a movie star, something that had already been suggested by so many magazine editors. Years later, she would make equivalent overtures to Rock Hudson.

She admitted that the Shah of Iran had known many women, but that she was still "the love of his life," despite the fact that he was divorcing her. "I cannot have children, so I must go."

She suggested that as a film producer and movie star, he might find a suitable property in which she could be featured. "I think you and I would be dynamic together on the screen."

He interrupted her. "Do you know I'm a Jew?"

"Your religion is of no importance to me," she said. "I was born a Roman Catholic and knew nothing of the Muslim religion and all its restrictions on women. I'm sure that you and I are people of the world, freed from silly prejudices and bigotry. My father, Khalil Esfandiary-Bakhtiary, was a Bahktiary nobleman and served as the Iranian Ambassador to West Germany. I do not plan to ever marry again. I want to be free…to follow the desires of my heart."

Her delivery was melodramatic, and her references were nostalgic. She told him that she'd been named after the constellation of seven stars, *Haft Peykar,* that's visible in the skies over Isfahan, the most beautiful city of ancient Persia.

She also spoke candidly about her marriage to the Shah, claiming that his first choice had been Grace Kelly. She described the Marble Palace in Tehran as politically and socially equivalent to a nest of vipers: "My life in the royal palace was a nightmare," she said. "It was made all the more so by Ernest Perron, the Shah's [*Swiss, French-speaking, and very odd, and occasionally suspected as a conduit to the British*] best friend and private secretary. He's a homosexual and detests all women, especially me. Actually, he's in love with the Shah, and worships him."

"In the palace, he stirred up vile gossip about me. He is cunning, perfidious, and Machiavellian. When conferring with me, he made very lewd remarks about my sex life with the Shah, revealing to me that he is hysterically jealous."

She discussed her trips to Hollywood, a town she said she adored, describing her encounters with Bob Hope, Grace Kelly, Esther Williams, Humphrey Bogart, and Lauren Bacall. After her most recent trip to Los Angeles, she flew to Miami, where she was photographed on the beach wearing a white bikini. The photos were widely circulated throughout Iran as part of a deliberate campaign to discredit her. She was widely condemned as "immoral."

She was staying in the royal suite at the Plaza Athénée, and she invited him to a catered dinner there on its terrace, overlooking the Eiffel Tower and the lights of one of Paris's most architecturally spectacular neighborhoods. He accepted her invitation not so much because he was attracted to her physical charms, but because of her links to the Royal House of Iran. As he later told Bresler, "If Queen Elizabeth had asked me to screw her, I would have said yes."

From Friday night until Monday morning, he was her boudoir companion.

He departed with only a vague promise that he would search for a suitable script as a co-starring vehicle for them, together, as factored through Bryna Production. That never happened.

[*Soraya spent a long time pursuing her dream of stardom, and Kirk kept abreast of whatever gossip was spread about her. She eventually got cast in a movie,* I Tre Volti *(1965), an Italian film released in English as* Three Faces of a Woman.

She became the lover of an ambitious young Italian director, Franco Indovina, who died in an airplane crash in 1972.

After his death, Soraya began a series of affairs, many of which were revealed by the scandal magazines. She had a fling with the hell-raising English actor, Richard Harris, the future King Arthur of Camelot, *and also with the Italian comic actor, Alberto Sordi.*

One of her serious romances was with the Austrian actor, Maximilian Schell ("We both had German roots"). That was followed by a fling with Gunter Sachs, the third husband of Brigitte Bardot. In a surprise affair, she ended up in the arms of TV's Wyatt Earp, Hugh O'Brian.

As Soraya aged, and as the high-profile movie stars like Kirk faded away, she began a series of one-night stands. By then, she lived in Paris at 46 Avenue Montaigne, across the street from the Plaza Athénée. She was frequently seen in the bar of that hotel, where she made many of her conquests. As she confessed, "As I got older, the men got younger until they disappeared from my life altogether, except for the gigolos. I've seduced so many fake princes in the Jet Set."

At the age of sixty-nine, Soraya died in Paris. She was buried in Munich where her gravesite was desecrated with the words "MISERABLE PARASITE."

There were published reports that she'd been murdered, but they were never officially confirmed.]

***

Kirk's homecoming in the wake of *The Vikings* wasn't the romantic interlude he had hoped for during those long, cold weeks of filming in Norway. He had abruptly come face to face with his wife, Anne Buydens, his son Peter, and another child on the way.

He and Anne began to argue over his business affairs, which he had turned over to Sam Norton, his attorney and business manager. Kirk always referred to him as "my best friend," and he dropped into his office sometimes just to chat or have dinner with him. "No matter what was on his schedule on any given day, he dropped everything and made time for me."

Whenever Kirk ran short of spending money, Norton would rush him two-hundred dollars immediately.

During his first week back in Los Angeles, Kirk engaged in confrontations over Norton. Anne was often unwell, suffering from her pregnancy, and sometimes, he didn't want to return home to face her.

Finally, under increasing pressure from her, he called Norton and asked him, "Just how much money do I have?

Norton assured him that he was a millionaire, and that night, Kirk passed the good news on to Anne.

She didn't receive it well and demanded proof. "I wouldn't take Norton's word for anything." She wanted to see bank statements, stock certificates, and deeds to real estate and properties such as the oil wells Kirk had often boasted about.

Before their wedding in Las Vegas, Norton had persuaded her to sign a prenuptial agreement which he now refused to show to her.

Her suspicions about Norton seemed to grow daily. Finally, after a bitter argument with Kirk, she shouted, "Sam Norton is a crook. He's robbing you blind. You're a fool not to see that."

Behind Kirk's back, she hired Greg Bautzer, the most high-profile lawyer in Hollywood. [*His promiscuous indiscretions had included sexual trysts with clients such as Joan Crawford and Lana Turner.*] Bautzer employed Price Waterhouse, the same accounting firm that tallied the Oscars, to investigate. The report they compiled devastated both of them.

Kirk had gone into exile in Europe for eighteen months as a vehicle that, in theory, at least, would allow him to avoid heavy taxes from the Internal Revenue Service. Yet on a technicality, his status as a bona-fide exile had been denied. As a result, he owed three-quarters of a million dollars to the IRS. With interest mounting, at that rate, and if not paid soon, it would amount to a million dollars.

The money in his bank account totaled $3,651.67. Even worse, all the investments he thought he owned had been transferred into Norton's name, including those oil wells.

Bautzer's report made clear that as Kirk's lawyer, Norton had taken ten percent of all his gross earnings, plus another ten percent as his agent.

"I had made good money, more than two dozen pictures, with nothing to show for it," Kirk lamented. "I was not only penniless, but at the bottom of a well of mounting debt, and with a wife and three sons to support, and another kid on the way."

Anne urged legal action against Norton, wanting to send him to jail. Kirk hesitated, saying, "He's been like a father to me." Then he reconsidered that statement. Actually, Norton had been like Kirk's real father, totally indifferent to him, the man who'd taken all his savings for college and never paid him back.

In Norton's office the next day, Kirk confronted his lawyer/agent with accusations of grand theft, calling him a "dirty son of a bitch and scumbag thief," and cut all financial ties with him. Then, through Bautzer, he blocked his ability to draw any funds about to come in from *The Vikings*.

Anne's assessments had been accurate, prompting Kirk to realize that he had married a "protective lioness." Eventually, with box office receipts coming in from *The Vikings*, he was able to settle his outstanding debt to the IRS.

Kirk claimed he'd learned his lesson: "The next time some lawyer in Tinseltown tells me to trust him and says he's my good buddy, I'm calling the police."

***

On June 21, 1958, Kirk's fourth son entered the world, this one from Anne Buydens. Her first words to Kirk at the hospital were, "Now Peter

412

has a playmate to grow up with."

In honor of the money pouring in from box office receipts from *The Vikings*, Kirk gave his new son a Norse name, "Eric," in honor of Eric the Red, the 10th-Century Norwegian navigator.

With the full name of Eric Anthony Douglas, he would have two half-brothers, Michael and Joel.

After this latest birth, Kirk announced, "No more kids for me." The following week, he went to his doctor for a vasectomy.

In the months that followed, he tried to put his financial house in order and plotted his next career moves. Then, devastating news arrived from his sisters, who asked him to fly East for an urgent visit to Albany, New York. His mother, Bryna, was dying in a local hospital.

As his last gift to her, he had taken her to Manhattan where he rented the largest limousine in town and had its driver take them to Times Square. There, in gigantic letters she read her name on a mammoth billboard: BRYNA PRESENTS THE VIKINGS.

"Oh, America!" she sighed. "Such a wonderful land, where dreams come true."

During Kirk's eastbound flight from L.A., he was glad that he had presented her with that final gift, her name glowing at the crossroads of the world.

He arrived at the hospital in Albany on December 9, 1958, his birthday. "Some birthday gift," he said. "A dying mother."

He found his mother under an oxygen tent, suffering from pneumonia, a heart condition, and diabetes. "My big-shot son," she said to him. "Come to see his old Ma."

Word spread quickly through the hospital corridors that Kirk Douglas was in the building. Many of the nurses wanted his autograph. As he signed his name, he didn't feel like a movie star, but more like poor little Issur.

He greeted each of his sisters as they arrived, pleased that each of them had managed to build productive, satisfying lives for themselves after their collectively horrible childhood. Each seemed grateful to Bryna for keeping them alive during those days of abject poverty with their brutal father.

As his sisters said their final words to Bryna, she was drifting in and out of consciousness. Kirk was left alone with her for an all-night vigil. He was holding her hand as she drew her last breath.

After her burial, he returned to Los Angeles. As he later relayed to Anne, "Issur is now dead, along with his Russian immigrant parents. What remains is a forty-two-year-old orphan, Kirk Douglas."

413

***

Producer Hal. B. Wallis had had such success with Burt Lancaster and Kirk in *The Gunfight at the O.K. Corral* that he wanted to craft another Western with them. Westerns were a genre to which he'd been long addicted.

To that end, he found a fast-paced action story by Lee Crutchfield and hired James Poe to craft a screenplay from it. Then, he opted to re-assemble, with a few minor differences, the same cast and crew from *O.K. Corral* for the fabrication of his newest Western, which he entitled *The Last Train from Gun Hill*.

For its leading character, Sheriff Matt Morgan, he first called upon Burt Lancaster, who turned him down because of another commitment.

Because of his upcoming appearance as *Ben-Hur* (a role Kirk had wanted), Charlton Heston wasn't available either. Kirk, therefore, was Wallis' third choice.

[Wallis had been put off by Kirk's salary demands of $325,000 up front, plus ten percent of the gross.]

When they finally hammered out an agreement on terms, the producer asked Anthony Quinn to take the second male lead, as he'd been impressed with the dynamic that had flourished between the two actors when they portrayed Van Gogh (Kirk) and Paul Gauguin (Quinn) in *Lust for Life*.

Charles Lang, Jr., who had photographed *O.K. Corral* so beautifully, was summoned back, as was Dimitri Tiomkin, the musical composer for other Kirk movies.

Wallis had already selected a film location near Tucson, Arizona. Summer had already come to the scrublands, covering them with green and wild-flowers. The cottonwood trees were already blooming.

The plot revolves around a theme about how the rape and murder of a beloved woman can turn old friends into deadly enemies. Craig Belden (Quinn) is a cattle baron, the richest and most politically powerful boss of the small "company town" known as Gun Hill. Marshal Matt Morgan, portrayed by Kirk, arrives in town to arrest his son. Kirk wants to haul him back to a federal court, where he'll stand trial for murder.

Earl Holliman, cast as Rick Belden, Quinn's son, has raped and murdered the marshal's (i.e., Kirk's) wife, a beautiful "squaw" from a local Indian tribe, as portrayed by Ziva Rodmann. Holliman's best friend, played

414

by Brian C. Hutton, had joined him in the rape and murder.

Born in Haifa, Israel, Rodmann became the first Israeli actress to ever be signed to a long-term contract with a major Hollywood studio—in this case, Universal-International. In time, she'd make forty movies with stars who included Barbara Stanwyck, Yul Brynner, and Elvis Presley.

After his mother is raped and murdered, her adolescent son, Petey (Lars Henderson), escapes by riding Holliman's horse for help from his father (Kirk), the town marshal. The horse Petey has taken has a distinctive, silver-studded saddle, which Kirk recognizes as belonging to the cattle baron, as portrayed by Quinn.

Kirk, as a U.S. marshal, has knocked out Rick Belden (Earl Holliman), the man who killed his wife.

In the photo above, Kirk waits for a train that will haul them back to the town where Belden committed the crime.

Kirk, as the town marshal and the bereaved husband of the raped and murdered woman, rides to the Belden ranch to confront his old friend, and ultimately, to arrest his son.

Then things get complicated: Kirk captures Belden's son and holds him as hostage in a hotel room until the scheduled departure of the train. Then Belden (Quinn) arrives with a heavily armed posse to demand the release of his son. When a stand-off develops, Kirk is aided by Belden's mistress (Carolyn Jones). Then, the other rapist, Lee, sets the hotel on fire as a means of smoking out Kirk. Kirk emerges from the burning building with a gun pointed at the young miscreant's head. During crossfire, Belden's son is killed.

That leads to a final showdown between Kirk and his old friend, Quinn. Just before the last train pulls out, with Kirk on board, Quinn is fatally shot. The venue ends as a cathartic tragedy.

During filming, Kirk became "very, very attracted" to Rodmann, who had been a member of the Israeli Army. Their budding friendship ended quickly. Her short but pivotal scenes were positioned at the film's beginning, and she was gone before he could move in on her.

During filming, Kirk made it a point to stay clear of the beautiful, hip, and very charming Carolyn Jones. She was married at the time to the powerful TV producer, Aaron Spellman.

Born in Amarillo, Texas, she had won a Best Supporting Actress nomination for her role in *The Bachelor Party* (1957). During the course of her career, she'd work with both Frank Sinatra and Elvis Presley before achieving her greatest exposure as Morticia Adams in the original black-and-white TV series, *The Addams Family* (1964).

Kirk bonded well with Brad Dexter, cast as the foreman at the Belden ranch. He'd been part of a quickie marriage to Peggy Lee in 1953. It had mostly ended even before the honeymoon.

Dexter was known for becoming "very, very close" to Marilyn Monroe, their affair beginning when they appeared together in *The Asphalt Jungle* (1950). In 1965, in a waterborne rescue, he saved Frank Sinatra from drowning off the coast of Kauai, Hawaii during their filming of *None But the Brave*.

In Kirk's summation, *Last Train from Gun Hill* "would not be my worst Western, certainly not my best, and most definitely, not my last."

The director told Carolyn Jones *(top photo)* to approach the handsome cowboy at the bar "like a woman of loose morals."

Lower photo: Here, Jones appears as Morticia Adams, in *the Addams Family*, the role that made her famous to generations of TV fans beginning in 1964.

***

After his filming in Tucson, Kirk's life would be invaded by other stars, notably Lord and Lady Olivier ("Heathcliff and Scarlett"), and "that lavender blonde," Kim Novak.

CHAPTER TWELVE

SCARLETT O'HARA IN LOVE WITH HEATHCLIFF ON THE ROAD TO HELL

KIRK'S ENCOUNTERS WITH LAURENCE OLIVIER AND VIVIEN LEIGH

SPARTACUS

KIRK LEADS A SLAVE REVOLT AGAINST THE ROMAN EMPIRE

LONELY ARE THE BRAVE

KIRK SEARCHES FOR A LOST EDEN WITH
ROCK HUDSON, DOROTHY MALONE, & KIM NOVAK

ELIZABETH TAYLOR

KIRK'S SUGGESTIVE FLIRTATIONS, IN ROME, WITH THE SLIGHTLY DRUNKEN
QUEEN OF THE NILE

"Hail Caesar, we who are about to die salute you!" is the theme from this scene played by Kirk, as leader (Spartacus) of the slave revolt, with Draba the Gladiator. As his antogonist, Kirk personally selected Woody Strode, a former decathlete, Army veteran, and football star, one of the first African American players in the National Football League.

The Devil's Disciple, a play by George Bernard Shaw, was never one of his best. Even the playwright himself said so. Referring to his 1897 comedy, he claimed, "My play will assuredly lose its gloss with the lapse of time and leave itself exposed as the threadbare popular melodrama it technically is."

Early in its life, Shaw had sanctioned its opening in Dublin, but after evaluating it onstage, he refused to greenlight a London production. However, he changed his mind when a celebrated English actor, Richard Mansfield, morphed it into a hit on Broadway.

As time marched on, Burt Lancaster became an ardent devotee of Shaw plays. Intrigued by *The Devil's Disciple,* he lobbied aggressively to adapt it for the screen, envisioning it as an $8 million blockbuster, a Technicolor extravaganza in which he'd be featured as one of its actors.

The Devil's Disciple is set in New Hampshire in 1777 during the American Revolution. British troops led by General Burgoyne ("Gentleman Johnny") are marching down from Canada to subdue the rebellious settlement of Springstown.

The British general has been ordered to quell unrest and to obliterate resistance. He begins by hanging a rebellious colonial named Timothy Dudgeon. A few days later, Dudgeon's estranged son, Dick, shows up to avenge his father's death.

The local pastor, Anthony Anderson, a solemn, no-nonsense man of peace, is discreetly sympathetic to the Rebel cause. He lives with his beautiful wife, Judith.

Dick Dudgeon ("The Devil's Disciple") is the black sheep of his family—a wicked rascal, an apostate, and an outcast.

Perhaps because she's unhappily married to such a stern, solemn husband, Judith is immediately attracted to Dick, who stays with her as a houseguest when her husband is away.

Then, Gentleman Johnny—with the intention of inspiring fear in the local populace—decides to hang another rebel. This time, he selects the outspoken pastor. When British soldiers arrive at his home to haul him away to be hanged, they mistake Dudgeon for the pastor and

arrest him instead. Dick (a role cherished by Lancaster but eventually portrayed by Kirk), for reasons murkily linked to his concealed idealism, doesn't tell them they've arrested the wrong man.

When the minister (a character eventually portrayed by Lancaster) returns, he's galvanized into action and becomes a firebrand. War erupts between the local rebels and the British forces.

All's well that ends well. Movie fans already know that the American rebels will win the day, and the Revolution, too.

***

Meeting with his friend Kirk, Lancaster ruefully informed him that financing he'd organized for the film adaptation of *Devil's Disciple* had collapsed.

Flushed with the recent success of Bryna Production's *The Vikings*, Kirk suggested that the two of them produce it themselves.

They devised a budget of about $1.8 million, with the understanding that their film would be shot in England, in black and white, as a means of cutting costs. The single biggest expense they'd face was the $600,000 that Bernard Shaw's Estate was demanding for the movie rights.

After reading the script, Kirk demanded the more flamboyant of the two roles for leading men, that of the family outcast, Dick Dudgeon, with Lancaster cast as the priest.

As the actor who'd portray "Gentleman Johnny," Kirk suggested the celebrated British actor, Laurence Olivier.

"I'm feuding with the stuck-up bastard, but, for the sake of the film, I'll make up with conceited ass," Lancaster said.

Then he explained the origins of his antagonism toward Olivier:

Lancaster and Olivier had feuded over who would play the lead in a drama, *Separate Tables*, the part going to Lancaster.

So whereas Lancaster's resented and disliked Olivier, Kirk was eager to work with him on *The Devil's Disciple* and demanded that Lancaster collaborate.

"At first," Lancaster said, "Olivier was hostile, but then I dangled a $200,000 salary in front of him for a relatively minor third lead. As it turned out, Sir Laurence was the only one who made any money from *The Devil's Disciple.*"

On a whim, Kirk and Lancaster spontaneously agreed that the role of the pastor's wife should be offered to the former child star, Natalie Wood. Each of them had been impressed with her performance in *Rebel Without a Cause* (1955), opposite the late James Dean. By 1957, she had clearly evolved into a mature adult. She had recently married the handsome actor, Robert Wagner.

Lancaster called her and invited her to Palm Springs for the weekend to discuss her onscreen portrayal of his wife. But as he later ruefully reported to Kirk, "She seemed more excited to be in a movie with Olivier than with two studs like us."

Kirk had first met Natalie and her mother when their cars had stopped side by side for a red light on a busy boulevard in Los Angeles. Mother and child had jumped out of their vehicle to introduce themselves to Kirk. At the time, as other cars blared their horns, he had gallantly but hurriedly promised to put her in pictures with him when she grew up.

Both actors were fully aware that Natalie had not been a sexual innocent at the time of her marriage to Wagner. Her mother had charged the minor actor, Nick Adams with the task of "taking my daughter's virginity." The director, Nicholas Ray, had also added his name to her list of pre-marital suitors. Rumors of escapades with Dennis Hopper, Elvis Presley, and Warren Beatty lay in her near-term future.

It was Lancaster who came up with a devilish scheme as an introduction to their weekend negotiation in Palm Springs.

When Natalie arrived, a servant, a 23-year-old black male, ushered her onto an outdoor terrace with a swimming pool. Waiting for her, reclining side by side on *chaises longues*, were Lancaster and Kirk. Each of them was (deliberately and consciously) "jaybird naked" (Lancaster's words).

Kirk had collaborated in Lancaster's scheme "Just to see how adult Natalie really was."

He later concluded, "She passed the 'adult' test. We conducted the negation of a possible screen role for her in the nude, but she turned down our invitation to take off her clothes for a swim."

"As Natalie got up to leave, she scored one on us," Lancaster said. "She gazed at our junk for a final time."

"Okay, guys," she said. "I've seen bigger and better."

"*Touché*," Lancaster said.

Natalie later rejected the possibility of any involvement in *The Devil's Disciple*. That upset Warners, which had her under contract at the time, and which didn't have any other immediate role for her. Her refusal (which led to her temporary suspension) meant they'd just lost $100,000 for not lending her to Lancaster and Kirk. Her official excuse was that she didn't want to be separated from her new husband during *The Devil's Disciple* location shoots in England.

But, as she confessed in an "exclusive" to Hedda Hopper, "I turned down the role because I didn't want to work with Mr. Kirk Douglas."

She didn't mention Lancaster.

***

Harold Hecht was hired as the producer to pull the messy package together. In England, he wangled permission to film at one of the Rothschild estates, The Mansion at Tring Park in Hertfordshire, and at the Estree Studios in the suburbs of London.

A New Yorker, Hecht was riding high at the time, having produced *Marty*, the Best Picture of 1955. *[That film had also brought its ugly star, Ernest Borgnine, a Best Actor Academy Award.]* Hecht was also a leading director, having worked with such stars as Bing Crosby, Cary Grant, Mae West, W.C. Fields, and Maurice Chevalier.

Lancaster, who for reasons associated with his ownership of the project's film rights, hired director Alexander Mackendrick, who had previously guided him through one of his best performances, *The Sweet Smell of Success*, in which Lancaster had played J.J. Hunsecker, the most powerful columnist in New York, a character modeled on Walter Winchell.

But after only two weeks of shooting in England, Lancaster fired Mackendrick because he was too meticulous and taking far too long. *[Lancaster later admitted, "The scenes Alexander shot were the best in the picture."]*

As director, Mackendrick was replaced with Guy Hamilton, born in Paris to English parents. From the 1950s to the '80s, he would direct 22 movies, including four James Bond flicks such as *Goldfinger* (1964).

As Hamilton recalled, "During the shoot, Kirk kept following Olivier around like a love-sick puppy dog, he was so in awe of his talent. Olivier told me he couldn't tell Burt and Kirk apart since they looked so much alike. He often referred to Kirk as Burt, which pissed off our boy."

A mostly English cast was hired, including Janette Scott as Judith, the pastor's wife.

"The boys would have preferred Natalie Wood, but they got Janette, who did reasonably well," Hamilton said. "She became better known after the release of *School for Scoundrels* (1960)."

[One of Scott's three marriages was to the high-profile singing star, Mel Tormé, from 1966 to 1977.]

The unusual inclusion in the cast of the great stage actress, Eva Le Gallienne, was Kirk's idea. He had met her during the early stages of his career as a struggling actor on Broadway through Katharine Cornell. As justified by Kirk, "Eva is to America what Sarah Bernhardt was to France, Eleanora Duse to Italy. I want her to play my mother."

Le Gallienne later recalled that she found "my scenes very few and

421

very unsatisfying. I had a lot of time off to attend shows in the West End, or to dine with John Gielgud or Margaret Leighton, or even with Larry (Olivier) on occasion."

She shared time with Kirk, too, during which she was very open about her affairs with Tallulah Bankhead, Beatrice Lillie, Laurette Taylor, Alla Nazimova, and Mercedes de Acosta.

"I was paid $20,000 for doing virtually nothing, but I pleased Kirk at least," she said.

Left to right, the four stars of *The Devil's Disciple:* Janette Scott, Kirk Douglas, Burt Lancaster, and Laurence Olivier

Near the end of filming, Olivier told Kirk, "I know I'm god damn awful in this disaster of a movie, and I'm not going to see it. I think it's my worst movie role."

After the wrap, Kirk came up for a temporary farewell to Olivier. "This, I hope, is not goodbye. I want you to play Crassus in my upcoming epic, *Spartacus.*"

***

In a biography of his father, Tarquin Olivier, the son Laurence had produced with his first wife, actress Jill Esmond, wrote with a petulance that probably reflected that of his father, "My fa-

Eva Le Gallienne..."What am I doing appearing in this disaster?"

ther was disenchanted with *The Devil's Disciple* and had convinced himself that Burt Lancaster was mad. He wished someone would tell Kirk Douglas for goodness sake to fill up that crater in his chin. Worse than that, he was furious that such a boring project should attract such expensive talent when his own far more important design for *Macbeth* had died. He felt he should be shredded by the critics as the only actor ever to have failed the fool-proof role of Gentleman Johnny."

Perhaps he was being falsely modest. In their reviews of *Devil's Disciple,* English critics went out of their way to praise Olivier, while, at the same time, they mostly mocked the performances of Lancaster and Kirk.

The most extravagant praise for Olivier came from the *London Evening Standard.* On its frontpage, it ran a review headlined "The Greatest Actor in the World."

"If you go to see The Devil's Disciple, *you will witness Laurence Olivier give the greatest performance of his life. In his superb self-confidence, he dared take the third lead to those American actors, Kirk Douglas and Burt Lancaster. Our Larry made those two actors look like stupid oafs who had wandered back from a Western into the world of the American War of Independence."*

Confronted mostly with hostile reviews, the movie flopped at the box office. A critic from *The Commonweal* referred to it as "The un-Shavian [i.e., *relating to or in the manner of G. B. Shaw]* mishmash that producer Harold Hecht turned out."

In America, reviews were bad, too. *Time* magazine claimed that it didn't find "a single even passably novel incident." *The New York Times* also expressed disappointment, stating that Kirk lacked "the requisite flourish and the air of tongue-in-cheek."

***

During the filming of *The Devil's Disciple*, Kirk became deeply involved in the troubled private lives of Laurence Olivier and his wife, Vivien Leigh. Their once-fabled marriage was crumbling, and he was there to watch the curtain going down on its final act. Later, he wished he hadn't appeared on the scene at all.

The director, Guy Hamilton, had noted—as previously stated—that Kirk frequently followed Olivier around the set. Responding to that, Kirk said, "It wasn't adoration, as Guy might have thought. I was trying to prevent Larry from committing suicide. On the verge of a nervous breakdown, he was very far gone. His relationship with his wife was taking a toll."

Olivier told Kirk, "I'm not myself. I pride myself on being capable of playing almost any role, but in the case of Gentleman Johnny, I feel at times that I can't perform. It's like I've lost touch with my actor's soul. I've never felt so miserable in any production, stage or film. I seem to be reliving the agonies of Heathcliff."

"Even though this silly little fop of a role is a mere passing fancy, I feel it's beyond me. Yet, I'm bubbling over with this ferocious energy, and acting is the only way to free my soul. It gives me a release I can't find elsewhere, certainly not in love relationships."

"I detest acting but can't live without it. Being a bit mad gives me a cutting edge in my performances. I'd die if I couldn't act. I'm like a cart horse with a collar around my neck. If my master takes it off, I start whinnying for him to put it back on again."

"To make matters worse, I've fallen in love with Joan Plowright. I'm

423

slipping around to be with her, making up excuses. I fear that if Viv finds out, she'll commit suicide. She's threatened that many times."

Olivier invited Kirk to dinner with him and Leigh at the Savoy Grill. Kirk had been enchanted by her since his first screening of *Gone With the Wind* (1939) and *That Hamilton Woman* (1941).

Before their introduction, Olivier had warned him, "She's often out of control, and I don't know how she'll be tonight. Sometimes, when she's consumed by the demons of her deepest depression, it arouses certain embarrassing desires in her. She becomes Mrs. Hyde. She's been known to wander around Soho at night picking up the most undesirable working class blokes. She takes them to this seedy hotel where they rent rooms by the hour—and does God knows what. I, along with all of her friends, are terrified she'll meet Jack the Ripper."

That evening at the Savoy, Leigh "naughtily" lived up to her reputation. Seated beside Kirk, with a flirtatiousness perhaps inspired by her character of Scarlett O'Hara, she placed her hand, concealed by the tablecloth, on his knee before beginning an exploration of points north.

The authors of this biography have a lot to say about the characters being described in this section. In 2011, they published the world's most controversial biography of Olivier and Leigh, with many insights into their rise, their anguish, and their decline.

Then, she suddenly announced, "Larry doesn't fuck me anymore. Even when I was a teen, and married, he fucked me, but not anymore. Now he seems to be raiding other honeypots, heaven only knows what gender."

Standing in front of their table, the Savoy's formally dressed *maître d'hotel* addressed her as "Lady Olivier."

In response, she quipped, "Her Ladyship is fucking bored with such formality and prefers to be known as Vivien Leigh, thank you."

Kirk could not help but notice that Leigh had put on weight and looked unwell. "Her beauty was there, but behind a faded mask. Her youth had gone with the wind. She wasn't the grand lady I had envisioned. I mean, she was crude, unfunny, and really vulgar…foul mouthed."

"I thought at first that I was talking to Elizabeth Taylor, who had replaced Vivien in *Elephant Walk* (1954). Everybody knows that darling Elizabeth had the biggest potty mouth in Hollywood. Vivien came very close."

Later, when they were alone, Olivier confided to Kirk that when Leigh met Peter Finch, cast as her co-star in *Elephant Walk,* she'd begun an affair with him.

"To complicate matters, Peter was also slipping around giving me a poke, too. Let's face it—in the circus they call the British theatre, I'm known as a bisexual. Why not admit it?"

"That's fine with me," Kirk said. "But don't ask me to mount you."

"Have no fear of that, dear boy," Olivier assured him.

During the collapse of their marriage, the Oliviers occupied a flat on Lowndes Place in Belgravia, a stylish neighborhood in the heart of London. Coincidentally, Kirk had rented a flat across the square. Unknown to Leigh, Olivier had also rented a hideaway in a mews house a block away for rendezvous with, among others, Plowright.

One night, Leigh, by now aware of her husband's affair with Plowright because of exposure in the tabloids, confronted him with it.

He confessed. "I figured that I might as well admit the bloody truth," he told Kirk later. "Actually, she took it very well, not becoming hysterical. She didn't ask the name of the woman, because I'm sure she already knew. She congratulated me on finding my next true love but warning that love is a very elusive thing."

But a few nights later, she became unhinged and began screaming, reeling from the full impact of her husband's confession.

According to Olivier, "It was the worst night of my marriage, an epic drama like your upcoming *Spartacus*. I was asleep, and suddenly this wet towel was slapped hard across my face. Then she tore into my face with her fingernails before pounding it with her fists. I jumped out of bed and fled into the study, where I locked the door. She almost broke it down, screaming vile denunciation—like a raging hyena—that I was only half a man, that Peter Finch was a better lover. Then I threw open the door, dragged her back to the bedroom, and hurled her across the room. But instead of hitting the bed, her head slammed against a nightstand, causing her to bleed from her temple. I was in no mood to offer care and comfort. I dressed and left the house, with her screams ringing in my ears for all the neighbors to hear."

Leigh, in a fit of madness and rage and bleeding from her head wound, ran out of the house clad only in her bra and panties. Heading across Lowndes Place, she pounded on Kirk's door until he finally answered it, finding her there, shivering, half-naked, and bleeding. He pulled her inside and tended to her like a male nurse, wiping the blood from her face and checking her for other injuries. She ferociously resisted his urging to call a doctor, afraid that word would get out to "those tabloid vultures."

"It's the end," she told him. "Vivien Leigh's fabled marriage to the dashing Laurence Olivier is over except for the burial. What a bloody beast he is to attack a defenseless woman."

He took her to bed and tucked her in beside him. He was asleep about an hour later when he felt her arms around him.

"I need to be in the arms of a strong, comforting man," she said in a flirtatious voice that evoked Blanche DuBois or Scarlett O'Hara. "A real man. A man like you."

As he later confessed to Lancaster, "That night, my heart wasn't in it, but another part of me was working quite well. I made love, not to Scarlett, but to Blanche."

[Kirk later claimed, "I didn't know it at the time, but Vivien was bipolar. I'm not sure that the term had been invented back then. Anne and I came to understand it better after learning that our son, Eric, suffered from the same affliction."]

***

Wounded by the hardships and inconveniences he'd suffered during filming of *The Vikings*, Kirk announced, "No more epics."

But when he learned that William Wyler was planning a remake of MGM's *Ben-Hur* for a release in 1959, he changed his mind.

In 1925, that studio had released the first version of *Ben-Hur*, a sweaty, bloody, dangerous-to-film, and very compelling silent film starring Ramon Novarro.

Kirk wanted the title role of Ben-Hur, but Wyler offered the role of Messala instead. Kirk rejected it. The role of Ben-Hur went to Charlton Heston.

The 1950s, a decade of epic grandeur in movie-making, had established a high bar for grand sagas of the screen. Examples had included Cecil B. DeMille's *Samson and Delilah* (1949), *Quo Vadis* (1951), *The Robe* (1953), and at least a half-dozen less successful others.

Miffed that he hadn't been cast into the title role of *Ben-Hur*, Kirk decided to produce his own epic based on a novel by Howard Fast entitled *Spartacus*.

Born to Jewish immigrants, like Kirk, Fast had joined the Communist Party in 1943. During McCarthy's Witch Hunt of the 1950s, Fast was summoned before the House Un-American Activities Committee, where he refused to disclose the names of contributors to a home for orphans of American veterans of the Spanish Civil War. *[As it turned out, one of its contributors was Eleanor Roosevelt.]*

For his refusal, Fast was sentenced to a federal prison. During his incarceration there, he began work on his novel, *Spartacus*, a saga about the uprising of Roman slaves a century before the birth of Christ.

No publisher at the time, including Doubleday and Random House, would publish it, so Fast published it himself, selling 50,000 copies, hardcover. One of them was sent to Kirk.

He became fascinated as he read about Spartacus, a rebellious Thracian, born and reared a slave. *[The ancient region of Thrace straddles modern-day Greece, Turkey, and Bulgaria.]*

Although Kirk thought *Spartacus* would make a great movie, he encountered more roadblocks than financing at the beginning. An avid reader of *Variety*, he read that Martin Ritt at United Artists was in pre-production on *The Gladiators*, a movie with many similarities, this one starring Yul Brynner.

Kirk called Ritt and proposed a joint deal wherein he would star with Brynner in the two leading roles. That plan collapsed after Ritt presented it to Brynner. "I talked to Yul, and he told me he hates your guts."

Kirk was left wondering why. "I should be the one pissed off at him. After all, he stole the Oscar from me for that silly *The King and I* (1956), and I deserved it more for how I handled Vincent Van Gogh in *Lust for Life* (also 1956)."

"Actually, I was fortunate to be alive and contemplating ANY movie," Kirk said.

[In March of 1958, Mike Todd had invited him to New York aboard his private plane, Lucky Liz, to accept an award. Todd's wife, Elizabeth Taylor, had been stricken with the flu and couldn't accompany him. As for Kirk, his wife, Anne, had a strange foreboding about the flight and talked him out of it, thereby saving his life. The plane crashed into a mountainside during a storm over New Mexico,

427

killing everyone aboard.]

In his struggle to put a package together before soliciting the financial backing of Universal, Kirk needed commitments from big-name stars and a prominent director.

First, he approached David Lean, who was still working on the final cut for *The Bridge on the River Kwai* (1957). Lean rejected him.

Kirk had optioned the film rights for Howard Fast's novel, and already hired him to craft its screenplay. When he returned from his failed outreach to David Lean, he found its 57-page first draft. After reading the first 15 pages, he defined it as "a disaster," and vowed to hire a different screenwriter.

Kirk had long admired the blacklisted Dalton Trumbo, a member of the notorious "Hollywood Ten" who had defied the House Un-American Activities Committee. For that he'd served eleven months in a Federal Penitentiary in Ashland, Kentucky.

Hiring Trumbo, Kirk realized, as a replacement scriptwriter would be dangerous, unwise, and possibly harmful to his own career. For years, no studio had openly hired Trumbo. but his uncredited scripts had already won two Academy Awards. *[They'd included* Roman Holiday *(1953) with Audrey Hepburn and Gregory Peck, and* The Brave One *(1956) with Michel Ray.]*

Kirk visited Trumbo at the scriptwriter's home. Trumbo, a noted eccentric, had configured his bathtub, with a tray positioned atop its edges, into an ersatz desk. As he wrote, a parrot rested on his shoulder, nibbling at his ear.

Trumbo, sometimes defined as a "swimming pool commie," was known for his distinctive and defiant personal style. He threw splashy parties, was driven around in a chauffeur-driven Chrysler, collected pre-Columbian art, and smoked six packages of cigarettes a day.

After some negotiations and snide comments about Fast ("I detest that son of a bitch"), he accepted the assignment of adapting his novel, *Sparta-*

cus, into a film.

In a daring move, Kirk decided to officially list Trumbo in the film's credits, despite dire warnings that doing that would threaten his own movie career. "I'll break the god damn blacklist," Kirk said. "Trumbo's name goes on the screen with the credits."

Screenwriter Dalton Trumbo's refusal to "name names of fellow communists in Hollywood" before the House Un-American Activities Committee ended up with a jail term for him.

[Otto Preminger followed suit, formally listing Trumbo as the screenwriter of his own epic, Exodus *(1960), which was released a year after* Spartacus.*]*

Fast was an enemy of Trumbo, so Kirk didn't immediately tell him who was actually writing the film adaptation of his novel. Eventually, with the assumption that Trumbo's identity was still unknown to Fast at the time, Kirk sent the novelist a rough draft of the script. Fast wrote back with the evaluation that "Your writer is a half-wit, a man of no talent, no imagination, a moron."

With Trumbo laboring over his script, Kirk approached the Hollywood super-agent, Lew Wasserman, who represented each of the three British actors he wanted for his film: Laurence Olivier, Peter Ustinov, and Charles Laughton.

Also, with the intention of tying up additional collaborators for his film, he chose, as producer of *Spartacus*, Edward Lewis, the Vice President of Bryna Production.

[During the course of his long career, Lewis would be closely associated with films that collectively garnered twenty-one Oscars or Oscar nominations.]

Kirk clashed with Trumbo several times over aspects of the script. A passionate Zionist, Kirk wanted the saga of *Spartacus* configured as a subsection within the centuries-long struggle of the Jewish people. In contrast, Trumbo interpreted it as a veiled critique of current American politics and the Cold War.

Wasserman phoned and said that he'd talked with "the boys over at Universal," and that they wanted Kirk to hire Anthony Mann as director. Around the Universal lot, Mann was known as "The Moneymaker."

[Born Emil Bundesman in San Diego in 1906, he had changed his name to Anthony Mann because his considered his birth name "too Nazi." He'd begun his career as a $10 -a-week messenger boy and eventually was promoted to the personal

429

staff of David O. Selznick. In fact, he'd cast some of the minor roles in Gone With
the Wind.

Mann was one of James Stewart's favorite directors, turning out such hits as
Winchester '73 *(1950). A producer once defined Mann's collaboration with Stew-*
art as "The most dynamic, if darkest, partnership to emerge in postwar Holly-
wood."]

Despite the approval Mann had generated with Universal's directors,
and his skill at directing the opening shots of *Spartacus [they were filmed at*
Death Valley, Nevada], Kirk considered his pace too slow and fired him,
telling the press, "Mr. Mann and I had artistic differences." He nonetheless
continued to admire his directorial skill and employed him again several
years later to helm *The Heroes of Telemark* (1965).

As a replacement for Mann, Kirk hired Stanley Kubrick, who had previously directed one of Kirk's greatest hits, *Paths of Glory.*

Wasserman reported that although Olivier had accepted the second
lead in *Spartacus,* the role of Marcus Licinius Crassus, he had refused a proposal to actually direct it. "It took a lot of persuading even to get him involved as one of the actors, because Olivier had actually wanted the lead
role, that of Spartacus himself."

Wasserman also reported on Charles Laughton's reaction to Wasserman's proposal that he join the cast as the hedonistic politician, Gracchus.
He called the first draft of Trumbo's script "A piece of shit."

"But he'll be great in the role," Wasserman said. "I'll talk him into it."

It was watching Peter Ustinov's performance as Nero in *Quo Vadis*
(1951) that convinced Kirk to hire him as Lentulus Batiatus, the slave trader.
Ustinov accepted the role immediately, as the actor's fee proposed to him
was generous.

"Ustinov is a great actor, but he'll insist on rewriting much of his dialogue," Wasserman warned. "He can also be a bit nasty. A few days ago,
he told the press, 'I have to be careful not to act too well so that I don't
make Kirk Douglas jealous.'"

During shooting, Ustinov remembered Laughton as "almost aggressively vulnerable and sometimes petulant. He seemed to sit around, waiting to have his feelings hurt, and there was no great love lost between Larry
and him, the result of some long ago animosity about which I was singu-
larly uninquisitive."

John Gielgud knew the source of the bitterness between them: "Back
in the 1930s, Larry angered Charlie by clearly rejecting his sexual advances."

Ustinov, in his own enigmatic way, called Olivier "The Vestal Virgin
to Laughton's whore."

Once, Laughton told Kirk, "I view acting as part art, part whoring, which is the much larger part. When Hollywood came calling, I sold my soul."

One afternoon, Kirk was sitting at his dressing table clad only in his jockey shorts, and with the door open. Suddenly, as he recalled, "Charles Laughton with his luscious, cocksucking lips appeared at my door, feasting his eyes on my basket."

After checking me out, he angrily announced that he was going to sue me, before fading into the afternoon."

[Laughton wanted to sue because in the first version of the script, the one he'd read before signing on, his role had been more prominent. Later, as filming progressed, rewrites diminished his part considerably.]

Kirk's friend, Tony Curtis, called and asked if there was a part for him in the new film. He owed Universal one more picture, and he felt that *Spartacus* might do it for him.

Kirk agreed to cast him as the poetic and comely slave boy, Antoninus, who attracted the lustful eye of Crassus, a powerful politician and bisexual, a sly epicene degenerate.

For the role of the slave girl Kirk tested Gene Tierney, his former girlfriend. It was an abject failure. "The spark in her eyes had dimmed," he said. "After all those electric shock treatments she'd endured for her mental health problems. I felt sorry for her but had to turn her down."

He turned instead to the sexy, blonde-haired Parisian, Jeanne Moreau,

AH, the ROMANS! In vivid contrast to the sufferings of the Empire's slaves and gladiators, two pros from the British stage, Peter Ustinov (left) and Charles Laughton, are depicted in this publicity photo from *Spartacus* as hedonistic gluttons who seem to be having a marvelous time, whom Orson Welles had proclaimed as "the greatest actress in the world."

"I got off on the wrong foot with her," Kirk said, "when I told her she had Bette Davis eyes. She hated Bette."

"I danced with her but didn't hold her too close for fear of getting an erection. At the end of the evening, she told me she could not accept the role because she could not stand to be away from her new lover for even one night."

"I'm addicted to him," she said.

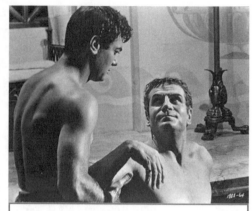

Coy and artful dialogue at the baths: Tony Curtis *(left)* as a comely slave ministering to the washday needs of Crassus (Laurence Olivier) playing a bisexual Roman Lord .

Moreau soon got over her addiction and began a series of other affairs, notably with director Tony Richardson, who left his wife, Vanessa Redgrave, for her.

She also sustained liaisons with fashion designer Pierre Cardin and with directors Louis Malle and François Truffaut. Jazz trumpeter Miles Davis was also a frequent visitor to her boudoir. "I never made it on her list," Kirk said.

Ingrid Bergman also rejected the role, as she had for the princess role in *The Vikings*. Kirk briefly considered Elsa Martinelli, with whom he'd had an affair and previously signed to a personal contract with Bryna. "Finally, I changed my mind. She'd had her chance with me, and after leaving me, her career was nose-diving."

After considering many other actresses, Kirk finally decided to cast Varinia, the slave girl, with an almost unknown 27-year-old beauty, the blonde-haired, blue-eyed Sabine Bethmann. He thought she would photograph fabulously in Technicolor.

Born in East Prussia, Sabine looked much younger than her years. She had made a German movie in 1956 called *Waldwinter*, and a few other less than spectacular screen roles. In 1959, around the time of the filming of *Spartacus*, the director, Fritz Lang, had cast her in two films, *The Tiger of Eschnapur* and *The Indian Tomb*.

Taking over the direction of *Spartacus*, Kubrick at once began to exert his control. He put Sabine through a screen test and when the result came through, she appeared to have no facial reaction at all.

432

After viewing the screen test, he ordered Kirk to fire her. Then, without soliciting Kirk's permission, he hired Jean Simmons, whom Kirk had originally rejected because of her British accent.

On the set, Simmons had a reunion with Olivier, with whom she'd starred as Ophelia to his *Hamlet* in the acclaimed 1948 film. Her performance in it had brought her a Best Supporting Actress Oscar nomination.

Seeing the rushes, Kirk concluded that she held her own against three of the leading actors of England: Olivier, Laughton and Ustinov.

She told Kirk that her husband, Stewart Granger, had threatened to kill the aviator/producer Howard Hughes for his sexual pursuit of her.

"I guess you're telling me this as a warning," he said to her. "Apparently, my reputation for seducing my leading ladies has reached you."

How did the celebrated Shakespearean actor, Laurence Olivier, articulate the acting technique he applied to his sometimes sexually ambiguous performance in *Spartacus*? "During its filming, I was passing through a patrician phase, but I gave my character of Crassus a touch of that flirting femininity of *Richard III*, the cool eyes suddenly aflame—second cousin to *Coriolanus*, several times removed," he wrote.

In this publicity picture, Laurence Olivier poses with Hollywood newcomer Sabine Bethmann (who was later fired and replaced with Jean Simmons) and Kirk Douglas

Unexpectedly, in ways that caused logistical problems with the production, two key players, Simmons and Curtis, each had to remove themselves from filming for a month. Simmons told Kirk she had to undergo "female surgery."

As for Curtis, during a game of tennis with Kirk, he split his Achilles tendon, in the aftermath of which his entire lower leg was put into a cast. His scenes had to be delayed until his leg healed, and the cast could be removed.

No sooner had Simmons and Curtis returned to work than Kirk himself got sick and was laid up for two weeks. "I was coughing up

Jean Simmons in *Spartacus*. Originally, Kirk had rejected her for the role of the slave girl because of her British accent.

blood with the world's worst case of the flu."

Kirk himself selected all the actors for the supporting roles, including Czech-born Herbert Lom as Tigranes Levantus. Suavely sinister in both looks and voice, he had an unfriendly glare that would melt butter. He had played Napoléon in *War and Peace* (1956).

As Spartacus, Kirk kills Charles McGraw, cast as Marcellus, who trains gladiators in how to kill. "Charles came to a bad end both in the movie and in life," Kirk said. "While taking a shower, he slipped and fell through a glass shower door, severing an artery."

Originally Kirk had wanted Orson Welles in the role, but he rejected it.

During the shoot, Laughton practically "adopted" the handsome young actor, John Dall, cast in *Spartacus* as Marcus Publius Glabrus.

[A New Yorker, Dall had a footnote in film history for his Best Supporting Actor Oscar nomination for his performance in The Corn is Green *(1945) opposite his teacher, as portrayed by Bette Davis.*

He was also the cold-minded intellectual killer in Alfred Hitchcock's The Rope *(1948) and the trigger-happy psycho in the film noir,* Gun Crazy *(1950).]*

"I'm not at all surprised that Laughton and Dall are bonding," Kubrick told Kirk. "Perverts like to stick together."

[Years later, Hollywood pimp Scotty Bowers revealed to the world that Dall had a most unusual fetish. He liked to be tied, nude, upside down to a tree in Laurel Canyon in the middle of the night.]

Kubrick cut out a lot of Trumbo's dialogue, especially the early love scene between Varinia (Simmons), the slave girl whose owner demands that she go to Kirk's cell to have sex with him. She's surprised when he doesn't rape her, as was the custom of that era.

Batiatus, the venal, conniving slave dealer portrayed by Ustinov, refers to his gladiators as "special animals." Crassus (Olivier) visits his gladiator school and spots Varinia, deciding he wants her for himself.

For the role of Draba the Gladiator, Kirk selected Woody Strode, who had been a decathlete and football star, one of the first African American players in the National Football League. An army veteran, Strode would be nominated for a Golden Globe as Best Supporting Actor in *Spartacus*.

Marcellus (Charles McGraw), Spartacus's trainer in everything related to how to kill.

He had posed nude for Hubert Stowitts' acclaimed athletic portraits displayed at the Berlin Olympics in 1936. When an enraged Josef Goebbels discovered that black and Jewish athletes had been depicted alongside Aryans, he ordered the exhibition shut down immediately.

Strode was already familiar with epics, having starred in *Androcles and the Lion* (1952) and *Demetrius and the Gladiators* (1954). He'd also played dual roles of a slave and the Ethiopian king in *The Ten Commandments* (1956).

John Dall attracted the lusty eye of Charles Laughton off-screen, but the gay actor said no.

In *Spartacus*, his character is forced into the arena to battle with Kirk to the death. He wins the conflict, but spares Spartacus' life and then attacks the patricians who ordered the fight. Draba is killed, setting off a slave rebellion.

"Nina Foch (as Helena Glabrus) was Kirk's piece during our shoot," or so said Kubrick in his rather ungallant way. That may or may not have been true, although they were often seen together. A beautiful, talented, Dutch-born actress, she usually played cool, aloof, sophisticates in such films as *An American in Paris* (1951) with Gene Kelly, and in *Executive Suite* (1954), which earned her a Best Supporting Actress Oscar nomination. Before working with Kirk, she had starred in another epic, Cecil B. DeMille's *The Ten Commandments.* (1956).

"Nina was unlucky in love," Kirk said. "I might have married her, but I was already wed. When she came into my life, she was divorcing her husband and getting ready to wed another. Poor Nina. None of her marriages, three in all, ever worked out."

As Julius Caesar, John Gavin, at the time, was competing with Rock Hudson for the title of the handsomest man in Hollywood. "John will be a treat for hot-to-trot gals and gay guys," Kirk predicted.

Gavin had just emerged from a performance opposite Lana Turner in a remake of *Imitation of Life* (1959). In the studio's attempt to

Nina Foch as Helena Glabrus in Spartacus.

Helena's favorite pastime was watching gladiators battle to the death.

configure him as a direct competitor of Rock Hudson, he'd also been assigned the lead in *A Time to Love and a Time to Die* (1958), based on the novel by Erich Maria Remarque.

[Although Gavin never achieved his hoped-for status as a major-league movie star, he eventually became President of the Screen Actors Guild (1971-73). Later, then-President Ronald Reagan appointed him U.S. Ambassador to Mexico (1981-86)]

Kirk had worked with John Ireland, the actor he privately called "Big Pecker" on *The Gunfight at the O.K. Corral*. He hired him once again in *Spartacus* as Crixus.

Into the minor role of Claudia, Kirk cast Joanna Barnes, a Bostonian who was also a novelist and journalist. Her research for an article on making movies let to her becoming an actress herself. She was often seen on "the little black box." Around the time Kirk met her, she was playing Lola on the NBC detective series, *21 Beacon Street*. He liked her so much, he was instrumental in getting her cast in his upcoming *The War Wagon* (1967).

Barnes' resumé also included her status as the 13th actress to play Jane, this time in *Tarzan, the Ape Man* (1959) opposite Denny Miller as Tarzan.

In the Roman tubs with John Gavin (Julius Caesar), later designated by Ronald Reagan as U.S. Ambassador to Mexico.

Some of *Spartacus'* scenes with Olivier were shot at San Simeon, the California estate of the late press baron, William Randolph Hearst and his mistress, the actress Marion Davies.

Kirk was involved in all aspects of *Spartacus'* production, even the hairstyles of the slaves. He went to his friend, Jay Sebring, a noted hairdresser, who devised a look that became a standard part of their costuming and wardrobe.

[Incorporating a "butch cut" on top, and left long in the back, and accessorized with a dangling pony tail, it became known as the "Spartacut." Adopted by many young men outside the movie colony, it enjoyed a popular vogue for a while after Spartacus *was released.*

In 1969, Sebring would be murdered along with the pregnant Sharon Tate, by the Charles Manson gang.]

There was almost no levity during the shoot, except once when Kirk encountered the identical twins, screenwriters Julius J. Epstein and Philip

G. Epstein, known as "Phil and Julie." They had written the screenplay for *Casablanca.*

They invited Kirk for lunch, where they discussed the possibility of one day writing a script for Bryna Production.

The twins were known as "the greatest lovers in Hollywood," or at least as the most durable. Phil revealed their secret to Kirk: "After Julie spends an hour in the saddle, he goes into the bathroom, gets dressed, and exits through a window. Then I emerge for the second round, fresh and raring to go. The gals just love the endurance, thinking all of it derived from just one man."

John Ireland as Crixus joined Kirk in the revolt of the gladiators.

A rumor circulated among the cast and crew that Curtis and Olivier—both known bisexuals—were having an offscreen affair. When Kirk heard that, he said, "Tony and Larry are just rehearsing for their upcoming scene together in a Roman bath."

In one of the most controversial scenes in the movie, Curtis, cast as Antoninus, is assisting his Roman master, Crassus (Olivier) in the bath.

As a coded signal to determine if Antoninus indulged in homosexual sex, he asked if he liked "Oysters or snails?"

The censors picked up on this subtlety and demanded that the scene but cut...or at least that the dialogue be changed to "artichokes or truffles?"

Before *Spartacus* went into release, the entire scene was cut, much to the frustration and disappointment of both actors. For the film's 1991 re-release, it was restored.

Two of the movie's most dramatic scenes occur near its end. Curtis and Kirk are forced into a gladiator fight to the death. As Spartacus, Kirk defeats Curtis as Antoninus.

"I love you, Spartacus," Curtis says, "as I loved my father."

"I love you like the son I'll never see," Spartacus responds, just before he plunges his sword into Curtis' heart.

After losing his battle/revolt against the Romans, Spartacus is crucified. In a melodramatic climax, he looks down from the cross and sees Varinia holding their newborn son at their final goodbye. He begins a prolonged death agony, evoking Jesus Christ on the cross. There's the prospect that his son will grow up to be a free man.

At Universal, Kirk was assigned the dressing room next to the one occupied by Mamie Van Doren, a clone of Marilyn Monroe who came off more as a clone of Jayne Mansfield.

"She suddenly appeared at my door, and I thought she was coming to seduce me, as she had so many other men. But then, Curtis appeared in a loincloth, winked at her, and told her, 'I'll see you later.'"

As the shooting for *Spartacus* dragged on and on, Curtis asked Simmons, "Who do you have to screw to get off this film?"

"When you find out, let me know," she shot back.

***

The movie's sound track of a crowd lustily cheering "SPARTACUS! SPARTACUS!" was recorded in 1959 at a football game in Spartan Stadium, home of the Michigan State University Spartans in East Lansing, Michigan. John Gavin flew to Michigan to direct the fans in the chant.

[Incidentally, perhaps because of Gavin's involvement as a cheerleader, Michigan State beat Notre Dame in that game 19-0.]

The musical score for *Spartacus* was composed by Alex North, a six-time Oscar nominee. It appears today on the American Film Institute's List of the greatest movie scores ever. North's score is big, brave, and epic, as such a movie needed. To create the exotic, ancient sounds he was looking for, he assembled bagpipes, a sarrusophone, a Chinese oboe, and a kythara. His prize instrument was the ondioline, a forerunner of today's synthesizers.

Spartacus was shot in 167 days with a cast of 10,500. They included 8,000 soldiers hired from the army of Generalíssimo Francisco Franco, the dictator of Spain. *[Franco mandated that not one of his soldiers could be depicted dying on the screen.]*

Spartacus cost more than $12 million, which made it one of the most expensive movies ever made at that point in time, although *Ben-Hur* (1959) ended up costing more.

It took in more than $15 million at the box office. Of all the actors, only Ustinov won an Oscar—in his case, as Best Supporting Actor.

Kirk was disappointed that he wasn't even nominated "for giving the performance of my life, equaled only by my performance as Van Gogh in *Lust for Life*. My buddy, Burt Lancaster, carried home the Oscar in 1960 for *Elmer Gantry*. I love Burt, but I was as jealous as hell."

Spartacus did win Oscars for costume design, cinematography, and set decoration.

Despite its stellar cast and critical and box office success, Bosley Crowther of *The New York Times* proved once again that he was no fan of Kirk's.

He defined *Spartacus* as "on the level of a lusty schoolboy. It is riddled

438

with a lot of romantic fiddle-faddle and historical inaccuracy. Kirk Douglas' *Spartacus* is heroic humbug, a spotty, uneven, drama that at times is pretentious and tedious. All in all, a romantic mish-mash, a blunt horse opera."

When it opened across America, the American Legion sent a letter to each of its 18,000 members, urging them to boycott it. "Don't go see *Spartacus*," it urged. "It's the work of communists. Kirk Douglas employed a blacklisted screenwriter who was jailed."

The right-wing columnist, Hedda Hopper, wrote, "The story was sold to Universal by a commie, from a book written by a commie. Don't go and see it if you're a true and patriotic American."

The newly elected U.S. president, John F. Kennedy, helped its box office a few days after *Spartacus* opened. He was seen defying the picket lines of the American Legion to attend a screening at the Warner Theater in Washington, D.C. He went to the performance with his former Navy buddy, Paul B. Fay, whom he'd nicknamed "Red" and had designated as the Under-Secretary of the Navy.

The American Film Institute ranks *Spartacus* as one of the Top Ten Epic Movies of all Time.

Kirk concluded, "*Spartacus* took three years out of my life, and Stanley Kubrick cut short my life by one year."

***

During the editing of *Spartacus*, Kirk starred in a modern-day soap opera, *Strangers When We Meet*, a Bryna Production that was released in 1960 and distributed by Columbia. He was looking forward to it, since his co-star would be the luscious "Lavender Blonde," Kim Novak. She had arrived at Columbia for grooming as the next Rita Hayworth, or at least the answer to Fox's Marilyn Monroe.

Kirk had first seen her emote with William Holden in *Picnic* (1955). He had warned Kirk, "Novak has absolutely no sense of humor. She's like ice water."

[His description had a humor of its own: Before becoming a movie star, Novak had been designated "Miss Deepfreeze" in a beauty contest sponsored by a refrigerator company.]

Tyrone Power, Novak's co-star in *The Eddy Duchin Story* (1956), had told Kirk, "She's a bitch and a spoiled brat. I will never make another picture with her."

Throughout most of the 1950s, Kirk was more interested in Hollywood gossip than he let on. He had followed Novak's escapades in fan magazines and tabloids. Frank Sinatra was rumored to have seduced her when they co-starred in *The Man With the Golden Arm* (1955).

The CEO of Columbia, Harry Cohn, had used organized crime to break up her affair with Sammy Davis, Jr. He had hired two members of the Las Vegas mob to kidnap him, drive him into the desert, threaten him, and dump him miles outside of town. "You've got only one eye now. Wanna try for none? DROP NOVAK! Beginning as of yesterday."

In contrast, Alfred Hitchcock, who had "this thing" for blondes, said, "The girl is the stuff of which real stars are made." That high praise for her was uttered during his direction of her in *Vertigo* (1958) opposite James Stewart.

While making another movie with Novak and Stewart, *Bell, Book, and Candle* (1958) about modern witchcraft, the director, Richard Quine, was said to have fallen hopelessly in love with his star.

***

The movie in which Kirk was featured, *Strangers When We Meet*, released in 1960, was a story of adultery between two otherwise married lovers, and based on a novel by Evan Hunter (aka Ed McBain). He is best known for his gritty *87ᵗʰ Precinct* novels, a series which began with *Cop Hater* in 1956. Over the course of his career, his books sold 100 millon copies, including his autobiographical novel, made into *The Blackboard Jungle* (1954) starring Glenn Ford.

The plot of the Douglas/Novak drama deals with Larry Coe (Kirk), an ambitious, idealistic, and brilliant architect who is married to a lovely wife, Eve, played by Barbara Rush. *[In private life, she had divorced screen heartthrob Jeffrey Hunter.]*

Larry meets with a client, a writer, portrayed by Ernie Kovacs, who wants him to design an *avant-garde* modern home for him on a mountaintop. The author is known for chasing after lovely young women.

Carrying out his assignment, Larry meets a stunning blonde neighbor, Maggie Gault (Novak). She is married to Ken (John Bryant), who is not interested in having sex with her—imagine that! Larry

The Heavens And Hells Of Marital Infidelity!

SOMEONE ELSE'S HUSBAND AND SOMEONE ELSE'S WIFE!

KIRK DOUGLAS / KIM NOVAK
ERNIE KOVACS / BARBARA RUSH
Strangers When We Meet

(Kirk) and Maggie (Novak) begin an affair.

Meanwhile, another unhappily married couple, Felix and Betty (as portrayed by Walter Matthau and Helen Gallagher), enter the picture. Felix considers all women, including Larry's wife, fair game, and tries to rape her. He has uncovered Larry's affair with Maggie.

The interconnected adulteries explored in the film come to a somewhat predictable ending as "those louses go back to their spouses."

Kirk had worked with Matthau before, not too satisfactorily, when they'd co-starred in *The Indian Fighter.*

The director, Quine, had assembled a strong supporting cast. It included Virginia Bruce as Mrs. Wagner. She was both a singer and actress who had been famously married to that long-ago idol of the silent screen, John Gilbert, Greta Garbo's lover on and off the screen.

Kent Smith, as Stanley Baxter, had a long screen career, appearing with A-list stars who included Susan Hayward, Marilyn Monroe, Gary Cooper, and Bette Davis.

Kovacs, married to Edie Adams, was one of the most talented actors with whom Kirk would ever work. He was also a hit on radio and television, having great influences on future TV stars such as Johnny Carson. He was rather eccentric, keeping pet marmosets and once wrestling a jaguar on live TV.

Although Kovacs and Kirk became close friends, their relationship was short, as Kovacs died two years after they met. At his funeral, Kirk joined pallbearers who included Frank Sinatra, Dean Martin, and Jack Lemmon, and which also attracted James Stewart, Groucho Marx, Milton Berle, and Charlton Heston.

Brooklyn-born Helen Gallagher was also a dancer and singer. She had won a Tony for her performance in the 1952 Broadway revival of *Pal Joey.*

On the set of *Strangers When We Meet,* Kirk's illusions about Novak were shattered before the end of his first day. "She and Quine were obviously a hot item, really in love, or so it seemed. It was obvious that he was, as director, going to devote all his attention to her. As for me, I felt, not like a star, but like the ragman's son all over again."

Novak must have thought she was the director," Kirk said. "She gave me

Kirk and Kim Novak perform a love scene in *Strangers When We Meet.* Off-screen, he referred to her as "The Ice Queen."

441

many unwanted suggestions about how I was to play a scene."

She later denied that. "I never told Douglas how to act, nor did I even try to give him direction. He was jealous of me. Dick was showering me with attention, not because he was my director, but because he was in love with me."

"I noticed that Quine and Novak seemed to be winding down near the last week of the shoot," Kirk said. "Soon, I was reading that he'd been seen around town with Judy Holliday and Natalie Wood."

Novak later said, "I'd be a terribly frustrated woman today if I'd married any of the men I ever loved."

[Like many of the men and women with whom Kirk worked during the course of many decades, Quine committed suicide by shooting himself at the age of 68 on June 10, 1989. He'd been through a long period of depression and failing health.]

Despite poor reviews, *Strangers When We Meet* made $3.5 million at the box office. Craig Butler in *Allmovie* found the screenplay "predictable, and Kirk Douglas out of place in his role of the architect."

Variety called *Strangers* "easy on the eye, but hard on the intellect, an old-fashioned soap opera that is pure tripe."

The New Republic interpreted the words flowing from the lips of Novak as "unvaried strangulation."

The Hollywood Reporter described it as "A rich, juicy melodrama, dealing with the sex life of the upper middle-class. It lacks nothing that money and imagination can lavish on a motion picture, except a point of view."

In his memoirs, Kirk wrote, "I enjoyed working with Novak." Privately, he told friends, "Appearing opposite her was the nightmare of my career. I detested every scene I had with her. Imagine having to make on-screen love to a woman you loathe. Of course, actors have to do that every day before the cameras of Hollywood."

***

Kirk's next film assignment was *The Last Sunset*, a Western eventually released in 1961 by Universal. As directed by Robert Aldrich, it would co-star Rock Hudson alongside Dorothy Malone, veteran actor Joseph Cotten, and Carol Lyn-

Richard Quine, the director, takes a stroll along the beach with his star, Kim Novak.

She got more attention from him than Kirk when they shot *Strangers When We Meet*.

ley. [*Lynley was actually Kirk's third choice. He'd originally offered her role to Sandra Dee and then to Tuesday Weld.*]

Its screenplay by Dalton Trumbo had been adapted from Howard Rigsby's novel *Sundown at Crazy Horse.*

Aldrich told Kirk that the movie would be filmed in cattle country near Aguascalientes, Mexico. Kirk found a detailed map of Mexico and located seven towns with that name, finally targeting the one Aldrich was talking about. Getting there required an overnight train ride from Mexico City.

The novelist on whose work the screenplay was based protested that his original title was more provocative and a better choice than what was eventually used. [*Actually,* The Last Sunset *was certainly better than other titles suggested (and rejected) by Universal:* All Girls Wear Yellow Dresses, Trigger Talk, Shoe the Wild Sea-Mare, *and* Two to Make Hate. *"Have you ever heard more atrocious titles?" Kirk asked.*]

Aldrich was a strong director, and whereas Hudson rarely conflicted with him, acquiescing to what was demanded of him, Kirk challenged him during the filming of almost every scene.

Critic John Patterson summed up Aldrich's directorial priorities: "He's punchy, caustic, macho, and pessimistic, depicting evil and corruption unflinchingly, and pushing violence. His aggressive and pugnacious filmmaking style, often crass and crude, but never less than utterly vital and alive, warrants—indeed will richly reward—your immediate attention."

Aldrich had previously directed *Autumn Leaves* (1956) with Joan Crawford and Cliff Robertson, and he was soon to use Crawford again, teaming her with Bette Davis in the classic 1962 horror film, *What Ever Happened to Baby Jane?"*

The director said, "I was dead broke when this offer came in from Kirk, having just made two 'box office bombs' in Europe."

"I knew that Kirk was making a political statement in rehiring Dalton Trumbo after *Spartacus,* but the bastard left us hanging to run off to finish *Exodus* for Otto Preminger. He fucked us."

The Last Sunset was the final movie that Hudson owed Universal under the terms of his contract. During the shoot, he signed a new contract calling for two Universal films a year for $100,000 per picture. If he had time left, he could work for other studios.

With two superstars in the same movie, there arose the thorny issue of billing. Although Kirk's film production company (Bryna) was making the movie and theoretically, at least, in charge of the creative content, Universal was financing and distributing it. Consequently, Ed Muhl at Universal demanded that Rock get first billing, and Kirk acquiesced.

He later asserted, "I had a problem working with Rock. He avoided any kind of direct contact with me. I was aware of how difficult it must have been for him—his co-star was also his boss. I tried everything I could to make him comfortable. But he always had a strange attitude to me, never dealing with me directly. He would make demands to Universal, and some executive would then come to me and say, 'You have to do this and this. Rock demands it.'"

"It never occurred to me that he was a homosexual," Kirk said. "I don't draw a line between masculine and feminine. We all have both sides. And we need them, especially artists."

In his capacity as the film's producer, during his pursuit of a suitable female lead, Kirk sent the script to Lauren Bacall, with whom he had co-starred, more than a decade before, in *Young Man With a Horn* (1950).

Bacall brusquely rejected the script for *The Last Sunset*, expressing indignation that Kirk had even offered it to her, although he could never figure out why. "She berated me for sending her the script. I said, 'Betty, it's the leading female role. You have Rock Hudson in love with you. He was in love with you in *Written on the Wind* (1956). Now you have Kirk Douglas in love with you. That's nothing new for you. I think it's a good part.' Bacall rejected the role anyway."

After that rebuff, Kirk sent the script to Dorothy Malone, whose character had been in love with Rock in *Written on the Wind*. Malone immediately and enthusiastically agreed to star in it.

She had recently married the French actor, Jacques Bergerac (also known as "Mr. Ginger Rogers.") so Kirk didn't move in on her. She and Rock were having a lot of laughs, having previously bonded on the set of *Written on the Wind* (1956), which had also starred Kirk's friend, Lauren Bacall. Dorothy had won a Best Supporting Actress Oscar for her performance.

[Ironically, Malone's last screen appearance was in Basic Instinct *(1992). It had co-starred Sharon Stone letting it all hang out in front of Kirk's oldest son, Michael Douglas.]*

Cotten was none too happy with his role. "Not only was I the cuckold husband of Dorothy Malone and the father of Carol Lynley (at least I thought I was), but I was a traitor, a rat who had deserted his command in the Confederate Army and carried a scar on one buttock eternally to stigmatize my shame. The script called for Kirk Douglas and Rock Hudson to sniff around the petticoat of Malone and take pleasure in humiliating her cowardly husband, namely, me."

Lynley, a former child model in New York, had graced the cover of Life magazine in April of 1957 at the age of 15. She'd appeared on Broadway and in the movie *Blue Denim*, a controversial stage play that had dealt with an unwanted pregnancy and subsequent abortion.

Character actors Jack Elam and Neville Brand played villains who ultimately want to sell Lynley and Malone into white slavery.

Kirk was cast as the neurotic gunman, Brendan O'Malley, a lonesome, tormented cowboy who dresses entirely in black and makes blarney-like observations about life. Perhaps for the first time in a Hollywood Western, the plot involves the potential for incest, a conundrum that seems to encourage his character's eventual suicide. O'Malley faces a shootout with Dana Stribling (as interpreted by Hudson), who has pursued him across the border and into Mexico for killing his brother-in-law, even though he has no jurisdiction to apprehend him South of the Border.

Rock Hudson Erotic Fire

Darwin Porter & Danforth Prince
Another Outrageous Title In Blood Moon's Babylon Series

In 2017, the authors and producers of this book published the most definitive, comprehensive, and unvarnished biography of superstar Rock Hudson in the history of Hollywood.

The Last Sunset (1961) wasn't the first film in which Dorothy Malone had appeared with Rock Hudson. In 1956, she had brilliantly portrayed a spoiled nymphomaniacal oil heiress in Rock's classic hit, *Written on the Wind*.

O'Malley (Kirk) has opted to visit his former sweetheart, Belle Breckenridge (Malone), with whom he'd had an affair sixteen years ago. He meets her daughter, Missy (Lynley), who, coincidentally, was born sixteen years ago. Belle is now married to an old drunk, John (Joseph Cotten), a garrulous and ineffectual gentleman rancher.

Herders and cowpokes are desperately needed to drive hundreds of cattle north from Mexico into Texas. For his involvement in the migration, O'Malley demands a fifth of the herd. When Stribling (Hudson) arrives on the scene, he agrees to join the ranchers, but only if he's designated as their trail boss. O'Malley, it appears, will travel northward with the herd, but only to Mexico's border with Texas, as he'll be arrested the minute he sets foot in U.S. territory.

Here, Trumbo turns up the heat: John (Cotten) is killed in a barroom brawl; Stribling falls in love with Belle, O'Malley (Kirk) develops the hots for Belle's teenaged daughter, Missy, and the group is attacked by Indians.

More trouble is on the way when a trio of nefarious bushwhackers join the group, supposedly as trail drivers. Their evil intentions are eventually thwarted.

Finally, with their cattle, the migrants reach the U.S. border, and O'-Malley—against his better judgment—crosses into Texas. Although he plans to escape with Missy after getting paid, Belle reveals that Missy is O'Malley's daughter from their love affair sixteen years before—a thorny problem, indeed, soaked with the potentiality for father/daughter incest.

Resolution to the dilemma comes in the aftermath of an armed confrontation between the "cowboy in black" (Kirk) and the vigilante sheriff (Hudson), who guns him down (perhaps with Kirk's collusion as part of a suicide pact, the script is unclear) as the sun sets in the West.

The critic for the Hollywood Reporter wrote: *"The Last Sunset* is a big, big Western. But like the men it celebrates, it gives indications of being a dying breed. It is not an exciting picture and is particularly disappointing considering the caliber of talent that went into its acting, writing, and directing."

***

For his next picture, a story set in West Germany during its uncomfortable military occupation by the U.S. military in the years after World War II, Kirk returned to Europe for location shooting in Munich and Vienna. Each of those cities had make remarkable recoveries since World War II, although some neighborhoods still carried traces of war-related devastations.

The film had been conceived as a co-production of Bryna with West Germany's Mirisch Corporation for a release in the U.S. in 1961 through

United Artists. He would be the only big name in the cast, which comprised a mix of European and American actors

He renewed his acquaintance with director Gottfried Reinhardt, who had helmed him as the trapeze artist in *The Story of Three Loves* (1953), the film in which he had co-starred and fallen in love with Pier Angeli. Its memory was still painful for him, but not working with Reinhardt, whom he respected.

His newest movie's plot, with many alterations, had been inspired by a German novel, *Das Urteil (The Verdict)*. Kirk changed its title to *Town Without Pity* and ordered the composition of a song with the same name, eventually sung by Frankie Laine. It became a big hit on jukeboxes in Europe and the U.S., even independent of the film itself.

Once again, he turned to his favorite screen writer, the formerly blacklisted Dalton Trumbo, for preparation of the screenplay's first draft before rushing off to work on Otto Preminger's *Exodus*. Eventually, three other writers were called in to polish and sharpen the plot.

A taut melodrama, *Town Without Pity* takes place in a small town in the American zone of Occupied West Germany in the aftermath of World War II. Four drunken U.S. soldiers have been accused of raping a sixteen-year-old German girl on the muddy banks of a nearby river.

Each of the young men faces the danger of a death sentence, as prescribed by the American Code of Military Justice at the time.

During a picnic together, the girl, Karen Steinhof (as played by Christine Kaufmann) quarrels with her 19-year-old German boyfriend, Frank Borgmann (as portrayed by Gerhardt Lippert). She runs away from him, and then begins changing out of her wet bikini, perhaps (but perhaps not) unaware that she's being lecherously observed by the quartet of U.S. soldiers.

When her boyfriend hears her screams, he rushes to her rescue, but is knocked unconscious by the U.S. soldiers. They're portrayed by Richard Jaeckel, Robert Blake, Mal Sondock, and Frank Sutton.

Arrested later that evening after the girl has returned, hysterical and allegedly gang raped, to her parents, the soldiers are defended by Kirk during a military trial. A "tiger in court," he faces an equally ferocious prosecutor, as portrayed by E.G. Marshall, who seeks the death penalty for all four of the defendants.

During his preparations for the case, he's followed around by a German writer, Inge, as played by Barbara Rütting, for a local newspaper.

Kirk approaches the father (Herr Steinhof, as portrayed by Hans Nielsen) of the victim, urging him to withdraw his daughter from the trial, warning that if his daughter takes the stand, her reputation might be shattered.

The girl's father, who happens to also be the local mayor, adamantly refuses, citing a need for these "evil men" to be punished by death.

In court, Kirk proves true to his word. Putting the girl on the witness stand, he exposes her as a willing and seductive co-participant in the sex acts she shared with the U.S. soldiers on the muddy banks of the river.

Kirk enters a not guilty plea for the men, overriding an unexpected guilty plea that Robert Blake insists he deserves. Blake's unusual request is voided when a psychiatrist testifies that Blake is his patient and that he is impotent. When that's aired in court, in front of witnesses, Blake becomes violent, and security guards have to restrain him and remove him from the court.

Karen collapses on the stand, three of the four soldiers are sentenced to long terms of hard labor, and Blake is sentenced to six years in prison. Later, the audience learns that Karen has committed suicide.

Kirk's character, horrified by the tawdry repression and venom he's seen, leaves, forever, this *"Town Without Pity."*

***

Early in his filming, Kirk was introduced to his leading lady, Christine Kaufmann, cast as the rape victim, Karen. She was born in Styria, Austria, the daughter of a Luftwaffe officer, during the final months of its Nazi occupation.

"She was beautiful and seductive," Kirk said, "But I didn't get the girl in this one. Tony Curtis did, and he wasn't even in the picture.

After *Town Without Pity*, Kaufmann starred in *Taras Bulba* (1962) with Curtis. She married him the following year, a union that lasted until 1968.

Before working with Kirk, she had just finished *The Last Days of Pompeii* (1959), with the bodybuilder/actor Steve Reeves, who had been Mr. Pacific, Mr. America, Mr. World, and Mr. Universe.

The prosecutor, E.G. Marshall, was one of America's finest character actors. Along with Montgomery Clift and Marlon Brando, he had been one of the founding members of the Actors Studio in New York City. Oddly enough, he switched from prosecutor to defense lawyer during his starring gig in the hit TV series, *The Defenders* (1961-1965).

The second female lead, that of a nosey reporter as portrayed by Barbara Rütting, was a Berliner who later evolved into a West German politician championing the rights of both humans and animals.

One of the soldiers, Richard Jaeckel had appeared with Burt Lancaster in *Come Back, Little Sheba* (1952). In it, he had played Terry Moore's athletic boyfriend. He had also recently appeared with Elvis Presley in a Western, *Flaming Star* (1960). He'd go on to win a Best Supporting Actor nomination for his role in the film adaptation of Ken Kesey's novel, *Sometimes a Great Notion* (1971), directed by Paul Newman.

Frank Sutton had the unattractive role of the most predatory of the American defendants, the sergeant who had first spotted the teenager stripping down on the riverbank.

Mal Sondock, another of the plots alleged rapists, had opted to remain in West Germany after his discharge from the U.S. Army in 1957. Evolving into a well-known radio host, broadcasting *Sondock's Hit Parade* in American-accented German, he eventually morphed into "the Father of German Disco."

The fourth soldier, Robert Blake, first entered show-biz as a child actor, portraying a young version of John Garfield opposite Joan Crawford in *Humoresque* (1946), and as a Mexican teenager opposite Humphrey Bogart in *The Treasure of Sierra Madre* (1948). As an adult, he starred in Truman Capote's chilling *In Cold Blood* (1967). In it, he bore striking resemblance to the real killer of a Kansas household, Perry Smith.

Blake achieved great success on television in the hit TV series *Baretta* (1975-1978), in which, as an undercover police detective, he specialized in disguises.

Playing the boyfriend of the rape victim, Gerhardt Lippert never became very well known in American cinema, yet evolved into a successful actor in Austria, Switzerland, and Germany.

The movie father of the teenaged girl, Hans Nielsen, made a career out of dubbing into German the English-language dialogue of many American actors in the German-language release of their films.

Once again for a Kirk movie, Dimitri Tiomkin wrote the musical score. The theme song, "Town Without Pity," as sung by Frankie Laine, was played on jukeboxes around America, ending with the line, "It isn't pretty, a town without pity."

With lyrics by Ned Washington, it was nominated for an Oscar for Best Song in a Motion Picture. Although it didn't win, it carried home a Golden

Globe.

At its preview in Hollywood, many viewers dismissed the film as "distasteful" or "repugnant" on the survey cards they were asked to fill out. That was a harbinger of what was going to happen at box offices, where attendance was poor, as were the reviews.

In the courtroom of a military trial, Kirk is the defense lawyer for four U.S. soldiers accused of raping a German girl, as played by Christine Kaufmann.

[Kirk was surprised when Robert Blake, years from the date they had worked together, was brought up on a charge of murdering his second wife, Bonnie Lee Bakley, in 2001. He'd married her only a year before.

Bakley was a notorious figure in Hollywood, and this was her tenth marriage. She had a reputation for exploiting celebrities for money. Right before Blake married her, she'd been sexually involved with both Marlon Brando and his son, Christian. Seeking damages when she got pregnant, she cited both of them as the father of her child.

On May 4, 2001, Bakley was fatally shot while seated in the front seat of a car. Her husband was later charged with her murder in one of the most-watched televised trials in America. Generating enormous media coverage, Blake faced a possible death sentence.

He was found not guilty. However, three of Bakley's children then sued him in civil court, winning a judgment of wrongful death for $30 million, forcing him into bankruptcy. An appeal court upheld the lower court's verdict.

"Another Hollywood case of horror," Kirk said. "At least in A Town Without Pity *I got him off on a rape charge with only six years in prison."]*

***

Although he never liked the title, *Lonely Are the Brave*, released by Universal-International in 1962, became Kirk's favorite film. It was a Western, but not really a Western in the sense of Roy Rogers or Gene Autry—and not a shoot-'*em*-up like *Gunfight at the O.K. Corral*.

It was produced by Joel Productions, the business entity named for Kirk's second son with Diana Dill. Edward Lewis, vice president of Bryna, was named producer once again. Both of them hired David Miller as director, a decision they'd later regret.

"He was miserable on location in Arizona, and not doing a good job,"

Kirk claimed. "I even pimped a girl for him, hoping to cheer him up, but to no avail. The rest of the cast and crew worked together in harmony—but not David. He and I clashed every day."

As a director, Miller had garnered several impressive credits, including *Billy the Kid* (1941) starring Robert Taylor, and *Flying Tigers* (1943) with John Wayne. One of his triumphs was *Sudden Fear* (1954), which had earned an Oscar nomination for Joan Crawford. He'd only recently directed Doris Day and Rex Harrison in *Midnight Lace* (1960).

Once more, Kirk hired Dalton Trumbo as the screenwriter. "The moment I read through the script, I thought it was perfect," Kirk said. "Never before in my career in Hollywood, and never again, would I ever read a first draft deemed ready to shoot."

The script was based on *Brave Cowboy*, a novel by Edward Abbey (not to be confused with playwright Edward Albee). That novel is today hailed as a classic within the genre of literature about the American West, a saga to wandering the canyons of a diminishing frontier. As its hero rides his trusty Palamino mare, "Whisky," airplanes fly overhead.

Abbey had created an "anarchist cowboy" who rode across a landscape riddled with highways. A critic defined it as "a tale of a stunted soul in drunken despair."

Location shooting was in and around Albuquerque, New Mexico, at such sites as the Manzano and Sandira Mountains and the Kirkland Air Force Base.

Jack appears for a reunion with his best friend, Michael Kane (Paul Bondi), now married to Jerry Bondi (Gena Rowlands); Jack is still in love with her. She tells him that her husband is in jail for having aided illegal immigrants. Jack plots to get himself arrested so he can join his friend in jail. He "cased the joint" and decided it will be relatively easy for both of them to escape.

He stages a barroom brawl with a one-armed war veteran portrayed by Bill Raisch. *[Raisch later became known for his role in the hit TV series* The Fugitive *(1963-67), in which he played the killer of the wife of Dr. Richard Kimble (David Janssen).]*

After Jack is arrested and jailed alongside his friend, Paul. Then he learns, to his dismay, that Paul's rebellious spirit has been extinguished, that he wants to serve out his sentence and return to his wife, and that he has absolutely no intention of becoming a fugitive fleeing with Jack to Mexico.

Kirk had worked with Walter Matthau in another Western, *The Indian Fighter*. This time, Matthau was cast as Sheriff Morey Johnson, a modern, high-tech lawman who uses helicopters and Jeeps in pursuit of Kirk as he

451

heads to the Mexican border.

George Kennedy was cast into the role of the sadistic deputy sheriff, Gutierrez. *[This brilliant character actor would go on to win a Best Supporting Actor Oscar for his performance opposite Paul Newman in* Cool Hand Luke *(1967).*

On a rainy night, as Whisky and Jack try to cross Highway 66, the horse is terrified of the headlights of an oncoming truck piloted by "Hinton" as portrayed by Carroll O'Connor. *[It was O'Con-*

Lonely are the Brave—This publicity still shows the jarring conflicts between the old, "Don't Fence Me In" West (as represented by Kirk and his horse, Whiskey, who is killed on a superhighway by a truck), and the modern urban world, as represented by the helicopter, representing restrictions, repression, and the law.

nor's film debut. The character he played was transporting a cargo of toilets. O'-Connor would go on to great acclaim playing the bigoted but lovable Archie Bunker in the hit TV series, All in the Family *(1971-79).]* His truck hits both Jack and his horse.

The film ends tragically. Jack is loaded into an ambulance, and Whisky is hauled away to be euthanized.

***

Kirk had great respect for the acting talent of his leading lady, Gena Rowlands. She was known for ten film collaborations with her actor/director/husband, John Cassavetes whom she had married in 1954. Their union lasted until his death in 1989.

Over the course of her career, she would receive two Oscar nominations for Best Actress—one for *A Woman Under the Influence* (1974), and another for *Gloria* (1980).

According to Kirk, "On the screen, Gena played the woman I was in love with," Kirk said. "That didn't take much acting on my part."

When Kirk later read a profile of Rowlands by Pier Carlo Talenti, he felt the writer had captured her look: "Rowlands has an undeniable butch quality about her. The way she chews her consonants, the way she says 'yeah' instead of 'yes.' Her smile is almost completely horizontal, curving neither upward or downward. When she grins, her eyebrows pinch up ever so slightly over the bridge of her nose."

James Horwitz in *They Went Thataway* wrote: "In *Lonely Are the Brave*, Kirk Douglas is a Brave Cowboy. But he is already an anachronism, a dinosaur. The time of the film is the present. The cowboy-hero races for the freedom of the mountains, pursued by sheriff's cars and walkie-talking-toting deputies, and he fires his Winchester at helicopters."

Kirk viewed *Lonely Are the Brave* not as a typical Western action adventure, but as an art film, and urged Universal to open it in a limited number of small, avant-garde art houses before moving it into larger, mass-market theaters nationwide.

But Universal opened it instead as a splashy, major release, and when it failed to attract big audiences quickly, they yanked it from theaters nationwide.

Today, it has had something of a revival, attracting aficionados and students of filmmaking as an art form. On lists, *Lonely Are the Brave* appears as one of the best Westerns ever made.

Most of the reviews—including those within *Time* and *Newsweek*—were raves, but film critic, Stanley Kauffmann, cast a dissenting vote. "The film's basic shortcoming is a lack of desirable alternative to what it seemingly deplores. Many of us uncharmed by neon and motels do not long for the old-time saloon binges and fist fights as the Lost Eden."

In November of 1962, a year before he was assassinated, President John F. Kennedy saw the movie at a screening in the White House. First Lady Jacqueline read off the names of new releases that had been made available there for screenings to the President and his entourage that night. According to Jackie, "All of us voted against it, but Jack selected a sadistic Western called *Lonely Are the Brave*."

***

The severely flawed film versions of *Two Weeks in Another Town,* starring Kirk, was a kind of send-up of Rome during its heyday as "Hollywood on the Tiber." Its plot had been based on a novel by the popular Irwin Shaw, one of his lesser efforts.

Gena Rowlands emotes with the last cowboy of his breed, as represented by Kirk, in *Lonely Are the Brave.*

A commemoration of the death of the best aspects of the Old West, it's one of the saddest movies Kirk ever made.

Metro-Goldwyn-Mayer eventually released the film in 1962.

Shaw had proven his merit again and again as a highly paid "quick fix script doctor" for many of the Hollywood films shot in Europe. As one observer wrote, "He simply wrote and wrote, the good and the bad, page after page, book after book, script after script. In time, he became a footnote in the literature of the time, not so much a hack, but a man of genuine talent. But for a man of his gifts, we expected more of him that *Two Weeks in Another Town*."

In another assessment of the script, a critic in 2014 wrote, "In the 21st Century, this work by Shaw would be judged as politically incorrect. Jack Andrus, a character played by Kirk Douglas, ruminates on his three wives in Rome. They come across as a collection of neurotic cheaters, liars, and manipulators. The producer's wife is an overbearing shrew, and Andrus' Italian lover turns out to be a nightmare."

Accused of being a communist, Shaw was blacklisted and fled America and remained abroad for twenty-five years, living mostly in Paris and Switzerland. He told Kirk, "My being on the Red Channels list only glancingly bruised my writing career."

[Originally, Sol Siegel, head of production at MGM, had wanted to release Two Weeks in Another Town *in 1960, two years before its actual release in 1962, and to "populate" its cast with Spencer Tracy and Clark Gable. But Gable suffered a fatal heart attack in 1960 after completing* The Misfits *with Marilyn Monroe, and by then, Tracy was no longer interested.]*

Hoping to replicate the success of *The Bad and the Beautiful*, MGM rounded up the "posse" from that film, including its producer, John Houseman, its director, Vincente Minnelli, its writer, Charles Schnee, and its composer, David Raskin.

Except for Kirk, the cast of actors differed from that of *The Bad and the Beautiful*. It would feature Edward G. Robinson, George Hamilton, Cyd Charisse, Dahlia Lavi, Claire Trevor, Rosanno Schiaffino, George Macready (who had had a far more significant role in Kirk's *Paths of Glory*), singer Leslie Uggams, and Erich Von Stroheim, Jr., the son of the fabled director of silent films.

Kirk came at a high price, charging MGM $500,000 plus ten percent of the gross.

During the shoot, Kirk encountered a teary Schnee, who had just heard news that his wife, Mary, had committed suicide. *[Fourteen months later, Schnee would himself die at the age of 46 after suffering a heart attack.]*

In *Spartacus*, Kirk had been a noble warrior, but in *Two Weeks in Another Town*, the role of Jack Andrus was that of a has-been actor, trying to make a comeback after three years confinement in a sanatorium for mental instability and alcoholism.

Robinson and Trevor had scored a big hit together in *Key Largo* (1948) with co-stars Humphrey Bogart and Lauren Bacall. The Brooklyn born actress won a Best Supporting Actress Oscar for her performance as Gaye Dawn, the boozy gun moll of the gangster portrayed by Robinson. Trevor specialized in playing hard-boiled, blonde-haired bad girls.

[In 1978, Kirk phoned her to express his sympathy after her son, Charles Dunsmore, died in the crash of PSA flight 182 in San Diego. Kirk called her again a year later when her third husband, Milton H. Bren, died of a brain tumor.]

Kirk, along with Robinson and Trevor, knew they were turning out a "cheesy potboiler" in the Eternal City. In the role of the director of the "movie within the movie," Maurice Kruger (Robinson) had once been the mentor to Kirk's character in their heyday in Hollywood. Now, he seems on his last legs.

He is in desperate need of Kirk's help to finish the picture

Low Camp from an American overview of Hollywood on the Tiber: Here's how the studio's press department described the scene in this publicity photo for *Two Weeks in Another Town*:

"Kirk and Edward G. Robinson try to separate Claire Trevor and Rosanna Schiaffino, who have started a nightclub brawl."

And perhaps as an insight into the insanity lurking just below the surface of *La Dolce Vita:*

"In a frenzy of despair and hate, Kirk takes his ex-wife, Cyd Charisse, on a ride of terror."

he's shooting with "that spoiled brat," Davis Drew (Hamilton). The young actor is hostile to Robinson and doesn't mind showing it.

Cast as Hamilton's leading lady is Barzelli, played by the Italian actress, Rosanna Shiaffino, who barely speaks English.

Hamilton complained to Kirk that he was horribly miscast "as a troubled, funky James Dean-type actor." Minnelli, or so it was rumored, had a crush on the handsome, forever suntanned, actor.

He had recently cast him in *Home from the Hill* (1960) with Robert Mitchum, and in the remake of *Four Horsemen of the Apocalypse* (1962). Hamilton would co-star with Kirk again in *Once is Not Enough* (1975).

He recalled Minnelli as "smoking cigarettes like Bette Davis and puckering his lips." Minnelli had continued to use Hamilton even though Bosley Crowther of *The New York Times* once reviewed him as "a bare cut above an idiot."

In 1966, Hamilton became consistently featured in the tabloids for regularly escorting First Daughter Lynda Bird Johnson to gala events. He also became embroiled in the excesses and scandals of Imelda Marcos, married to President Ferdinand Marcos of the Philippines.

A note of romance is added in the movie when Kirk, as Jack, meets Veronica (Dahlia Lavi), cast as a beautiful, charming young woman. When he shot *The Juggler* in Israel, he had met Lavi when she was only ten years old, dreaming of becoming a ballet dancer.

In 1965, she tried to shoot to stardom opposite Peter O'Toole in *Lord Jim* (1965), but fame eluded her. She ended up playing scantily clad *femme fatales* in a number of lackluster films.

During the making of *Two Weeks*, two underground Roman tabloids speculated that she had had, at an indefinite time in her past, a brief fling with Kirk, perhaps working him in among her four husbands.

In a non-dancing role, Cyd Charisse was cast as Carlotta, Jack's ex-wife. She is spoiled, aggressive, and destructive, and may have contributed to her husband's downfall. It appears she wants to resume her role in his life.

Privately, Kirk told Robinson that he was having "wet dreams" about Charisse. "Those legs! Better than Betty Grable's." Apparently, the *Guinness Book of World Records* agreed with him, since a company insured them for a record $5 million.

[She had starred with Gene Kelly in the "Broadway Melody" episode in Singin' in the Rain (1952), hailed as the greatest musical ever made.]

Upon his return to Hollywood, Kirk met Charisse again when she was shooting the never-finished *Marilyn*

Edward G. Robinson and Claire Trevor in *Key Largo* (1948)

Monroe movie, *Something's Got to Give* (1962), partially shot near the time of Monroe's death.

Although Kirk admired Charisse's talent as a dancer, he had objected to casting her in such a dramatic role. "This is heavy drama. Bring back Lana Turner. We sizzled in *The Bad and the Beautiful*, both on and off the screen."

"Another thing I had against Cyd was that she was a staunch Republican. In the 1968 race for the White House, she was salivating over Richard Nixon."

Leslie Uggams...the new Lena Horne.

In contrast, Edward G. Robinson was an ardent liberal, too much for some people. After he refused to name names before the House Un-American Activities Committee, he was blacklisted. "But to put food on the table and a roof over my head, I returned to the committee and cited such communists as Dalton Trumbo," he said.

Later, he claimed, "I was duped by the commies. He wrote an article, "How the Reds Made a Sucker Out of Me."

Dahlia Lavi...dreams of stardom.

During the course of his career, Robinson (aka "Little Caesar"), who was born in Bucharest, Romania, made a hundred films.

Also in the cast was Erich Von Stroheim, Jr, who played an assistant director in *Two Weeks*. Minnelli had also recently cast him in that flop, *Four Horsemen of the Apocalypse* (1962). Von Stroheim had both the good fortune and bad luck to be the son of the autocratic silent screen director, Erich Von Stroheim, who had immortalized himself in "that damn butler part," in *Sunset Blvd.* (1950) with Gloria Swanson. Von Stroheim, Sr. had died in France before Kirk ever met and worked with his son.

George Hamilton in 1969...working with legends.

Leslie Uggams, born in Harlem, added a grace note to the film with her rendition of the song "Don't Blame Me." Stardom came to her in the Broadway musical *Hallelujah, Baby!* In 1967 after Lena Horne turned it down.

Two Weeks in Another Town ran into trouble with both MGM and the censors. Joseph Vogel had taken over the studio in October of 1956, proclaiming, "MGM will start turning out pictures for the entire family."

Cyd Charisse with Kirk in *Two Weeks in Another Town*. Hollywood's greatest pair of legs.

MGM's former CEO, Louis B. Mayer, called him "a fool" and attempted a hostile takeover. Vogel and his production manager, Sol Siegel, turned out such big hits as *Gigi* (1958) and *Ben-Hur* (1959).

The MPAA (Motion Picture Association of America), still a bastion of Hollywood censorship, claimed that *Two Weeks in Another Town* "portrayed free and easy sexual intercourse graphically depicted. Any pretense presenting it in a moral light would appear to be almost ludicrous."

In the words of one critic, "*Two Weeks in Another Town* was mangled by MGM, roasted by film critics, and spurned by movie-goers."

Both Kirk and Minnelli objected strongly to the cuts ordered by Vogel, Kirk sending him a scathing letter of protest. Margaret Booth, MGM's supervising editor, was blamed for a "hatchet job," but she told Kirk that she was merely following Vogel's mandate.

Emanuel Levy, Minnelli's biographer, said, "Booth's merciless, brutal cuts made the film's already neurotic characters even more sordid and unsympathetic than they had been in the original."

"The picture that was released should have been better than it was," Charisse said. "After Vincente made his cuts, someone else took over and chopped it to shreds. My best scenes ended up on the cutting room floor. When I finally went to see it in a theater, I couldn't make heads or tails out of it, it was so disconnected. It was a shame. There had been so many good scenes. I enjoyed working with Kirk and getting to know his charming wife, Anne."

Peter Bogdanovich, writing in *Film Culture*, had praise, finding the movie "a gaudy, flashy, cynical, and debauched look at the Roman world, a picture of perversion and glittering decay, making Fellini's *La Dolce Vita* look pedestrian and arty.

Minnelli later said, "*Two Weeks* left ashes in my mouth. Vogel found our film immoral at the same time he was greenlighting *Lolita*, a film about child molestation. I will never forgive him for taking a meat cleaver to what might have been a second great film about the movie industry in the tradition of *The Bad and the Beautiful*."

Stephen Harvey wrote: "*Two Weeks in Another Town* has got satyriasis,

458

nymphomania, latent homosexuality, suicidal episodes, and paranoid hysteria, both acute and chronic, when just one mental malady per customer would have sufficed."

He also suggested that Charisse played Carlotta like "a transvestite in heat" and that Trevor "rants and brays to the point of apoplexy."

Bosley Crowther of *The New York Times* delivered the most devastating attack, using such charges as "a picture of Hollywood rejects…a drippy drama on a theme of degradation…a lot of glib trade patter…the story of a Hollywood actor/director who wallows in a slough of dull self-pity and spurious sentimentality."

He concluded that Kirk is no more intelligible or convincing than Steve Reeves as Hercules.

He also attacked the supporting cast, calling Trevor a "rasping cliché of a wife; Lavi "empty headed"; and Charisse a woman character "devoid of brains or morals."

"Robinson storms and snarls and gives the barest impression of a human being in genuine distress," he concluded.

***

Elizabeth Taylor and her husband, Eddie Fisher, were in Rome for her starring performance in the ill-fated *Cleopatra* (1963).

Richard Burton had been cast as Marc Antony, with Rex Harrison taking the role of the older Julius Caesar.

Kirk and Elizabeth had been friends ever since her marriage to Mike Todd, who had died in that plane crash in New Mexico.

She was living in a rented villa with Fisher and her children. She called Kirk after hearing that he'd arrived in Rome. Both of them lamented Todd's death, and each of them speculated about how close they had come to death itself if either of them had accepted his invitation to fly with them aboard his airplane to New York.

In honor of the first anniversary of the release of *Spartacus,* she tossed a lavish party in the ballroom of the Grand Hotel, inviting two hundred guests. Many of them were movie stars visiting Rome or working on films in other parts of Italy.

Kirk showed up with his wife, Anne, who remained discreetly in the background as he worked the party.

Cyd Charisse recalled, "Richard Burton was there with his wife, Sylvia, and I think Elizabeth met the Welsh actor for the first time. I danced with Tony (Martin), watching Burton and Elizabeth dance so close together that their bodies seemed held together by glue. I noticed Eddie looking on with the most forlorn expression on his face."

"Kirk was there, and he also danced with Elizabeth, crotch to crotch," Charisse said. "I wasn't sure, but I think Elizabeth was getting ready to take on a lover. Was it going to be Kirk? Or perhaps Burton? Eddie was going to be the cuckold locked out in the cold."

"From the night of that party, I knew that a chapter in cinema history was going to be written before *Cleopatra* was wrapped," Charisse said.

As she observed, "Kirk made the rounds, dancing with all the beauties. In spite of his marriage, he seemed to be paying a lot of attention to other women, beginning with Joan Collins."

As Kirk remembered it, he encountered Collins, who had a certain bitterness, telling him that originally, Fox had cast her as the female lead in *Cleopatra.*

"You feel left out," he said. "So do I. I'm furious at Fox for not casting me as Marc Antony. I've kept in shape, and would look great in a Roman toga."

He renewed his friendship with Anthony Quinn and speculated about when they would be cast together again in another picture. Quinn was entering the final months of his marriage to his first wife, Katherine DeMille, the adopted daughter of Cecil B. DeMille.

"It's okay to have a little woman waiting at home with a stiff drink and your bedroom slippers, but my Latino dick belongs to the world's most beautiful woman," Quinn said.

An old rival, Charlton Heston, was there, too. He and Kirk began discussing Hal B. Wallis, Kirk claiming, "He sure did more for your career than mine."

Heston said, "I read in *Variety* that you wanted *Ben-Hur.*"

"I thought about it, but I made *Spartacus* instead, a better role for me. No hard feelings."

Jack Palance was another rival in the sense that Joan Crawford had preferred him as her leading man in *Sudden Fear* (1952). Kirk congratulated him and asked him to transmit his regards to Gloria Grahame. Palance's co-star in *Sudden Fear.* "I knew Gloria rather well."

Robert Wagner was at the party and rather confrontational. "I heard you fucked Natalie (Wood)," he charged.

Liz and Dick: They were everywhere. Here's the front cover of LIFE's edition of April 13, 1962

"A god damn lie," Kirk said. "I never touched her."

He found meeting Elsa Martinelli rather embarrassing, as he had been her on- and off-screen lover during their filming of *The Indian Fighter*.

Her English had greatly improved. He had offered to put her under personal contract for Bryna Production, but she had turned him down.

Now, with a film career going seemingly nowhere, she said, "I made a mistake. How about giving me a second chance?"

"Too late, babe," he answered. "I've moved on." Then he turned from her and headed across the room to invite Elizabeth for another crotch-to-crotch dance.

After more interchanges with Elizabeth, Lex Barker approached him, but Kirk wasn't glad to see him—based on many earlier encounters with him, Kirk had already evaluated him as an anti-Semite.

Barker's two marriages to the most beautiful women in Hollywood—Arlene Dahl (1951-52) and Lana Turner (1953-57)—were over. He had come to Rome to play Anita Ekberg's husband in Fellini's *La Dolce Vita* (1961).

"Do you still hate the Jews?" Kirk asked.

"C'mon, Kirk," Barker said. "I've changed since them. Living in Europe has made me more international, more tolerant."

"Good for you, kid," Kirk said. "Now go swing on a vine, Tarzan." Then he walked away.

He ran into a drunken Rory Calhoun, who had made two movies with Marilyn Monroe, *How to Marry a Millionaire* (1953) and *River of No Return* (1954). "I asked Marilyn what kind of lover you were," Calhoun said. "She came up with the oddest answer. She said, 'He's clean.'"

It was good seeing Dorothy Malone again, as she and Kirk had worked harmoniously together on *The Last Sunset* (1961), a movie in which they had co-starred with Rock Hudson.

He asked her, "Do you think Rock will ever find the right guy and settle down?"

"Not likely," she said. "He's the kind who likes to play the field, probably afraid of commitment."

Another of Kirk's co-stars, Barbara Rush, was at the party, too. They had co-starred with Kim Novak in *Strangers When We Meet*. "I didn't like the role," she said. "Cast as the wife of a husband who has to turn to another woman for satisfaction."

"If I were married to you, my eyes would never wander," he promised, with an insincere wink.

Another talented actor, Hume Cronyn, husband of actress Jessica Tandy, chatted pleasantly with Kirk. He had a role in *Cleopatra* at the time, and in the future would appear in two movies with Kirk.

Anthony Franciosa, the third husband of Shelley Winters, then came up to Kirk.

"Shelley told me that in London, she stayed on the same floor with you at The Dorchester. She said Elizabeth had a suite on the floor, too, when she was trying to shoot the first version of *Cleopatra*, back when Peter Finch had been (temporarily) cast as Marc Antony. Shelley said she needed a really good fuck and knocked on your door at 2AM. How did that go?"

"I honestly have to say that I don't remember."

"Yeah, right," Franciosa answered. "How could any man forget Shelley Winters?"

Kirk was stunned by the beauty of Gina Lollobrigida, later telling Vincente Minnelli, "Gina looked good enough to eat, but fortunately, I maintained my virginity, and Anne steered me to the twenty-pound cake Elizabeth had ordered for the occasion. I ate cake instead of Gina."

Before exiting from this grand party at Rome's Grand Hotel, he thanked his hostess, Elizabeth, who had paid for this lavish *fête*, and wished her luck in her portrayal of the Queen of the Nile. He was fully aware of the health issues she'd endured in London when Fox had tried to shoot the movie there.

As he remembered it, "She was tipsy, drunk, actually, but adorable. I told her, 'Till we meet again, 'lil darling,'" kissing her on the lips.

"I've got an idea," she said. "As soon as I go through all this pomp and get in and out of all that Cleopatra drag, let's you and I co-star in a romantic movie, maybe with a nude scene together in bed. I'll wear nothing under the sheet. I hope you'll do the same."

"That's a fabulous suggestion," he answered. "A Jew fucking a Jew."

[Elizabeth had converted to Judaism.]

Her lips brushed his for a final time.

No doubt in the coming months, you'll read about what a scarlet woman I am," she said. "That's a god damn lie. Color me purple, sweetheart."

CHAPTER THIRTEEN

JOHN F. KENNEDY

How Kirk's Fellow Horndog Wanted Him to Make a Movie About an Attempt to Overthrow the U.S. Presidency

THE HOOK

Notorious Nick Adams and Robert Walker, Jr. with Kirk in a War Movie

"KILLER DOUGLAS"

Why Members of an African Tribe Called Him That During a Safari

KIRK'S ROLE AS AMERICA'S GOOD WILL AMBASSADOR

Getting Groped in Brazil and Shot at in Istanbul

The plot of Kirk's *Seven Days in May* seemed oddly prescient in the months that followed JFK's assassination in November of 1963.

Kirk always cited the President's approval of the film project as important to its eventual box office success—and its fiming as an act of patriotism that specificlly reverberated with the memory of JFK.

In his memoirs, Kirk admitted that Nick Adams "was a good friend of mine." And so he was, a memorable player in one of Kirk's strangest relationships. Born in a depressed region of northeastern Pennsylvania, the son of a Ukrainian-born coal miner, Adams is the centerpiece of a bizarre footnote in Hollywood history. Today, many of the details of his life and early death have morphed into subjects of lurid speculation.

The noted biographer, Albert Goldman, wrote, "Nick was forever selling himself, a property which, to hear him tell it, was nothing less than sensational, the greatest little actor to hit this town in years. In fact, he had very little going for him in terms of looks or talent or professional experience. He was just another poor kid from the sticks who had grown up dreaming of the silver screen."

"Movies were my life," he told Kirk. "I've seen every film you ever made. You're dynamite on the screen, you bring a force and vigor to a role that makes even Marlon Brando jealous. Let Steve McQueen worry about being cool. You bring energy, intensity, a jut-jawed strength, to every role you play. You throw everything you've go into it. You make Robert Mitchum look like a mannequin in a department store window."

"Who wouldn't love a guy like this little fucker?" Kirk asked. "He could charm hell out of you by lavishing praise that was music to my ears. From the first night we met, we became friends. Of course, I knew he was hanging onto my every word, laughing at my worst jokes and telling me such shit that I was the single most beautiful face and body that had ever graced the silver screen."

"I'm no fool, not Issur. I was aware that he was brown-nosing me just to get cast in one of my upcoming movies, but that was all right with me. I found him a lot of fun to hang out with."

Nick entered Kirk's life after a stint in the Coast Guard that had begun in 1952. Kirk heard that he was devoting most of his act at the Mocambo nightclub in Hollywood to an impersonation of him. For $25 a night, Nick had been hired as an impersonator of Hollywood stars, notably James Cagney, Humphrey Bogart, and James Stewart. On the night Adams was hastily booked because the regular

Nick Adams, as Johnny Yuma in the hit TV series *The Rebel* (1959-1961)

act, singer Pearl Bailey, had fallen sick with the flu, Kirk went to see him.

Sitting near the stage, Kirk was astonished that Nick opened his act with his replication of Kirk as "The Gentleman Caller" from *The Glass Menagerie*. Kirk later said, "I couldn't believe it. He nailed me. He even distorted his face to look like mine. His voice was perfect. I've heard myself on the screen long enough to know what I sound like. Then Nick followed with scenes from some of my most aggressive performances—like *Champion* and *Ace in the Hole*."

"After the show, I was directed backstage. As Bogie said, and I often repeat, 'It was the beginning of a beautiful friendship.'"

Kirk got to know only the sparse details of Nick's notorious life, although he'd heard plenty of gossip, especially about his link to James Dean.

"I knew Nick was gay, although I'd call it bi-. After all, he got married one time and also took Natalie Wood's virginity. But he never shared all that gay stuff with me. Our friendship was about having fun—not sex."

"I'll tell you one thing, though. He didn't mind showing off his junk. If anyone, male or female, got too inquisitive, like on the set or at a party, Nick would take them to the rest room or to his dressing room and unzip. In a town of whoppers, he marked right up there with the biggest."

Although Nick got involved

How did Kirk relate to a new generation of wannabe male stars? Perhaps with touches of anger. Here he is with Robert Walker, Jr.

...and with Nick Adams, in *The Hook*

with a string of Hollywood's mostly gay actors, including Montgomery Clift, Rock Hudson, and Sal Mineo, he also became involved in the private lives of supposedly straight men, too, notably Rory Calhoun, Forrest Tucker, John Wayne, and director John Ford. He could service both men and women, not just Natalie Wood, but a string of other Hollywood beauties, too. He soon became one of Tinseltown's leading acolytes and "star fuckers."

The two actors with whom Nick was most closely linked, becoming their best friends, were James Dean and Elvis Presley. "Tongues were wagging all over Hollywood about those liaisons," Kirk said. "But I never pried."

Hot, Unauthorized, and Unapologetic!

HOLLYWOOD BABYLON

It's Back!

Volume #1

All Those Celebrities!

All That Nudity!

All Those Scandals!

...and All That Sin!

BY DARWIN PORTER & DANFORTH PRINCE

Wanna read the tragic and traumatized full story of Nick Adams? It's all here, in a title Blood Moon published in 2008

To date, the most complete story of Nick's life appeared in Blood Moon's *Hollywood Babylon, It's Back* (2008).

Another overview of his life, this one detailing Nick's complicated friendship with James Dean (each had been a hustler on Santa Monica Boulevard), was incorporated into Blood Moon's *James Dean, Tomorrow Never Comes* (2016).

Elvis Presley had been a huge fan of the screen image of James Dean, and was sorely disappointed when Dean died in a car crash in 1955. When Elvis moved to Hollywood in 1956 for the filming of *Love Me Tender,* he spent lots of time with Nick Adams, pumping him for information about Dean's private life and personal quirks. Soon, Elvis assumed the role that Dean had occupied in Nick's life—that of a supportive star he could hang out with. They were seen living together at Graceland, and riding around Memphis on a motorcycle together after midnight.

As time went by, although Nick's career as a movie star continued to elude him, his circle of friends grew, and he nabbed an occasional role. Eventually, Rock Hudson steered him into a small part in *Pillow Talk* (1959), that romantic comedy in which Hudson, a gay man, played a straight man impersonating a gay man in his most successful appearance in a comedy.

Also in 1959, Nick was cast as the star of the hit ABC TV series, *The Rebel*, the most visible role he'd ever play. In it, he played Johnny Yuma, a wandering ex-Confederate soldier with a sawed-off shotgun, a "trouble shooter" looking for action and adventure in the Old West.

At last, Kirk was on hand, on the verge of delivering what Nick had been hoping for—an entrée into a bigger league of films.

***

The role eventually offered to Adams was in *The Hook* (1963), a war movie in which Kirk had been cast as a soldier. Set at the time of the Korean War in 1953, the film was being produced as a (minor) collaboration between its producer William Perlberg, and its director George Seaton. The Perlberg-Seaton collaboration was already famous for *The Miracle on 34th Street* (1947), that's still shown on television every year at Christmas. As such, everyone seemed to know in advance that *The Hook* would not rival their very famous earlier classic.

[Seaton and Perlbeg had also produced The Country Girl (1954), that had brought Grace Kelly her Best Actress Academy Award when she appeared opposite William Holden and Bing Crosby.]

In a nutshell, *The Hook* tells the story of Sergeant P.J. Briscoe and his fellow soldiers, private O.A. Dennison (Robert Walker, Jr.) and Private V.R. Hackett (Nick Adams). Along with some fellow soldiers, they're preparing to evacuate from a battle, but a North Korean plane attacks and kills all but the three of them.

Kirk plays the hard-nosed, hard-driving sergeant, who's conflicting with Walker's more sensitive type. Adams portrays the sergeant's "flunky."

As the trio maneuver their way from the beach to a freighter standing by, they swim past the North Korean pilot of the plane they've just shot down. Portrayed by Enrique Magalona, he's floating in the water unconscious. Kirk wants to "leave the bastard to die," but Walker insists on rescuing him.

On board the freighter, U.S. Captain Van Ryan (Nehemiah Peersoff) informs them that all four of them (Kirk, two army associates, and the rescued enemy pilot) will have to share the same tiny cabin.

On a phone, Kirk reaches his headquarters in South Korea, where the staff there orders him to kill the prisoner. He is willing to carry out that order, but Walker insists on saving his life.

Unable to understand English, the prisoner awaits his fate, but eventually, he escapes and tries to ignite gasoline as a means of destroying the ship. Kirk discovers the plot and kills him with a wrench.

After a screening of Robert Walker, Jr.'s film test, Kirk was amazed at how closely he resembled his famous father, actor Robert Walker, Sr.

[Junior was the son of Walker, Sr., and the famous brunette, Jennifer Jones.

The son had been conceived during their ill-fated marriage before David O. Selznick stole Jones for himself.

After that, Walker, Sr., got involved with Judy Garland during their co-starring together in The Clock *(1945), and with Ava Gardner during the filming of* One Touch of Venus *(1948).*

A bisexual, Walker, Sr., became intimately involved with both Peter Lawford and Nancy Davis (Reagan) in a ménage à trois.

Walker, Sr. eventually descended into alcoholism.

FATHER AND SON

On the left is Robert Walker Sr. (1918-1951), and on the right is his son, Robert Walker Jr., the actor who worked with Kirk on two movies. Born in 1940, he made clear to Kirk some of the difficulties faced by the children of famous movie stars.

That was something that Kirk became painfully aware of through the life of his own children in the decades to come.

In 1951, in an attempt to calm what his psychiatrist defined as psychotic and violent behavior, he was injected with a sedative, sodium amytal. Reacting to alcohol and other drugs already in his system, it was fatal.

Kirk, perhaps motivated by a sense of how difficult life could be for the actor sons of famous movie stars, eventually got Walker, Jr., cast in The War Wagon, *a picture, released in 1967, they'd make together a few years later with John Wayne.]*

As the Korean prisoner, Enrique G. Magalona, Jr., delivered—without a single word of dialogue—one of the best performances in the film. He was not Korean, but from the Philippines, where he and his wife, Tita Duran, had appeared in several movies as a popular love team in the 1940s.

Variety claimed that Kirk's *The Hook* had a tendency to stray "beyond pertinent, basic issues into artificial tangents and melodramatic postures."

Bosley Crowther of *The New York Times* found *The Hook* to be "of such doubtful occurrence and so little urgency that one finds it hard to get involved. The whole thing has the nature of a contrived hypothesis."

***

"Once again, I made a final attempt to play Cary Grant," Kirk claimed, "in *For Love of Money* (1963)." It was a romantic comedy, released by Universal, in which he would play the male lead. He was given strong support by Mitzi Gaynor, his leading lady, and such stars as Thelma Ritter, Julie Newmar, Gig Young, William Bendix, Leslie Parrish, and Dick Sargent.

Robert Arthur, the film's producer, was also well-known as a screenwriter, a force behind the corny hit series devoted to Francis "the Talking Mule," and to slapstick comedies by Abbott and Costello. In time, he'd work with such names as Cary Grant, Shirley MacLaine, James Stewart, Doris Day, and Tony Curtis.

[Robert Arthur, the producer of this film, is not to be confused with another Robert Arthur, the young actor who had portrayed Kirk's photographer/sidekick in Ace in the Hole.]

Kirk had high hopes for this comedy, especially because Arthur, as producer, had selected Michael Gordon as its director. Kirk always viewed working with a previously blacklisted director or writer as a badge of honor.

[Gordon had previously directed José Ferrer as Cyrano de Bergerac (1950), which brought him a Best Actor Academy Award. Following that, he was blacklisted until Ross Hunter called him back to direct Doris Day and Rock Hudson in Pillow Talk (1959), one of the biggest box office comedies of that decade.

Kirk told Gordon, "I hope lightning strikes twice."]

The improbable script by Larry Marks and Michael Morris asks you to believe that a bachelor matchmaker, Deke Gentry (Kirk), is needed to find husbands for three rich and luscious sisters who can't seem to get a date. There's Kate Brasher (Gaynor), Bonnie (Newmar), and Jan (Leslie Parrish). Their mother is the forever wonderful Thelma Ritter as Chloe. In *Pillow Talk,* she had stolen every scene she was in.

Each member of the sisterly trio has a different personality. Gaynor portrayed a headstrong "motivational researcher," bright and capable. The other sisters are beautiful numbskulls, Newmar a ditzy health addict and fitness guru, and Jan, a bohemian artist, hanging out with a coven of hippies. Kirk claimed, "Mitzi and I were cast as 'Rock and Doris' types."

[For Love or Money would mark the final screen appearance of the very talented Mitzi Gaynor. Although she'd made seventeen movies during the course of her career, she told Kirk, "I feel I'm too ordinary for film. From now on, I'm going

to do nightclub acts and television appearances."

Among others, *Gaynor had starred in the biopic of Eva Tanguay entitled* The I Don't Care Girl *(1952); in* There's No Business Like Show Business *(1954), starring Ethel Merman, Marilyn Monroe, Donald O'Connor, and Johnnie Ray; and* The Joker is Wild *(1957) opposite Frank Sinatra. Her greatest triumph had been as Ensign Nellie Forbush in the film adaptation of Rogers and Hammerstein's* South Pacific *(1958).]*

Another sister, the fitness guru, Bonnie, was portrayed by Julie Newmar. During her career, she'd already had many professions: actress, dancer, singer, writer, real estate mogul, and, of all things, a "lingerie inventor." Her pantyhose, known as a "Nudemar," was said to bring *"derrière* relief." She had also designed and marketed a popular bra described as "nearly invisible" in the style of Marilyn Monroe.

TV audiences came to know her for her appearances on *Batman* (1966-67). She reprised her role as Catwoman half a century later. She also was in the camp classic, *To Wong Foo, Thanks for Everything! Julie Newmar* (1995).

According to Kirk, "Julie was a reigning sex symbol, a seductive temptress, and an Amazonian beauty—too much woman for me. I didn't even try to climb that mountain."

In *For the Love of Money,* as a matchmaker, Kirk plans to arrange a

Kirk, as a matchmaker, has to find husbands for (left to right), Julie Newmar, Leslie Parrish, and Mitzi Gaynor.

Left to right, Mitzi Gaynor, Julie Newmar, and Leslie Parrish. The writer of this absurd plot asks us to believe that these beautiful (and rich) women have trouble finding husbands.

marriage between Gaynor and his best friend, Sonny Smith (Gig Young), a rich playboy. As for Newmar, Kirk pairs her to Harvey Wofford (Dick Sargent), an IRS agent. The third sister, as portrayed by Leslie Parrish, gets "matched" with her friend from childhood, Sam Travis (William Windom).

By now, the audience already knows the ending: Gig Young will move out of the way, and Gaynor will fall into Kirk's arms instead, and a triple wedding will ensue.

Although Kirk worked smoothly with the other actors, he became especially impressed with Leslie Parrish, a New Englander, who, after being a model, became a writer, producer, and, in time, a political activist, campaigning for civil rights, protesting against the Vietnam War and a defender of the environment in an era when heavy smog often blanketed Los Angeles.

Sargent received his widest exposure cast opposite Elizabeth Montgomery, as her husband in ABC's hit fantasy comedy, *Bewitched*. On "National Coming Out Day," in 1991, he declared his homosexuality and his support of gay rights.

The ever-lovable William Bendix, cast as Joe Fogel, played a chief of detectives, following Kirk around. Frequently cast as rough, blue-collar types in films and on television, he'd received a Best Supporting Actor Oscar for *Wake Island* (1942). He later nabbed the third lead in *Detective Story* (1951) with Kirk.

One day on the set, Kirk spotted Billy Halop, who'd been assigned a small, uncredited role in *For the Love of Money* as an elevator operator. In the late 1930s, he'd become a famous star cast in the *Dead End Kids* movies. He told Kirk that between gigs (which were rare), he worked as a registered nurse.

The saddest fate awaited Gig Young. Kirk had first seen him as Bette Davis' young beau in *Old Acquaintance* (1943). Young's best performance had been as an alcoholic in *Come Fill the Cup* (1951) with James Cagney. For

Left to right: Thelma Ritter, Gig Young, Dick Sargent, and Billy Halop. Thelma Ritter will become the mother-in-law of only one of these men.

471

it, Young was nominated for a Best Supporting Actor Oscar. He went on to co-star with Elizabeth Taylor in *The Girl Who Had Everything* (1953); *Torch Song* (1953) with Joan Crawford, and *Teacher's Pet* (1958) with Clark Gable and Doris Day.

In 1969, Young won the Best Actor Oscar for portraying the dance marathon emcee in *They Shoot Horses, Don't They?*

Alcohol finally took its toll in October 1978 in a Manhattan apartment. Young shot his fifth wife, Kim Schmidt, before fatally shooting himself. No motive for the murder/suicide was ever made clear. Kirk said, "The news passed over me like a shock wave."

***

For his company, Joel Productions *[a subsidiary of Bryna Production]*, Kirk acquired the screen rights for a murder mystery written by Philip MacDonald, one of the most widely read author of "whodunits" of the 1930s and 40s. The novel was entitled *The List of Adrian Messenger. [In other words, if your name was on that list, you were a target for murder.]*

Kirk turned to Edward Lewis, one of the chief officers of his subsidiary company, to produce it.

John Huston was intrigued with the project and agreed to direct it if some of the fox-hunt scenes were shot in Ireland, where he owned a country house. *[Huston was anxious to move quickly through this project because of his commitment to begin the filming of Tennessee Williams'* The Night of the Iguana *(1964), starring Richard Burton and Ava Gardner, in Mexico.]*

Many screen adaptations of MacDonald's murder mystery were submitted, but Kirk and Huston rejected all of them. Huston thought the veteran writer, Anthony Veiller, might be the man to adapt this complex novel into a script, but there was a problem: Huston was feuding with Veiller because he'd run out on him in Italy during the filming of *Beat the Devil* (1954), starring Humphrey Bogart and Jennifer Jones.

[Veiller and Huston had also pulled off a big hit movie, Moulin Rouge *(1952), starring José Ferrer as Toulouse-Lautrec.]*

Huston called a truce with Veiller, met with him, and discussed the complicated story line of *Adrian Messenger*. From the beginning, it was understood that many members of the cast, including Kirk, would be disguised and in some cases, cast into multiple roles.

A stew of intrigue and an outrageous melodrama, *The List of Adrian Messenger* boiled over with "accidents" that led to sudden deaths, a web of obscure clues, double-edged verbal sparrings, fox hunts, an airplane crash, and many detours in the story line, all of them rendered more complicated because of all those disguises.

Kirk was so intrigued with the artistic implications of his makeup that he went home after work one day, in disguise, and wasn't recognized either by his maid or by his sons, Peter and Eric. Anne, however, was far too smart to fall for his disguise.

Strong supporting players were lined up by Huston, notably George C. Scott, cast as a detective from Scotland Yard. The leading female character was portrayed by Dana Wynter, portraying Lady Jocelyn Bruttenholm. Herbert Marshall would play Sir Wilfrid Lucas, with Clive Brook as the Marquis of Gleneyre.

Cameo roles were often played by major-league actors in disguise. Frank Sinatra impersonated a gypsy. Robert Mitchum was a scheming Englishman who gets dumped into a river. Tony Curtis did double-duty as an Italian with an accordion and an organ grinder with a monkey.

Lancaster performed in drag as a matron protesting the fox hunt as cruel to animals. Under a wig and with heavy makeup, and looking large, he delivered one of the best lines in the film: *Read what Oscar Wilde says of a fox hunt: The unspeakable after the uneatable. That's what the so-called Gentry are, the unspeakable.*

[The List of Adrian Messenger *would be the fourth of seven films that Kirk would make with Lancaster.*]

The best makeup man in Hollywood at that time was Bud Westmore. He was charged with creating disguises for each of the big-name stars in the film. He arrived on the set with an arsenal of false chins, contact lenses, hairpieces, and "tons" of makeup.

At the end of the film, footage of each of them removing their masks was inserted as a revelation of their true identities. The effect was shocking for whichever fans had not yet figured out who they were.

In the most outrageous casting Kirk had ever conjured, he wanted Elizabeth Taylor to appear in a cameo as a grizzled, foul-mouthed old sailor. On the phone from Switzerland, she agreed to do it, and he flew a makeup artist to Gstaad for early rehearsals of her transformation.

He succeeded, but when everyone involved was confronted with the time and effort it would require, she decided not to go through with it. "Get Joan Crawford," she advised Kirk.

Kirk had first seen George C. Scott on Broadway in a drama, *The Andersonville Trial*. It had been produced by Bill Darrid, who had married Diana Dill, Kirk's first wife.

He was impressed with Scott's stage presence. An actor of rather unattractive features, he looked tough and had a gravelly voice. Growing up on the rough streets of Detroit, he would be asked to portray an English detective. Critics later pointed out that Scott, in the company of such Britishers as Clive Brook, Herbert Marshall, and Gladys Cooper, sounded "about as English as Nelson Rockefeller."

George C. Scott...beating up on Ava Gardner.

Scott startled Kirk when they first met by telling him that he'd learned all he needed to know about acting by watching Bette Davis on the screen.

He was still married to the very talented actress, Colleen Dewhurst. Kirk later met her a at a party following her divorce. "Scott's a fine actor," she said. "Heavy drinker. Wife beater. What else is there to know?"

Huston told Kirk, "Scott is one of the best actors alive, but my opinion of him as an actor is much higher than my opinion of him as a man. He told me he became an actor to escape his own personality."

By 1966, Scott would be directed by Huston in *The Bible*. In it, he'd be co-starring with Ava Gardner and beating her up at night.

Scott, in 1970, would win the Best Actor Oscar for his portrayal of General George C. Patton in the movie *Patton*. He'd become the first actor to reject an Oscar because he felt that all performances were unique, and that actors should not compete with each other based on such limited criteria.

Dana Wynter was *The List of Adrian Messenger's* leading lady. Born in Berlin to a British father and a Hungarian mother, she'd spent part of her youth in South Africa. A dark and elegant beauty, she had starred in the classic film, *Invasion of the Body Snatchers* (1956). Before working with Kirk, her co-stars had included Robert Taylor, Rock Hudson, Mel Ferrer, James Cagney, Robert Wagner, and Danny Kaye.

What most impressed Kirk about her was her marriage to Greg Bautzer, the celebrity attorney who had exposed Kirk's business manager, Sam Norton, as a crook. This "oasis of elegance," as Wynter had been called in the press, managed to snare Bautzer from the leading beauties of Hollywood, including Joan Crawford and Lana Turner. "She must have something concealed," Kirk said.

He told Wynter, "I will never divorce my wife, Anne, because she'll go to your husband, and I'll end up on the street after he finishes with me."

At the beginning of his newest film, the character portraying its namesake, Adrian Messenger (played by the Canadian actor, Jack Merivale) approaches Detective Gethryn (George C. Scott) of Scotland Yard. Messenger (Marivale) carries a list with eleven names of persons either already murdered or likely to be murdered soon. Each was or is in line to inherit a large fortune.

Then Merivale boards an airplane, which explodes and crashes into the ocean. Before dying, he whispers an important clue to the only surviving passenger, a former espionage agent, portrayed by Jacques Roux. Roux teams with Gethryn (Scott) to ferret out the murderer.

Dana Wynter...the actress who snared Hollywood's most eligible bachelor.

Early in the shoot, Merivale was invited to lunch by Kirk. He had previously been married to Jan Sterling, Kirk's co-star in *Ace in the Hole*. Since 1959, he'd functioned as the lover and caregiver of Vivien Leigh. "Viv has her good days and her bad days," Merivale told Kirk. "Mostly bad. But I love her and will always be at her side."

"I admire you for your loyalty and courage," Kirk said.

Coincidentally, Merivale was cast in *Adrian Messenger* alongside his stepmother, the distinguished and very formidable actress Gladys Cooper, playing Mrs. Karoudjian. Born in 1888, Cooper had begun her theatrical career in English music halls, advancing from there to appearances on the stage and screen in a career that thrived for seven decades.

Kirk had been impressed with her skill as an actress ever since he'd seen her cast as Bette Davis' domineering mother in *Now, Voyager* (1942).

After finishing *Adrian Messenger*, Cooper starred as the mother of Henry Higgins in *My Fair Lady* (1964), for which she won an Oscar nomination for Best Supporting Actress.

On the set, Kirk bonded with Mitchum, with whom he'd co-starred in *Out of the Past*. As a trio, with Huston, they discussed the tragic death of Marilyn Monroe, in August of 1962. All three speculated grimly that her death was not a suicide, but a murder.

Whereas Huston had directed Marilyn in *The Asphalt Jungle* (1950), Mitchum had co-starred with her in *The River of No Return* (1954). Kirk never made a film with the doomed star but had seduced her when she had wanted to co-star with him as the slutty waitress in *Ace in the Hole*. Ironically, all three of the men (Huston, Mitchum, and Kirk) had bedded

Marilyn at one point or another during her career.

Mitchum apologized to Huston for rejecting the role of the male lead in Marilyn's last picture, *The Misfits* (1960), the part going to Clark Gable.

"I hear Marilyn drove Gable to his early grave," Mitchum said. "If I'd taken the role, I might have saved Gable's life. If I'd worked with her, I could have kept her in line."

Incidentally, that was the day Mitchum demanded $75,000 for his brief cameo in *Adrian Messenger*. Huston countered by offering him an original painting by Paul Klee.

"No way!" Mitchum retorted. "The money, baby!"

Both Herbert Marshall and Clive Brooks had been big stars in their day, but the sun was setting on their lives and careers.

A Londoner, Marshall had been cast as Wilfrid Lucas. His heyday had been in the 1930s and '40s. Married five times, he had had a torrid affair with the vamp of the silent screen, Gloria Swanson. His co-stars had included Greta Garbo, Bette Davis, Marlene Dietrich, Katharine Hepburn, and Joan Crawford.

In World War I, a German sniper had shot him in the knee during the 2nd Battle of Arras in northern France. Doctors had to amputate his leg. With a prosthetic limb, he learned to walk without a limp, and went on to seduce all those ladies of the screen—and some off the screen—not just Swanson.

Another Londoner, Clive Brook, playing the Marquis of Gleneyre, made his farewell to the screen in *Adrian Messenger*. During his heyday, he'd been Dietrich's leading man in *Shanghai Express* (1932), and in time, he'd play Detective Sherlock Holmes on the screen three times.

As the plot grinds on, the remaining heir, who stands in the way of the

Clive Brook — Marlene Dietrich

Herbert Marshall with Gloria Swanson during his leading man heyday in the late 1930s	Clive Brook with Marlene Dietrich in a publicity still for *Shanghai Express* (1932)

villain's (i.e., Kirk's) inheritance of the fortune, is portrayed by Tony Huston, the first-born son of the director.

He told Kirk, "I can't remember when I was growing up of my daddy ever hugging me. But last night he let me sit on his lap."

In their reviews of *Adrian Messenger*, most of the critics were harsh. Although *Newsweek* defined it as "clever," *The New York Times* appraised it as "mediocre." John Russell Taylor pronounced it "a small joke of a film. The director was just amusing himself with a cheery disregard of his audience."

Judith Crist was kinder: "A fine first-rate murder mystery/suspense thriller to delight aficionados and to offer movie buffs added jolts of an encore."

Some critics denounced all those disguises as Huston's "gimmickry," complaining that the ploy detracted from the intricate murder plot.

Critic Andrew Sarris suggested that Huston "has gone sour, a forgotten man with a few actors' classics behind him."

***

"Frank Sinatra might have hosted JFK's inauguration gala *[January 19, 1961; one of the biggest parties ever held in Washington, D.C.]*, but Gene Kelly and I were co-masters of ceremonies for the event marking his second anniversary *[on January 18, 1963]* of JFK's presidency." Kirk said.

For that night in 1963, Kelly and Kirk had tapped A-list entertainers, including both Carols (Channing and Burnett), as well as Shirley Bassey, Yves Montand, opera diva Joan Sutherland, Peter, Paul & Mary, and others.

Kirk and Anne had planned to fly back to Los Angeles, until stormy skies over D.C. cancelled all outgoing flights. In a surprise move, Jacqueline and JFK invited special guests back to the White House for an impromptu party. Bobby and Ethel Kennedy drove Kirk and Anne to the party.

"It was very informal," Kirk said. "Most of us sat on the floor, and some of us, including myself, entertained."

Carol Channing sang, "Diamonds Are a Girl's Best Friend," and "Bobby and Jack" sang a song they'd learned in boy's camp so long ago," Kirk said.

Then their younger brother, Teddy, sang, accompanied on the piano by his wife, Joan.

"Stage fright be damned. I, too, was called upon to sing," Kirk said. "What else? Act?"

With his eyes directly focused on the regal-looking First Lady, Jacqueline, Kirk sang "I'm Red Hot Harry Brown, the Hottest Man in Town."

Anne always remembered the President stopping by her table and flirtatiously asking, "Aren't you with the wrong guy?"

That night in 1963, Kirk got to chat with the President for about fifteen minutes before he was summoned away. "He was completely unguarded," Kirk said, "Amazing in his candor."

"We have two titles in common," JFK said to Kirk. "You are called the Horndog of Hollywood. Well, I'm the Horndog of Washington."

The press didn't write about JFK's extramarital affairs then, but much of the Washington gossip vine and also the Hollywood vine knew about them. So did Kirk. He was aware they had even shared some of the same women: Marilyn Monroe, Marlene Dietrich, Gene Tierney, Joan Crawford, Hedy Lamarr, and Lana Turner.

Certain women had eluded Kirk's net but were caught up in JFK's trap: Janet Leigh, Jean Simmons, Kim Novak, and Audrey Hepburn.

Although he bragged in song that he was the "hottest man in town" to Jacqueline, he later admitted that he never achieved the woman of his dreams even after her divorce from Aristotle Onassis, when she was entertaining a number of beaux. "My fellow actors—William Holden, Marlon Brando, and Paul Newman—succeeded where I failed, even though I tried to reach her several times."

***

In February of 1963, Kirk and Anne flew to Rio de Janeiro for the annual Mardi Gras celebration. This was his first real exposure to how worldwide his fame and adulation were. "I was mobbed wherever I went. The world had seen my films. I wasn't used to this, but it seemed that everybody, both men and women, felt compelled to put their hands on a movie star."

One case stood out. As he and Anne got out of their limousine in front of a large reception hall for a costume ball, they tried to walk up the steps to the entrance, but a mob had formed. He was dressed in a skimpy *Spartacus* toga. Five muscular Brazilians had been hired to escort Anne and himself inside the hall.

"In spite of the guards, I was practically devoured by the crowd. Anne tried to hang on to me but was swept away by the mob. The guards pushed forward with me and had to lift me up a bit. I felt this strong hand groping me. I mean not only merely groping but feeling me up as intensely as masturbation. I'm sure such fondling could determine if I were cut or uncut."

"I was finally able to push away the hand of this groper only to stare into the face of one of my bodyguards. I hoped he'd enjoyed copping a feel. But who was going to protect me from the guards?"

"After that sexual assault, the burly guard assumed his duties and, along with his fellow guards, got me safely into the ballroom, with Anne following soon thereafter. My outfit went over great. No more groping for the rest of the night."

[Weeks later at a White House party, Kirk was introduced to Senator George Smathers of Florida. Standing tall and handsome, he was known in the U.S. Senate as "Gorgeous George." He also was the best friend of JFK.

Kirk was surprised at how candidly the senator talked about the President. "He must have trusted me," Kirk said.

"I love Jack," Smathers said. "But no one is off-limits to him—not your wife, your mother, or your sister. He told me he's not through with a woman until he has had her three ways."

"The Secret Service really has to protect him from his more voracious women admirers. Many of the hot-to-trot bitches try to grope him. The same thing happens to me. You see, I have a certain reputation for a certain asset of mine."

It was at this point that Kirk relayed the groping incident with the guard back in Rio.]

***

Back in Brazil, in Rio, Kirk received a telegram from Robert Kennedy, Attorney General of the United States. Since he was still in South America, RFK asked Kirk if he could represent the United States at a film festival coming up in Cartagena, Columbia. Kirk wired back that he'd be delighted.

Before that event, he and Anne had time for stopovers in both Belo Horizonte and its capital, Brasilia, Brazil's sixth and third most-populous cities.

As their plane was coming in for a landing in Belo Horizonte, Kirk looked out the window and spotted a large mob gathering at the airport, evocative of the newsreel footage he'd seen of Charles Lindbergh's landing in Paris after his historic flight across the Atlantic.

He asked a young male flight attendant, "What's all the excitement—all those people below?"

The steward must not have been much of a movie fan. He said that the mob had formed to greet the American movie star, Kirk Douglas."

"The little fucker didn't know who I was, but he soon found out."

A few days later, the reception that awaited him in Cartagena was even larger. Kirk was mobbed wherever he and Anne went.

When he returned home, he heard from both JFK and RFK, thanking him for such fine representation of the United States. He was asked if he would continue to be America's representative abroad in many other countries as part of other goodwill trips.

"I was more than willing to participate," Kirk said. "At his inauguration speech, the President had told us not to ask what our country could do for us, but what we could do for our country."

"When I wasn't shooting a film, I wanted to participate in these cultural exchange programs. I agreed to pay my own fare and not visit just to promote my latest film—that was just too commercial. Instead of an ambassador or a congressional delegation, people abroad wanted to see an American movie star."

***

For his next film, Kirk flew to Washington to acquire the screen rights to the controversial political thriller, *Seven Days in May*.

There, he was to meet with the authors of the book, Charles W. Bailey and Fletcher Knebel. Published in 1962, it became a best-seller, as defined by *The New York Times*.

During his time in Washington, the Vice President, Lyndon B. Johnson, invited him to a lavish buffet, along with many others, at his residence.

As a hungry Kirk was loading up a platter of hot food, he heard a familiar voice behind him.

"Are you really going to make *Seven Days in May* into a film?"

Kirk spun around with a certain embarrassment. After all, the plot revolved around a group of U.S. military leaders plotting to overthrow the U.S. President because he supported a nuclear disarmament treaty—and they feared a Soviet sneak attack.

"Yes, Mr. President," Kirk said.

JFK smiled. "Good, I want to see it on the screen. We'll even cooperate here at the White House. Jackie's against it, though."

***

Kirk had read *Seven Days in May* and thought it "will make one hell of a movie…and it's a chance to put a nail in the coffin of witch-hunting Senator Joseph McCarthy." He set about to acquire the film rights and made a deal between Seven Arts and his own Joel Production to finance it for $2,200,100 and for its distribution to be through Paramount. *[Ultimately, it was released in 1964.]*

His favorite producer, Edward Lewis, who had run Bryna Production, was tapped once again as producer of *Seven Days*. "I should have made him a partner. Maybe then he wouldn't have run away. He would listen patiently to all of my suggestions, and then wander off and do a scene his way."

In Washington, Kirk lunched with the authors of *Seven Days in May*, Bailey and Knebel. "They seemed skeptical of me."

At one point, Knebel mockingly asked him, "Why not call the film *Spartacus Goes to Washington?*"

Then Bailey wanted to know if Kirk "would make another of those political thrillers that had become such a cliché?"

Those remarks angered Kirk, and he stood up and tossed fifty dollars on the table. "I'm going to shoot a much better film than your god damn book." Then he stormed out of the restaurant, never to see the writers again.

Kirk personally selected Rod Serling to adapt the novel to the screen. The playwright, TV producer, narrator, and screenwriter was best known for his hit TV series, *The Twilight Zone* (1959-64).

Kirk thought he'd be ideal to tackle this controversial script, which the Pentagon did not want made. *[Serling was known in Hollywood as "the angry young man," having many issues opposed to censorship, racism, and war.]*

Kirk wanted to hire John Frankenheimer, a film and television director known for his social dramas and action/suspense movies. *[Kirk and been mesmerized by his latest political thrill, The Manchurian Candidate (1962), starring Frank Sinatra and Laurence Harvey. Nearly every major studio in Hollywood had turned down The Manchurian Candidate, but United Artists had taken a chance. It was the story of a Korean War veteran who had been brainwashed by Chinese communists to assassinate the U.S. President.]*

Frankenheimer wanted Paul Newman to play the scheming General Scott, but Kirk demanded—and got—Burt Lancaster cast into the role instead. It would be the fifth of their seven movies together.

After casting Lancaster, Frankenheimer threatened to walk off the picture, since he had just helmed him in *Birdman of Alcatraz* (1962), during which they had clashed bitterly. The director had vowed never to work with Lancaster ever again.

Kirk moved in as the peacemaker and assured Frankenheimer that he could control Lancaster's famous temper.

"But who will control Kirk Douglas' famous temper?" the director asked.

"As peacemaker, I succeeded brilliantly," Kirk said. "At the end of the shoot, I spotted Burt and Frankenheimer walking off the set hand in hand to make *The Train* (1964)."

To cement a deal with Lancaster, Kirk offered him his choice of two key roles: That of the chief of staff, General Scott, plotting treason, or else that of Colonel "Jiggs" Casey, who discovers the military's plot to overthrow the President because of his agreement to reduce the U.S. arsenal of nuclear arms, as proposed by the Soviets.

"I wasn't surprised when Burt took the role of the right-wing general, since it was a stronger part. Not only that, but, always, he would get star billing with me tagging along

Burt Lancaster and Kirk, a U.S. General and a Colonel at war (with each other) in *Seven Days in May.*

in second place. I hadn't often played nice guys, so this was a good change for me. Besides, I get to be the hero who discovers the plot to overthrow the President."

Lancaster's character as the general was best described by the *Daily Express:* "Burt Lancaster is the megalomaniac four-star general, crazy with patriotism, a crisp-talking Napoleon of the Atomic Age."

Frankenheimer claimed that the character portrayed by Lancaster was an amalgam of General Douglas MacArthur and Curtis LeMay (the real-life Air Force Chief of Staff), who was angry at President Kennedy for having refused to provide air support for the Cuban rebels during the American-supported Bay of Pigs invasion of Cuba.

The director recalled that he sustained many conflicts with Kirk during filming. "He was jealous of Burt. He felt he was playing a secondary role to him. I told him before we went in, he would be. He wanted to be Burt Lancaster all his life. In the end, it came to sitting down with Douglas and saying, 'Look, you prick, if you don't like it, get the hell out.'"

As for the rest of casting, Kirk and Frankenheimer were more or less in agreement. Both of them got Fredric March to play the weak, peace-loving President, Jordan Lyman.

[Kirk had long been a devotee of the films of Fredric March, considering him one of the finest actors on the screen. His heyday had been the 1930s and '40s when he had been a leading man cast opposite such screen legends as Carole Lombard. He had starred with Janet Gaynor in the original A Star Is Born *(1937). One of his biggest successes was in Samuel Goldwyn's* The Best Years of Our Lives *(1946).*

*In a bit of irony, Kirk would star in the remake of two of March's most famous roles—*Dr. Jekyll and Mr. Hyde *(1932) and* Inherit the Wind *(1960).]*

Another key role, that of Raymond Clark, went to Edmond O'Brien as an alcohol-addicted U.S. senator, a friend of the President. He flies to Fort Bliss, outside El Paso in Texas. From there, he drives into the desert to locate the secret military camp where the coup against the President will be launched. The senator is imprisoned.

[In 1948, O'Brien and March had co-starred in two movies together: Lillian Hellman's Another Part of the Forest *and* An Act of Murder.*]*

Despite three superb performances—Kirk, Lancaster, and March—only O'Brien received a Best Supporting Actor Oscar nomination.

Fredric March, looking presidential.

Character actor Martin Balsam, cast as the President's trusty assistant, Paul Girard, had been born in the Bronx Like Kirk, his parents were Russian Jews. Balsam would be forever remembered for playing Detective Arbogast in Alfred Hitchcock's *Psycho* ((1960), starring Anthony Perkins. Balsam would go on to win a Best Supporting Actor Oscar in *A Thousand Clowns* (1965).

Balsam, as Girard, flies to Gibraltar to confront Admiral Farley C. Barnswell, the commander of the Sixth Fleet, who had refused to join the conspirators against the President. He informs Girard of the plot and names the conspirators. Carrying this information back to Washington, Girard dies in a plane crash over the Atlantic.

John Houseman had produced many of Kirk's movies, but this time, he wanted to be an actor on the screen. In *Seven Days in May,* he was assigned the key role of Admiral Barnswell.

Kirk also had a reunion with two actors with whom he'd worked before: Richard Anderson was cast as Colonel Ben Murdock, one of the conspirators, and George Macready played Chris Todd, one of the members of the President's cabinet.

Hugh Marlowe, who had been the playwright husband of Celeste Holm in *All About Eve* (1950), was cast as Harold McPherson, a TV commentator, one of the conspirators.

"I thought Burt was my best friend, and I looked forward to spending time with him," Kirk said. "But, temporarily at least, Marlowe seemed to have taken my place as Burt's buddy-buddy." The two actors had bonded when they'd made two films together: *Elmer Gantry* (1960), and *Birdman of Alcatraz* (1962).

"Marlowe was a good-looking guy, and Burt was a bisexual," Kirk said. "From what I heard, Marlowe was a straight arrow, and I wondered if Burt were trying to convert him, at least during the shoot, to the other team. At any rate, Marlowe shared Burt's dressing room, and they seemed very, very cozy together."

"Poor Marlowe," Kirk said. "He was always being mistaken for another actor, Richard Carlson. They weren't related but looked like twin brothers. Naturally, they were always competing for the same roles."

The female lead for *Seven Days,* actually a minor role, was the character of Eleanor Holbrook. The authors based her on a real person, the 1930s mistress of General Douglas MacArthur, a beautiful Eurasian woman, Isabel Rosario Cooper.

Almost any name actress in the Hollywood Hills could have been summoned to play her, but Kirk wanted Ava Gardner. His passion for her had faded, but the friendship lingered on.

Many years had gone by, and she was not eager to return to Hollywood based on (her words) "so many bad memories." Kirk lured her back by dangling a six-figure salary for a six-day shoot.

Her role was almost type cast, that of a faded beauty of yesterday who was still alluring. She would play the former mistress of General Scott (Lancaster) who becomes involved with Kirk's character of Jiggs. [*Actually, he's seeking some indiscreet and politically compromising love letters Scott had written to her during the peak of their affair.*]

On the set, Ava had a reunion with Lancaster, her former lover and co-star in *The Killers* (1946), his film debut. Gardner would also be working again with Edmond O'Brien, her former co-star in *The Barefoot Contessa* (1954), which had also starred Humphrey Bogart. [*For his performance, O'Brien had won the Best Supporting Actor Oscar.*] Before heading to Hollywood, Ava told her sister, Bappie, "Perhaps I'll have a three-way with Burt and Kirk. None of us is getting any younger. Better do it now while the sun is still shining."

Although he embraced her warmly and was delighted to see her again, Kirk was alarmed to note that Ava's physical and mental state had deteriorated. She was no longer the love goddess of the world. Rita Hayworth, her rival, was experiencing even rougher conditions.

On the set, Ava's moods became mercurial and unpredictable. Her temper flared, often directly at Frankenheimer. Diplomatically, Kirk avoided getting in the middle of their fights, which turned raw and verbally violent. She demonstrated a potty mouth even more foul than that of Elizabeth Taylor.

Without proof, she accused the director of having a homosexual relationship with Kirk. "Is that why you favor him in every scene?"

When she saw the rushes, she was horrified. "Do you have to show every line in my face?" she screamed at him. "You went out of your way to show every imperfection. I look like shit. In a town populated with assholes, you win the dingleberry prize."

In her goodbyes with Kirk, she hugged and kissed him. Her final words to him were: "Yesterday is dead and gone, isn't it, *honey chile?*"

Two days before Ava's departure, reporters and a photographer from *Life* magazine invaded the set. When she saw them coming, Ava fled to her dressing room, claiming, "I hate that damn magazine." She had objected to the way *Life* had covered her affair and subsequent marriage to Frank Sinatra.

Lancaster, however, stayed behind and talked to the reporters. "I know you've heard about me. That I'm always difficult and grab the broads. I'm only difficult some of the time, and I grab only some of the broads."

"What about Kirk Douglas?" a reporter asked. "Is he the horndog everyone says?"

"Don't ask me, ask him," Lancaster responded. "He's never fucked *me.*" Then he paused. "Don't print that."

Pierre Salinger, press secretary to JFK, allowed a riot peopled with extras to be staged in front of the White House. But he made sure that the Kennedy family was in Hyannis Port the weekend of its filming.

Seven Days in May was shot during the summer of 1963, the last such season JFK would ever live to see. In addition to Washington, interiors were also shot in the Paramount Studios with location shooting in Paris, San Diego, Arizona, and California's Imperial Valley.

Lancaster hosted the award ceremony for the American Academy of Dramatic Arts. Before presenting Kirk, he said, "Kirk Douglas would be the first to admit that he is a very difficult man to work with." He paused. "And I would be the second."

For the most part, reviews of *Seven Days in May* were favorable, even though some critics found the plot unbelievable. *The New York Times* wrote: "It is a taut and exciting melodrama, as loaded as a Hitchcock mystery film and as seemingly documentary as Carol Reed's *The Third Man.* Kirk Douglas is sturdy and valiant as the colonel who smells out the plot."

The magazine, *Commonweal,* interpreted *Seven Days* as

Ava Gardner, a grand allure and beauty in decline, with Kirk in *Seven Days in May.*

485

"One of the most exciting films in years. Kirk Douglas stands out as the Marine colonel who discovers the plot."

Senior Scholastic predicted, "It might turn out to be the most exciting movie of the year."

Many conservatives attacked the film, including Harrison Carroll for the *Los Angeles Herald-Examiner:* "The advisability of such pictures, especially for the American image abroad, is controversial. I don't think the movie should have been made. The world is on too short a fuse."

"*Seven Days in May* is a perfect example of its kind, and I salute everyone who helped bring it about," wrote a critic for the *New Yorker.*

[The studio delayed its premiere to February 1964 so as not to look like it was capitalizing off the assassination of John F. Kennedy that previous November in Dallas.]

***

Like most Americans of that time, Kirk would remember where he was on November 23, 1963.

The night before, in Manhattan, he'd attended a dinner party with Frank Sinatra and his young wife, the very talented and smart Mia Farrow. "Ol' Blue Eyes is one lucky dude," Kirk said.

The next afternoon, he hailed a taxi and got into it. "Have you heard the news?" the driver asked.

"What about?" Kirk said.

"The President's been shot in Dallas."

Forgetting where he was going, Kirk exited from the cab and returned to his hotel suite. There, he remained inside for the next three days and nights, glued to the television set.

"I'm not ashamed," he recalled. "I cried and then I cried some more."

During the weeks ahead, he decided to honor the memory of a man he respected. He would carry through on a promise he'd made to JFK, who had entertained him at the White House.

In the interims between filmmaking, he would represent America on goodwill tours. In the years ahead, he'd tour with them in forty different countries.

Along with his multi-lingual wife, he would visit not just democracies, but communist nations, too. Even countries under the iron fist of dictators.

"We toured in both West Berlin and East Berlin," he said. "The people were free in the West, although always living with the fear of a possible invasion from the Russians. In East Berlin, a spy trailed us everywhere we went."

Kirk continued these tours under future President Lyndon B. Johnson, Richard Nixon (whose policies he deplored), Gerald Ford, and Jimmy Carter, who presented him with a medal of Freedom Award.

As time went by, details of this massive travel became a bit of a blur. As always, though, certain events stood out, as when Margaret Thatcher in London, "The Iron Lady," locked an iron grip on his arm, directing him along.

In India, he remembered Mrs. Ghandi, who kept looking at her watch as if she could not wait for their afternoon tea to be over. In what was then Yugoslavia, Marshal Tito sent a limousine to transport him to his villa in Ljubljana. There, the dictator confessed to him that his alltime favorite film was *Gunfight at the O.K. Corral.*

In London, *en route* home to L.A., he received a sultry, seductive phone call from Diana Dors, England's answer to Marilyn Monroe. She invited him "to come up and see me sometime."

"I wonder where she got that line?" Kirk asked.

In Athens, he discovered that the Queen of Greece (Anne-Marie of Denmark) was a devoted movie fan. "She was like a star-struck bobby soxer, of the type that chased after Frank Sinatra on Times Square in 1942."

Queen Anne-Marie seemingly adored Kirk and asked many questions about Hollywood movie stars. At dinner that night, Kirk was introduced to Constantine II, who had assumed the throne after the death of his father in 1964. Over the next decade, Kirk became friends with the King and Queen and was saddened when they were forced into exile after the abolition of the Greek monarchy in 1973.

"The King was a first-class sailor, the winner of an Olympic gold medal—and he took me sailing," Kirk said.

The last time he saw the King, Constantine had said, "Anne-Marie and my children are people without at country."

Kirk remained a strong supporter of Israel, a nation he defined as his favorite country outside the U.S. He had formed friendships there and met with its leaders.

He was fêted in Japan and met the King and Queen of Thailand. He bombed in a conversation with the King when he said, "What did you think of Yul Brynner as *The King of Siam*?

The King looked at him and said, "Our nation is Thailand. We don't call it Siam anymore."

In the Philippines, a young communist student stood up in the audience and asked, "What are you doing in our country? We're not your colony anymore."

"I'm here to let you know that America will stand behind you like it did in World War II when you needed American soldiers to lay down their lives for your freedom."

Once, in Istanbul, he encountered fifteen young and militant communists. They surrounded him unexpectedly, threatening him with violence.

Three security guards in plain clothes grabbed him and rushed him forward, shoving him into the rear of a limousine, into which they piled on top of him. A bullet was fired, shattering the rear window.

He found out later that the would-be assassin was arrested and never heard from again.

As Kirk told the press, "Let's face it. As you travel the globe, you won't be adored everywhere."

***

Born in Colorado to a dairy farmer who moved his family to Oregon, Ken Kesey was a countercultural novelist viewed "as a direct link between the Beat Generation of the 1950s and the hippie movement of the 1960s."

In 1960, he began work on his most famous novel, *One Flew Over the Cuckoo's Nest.* His inspiration derived from working the night shift at Menlo Park Veterans Hospital. He did not believe that all the inmates there were insane, but instead under the influence of hallucinogenic drugs.

Published in 1962, his novel was sent to Kirk in galley form. At first, he thought he was too busy to read it, but when thumbing through it he became intrigued.

Eventually, he paid Kesey $47,000 for the film rights. Kirk envisioned it first as a Broadway play and later, as a movie. Ironically, Jack Nicholson, who would later star in the movie, also wanted to option it but could not match Kirk's price.

Kirk suffered many setbacks in acquiring financing, but his belief in the story survived. The passage of the years have proven him right, especially when *Time* magazine named the book one of "the 100 Best Novels in the English language from 1923 to 2005."

Kirk hired Dale Wasserman to write the stage play, having known him since he wrote the first draft of *The Vikings.*

After tryouts in Boston, *One Flew Over the Cuckoo's Nest* opened at the Cort Theatre on Broadway on November 13, 1963, where it was not successful, running for eighty-two performances.

Kirk played the lead, the role of Randle Patrick McMurphy, with a supporting cast that included Gene Wilder, William Daniels, Ed Ames, and Joan Tetzel as the wretched Nurse Ratched. The cast had completed only nine performances before the world learned of the assassination of John F.

Kennedy in Dallas.

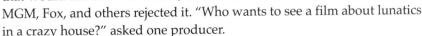

Two of New York's leading film critics more or less sounded the death knell for the play. Walter Kerr claimed, "It was written from the gut down." Howard Taubman of *The New York Times* dismissed it as "a crazy quilt of wisecracks, cavortings, violence, and historic villainy."

Undaunted by its failure on Broadway, Kirk struggled for the next ten years to find a studio that would finance it as a film, but Paramount, MGM, Fox, and others rejected it. "Who wants to see a film about lunatics in a crazy house?" asked one producer.

Finally, Kirk turned the project over to his oldest son, Michael, who had much better luck with it, despite some epic early struggles.

In a nutshell, *Cuckoo's Nest* was the story of a supposedly sane man who gets himself committed to a mental institution as an escape from criminal prosecution., Michael Douglas made a deal for its production with Fantasy Films, with distribution by United Artists, something Kirk was never able to pull off.

The producers, however, did not want Michael's father, age sixty, as its male lead, and ordered Michael, as the dealmaker, to come up with a younger actor. Marlon Brando was his first choice, but he rejected it. Gene Hackman and James Caan didn't go for it either. At one point "the cheap charisma" of Burt Reynolds was viewed as an asset, but no firm offer was ever made to him.

Finally, Jack Nicholson was cast into the role. He had been the first actor, other than Kirk, who recognized the dramatic possibilities of the character and the plot.

The next casting problem was the all-important role of the relentlessly hostile Nurse Ratched. A number of actresses were considered: Jane Fonda, Anne Bancraft, Faye Dunaway, and Geraldine Page. A relatively unknown actress was finally hired, Louise Fletcher, who had just completed Robert Altman's *Thieves Like Us* (1974).

It must have been a painful moment in Michael's life when

Kirk on Broadway in 1963 in a performance of the stage version of Kesey's novel. With him is Joan Tetzel as the evil Nurse Ratched.

he had to confront his father, informing him that he would not be assigned the role he had coveted for so many years and had virtually nursed for almost a decade.

When he heard this, Kirk exploded. "My own son has betrayed me. The part was *me*. I discovered it. It was my creation."

Whereas Kirk had failed, Michael succeeded, perhaps beyond his wildest dreams. The film version was both a critical and box office hit. The American Film Institute now lists it as No. 33 on its roster of "the 100 Best Movies Ever Made."

At Oscar time, it won for Best Picture, Best Actor, Best Director, and Best Screenplay. That had not occurred since *It Happened One Night*, in 1934, starring Clark Gable and Claudette Colbert.

"At first, I didn't understand why my desire to make this movie was being thwarted," Kirk said. "Why was God telling me 'no' over and over again?"

"But when Michael went up there to pick up his Oscar, I knew the answer was God laughing again: 'Dummy, this one is for your son.' Thank God for unanswered prayers."

He later recalled, "I made more money from *Cuckoo* than I did for any film in which I starred. But, get this, I would have happily given every red cent to have starred in *Cuckoo*. It was my baby."

***

As the 1960s rolled on, Kirk hustled a script by the once-blacklisted writer, Dalton Trumbo. Called *Montezuma*, it was the epic saga of how Hernando Cortéz conquered the once powerful Aztec Empire and held its ruler, Montezuma, captive. Even with John Huston signed on as director, Kirk could not sell it to any studio.

Around the same time, he was offered the lead in an upcoming film, *The Fall of the Roman Empire* (1964). His agents were shocked when he turned down an almost record $1.5 million.

Even without Kirk, it became a successful movie, starring Stephen Boyd in the role Kirk rejected opposite Sophia Loren. Anthony Mann directed with strong supporting players: James Mason, Alec Guinness, Christopher Plummer, Anthony Quayle, John Ireland, Omar Sharif, and Mel Ferrer.

Another more dubious offer came in from Timothy Leary, who wanted Kirk to star in a film about the story of his life and his sudden rise to fame in the 1960s.

A clinical psychologist at Harvard University, Leary was all the rage for his advocacy of the therapeutic potential for psychedelic drugs such as the "mind-expanding" LSD, under controlled conditions. Among celebrities, Cary Grant had become an early devotee.

Leary had already devised a title for his projected movie, *Turn On, Tune In, Drop Out*. Leary's odyssey was filled with lots of drama, including his seeing a jail cell thirty-six times.

Kirk was involved in other projects, and had no time to meet with Leary, although LSD intrigued him.

"Mind expansion?" he asked. "What man wouldn't get off on that?"

For years to come, Leary was referred to in other films, including Johnny Depp's *Fear and Loathing in Las Vegas* (1998). The film refers to heavy psychedelic drug use and mentions Leary.

Leary's *The Psychedelic Experience* (1964) was the inspiration for the John Lennon song, *Tomorrow Never Knows* (1966).

Later, Kirk felt he missed a chance to stay *au courant* by starring in the Leary movie. The public was turning to a new set of actors such as Paul Newman, Robert Redford, Clint Eastwood, Jack Nicholson, and Steve McQueen.

Although he had experimented briefly with marijuana, Kirk feared that his sons might become drug addicts. In the backyard, he destroyed the marijuana they had planted. His zealousness was based on fear for the life of his sons, as he reflected on the deaths of the sons and daughters of stars who had died of drug overdoses or committed suicide.

"The offspring of stars live in a fishbowl," he said. "They are envied by most of the world, given luxury, the most expensive education if they want it, vacations, sports cars, a wardrobe of their fantasy. In spite of that, children of stars don't have an easy life—and that's why so many of them want to end it."

A self-inflicted bullet had ended the life of Gregory Peck's son when he was thirty-two. Kirk knew the son of his close friend, the producer Ray Stark. He jumped out of the window of a tall building. Paul Newman's son had died of an overdose after years of drug abuse and erratic behavior. Marlon Brando's son Christian murdered his sister's lover, and she committed suicide. The son of Louis Jourdan chose drowning. The daughter of Carol Burnett overdosed on drugs.

Charles Boyer's son also committed suicide, as did his father. Carroll O'Connor's son killed himself. Perhaps most tragic of all, two of Bing Crosby's sons committed suicide. "Bing may have had something to do with that," Kirk said. "He was an awful father."

Kirk told the press, "I hope that fate doesn't happen to one of my sons."

Ironically, Kirk himself would one day contemplate suicide.

But at this point in 1964, he wasn't thinking of ending his life, but that of the wild beasts of Africa.

***

True, the Man's Magazine, had the largest circulation of all such competing periodicals. For publicity purposes, the editors decided to offer Kirk an all-expense-paid safari to hunt big game in Tanganyika and Kenya. He gleefully accepted the invitation and went out the next day to shop for "Ernest Hemingway drag."

Before embarking, two experts were assigned to teach him how to shoot. It came as a surprise that a man who'd made so many Westerns didn't know how to fire a gun. He proved to be not only a fast learner, but soon developed into a crack shooter, always hitting the bull's eye.

Off he went to what used to be called "The Dark Continent." He would later admit to being bloodthirsty, as he shot oryx (a species of antelope), gazelles, zebra, and a 1,200-pound eland. *[An elegant animal, an offshoot of the antelope family, an eland is often domesticated for its rich, nutritious milk. Africans also use its skin to make leather coats.]*

In ways later denounced by animal rights advocates, Kirk earned a reputation as "Killer Douglas," a title bestowed on him by the Masai tribe. For most of their existence, this Nilo-Saharan ethnic group of nomads became famous for their fearsome skills in battle and for their cattle-rustling. Protected by shields, they used spears for killing.

The Masai are one of the tallest ethnic groups on the globe, with an average height of six feet three inches. Impressed with Kirk's ability to kill animals, they made him a "blood brother" of their tribe.

He had already heard many stories of white hunters in Africa. One of his favorite movies had been *Mogambo* (1953), starring Clark Gable, Grace Kelly, and Ava Gardner.

Some of the tales he'd heard sounded preposterous. A tribesman told him that on occasion, some of the rich females on safari would demand that their white hunter/guide seduce them on top of a dying or dead animal recently slaughtered.

He was reminded of the Nina Foch character in *Spartacus,* who selected the most muscular of the gladiators to battle to the death for her amusement.

"Killing animals, at least for some, seems to be an aphrodisiac," he said.

Near the end of his safari, Kirk and his fellow hunters camped near the habitat of the Borana Oromo people. He was captivated by some of the young women, who walked about in topless sarongs, their beautiful, dark-skinned breasts exposed.

The males of the tribe led a leisure life, lying about as the women did all the work, gathering the food and even building their primitive huts. One day, Kirk joined the females and helped with their tasks. This caused him to be mocked by the males for doing "women's work."

At one point, he went really native and squatted with the local tribesmen to suck on the bones of a recently killed wildebeest.

The hunters wanted to show Kirk a herd of elephants, and they followed a trail of dung heaps until they came upon about 500 of these beasts. He was hoping to bring home tusks weighing about 125 pounds each.

As he trained his gun on one of the largest elephants, his guide yanked his rifle down. "Don't be a fool! Don't shoot! You'll start a stampede, and we'll be trampled to death!"

Kirk wanted to kill a leopard and use its skin to have a coat made for Anne. After waiting for hours, he stalked one, shooting and killing the animal in a tree. But then his guide told him he'd need four more leopards to make a coat. Instead of trying to shoot four more, he bought the skins from a tribesman who sold them to him, thereby, according to critics, encouraging an ongoing cycle of poaching and, ultimately, in some cases, extinction.

One of the highlights of his trip was a preview of *Spartacus,* screened at the largest theater in Nairobi.

Back in the safety of his California home, Kirk decorated his study with the mounted heads of some of the wild game he'd killed in Africa.

Months later, he was overcome with guilt for killing such beautiful animals, whose eyes seemed to be staring down at him, accusingly. He donated his trophies, including Anne's leopard coat, to the Museum of Natural History in Manhattan.

***

"Otto the Terrible"—that is, director Otto Preminger—set out to re-enact the Japanese attack on Pearl Harbor. The day it happened (December 7, 1941), according to Franklin D. Roosevelt, was "a day that will live in infamy." The film that emerged from that horrifying "binding-together" of the American spirit of war eventually emerged in 1965 as a movie starring Kirk, *In Harm's Way.*

As biographer Foster Hirsch noted, "Nothing about Preminger was small, trivial, or self-denying, from his privileged upbringing in Vienna as the son of an improbably successful Jewish lawyer to his work in film and theater in Europe and later, in America."

Like Kirk, Preminger had helped break the Hollywood blacklist when he hired Dalton Trumbo, the accused communist, to write the screenplay for his epic movie, *Exodus* (1960).

For his upcoming memorial to the events of December 7, 1941, Preminger did not intend just to focus on battle scenes. Instead, he compiled an anthology of personal stories that embraced themes associated with father/son generational gaps, adultery, rape, and suicide.

Its title derived from a famous quote by John Paul Jones, the Revolutionary War hero. "I wish to have no connection with any ship that does not sail fast, for I intend to go *in harm's way.*"

Preminger acquired the rights to the novel, *In Harm's Way*, from James Bassett, a columnist for *The New York Times*. During World War II, he had been a press aide for Admiral William F. Hasley. He'd also run two political campaigns for Richard Nixon—first, when he ran for a second term as Eisenhower's Veep in 1955, and again when he ran for President in 1960, but was defeated by Senator John F. Kennedy.

Preminger, as both producer and director, worked with Wendell Mayes to fashion a suitable screenplay for Sigma Production, with a distribution deal made with Paramount for a general release in 1965.

For the two male leads, he wanted John Wayne in top billing, with Kirk Douglas in the second lead. For the rest of the cast, he assembled an amazing list of yesterday's "has-beens," matched with some fresh new talent, too.

The movie opens on the Saturday night of December 6, 1941, hours before the unprovoked attack, early the next morning, on Pearl Harbor, home of America's Pacific Fleet. The plot moves along through the first year of the war, depicting infighting among the Navy brass with occasional "disreputable private acts by individuals."

Preminger was a left-wing liberal, and he knew in advance that Wayne was a champion of the Alt-Right. The Duke viewed Preminger's politics as Red [*i.e., dangerous and ultra-liberal to the point of communist.*] Yet each of the two men were dedicated professionals and planned to put politics aside and concentrate on making a good movie.

Cast as Captain Rockwell Torrey, Wayne commands a heavy cruiser known only as *Old Swayback*. Some twenty years ago, he bolted from his wife and son, preferring to roam the world as an enlisted man in the U.S. Navy.

His love interest in the movie is an "earth mother nurse," Lieutenant Maggie Haynes.

Wayne had been horrified when Gary Cooper, age fifty-five, had been cast as the romantic interest of Audrey Hepburn, twenty-six, in *Love in the Afternoon* (1957). "Coop looked like a grandfather making love to his granddaughter," Wayne told Preminger. "I don't want to make an ass of myself like he did."

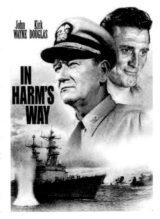

At first, the director had considered Deborah Kerr, who had done such a fine acting job as the adulterous Army wife in love with Burt Lancaster in *From Here to Eternity* (1953).

Preminger finally decided that he wanted to hire Patricia Neal for $130,000, even though she was recovering from a stroke. She was thirty-eight years old and Wayne was fifty-seven. He approved the choice because he had co-starred with her in 1951 in *Operation Pacific*. His appearance with her would mark the last time he made on-screen love to a younger woman.

[When Neal was coming down from her unhappy love affair with Gary Cooper in the early 1950s, she had dated both Preminger and Kirk.]

Kirk had been cast in the film as Commander Paul Eddington, Jr., chief aide to Wayne, his commanding officer, Rockwell Torrey. He was apprehensive about working with the Duke, fearing a clash of temperament and egos. Not only that, but he wondered if he and Preminger were compatible, too.

When Kirk arrived on the set to greet Wayne, whom he already knew, he would later agree with the description of him written by the biographers Randy Roberts and James S. Olson.

Wayne *"had turned fifty-seven before boarding the USS St. Paul on its voyage from Seattle to Hawaii, and he appeared every year of it. He was no longer middle-aged and fit. His eyes reflected a wet, cloudy luster, and the thick, heavy eyelids and jowly cheeks were those of an older man. At 260 pounds, he was corpulent, and he battled a vicious cough all through the summer of 1964. Loud, hacking, and persistent, the cough often interrupted shooting."*

The U.S. Navy hauled the cast, the crew, and most of their equipment aboard the *USS St. Paul* to Pearl Harbor. En route, Preminger shot several scenes on board. Once in Honolulu, he used the Pearl Harbor Naval Base as a virtual set for *In Harm's Way.*

Aware of Preminger's reputation as a tyrant, Kirk was prepared to stand up to him. On the third day of shooting, Preminger bellowed: "Douglas, get your ass over here. You fucked up that scene."

Kirk strode over to the director and confronted him, "nose to nose."

"Did you call me?" he asked, defiantly.

Preminger seemed to realize that, like Wayne, Kirk was not an actor to be bullied. After that, he accorded him the same respect he delivered to Wayne.

In the plot, Torrey (Wayne) defies orders and leads his crew in a disastrous attack on the Japanese invaders. But an admiral gives him a second chance, and this time, he succeeds, finding "redemption."

After the attack, Kirk's character of Eddington grabs Torrey's shoulder and with jubilation exclaims, "Oh, Rock of Ages! We've got ourselves another war! A gut-bustin', mother-loving Navy war!"

In this movie, Kirk was not the honorable soldier he'd been as Colonel Dax in *Paths of Glory*. His character, tormented and haunted by demons, is a cuckolded husband whose wife is nymphomaniacally involved in indiscretions with soldiers and sailors.

At the moment of the actual attack, she is killed on the beach, where she has gone to make love to Hugh O'Brian (TV's Wyatt Earp), an Army Air Force Major.

That drives Kirk into a rage, and he gets involved in a drunken barroom flight with Air Force officers. That lands him in the brig.

After his release, he's put in charge of piers and warehouses, a post he defines as "a backwater island purgatory."

As a subplot within the film, Wayne's son, Ensign Jeremiah (Jere) Torrey, arrives in Honolulu and Wayne doesn't even know him—he last saw him when he was a baby. Jeremiah loathes his father and is more dedicated to Commander Neal Owynn, to whom he has been assigned as an aide. The young man seems like an opportunist (and even worse), a pacifist, attacking "Roosevelt's trumped-up war."

At first, Preminger asked actor Keir Dullea to portray the young ensign, but he rejected the part. "I'd just made a war movie, and I didn't want to work with John Wayne."

In Dullea's place, Preminger hired Brandon De Wilde. He had impressed Preminger with his performance in Paul Newman's Western, *Hud*, with Patricia Neal. De Wilde was also remembered for playing Joey Starrett in the memorable Western, *Shane* (1953), opposite Alan Ladd.

Tragedy befell De Wilde both on the screen and in his private life. His girlfriend in the movie is Ensign Annalee Dorne, as portrayed by Jill Haworth. She is raped by Kirk's character, which leads to her suicide.

Afterward, consumed with guilt, Kirk embarks on a suicide mission to locate the Japanese fleet. He transmits its location before he is shot down, disappearing with his plane into the murky sea.

De Wilde comes to respect his father, but he, too, is killed tragically by Japanese gunfire.

[In his private life, De Wilde at the age of thirty was killed in a car crash in Colorado on July 6, 1972.]

An English actress, Jill Haworth, had worked with Preminger before, when he'd cast her into the role of Karen, the ill-fated Jewish refugee in love with Sal Mineo in *Exodus* (1960).

She later told the press, "John Wayne is the meanest, nastiest man with the worst attitude of any man I've ever worked with."

"Surely no actor was ever abused as much by Preminger as Tom Tryon," Kirk said. In his role of lieutenant William ("Mac") McConnell, he was attacked violently by Preminger for every scene he tried to perform. He had recently starred in Preminger's *The Cardinal* (1963).

Tyron told Kirk, "Making that movie was living hell. At times, I wanted to kill the Austrian bastard. My parents came to visit me on the set, and he fired me right in front of them just to humiliate me. He hired me back later that night."

In *In Harm's Way*, Tryon portrayed the frantically overburdened "Deck Officer" aboard the destroyer *Cassidy* on the morning of the Japanese attack. Later, his character is awarded with a thirty-day leave to return to San Francisco for a reunion with his wife, Beverly (Paula Prentiss), who feared that he'd be killed in battle.

[Tryon had served in the Pacific as a sailor from 1943 to 1946. Eventually, he would abandon movies altogether and become a best-selling novelist, many of his books adapted into films.]

The Belle of San Antonio, Texas, the statuesque Prentiss had her first big success in *Where the Boys Are* (1960). Her co-star was Jim Hutton, and they were so successful that MGM cast them together in three more romantic comedies. They were among the tallest stars on the MGM lot.

That same year, she'd starred with Peter Sellers in *What's New Pussycat?*. During its filming, she suffered a nervous breakdown and called a temporary halt to her movie career.

Since 1961, she'd been married to the actor/director Richard Benjamin.

Dana Andrews, suffering from alcoholism in real life, was given the role of Admiral "Blackjack" Broderick, a super cautious officer and not the most competent in the U.S. Navy.

Brandon De Wilde...doomed to an early death.

He'd been a major star in the 1940s, appearing in such hits as *Laura* (1944) and *The Best Years of Our Lives* (1946).

In real life, he had a sad end. Having suffered from Alzheimer's disease for years, he died in a clinic in Los Alamitos, California.

Another has-been, Bruce Cabot, played Quartermaster Quoddy. Cabot is still remembered for his portrayal of Jack Driscoll in *King Kong* (1933), opposite Fay Wray. He often appeared in Wayne's movies as one of Duke's "regulars." For years, Cabot had been one of the

Tom Tryon. Otto Preminger called him "a slimy faggot."

closest friends of Errol Flynn, living with him and attending the same orgies.

Yet another has-been, Franchot Tone, cast as Admiral Husband E. Kimmel, had been a big star in the 1930s, especially when he was married (1935-1939) to Joan Crawford. Tone had been nominated for an Oscar for his role in *Mutiny on the Bounty* (1935) opposite Clark Gable. In *In Harm's Way*, Tone played a politically motivated admiral, cautious of his reputation in Washington.

In a chat with Kirk, Tone said, "I guess you've had my former wife, Miss Crawford. Everybody else has had her, too. You've heard the joke about how First Prize is four years with Joan Crawford, and second prize is eight years with her."

[In spite of his put-down, Crawford came to Tone's aid in his final years, paying all his bills, including medical treatments. A chain smoker, he died of lung cancer in 1968.]

In a role inspired by Admiral Nimitz, Henry Fonda would star as the Pacific Fleet's Commander-in-Chief, the officer who gives Torrey (John Wayne) his second chance. "The role requires guts and gallantry, and Torrey is the man"

Kirk talked to James Mitchum, the oldest son of Robert Mitchum. James had been cast as Ensign Griggs. Kirk told him about having worked with his father in one of his first movies, *Out of the Past* (1947). Both of them related to the difficulties for sons of famous stars trying to follow in their father's footsteps.

Larry Hagman, cast as Lieutenant Cline, was the son of the fabled Broadway star, Mary Martin. His greatest fame would be in the future when he was cast as J.R. Ewing in the hit TV soap opera, *Dallas* (1978-91).

Hagman told Kirk, "I have the most gorgeous legs of any actor in Hollywood. I'd be great as an underwear model."

[The executives at BVD must have been alerted to his claim, because in the early 1980s, they hired him, outfitted in full J.R. Ewing drag, as a spokesperson for their underwear.]

Patrick O'Neal was cast in *In Harm's Way* into the unattractive role of Commander Neal Owynn, a former U.S. Congressman intent on doing as little as possible in combat. His goal is later to embellish his record, hoping to return to Congress as a war hero.

O'Neal had recently been tentatively cast as the male lead in Tennessee Williams' *The Night of the Iguana* (1964), losing the movie role to Richard Burton.

Franchot Tone with his wife, Joan Crawford, in the late 1930s

On the set, Kirk had a reunion with Carroll O'Connor, cast as Lieutenant Commander Burke. "I thought I killed you off in *Lonely Are the Brave*," O'Connor quipped.

Kirk and O'Connor also hooked up again with George Kennedy, who had also appeared with them in *Lonely Are the Brave*, a film that remained Kirk's favorite Western. In *In Harm's Way*, Kennedy played Colonel Gregory.

Burgess Meredith as Commander Egan Powell had only recently been directed by Preminger in *Advise and Consent* (1962) and *The Cardinal* (1963). He would soon be co-starring with Kirk in another movie.

An English actor, Stanley Holloway (playing Clayton Canfil), had just emerged triumphant from his Oscar-nominated role as Liza Doolittle's father (Alfred P. Doolittle) in *My Fair Lady* (1964).

Slim Pickens, as C.P.O Culpepper, is best remembered for his memorable role in *Dr. Strangelove* (1964).

Kirk was offended by the review that appeared in *Variety*: "John Wayne, not Kirk Douglas, is the big gun in *In Harm's Way*. Spartacus has met his match in the Duke."

In Kirk's final conclusion about Preminger, he said, "He's a bully and, as a director, only mediocre."

Movie critics then and now tend to agree that all three of the "big guns" bat-

Larry Hagman, star of *Dallas*, advertising men's underwear.

tling on and off screen in this movie—John Wayne, Kirk Douglas, and Otto Preminger—would be remembered decades later for films better and more powerful than *In Harm's Way*.

***

Back in California, Wayne called Kirk and asked him if he'd go for a long drive up the coast with him. He had something he wanted to discuss.

Kirk was surprised by the invitation—perhaps an offer of another co-starring role.

From behind the wheel, Wayne drove mostly in silence, as if not wanting to reveal what was on his mind. He stopped at the beach in Malibu and asked Kirk to go for a swim with him.

"I've come from the doctor," Wayne said. "I've got the Big C."

Kirk was shocked. Weighing 260 pounds, Wayne looked fairly robust, with red cheeks.

At first, Kirk couldn't speak. "I was too stunned by the news."

Duke said that he had submitted to detailed tests at the Scripps Clinic in La Jolla. "The doctors found cancerous lesions in one lung."

Kirk recalled that "I mumbled and fumbled, not knowing how to respond. Finally, he asked, "Are you going to go for cobalt treatments?"

"None of that shit," Wayne said. "I've ordered the doctors to remove one of my lungs. I undergo surgery in the morning."

"I didn't let on at the time, but I thought the sun was setting in the West for the Duke, who was coming to the end of a long trail that had begun so long ago in Winterset, Iowa, in 1907, when the world was a very different place."

"Duke not only survived, but the two of us would appear in two more movies together," Kirk said. "I thought of the Johnny Cash song about a father who names his son 'Sue.' Wayne's father had named him Marion, and his son learned to use his fists, growing up to face the taunts of boys who mocked him for having a girl's name."

CHAPTER FOURTEEN

IS PARIS BURNING?

KIRK HELPS SAVE THE CITY OF LIGHT
IT GENERATES LACERATING REVIEWS AND PLEASES NOBODY

HEROES OF TELEMARK

HEAVY WATER, HEAVY SNOWFALLS, HEAVY DRAMA

JOHNNY CASH

HOW THE COUNTRY MUSIC SUPERSTAR HANDLED
A GUNFIGHT WITH KIRK

THE LIGHT AT THE EDGE OF THE WORLD
& A KISS BEFORE DYING

VILLAINOUS FOES, HIGH DRAMA & THE MOB

THE ARRANGEMENT

KIRK TACKLES AN UNCONVINCING ON-SCREEN IMPERSONATION OF
ELIA KAZAN ALONGSIDE DEBORAH KERR & FAYE DUNAWAY

THE WAR WAGON

PLAYING TO THE ALT-RIGHT WITH JOHN WAYNE

Although some of his films—including one based on Elia Kazan's autobigraphical novel, *The Arrangement*—bombed at the box office, Kirk was still flexing his muscles as an actor and working to broaden his range.

In the scene above, he shares a drink with his character's mistress, as portrayed by Faye Dunaway, in a movie almost universally ridiculed by every critic in Hollywood.

Although a few years before, Kirk had fired Anthony Mann as the director of *Spartacus* (1960), there were apparently no hard feelings because an unexpected call came in from him offering Kirk the lead in a World War II drama, *The Heroes of Telemark*. It was the saga of a real-life World War II expedition in which Norwegian Resistance fighters sabotaged a crucial manufacturing plant in which the Nazis were making "heavy water." At the time, it was a key ingredient in their research for the development of atomic bombs, with the intention of destroying London, New York, and Washington.

Produced by Benjamin Fisz, the British movie, eventually released by Columbia in 1965, would be shot on location during the cold Norwegian winter. In addition to Kirk, leading roles had been assigned to Richard Harris, Ulla Jacobsson, and Michael Redgrave. *The Heroes of Telemark* would be the last film Mann ever completed. He died during the direction of his next picture, *A Dandy in Aspic* (1968), a Cold War spy thriller starring Laurence Harvey and Mia Farrow.

The plot had already been laid out more than once in book form, most importantly in *Skis Against the Atom*, the memoir of a Norwegian Resistance fighter named Knut Haukelid. Some additional scenes within the film were drawn from another published account, *But for These Men*, by John Drummond. The screenplay for the film was written by Ivan Moffat and Ben Barzman, with input from playwright Harold Pinter.

Kirk was cast as Rolf Pedersen, a Norwegian professor of physics, who prefers to "wait out the war," believing that the Allies will ultimately prevail. But he is drawn into the epic struggle by the local Resistance leader, Knud Straud (Richard Harris).

Together, they plot a commando raid to sabotage a Nazi-controlled facility for the manufacture of heavy water.

[Heavy water is a compound in which the hydrogen within a water molecule is partly or wholly replaced by the isotope deuterium. Whereas today, heavy water is used as a moderator in nuclear reactors, it was, during the early days of atomic research, something whose properties the Nazis were using in their development of an atomic bomb.]

Together, the Norwegian commandos plot a raid to sabotage a heavy water plant in the mountains. After they damage it, the Nazis quickly repair it and continue manufacturing heavy water. The Resistance plans a second sabotage and pull this one off when a ferry carrying the heavy water drums is blown up in the deepest part of a fjord.

Only after filming began did Kirk learn that Mann had wanted to cast

Stephen Boyd in his role. Coincidentally, Boyd had starred in *The Fall of the Roman Empire* (1964), a role originally offered to Kirk. *[At one point, the part was also offered to Anthony Perkins, and the Harris role was originally given to Cliff Robertson.]*

Boyd later sued Mann for $500,000, when the initial financing fell through. He claimed he could have taken four roles for "plenty of money" after signing with Mann.

The female lead in *Heroes of Telemark* went to the Swedish actress, Ulla Jacobsson, whose major claim to fame was that she had had the only female speaking role in *Zulu* (1964). She had also performed a nude scene in *One Summer of Happiness* (1951). When Kirk met her, and in reference to the brutal Norwegian climate, he jokingly told her, "You'd better keep your clothes on in this one. Baby, it's cold outside."

On the set, Kirk had a reunion with his former co-star, Michael Redgrave. Cast as "Uncle," the bisexual actor was the father of two actresses, Vanessa and Lynn. The actors had appeared together in Kirk's early film, *Mourning Becomes Electra* (1947), with Rosalind Russell.

An Irish actor, Richard Harris, competed with a fellow Irishman, Peter O'Toole, for which was the bigger boozer and womanizer. For *The Sporting Life* (1963), Harris had been nominated for a Best Actor Oscar.

Kirk and Harris hardly bonded, and Mann recalled that directing them was like "working on the slopes of an angry volcano. They didn't get along, as they were two different animals."

The Tourist Authorities of Norway defined *The Heroes of Telemark* as a useful representative of the best aspects of their nation.

As such, they illustrated the front cover of one of their tourist brochures with a likeness of Kirk and his (Swedish) co-star, Ulla Jacobsson,

"It was a battle from the beginning to the end," Jacobsson said. "They fought over camera position and to see which one could hog the scene. Harris constantly referred to Kirk as 'granddaddy.'"

"I'm bloody tired of you boasting about all the birds you've seduced,"

Harris told Kirk. "I'm fucking higher on the A-list that you. Right now, I'm banging Princess Margaret, who has agreed to sell me her Rolls-Royce Phantom at a very good price for services rendered."

Harris' final advice to Kirk was to say, "You've got to grab life by the balls."

The Heroes of Telemark did not do well at the box office. Audiences in the 1960s had grown bored with the endless round of movies about World War II. However, critics praised the film for its beautiful winter scenery in Norway and for its breathtaking skiing.

Richard Harris...boasting to Kirk of a brief fling with Princess Margaret.

***

"In the 1960s, I appeared in so many war movies, I was jokingly nicknamed 'General Douglas,'" Kirk said. "I saved the world a few times in *Seven Days in May, The Heroes of Telemark,* and in *In Harm's Way.* And later, I kept Paris from burning and liberated the State of Israel."

In London, Kirk was shooting the final interior shots for *The Heroes of Telemark* when a call came in from John Wayne. He wanted Kirk to play the lead of General "Mickey" Marcus, the military hero of the Israeli-Arab War of 1948. Wayne had already accepted a smaller role in this film, *Cast a Giant Shadow* (1966), a cameo appearance as the American General Mike Randolph.

The Duke told Kirk, "It's a real American story, a U.S. General who comes to the aid of a struggling little country."

After Duke made his pitch, Kirk accepted. "I'm a Jew. How could I not accept?"

The next day, Kirk read some biographical material about David ("Mickey") Marcus, an American-born Jew who emerged as a military hero in years that immediately followed the establishment of the Nation of Israel. Born on the Lower East Side of New York, Marcus went on to be graduated from West Point in 1924. For six years, he was stationed at Governors Island attending night classes at the Brooklyn Law School.

During the administration of Mayor Fiorello La Guardia, he was the New York City Commissioner of Corrections.

In World War II, on D-Day (June 1944) he parachuted onto the coast of Normandy as part of the invading Allied forces.

That same year, he assisted the American delegation when President Franklin D. Roosevelt met with Josef Stalin and Winston Churchill in Yalta, and again when President Harry S Truman negotiated with the same leaders at Potsdam in 1945.

Mickey was already retired when David Ben-Gurion asked him to help regiment the rag-tag Israeli Army. He'd be tasked with uniting two diverse forces— the *Haganah* and the *Palmach*—into a state-of-the-art fighting force. As a Jew, he felt duty-bound to answer the call.

In Israel, Ben-Gurion appointed him to the rank of *Aluf,* pointing out that he was the first general to lead a Jewish Army in two millennia. Mickey would eventually be honored as "the general who liberated Jerusalem."

A Mirisch-Llenroe-Batjac Production, with screenplay and direction by Melville Shavelson, the war movie was eventually distributed in 1966 by United Artists. Its story was based on the book by Ted Berkman, which had received rave reviews.

"Catch a Giant Shadow, was Melville's baby," Kirk said. "He was the force behind getting me cast."

MGM had originally optioned it, but gave way to mounting pressure from the Arabs, since the script presented them as "savages." Paramount also rejected it, an executive, Jack Karp, asking, "Who wants to go see a movie about a Jewish general?"

Shavelson answered the challenge by casting the movie so "It won't be too Jewish. That's why I brought in Wayne, and why I'm featuring other non-Jewish stars too, including a cameo by Frank Sinatra and the female roles going to Angie Dickinson of North Dakota and Senta Berger of Vienna. Yul Brynner also has a key part."

Kirk had long been a friend of Sinatra, and he was there to greet him when he landed at Lod Airport (now the Ben-Gurion). After he hugged and kissed Kirk, Sinatra asked him, "Have you lined up some hot Jewish broads for me?"

"It can be arranged," Kirk said. "I've got more than I can handle. Jewish girls are very beautiful."

Sinatra's role took only days to shoot. For his finale, his character (Vince, a "pilot of fortune") flies on a suicide mission over Arab tanks. Since he lacks an arsenal of explosives, during his flights over enemy territory, he drops clusters of soda siphons as "bombs. They go "bang" when they hit the earth. Many critics in their evaluations of the film called his flight "absurd."

Kirk met with Sinatra on his final night in Tel Aviv when a party was hosted in his honor. He told Kirk that an officer in the Israeli Army had lined up "two young, hot broads for me tonight," and that "I've fallen in love with this twenty-year-old chick, Mia Farrow."

Kirk met his two leading ladies, including Angie Dickinson, cast as his wife Emma.

[Dickinson, very famous at the time, was quoted as saying, "I dress for women, and I undress for men. I've never knowingly dated a Republican."

Her affairs had ranged from Sinatra himself to Johnny Carson. "She was getting ready to marry Burt Bacharach [composer and singer], so I didn't move in." Kirk said.

Dickinson's most prized possession was an autographed photo of the assassinated John F. Kennedy. It was inscribed to "Angie, the only woman I've ever loved."

Angie told Kirk that she'd just made The Killers (1964) in which Ronald Reagan, in his last movie role, played a villain.

Based on an Ernest Hemingway short story, it was a made-for-TV movie, but when viewed, it was evaluated as too violent and was released into theaters instead. It was a remake of the 1944 The Killers that had starred Kirk's friends, Ava Gardner and Burt Lancaster.]

In an attempt to attract more business at the box office, the screenplay of *Cast a Giant Shadow* included an adulterous love interest for Kirk in his portrayal of Mickey. Senta Berger, Austria's answer to Sophia Loren, was cast as Magda Simon. "Senta was gorgeous, but she was on the dawn of marrying the German film director, Michael Verhoeven."

Yul Brynner had been cast as Asher Gonen, a role clearly based on Moshe Dayan without an eye patch. Ferociously competitive, Brynner surprised Kirk by suggesting that when *Cast a Giant Shadow* was wrapped, the two of them should co-star in yet another movie together.

Kirk dismissed the idea, but by 1971, he and "Baldy," as he called Brynner, would be co-starring together in *The Light at the Edge of the World*.

The veteran actor, Luther Adler, played "Jacob Zion," his character obviously based on Ben-Gurion, the first Prime Minister of Israel, the familiar white hair projecting from both sides of his head.

On the set, Kirk had a reunion with the Scottish actor, James Donald, who had played his brother, Theo Van Gogh, in *Lust for Life*. Another British actor, Michael Hordern, known for his Shakespeare roles, portrayed the British ambassador.

As its director and producer, making this movie evolved into a nightmare for Shavelson. He later wrote a rather cynical book, *How to Make a Jewish Movie*.

Both of Kirk's sons flew to Israel to observe and help with the filmmaking. Joel became a sort of bodyguard, and Michael appeared on the screen in an uncredited role as the driver of a Jeep.

Gary Merrill was cast as the Pentagon's Chief of Staff, but all of his scenes were later deleted. He had divorced his second wife, Bette Davis, about four years earlier.

In spite of its good intentions and high hopes, *Catch a Giant Shadow* failed at the box office. "Our movie got to be pretentious," Kirk said. "It was top heavy with stars. I think in a sense they twisted the simplicity of the story. It had a wonderful subject, but I think we blew it."

The New York Times defined it as "a confusing, often superficial biography that leans a good deal on comedy and extremely salty dialogue and effects."

The *New York Sun* praised its "pro-Jewishness. Even so, it's an awful film from a technical standpoint and for its fictitious love interest subplot."

***

"There were just too many movie stars in *Is Paris Burning?*," Kirk claimed. "It was a great story, but we botched it up."

The saga of the 1944 liberation of Paris from the Nazis was one of the great dramas of World War II, with nuances that will be discussed by historians many centuries from now. Hitler ordered the retreating Germans to raze Paris to the ground, like Warsaw. But his own general defied the mandate.

Based on a book by Larry Collins and Dominique Lapierre, its script was written for the most part by Gore Vidal and Francis Coppola. It was financed by Transcontinental Films and Marianne Productions and pre-

sented by Paramount-Seven Arts-Ray Stark as a release in 1966. Producer Paul Graetz pulled off the almost impossible, winning the approval of the Mayor of Paris to shut off large sections in the heart of the city during the summer of 1965 for location shooting.

To re-enact the epic struggle, Graetz even "enrolled" the assistance of the French Army and use of the Jeeps and tanks that were deployed in the historical events associated with the film. He also hired thousands of extras outfitted in 1940s clothing.

All this may have been too much for Graetz, who died at the age of 65 before the film's completion.

As his replacement, René Clément, one of the most acclaimed directors in France, was hired. He'd already won two Oscars for "Best Foreign Language Films," *Walls of Malapaga* (1950) and *Forbidden Games* (1952). "I predict that the story of the liberation of Paris will be my crowning glory." *[Regrettably, he had no talent as a fortune teller.]*

Once again, Kirk was cast as a ferociously strong-willed military leader—in this case as General George S. Patton. Ray Stark offered him $50,000 for a day's shoot, for which he delivered an electrifying performance as the egotistical, foul-mouthed Allied commander.

[An odd coincidence unfolded four years later, when Coppola, as screenwriter, crafted a film treatment for a biopic about the famous general as portrayed in the 1970 film, Patton. *It led to Coppola's Oscar for Best Original Screenplay. George C. Scott would also win an Oscar as Best Actor. Kirk, always competitive, was jealous.*

Coppola would soon follow all that with his directorship of The Godfather *(1972), starring Marlon Brando. It revolutionized movie-making in the gangster genre.]*

In *Is Paris Burning?*, a grizzled and corpulent Orson Welles portrayed the Swedish counsel general, urging restraint from the retreating Nazis.

A French real-life husband-and-wife team, Simone Signoret playing a café owner and Yves Montand as Marcel Bizien were also in the film, with Billy Frick cast as Hitler. Glenn Ford portrays U.S. General Omar Bradley.

The French heartthrob, Alain Delon, cast as Jacques Chaban-Delmas, captures the brutish Nazi general. One critic compared Delon's acting to that of Frank Sinatra in one of his military roles.

Anthony Perkins, [aka psychotic Norman Bates of the Bates Motel], appeared briefly as the owner of a café. Charles Boyer, the French former matinee idol, also appeared in a cameo as Dr. Monod. His memorable screen roles, for which he'd been nominated for four Best Actor Oscars, were a distant memory.

Jean-Paul Belmondo, as the historic figure of Yvon Morandat, leads the French Resistance. During the course of the fighting, he commandeers the Hotel de Matignon, the official residence of the French Prime Ministers, and declares it the seat of the provisional French government.

In an odd but poignant cameo, Leslie Caron portrays Françoise Labe, the frantic wife of a political prisoner. As he's being herded onto a train headed for Buchenwald, despite her valiant efforts to enlist the support of bureaucrats who might get him released, he's shot down on the platform of a railway station.

In a brief appearance on screen as General Edwin Sibert, Robert Stack could speak to the crew in French. [Although born in Los Angeles, his parents moved to France and he learned French before he learned English.]

George Chakiris, known for his role in West Side Story (1961), has a brief cameo as a character identified only as "G.I. in a tank."

One of the key roles, that of the Nazi General in control of Paris, was an actual German, Gert Fröbe, who played Dietrich von Cholitz. He's been ordered by Hitler to raze Paris before the Nazi retreat. To that effect, bombs have been positioned at key points throughout the city, ready to be detonated on command.

Von Cholitz ultimately decides that he doesn't want to be remembered as the man who destroyed Paris, and after lots of jockeying, he passively waits for his arrest by the Allies.

[Fröbe had joined the Nazi party in 1927 and was later drafted into the German Army

Before tackling the role of Von Cholitz, Fröbe had earned international "bad guy" acclaim for his performance in the title role of Goldfinger (1964), the James Bond thriller.]

As the high drama comes to an end, the streets of Paris are filled with the cheering of newly liberated masses. In the general's headquarters, a phone receiver is off the hook. Through it, far away and enraged, we hear the voice of the Führer bellowing "Brennt Paris?" ["Is Paris Burning?"].

509

In London, Alec Guinness went to see the film at a movie theater in Leicester Square, later remarking, "All that the audience did was spot the celebrities, calling out their names."

Is Paris Burning? flopped at the box office.

***

A.B. Guthrie, Jr. wrote a Western novel, *The Way West,* in 1949. It won the Pulitzer Prize for Fiction the following year. In 1967, it became the basis for a film of the same name, starring Kirk, Robert Mitchum, and Richard Widmark.

The novel was one of a series by Guthrie dealing with the Oregon Trail and the development of Montana beginning around 1830, with a close look at the rise of the cattle empires of the 1880s and beyond. *[The first novel published in the Guthrie series was The Big Sky, which had already been adapted to the screen in a film starring Kirk back in 1952.]*

Producer Harold Hecht *[not to be confused with Ben Hecht, the Hollywood writer]* acquired its screen rights and made a distribution deal with United Artists. He hired Ben Madlow and Mitch Linderman to write the brawling, two-fisted screenplay.

Hecht in the 1930s had been one of the leading producers, dance directors, and talent agents in Hollywood. Eventually, he formed a production company with Burt Lancaster, who had remained Kirk's best friend. That had led to Hecht casting the two macho stars together in *The Devil's Disciple* (1959) alongside Laurence Olivier.

Hecht now found himself director of *The Way West.* He hired London-born Andrew V. McLaglen, the son of Victor McLaglen, a famous star of early films who had won a Best Actor Oscar for *The Informer* (1935).

Andrew, despite his British heritage, was known for his directorship of American Westerns and adventure films, many of which starred James Stewart or John Wayne.

Kirk had been cast as the male lead, a former senator, William Tadlock, who leaves his home in Missouri in 1843, heading west on the Oregon Trail in a covered wagon.

Robert Mitchum accepted a role in it too. Although he had made a brief appearance with Kirk in *The List of Adrian Messenger,* the two men hadn't worked together in any big way since *Out of the Past* when Mitchum was the star and Kirk the lead supporting actor. In *The Way West,* the situation was reversed, with Kirk getting star billing.

Mitchum was cast as Dick Summers, a hired guide who presumably knows the tricks, traps, and layout of the Oregon Trail. He is reluctant to

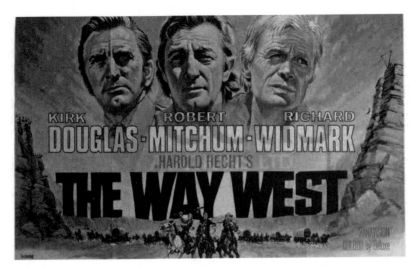

go along, but finally accepts, appearing on the screen surly and droopy-eyed.

Director McLaglen said, "Kirk and Bob were miles apart personally. Bob was an easy-going type of guy, and Kirk very temperamental and volatile, quick to explode, while Bob sat by enjoying his weed. There was no feud between them, but I felt Bob was definitely not one of Kirk's favorite guys like Burt Lancaster. The two stars never expressed to me their resentment of each other, but I knew it seethed beneath the surface."

In his memoirs, Mitchum painted an unflattering portrait of Kirk: "I learned my lines, and every now and then some guy would show up with new lines Kirk wrote last night. I would drop them on the floor. To hell with his new stuff. He threw his tirades, a lot of bullshit. He was the asshole of the company, but not dumb enough to provoke a confrontation with me. All I had to do was whack him one between the horns, and it'd be all over. *And he knows that!*"

According to McLaglan, "Bob lobbied to get his younger brother, John, a small role in the movie, playing little Henry."

"John became better known for appearing in the first three *Dirty Harry* movies," McLaglen said. "I had dinner with the two brothers one night, and they talked of their early struggles, rising out of poverty. When they hit Hollywood, John confessed, 'we hustled the queers, with Clifton Webb being our best paying customer.'"

Richard Widmark's rivalry with Kirk had begun during their early years on the stage in New York when they were up for the same roles. "There was no love lost between those two," McLaglen said. "They didn't fight, but the tension between them was obvious to the other cast members and crew."

Acrid and aggressive, Widmark played the third male lead, Lije Evans, a farmer. "He knew his day as a leading man was fading, and he was taking whatever roles he could get," McLaglen said.

In the plot, Widmark is married to the character portrayed by Lola Albright.

"Lola had been one of Kirk's early conquests when they had co-starred in his hit, *Champion*."

Lola Albright (left) and Sally Field, as they appeared in *The Way West.*

McLaglen said. "They were friendly at their reunion, but whatever passion they had back in the 1940s now seemed at low tide."

Albright was nearly killed during filming of a dangerous river-crossing scene. Her wagon tipped over in the raging waters, trapping her underwater when part of its load fell on her. Three men on the shore jumped in to save her life.

Pulled out of the water, semi-conscious, she was rushed to the nearest hospital. When she recovered, she was informed that her scene had been reshot with a stunt woman. She later told the press, "I'm still traumatized by my near-death drowning. I'm haunted by it. I came very, very close."

Evans' [i.e, Widmark's] teenaged son, Brownie, was played by Michael McGreevey. He falls for a young girl, Mercy McBee, portrayed by Sally Field, who is sexy, saucy, and flirtatious. At this point in her career, Field was trapped in 1960s sitcoms that included *Gidget* (1965-1966) and *The Flying Nun* (1967-1970), a TV series defined by Paul Mavis at *Drunk TV* as "one of the most noxious sitcoms to ever come down the pike."

Her character is raped by a sexually frustrated young farmer, Michael Whitney, cast as Johnnie Mack. *[Whitney had just starred as Wild Bill Hickok in a 1965 episode of* Death Valley Days *hosted by Ronald Reagan. In 1983, as the estranged husband of the British actress and model Twiggy, he died of a heart attack in a Manhattan restaurant at the age of 52.]*

While assaulting Field, Whitney fires his rifle at what he thinks is a wolf, but which turns out to be an Indian boy hiding in a wolf's skin. His father, an Indian chief, wants revenge or else his tribe will attack the wagon train. Kirk, as Tadlock, has the rapist hanged as a means of saving the other pioneers. This leads to an undying hatred from the rapist's wife, Amanda, cast with Katharine Justice. She gets her revenge on Tadlock when he's making a descent by rope down a steep gorge. Brimming with venom, she cuts the rope, and Tadlock (Kirk) plunges to his death.

The Way West was the first big budget Western since John Wayne's *The Big Trail* (1930) to depict pioneers lowering a wagon train over a cliff with ropes.

Two leading men of yesteryear, Patric Knowles and William Lundigan, both survivors of Errol Flynn's casting couch, had a reunion during the filming of *The Way West*. Knowles was cast as Colonel Grant and Lundigan played Michael Moynihan. Nostalgic for old times, they spent nights together on location in Tucson, Arizona and in Oregon at sites that included the Crooked River Gorge.

[An English actor, tall and handsome, Knowles enjoyed his heyday in the 1930s as a secondary leading man. The swashbuckler (Flynn) introduced him to same-sex parties and drunken bashes, and cast him in many of his movies, including The Charge of the Light Brigade *(1936) and* The Adventures of Robin Hood *(1938).*

Although rather bland, Lundigan, too, had had a brief reign as a leading man, appearing in Love Nest *(1951) with Marilyn Monroe and in* I'd Climb the Highest Mountain *(also 1951) with Susan Hayward. He'd been in other wagon train Westerns before working with Kirk. Flynn had cast him as the reckless brother of Olivia de Havilland in* Dodge City *(1938).*

It was widely known that William Lundigan also ended up in Flynn's bed on numerous occasions. When he met Lundigan for the first time at a party, he was very blunt: "You're my type, sport. I'm taking you home tonight."]

The Way West had a lot of minor supporting players whose faces were familiar to movie-goers at the time. Kirk encountered Jack Elam—"the creepiest face I've ever seen"—with whom he had worked in a previous western, *Gunfight at the O.K. Corral* (1957).

In the role of Sam Fairman, Stubby Kaye, a comedian, is best remembered for playing "Nicely-Nicely" in *Guys and Dolls* (1955) with Marlon Brando.

Nick Cravat, cast as "Calvelli," was one of Burt Lancaster's closest friends. He often appeared in his movies such as *The Crimson Pirate* (1952).

Harry Carey, who played "Mr. McBee," was the son of the veteran character actor Harry Carey, Sr. (1878-1947). As a child, he learned to speak Navajo and was nicknamed "Adobe" because of the color of his hair. In 1944, he'd married Marilyn Fix and was still wed to her at the time of his death in 2012. In all, he appeared in some ninety films, including two with Marilyn Monroe: *Monkey Business* (1952) and *Gentleman Prefer Blondes* (1953).

He told Kirk, "I heard you once banged her. I never did."

Ken Murray, cast as "Hank," was a comedian and radio/TV personality. His most remarkable screen performance had been in John Ford's *The Man Who Shot Liberty Valance* (1962), starring John Wayne and James Stewart. Murray became better known for shooting home movies of the stars, catching them at leisure, as he did with Jean Harlow, Charlie Chaplin, and Mary Pickford. Murray asked to film Kirk in the shower, but his request was rejected.

The Way West came under fire from critics and did not perform well at the box office. However, the scenery of Oregon won high praise.

Roger Ebert wrote, "All these pioneers weren't clean-cut heroic types with a yen for adventure. They were marginal farmers, bankrupt businessmen, religious zealots, parolees, visionaries, con men, and, of course clean cut, heroic frontier types once in a while. Some of them went west to be tin hat Napoleons and two-bit empire builders."

Bosley Crowther of *The New York Times* denounced it as "hackneyed hash from Guthrie's novel. It is so stagy and unrealistic that it makes an old Western fan want to scream. Kirk Douglas, high-minded and hammy, stands on elevator shoes and delivers speeches about establishing a Utopia in Oregon."

***

John Wayne continued to lure fans into movie houses across the country and abroad. Despite his poor health, he had decided to endure an involvement in yet another rigorous Western, in this case, the project that evolved into *The War Wagon*.

He had long considered Clair Huffaker as the best Western author in the business, and he read his 1957 novel *Badman*. Then he contacted him to purchase the screen rights and to hire him as the scriptwriter, providing he would agree to change its film adaptation to *The War Wagon*. A deal was also struck with Universal-International for its release and distribution in 1967.

Naturally, Wayne cast himself in the lead role of "Taw" Jackson, an infamous gunfighter wrongly jailed for three years. Fresh out of prison, he seeks revenge on the man who put him there. "I'm tired of playing good guys," Wayne told Huffaker.

Jackson (i.e., Wayne) had been double-crossed by Frank Pierce (Bruce Cabot), a corrupt businessman who had stolen Wayne's land while he was in jail, and then discovered gold on the property.

Wayne and Cabot were close friends, even though in *Angel and the Badman* (1947), he had tried to kill Duke. Wayne used Cabot in his movies whenever he could, including their upcoming *The Green Berets* (1968).

Kirk also had worked with Cabot before, when they made *In Harm's Way*.

Pierce (Cabot) needs to ship the gold that by rights belonged to Jackson (Wayne). Aware of what a tempting target the gold shipment would be, he plans to transport it to a nearby city's bank in an iron-plated stagecoach that's protected with a Gatling gun and with four guards inside. Riding along is a rifleman on top, plus a "posse" of twenty other cowboys.

The "Iron Stagecoach" was constructed as a prop from plywood that was painted to look like metal. Metallic sound effects emanated from it during the opening and closing if its "heavy iron doors."

To pull off the robbery, Jackson knows that he'll need another sharpshooter/gunfighter like himself. He turns to a former enemy, "Lomax," as portrayed by Kirk. *[Lomax is weighing a simultaneous offer from Pierce (Cabot), wherein he'd promised $12,000 if he'd kill Wayne. Lomax weighs both offers and decides that a life of crime would be more profitable and opts for an alliance with Wayne, instead.]*

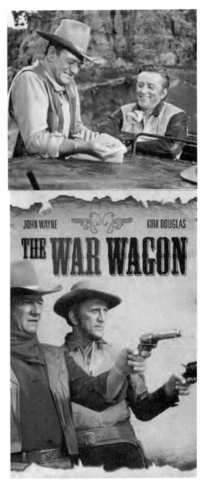

When Wayne offered Kirk the role of Lomax, he was amazed at how quickly he accepted, even agreeing to second billing.

As a team, Wayne and Kirk round up some fellow thieves and castaways to help them steal the gold. The other robbers include Robert Walker, Jr. as an alcoholic explosives expert; and Keenan Wynn as a mean old codger with a beautiful young wife, as portrayed by Valora Nolan.

[The battered hat, a design associated with the Confederate Cavalry, that Wynn wore in many of his scenes in The War Wagon *had, years before, been worn by Leslie Howard when he'd starred as Ashley Wilkes in* Gone With the Wind *(1939). Wynn had purloined it from MGM's wardrobe department and wore it in his 1942 screen test for MGM. He tried to work it into every picture he made, with the belief that it was a good luck charm. As the film's "crazy old man," Wynn was*

actually nearly a decade younger than Wayne.]

A casting oddity in *The War Wagon* involved Howard Keel portraying an Indian chief, "Levi Walking Bear." When Kirk heard that, he couldn't believe it. "Howard Keel, an Indian! You gotta be kidding!"

[He had known this former MGM musical sensation whose bass-baritone had rung out in Annie Get Your Gun *(1950) and in* Seven Brides for Seven Brothers *(1954).]*

On the set, Kirk had a reunion with character actor Gene Evans, cast as Deputy Hoag. They had worked together on *Ace in the Hole.* "Those Arizona boys are tough *hombres,*" Kirk said. He congratulated Evans on his recent performance as "Bat" in *Dr. Strangelove* (1964).

The film's leading female role, such as it was, starred Joanna Barnes as "Lola," a woman of easy virtue.

Flying to Durango, Mexico, for location shooting, Kirk had not seen Wayne since he'd had his lung removed. Seated next to him on the plane, he noticed that the Duke, midway through the flight, had to rely on an oxygen mask.

In Mexico, the two actors met their director, Burt Kennedy, who specialized in the Western genre. Critics charged that he always went for the easy laugh.

On the second day of shooting, Kirk noticed that Wayne seemed to be taking over all aspects of the film. A few days later, alert to the trend, Kennedy told Kirk, "From now on, I plan to let him direct himself."

Barroom antics and macho posturing lead to fist fights in a hellish barroom brawl. Wayne estimated that it was his 500th on-screen fight.

Kennedy also told Kirk that he was getting ready to help Henry Fonda in his next picture, *Welcome to Hard Times* (1967). *[Kirk would also be starring with Fonda in the near future.]*

Back in the early '50s, in preparation for his role in *The Juggler* (1953), Kirk had learned to juggle. In *The War Wagon,* he demonstrates his skill at juggling six-guns. He also made some great leaps onto the back of his horse, although he had to use a tambourine *[i.e., springboard]* to get airborne. "Not bad for a guy who's reached the Big 5-0," Kirk said to Kennedy.

[The director later told the press that he surrendered half his salary to be able to afford Kirk.]

To add a touch of flamboyance to his character, Kirk decided to wear a black glove, on one finger of which he placed a large ring.

When Wayne saw that, he asked, "Are you gonna play a queer?"

During the snapping of publicity shots in Hollywood, Kirk held up production to film a commercial endorsement of Democratic Governor Edmund G. Brown. To retaliate, Wayne showed up late for work the next day, having taken time out to shoot a commercial for Brown's Republican opponent, Ronald Reagan.

For its era, *The War Wagon* did well at the box office, taking in $10 million in domestic sales. It reigned briefly as one of the biggest-grossing films of the season.

Critic Roger Ebert gave it three out of four stars, noting that it had was "that rarity, a Western filmed with quiet good humor." The critic also claimed that the picture set a first for nudity in a Western, depicting Wayne in his long johns and Kirk wearing only his gun belt.

After the movie was wrapped, Kirk said, "John—I never called him Duke—and I never became friends. We didn't see eye to eye on most things, especially politics. He gave Kennedy a lot of trouble. Very very bossy."

Kennedy recalled, "There was a definite rivalry between the Duke and Kirk. They were two roosters fighting over only one chicken. Both of them tried to hog the camera, and each of them wanted to be the center of attention, always trying to upstage the other. I doubt very seriously if they'd ever work together again."

In spite of these negative comments, Wayne later was asked which male actors he found most compatible to star in a film with. "I can answer that," he said. "In overall favorability, I'd name (in this order) Dean Martin, Robert Mitchum, and as a distant third, Kirk Douglas."

***

As the turbulent 1960s neared its inglorious end, Kirk was one of the busiest actors in Hollywood, turning out one film after another. None of them was memorable.

Richard Barton Lewis, the film producer, writer, and co-founder of Trilogy Entertainment, offered Kirk the lead in a routine police drama, *A Lovely Way to Die*, a film released through Universal in 1968.

["Lewis was one big shot," Kirk said. "In his career, he would generate more than $1.2 billion in revenue from sixteen major movies such as Robin Hood: Prince of Thieves *(1991), starring Kevin Costner, and more than 300 hours of primetime television. His pictures would win more than 135 Oscar, Emmy, Golden Globe, and other entertainment awards. In 2007, he was still going strong, with such pictures as* August Rush, *starring Robin Williams.]*

A Lovely Way to Die was a fairly routine police drama that could have starred any number of actors in Hollywood—Richard Widmark comes to mind, even Tony Curtis.

David Lowell Rich was hired to direct Kirk in the role of Jim Schuyler, a cop who quits the force rather than face a grilling about how tough he was on criminals.

The script by A.J. Russell evoked the role Kirk had played way back in 1951 in *Detective Story*. The tough, world-weary cop in *A Lovely Way to Die* (1968) was based, however, on a much weaker script.

[In an era of political upheaval marked by, among many other tragedies, the assassinations of both Robert F. Kennedy and Martin Luther King, Jr. theaters were awash in roughly similar films. In the same year as A Lovely Way to Die, *Clint Eastwood starred in a crime drama,* Coogan's Bluff, *and George Peppard filmed* P.J. *In both of them, in ways similar to the plot of Kirk's film, a bodyguard was needed to protect the life of an endangered woman.]*

In *A Lovely Way to Die*, Kirk meets with a quick-talking criminal lawyer (Eli Wallach) named Tennessee Fredericks. He hires Kirk to protect the life of Rena Westbrook (Sylvia Koscina), the wife of a recently deceased multi-millionaire. She's about to go on trial on a charge of murdering her husband for his money. Her lover, Jonathan Fleming (portrayed by the English actor, Kenneth Haigh) is also implicated.

Brooklyn-born Wallach, with his raspy voice, could play almost any role he wanted. He was a graduate of the Actors Studio and fascinated Kirk with stories of working with Marilyn Monroe and Clark Gable on their last picture, *The Misfits* (1961).

Kenneth Haigh had stories to tell about appearing with the Beatles in *A Hard Day's Night* (1964). He had come to prominence playing Jimmy Porter in the premiere of John Osborne's play, *Look Back in Anger* (1956), but lost the movie role to Richard Burton in 1959.

The year of 1968 was a high point in the career of the beautiful Yugoslav actress, Sylvia Koscina. In addition to co-starring with Kirk, she played opposite Paul Newman in *The Secret War of Harry Frigg* (also 1968). She's also remembered for her role as the bride of *Hercules* (Steve Reeves) in 1958.

Koscina had been uninhibited about stripping, which she did for a photo layout in the American edition of *Playboy* in 1967. She'd go on to star in *l'assoluto naturale* (1969), featuring a notorious nude love scene that made the movie famous in Europe.

Cast and crew noted that Kirk, though happily married, was spending a lot of time in Koscina's dressing room.

As her on-screen lover, Haigh noted, "Kirk was probably needed to help Sylvia get undressed. What man wouldn't? She was a doll."

Ali MacGraw made her film debut in this routine melodrama in an uncredited walk-on.

Critic Roger Ebert wrote: "The screenplay of *A Lovely Way to Die* has holes in it large enough to slip Sidney Greenstreet through sideways. Kirk Douglas, who has run into some bad movies lately, does a better job than this one deserves. Director Rich must be responsible for a shot that many people thought belonged in the Old Cliché's home. While the lovers embrace, the camera coyly pans to a window. And—yes—the curtains are waving in the breeze."

***

Executives at Paramount were so disappointed with the box office receipts of Kirk's next movie, *The Brotherhood* (1968), that they were reluctant to make any more organized crime movies. *[Frequently skeptical, partly as a result of the dim performance of* The Brotherhood, *it took enormous work to persuade them to shoot* The Godfather *(1972), starring Marlon Brando. As the world knows, it became an international triumph. Kirk did not have such luck.]*

The original draft for *The Brotherhood* was written by Lewis John Carlino. Kirk asked Martin Ritt, a rival from yesteryear, to direct it.

Ritt was no friend of Kirk's, their feud dating from when both of them had tried to launch a film about Spartacus. When Kirk barged ahead and began shooting, Ritt had abandoned his attempt to shoot *The Gladiators* with Yul Brynner as his star.

Even though he didn't like Ritt personally, Kirk admired his talent, as had been evident in his direction of *Hud* (1963) starring Paul Newman and Kirk's friend, Patricia Neal. Ritt had also directed Richard Burton in *The Spy Who Came In From the Cold* (1965).

Kirk admired Ritt for surviving the Hollywood blacklist. He'd bounced back after five years in exile from the film colony, during which time he taught acting at Actors Studio.

At first, Ritt refused Kirk's offer, but when Kirk—as producer of the film—devised a revised screenplay, Ritt finally signed on.

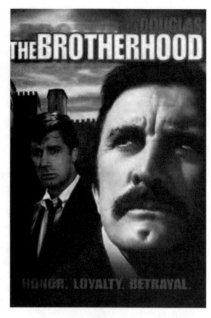

Kirk admitted, "We never became buddies—far from it, and we certainly had our artistic differences. But we got through the picture with no internal injuries."

Before flying to Italy, Kirk began to transform himself into the persona of his character, a Mafia gangster, Frank Ginetta. He dyed his hair jet black and grew a mustache.

From Rome, he booked a flight to Naples and rested for three days on Capri before taking a boat to Palermo, the capital of Sicily, where most of the film would be shot. As he stood on the deck as the boat approached that island, he was disappointed by the sight of all the floating defecation, garbage, and used condoms in the polluted waters of the harbor.

He had lined up an impressive cast, headlined by Irene Papas cast into the role of his character's first wife, Ida. A child of Greece, she would have a career that stretched over half a century and seventy films, including *The Guns of Navarone* (1961), *Zorba the Greek* (1964), and *Z* (1969).

She was a tall woman, and he feared she would tower over him. He had known of her "secret affair" with Marlon Brando in 1954, and he wondered if she'd be sexually attracted to him.

As it turned out, she was not, although she did say she admired his acting, having seen some of his movies.

Roger Ebert, in print, had evaluated her looks and talent: "She is a great actress, her unusual beauty not the sort of your typical superstar. Ordinary actors have trouble sharing the screen with her. Her presence in movies inspires a cult following."

[Years after co-starring with Papas in The Brotherhood, *Kirk learned she was*

Irene Papas portraying Helen of Troy in *The Trojan Women* (1971) *still alive and inquired about her, hoping she was still in good health. Her aide informed him that for the last five years, Papas had been suffering from Alzheimer's disease.]*

The third lead, that of Kirk's younger brother in the film, Vince Ginetta, starred Alex Cord. He later became well known for appearing in fifty-five episodes of the hit TV series, *Airwolf* (1984-85). Stricken with polio at the age of 12, Cord had bounced back by horseback riding in the wilds of Wyoming.

In *The Brotherhood*, the Mafia ordered Cord to seek out his older brother (Kirk), in exile at the time in Sicily, and murder him.

The movie poster advertising *The Brotherhood* depicted Alex giving Kirk the Mafia "kiss of death." That led to stupid protests about the movie's alleged homosexual overtone, which infuriated Kirk. "My younger brother is about to assassinate me, not fuck me."

One critic called Cord "a lightweight actor, but he does have one thing going for him: The beginning of a chin dimple much like that of Kirk Douglas."

In an extended flashback, happier times are depicted. Kirk welcomes his brother back from Vietnam, where he'd served in the Army. He subsequently marries Emma Bertolo (Susan Strasberg). The father of the bride is Dominick Bertolo (Luther Adler), a Mafia don. Kirk's character had also been a Mafia don. *[Kirk had previously worked with Adler when he'd played David Ben-Gurion in* Cast a Giant Shadow.*]*

One critic noted that Adler's "Sicilian sounded Yiddish."

Kirk engaged in several talks with Susan Strasberg, the hard-driving daughter of Lee Strasberg of the Actors Studio. She had once been one of Marilyn Monroe's close friends.

When he met Susan, she was coming down from a disastrous, drug-soaked marriage to screen heartthrob Christopher Jones, voted by one gay magazine as "The Sexiest Man Alive."

The Brotherhood ends tragically. Kirk, no longer in favor with his Mafia bosses, dies when his brother shoots him. Many viewers objected to the tragic ending.

Kirk enjoyed meeting character actor Eduardo Ciannelli, who played an aging Mafia don. Kirk said to him, "I've spent many a Saturday afternoon in a dark theater, munching popcorn and watching you emote with Joan Crawford, Clark Gable, Bette Davis, Anthony Quinn, Sophia Loren, Marlon Brando, and Robert Taylor."

Vincent Canby of *The New York Times* wrote that "Douglas' Italian accent is not easy on the ears, but he is always in command of a tremendous, effective vitality." That faint praise hardly attracted hordes to the box office. *The Brotherhood* opened and closed in most theaters quickly. If that weren't disappointing enough, Kirk, its star and producer, suffered personal condemnation for having made it in the first place.

The Americans of Italian Descent defined *The Brotherhood* as "a disgraceful spectacle that denigrates, slurs, defames, and stigmatizes 22 million Americans of Italian descent."

The National Italian League to Combat Defamation filed protests that were even stronger.

***

The Arrangement, released in 1969, began as a novel, published in 1967 and authored by the noted director, Elia Kazan, the driving force behind the stage versions of many of Tennessee Williams' plays. An unexpected runaway best-seller, it was a semi-autobiographical story of an advertising executive whose life is falling apart.

Living with his wife, Florence, in an affluent suburb of Los Angeles, Eddie Anderson, portrayed by Kirk, suffers a nervous breakdown and drives his sports car into an oncoming truck. Miraculously, he survives the crash and enters a period of long convalescence where he begins to examine his life.

"Life," he muses, "is only a series of arrangements"—hence, the title.

In a memorable scene with Florence, Kirk tells her, "I don't like my life. I don't like what I've done with my life. I don't like my home."

Much of the novel was torn from the pages of Kazan's own life. Born in Constantinople (now Istanbul) in 1909 under the Ottoman Empire, he eventually moved to America. Here, he became, in the words of *The New York Times*, óne of the most honored and influential directors on Broadway and in Hollywood."

During the course of his career, Kazan would direct 21 actors to Oscar nominations, resulting in nine wins. He'd first won a Best Director Oscar for *Gentleman's Agreement* (1947), which dealt with anti-Semitism and starred Gregory Peck.

He'd had spectacular success directing James Dean in *East of Eden* (1955), and had even more success helming Marlon Brando in *A Streetcar Named Desire* (1951); *Viva Zapata!* (1952), and *On the Waterfront* (1954).

Originally, Brando accepted the lead in *The Arrangement* and even told Kazan to order special wigs from a wigmaker in Rome. Kazan had not seen him in some time, but to judge from his photos, Brando needed to take off some weight so that, as Eddie, he would look "lean and mean."

After the assassination of Martin Luther King, Jr. in 1968, Brando summoned Kazan to "drive up the hill and see me."

When Kazan pulled into the parking area of Brando's house, the actor was already waiting for him out front. He didn't invite Kazan inside, but talked to him briefly.

Walking Kazan back to his car, Brando informed him

Elia Kazan's
The *Arrangement*

The girl knew about the wife...
The wife knew about the girl...
It was all part of the arrangement!

so frank, so daring,
so shocking, so brilliant.

elia kazan's **the arrangement** x

a film written and directed by elia kazan starring **kirk douglas · faye dunaway**
deborah **kerr · boone · cronyn**
music composed and conducted by david amram · produced by elia kazan from his novel 'the arrangement'
technicolor® panavision® from warner bros.

Warner LEICESTER SQUARE 437 3423 **NOW**

that he was dropping out of *The Arrangement* because he wanted to devote all his time to the civil rights movement. Then Brando kissed Kazan long and passionately—perhaps in tribute to the creative work they'd accomplished during the course of their early careers—and walked alone back toward his house. That was the last time Kazan ever saw him.

"I was deeply disappointed, considering how successful Marlon and I had been working together," Kazan said. "He was the heart and soul of my best work."

The title role called for Eddie to undergo endless scenes of blame, guilt, disintegration, hysterics, and self-analysis, and Kazan felt that only Brando could pull all of that off.

Then an unexpected call came in from Kirk, informing Kazan he wanted the role. After mulling it over, the director acquiesced.

"Brando could suggest depths of feelings that Kirk could not—and I knew that, but I didn't have any other actor in mind. Shooting had to begin."

"*The Arrangement* was my baby," Kazan said. "Not Kirk's. I was the producer, director, and writer of the screenplay. He was known for trying to direct every picture he was in—but not this time."

Kazan had assigned the role of Eddie's wife, Florence, to the Glasgow-born actress Deborah Kerr.

Although she seemingly tolerates his having a mistress, she's not without her schemes. She goes to the family lawyer, Hume Cronyn, cast as Arthur, and then maneuvers Kirk into designating her as his agent with power of attorney over his business affairs. Then she commandeers the

Even if the critics (and Kazan, too) didn't appreciate how Kirk handled his role in *The Arrangement*, there was by now a soulfulness in his demeanor that could only be the result of oceans of pain and a new world-weariness that some fans believe added to his allure.

On the left side is Deborah Kerr, cast as his wife.

family's home on Long Island and immediately evicts Kirk's father. In retaliation, Kirk goes wild and burns down the house.

[*Cronyn, long married to actress Jessica Tandy, would soon be co-starring with Kirk in his upcoming film,* There Was a Crooked Man.]

[*Kerr was one of the best actresses with whom Kirk would ever work. During the course of her career, she would be nominated six times for a Best Actress Oscar. One of her biggest hits had been* The King and I *(1956) with Yul Brynner.*

One of Kirk's favorite movies was From Here to Eternity *(1953) in which Kerr had appeared in that iconic beach scene, making adulterous love to Kirk's friend, Burt Lancaster.*

At this stage in his life, Kirk didn't plan to go after her like Lancaster did. He did say, however, "I have never appeared with an actress of such grace and beauty."]

In the role of Gwenn, Kazan cast Faye Dunaway. Critic Vincent Canby said, "She looked so cool and elegant that the sight of her almost pinches the optic nerve. She plays what's described as 'the office tramp.'"

In the beginning of *The Arrangement*, Dunaway is separated from Kirk, but he wants her back as his mistress. There's a problem: She's taken a new lover, Charles (John Randolph Jones).

It was with some misgiving that Dunaway accepted the part. Described as a "bullshit detector," her most memorable line was "The fucking I'm getting is not worth the fucking I'm getting."

Kazan based her role on the second of his three wives, actress Barbara Loden, to whom he was married from 1967 to 1980. [*He had married her at around the same time as the publication of the novel on which his film was based, and it can be argued that she had encouraged and inspired at least some of its content.*] She was visibly furious at him for not standing up to the brass at Warner Brothers and for "caving in" to their demands that Dunaway portray the character she had desperately wanted to play onscreen.

[*Loden had starred on Broadway in Arthur Miller's* After the Fall, *based on the life of Miller's late ex-wife, Marilyn Monroe. Ironically, in 1974, Dunaway would star in the Loden role in a made-for-TV remake of that same play.*]

Kirk had some provocative nude scenes with Dunaway in both a bed and on a beach, "I feared I might get an erection," he said.

Variety was the first to headline a story that Kazan was going to break A-list movie ground by presenting his stars—Kirk, Kerr, and

The mistress: Faye Dunaway

Dunaway—frontally nude. They would be naked but would not reveal their genitalia. Or would they?

In a beach scene, Kirk saw Dunaway strip down. She had covered the nipples of her breasts and her vagina with pasties. "He roared at me like Spartacus," she said, "claiming that my pasties were just going to get in the way. I decided he was right, and off they came."

"I didn't make any headway with Faye," he claimed. "She was madly in love with the Italian heartthrob, Marcello Mastroianni."

Kazan had told both Kirk and Dunaway that the role he'd written would be their crowning achievement. He was wrong. Some critics thought *The Arrangement* was one of Kirk's worst pictures.

Of course, Dunaway would achieve far greater glory for her roles in *Bonnie and Clyde* (1967), *Chinatown* (1974), and *Network* (1976).

In the tabloids, Dunaway was also splashed across the pages for her love affairs, notably with Marlon Brando, Michael Caine, Steve McQueen, and Jack Nicholson.

She once said, "I have had work, possessions, love, sex, and men. I work during the day, and I share my bed at night because I need love and sex—but never one without the other."

In Rome, Mastroianni told a reporter, "I have loved many women, but Faye Dunaway was the one I loved the most."

As dictated by the plot, as the price his character paid for loving Gwenn (Dunaway), he gets shot by her jealous lover, Charles. He survives.

Kazan was only ten days into the shoot when he realized how perfect Kerr and Dunaway were in their roles, and "how wrong Kirk was. But we were too far gone into production for me to find a new leading man. I survived. But would my film?"

In New York, the character played by Kirk visits his sick and dying father, Sam (Richard Boone), who was actually a year younger than Kirk. "Both of those scene-stealers tried to see who could hammy the other," Kazan said.

The plot reveals that the father (portrayed by Boone) had been a tyrannical father to his son (Kirk), and that his mother Thomna (Anne Hegira) had been overly protective.

[Kirk and Boone had co-starred together before in Man Without a Star.*]*

Cast as "Finnegan" by Kazan, Charles Drake had dreamed of stardom but never graduated from the status of a supporting player. His peak year was 1950 when he'd appeared in two hit movies, each starring James Stewart: *Winchester '73* and *Harvey.* As major stardom had eluded him, he took what roles he could get before his ashes were scattered in the Pacific in 1994.

On the set, Kirk had a reunion with Barry Sullivan, his former co-star in *The Bad and the Beautiful.* He was shocked to find him appearing in an uncredited role as Chet Collier. In his heyday, he'd been a leading man to Lana Turner, Joan Crawford, Bette Davis, and Jane Wyman. "When you climb the Hollywood ladder, you must descend rung by rung sometime," he told Kirk.

When *The Arrangement* was released, critics sharpened their nails. Vincent Canby of *The New York Times* called it "slightly absurd" and compared it unfavorably to Kirk's *Two Weeks in Another Town.* "A mess of borrowed styles" was another charge against Kazan.

Variety pronounced it "dead on arrival—confused, overly contrived, and overlong, peopled with characters about whom the spectator could care less."

The Cleveland Press defined it as "A bad novel that didn't improve much in its transfer to film." *The Monthly Film Bulletin* claimed that "Kazan's film turns out to have said no more in 125 minutes than it stated during the first six."

Long after the film opened to failure, Kazan wrote a note to Kirk. "*The Arrangement* was a disappointment to me, as it must have been for you. I say what I have to say in my novel."

The Arrangement marked the end of Kazan's own career as an A-list player in Hollywood. Sadly, the same could be said about Kirk, who would go on to appear in more than thirty-five more films. But although he continued to work, even after a stroke, until 2011, his glory days were over.

60¢ Paperback Library 63-522

Once upon a time
there was a crooked man.
When he was good,
he was very, very good.
And when
he was bad...
it was
murder.

THERE
WAS A
CROOKED MAN

A Novel by David King
Based on a screenplay by David Newman and Robert Benton

NOW A SPECTACULAR WARNER BROS. MOTION PICTURE
STARRING Kirk Douglas AND Henry Fonda

***

Kirk had not talked with director Joseph L. Mankiewicz since the late 1940s when he had helmed him in *A Letter to Three Wives.* Since then, he'd gone on to direct such classics as *All About Eve* (1950). Not only that, he was behind the success of some of Kirk's favorite movies, including *The Barefoot Contessa* (1954), starring Humphrey Bogart and Ava Gardner, as well as *Suddenly, Last Summer* (1959) with Montgomery Clift, Elizabeth Taylor, and Katharine Hepburn.

At first, Kirk thought Mankiewicz was calling to cast him in a first-rate melodrama, perhaps within a Hollywood setting. "But after five minutes, I believed I had John Ford on the wire. Joe wanted me to star with Henry Fonda in a very gritty, very cynical Western set in the dying days of the Old West in the 1880s. Released in 1970, its title was *There Was a Crooked Man*.

"When I read the script two days later, I accepted." It was the first film script written by David Newman and Robert Benton since their success with *Bonnie and Clyde* (1967).

Kirk repeatedly read and re-read his role of Paris Pitman, Jr., a ruthless villain and bandit who wears steel-rimmed glasses and is a bundle of explosive energy, plotting and scheming.

Although the script did not call for it, he dyed his hair red. As a post-Civil War scoundrel, he lines up a small group of masked marauders.

He plays this roguish criminal with a deadly charm, and did so with a certain relish, as if actually enjoying being such a nefarious character, spinning an intricate cobweb of confidence trickery—and not afraid to murder his own men.

In his memoirs, Henry Fonda does not even mention Kirk or *Crooked Man*. Fonda had agreed to accept second billing for his portrayal of a former sheriff, Woodward W. Lopeman, who becomes the warden of a notorious hell hole prison isolated in the desert.

[Fonda had already appeared in the brief role of a World War II Admiral in Kirk's In Harm's Way.]

Kirk revealed in a memoir that back in the late 1940s, he had first resented Fonda when he escorted, as his date, a beautiful young starlet to his first Hollywood party. She later disappeared, without telling him, but not before he spotted her exiting through a rear entrance with Fonda and his best friend, James Stewart.

"It was obvious that the bitch was a star-fucker and had tossed me aside for these two big stars. Perhaps they were fading into the night for a three-way. Fonda and Stewart had lived together as aspiring actors in a small room in Manhattan, and Hollywood gossips have buzzed about what went on between them back in those Depression days."

"I should have long ago recovered from that insult and let it die. But I was still mad as hell, even though today I'm the big star stealing beautiful trophies from lesser mortals."

There Was a Crooked Man was shot in the high desert country of the

Joshua Tree National Monument, some 45 miles northwest of Indio, California. To construct the remote and isolated 1880s "hell hole" of a prison, one of the leading art directors in Hollywood, Edward Carrere, was hired. *[He had already won an Oscar for his set decoration of* The Wild Bunch *(1969).]*

For *Crooked Man,* he was given his biggest assignment to date. It involved creating a desert prison with thick walls, and more than a dozen buildings. They would include a barracks, a mess hall, seven lookout towers, a mule shed, a blacksmith shop, and a gallows. He even had to bring in large rocks for the prisoners to split. One of those prisoners was a shirtless Kirk.

Kirk, as Pitman, leads his gang in pulling off a $500,000 robbery of a rich rancher, Mr. Lomax (Arthur O'Connell).

In fleeing from the scene of the crime, Kirk's men are shot, except for one, who Pitman shoots so that he can escape with all the loot. He placed the swag, wrapped in a pair of women's bloomers, in a rattlesnake pit in the desert and then heads into town to patronize the local brothel.

Kirk and two nude women are shown in a bordello bedroom, enjoying a night of lust.

There, he is spotted by the rancher he'd robbed, who turns him in to the sheriff.

O'Connell was very effective in the role of the rancher. He had already been nominated twice for a Best Supporting Actor Oscar—first, for *Picnic* (1955) starring William Holden, and second, for *Anatomy of a Murder* (1959) with James Stewart.

Arrested and tried, Kirk is sent to the most notorious and isolated prison in the entire Southwest. There, he joins a coven of depraved convicts.

Kirk charms his way into a relationship with the warden, Francis LeGoff (Martin Gabel), who wants to make a deal with him. He will allow him to escape if he'll split the loot with him.

Kirk had never worked with Gabel before, although he was a familiar figure to him on television, appearing as a frequent guest panelist on the hit TV series, *What's My Line?* His glamorous, blonde-haired wife, Anne Francis, was also a regular

Rainbarrel bathtime with Kirk (left) and Henry Fonda

529

panelist on the show.

The warden's plan goes awry when he's killed in a prison uprising. Replacing him is Woodward W. Lopeman (Fonda), who seems to be decent and uncorruptable. Kirk, as Pitman, ingratiates himself with the new warden, ostensibly to improve prison conditions while plotting his escape from a ten-year sentence.

The Fonda and Kirk characters become so friendly that in one scene they're depicted bathing in the nude in two large wooden barrels.

Kirk and the warden cooperate to inaugurate a new dining hall, to which the governor of the state is invited, along with many distinguished guests, some of whom are women. The prisoners hadn't seen a woman in months, and they feast their eyes on Lee Grant, cast as Mrs. Billard.

Kirk had not seen her since she co-starred with him in *Detective Story* (1951), almost twenty years before. She told him about what had happened in the interim. She had been blacklisted by the House Un-American Activities Committee.

Pitman certainly lives up to his reputation as a crooked man, as he manipulates everyone around him with his personal charisma.

Burgess Meredith has the most colorful role in the move, playing "The Missouri Kid," a grimy old pot-smoking codger who takes a bath once a year and wears the dirtiest long johns in the history of Arizona.

"Burgess looked totally repulsive," Kirk said. "A great character role, I could hardly believe that he was once married to the screen goddess, Paulette Goddard after Charlie Chaplin dumped her." Burgess had recently worked with Kirk and John Wayne on the set of *In Harm's Way*.

Mankiewicz selected a talented array of supporting players, including Hume Cronyn, who had co-starred with Kirk in *The Arrangement*. He was cast as a homosexual con man and religious fake, Dudly Whinner, always sticking close to his lover, Cyrus McNutt (John Randolph).

Alan Hale, Jr. played "Tobaccy," a prison guard. He had last worked with Kirk on location in Oregon shooting *The Indian Fighter*.

Kirk also found himself speaking again with Gene Evans, cast as Colonel Wolff. They had worked on location together in *The War Wagon*.

Warren Oates played an oafish gunman, Floyd Moon, who shoots the sheriff in the leg. Kentucky born, he had appeared in several films directed by Sam Peckinpah, including *The Wild Bunch* (1969).

Making his film debut was Yang Chuan-kwang [*also known as C.K. Yang*], an Olympic decathlete from Taiwan, known as "The Iron Man of Asia." As a murderous Chinaman, he was one tough inmate who did not speak.

Michael Blodgett, as Coy Cavendish, had a tragic role. His character learns of his fate, a walk to the gallows, where he is to be hanged for accidentally shooting his girlfriend's father, who stumbled upon them making love.

When Blodgett got back to Hollywood, with some excitement, he told gossip columnist Marilyn Beck about the nudity being filmed in Kirk's latest movie. "Kirk stripped buck-assed naked. He sure isn't ashamed to pull off every stitch. I don't know what the censors will allow on the screen."

Barbara Rhoades in *There Was a Crooked Man.* In one scene, she showed more than the censors could tolerate.

What might have become the most controversial scene in *Crooked Man* ended up on the cutting room floor, even though Hugh Hefner of *Playboy* wanted stills from it.

Love-starved prisoners attack starlet Barbara Rhoades and strip off her clothing. She is seen fleeing with "jiggling jugs," a decorative hat, and one full-length glove.

In the same year, Blodgett went on to greater but dubious fame when he played the gigolo, Lance Rocke, in Russ Meyer's cult classic, *Beyond the Valley of the Dolls* (1970).

The roles he was offered got so bad that he finally gave up acting altogether and became a novelist and screenwriter, turning out scripts for Tom Hanks and Burt Reynolds.

Near the end of *Crooked Man*, Kirk engineers his escape and returns to Rattlesnake Mountain to retrieve the swag he wrapped in that pair of women's bloomers and buried. He shoots all the rattlers and jubilantly lifts up the money. However, one snake has hidden within it. Disturbed, it lunges toward his neck with fangs exposed, and bites. Pitman dies shortly thereafter, an ironic twist to a plot riddled with ironies, deception, striving, and pain.

His body is found by Fonda, who has trailed him. He hauls it back to the gates of the prison, where he dumps it.

Then the rather decent, morally upright warden turns crooked, riding off with the $500,000 to destinations south, beyond the Mexican border, no doubt spending the rest of his days in grand luxury. [*One estimate evaluates the equivalent of $500,000 in the dollars of that era to $25 million in today's cur-*

531

rency.]

There Was a Crooked Man opened on Christmas Day of 1970. "What a stupid time," Kirk said. "No wonder it did poorly at the box office and in the weeks to come. On Christmas, most Americans wanted to watch Jimmy Stewart, the 'plucker' of my girlfriend at that party back in the '40s, perform onscreen in *It's a Wonderful Life* (1946)."

Vincent Canby, of *The New York Times*, wrote, "*Crooked Man* is rather low-eyed and takes its own sweet time to reveal itself. It is a movie of the sort of tastes, intelligence, and somewhat bitter humor associated with Mankiewicz, who, in real life, is one of America's most sophisticated, least folksy raconteurs."

***

In a rare move prompted by fiscal and tax issues, the chiefs of the Jacarilla Apache Tribe in New Mexico contacted Kirk and his Bryna Production Company, wanting to invest $2 million in a Western. The Apaches had garnered a huge burst of cash from deposits of uranium discovered on their tribal lands.

At first, he thought they wanted a new twist on the Western genre, wherein the Indians would triumph over cowboys. But to his surprise, the script they were backing, *A Gunfight*, was completely devoid of Native Americans. It was the saga of two famous gunfighters of the Old West, coming together for a reunion in the little town of Bajo Rio.

Its producers were Ronnie Lubin and Harry Jack Bloom, who had already written the screenplay. Kirk (with Bryna Production) joined forces with Harvest-Thoroughbred Pictures for its filming, having designated Paramount as its distributor. Lamont Johnson was brought in as its director.

Johnson, a Californian, was both an

532

actor and director in television and for the big screen. He'd go through the inevitable clashes with Kirk, who always maintained strong ideas about how any picture he was in should be helmed. Behind the scenes, Kirk was instrumental in rounding up a topnotch cast.

Johnny Cash in *A Gunfight*...."Even if I win, I will lose."

This story is about two aging gunfighters, each in need of dough and each already famous as a legend of the Old West.

[Kirk, as Will Tenneray, had been a notorious gunslinger in Dodge City. It's established that he's living in peace with his wife, Nora, played by the talented and prestigious actress, Jane Alexander. A daughter of Boston, she'd go on to greater glory as an award-winning star nominated eight times for an Emmy. Her first major acclaim derived from Eleanor and Franklin *(1976), in which she had to age from 18 to 60.*

When Bill Clinton became President, he would name her chairwoman of the National Endowment for the Arts.]

Kirk's character is bitter. His glory days behind him, he's world-weary, sick of life but perhaps afraid of dying. He works in a saloon run by Francisco Alvarez (Raf Vallone). Since Kirk's character is a local celebrity, he stands at the bar, luring "sucker fools to buy a drink."

Riding into town is another gunfighter, Abe Cross, whose reputation as a gunfighter is almost as widely known as that of Tenneray's. Cross, a laconic drifter, has not come to town for a showdown with Tenneray. In fact, to everyone's surprise, the two gunslingers seem to like each other.

But it is the gossipy and voyeuristic townspeople who want a confrontation to explode between the gunmen. They're are willing to pay a lot of money to see them go at it at the Plaza de Toros, a bullring across the border in Mexico.

Kirk was instrumental in an odd choice of casting. He phoned Johnny Cash, one of the most iconic musicians of the 20th Century and persuaded him to sign on as his co-star. The character he'd play has failed at prospecting for gold, and like Tenneray, he's in need of money.

Cross's arrival in town is announced onscreen by Eric Douglas in his film debut. He cries out, "Paw, Abe Cross is in town."

Although Kirk had been the force behind the enrollment of his son as a player in the film, he warned the boy that he didn't want him to grow up to become an actor.

Cross, astride a trusty horse, makes his entrance into town against the background music of a Johnny Cash song, "It's an Evil Wind that Blows."

At first, the townspeople seem to be waiting for each of the gunslingers to blast the other's head off. But that doesn't happen. They bond and become friends...of a sort, although under pressure, they'll eventually duel—for the money.

[As millions of Americans knew, Johnny Cash in real life was "The Man in Black," the quintessential American troubadour of the South, born in the cottonfields of Arkansas. In time, he would sell 90 million records, singing such mega-hits as "Folsom Prison Blues," "I Walk the Line," and "Ring of Fire."

Karen Black in *Five Easy Pieces* (1970)

Kirk, at the time, was only vaguely aware of Cash's past, a turbulent background of clashes with the police and struggles with liquor and drugs.]

"In time, both Johnny and I would go on our own spiritual odysseys, but in doing so, we were marching to different drummers," Kirk said. "For one thing, he was an ardent Christian and I, a Jew. But we worked in harmony."

Karen Black was cast as a dance hall girl, Jenny Simms, who falls for Cash, perhaps realizing how hopeless that was.

[Before working with Cash and Kirk, Black had starred in Easy Rider *(1969) and in* Five Easy Pieces *(1970), for which she won a Best Supporting Actress Oscar. Before cancer overcame her in 2013, she would generate 200 film credits, and become a cult horror icon.]*

As a prelude to the big showdown between the "vintage gunfighters," another young cowboy, perhaps wanting to make his own reputation, challenges Tenneray (Kirk) to a battle, and is killed. *[That character was portrayed by Keith Carradine, son of the famous actor, John Carradine. During the shoot, he told Kirk, "My dad was a born alcoholic and my mom was a manic depressive paranoid schizophrenic catatonic."]*

At last the gunfight between Cash and Kirk is staged at a bullfight arena across the border. Unlike Kirk's *Gunfight at the O.K. Corral,* the action in *A Gunfight* is low key, and the actual shoot-out is over only a few moments after it begins. A single, "lightning-fast shot" from Cross fatally kills Tenneray. The disappointed spectators exit from the Plaza de Toros in silence.

The director inserted a confusing and totally unnecessary fantasy sequence at the end, showing what might have been if the gunfight had been depicted with Tenneray as the victor.

Critics described the face of Johnny Cash, enlarged on the screen as, "corrugated, his voice rumbling and gravelly."

Mel Gussow of *The New York Times,* commented that Kirk's "aging chin-dimple more and more was resembling a bullet wound." Gussow went on to say that *A Gunfight* reminded him of *Ride the High Country* (1962), a Sam Peckinpah classic Western starring Joel McCrea and Randolph Scott as the antagonists. "McCrea and Scott were not tintype cowboys but real, salty people, trapped by their choices in life. *A Gunfight* merely goes through the motions."

Paramount, as the film's distributor, quietly "dropped" the picture into a scattering of movie houses for a very limited release, perhaps showing what studio executives thought of it. It made enough money to recoup the investment of the Apaches but did not cause much excitement among fans of Westerns.

Variety wrote, "In its commentary on the less-than-noble aspects of mob psychology, the film resembles Kirk Douglas' *Ace in the Hole.*"

***

It should have been another spectacular hit movie like Kirk's version of *20,000 Leagues Under the Sea* (1954) by Jules Verne. Based on another of Verne's novels, *The Light at the End of the World,* written in 1905, suffered in its transition to the screen, even though it starred two major box-office draws, Kirk and Yul Brynner.

Each of them shared a long history of rivalry off screen. That competitive edginess would be depicted on camera in this saga set at Cape

Horn, Tierra del Fuego, "The Edge of the World" in 1865. Argentina had installed a lighthouse there, at the southernmost tip of South America, beside a major shipping route that flourished before the opening of the Panama Canal.

The dream of making a movie based on the Verne novel had been kicking around Hollywood since 1962, when Columbia announced its intention of filming a version starring Jean Marais and Hardy Kruger. That movie was never made.

Kirk and Anne were vacationing together at one of their favorite spots, Cap d'Antibes on the French Riviera, when the offer came in. At first, he was not interested in starring in another Jules Verne adventure, but after reading the script by Tom Row, he took the bait.

He agreed to make it a Bryna Production, which would join forces with a consortium of Spanish companies that included Jet Films. Kirk also raised $11 million from Spanish banks and arranged a distribution deal through National General Pictures for a 1971 release.

Kirk reportedly took in a million dollars for his appearance in the film.

Kevin Billington was hired as its director. Son of an English factory worker, he had carved out a career with the BBC making films and documentaries for the most part filmed in London. Some of his previous films had been based on plays by Harold Pinter, his brother-in-law.

Billington decided it was too costly to fly cast and crew across the world to Argentina, so he selected Spain's rugged Costa Brava as the location, settling into the quaint little resort of Cadaqués, near the French border. *[Cadaqués was the site of the home and studio of the surrealist genius, Salvador Dalí, from 1930 till 1982.]*

He also shot some scenes farther to the south, along the Mediterranean coast near Alicante and Murcia.

Before driving west from France into Spain, Kirk studied his role, that of a soldier of fortune, Will Denton, a jaded expatriate American adventurer with a past. During the California gold rush, he'd failed as a prospector. He'd also suffered a broken romance and shot a man in a gunfight. The plot reveals that with an intention of living in solitude, he's been hired to live in and maintain a lighthouse by its supervisor, Captain Moriz (Fernando Rey).

Born in Galicia, Spain, Rey evolved into a suave international star known throughout Eu-

Fernando Rey...cast as a fanatical ex-sea captain.

536

rope. His most famous early work had been directed by the surrealist Spaniard, Luis Buñuel. He'd also portrayed a drug lord in *The French Connection* (1971), perhaps the most famous of the 150 films in which Rey would appear over the course of his 50-year career.

Although he did not like the actor, and viewed him as a rival, Kirk thought Yul Brynner would be ideal cast as the villain, a ruthless sea captain and "diabolical fiend," Jonathan Kongre. His motley crew arrives to commandeer the lighthouse with the intention of rigging it to misdirect ships onto rocks so that they can murder their crews and plunder their cargoes.

The scenes of the sadistic crew whacking bodies with swords, knives, and clubs would be rated as too bloodthirsty for family audiences.

[Brynner came from a mysterious past and had deliberately confused Hollywood writers with false information about his origins. As best as can be ascertained, he was born in 1920 in Vladivostock in the Far Eastern Republic (also known as the Chita Republic), a puppet state controlled by the Soviets. (Two years later, it merged into the U.S.S.R.) Brynner falsely claimed a part Mongol heritage, although it appears he was of Swiss, German, and Russian origins.

It's believed that he worked for a French circus troupe for five years as an acrobat and that he later earned a doctorate at the Sorbonne in Paris, later fighting on the side of the Loyalists in the Spanish Civil War.

During World War II, Brynner worked for the U.S. Office of Information, broadcasting in French into occupied France. In New York, he became a stage actor, and later posed nude for Andy Warhol in all his uncut glory.

After shaving his head for his 1951 role on Broadway as King Mongkut in The King and I, he made his bald head a trademark for the rest of his life. Over the years, he would deliver 4,625 performances of that Rodgers and Hammerstein musical.

Married four times, he was more famous for his long affair with the screen goddess, Marlene Dietrich, who was nearly twenty years his senior.

An inveterate smoker, he was diagnosed with throat cancer, having dumped Dietrich years before. She reacted strangely to the news, saying "Goody, goody!"]

Yul Brynner...overly flamboyant acting.

During the filming of *The Light at the End of the World*, Kirk and Brynner concealed their resentment of each other and were quite respectful.

One night, Brynner entertained Kirk at his own rented villa, the largest in the immediate vicinity. He'd hired a chef from Barcelona to prepare a lavish seafood dinner with oysters and lobster. At that dinner, Kirk learned that Brynner was addicted to opium.

[In a kind of one-upmanship, Brynner named many stars he'd seduced, including Dietrich, and wondered out loud how many of the same women Kirk had been intimate with.

Samantha Eggar...a "present" for love-starved sailors.

On Brynner's seduction list were Tallulah Bankhead, Anne Baxter, Ingrid Bergman, Claire Bloom, Joan Crawford, Yvonne De Carlo, Judy Garland, Gina Lollobrigida, Marilyn Monroe, Maria Schell, and a surprise, Nancy Davis in her pre-Reagan days.

Maybe it was the opium, but Brynner also confessed a fondness for young boys, naming a pubescent Sal Mineo, who had appeared in many performances on Broadway with him in The King and I.*]*

As dictated by the plot of *Lighthouse,* when an Italian ship is wrecked nearby, Kirk, as Denton, saves a member of its crew. His name is Montefiore (Renato Salvatori), and he evolves into Kirk's sidekick, hanging out with Kirk in his cave and staging guerilla attacks against Kongre's cutthroats who are now in control of the lighthouse.

For his own pleasure, it's revealed, Kongre kept one of the passengers from the Italian wreck alive, a beautiful Englishwoman named Arabella (Samantha Eggar).

She stood out as the only female in a cast otherwise comprised entirely of men. A Londoner, she'd launched her career in Shakespearean theater and had received acclaim for her performance in William Wyler's thriller, *The Collector* (1965).

Kirk liked appearing with Salvatori, an Italian actor who began his film career as a juvenile and went on to work with some of the leading directors of his home country, including Roberto Rossellini, Vittorio De Sica, and Luchino Visconti. In time, Salvatori became known for his successful portrayal of grim, realistic characters.

He told Kirk, "On the day I met my future wife, *[the French actress]* Annie Giradot, she was a prostitute, but I raped her anyway." *[Only later did he explain that both of them were playing roles in* Rocco and His Brothers *(1960), starring Alain Delon.]*

In one of the worst accidents he ever had, Kirk was directed to fall from the roof of a hut onto the jagged rocks below. A stuntman could have done it convincingly, but Kirk insisted on performing the dangerous act himself. To break his fall, an assistant stuntman was concealed, out of camera range, standing on a mattress, with the intention of catching Kirk and breaking his fall.

Kirk landed on the stuntman so hard that both of them fell onto the rocks below. Kirk hit his head on a flat rock. Had it been jagged, it no doubt would have split his head open. For a week he lay in bed with a concussion.

Near the end of filming, Montefiore is captured by Kongre's thugs while creating a diversion so that Denton can rescue Arabella. Kongre orders that his prisoner be flayed alive aboard his ship, hoping to draw Denton out of hiding. To save his friend from further agony, Denton shoots him from afar.

Kongre then turns Arabella over to his motley crew and withdraws to the lighthouse, presumably leaving Arabella to face a gang rape "worse than death."

Denton uses the pirates' cannon to sink their ship and also sets the lighthouse on fire. At the finale, he faces a showdown with Kongre that ends with the villain's death.

In Cadaqués, Kirk's lodgings were next door to the fabled surrealist artist Salvadore Dalí, who visited the set several times to watch the filming. One night, Dalí invited Kirk to dinner along with a handsome young French actor who had caught his eye: Jean-Claude Drouot, cast as Virgilio, agreed to accompany Kirk to dinner.

Inside Dalí's home the actors were introduced to a beautiful young woman (name unknown). Dalí began showing them his paintings and *objets d'art.*

He took them into a small, dark room where he showed them a film clip that illustrated all the things a woman in heat could do with a banana. It was a very large banana. After that, he invited them into a room filled with plaster casts of various parts of the male and female anatomy. Then he demonstrated how two plaster penises could be inserted simultaneously into the same plaster vagina.

The suggestion was obvious: A noto-

Salvadore Dalí, snapped at the Hotel Meurice in Paris in 1972. He wanted to see Kirk perform a sex act with another man and a beautiful woman.

WIKIMEDIA COMMONS COURTESY ALLAN WARREN

539

rious *voyeur*, Dalí wanted Kirk and Jean-Claude to replicate that illustration in a live act with the young woman.

Kirk grabbed the French actor's arm, telling Dalí that they had to retire to bed early for 5AM call on the set. He noted the disappointment on Dalí's face as they hastily retreated through the front door.

***

Although at first he didn't seem to want to go, Kirk took his son, Peter, then 14 years old, to the Spanish coast during his filming there. Together, they occupied a small house, the abode of a fisherman and his wife who had moved out for the duration of the rental.

"It was wonderful for Peter. He bonded with some English sailors, having dinner with them every night on their boat. Not only that, but he got drunk for the first time and lost his virginity when he accompanied two sailors to a bordello in Barcelona. He arrived in Spain a boy, but left as a man," Kirk said.

Upon its release, the movie got roses for its cinematography, but thorns for its story line and hideous violence. Tony Mastroianna in *The Cleveland Press* noted that Kirk's "teeth were still flashing brightly above his cleft chin."

Variety called it "good action-adventure escapism," but issued a warning that "it might be too brutal for families."

Brynner was displeased with its final cut. "I admit the original Jules Verne story was butchered, but the critics ignored some superb scenes, especially where Kirk and I have a confrontation on top of a burning lighthouse. In its own way, that bit of action was a little masterpiece. The director, a newcomer, wanted us to talk. I disagreed. Our facial expressions and body movements told how we felt. Words were not essential. I wanted silence instead of silly dialogue. But I was overruled."

***

A comedy/drama about espionage, *To Catch a Spy,* marked a turning point in Kirk's career as it moved into the 1970s. Hollywood was radically different from the place he had conquered in the 1940s. By now, he was actively and aggressively involved—in addition to acting—in film production and financing.

Baby boomers were watching more and more television, having long ago stopped visiting movie houses once or twice a week, and fewer films were emerging from big studios like MGM, Paramount, Fox, or Warners.

Most of the smaller studios on "Poverty Row" had disappeared.

Inspired to some degree by Kirk's success with Bryna Production, stars like John Wayne and Burt Lancaster had also set up production companies, joining forces with local filmmakers (in Europe or elsewhere) whenever location shoots abroad were called for.

Such was the case with *To Catch a Spy* when it was determined that sections needed to be filmed (through Ludgate Films of London) in the U.K and (through Capitole Films of Paris) in France.

Film rights to the novel by George Marton and Tibor Moray were acquired, and a relatively unknown director, Dick Clement, was hired.

[To Catch a Spy wasn't this film's only title. It would also be released as Catch Me a Spy *and as* Keep Your Fingers Crossed.*]*

Kirk's male co-stars were mostly English. Trevor Howard played Sir Trevor Dawson, Tom Courtenay portrayed Baxter Clarke, and Patrick Mower was James Fenton. A French national, Marlène Jobert, became Fabienne.

Its plot was a tangled spider web of intrigue. Location filming was in Bucharest, Romania, and at Lochs Etive and Awe in Scotland. Noteworthy scenes would include a gunboat battle and views of Kirk running through a herd of Highland cattle.

Cast as André, Kirk is a spy posing as a Romanian waiter. He becomes emotionally involved with a young British schoolteacher, Fabienne (Jobert), who is trying to locate her husband, James Fenton (Mower), who has gone missing. It turns out that he has been detained by Soviet intelligence and charged with spying. This is merely a ruse to contact him as he, himself is, in fact, a Soviet agent.

Unable to find him, Fabienne returns to England to seek advice from her uncle, Sir Trevor Dawson (Howard), a diplomat in the Foreign Office.

He suggests that a trade could be made if England released a Soviet spy to the Russians. That's how Andrej enters the picture, as he's in London trying to locate her since he'd stashed the results of his spying on the Soviets in her suitcase. The plot boils over from there, and, as might be expected, he becomes more deeply involved with Fabienne.

Except for Trevor Howard and Tom Courtenay, the international cast was unknown to Kirk. Also unknown to him was that Howard had long resented him, as he had wanted to play the musician, Bix Beiderbecke, in *Young Man With a Horn* (1950).

In the 1940s, Howard had been one of the leading box office attractions in England, known for such films as *Brief Encounter* (1945) and the very popular hit, *The Third Man* (1949). Although not traditionally handsome, he and Kirk had appeared with some of the same leading ladies, notably Jean Simmons and Deborah Kerr.

Kirk's leading lady, Marlène Jobert, had been born in Algiers into a Sephardic Jewish family. In the 1970s, she had become one of the leading film actresses of France, playing opposite such co-stars as Charles Bronson and Jean-Paul Belmondo. After appearing with Kirk, she accepted the lead in *Ten Days' Wonder* (1972) with co-stars Orson Welles and Anthony Perkins.

Cast as Baxter Clarke, Tom Courtenay was an English actor from Yorkshire who had initially struggled to get over his thick accent of the north. In the early 1960s, he had risen to prominence in such hits as *The Loneliness of the Long Distance Runner* (1962), *Billy Liar* (1963), and *Dr. Zhivago* (1965), for which he was nominated for a Best Supporting Actor Oscar. He told Kirk, "I don't particularly like appearing in films. I prefer the stage."

Another English actor, Patrick Mower, was already familiar with playing a secret agent or detective on TV or the big screen. He was best known for portraying a secondary character in the British TV spy series, *Callan* (1967-1972).

The reviews were hardly raves and the box office was disappointing. *Britain's Monthly Film Bulletin* wrote, "Things pick up briefly toward the end, with some cat-and-mouse scenes in a deserted Scottish hotel, and there are enjoyable performances from Kirk Douglas and Marlène Jobert. But on the whole, it's one of those films that was obviously more fun to make than to watch."

TV Guide said, "*To Catch a Spy* has a good cast, an exciting speedboat chase, a few chuckles, and every spy cliché in the book."

Radio Times claimed, "It sometimes has a clever and witty script. However, it is let down by Dick Clement's uncertain direction. Another problem is that Kirk Douglas, as a Bucharest waiter who is actually a spy, isn't suited for comedy."

***

The Master Touch, also released as *A Man to Respect*, was a 1972 Italian-West German crime film, starring Kirk and the voluptuous Brazilian

542

beauty, Florinda Bolkan. After its release, it was described as "a versatile legend of arthouse and grindhouse Italian cinema."

Four writers created this crime drama, financed by Verona Cinematografica in Rome and Paramount-Orion in Munich, with distribution by Warners. An Italian, Michele Lupo, was hired to direct it. He'd previously helmed his own version of *Spartacus*, calling it *The Revenge of Spartacus* (1965).

Steve Wallace (Kirk) has just been released from prison. Before that, he was a master safecracker. He returns to his wife, Anna (Florinda Bolkan), in Hamburg, Germany.

He is soon approached by Müller (Wolfgang Preiss), for whom he was working before he was arrested. The gangster wants him to join in a big heist, robbing an insurance company of a million dollars that's guarded in a building with good security. He rejects Müller's offer, but later decides to steal the money by himself, since he is penniless.

When Muller hears of this, he has one of his thugs attack Wallace, but he's rescued by Marco (Giuliano Gemma), an out-of-work circus acrobat, who intervenes and beats up the gangster. Wallace is so impressed that he invites Marco to join him in his daring heist.

Wallace and Marco embark together on this dangerous crime and reach the money stored in the thought-to-be-impregnable vault. Wallace sends Marco off with the loot and allows himself to be arrested, planning to spend a short time in prison before joining Anna to live it up with all that money.

But there's a hitch: Marco and Anna try to run off together, taking the money with them. Wallace eludes the police, catches up with Marco, and murders him. The police, led by Detective Hoffman (Reinhard Kolldehoff), close in on him. Wallace faces life in prison.

Filmed in Hamburg, still recovering from the bombings of World War

II, *The Master Touch* contains one of the most alarming high-speed car chases ever recorded on film. Not shown in the United States until two years after its release in Europe in 1972, Kirk's film played only in some large cities before disappearing.

Kirk had to introduce himself to most of the cast, including the German film actor Reinhard Killdehoff. A Berliner, he was the star of some 140 films. In 1978, he would appear in Marlene Dietrich's last film, *Just a Gigolo*, with David Bowie.

Giuliano Gemma (Marco) was an actor known for spaghetti Westerns, at least one of which *Arizona Colt* (1966) was helmed by his present director, Michele Lupo. His most prestigious film was Luchino Visconti's *Il Gattopardo*, where he'd played one of Garibaldi's generals. Released in America as *The Leopard* (1963), it had starred Burt Lancaster.

A Bavarian, Wolfgang Preiss (Müller) was already known to Kirk, as both of them had worked on *Is Paris Burning?* Preiss had made his film debut for UFA in wartime Berlin of 1942, appearing opposite Zarah Leander in *Dei Grosse Liebe*.

Twenty years later, he was starring with Burt Lancaster in *The Train* (1965). He'd also worked with some other big stars, notably Frank Sinatra, Robert Mitchum, Richard Widmark, and Gregory Peck.

He also worked as a "voice-over" actor, dubbing the voices of American actors into German: Christopher Lee, Claude Rains, Anthony Quinn, Lex Barker, Widmark, and Conrad Veidt as "Major Strasser" in the remastered version of Bogie's *Casablanca*.

In a review, Ben Meyers wrote, *"The Master Touch*—predictable story accompanied with weak acting—contains one hook to keep an audience engaged: Will Kirk Douglas and Giuliano Gemma's characters get caught? The fact that we care is an ode to the charisma that drove Douglas' career throughout his long and prolific life."

Kirk had been captivated by the beauty and charm of Florinda Bolkan, the daughter of a Brazilian father and an Indios mother. Florinda visited Rome in 1967, where she met producer Marina Cicogna, who became her lover for the next two decades.

Cicogna introduced her to the Italian director, Luchino Visconti, who persuaded her to take up acting in films. She had one of the roles in his most controversial film, *The Damned* (1969). Before that, she had played Ringo Starr's sister in *Candy* (1968), a film that starred Marlon Brando and Richard Burton.

During the shoot, she made an astonishing confession to Kirk about a belief that she had nurtured and ferociously maintained. "John F. Kennedy was handsome, young, rich, intelligent, and at the height of his power when I met him. He could have any woman he wanted. We were so close in that short time before his death. I believe he has watched over me ever since. There was something strangely supernatural in our meeting. He was my first love…and my last."

***

Most directors who worked with Kirk later claimed he never wanted to take direction but wanted to direct—not only himself but all the other actors, too.

At last, he got his chance when he decided to produce, direct, and star in *Scalawag* (1973), an adventure film in which he would play Captain Peg, who in his words, "wasn't born to die in bed." Produced by himself and Bryna Production in collaboration with the Inex-Oceanic Company, it was eventually released by Paramount.

Shot in Yugoslavia during the summer of 1972, it ran into so many disasters, including financial trouble (it had only a $500,000 budget), that he finally had to designate Anne as its producer. She managed to pull it off, whereas Kirk could not. "Nonetheless, I kept my day job," he said, a reference to his remaining associated with the project as its director and star.

Albert Maltz, one of the infamously blacklisted "Hollywood Ten," was one of the first writers to sign on. He was instructed to concoct an adaptation of Robert Louis Stevenson's *Treasure Island*. Kirk as a salty cutthroat, a peg-legged pirate, would obviously be based on Long John Silver, a character who had been depicted in films before. *[In 1934, Wallace Beery had starred in* Treasure Island, *and in 1950, Walt Disney had brought it back in Technicolor with Robert Newton.]*

It would be the first film in nineteen years for which

Maltz would receive screen credit. But his "rise from the ostracized grave" happened only with a lot of additional anguish.

When Maltz turned in his script, Kirk told Anne, "Of the Hollywood Ten, only two have talent. One of them, of course, is Dalton Trumbo." Then he hired another writer, Albert Sidney Fleishman, who Kirk guided in the revision of Maltz's script.

When Maltz read the revisions, he was enraged, demanding that his name be removed. Obviously, he later changed his mind. After he appealed to the Screenwriters Guild for arbitration, his name was restored to the screen credits.

Scalawag would become a family affair. Anne produced it, and their sons were hired, too—Peter as a still photographer and Eric as the office boy. Kirk told the press, "My phone doesn't ring any more from producers offering me work, so I have to create acting jobs for myself. I'm using the Douglas clan on the film so if it flops, all of us are to blame. In *Scalawag*, I wanted to get back to the old feeling I'd experienced as a kid…you know, all those dashing Errol Flynn movies…pirates, derring-do, people getting slaughtered."

"It's a version of *Treasure Island* but set in the Old West on horseback," Kirk said. "There's adventure, violence, romance. A girl sings a ballad while dreaming of a good-looking guy. Yes, it's old fashioned, but that's what I liked as a kid. I guess I haven't lost either my love of romance or my sense of innocence. You see old movies on *The Late Show* and everybody wants to know why they don't make films like *Captain Blood* anymore. Critics have made it fashionable to be pretentious with actors mumbling like Marlon Brando."

Although the script of *Scalawag* was inspired by *Treasure Island*, it made many radical departures. Unfolding in 1840 in Baja, California, it includes circus performers. Kirk hired John Cameron and Lionel Bart to compose songs, including "Silver Fishes" and a rousing pirate ditty, "When Your Number's Up, You Go."

As Captain Peg, Kirk ferociously pursues treasure and doesn't mind killing a man if he feels it's necessary. He rounds up a gang of cutthroats, one of whom was Neville Brand in a dual role of the murderous twins, "Mudhook" and "Brimstone."

Kirk and Brand had previously worked together with Rock Hudson on *The Last Sunset* (1961). In World War II, Brand had been the second most-decorated soldier after Audie Murphy.

Kirk found him to be a heavy-drinking hellraiser, who got out of control at night. "He fell for a local girl, much to the horror of her parents, who hid her from our cowpoke," Kirk said. "Neville would go ballistic searching for her, screaming and shouting, 'I've got to fuck the *puta!*'"

"Even though he was a big-time war hero, I stood up to him and brought him under control, which I had to do almost nightly."

"By morning, Brand sobered up and played both of the twins perfectly," Kirk said.

[At one point, Kirk, as Captain Peg, murders Brimstone to punish Mudhook.]

Kirk was horribly uncomfortable with the device his wardrobe staff devised to give the impression that he had lost his left leg. Friends sometimes asked him what he did with that "missing leg."

"I stuffed it up my ass," he answered.

[Actually, using great dexterity, he twisted one leg up and strapped it to his rear. It required great skill whenever he had to jump on a horse. "Mounting a horse was one of the hardest damn things I ever had to do in a movie, with my leg tied up like that."]

As Captain Peg, Kirk meets a beautiful orphan boy, Jamie (Mark Lester), and his even more beautiful sister, Lucy-Ann (Lesley-Anne Down). The voice of their saucy parrot is that of Mel Blanc.

As the plot guides along, Lucy-Ann's suitor, Don Aragon (George Eastman), hires Captain Peg to guide him to hidden treasure, not knowing that Peg plans to take it for himself.

One by one, the other treasure hunters are knocked off, and Peg escapes with Jamie and Lucy-Ann in a hot-air balloon made from bolts of silk.

Eastman (Don Aragon), was an Italian actor whose birth name was Luigi Montefiori. Standing six feet, nine inches, he towered over Kirk. *[A star of "Spaghetti Westerns," he was known mainly for his collaborations with the notorious director, Joe D'Amato. In the future, Eastman would appear in the gory horror flick* The Grim Reaper *(1980), playing a cannibalistic serial killer.]*

As the voice of the parrot, Blanc was nicknamed "The Man of a Thousand Voices," providing the vocal animation of screen creatures who included Bugs Bunny, Porky Pig, Yosemite Sam, and Tweety Bird.

When Kirk met him, he said it was hard to believe that the sounds of those different "personalities" all derived from the same actor.

[Later, Kirk and Blanc did public service announcements and commercials together. Blanc also worked with Lucille Ball, Phyllis Diller, and The Who.*]*

For comic relief, Danny DeVito was cast as "Fly Speck." Standing only five feet, he was told by Kirk, "You're the only actor in Hollywood who makes me feel like a giant."

"Danny was a damn good actor," Kirk said.

[As the years rolled on, Kirk was an eyewitness to the emerging friendship "between my son Michael and this talented little gnome."]

DeVito starred with Michael in several future films, including One Flew Over the Cuckoo's Nest *(1975),* Romancing the Stone *(1984),* The Jewel of the Nile *(1985), and* The War of the Roses *(1989).]*

The moppet actor, Mark Lester, in the role of "Jamie," was born in Oxford, England, and was a successful child actor in the 1960s and '70s, garnering his most fame in the musical, *Oliver!* (1968).

[A close friend of Michael Jackson, Lester later claimed in an interview in News of the World *that he was the biological father of Paris, the singer's daughter. "Michael asked me in 1996 to be the sperm donor, and I agreed. I willingly volunteered for a paternity test, but his lawyers didn't want me to."]*

Anne and Kirk discovered a young actress, Lesley-Ann Down. Born in London, she was also a model and singer. At the age of fifteen, she'd been voted *Most Beautiful Teenager of Britain*. She was only seventeen when they cast her in *Scalawag*.

Peter Douglas fell for her and got her to sign a contract with him. It allowed him to orchestrate a nude photo layout, which he later sold to *Playboy's* Hugh Hefner.

As Down's fame grew, she didn't want the pictures released, but it was too late—they'd already been sold. She became enraged and denounced Peter. "However, those two lovebirds made up," Kirk said. "Peter was only seventeen when he 'flew the coop' and went to live with Lesley-Anne."

Many critics claimed that the best feature of *Scalawag* was the brilliant Technicolor photography of Jack Cardiff, one of the best cinematographers in the business.

Most reviewers found Kirk's movie "too gory" for family audiences. The critic for the *Los Angeles Times* suggested that it would even give director Sam Peckinpah, famed for his gory Westerns, "the shakes."

Kirk with Mark Lester (left) and Lesley-Ann Down in *Scalawag* (1972)

CHAPTER FIFTEEN

BEFORE I FORGET,
"ONCE IS NOT ENOUGH"

"IT TAKES COURAGE"

In Multiple "Ode to Nostalgia" Films, None of them Blockbusters, Kirk Depicts a Wise, Dying Man with a Foot in the Grave

ALMOST DEAD: A DOUBLE WHAMMY

A Helicopter Crash and Stroke. Kirk Nearly Dies (Twice)

FOUR SCORE AND SEVEN YEARS AGO:

Kirk's Reinvention as an Actor

SWAN SONG TRENDS

Whereas Kirk's Tenacity as an Actor is Applauded, Critics Tend to Dismiss the Films He's In

Lancaster Blasts Kirk for His Tell-All Memoir

HOW KIRK DOUGLAS, A GOLDEN STAR OF YESTERYEAR, LENT CACHET TO:

Dr. Jekyll & Mr. Hyde, Mousey, Posse, Victory at Entebbe, The Chosen, The Fury, The Villain, Saturn 3, The Final Countdown, Man from Snowy River, Remembrance of Love, Draw!, Tough Guys, Queenie, Oscar, The Secret, Greedy, Take Me Home Again, Diamonds, It Runs in the Family, Illusion,

AND OTHERS THAT EVEN DIE-HARD FANS FIND HARD TO REMEMBER.

At first, the idea sounded absurd, even laughable—a musical version of Robert Louis Stevenson's fabled horror tale, *Dr. Jekyll and Mr. Hyde*. When Kirk was told he'd get to sing if he starred in it, something he had always wanted to do on film but rarely was given the chance, he signed for both of the two title roles.

It was his first dramatic role for television, set for a showing on NBC early in 1973 as a Timex Special. David Winters was assigned to direct it from a screenplay by Sherman Yellen. Music and lyrics would be composed by Lionel Bart, who had composed the music and lyrics for the highly successful *Oliver!*, a play that had opened in London in 1960.

As a straight drama, *Dr. Jekyll and Mr. Hyde* had been filmed before, notably by John Barrymore in 1920, Fredric March in 1932, and Spencer Tracy in 1941, the latter co-starring Ingrid Bergman and Lana Turner.

Kirk's own company (Bryna) co-produced this oddity. "I need to stretch myself as an actor to avoid being stereotyped," he told the press.

Susan Hampshire with Kirk in the 1973 TV musical special, *Dr.Jekyll & Mr. Hyde*

The basic plot would remain the same: Dr. Henry Jekyll's experiments reveal the dark, hidden side of man, and he unwittingly unleashes the hideous Mr. Hyde, a homicidal maniac who dwells within himself.

Kirk opted to more or less replicate the makeup—grotesque and with widened mouth and eyes—that had been developed for Spencer Tracy's 1941 manifestation of Hyde.

On the set with other members of his cast, Kirk was awash in a sea of British accents. To explain his noticeable lack of a British accent, his character is defined as an immigrant to London from Canada.

Michael Redgrave was among the supporting players. Kirk had worked with the distinguished English actor twice before, in *Mourning Becomes Electra* (1947) and *In Harm's Way* (1965). In spite of Redgrave's high stature as an Shakespearean actor, Kirk found his brief performance wooden.

Susan Hampshire was cast as Isabel, Redgrave's daughter, the fiancée of Dr. Jekyll. A Londoner, she had recently won three Emmy Awards for performances in *The Forsythe Saga* (1970), *The First Churchills* (1971), and *Vanity Fair* (1973).

The more colorful role of Anne went to another Londoner, Susan George. She played a prostitute and the "sex slave" of Mr. Hyde. Critics found her better in the role than the actresses who had attempted it in earlier versions: Miriam Hopkins or Ingrid Bergman.

Susan George in the 1970s...a sexy siren enslaved by the hideous Mr. Hyde.

[Susan George had recently appeared in Sam Peckinpah's Straw Dogs (1971) and in Dirty Mary, Crazy Harry (1974) with Peter Fonda. Presented in the tabloids as a "sexpot" she had been romantically linked to Prince Charles.]

As the butler, Poole, Stanley Holloway, an English star of stage and screen, seemed right at home in a musical. A humorist, poet, and monologist, he had won a Best Supporting Actor Oscar for his performance as Alfred P. Doolittle in *My Fair Lady* (1964).

Another English actor, Donald Pleasance, was cast as Fred Smudge, Hyde's lowbrow aide, bouncer, and enforcer, and Anne's jailer. He reveals a good singing voice. He escorts Hyde on a tour of some of the fleshpots of London's Soho. He is the character who eventually blows Dr. Jekyll's cover. In what one critic called "the mother of all meltdowns," Kirk transforms himself into Mr. Hyde and then lunges for Susan Hampshire's throat.

[Kirk had seen Pleasance on the screen in the James Bond film, You Only Live Twice *(1967).]*

Most critics found *Dr. Jekyll and Mr. Hyde* well-orchestrated but the lyrics to the songs inane. Kirk hardly had a great singing voice, and one reviewer called his attempt to sell a song, "very, very silly."

Another critic noted, "A child could have scribbled the rhyming passages during a jelly-bean high—and the songs break up any *gravitas* Douglas is trying to maintain."

Variety wrote, "Kirk Douglas' idea of dramatic contrast is to prance about like a superannuated schoolboy as Jekyll while impersonating a bumptious, braying loudmouth as Hyde."

551

***

Kirk's next film, *Mousey*, opened in England, where it was called *Cat and Mouse*. It got a modest send-off featured as part of a double bill with *Craze* (1974), in which Jack Palance played a demented antique dealer.

When it was shown later in America, it was presented on television without a lot of advance buildup or publicity.

Kirk, as George Anderson, was a mild-mannered school teacher who his students call "Mousey."

He's married to Laura (Jean Seberg). When he returns home one afternoon, he learns that she has bolted, and taken their son with her.

Although he knows that the boy is not his, he was like a real son to George.

He quits his job and heads for the big city with revenge on his mind. He carries a throat-slitting razor.

Kirk with Jean Seberg in *Mousey* (aka *Cat and Mouse*)

Director Daniel Petrie, Jr. was best known for his "buddy cop" movies, including *Beverly Hills Cop* (1984). When he met Kirk, he had just filmed *Buster and Billie* (1974), starring Jan-Michael Vincent. *[It was one of the first major motion pictures to depict a frontal male nude, with Vincent seen bare-assed naked running through the woods. Hey, it was the 1970s.]*

John Vernon, as David Richardson, is actually the boy's biological father. The Canadian actor is better known for his appearance with Clint Eastwood in *Dirty Harry* (1971).

In *Mousey*, Sam Wannamaker played the police inspector. *[A son of Chicago, he had fled to England to escape the McCarthy witch hunt. In time, he became one of London's favorite American actors and was instrumental in the re-creation in London of Shakespeare's Globe Theatre on its original site on the South Bank of the Thames.*

During the course of his career, Wannamaker had played many distinguished roles. They had included starring with Ingrid Bergman onstage in Joan of Lorraine *(1942).]*

552

Beth Porter, as Sandra, befriends the stranger, George, and ends up getting her throat slit. The multi-talented actress was born in America but found that her heart was in England. In reference to the movie *Futz* (1969), a critic wrote, "Miss Porter makes the Whore of Babylon look like the Singing Nun."

Kirk was mildly surprised when Petrie introduced him to an actress named Bessie Love, whom he'd cast as Mrs. Richardson. He'd never seen one of her pictures, but knew her name, as she'd been a legendary star of the silent screen and early talkies. Now she was a relatively forgotten name of yesterday.

Love goddess of the silent pictures, Bessie Love vied with Mary Pickford for the title of America's Sweetheart.

[*Born in 1898, she'd worked with the most famous cowboy star, Tom Mix, and the best known director of that era, D.W. Griffith, who had cast her in his classic,* Intolerance *(1916). Love was often compared to Mary Pickford, once known as America's Sweetheart. Love became one of the first actresses nominated for an Academy Award—in her case, for her performance in* Broadway Melody *(1929). As a silent screen flapper, she was the first actress to dance the Charleston (not Joan Crawford) on the screen. When her career faltered in 1932 with the coming of the talkies, she moved to England.*]

When Kirk shook her hand, he parodied William Holden meeting Norma Desmond (Gloria Swanson) in *Sunset Blvd.* (1950). "You used to be big."

"I'm still big," she answered. "Only the pictures got small."

As a critic of *Mousey* noted, "Douglas is in 95% of every frame, and dominated the screen with a disturbing portrayal of a man who goes from being a cry-baby to a serial killer like a god damn yo-yo—and he makes a convincing character all the way."

***

Kirk had somewhat dreaded—yet, in contrast, looked forward to meeting—his leading lady, Jean Seberg. Although she'd actually been born in Iowa, because of her long residency in France, many movie-goers thought she was French.

At the time she was interacting with Kirk, she was already something

553

of a legend, certainly mysterious, most definitely an enigma. Stories were spread about her and Jane Fonda concerning their widely broadcast support of the Black Panthers.

Otto Preminger, Kirk's former director, had cast Seberg in George Bernard Shaw's *Saint Joan* (1957) when she was only seventeen. Her performance as its star became one of the most famously lambasted in cinema

Jean Seberg with Jean-Paul Belmondo in Jean-Luc Godard's seminal art film, *Breathless* (1960)

history. The director stuck by her and cast her again in *Bonjour Tristesse* (1958).

Kirk had seen only one of her films, Jean-Luc Godard's *À bout de souffle* (*Breathless;* 1961), in which she'd co-starred with Jean-Paul Belmondo, whom Kirk remembered from the set of *Is Paris Burning?*

The French director, Yves Boisset, claimed, "It was important to Seberg to feel, well, excuse the term…'fuckable.' In her depression, she turns to men for reassurance. Jean could have sex in an elevator between the third and fourth floor."

Seberg's sexual reputation had long intrigued Kirk. He wondered if she were as free and easy with her favors as had been rumored. Might she find him, already in his fifties, attractive? Would he be numbered among the leading men she'd seduced? They'd already included Warren Beatty during their filming of *Lilith* (1964) and Clint Eastwood during their work together on *Paint Your Wagon* (1969). Burt Lancaster told Kirk that he'd become intimate with Seberg when she'd portrayed his mistress in *Airport* (1970).

Many of Seberg's conquests were exotic, and often, she gravitated to interracial affairs with men who included Sammy Davis, Jr. "After Sammy," she told friends that "Dennis Hopper was a disappointment."

Some of her more controversial affairs were with Masai Hewitt, the leader of the Black Panthers, and with Carlos Navarra, the Mexican revolutionary, plus many African Americans. Algerians in Paris were said to have been one of her specialties.

As Kirk later told Petrie, his director, "Jean came to my dressing room on the second day of the shoot, ostensibly for help with her lines. We did it. I don't think she was in it just for the sex. She needed to be held and appreciated. I don't think I've ever met an actress this insecure. She needed to be reassured of her beauty and appeal, even her ability to act. An involvement with her calls for tenderness and compassion."

As Petrie noted, "Kirk must have provided both of those qualities… and more. Jean visited his dressing room every day for the rest of the shoot."

"She lived in terror of the FBI," Petrie continued. "G-Men were hounding her, presumably on her trail day and night, because of her association with the Black Panthers."

After the end of filming, Kirk never saw Seberg again. He heard that she'd returned to live in France.

[On September 8, 1979, two French policemen on a quiet street in Paris came upon a white Renault that had been parked there for ten days. They looked inside and noticed the decomposing body of a young woman slumped over in the front seat. They forced their way into the car and were overpowered by the stench. A bottle of barbiturates was found, and an autopsy confirmed that she had committed suicide by overdosing.

Or had she been murdered? Rumors about her untimely death persist to this day.

Seberg's second husband, Romain Gary, the novelist and former French Resistance fighter, called a press conference. He blamed her constant hounding by the FBI for "creating paranoia in Jean…in fact, making her psychotic. She was spied upon."

When Gary learned that Clint Eastwood was having an affair with Seberg, he challenged him to a duel, an idea that the movie star rejected.

On December 2, 1980, Gary himself died of a self-inflicted gunshot wound. He left a note asserting that his death was not connected to the suicide of Seberg. Scion of a long, adventurous, and ultimately tragic life, he was cremated and his ashes scattered into the sea near Roquebrune-Cap Martin on the French Riviera.]

***

Kirk and his son Joel flew to Tucson to film another Western, this once called *Posse*. In it, Kirk had been cast as a fiercely ambitious U.S. Marshal with a grand ambition: He wants to hunt down a "most wanted" outlaw who robbed a train, hoping to gain publicity for his upcoming race for the U.S. Senate. His ultimate goal involves becoming President of the United States.

It was clearly understood that Kirk would be the film's producer, director, and star. Its plot was based on a novel by Christopher Knopt.

"After I bombed as director of *Scalawag*, I swore I'd never try that again. So much for my vow." In his capacity as chief of Bryna, before leaving for location shooting in Arizona, he'd persuaded Paramount to release it in 1973.

As his co-star, and to play the outlaw, Kirk hired Bruce Dern. He had admired Dern's talent during the filming of *The War Wagon*. "I always thought Dern was handsome enough for leading man status, but he never could seem to get rid of that god damn squint," Kirk claimed.

"Posse" begins like most Westerns. It ends like none of them. It will knock you off your horse.

In *Posse*, Dern (as Strawhorn) upsets the plan of Kirk (as Nightingale, the "conquering hero") to haul him off to prison in handcuffs. Instead, Dern ends up capturing Kirk and holding him for $40,000 ransom. To raise the money, Kirk's posse robs the townspeople, which turns them against the Marshal. There goes Kirk's hope for a political career.

As "Wesley," Bo Hopkins held the third lead. [*A native of South Carolina, he had co-starred with Burt Reynolds in White Lightning (1973). That movie is now a cult classic. In time, Hopkins would be cast in 100 film and TV roles, including* The Wild Bunch *(1969) and* Cat Ballou *(1971).*]

Kirk in *Posse*. The poster within the frame displays the image of Bruce Dern

A descendant of Calamity Jane, David Canary was cast as Pensteman, one of Dern's men. He was better known for playing Adam Chandler in the hit TV soap opera, *All My Children*. Broadway audiences had seen him on stage opposite Geraldine Page in *Clothes for a Summer Hotel* (1980).

Kirk's son, Joel, didn't stay in Arizona for very long. A call came in from his older brother, Michael, who wanted him to work with him on *One Flew Over the Cuckoo's Nest*, which Michael was producing, starring Jack Nicholson. There was irony here: The lead role had been coveted by Kirk for so many years that he'd grown too old to convincingly play it.

Another candidate for stardom had been James Stacy, who was known for co-starring in the hit TV Western, *Lancer*, in the late 1960s. From 1963 to 1966, he'd been famously married to the singer, Connie Stevens, once wed to singer Eddie Fisher.

In 1973, he took a motorcycle ride through Benedict Canyon with his girlfriend, Claire Cox, on the seat behind him. A drunk driver crashed into them. Whereas Cox was killed, Stacy was rushed to the hospital, where surgeons had to amputate his left leg and arm.

During his long, agonizing recovery, a charity fundraiser, hosted by Barbra Streisand and Frank Sinatra, was staged, netting $120,000 for his medical bills and rehabilitation.

In a campaign to find work for him, Kirk was asked to create a role for Stacy in *Posse*. With that intention, Kirk crafted and inserted into the script the character of Hellman, editor of the town newspaper who happens to also be missing an arm and a leg. "Stacy was a son of a bitch to work with," Kirk remembered. "He was rough, but I was rougher."

The drunk driver who had hit him did not have any insurance, so Stacy sued the Melting Pot Restaurant, where the bartender had allowed him to drink too much. Patrons had seen him stagger out the door and into his car.

Kirk was summoned as a key witness. During his testimony, he suggested that Stacy had been headed for stardom before the accident deprived him of his goal and went on to suggest that the insurance company should award Stacy two or three million dollars for the obliteration of that dream. The court awarded $1.9 million instead.

[There is a sad note to the life and death of James Stacy. He had a Lolita fixation, and was arrested twice as a Peeping Tom, spying through windows at little girls.

In November of 1995, he was arrested, tried, and convicted of molesting an 11-year-old girl. He fled to Honolulu to avoid sentencing. After a suicide attempt there, he was arrested and brought back to Los Angeles.

He was sentenced to the California Institution for Men at Chino, where he served a six-year prison term. At the age of 79, in 2016, his tragic life came to an end.]

Two of the stars from the long-running TV soap opera, *All My Children*, included David Canary, who appeared in *Posse*- with Kirk, and TV talk-show host Kelly Ripa (right), who acknowledged Canary's death in 2015 by posting this photo on her Twitter account.

The sad and tragic James Stacy with Kirk in *Posse*.

***

The Valley of the Dolls, the first novel Jacqueline Susann ever wrote, released in 1966, became one of the best-selling books in publishing history.

Her third novel, *Once Is Not Enough*, became the best-selling novel of 1973, remaining for thirty-six weeks on *The New York Times* bestseller list.

Naturally, Hollywood wanted to adapt the novel into a movie. A deal was struck for a 1975 release from the Sujac-Aries company with a tie-in to Paramount.

As with all Susann novels, reviews were mostly negative, the *Times* defining it as "nearly five hundred steadily monotonous pages." Gore Vidal claimed, "Susann doesn't write, she types." On *Johnny Carson's Tonight Show,* Truman Capote said, "Susann looks like a truck driver in drag."

Irving Mansfield, who many defined as a genius when it came to book promotions, was Susann's husband, having married her in 1939. He took over the post of the film adaptation's executive producer. A brilliant organizer, he devoted his entire life to promoting his wife. He hired Howard W. Koch as the film's producer, Guy Green as its director, and Julius J. Epstein to author the screenplay. *[Years before, Epstein, in collaboration with Koch had written the screenplay for Bogie's most famous picture,* Casablanca *(1942).]*

The Hollywood producer — the husband bought for $3 million and — he earned every penny of it.

Epstein told Kirk, "There wasn't one moment of reality in *Casablanca.* We weren't making art, we were making a living. Movies in those days were prevented from reality. Every leading man had to be a great sexual athlete. Every boy and girl had to 'meet cute,' and the girl had to dislike the hero when they met. If a woman committed adultery, she had to die. Now, the woman who commits adultery is your heroine."

Unless she was writing about her beloved poodle, Susann drew on living people to create the fictional portraits in her novels. For *Once Is Not Enough,* Howard Kock, the film adaptation's producer, was said to have been the model for Kirk's lead role of Mike Wayne.

The heiress, Deidre Mildred Granger (as portrayed in the film by Alexis Smith), was inspired by Barbara Hutton, the Woolworth heiress. The reclusive actress and her on-screen lesbian lover, Karla, were obviously based on Greta Garbo.

The novelist, Norman Mailer, was used as the inspiration for Tom Colt (portrayed by David Janssen). The character of Linda Riggs (as portrayed by Brenda Vaccaro) was ripped off from the life of Helen Gurley Brown, the editor of *Cosmopolitan*. For her performance, Vaccaro won a Best Supporting Actress nomination.

An Englishman, Guy Green, was the film's director. He had been a noted cinematographer, having won an Oscar for his work on *Great Expectations* (1946), the Charles Dickens classic. After Green turned to directing, he helmed *A Patch of Blue* (1965), starring Sidney Poitier and Shelley Winters.

Jacqueline Susann with TV Talk Show host Merv Griffin in 1973.

The title of Susann's novel had been borrowed from a remark made by the comedian, Joe E. Brown, who's mostly remembered for his portrayal of the captain of *Show Boat* (1951).

Susann visited him on his deathbed. As she stood beside it, she said, "C'mon, Joe, didn't you always say, 'We go around once, but if you play your cards right, once is enough?'"

He looked up at her and, in a weak voice, answered, "I was wrong, Jackie. Once is not enough."

[Susann herself died of cancer at the age of 56 before production began on the film adaptation of her novel. From her bed at Doctors Hospital in Manhattan, in the last words she uttered to Mansfield, her husband, she said, "Hey, doll, let's get the hell out of here."]

After five years of shooting multiple films on location, Kirk returned to the sound stages of Hollywood. Although he knew that the Susann picture was kitsch, he concluded, "It pays well, and besides, William Holden told me, 'all actors are whores.'"

Susann's plot defined Mike Wayne (Kirk) as an over-the-hill movie producer whose career has fallen on bad days. He enters into a loveless marriage with Diedre (Alexis Smith) who is secretly involved in a lesbian affair with Karla, as portrayed by Melina Mercouri.

Wayne (Kirk) has a pampered daughter, educated in Switzerland. Her name is January (as cast with Deborah Raffin) because she was born on New Year's Day. According to Wayne, "I swore I would give her the earth."

Once, during an argument with his wife, Kirk shouts, "You just cut off my balls in front of my daughter."

January's stepmother, Dierdre, lures her into an affair with her sleazy playboy cousin, David Milford (George Hamilton). After he takes her virginity, she drops him for a novelist, Tom Colt (David Janssen), an enemy of her father.

Deidre and Wayne agree to eventually divorce, but while flying aboard the same airplane, it crashes and kills both of them. Meanwhile, January has renewed her friendship with Linda Riggs (Brenda Vaccaro), the editor of a trendy, gossipy magazine. She hires January to work for *Gloss,* a magazine inspired by *Cosmopolitan.* In time, Riggs is fired for an affair with her boss.

Before the end of *Once Is Not Enough,* January receives a $3 million inheritance and wanders alone into the foggy Manhattan night, perhaps hoping for a better world. As a "poor little rich girl," she will probably not be alone for long.

On the set, Kirk had a reunion with the man with the perpetual tan, George Hamilton. They had once starred together in *Two Weeks in Another Town* (1962).

The Greek actress, Melina Mercouri, had received an Oscar nomination for her role in *Never on Sunday* (1981). She was married at the time to the American director, Jules Dassin, who often cast her in his movies.

In 1981, she'd become the first female Minister of Culture and Sports in Greece. During her tenure, she would lobby for the return of the Parthenon Marbles (aka the Elgin Marbles) from the British Museum.

Kirk found Alexis Smith ideally cast. [*Reportedly, he said, "It takes a lesbian to play a lesbian."*] A Canadian, she had a film career in Hollywood in the 1940s, and in time, would co-star with Errol Flynn, Clark Gable, Humphrey Bogart, Fredric March, Cary Grant, Bing Crosby, Paul Newman, Dean Martin, and her husband, Craig Stevens.

David Janssen easily fitted into the role of the novelist. His greatest fame came from playing Richard Kimble in the TV series, *The Fugitive* (1963-1967). *TV Guide* ranked him no. 36 on the list of the 50 Greatest TV Stars of All Time.

A native of Los Angeles, Raffin had graced many a magazine cover, including *Seventeen* and *Good Housekeeping.* She was a minor actress in films of the 1970s and later became an audiobook publisher.

Brooklyn-born Brenda Vaccaro had a special place in Kirk's heart, as she was his virtual daughter-in-law because of her long-running relationship with his son, Michael. Her on-screen credits had included starring in *Midnight Cowboy* (1969), with Jon Voigt and Dustin Hoffman. She once was quoted as saying, "Michael just doesn't want to get married."

Upon the release of *Once Is Not Enough,* one viewer wrote, "Kirk looked like he was ready to stalk off the set any minute."

Another critic noted, "No one can impersonate Kirk Douglas better than the man himself."

***

Resting after the film was wrapped, Kirk fell asleep early one night but was awakened by one of the world's most recognizable voices.

Over the phone, Elizabeth Taylor told him, "I want to be in your next picture."

The following evening, he drove to her house, where she greeted him in her living room wearing a purple kaftan. Perhaps in the back of his mind, he didn't know if she really wanted to talk about a movie—or whether seduction was on the menu. He'd known her for a long time, particularly during the course of her marriage (1957-1958) to Mike Todd.

She kissed him on the lips. "I want you to be my husband."

"You mean, I'm next in line?" he asked. "If you keep going, you'll have a football team. At last, I get my chance at the Queen of the Nile. I've brought my own snake."

"Oh, darling, you slay me," she said. "This is serious. As one Jew to another Jew, I want you to do a cameo with me in an upcoming movie, *Victory at Entebbe*. We'll be man and wife."

"I swore I'd never do another cameo, but since it's for you and for Israel, I can be persuaded to change my mind."

"That's wonderful. As you can see, the champagne is chilling, and I'm already hot."

As the evening progressed, he learned the details of the upcoming movie, including the names of its all-star cast. Its executive producer, David L. Wolper, in an agreement with Warners, wanted to film a re-enactment of *Operation Entebbe*, a made-for-TV movie to be broadcast over ABC.

It would be based on that daring counter-terrorist hostage-rescue mission executed by Israeli commandos at Uganda's Entebbe airport on July 4, 1976.

So far as it is known, neither Elizabeth nor Kirk spoke publicly about what happened that night at her home. Perhaps they did more than discuss Entebbe. If these two survivors of the Golden Age of Hollywood did more than converse, the details have been lost to history. However, her name often appears on the list of Kirk's sexual conquests.

He did say, "Elizabeth is the world's most beautiful woman, and I've had Hedy Lamarr."

He took home Ernest Kinoy's script for *Victory at Entebbe,* which was to be directed by Marvin J. Chomsky. A Jewish New Yorker, Kinoy had been a prisoner of war in the Berga-Elster subdivision of the Buchenwald concentration camp during World War II. After the war, he returned to America and became a script writer for NBC, turning out both radio and television dramas.

Kirk with Elizabeth Taylor in *Victory at Entebbe*

Kirk had read extensively about Operation Entebbe, and the script he'd received more or less accurately reflected its true events. On June 27, 1976, an Air France jet with 248 passengers had been hijacked by two members of the Palestine Liberation Force and two members of the German Revolutionary Cells.

The plane had originated in Tel Aviv, bound for Paris, but was diverted after a stopover in Athens. The dictator of Uganda, Idi Amin, supported the terrorists, welcoming them to Uganda.

At the Entebbe Airport, Jews and non-Jews were separated. The non-Jewish passengers were allowed to continue onward to Paris, but the Jews were held under guard along with a dozen Air France crew members. There were rumors that they'd be executed.

Quickly but efficiently planned, Israeli transport planes flew on a 2,500-mile rescue mission. After quietly landing at Entebbe, they rescued 102 hostages, with only three killed. Five Israeli commandos were wounded and one was fatally shot. Ugandan soldiers suffered the heaviest toll. When the Israeli planes departed, they left behind 43 dead Ugandan soldiers.

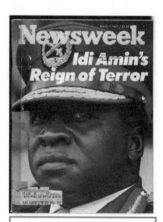

Amin, the sociopathic president of Uganda from 1971-1979, was one of the most notorious rulers in the history of Africa, with a horrifying record of brutality, genocide, and oppression. His autocratic reign was characterized by the most hideous of human rights abuses, political repression, extra-judicial killing, nepotism, corruption, and gross economic mismanagement.

The cover of *Newsweek* (1977) depicted the brutal face of Africa's most notorious dictator and murderer.

A Philadelphia native, Julius Harris,

562

played Idi Amin. James Bond fans remembered him as the villainous, steel-armed "Tee Hee" in *Live and Let Die* (1975) starring Roger Moore.

The director of *Victory at Entebbe,* Chomsky, had lined up one of the most impressive all-star casts of any movie made in the 1970s. Since all of them were stars, he billed them on movie posters in alphabetical order: Helmut Berger, Linda Blair, Kirk Douglas, Richard Dreyfuss, Helen Hayes, Anthony Hopkins, Burt Lancaster, Christian Marquand, and Miss Elizabeth Taylor.

After the hijacking, Hershel and Edra Vinofsky (Kirk and Elizabeth) go to Israel to plead for the rescue of their daughter, Chana, a character portrayed by Linda Blair. *[Blair had made a screen sensation as the demon-possessed child, Regan, in* The Exorcist *(1973), for which she was nominated for an Academy Award.]*

In Tel Aviv, the characters portrayed by Kirk and Elizabeth are granted an audience with Yitzhak Rabin (Anthony Hopkins).

During the shoot, Kirk caught up with Burt Lancaster, cast as Shimon Peres, the Israeli Minister of Defense and later—among many other positions of leadership—the nation's President. Kirk also met the distinguished actress, Helen Hayes, cast as Etta Grossman Wise. They discussed their mutual friend, Katharine Cornell. *[Kirk was clearly aware that his former theatrical mentor and Miss Hayes vied for the title of First Lady of the American Theater.]*

Christian Marquand...lover of Marlon Brando.

Kirk lunched with the French actor Christian Marquand, who played Captain Dukas. *[Marquand had been the heartthrob of French cinema in the 1950s and the longtime lover of Marlon Brando. He and Brando were so close that the American actor named his son, Christian, in Marquand's honor. Kirk had first admired Marquand onscreen in* And God Created Woman *(1956), the film that launched Brigitte Bardot as an international sensation.]*

The actor who most fascinated Kirk was the German star, Helmut Berger, long a *protégé* of the Italian director, Luchino Visconti. Self-identified as bisexual, he'd had international affairs that kept tabloid writers busy: Elizabeth Taylor, Rudolf Nureyev, Tab Hunter, Ursula Andress,

Helmut Berger in 1974...lover of Luchino Visconti

Florinda Bolkan (Kirk's former co-star), Jerry Hall, Britt Ekland, and both Bianca and Mick Jagger.

Victory at Entebbe led to radical pro-Palestinian activists placing bombs in Italy and Germany and loud denunciations of the film as "Zionist propaganda."

A critic wrote, *"Victory at Entebbe* has a surprising number of star names, especially when you consider this was made-for-TV. But none of the characters feels real. Instead, it has the feel of a collection of marquee names called upon to give their parts some gusto, to shout their lines to try and create tension, but without good dialogue, it comes across as noise."

***

The producer and exhibitors of Kirk's next film, a sci-fi horror movie, couldn't agree on a title. A joint British and Italian company, Embassy-Aston, released it in 1978 using three different titles at different times for various markets: *The Chosen, Holocaust 2000,* and *Rain of Fire.*

The Italian director, Alberto De Martino, gave Kirk the script by Sergio Donati and after his first reading he agreed to star in it. Of course, he immediately recognized that it had been "inspired" by *The Omen* (1976).

De Martino, the Roman director, had begun his career as a child actor. Later, as an adult, he directed Italian movies. His specialty involved replicating (some said "copying") the plots of American hit movies, and recrafting them into "Spaghetti Westerns" and horror films. He also made "sword-and-sandal" movies when that genre became popular.

Kirk's role was that of Robert Caine, an American industrial tycoon and specialist in nuclear power. He lives in London and is married to an elegant English wife, Eva (Virginia McKenna). They are parents of a devilish son, Angel (Simon Ward).

Caine makes a controversial decision to erect a nuclear power plant near a sacred cave in a country in the Middle East. As the plot unfolds, he discovers that his son, Angel, is the Antichrist. He's plotting to use his father's discoveries to take over the world by launching a nuclear Armageddon.

Caine is warned he might wake up to a monster with seven heads and ten horns if he carries out his plan to build the nuclear plant. He dismisses such assertions as superstition.

According to legend, the cave near the construction site is inhabited by one of the prophets of the Apocalypse. Caine and Sara Golin (Agostina Belli), a local government employee, discover the cave and its prophetic contents.

There's a lot of blood and gore in *The Chosen,* including a series of horrible deaths. Caine's wife, Eva, is knifed at a party. A prime minister is decapitated by a whirling helicopter blade. Caine's associate, Professor Griffith (Anthony Quayle), is murdered after discovering that Angel, Caine's son, is a manifestation of Satan.

In a dream sequence, Kirk, in spite of his age, appears totally nude, as he had in others of his films. As he's stranded on a beach, a lot of weird images appear by the power of backprojection.

When Sara becomes pregnant, Caine fears that her child is the spawn of Satan and whisks her off to an abortion clinic.

The English actress, Virginia McKenna, was known for her cinematic collaborations with her husband, Bill Travers. Often, they co-starred together, as they did in one of their most popular films, *Born Free* (1996).

Kirk worked smoothly with his fellow actors, including Alexander Knox, cast as Meyer, with whom he'd appeared in *The Vikings.* Kirk had also appeared with Anthony Quayle in *Victory at Entebbe.*

Cast as Sara was the Italian actress, Agostina Belli, who in time would appear in some fifty films, most of them Italian.

The British actor, Simon Ward, was best known for his performance as Winston Churchill in *Young Winston* (1972). *[Ward's career temporarily suspended in 1987 when he suffered a serious head injury during a violent street attack by a gang of thugs. His assailants were never identified but left him with a broken skull requiring brain surgery, and a blood disorder (polycythemia) that remained with him for the rest of his life.]*

One reviewer got nasty in his references to the film's director, De Martino, calling him a "certified copycat piggy-backing on popular U.S. films

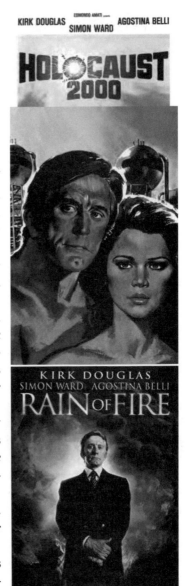

that had been box office bonanzas. *"The Chosen* is a dark tale of murder, sex, and power gone completely mad."

The monthly *Film Bulletin* defined *The Chosen* as "the wildest farrago yet to come out of the demonology genre. The religious allegory adds little weight to the confusion of the plot."

AllMovie claimed it "offers some creepy fun for fans of Euro-horror."

***

Kirk was eager to work with director Brian De Palma, and he got his chance when he was cast as the lead in *The Fury* (1978), a complicated drama greenlighted by 20th Century Fox. Screenwriter John Farris based it on his novel, which was much easier to understand than the fast-moving film.

Kirk met with De Palma, whom he'd admired for psychological thrillers, suspense movies, and crime dramas. Critics often attacked him for his violence and sexual content, but that was no problem for Kirk. After seeing *Carrie* (1976), Kirk was convinced that he and De Palma would make an ideal team.

The Fury is the story of a former CIA agent, Peter Sandza, who is hell-bent on rescuing his son, Robin (Andrew Stevens), who has been kidnapped by sinister officials hoping to take advantage of his powerful psychic abilities, perhaps as a tool for use against the Russians.

The villain of the film is a sinister government agent Ben Childress (John Cassavetes), who gathers up children with parapsychological abilities and trains them to become killers.

It takes Peter almost a year to track down where Robin is being held. While doing so, he has to avoid Childress and his agents, who want him dead.

In captivity, Robin enjoys a luxurious lifestyle, and is even provided with an elegant doctor who becomes his mistress. All this has spoiled him, and he's become a mercurial egomaniac with a violent temper.

After years of voluntary retirement, Carrie Snodgress came out of retirement to play Hester, an institute researcher with whom Peter falls in love. She becomes embroiled in his schemes, and it costs her her life.

To get his son back, Peter is helped by a young girl, Gillian Bellaver (Amy Irving), who has strong psychic powers, too. He gains her trust, and then tries to save her from kidnapping by government agents under the direction of Childress.

Charles Durning, as Dr. Jim McKeever, is director of an institute investigating psychic powers. He turns out to be in league with Childress.

For a short while, at least, John Belushi was hired for a minor role, but when he showed up drugged, he was fired.

The Fury also marked the screen debut of Daryl Hannah, who for a time was the girlfriend of John F. Kennedy, Jr.

At the end, Robin is driven insane, and he jumps out a window to his death. A distraught Peter (Kirk) follows him, falling out of the window, too. To avenge the death of Kirk and his son, Gillian (Irving) uses her psychic abilities to cause Childress' body to explode.

For the most part, Kirk always had good luck in getting backed up by strong supporting players. In *The Fury,* they included Snodgress whose *Diary of a Mad Housewife* (1970) had earned her an Oscar nod.

Amy Irving had begun her career in the 1976 horror movie, *Carrie,* following that with her role with Kirk in *The Fury.*

[From 1985 to 1989, Irving was married to producer Steven Spielberg. At their divorce settlement, she was awarded $100 million after a judge controversially vacated a prenuptial agreement which had been written on a napkin.]

Before working with Kirk in the role as his son, Robin, Andrew Stevens had had a substantial role in *Shampoo* (1975), co-starring with Warren Beatty. When Kirk met him, he was married to the actress, Kate Jackson.

Of them all, Charles Durning was the most veteran performer, having over the course of his life appeared in some two hundred movies, including *The Sting* (1973) and *Dog Day Afternoon* (1975).

A Greek actor, John Cassavetes, as the villainous Childress, was a pioneer of American independent filmmaking, and in time, he would both write and direct more than a dozen movies. Kirk had admired his performance in *Rosemary's Baby* (1968). He was married to Gena Rowlands, Kirk's former co-star.

Roger Ebert wrote, "De Palma's almost nonstop action carries the film along well (and distracts us from the holes in its plot). Kirk Douglas was a good casting choice as the avenging father. In his best roes, he seems to be barely in control of his manic energy, and this time, being chased down, he seems just right."

***

In a radical change of pace, Kirk was cast as the human incarnation of the cartoon character, "Wile E. Coyote," the nemesis of another cartoon character, "The Road Runner," in *The Villain* (1979). [*It was marketed in the U.K. and Australia as* Cactus Jack.] Raster Production financed it for a release by Columbia. The movie was a parody, in general of Western films, and specifically of Warner Brothers "Wile E. Coyote" cartoon episodes.

The Villain: Kirk, Ann-Margret, and Arnold Schwarzenegger

Kirk, as Cactus Jack, is a bumbling badman with a penchant for slapstick. He falls off cliffs, lights the wrong end of a dynamite stick, and glues himself to railroad tracks in front of a fast-approaching train. As such, he gets more hee-haws than laughs.

A wealthy rancher, Parody Jones (Strother Martin) gives a large sum of money to his beautiful and sexy daughter, Charming Jones (Ann-Margret). She has to transport the

Kirk, living dangerously, in *The Villain*

loot by stagecoach to a bank in the nearest town. As a bodyguard, she hires a big, handsome bodybuilder, known as "Handsome Stranger" (Arnold Schwarzenneger). Although she's seductive and flirtatious, he seems indifferent to her charms. She is dressed like Daisy Mae attending a formal barbecue.

Bad guy Avery Simpson (Jack Elam) hires Cactus Jack to rob the stagecoach. He lays one trap after another, but each of his schemes backfires. At one point, he hires an Indian, "Nervous Elk" (Paul Lynde, the ultimate "over the top Queen"), whose bitchy humor emerges as relentlessly unfunny.

Born in Sweden, Ann-Margret is still remembered for her contributions to movies that included *Bye Bye Birdie* (1963). Her sexy, sultry, throaty contralto cause invited comparisons to "the Female Elvis Presley." The two came together when they co-starred in *Viva Las Vegas* (1964). In 1967, she married actor Roger Smith, who became her business manager.

Minor roles were played by Ruth Buzzi as "Damsel in Distress" and Mel Tillis as "Telegraph Agent." [*A singer and comedian, Buzzi was best known for her appearances on* Rowan & Martin's Laugh-In *from 1968 to '73. A country music singer and songwriter, Tillis had a speech impediment. Surprisingly, it did not affect his singing voice.*]

This runaway film, which contained many dangerous stunts, did nothing for Kirk's career. It was helmed by Hal Needham, a former stuntman himself. As he told Kirk, "I have forty-two broken bones, a token from my heyday as a stuntman." He was most famously known for his frequent collaborations with Burt Reynolds in such hit movies as *Smokey and the Bandit* (1977).

Janet Maslin in *The New York Times* summed up *The Villain* in a nutshell: "The movie is almost as dopey as it is interminable."

***

As the 1970s hurried to its exit, Kirk's sons were growing up and becoming men, clinging to the movie industry for the most part.

Michael had already become a movie star and producer, especially after the release of *One Flew Over the Cuckoo's Nest* (1975), a role that Kirk had coveted for so long.

Before the decade's end, he had another big hit, *The China Syndrome* (1979), about a nuclear power accident. The Three Mile Island nuclear power plant disaster occurred only twelve days after the movie's release, incredible timing that added to its box office allure.

Kirk loved his sons and was pleased that they wanted to work and succeed. Burt Lancaster weighed in with a privately held opinion. "There had to be some father-son jealousy between Kirk and Michael. Kirk realized that the torch of stardom had passed. Michael, I'm certain, will go on to make even greater films. Kirk was currently appearing in crap, with more on the horizon. His glory days were fading fast."

In March of 1977, Michael, age 32, married Diandra Luker, the 19-year-old daughter of an Austrian diplomat. A year later, they had a son,

Cameron, whose life veered frequently into the tragic.

When Kirk heard of his birth, he said, "It had to happen. Now I'm a grandfather, I pray Cameron doesn't call me Gramps. God, does time move on so swiftly. It seemed only yesterday that I was the horndog of Hollywood, seducing all the movie goddesses…well, most of them, at least."

He later wrote, "My Jewish dream of being the patriarch, with my children working together with me, will never be fulfilled. My need to have them sitting around me at the dinner table once a week will never be satisfied. I always wanted that to happen with my Pa. My sons have expressed to me so much love and much resentment. Whatever I might say about all four of them—Michael, Joel, Peter, and Eric—those kids are never dull."

***

Kirk launched a strange interlude in his career as an actor and film producer when he got involved with Brian De Palma again after the release of *The Fury* (1978). The director was teaching a course in filmmaking at his alma mater, Sarah Lawrence, a liberal arts college in Bronxville, New York, and he prevailed on Kirk to lend his star presence to what had been conceived as a work/study training exercise for students desiring a career in the film industry.

De Palma laid out the challenges associated with filmmaking before his students: Raise the money to produce this experimental film, shoot it, edit it, and promote it as a 90-minute experimental film entitled *Home Movies*.

It was clearly understood that Kirk would play the male lead, but the role eventually degenerated into an extended cameo. Kirk played "The Maestro," a distracted and egocentric professor teaching filmmaking—clearly a spoof of De Palma himself. As a college professor, "The Maestro's" film course was entitled "Star Therapy." It promoted, perhaps satirically, a state of affairs that few filmmaking students will

ever attain: "Publicize your name before the title of the film."

Most of the events that unfold as part of the plot were inspired by De Palma's own life growing up in an eccentric family.

Denis Byrd (Keith Gordon) is an archetype for De Palma himself. As a young man, he films everything that is happening at his home. His domineering mother, Mrs. Byrd, was cast with Mary Davenport, and his philandering father, Dr. Byrd, starred Vincent Gardenia.

During the course of the film, sibling rivalry raised its nasty head when brother Denis competes with James (Gerrit Graham) for the affection of the beautiful Kristina (Nancy Allen), who was married to De Palma at the time.

Actually, much of the cast was quite talented and would go on to successful careers. Allen had appeared in her husband's *Carrie* (1976) and would soon star in his *Dressed to Kill* (1980), in which Keith Gordon would also be cast.

Gerrit Graham would also appear in other De Palma movies and in two different *Star Trek* episodes.

A Neapolitan, Vincent Gardenia had been nominated for a Best Supporting Actor Oscar for *Bang the Drum Slowly* (1973), and again for the same award for *Moonstruck* (1987).

Home Movies cost $400,000 to make and took in $90,000 at the box office. Although a few viewers found it "an undiscovered gem," the majority seemed to feel it was "boring and forgettable."

As a training exercise for the film students at Sarah Lawrence, however, the experience was probably invaluable.

***

With the decline of Westerns, science fiction became a popular film genre in the late 1970s and early '80s. A British film company, Transcontinental Film Production, greenlighted a sci-fi movie, *Saturn 3* (aka *Saturn City*). Its producers set out to sign two American stars, Farrah Fawcett and Kirk Douglas.

Since the blonde-haired goddess, Fawcett, was all the rage at the time, it was understood that she'd take star billing

Detail from a movie poster for *Saturn 3* with Farrah Fawcett, Harvey Keitel (inset), and Kirk

because of her marquee name. Although Kirk was a bit old to play her lover, he wanted to star in it anyway.

She had risen to international fame when she'd posed in a red swimsuit for a full-body portrait that morphed into the best-selling poster in the world. She had starred as a private investigator in the hit TV series, *Charlie's Angels* (1976-77).

At the time Kirk met her, she was being featured on many magazine covers. In 1973, she'd married Lee Majors, but six years later, they separated, and she became involved in a romance with heartthrob Ryan O'Neal.

She was quite candid during lunch with Kirk. "Sometimes, Ryan breaks my heart, and I can't trust him not to run off with other women, but he gives me confidence in myself. He does have a terrible temper and can be violent at times. He sent a warning to you that you're not to touch me unless required by our director."

In *Saturn 3*, she made a brief appearance topless, but she steadfastly refused to sign a release for the nude photographs to be replicated in magazines. Hugh Hefner, the *Playboy* publisher, was said to be "salivating" to get hold of them.

The screenplay for *Saturn 3* was written by Martin Amis, based on a story by John Barry. The director-choreographer, Stanley Donen, was signed to helm the movie.

[As a former chorus boy and "the King of Hollywood musicals," Donen was an odd choice for a sci-fi flick. He was better known for his frothy show-stoppers, none more notable that Singin' in the Rain *(1952), starring Gene Kelly and Debbie Reynolds. He had also been a key player in the career of Kelly, helming him in such musicals as* On the Town *(1949).]*

When Kirk met him, he jokingly asked, "Do Farrah and I have to dance? I'm no Gene Kelly, but I can do a great Debbie Reynolds."

The plot of *Saturn 3* was far-fetched. Lovers, portrayed by Kirk and Fawcett, are stationed at a remote base on Saturn's third moon, Titan. Their mission involves research associated with food production for the starving, overpopulated Planet Earth.

Their bizarre but relatively tranquil life is interrupted by the arrival of Bensom (Harvey Keitel), a deranged killer masquerading as a visiting tech expert. He invades this lonely outpost in space and takes over. Shades of Frankenstein: He creates a monster robot, a lethal "artificial intelligence" that towers eight feet tall, with murder as its ultimate goal.

Benson had lied to Kirk and Fawcett about his identity, claiming that he was Captain James, the shuttle commander, whom he had murdered. To complicate matters, Benson begins to show a sexual obsession with Fawcett, Kirk's girlfriend. Disturbingly, she also arouses lust in the robot.

In time, both Benson and Kirk will be killed, and the robot destroyed. That leaves lonely Fawcett to prepare for her solo flight to Earth, a planet she has never visited.

When Kirk saw the final cut of *Saturn 3*, he turned to Donen and said, "Let's face it…The robot is the fucking star of the picture."

Colin Chilvers, incidentally, modeled the monster, Hector, on a 16th Century drawing by Leonardo da Vinci.

***

One of the most intriguing of Kirk's films in the 1980s combined aspects of a World War II drama and a sci-fi movie. Most of the action in *The Final Countdown* (1980) takes place aboard a modern and fully equipped aircraft carrier. The vessel is suddenly caught up in a violent storm, which transports it through time and space to December 6, 1941, only hours before the unprovoked Japanese attack on U.S. Naval facilities at Pearl Harbor.

Kirk's third son, only twenty-three years old at the time, Peter Vincent Douglas, pulled off the film production of this daunting project with a team of writers. He even got permission from the U.S. Navy to shoot for three weeks aboard the U.S.S. *Nimitz*, the nation's oldest and finest aircraft carrier, a "flagship" loaded with jets, bombs, and the most sophisticated military equipment of its era.

Kirk was cast as Captain Matthew Yelland, the ship's commanding officer. When he and his crew come to accept that they're in 1941, not 1980, a major decision will have to be made that will alter the course of world history. Should they counterattack and destroy the Japanese forces before they descend on Honolulu?

The Final Countdown's director was Don Taylor, whom Kirk had known first as an actor through his appearances in some classics of the 1940s and '50s, *Father of the Bride* and *Father's Little Dividend*. He'd also had a key role in *Stalag 17* (1953) starring William Holden. Taylor's final film appearance was in *I'll Cry Tomorrow* (1955) with Susan Hayward.

[As a director, Taylor churned out

such films as Escape from the Planet of the Apes *(1971).]*

The second lead was that of Warren Laskyu, a civilian systems analyst assigned as an observer aboard the *Nimitz*. Kirk had wanted to cast his son Michael into the role, but he was too involved with another production at the time. The role then went to Martin Sheen, who had delivered such a strong performance in *Acopalypse Now* (1979).

As a subplot, the crew of the *Nimitz* rescue the survivors of a Japanese attack on their yacht. Coming aboard was Senator Samuel S. Chapman, in a role cast with Charles Durning, with whom Kirk had worked before. With him is his assistant, Laurel Scott (Katharine Ross), her dog, Charlie, and one of the surviving Japanese Zero pilots, Shimura (Soon-Tek Oh).

[The real-life figure of Senator Chapman is a curious footnote in world history, as he disappeared at sea right before the attack on Pearl Harbor. Had he lived, he might have been Franklin D. Roosevelt's running mate in the 1944 presidential elections. That would mean that he, not Harry S Truman, would have become President of the United States in 1945.]

In one of the movie's most dramatic scenes, the pilot of the Japanese Zero grabs a weapon and kills a guard, threatening the others. He wants to send word to the Japanese fleet about the presence and the power of the *Nimitz*, but he is eventually overpowered.

Chapman demands to be taken at once to Pearl Harbor to warn of a possible attack, but the captain drops him and Laurel off on a remote Hawaiian island where he knows that they will be discovered and rescued. Kirk places them under the supervision of Commander Richard Owens (James Farentino) and some sailors.

Captain Kirk then decides to advance toward a military engagement to protect Pearl Harbor, but the mysterious storm suddenly returns and the carrier is swept through time back to 1980. History will not have to be rewritten, and the *Nimitz* will not be able to stop the Japanese bombers.

Actually, World War II buffs found its premise fascinating, as they speculated about "what might have been." But many movie-goers found the plot of *The Final Countdown* a rip-off of themes from an episode of *The Twilight Zone*.

Katharine Ross, as Laurel, had starred as Elaine Robinson in *The Graduate* (1967) with Dustin Hoffman, and she also received a Best Supporting Actress Oscar nomination for her performance in *Butch Cassidy and the Sundance Kid* (1969) with Paul Newman and Robert Redford.

She surprised Kirk by telling him "I'm not a movie star. The system is dying, and I'd like to help it along."

As Captain Owens, a Brooklyn-born Italian actor, James Farentino, would eventually star in a hundred films, TV, and stage roles. After working with Kirk, he was slated to play Juan Perón opposite Faye Dunaway in a 1981 made-for-TV movie, *Evita Perón*. At one time in the 1960s, Farentino had been the husband of actress Elizabeth Ashley.

The Final Countdown received mixed reviews and wasn't the summer blockbuster that Bryna-United Artists hoped it would be.

Vincent Canby of *The New York Times* reserved his praise for the movie's sweeping overviews of the *Nimitz*. Roger Ebert claimed that "logic doesn't matter in this *Star Wars*-like movie." He, too, thought the film's chief interest centered on the aircraft carrier itself.

Critic Gene Siskel cited *The Final Countdown* as "one of the dogs of 1980."

***

In 1982, when *The Man from Snowy River* was released, it was the most expensive movie ever made in Australia, costing $5 million. The movie was based on the storyline of a beloved Australian poem, the work of A.B. ("Banjo") Patterson, a journalist and entertainer long associated with the song "Waltzing Matilda."

[Patterson (1864-1941), sometimes defined as a "bush poet," is so deeply associated with the Australian psyche that he appears on some editions of Australia's ten-dollar banknote.]

To attract an international audience, the producers needed a top star, and turned to the limited number of American actors who might be able to pull it off—Burt Lancaster, Robert Mitchum, and Kirk Douglas, in that order. Gregory Peck and Charlton Heston were runners-up.

Lancaster and Mitchum had other plans, but Kirk accepted the challenge, mainly because he could play two of the roles, those of two alienated brothers, Harrison and Spur. When it was announced that an American movie star would play a key role in this insight into the Australian psyche, there was much resentment expressed in the "Down Under" press.

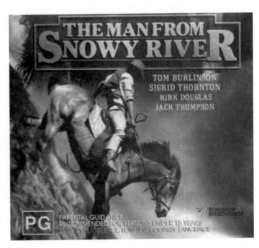

Harrison is a rich cattleman and landowner, and Spur is a grizzled old miner walking around on a peg leg, a *persona* that evoked Kirk's performance in *Scalawag*. "Once again," Kirk said, "I had to hide my right foot up my ass."

After an 18-hour flight, a jet-lagged Kirk faced some rather belligerent reporters at the airport in Sydney, but he won them over with his charm.

Sigrid Thornton and Tom Burlinson, the romantic protagonists of *The Man from Snowy River*

Actually, Kirk's involveent in *The Man from Snowy River* might be defined as that of the third lead. The stars of the picture were Tom Burlinson (portrayed by Jim Craig) and his girlfriend, Jessica Harrison (played by Sigrid Thornton). They fall in love despite the objections of her father. Or is he her real father? Her aunt, Rosemary (Lorraine Bayly), suggests that Spur, the grizzled miner, might be her biological father. It seems that years ago, the brothers fell in love with the same woman.

Many Australians believe that the essence of Banjo Peterson's poem—the one that inspired the production of this film—is captured in this sequence...the precarious, terrifying ride down the mountain.

As such, Australia's National Film and Sound Archives define *The Man from Snowy River* as a film that's of historic importance to the national identity of "Down Under."

Clancy (Jack Thompson) is a celebrated horseman, who is called upon to lead a posse of locals in a chase to capture a prized wild stallion.

George Miller, an Australian of Greek origin, was hired as its director. He would, in time, become one of the most successful and most awarded filmmakers in the country, having gained international fame by launching the *Mad Max* franchise in 1979, starring Mel Gibson.

Tom Burlinson was actually born in Toronto but his family emigrated to Australia. His big break came when he was cast in *Snowy River,* and he

Kirk played two characters in *Man from Snowy River*. Here's the scruffier of the two.

would go on to stardom. There was a problem: He had to be an expert horserider in the film, and he didn't know how to ride a horse. He learned, however, before the debut of filming.

Sigrid Thornton, a daughter of Canberra, was on her way to becoming a popular actress in Australia in both films and TV. Burlinson and Thornton—but not Kirk—would appear in the sequel, *The Man from Snowy River II*.

The movie went over big in Australia and had a certain international success, but without critical acclaim. In his review, Roger Ebert found the troubled romance of Burlington and Thornton "plundered from some long-shelved Roddy McDowall script."

"But the film has good qualities, too," he wrote, "including some great serial photography of thundering herds of horses, and the invigorating grandeur of the Australian landscape. However, I quickly tired of Douglas' grizzled old miner. He's a great screen personality and often an effective actor, but he has a tendency to overact. You're asking for trouble if you give him a beard, a pickax, a whiskey bottle, and a wooden peg leg. The whole rivalry between the two brothers is a set-up anyway, meaningless to the plot."

***

Remembrance of Love was a 1982 made-for-television movie in which Joe Rabin (Kirk), a middle-aged widower, returns to Israel for a reunion of Holocaust survivors. He is accompanied by his daughter, Mary, as portrayed by Pam Dawber. *[Dawber was an American actress known for her TV sitcom success as Mindy in* Mork & Mindy *(1978-1982), opposite Robin Williams.]*

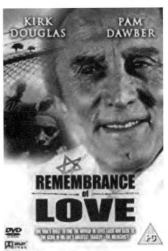

Producer Doris Quinland, working for NBC, shot the film entirely in Israel. It was based on a teleplay by Harold Jack Bloom, with direction by Jack Smight. His screen credits included such hits as *Airport* (1975).

Rabin (Kirk) has another motive for flying to Israel: He hopes to encounter the girlfriend he left behind, pregnant with his child, in Poland just before the Holocaust. Her name was Leah. Eric Douglas, Kirk's youngest son, played Rabin as a teenager in Poland.

Kirk eventually locates Leah, and they

share tender moments together, but, of course, both of them realize they have moved on with their lives and can't replicate what might have been had they escaped the Nazis together.

As one reviewer wrote, "While melodramatic, the movie does not descend into mush. Much of this is thanks to the casting of Kirk Douglas, who treats his character with the appropriate respect and sensitivity to make it a mature performance rather than an over-the-top one."

***

Eddie Macon's Run, a Martin-Bregman-Universal Production set for a 1983 release, was an American action-thriller-drama. It was more important to Kirk's co-star, John Schneider, than it was to Kirk himself. This was Schneider's first feature film after his long-running (1979-'85) TV hit, *The Dukes of Hazzard* that ran for seven seasons. The young actor and country music singer was hoping that success with this picture would lead to his being cast as a leading man in future movies.

The film is burdened with too many flashbacks. Schneider is a young man harshly sentenced for a few minor infractions. In jail in Alabama, he plots his escape and flees to Laredo, Texas, where he hopes to cross the border into Mexico for a reunion with his wife, Chris (Leah Ayres), and his infant son.

The Jewish-American director, Jeff Kanew, not only directed the film, but wrote and edited it, too. He would appear in Kirk's life once again as the director of the final film that paired Burt Lancaster with Kirk.

Eddie Macon is running from a nightmare... running to a dream....and running for his life.

EDDIE MACON'S RUN

KIRK DOUGLAS · JOHN SCHNEIDER
A MARTIN BREGMAN Production
EDDIE MACON'S RUN
Screenplay by JEFF KANEW Executive Producer PETER SAPHIER Produced by LOUIS A. STROLLER
Directed by JEFF KANEW A UNIVERSAL PICTURE

A daughter of Baltimore, Ayres was better known for her role as Valerie Bryson in the daytime soap opera, *The Edge of Night.*

Her competition is Jilly Buck (Lee Purcell), the rich niece of the governor of the state. Eddie rescues her from a gang of thugs, and she seems to fall for him, but he remains faithful to his wife, which she admires. She aids him in his escape. *[Coincidentally, in 1969, Purcell had co-starred with Michael Douglas in* Adam at Six A.M.*]*

Hot on Eddie's trail is Buster Marzack (Kirk), a former New Jersey policeman now working as a corrections officer in Texas whose job it is to track down escaped prisoners. He does finally catch his man, but shows that he has a heart, letting him go free.

We last see Eddie walking across a bridge spanning the Rio Grande into Mexico to join his wife and son.

***

During the course of his career, a Canadian director, Steven Hilliard Stern, would helm some sixty motion pictures and TV mini-series, working with some of the world's most famous stars. One of them was Kirk's son, Michael Douglas, whom Stern directed in *Running* (1979). Stern also directed Tom Hanks, Keanu Reeves, Christopher Reeve, Kim Basinger, Tony Curtis, Holly Hunter, Tommy Lee Jones, Kate Jackson, and Bill Cosby.

Stern came across a Western drama, *Draw!* by Stanley Mann, and made a deal with Kirk's Bryna Production and Astral Films of Canada to adapt it into a made-for-TV saga. It was eventually released in 1984.

Its theme was already familiar to Kirk—"Been there, done that," he said. "It was the tale of two old gunslingers, Kirk as Harry H. Holland and James Coburn as Sam Starett.

Kirk had never worked with Coburn before. Throughout his career, this son of Nebraska would appear in 70 films and dozens of TV appearances. He would go on to win a Best Supporting Actor Oscar for his performance as Glen Whitehouse in *Affliction* (1999). With his toothy grin and lean physique, Coburn was perfectly cast as one of the aged and alcoholic gunslingers in *Draw!*.

As Holland, Kirk wants to get out of Bell City with the loot he's picked up at a poker game. Reggie Bell (Derek McGrath) is he gambler who lost all that money to Kirk and he wants it back. He is aided by Sheriff Harmon (Richard Donat) and his deputy, Wally Blodgett (Graham Jarvis). In a shootout, the sheriff is killed, Holland is wounded, and Starret (Coburn) is dragged out of a drunken stupor to make everything right again. The two aging gunslingers bond and return to clean up crooked Bell City.

There's a lot of tongue-in-cheek in *Draw!*, as if Kirk and Coburn are each spoofing their many involvements in Westerns.

***

Peter Douglas was given Richard Kramer's screenplay of *Amos*, set to be aired on CBS in September of 1985. When his son showed it to Kirk, he said, "Here's a role you're too young to play." It evoked memories of *One Flew Over the Cuckoo's Nest*, a play that Kirk had been a part of on Broadway. *[A movie role in that, however, had escaped him]*

Kirk avidly read the script that night and wanted to star in it as Amos Lasher.

Within a few days, he met with the British director, Michael Tuchner, who told Kirk, "In the summer of 1978, I was the hottest director in Hollywood for fifteen seconds." Kirk had admired his remake of *The Hunchback of Notre Dame* (1982), in which its star, Anthony Hopkins, had spent five hours every morning being physically transformed by the makeup and costuming departments.

Kirk would later look back on *Amos* and express his delight in accepting his role. "No doubt, it was my best performance on television...one of the best."

Before the debut of filming, he read the novel the screenplay had been based on. Written by Stanley West, it was entitled *Amos: To Ride a Dead Horse*. It had been a self-published novel and, like John Grisham, West started out by selling his books from the trunk of his car.

"I began writing *Amos* on an old, beat-up typewriter," West told Kirk. "I sent it to many publishers, and it was returned many, many times, so I published it myself in 1983."

Unlike some of his recent films, where on occasion, he had never heard of his co-stars, Kirk was delighted the both of his leading ladies were already known to movie or TV audiences from coast to coast. Eliza-

Kirk with Elizabeth Montgomery, who, in *Amos*, is now playing a witch who's more malignant that what she portrayed as Samantha in *Bewitched*.

580

beth Montgomery was cast as a dreaded nurse in a retirement home, alongside Dorothy McGuire as Hester Farrell.

Amos (Kirk) has lost his wife in a car accident and has been sent to live at the Sunset Nursing Home. The place evokes a dark version of Sunny Pines in the TV sitcom, *The Golden Girls.*

The supervisor there is Daisy Daws, a toxically belligerent nurse who evokes the monstrous Nurse Ratched in *Cuckoo's Nest.* She rules with an iron fist, abusing her patients and actually hastening their deaths so that she can collect on their insurance policies whenever the nursing home is named as the beneficiary.

Partly because he's in better physical shape than most of the other residents, Amos, a former baseball player, is abused by the staff.

McGuire, a daughter of Nebraska, had never been known to give a bad performance. She's a lonely widow who falls for Amos. She had starred in a number of Hollywood classics, including *Gentleman's Agreement* (1947) with Gregory Peck and *Friendly Persuasion* (1956) with Gary Cooper.

As a shock to many viewers, Elizabeth Montgomery played the evil villain. The daughter of actor Robert Montgomery, she is best remembered for her role as the lovely witch, Samantha Stephens, in the hit ABC-TV sitcom, *Bewitched.*

As one reviewer noted, "The famous gladiator meets the small screen's famous witch." Another noted, "Miss Montgomery has buried the Samantha image forever."

As the film's conclusion, Amos gets his revenge on the nurse by committing suicide and leaving behind clues suggesting that she had engineered his death.

In the aftermath of the airing of *Amos,* Kirk investigated some of the many abuses in the nation's nursing homes and wrote a blistering editorial that appeared in *The New York Times.* He also flew to Washington to testify before Florida Representative Claude Pepper's Select Committee on Nursing Homes.

Many nursing homes attacked Kirk viciously, claiming that his conclusions were wrong. But hundreds of patients swamped him with letters, citing abuses so horrible that he turned whatever documentation they provided over to the police. Many of his fans thought he had power to fix whatever was wrong.

"I may be Spartacus, but I'm not Superman," he responded.

***

In their swan song together, Burt Lancaster and Kirk appeared for a

581

final time on the screen together in *Tough Guys* (1986). It was the last film released by Kirk's Bryna Production.

Before filming began, Kirk was asked to comment on his love/hate dynamic with Lancaster. "Sometimes we don't see each other for years at a time. We go our different ways, but our friendship is still there. We fight a lot, and we disagree on most things. That's what keeps our friendship going. Burt knows that he can always count on me, and I can always count on him."

Can any other team of actors claim as long an onscreen relationship as Douglas and Lancaster? Here they are, paired up again, in *Tough Guys*, a testimonial to their enduring talent to survive.

[The two actors had last performed together not in a film, but in a play. In 1981, they had co-starred in the Bernard Sabath play, Boys in Autumn. *It had been an "as imagined" rendezvous of Tom Sawyer (Kirk) with Huckleberry Finn (Lancaster) on the banks of the Mississippi River.*

Most critics found it "a dreadful bore," but because of the actors' star power, it filled all the theaters' seats during its month-long run at the Marines Memorial Theater in San Francisco.]

Jeff Kanew, who had just directed Kirk in *Eddie Macon's Run*, met with him and gave him a copy of a new script by James Orr and Jim Cruickshank, two young Canadian writers. The team had written their screenplay with the specific purpose of reuniting Lancaster and Kirk on the screen for a final time. It had been nearly two decades since their last joint on-screen appearance in *Seven Days in May* (1964).

According to the plot, Harry Doyle (Lancaster) and Archie Long (Kirk) are being released from prison after serving thirty-year terms for a train robbery. These two bandits, it's revealed, had been the last in America to hold up a train. Archie had two immediate goals: to devour some Chicken McNuggets and to "hold a woman for five years."

Greeting them outside the prison's gate is a young man, Richie Evans, played by Dana Carvey in his film debut. He is their parole officer, yet he has some hero worship of them as two towering figures from America's roguish past.

Strictly for comic relief, another man is waiting for them to get out of prison, too. Almost immediately after they emerge into the world as civilians, Leon B. Little (as portrayed by Eli Wallach) shoots at them. Because he's nearsighted, he misses. He'll be on their trail until the end of the picture, as he is still trying to fulfill a contract he made three decades earlier to assassinate both of them.

Now that they're free, they're like Rip Van Winkle, emerging from a long slumber into an environment that's unfamiliar to them. Before separating, they stop in at their former saloon only to discern that it's now a gay bar.

Freedom isn't what they'd envisioned. Because he's older, Harry (Lancaster) is checked into a retirement home to live on Social Security. There, he united with his old girlfriend (Alexis Smith). One reporter later wrote, "It was just great for fans of Miss Smith to see her still looking sharp, saucy, and sexy after all these years."

The parole officer has arranged a job for Archie (Kirk). He'll work in an ice cream parlor and live in a seedy hotel. His job stint ends disastrously.

Sex re-enters his life in the shapely form of Sky Foster (Darlanne Fluegel), a hip feminist and aerobics instructor. She is attracted to him, asserting, "You're the only real man in the gym." She sets about to transform him, even changing the style of his clothing to reflect something more current. But at his age, he finds it difficult keeping up with her sexual demands.

In the meantime, the two ex-cons are being trailed by Deke Yablonski (Charles Durning), an aged cop, who was responsible for sending them "up the river" in the first place. He suspects they'll return to their old penchant for robbing trains.

He's right.

Kirk and Lancaster's goal involves a holdup aboard the Gold Coast Flyer during its final run and at the moment it pulls into the railyard in Los Angeles. It's made clear that it will be loaded with members of the press and local dignitaries.

They commandeer the train and ride with it toward the Mexican border. Their would-be assassin, "Mr. Magoo" (Wallach) is still on their trail.

The train speeds south as Harry and Archie stage their Last Hurrah, each of them aware that it's the end of the line. They want to exit from life with a rousing finale—in this case, in a volley of bullets. Their wish comes true.

As could be anticipated, reviews of *Tough Guys* were mixed. Longtime fans, still loyal to both of them, went to see the film as a final *adieu*. It grossed about $22 million at the box office, *Time* magazine calling it "*Cocoon* with *cojones*," a reference to Don Ameche's sci-fi adventure / comedy, *Cocoon* (1985) about a group of elderly people rejuvenated by aliens.

Roger Ebert wrote, "Watching *Tough Guys*, you begin to meditate. You look at Kirk Douglas and Burt Lancaster, and you remember years and years of movie-going. *Tough Guys* might have been better if they played characters who were a little more fallible, humble, and realistic."

A critic for the *Washington Post* wrote: *"Tough Guys"* would like to think it's making a statement about the way we treat our old, but the movie itself makes that statement far more eloquently by paradoxical example—its comedy is based on the shock of seeing two old men behave like jackasses. The movie gives us two actors who, whatever their deficiencies, have generally displayed remarkable daring and integrity in choosing their roles. That they now find themselves grotesquely mired in a movie so crass may be seen as telling commentary on the state of mainstream Hollywood culture."

Lancaster recalled his final meeting with Kirk. After a dozen phone calls, Kirk finally persuaded him to come by his home to read "one of the best scripts I've ever seen, *Haiti Nocturne.*"

Lancaster later said, "Kirk loved it. I thought it was a piece of crap. It was about two mercenaries who descend on Port-au-Prince dressed like buccaneers. We beat the shit out of all the bad dudes; we fuck all the bare-breasted beauties in a seedy bordello run by a black version of Mae West; and we swing out of trees like Tarzan to avenge our enemies. I had to tell Kirk to wake up and face reality. I told him, 'Listen, Spartacus, aren't you aware that our fans, at least the few diehards we have left, are happy to hear that we wake up in the morning?'"

In the months ahead, Kirk presented Lancaster with a copy of his memoir, *The Ragman's Son*, with this inscription: "A lot of these girls will be familiar to you," a reference, perhaps, to Ava Gardner, among many others.

The book became a best-seller, but Lancaster told his friends, "I'm not going to read it. You don't go around banging all the gals and then have the bad taste to write about it. How vulgar can you get?"

***

Kirk had visited India once before as a kind of unofficial ambassador of goodwill from the United States. He returned again in January of 1987 to shoot scenes from an upcoming ABC-TV mini-series, *Queenie.*

It was based on Michael Korda's best-selling novel of the same name, which itself was a *roman à clef* about his aunt, Merle Oberon, who had married his uncle, the British producer, Alexander Korda. Kirk still had memories of the former screen goddess, Oberon, with whom he'd had a long-ago affair.

Ironically, during his time in India, Michael Korda, from within an office at Simon & Schuster Publishers, was editing Kirk's autobiography, *The Ragman's Son*. From reports, the editors didn't like Kirk's strong emphasis on "the little Issur inside my belly" (Kirk's words), but he held steadfast to the original wording of his manuscript.

In the "Pink City" of Jaipur, Kirk dined with the Maharajah of Jaipur. *[Flamboyant, very wealthy, and known for his influential role in Indian politics, Brig. Maharaja Sawai Bhawani Singh Bahadur MVC (1931- 2011) became famous for retrofitting his ancestral seat of power, the Rambagh Palace, into a world-class hotel, today administered by Taj Hotels. His nickname was "Bubbles," a name given by his English nanny because of all the champagne that had flowed at the announcement of his birth. He numbered Bill Clinton and Mick Jagger among his friends.]*

Kirk was not the star of *Queenie*, but a featured player. Cast as producer David Konig, it was a character clearly based on Sir Alexander Korda.

Its script was by April Smith and Winston Beard, a pseudonym for James Goldman. Bronx-born Larry Peerce was assigned to direct.

[Peerce had made a name for himself in One Potato, Two Potato *(1964), a ground-breaking drama about interracial marriage, the first major U.S. movie to do so. He'd also directed Philip Roth's* Goodbye Columbus, *starring Richard Benjamin and Ali MacGraw, and* Ash Wednesday *with Elizabeth Taylor, Henry Fonda, and Helmut Berger.]*

For the historic re-creation of Queenie (Merle Oberon) herself, Kirk just assumed that one of the top box office stars of the 1980s had been selected. Instead, Peerce cast Mia Sara, an actress unknown to Kirk at the time. *[Two years before, Sara had made* Legend *(1985), a lavishly mounted fairytale inspired by Grimm's, with Tom Cruise. In 1996, she would marry James Connery, the son of Sean Connery.]*

The series opens with Queenie, of mixed Irish and Indian background, growing up in Calcutta. The snobby English who rule the place refer to her derisively as "chee-chee" and refuse to welcome her into upper-class society. Her mother "Vicki Kelley" (portrayed by Claire Bloom) is a Hindu who has been abandoned by her Irish husband. She desperately wants Queenie to evolve into a proper English lady.

Prunella Runsey learns about Queenie's mixed racial background and spreads the word among her snooty classmates. That unattractive role was assigned to Serena Gordon, a Londoner who eventually starred in the James Bond spy thriller, *GoldenEye* (1985).

The very talented English actress, Sarah Miles, is seen far too briefly in her role of "Lady Sybil." However, she did confide to Kirk one of her health and beauty secrets, suggesting that he follow her daily ritual, "Drink a cup of your own urine."

Queenie's life is fraught with hazards, including fleeing from the clutches of a "dirty old man," Sir Burton Ramsey, played by Joss Ackland, a Londoner who would appear in more than 130 films and TV roles. Part of the Old Vic troupe, he once ran a tea plantation in Kenya before deciding it was too dangerous.

The character he portrayed tries to seduce Queenie. He is also the father of Prunella, Queenie's enemy. Queenie is accused of his murder. Prunella swears vengeance.

Queenie's uncle is Morgan Jones (Leigh Lawson), a British film and stage actor, director, and writer. At the time Kirk met him, he was the partner of Hayley Mills, the English actress, and mother of his son. By 1988, he married Twiggy, the most famous model in London.

According to the plot, Queenie's uncle is the lover of a rich, jaded socialite. Together, he and Queenie plot to steal a diamond bracelet from her, which they pawn and use to pay their transport to England. There, as a means of supporting herself, Queenie becomes a stripper, a sort of Sally Rand fan dancer in a seedy dive in London's Soho district.

A seemingly long time into the run of the episode, Kirk enters the scene as producer David Konig and meets Queenie. A critic noted that Kirk appears on the screen "with a clenched jaw that has assumed a set-in-concrete life of its own." He's enchanted with her, changes her name to Dawn Avalon, and sets out to morph her into an international celebrity and star, casting her first in an epic to be shot in her native India.

Back in India, the dreaded Prunella is still plotting revenge. As the series comes to an end, expect a final showdown in the colorful but poverty-soaked city of Calcutta.

John J. O'Connor, writing in *The New York Times*, suggested that the casting of Queenie was not politically correct. "The details show an insensitivity to today's global village. Why, for instance, when so many Indian actors have excelled in such productions as *A Passage to India* and *The Jewel in the Crown*, do we still find Indian characters using dark makeup and a singsong voice?"

***

Kirk's most prestigious made-for-television movie was a courthouse drama, *Inherit the Wind*, aired on NBC on March 18, 1988. It was directed by David Greene, with Kirk's son, Peter, the executive producer.

[The teleplay was a shorter version of the 1960 Stanley Kramer movie, Inherit the Wind *that had famously starred Spencer Tracy, Fredric March, and Gene Kelly.*

Inherit the Wind *had already been a teleplay in 1965, starring Melvyn Douglas and Ed Begley. Yet another teleplay, this one with George C. Scott and Jack Lemmon, would be broadcast in 1999.]*

The drama, though highly fictionalized, was based on an actual trial, that of John T. Scopes, a schoolteacher convicted and penalized for teaching Charles Darwin's Theory of Evolution to a high school science class—a violation of Tennessee law. It became notorious as "The Scopes Monkey Trial."

'Inherit the Wind'
Kirk Douglas updates the Scopes 'monkey trial' with issues still vital today

In the 1988 version of the drama, Kirk was cast as Matthew Harrison Brady, a corruption of the actual lawyers at the original trial, the Bible-thumping William Jennings Bryan. Jason Robards portrayed Harry Drummond, a character based on the flamboyantly liberal lawyer, Clarence Darrow. Actor Kyle Secor was cast in the role of the unfortunate Scopes.

Kirk's wife was portrayed by Jean Simmons, with whom he had made *Spartacus* twenty-eight years before. Another major player in *Inherit the Wind* was actor Darren McGavin, as E.K. Hornbeck, a character patterned after Henry L. Mencken, a famous opinion writer for *The Baltimore Herald,* and one of the most influential journalists of his era.

The English director, David Green, was known for having had seven wives. Before working with Kirk, he made *Liberace: Behind the Music* (1988). Ironically Kirk's son, Michael, would portray the flamboyant entertainer in the 2013 film, *Behind the Candelabra.*

Greene had also directed a TV re-

INHERIT THE WIND: Three pros (Kirk, Jean Simmons, and Jason Robards) prove their late-life endurance and durability by reprising (at least for Kirk and Jean) their collaborations in movies from other venues and other eras—*Spartacus,* for example—when screens and movie budgets were bigger.

587

make of *What Ever Happened to Baby Jane* in 1991, the original having been cast with Bette Davis and Joan Crawford.

Robards had been married to Lauren Bacall from 1961 to 1969, and he and Kirk talked about his former wife, Kirk expressing his extreme gratitude for her efforts to help make him a movie star.

Many viewers hailed Kirk's performance as Brady, a Biblical scholar and staunch foe of evolution. He is slowly beaten down and becomes almost apoplectic at the end, defeated in spirit and mind. Kirk's fans seemed to think he should have won the Emmy instead of Robards.

Reviewer Michael Elliot wrote, "Douglas really gets into character so much you feel as if you're watching the real guy and not the actor performing. His speech in the church is among some of the best preaching I've seen from any actor or any real preacher."

[Fans of Burt Lancaster might disagree. Some of them believe that Lancaster, in Elmer Gantry *(1960), had delivered an even more outstanding performance within roughly equivalent settings and circumstances. In that iconic film, in the role of a silver-tongued, hard-drinking, and womanizing preacher, Lancaster developed a role that brought him an Oscar.]*

***

Director John Landis came to Kirk and asked him to play the dying father of Sylvester Stallone in *Oscar,* a slapstick crime comedy released in 1991. At first, Kirk wasn't interested. But after reading the brief script, he accepted.

"I get to crack Stallone in the face," Kirk said. "I'm this dying Italian papa, and he's a gangster. I accuse him of bringing shame to our family. Then I give him another crack."

"We had to do several takes before we pleased the director, and I enjoyed slapping his face. He told me he could take it."

Stallone later told Landis, "Douglas gave me brain damage."

Cast into minor roles were Don Ameche, Eddie Bracken, and Yvonne De Carlo.

Only later did Kirk learn that he had been the second choice to play Stallone's father. Victor Mature had been asked to do it first.

For his performance as the film's kindhearted mobster, Stallone won the Razzie as Worst Actor of the Year. Landis won one, too,

588

as the year's worst director, as did Marisa Tomei as the Year's Worst Supporting Actress.

***

In his next film, *Veraz [also released as* Welcome to Veraz*]*, Kirk played the lead role of Quentin, a long-haired and bearded old coot. He called it "The movie you never saw. A lot of its acting went to waste—from me, not the bear. *[He was referring to a scene in which he feeds a big grizzly bear. As it's sprawled on its back, Kirk's fingers are practically inserted into its mouth.]*

Years later, Kirk would not remember the plot, and no exhibitor seemed to want to touch it. Its director, Xavier Castano, wrote the screenplay.

***

Kirk later sarcastically called it "A Valentine's Present." He was referring to his having survived a helicopter crash on February 13, 1991. "I escaped from the jaws of death. Let me restate that. Come to think of it, it was a great present. God gave me life, the most precious gift of all. Regrettably, others had to die."

Kirk, then aged 74, was at the Santa Paula airport, a simple regional landing strip without a flight tower or air traffic controller about fifty miles northwest of Los Angeles. He boarded a silver-painted Bell Jet-Ranger helicopter with Noel Blanc, its pilot, and a Beverly Hills police officer, Michael Carra. Their itinerary called for a flight plan to Santa Monica.

The crash occurred at 3:30PM. Their craft lifted off the helipad and, instead of heading south over the Santa Clara Riverbed, the mandated and officially recommended route, Blanc flew north, crossing above and across the airport's only runway. That put them directly into the path of a Pitts Aerobatic stunt plane, also taking off. Colliding at a height of about 40 feet above the ground, the helicopter lost a rotor, causing it to free-fall, hitting the runway and turning violently over onto its side. Airport workers rushed to retrieve its pilot and his two passengers, Kirk and the cop. All of them, though badly injured, survived.

About 200 feet away, the stunt plane crashed and exploded in a fiery blast, burning its veteran stunt pilot, Lee Manelski, 46, of Santa Paula, and his student, David Tomlinson, 18, of Thousand Oaks. Their charred bodies were later removed from the wreckage. The episode launched a flurry of lawsuits.

A paramedic, rushed in an ambulance to the scene, later reported, "Mr.

589

Douglas was in a complete daze. He didn't seem to know what had happened. He said, 'I think I've broken my spinal cord.' He had not, but he was very seriously injured."

All three survivors were rushed to the Santa Paula hospital. Later, Kirk was transferred to the Cedars-Sinai Medical center in Los Angeles.

After treatment for his injuries the police officer was let go.

Noel Blanc was put under a breathing machine, as he suffered from the most injuries of all: a fractured leg, broken ribs, a bruised kidney, and a ruptured lung.

[Kirk had worked in a film with his famous father, Mel Blanc, the legendary master of the cartoon voices of Porky Pig, Elmer Fudd, Bugs Bunny, and other Warner Brother's Looney Tunes characters. He had died at the age of 82, and Noel had taken over his father's job.]

Anne, with her sons, Peter and Eric, rushed to Kirk's bedside. The next day, Michael also arrived. He had been somewhat alienated from his father, but Kirk's life-threatening injuries seemed to bring them together again as a loyal father and son.

The two actors even promised to make a picture together. *[That promise waited a dozen years, until the 2003 release of* It Runs in the Family.*]*

Michael was forty-six at the time of Kirk's helicopter accident. As Kirk, in his hospital bed, hugged and kissed him, he noticed the beginning of gray hairs on his son's head.

He asked Michael what script he was working, and his son told him it was a movie called *Basic Instinct*, an in-your-face sex thriller that would co-star Sharon Stone.

***

As the 1980s churned to an end, Kirk, for the most part, had been disappointed with the roles he'd delivered during that decade. In contrast, he was dazzled by his son Michael's movies, notably *Romancing the Stone* (1984), *The Jewel of the Nile* (1985), *Fatal Attraction* (1987), *Wall Street* (1987), and *Black Rain* (1989). Michael's winning streak was capped off with *The War of the Roses* (1989).

Kirk later asked, "Why did God spare me and doom those other two guys? I came down with a bad case of survivor's guilt."

***

Six months after Kirk's near-fatal helicopter crash, he accepted the lead in a low-budget film to be shot in Nova Scotia, the made-for-television movie, *The Secret*, was set for a broadcast on CBS on April 19, 1992. It was the story of a grandfather and his grandson, both of whom struggle with dyslexia.

Kirk had been cast in the role of Mike Dunmore, a store owner in a small town who conceals the fact he can't read or wrote. That's his secret.

Since his grandson, Danny (as portrayed by Jesse R. Tendler), also suffers from dyslexia, the man and boy are drawn together by their shared dilemmas.

Kirk had an affinity for the story because he claimed that his son, Joel, suffered from the same affliction.

The day before Kirk's scheduled departure for Canada, his doctor delivered some bad news: During the helicopter crash, the aerial wire in his pacemaker had become disconnected. He consulted a heart specialist, who told him that he could continue with his normal routine because the aerial wire was a backup. The ventricle wire, a more important piece of hardware, was still in place and functioning normally.

Although at first glance, that was good news, the discovery affected Kirk's insurability as a key element of the film about to be shot. Its producer, Robert Halmi, was a longtime friend who took the risk of continuing his commitment to Kirk's involvement in the film, even though he could not afford the suddenly much more expensive insurance premium. So he agreed to shoot the film anyway, with some aspects of Kirk's involvement remaining uninsured.

"I flew to Canada feeling like a bird with only one wing," Kirk said.

Except for his aches and pains, shooting went smoothly. When it was over, he returned to California and Anne.

One review of *The Secret* read: "Kirk Douglas puts in a great performance, as usual. You really feel for him. The only weakness is the grandson, who seems a little too coached for his lines. It's the type of feel-good fare you'd catch on the Hallmark Channel in between repeats of *Matlock* and *McBride*. *The Secret* is a fine drama."

***

Paul Newman was offered the lead in an upcoming comedy called *Greedy* (1994), an apt title for the story of scavenging relatives descending on their wealthy Uncle Joe, who is in frail health. His treacherous family is eager for him to die and leave them his money. Newman wisely rejected the part. So did Jack Lemmon and Kirk's former co-star, Anthony Quinn.

Working for Imagine Entertainment, the English director-actor, Jonathon Lynn (*My Cousin Vinny*), turned to Kirk, who read the script by Lowell Ganz and Babaloo Mandel, known for such comedies as *Cocoon* (1985), *Parenthood* (1989), and *Mr. Saturday Night* (1992). Kirk then phoned Lynn and accepted the second lead in a picture that would star the much younger Michael J. Fox.

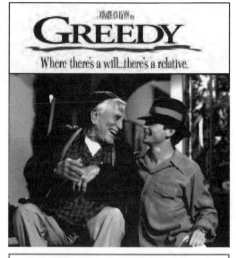

Kirk with Michael J. Fox...Actors of different eras collaborating beautifully.

As Uncle Joe, Kirk portrayed a wheelchair-bound scrap-metal tycoon, an old reprobate with a sharp eye on his "hottie" nurse. He is also still "foxlike" about the venal schemes and manipulations of the McTeague clan, whose members have descended on him like vultures waiting to feed off his corpse.

In 1991, three years before the debut of his filming with Kirk, at the age of twenty-nine, Fox had been diagnosed with Parkinson's Disease. He had learned about his debilitating chronic illness during his filming of *Doc Hollywood*, and he had bravely carried on.

In *Greedy*, Uncle Joe has always had a special affection for Daniel, the character portrayed by Fox, and the son of the family's black sheep. His father, a "do-gooder," had abandoned his brother long ago.

Daniel, when summoned, dutifully returns and amuses his elderly uncle (Kirk) with a Jimmy Durante impersonation. He is a bad professional bowler and wants Uncle Joe to finance the purchase of a bowling alley for him.

Romantically, he's involved with Robin, a level-headed TV sports producer, as portrayed by Nancy Travis. *[A New Yorker, Travis was best known for playing Sylvia Bennington in the 1987 comedy,* Three Men and a Baby.*]*

The family is worried that Uncle Joe will leave his fortune to his sexy nurse, Molly (Olivia d'Abo), a former bikini model and pizza deliverer. She is said to have "her tongue in Uncle Joe's wallet."

As Carl, Ed Begley, Jr., seems to be the leader of the fortune-hunting clan. Its members are venomous even to each other. They arrive with stuffed birds of prey, which Uncle Joe is said to like. The family members flatter and indulge Joe, even naming their ill-mannered children after him.

The movie ends on a sneaky note, so we won't give the plot away.

Janet Maslin of *The New York Times* noted that "Douglas has great fun in the role of the aging Uncle Joe, and he and Michael J. Fox work well together even when the material shows its maudlin side."

***

By the mid-1990, movie roles were getting harder and harder for Kirk to find. Yet instead of retiring, he still wanted to work.

He had been given a script entitled *Take Me Home Again,* a father-and-son drama that he thought would be ideal for him and his son, Michael, as the co-starring vehicle they had each vowed to find.

NBC greenlighted the project for the father-son team and committed it to an airing date on their network of December 18, 1994.

[In Britain, it was released as The Lies Boys Tell.*]*

Michael, however, had to disappoint his father because he was shooting *Disclosure* (1993) with Demi Moore and Donald Sutherland.

Therefore, as Kirk's estranged son, Larry, the director of *Take Me Home Again,* Tom McLoughin, hired Craig T. Nelson, an actor who, at six feet five inches, towered over Kirk. Screenwriter Ernest Thompson based his script on a novel by Lamar Herrin.

In this mawkish plot, Kirk was cast as Ed Reece, who's been stricken with terminal cancer. He becomes obsessed with the idea of dying in the bed in which he was born. That involves a cross-country road trip filled with adventures, including a brawl with some menacing rednecks.

Kirk found Nelson a brilliant actor. "I made a mistake, however, in in demanding that I perform a wrestling scene with him instead of faking it and using a stuntman," Kirk said. "After take after take, my back felt worse than it did after that god damn helicopter crash."

As his estranged son, Larry, Nelson plays a draft-dodging bastard who has deserted his family but agrees to escort his father on his final sentimental journey.

In one scene, Kirk visits an old flame, Sada (Eileen Breenan). He also tries to broker a reconciliation between Larry and his deserted spouse, Connie (Bess Armstrong).

Kirk's big moment is his deathbed scene. "Since that helicopter crash, I'd been thinking a lot about death," he said. "I didn't need a director to tell me how to play the scene. A seventy-seven year old actor sure knows how to play a dying man."

***

On January 28, 1996, at the age of 80, Kirk once again "almost walked into the jaws of death with that bastard's shark-like teeth." Without warning, he had a near-fatal stroke, losing his ability to speak.

He remembered it being a sunny afternoon in Los Angeles, not unusual for a winter day there. He was getting his nails filed and buffed by his manicurist, Rose. "The only way Anne could bear my peasant hands on her was if they were manicured."

It came without warning, beginning with a peculiar sensation in his right cheek. Rose noticed that something was wrong, but only gibberish came out of his mouth.

She rushed to call Rock Gold, his doctor, and then to summon Anne, who was playing bridge at the home of Barbara Sinatra. When Anne arrived, he had just examined Kirk, and told her to drive him to the hospital, as "an ambulance will take too long."

At the rear entrance of the hospital—Anne did not want to alert the press—he found that his legs were not paralyzed, and that he could stagger into the building. That was especially difficult because he was recovering from recent back surgery.

No words the medical team could understand came out of his mouth. He was asking himself, "A stroke? ME? I am only eighty years old."

After a week, he was discharged from the hospital and returned home. There, he was told to begin daily lessons with a speech therapist. It was slow going at first. He wanted to speak like he did in such pictures as *Top Secret Affair* in 1957. He asked the therapist (in writing) when his old voice would return, and how much longer would they be working together?

Her answer was blunt: "Until the day you die."

One late afternoon after she left, he entered the worst depression of his life. He was an actor. An actor needed his voice unless he was playing a deaf mute like Jane Wyman in *Johnny Belinda* (1948).

Privately, Anne was given a dim forecast by his doctor. They told her that unless he showed rapid improvement, there was a strong chance his loss of speech would be permanent. She didn't want to hear that.

He later publicly thanked her for being "a fantastic woman who did not coddle me. Whenever I bemoaned my fate, she told me to get my ass out of bed and keep working with that speech therapist."

Had it all come to an end? The camaraderie of film sets? All the *joie de vivre* of traveling the world as an ambassador of goodwill? The glitz and glamour of the awards ceremonies where he was often an honored guest? What could he do? Sit around and wait for the return of Silent Pictures? Would he become a Norma Desmond on *Sunset Blvd.*, listening to the sound of traffic that passes her by?

He would sit silently for hours, thinking of all the movies he'd made, the women he'd loved. Many were gone, their lives ending tragically like Linda Darnell in a fire. There was Rita Hayworth, gone. Lana Turner, gone. So was Marlene Dietrich. Marilyn Monroe so long ago. Near the end of her life, Joan Crawford could face the world no more and decided one day never to be seen in public again. Death came months later.

One afternoon when the speech therapy lessons had gone particularly bad, he contemplated suicide. In his wheelchair, he maneuvered over to his desk, from which he removed a gun, the one he'd used in *Gunfight at the O.K. Corral* (1957). He also removed a box of bullets and loaded the gun, trying to decide if he should shoot into his temple or into his mouth, the mouth winning out as the target.

As he moved the gun toward his mouth, he banged the barrel against his famous teeth, causing great pain. Right then and there, he decided he couldn't go through with it. He later claimed, "It was that damn toothache that saved my life."

After his flirtation with suicide, he vowed to learn to speak again.

In March of 1996, only two months after his stroke, he was able to appear at the Academy Awards presentation to accept a Lifetime Achievement Oscar for his long career in films. He was also able to thank the audience.

In the days that followed the ceremony, he was overwhelmed with letters from all over the world, even an invitation from the King of Jordan to visit his country.

More awards were in store for him, too, including a U.S. Medal of Freedom, plus honors from many international organizations.

Months later, he would release a special autobiography, *My Stroke of Luck*, which he hoped would become an "operating manual" about how a family should handle a stroke victim in their midst.

He wrote, "My stroke was a blessing in disguise. I learned that we take too many things for granted in this world—even speech. I am lucky, even though my speech is impaired. I suffer no paralysis, and I didn't die. I began to appreciate the gift of life."

***

The 20th Century neared its end. During its turbulent latter half, Kirk had become one of the most outstanding movie stars of the Golden Age. He was already back at work on yet another movie. He'd be co-starring with Lauren Bacall. "She was that marvelous dame who got me started in this damn business in the first place."

Kirk with Bacall—always a winning team, with long movie antecedents to prove it—in *Diamonds*.

Kirk had found what he defined as the perfect vehicle for his comeback. *Diamonds* was an American comedy directed by John Mallory Asher and written by Alan Aaron Katz, with distribution by Miramax. In it, Kirk's speech impediment was deftly handled by having his character of Harry Agensky depicted as infirm and recovering from a recent stroke.

In this bittersweet *schmaltz*, he's a grumpy old man who doesn't want to be sent off to a retirement home. Instead, he hopes to buy a ranch. He is seen living with his favorite son, Moses (Kurt Fuller), in Canada.

Harry has known finer days back when, as a welterweight boxing champion, he was called the "Polish Prince." Scenes from Kirk's 1949 boxing film, *Champion,* were inserted into the context of *Diamonds,* depicting him, years before, in all his power and glory.

The role is a *tour de force* for Kirk, still recovering in real life. He displays emotions which, in the words of one critic, range "from feisty, weepy, and crazily reckless to an old man mired in a puddle of disappointment and confusion."

Arriving for a visit is Harry's estranged second son, Lance (Dan Aykroyd), a pudgy, fussbudget sportswriter. With him is Lance's rebellious, back-talking 15-year-old son, Michael (Corbin Allred).

Harry wants them to drive him to Reno, where he claims he once stashed thirteen priceless diamonds in the home of a bigtime gambler, "Duff the Muff." Harry had been given the cache of jewels as a reward for throwing a fight. He insists that the gems are still hidden in the gangster's home.

Although Lance is skeptical of his father's claim, the three of them (grandfather, son, and grandson) head south from the Pacific Northwest of Canada. Adventure and mishap follow, reaching a dramatic crescendo when grandfather, son, and grandson visit a brothel. They haven't found the diamonds yet, but they come across prostitutes "with hearts of gold."

If Harry can recover these diamonds, he can buy the ranch and a vast tract of land, too.

As it happens, the Madam of the brothel *[she bears the unlikely name of "Sin-Dee"]* is Lauren Bacall, still looking serene and glamourous after all these years. She and Kirk had a reunion, confiding in each other their respective triumphs and tragedies.

[Bacall and Kirk had not worked together since they last starred in Young Man With a Horn *(1950). His affection and attraction for her dated back to their early days in Manhattan when both of them were struggling for their place in the sun. At the time, she was identifying herself as "Betty Bacall" and working as a model. Sexual attraction was no longer a theme song for either of them, except in their current screen roles. Bacall glided perfectly into her role, having nursed an ailing John Wayne character back to life in* The Shootist *some twenty-five years before.]*

In the brothel, Harry warms to Sin-Dee; a divorced Lance rediscovers the joy of sex; and Michael meets a sexy young bombshell, "Sugar" (Jenny McCarthy), who takes his virginity. She tells him that he reminds her of her first love, a high school sweetheart.

A Canadian-American, Aykroyd, had previously appeared in such movies as *The Blues Brothers* (1980) and *Ghostbusters* (1984). In 1989, he'd been nominated for a Best Supporting Actor Oscar for *Driving Miss Daisy.*

Allred had been acting since he was twelve, getting his start in Mormon cinema in his native Utah. When Kirk met him, he had just starred in the TV series, *Teen Angel* (1997-1998).

Reviewers tended to hate the movie and love Kirk's contribution to it. Roger Ebert wrote, "*Diamonds* is a very bad movie, but a genuinely moving experience of three generations. It is unbearable junk. But as a demonstration of Kirk Douglas' heart and inspiration, it is inspiring."

In *The New York Times*, Stephen Holden asked, "What about those diamonds? Do they really exist? Let's put it this way: The only thing about the movie that isn't a transparent paste imitation is Douglas' hard, gleaming performance."

***

It Runs in the Family had long been a dream of Michael Douglas. He had plotted working in the same movie with his father and his son, Cameron, for years. Several times in the past, it had been announced that something like it was on the verge of being launched, but nothing ever got airborne. But finally, something was underway.

Michael was in charge in a co-production deal with MGM and Buena Vista International. Fred Schepisi was named as director. An Australian, he was known for having directed *Six Degrees of Separation* (1993). From the beginning, Michael asserted his authority. When Schepisi wanted to cast the role of Michael's wife in the film, Rebecca, with Sigourney Weaver, Michael hired Bernadette Peters instead.

MICHAEL DOUGLAS KIRK DOUGLAS
IT RUNS IN THE FAMILY

Some families can survive anything.
Even each other.

Even Diana Dill, Kirk's first wife, got included in the film version of the Douglas family saga. In the photo above, she's symbolically positioned between her son, Michael (upper right) and her ex-husband, Kirk.

As Evelyn, Kirk's wife in the film, Michael cast his own biological mother, Diana Dill, the real-life ex-wife of the film's star, his father.

[*Diana had co-starred with Kirk, post-divorce, once before in* The Indian Fighter *(1955). On seeing him after all these years on the set of* It Runs in the Family, *she said, "Do you realize it's been more than fifty years when we were married?"*

"Don't remind me," he answered.]

Kirk was already used to taking second billing in all those movies he'd made with Burt Lancaster. Now, he was taking second billing to his son, Michael, by now a bigger marquee name than he was.

Cameron didn't seem that happy to be working as an actor. Perhaps he'd decided that if he'd be constantly compared to two bigtime stars like his father and grandfather, an acting career was not for him. Consequently, although he appeared briefly in it, Cameron devoted a lot of his time during this era to contemporary music and DJ-ing.

It Runs in the Family, an overview of the Jewish Gromberg family, seems torn from the lives of the real-life Douglas family. As Alex Gromberg, the founder of a powerful law firm, Kirk's character has a speech impairment from a recent stroke. In charge of the law firm is Alex's son, Mitchell

Gromberg (played by Michael Douglas), who has problems with marital fidelity. *[Michael had openly admitted to a reporter that he was a "sex addict."]* Mitchell's son, portrayed by Michael's son, Cameron, has an ongoing problem with drugs, as he did in real life and for which he'd later be imprisoned.

Alex (Kirk) is married to Evelyn (Diana Dill), and Mitchell (Michael) is married to Rebecca, a psychologist (Bernadette Peters). Mitchell and Rebecca have two sons, Eli (Rory Culkin), and Asher (Cameron).

Asher is an "arrogant, girl-crazy, part-time DJ, with a macho hip-hop attitude." Failing in college, he deals in home-grown marijuana. His eleven-year-old brother, Eli, is a brash martial arts whiz, and appears to be going down the same reckless path as his older brother.

[In real life, Rory Culkin had a far more famous older brother, Macauley, the Home Alone *(1990) star, who was for a while the apple of Michael Jackson's eye. Ironically, their other brother, Kieran, had, in 1994, starred in a film which had the same title but had nothing to do with the Douglas family production.]*

It Runs in the Family, eventually released in 2003, was a flop at the box office, generating only $7.5 million in receipts. That compared unfavorably to Michael's other film that year, *The In-Laws,* which earned $21 million. Its co-stars were Albert Brooks and Candice Bergen.

The Douglas family's labor of love came and went fast. Most theaters didn't book it, as reviews were either unfavorable or mixed. Stephen Holden in *The New York Times* called the film "surprisingly complex and a subtle portrait. Besides its reluctance to tie up loose ends, the most courageous thing about it is its refusal to make you love its aggressive, strong-willed characters."

Rotten Tomatoes was less diplomatic, saying that in spite of "its gimmick casting, the film ultimately goes nowhere."

Roger Ebert claimed, "The movie is simply not clear about where it wants to go and what it wants to do. It is heavy on episode and light on insight, and although it takes courage to bring up touchy topics, it would have taken more to treat them frankly."

During the shooting of the film, Michael's real wife, Catherine Zeta-Jones, was at home, pregnant. However, in a maternity gown, she appeared at the Academy Awards presentation that March of 2003. She walked away with the gold for Best Supporting Actress for her performance as Velma in the hit film, *Chicago.*

At the ceremony, Kirk, with his impaired speech, and Michael appeared together on stage before millions of TV viewers to present the Best Picture Oscar. *Chicago* walked off with that prize, the musical winning six Oscars that night.

[Diana's last screen appearance was in It Runs in the Family. *Previously, she had starred in about twenty movies, including* The Indian Fighter *with her former husband. Her second husband, Bill Darrid, had died in 1999.*

In her memoir, In the Wings, *she expressed her philosophy of life: "Be courageous, be compassionate, and for God's sake, have fun!"*

A breast cancer survivor, Diana died on July 3, 2015 at the age of 92, from an undisclosed form of cancer. She was living at the time at the Motion Picture and Television Country House and Hospital in Woodland Hills, Los Angeles.]

***

In 2004, on the 50th anniversary of their marriage, Kirk Douglas and Anne Buydens renewed their marriage vows. He was fulfilling a promise of long ago, when he had held out the prospect of giving her a real wedding.

[The first had been a casual affair in Las Vegas presided over by a redneck justice of the peace. Not yet that familiar with colloquial English, and a bit rattled at the time, Anne had accidentally said, "My awfully wedded husband."]

That same year marked a milestone in Kirk's life. At the age of 87, he announced that he was appearing for the last time on screen in a movie. Its title was *Illusion* (2004). In such a role, he became one of the oldest leading men to star in a movie.

Michael Goorjian, the *wunderkind* producer, writer, director, and co-star, had spent nearly seven years working to bring about this film.

As the lead in this, his final movie, Kirk, then 87, was cast as Donald Baines, a once-powerful but now ailing movie director. Facing the end of his days, he is bedridden, with only one foot and only four toes.

Awaiting the Grim Reaper, Kirk is visited by the ghostly image of a film editor who died 35 years ago. Stan (Ron Marasco) shows him a trio of film snippets from the life of his illegitimate son, whom he (Kirk's character) had abandoned thirty years before.

Goorjian, a son of San Francisco, had won an Emmy as Outstanding Supporting Actor in a miniseries for his performance as David Goodson in the TV film, *David's Mother* (1994).

Illusion would be his first major independent film. This multi-talented young man was also a dancer. He had previously starred with a number of well-known actors, who included Kirstie Alley, Christian Bale, Robert Duvall, Mel Gibson, and Morgan Freeman.

In addition to its star, Kirk, *Illusion* features Karen Tucker, a young woman he loves but loses in a brutal twist of fate; and Bryan Cranston, who would go on to greater things in the 21st Century, including an Oscar

600

nomination for his performance in the title role of *Trumbo* (2015).

In *The San Francisco Chronicle*, Mick LaSalle wrote: *"Seeing Douglas so frail and infirm is still a jolt that brings a mix of contradictory feelings. His speech is so impaired (from a stroke) that it's not much fun to see him act; nor is it a pleasure to feel the strain of a performer's effort to blast through infirmity to inhabit a role."*

"It partly feels like this is a private misfortune being inflicted on the public, something viewers are obliged to accept either out of past regard or some vague sense that spectacle is somehow good for them. If anybody is going to be the vehicle by which audiences encounter the not-very-pretty sight of Father Time doing his dirty work, why not Kirk Douglas?"

***

As it turned out, *Illusion*, as announced, was not Kirk's *adieu* to the screen. He was seen once again in *Empire State Building Murders* (2008), an experimental French-made mock documentary by director/writer William Karel.

The creative force behind Kirk's *Illusion*—Michael Goorjian.

It starred, among others, Ben Gazzara, Mickey Rooney, Kirk, Cyd Charisse, Richard Erdman, Anne Jeffreys, and Marsha Hunt. The whole picture was a spin-off of the 1982 *Dead Men Don't Wear Plaid*.

The 88-minute movie was released with a *film noir*-like narration by Patrick Floersheim. It begins in December of 2007 when an old long-lost letter from 1949 *[we learn that it was written by Penny Baxter, a character portrayed by Sara Sumara]* turns up at the New York City Post Office. The audience learns that in it, she claims that her husband, Mafia boss Tony Carlucci (James Cagney) is plotting to kill her.

The letter had been sent to police chief Jim Kowalski (Kirk), who is now an old man when he finally receives the letter. He is one of the few people who has first-hand knowledge of the doomed romance between

Penny and Carlucci.

Here, nostalgia and an ode to the Hollywood of Yesteryear take over the plotline. Movie clips of Lauren Bacall—drawn from *Key Largo* and *To Have and Have Not*— depict Penny Baxter as a beautiful young woman. James Cagney lives again in *The Public Enemy*, Bogie again in *Casablanca*, Even *King Kong* and *Singin' in the Rain* are woven in, as are appearances by Van Heflin. Edward G. Robinson, Lizabeth Scott, Lawrence Tierney, and Richard Widmark.

Critic Rob Nelson called *Empire State Murders* "Ambitious and intriguing, but inept enough to desecrate the memory of many great classics. Snippets don't begin

Meurtres à l'Empire State Building

to match in Karel's ham-handed recontextualization. Buffs are hereby warned."

***

Despite many previous denials that he'd ever make another movie, in 2009, Kirk appeared on video as the centerpiece of a live stage show he was in. Produced by his wife, Anne, it was filmed onstage at a theater named after him in Culver City, California. His three sons were there on opening night and depicted in the film paying tribute to their then-92-year-old father. The footage was packaged and marketed as *Before I Forget* and released in November of 2009.

According to Kirk, "What does a guy of 92 do when he has impediment in his speech? He does a one-man show."

"I have discovered that when you have a stroke, you must talk slowly to be understood," he said. "and I've discovered when I talk slowly, people listen. They think I'm going to say something important."

As revealed to the audience, he had forgotten very little about his career, his disappointments, and his triumphs. He recalled one of the few times his father ever saw him perform. It was his first acting gig, a role in a kindergarten play.

"After the show, he didn't say a word, but he took me and bought me an ice cream cone. That was my Oscar. From that day on I was determined to be an actor."

His dialogue onstage covered a wide range of topics, including how he broke the Hollywood blacklist by designating Dalton Trumbo as the screenwriter of *Spartacus;* his deepening spirituality; and his considerable role as a philanthropist.

The show touched on the theme of fathers and sons—Michael, Joel, and Peter. There was also talk and archival footage of Eric, who had died from a drug overdose five years earlier.

A film clip shows Kirk at Eric's grave, one of several clips that allowed the elderly actor a chance to sit down and rest during the performance.

The most extended clip is from an HBO documentary about Kirk's sometimes strained relationship with his oldest son, Michael.

His son was sitting in the audience during his father's delivery. From the stage, Kirk poignantly asked him, "Was I a good father?"

Michael stood up: "You ultimately have been a great father."

Kirk's live stage performance that night, as the film demonstrates, was met with uncritical adoration and a standing ovation. Kirk seemed to let the applause sweep over him like a warm bath.

Suddenly, Michael appears on stage and hands his father an ice cream cone.

***

When a reporter asked Kirk about why he was still working at his age, he answered, "What the hell! Being old has its advantages. Now I can say anything I damn please. There's plenty of life in the old carcass yet. The last time I was walking the streets of Manhattan, construction workers called down to me: *'Koik! Koik!'"*

He was also asked about how he felt that his sons had gone into the family business, especially bigtime movie star, Michael.

"The first time it dawned on me that the acting torch had been passed was one sunny afternoon when I was walking along Wilshire Boulevard in Los Angeles…I'd had a good workout that morning, and I felt in tiptop shape, the best of health."

"This beautiful girl was walking toward me, reminding me of how

Sandra Dee looked in 1959. As she approached me, she studied my face carefully and looked me up and down. I thought she wanted me to take her home."

"'Aren't you Mr. Douglas?' she asked. 'I saw your picture in a magazine.'"

"'Yes, I am, you sweet thing,' I said. 'Want an autograph?'"

"'Wow! Wow!' she said. 'I can't wait to tell the girls at school that I ran into the father of Michael Douglas.'"

***

In the late spring of 2014, Kirk described, in the *Los Angeles Times*, his sixty-year marriage to Anne Buydens. "I don't know why Anne stuck with me through those early decades. If anyone I worked with is still alive, they will attest that I wasn't Mr. Popularity. I had a lot of anger matched by a lot of arrogance. Some people put up with me, I think, simply because I had such a wonderful wife."

***

On December 9, 2016, Kirk Douglas became a member of a select group, centenarians, 100-year-olds who had seen the world radically change many, many times.

He celebrated his birthday at the Beverly Hills Hotel, where he was joined by Anne, of course, along with his son Michael and his new daughter-in-law, Catherine Zeta-Jones.

A coterie of friends included Jeffrey Katzenberg, Steven Spielberg, and Don Rickles.

At the end of the gala evening, Rickles rose to deliver his usual take-no-prisoners toast. "You won't die, you Jew bastard, until you turn 150. By that time, you'll be calling yourself Grandpa Moses. I guess we'll have to put up with you until that Great Day in the Morning comes. All of us will go to your funeral to make sure you're dead. Give people in Hollywood what they want to see—and they'll show up."

POLLUTED, BITTER WINDS BLOW IN A
NEW MILLENNIUM
MARRED WITH TRAGEDY

IT RUNS IN THE FAMILY

In addition to the collapse of his health and the age-related sidelining of his film career, some of the tragedies that befell Kirk in the new millennium derived from anguish associated with his family.

Some of the publicity associated with a film that insiders viewed as particularly revelatory included this view of three generations of his gene pool: Kirk (left); Michael (center); and Cameron. Like American society itself, they evolved in ways that no one, especially Kirk, could have predicted back in the heyday of Hollywood's Golden Age.

In 2000, as if to celebrate the arrival of the new millennium, the Douglas family added a glamourous new addition to their clan in the shapely form of Welsh actress Catherine Zeta-Jones. Michael Douglas married her five years after his divorce from his first wife, Diandra Luker.

Their engagement had lasted eleven months, during which time he had lived with her and fathered a son. Each of them had been born on September 25, albeit with an age difference of twenty-five years.

The actress had met her future husband in Deauville, an exclusive, nostalgia-soaked resort on the northern coast of France. His first words to her were, "I want to father your children."

Catherine had been born in 1969 in Swansea, on the southern coast of Wales, the same town where that country's most celebrated writer, Dylan Thomas, had lived.

At the age of fifteen, she was performing onstage in such musicals as *Pajama Game*. Her first major success came when she starred in the Yorkshire Television comedy/drama series, *The Darling Buds of May* (1991-1993). In her role as the eldest daughter of a raucous English family, she was hailed for being "drop dead" gorgeous, and the press soon designated her as "Britain's Newest Sweetheart."

Soon, Hollywood beckoned with a breakthrough role in *The Mark of Zorro* (1998), co-starring Anthony Hopkins and Antonio Banderas. "Banderas and I competed to see which one of us the fans would find the most beautiful," she reportedly said.

Big blockbusters followed, and in 1999, she was co-starring in *Entrapment*, a stylish art theft caper opposite Sean Connery. She told the producer, "Sean is the most fabulous thing in the world. He's a cake. You could eat that."

The year they were married, Michael and Catherine co-starred together in *Traffic* (2000), an exploration of the international drug trade from multiple perspectives, for Steven Soderbergh. Many of her fans thought she should have received an Oscar nomination, but that would come later for

Catherine Zeta-Jones and Michael Douglas arrive at the *Vanity Fair* party during the 2012 Tribeca Film Festival.

BY DAVID SHANKBONE, THROUGH WIKIMEDIA COMMONS

606

her role of Velma in *Chicago* (2002).

Reviewers hailed Catherine not only for her prodigious talent, but for her "trademarks," especially a deep, seductive voice that in time would see her hailed as among the "100 sexiest women in the world."

When Kirk was introduced to Catherine, he told her, "You're taking up with the wrong Douglas. It should have been me."

"But you're already married, Mr. Douglas," she said, demurely.

"So I am," he answered. "Thanks for the heads-up."

Everyone in the Douglas clan, especially Kirk and Anne, welcomed Catherine to their growing family—that is, everyone except Eric, Kirk's youngest son, who seemed to resent her from the beginning. Eric and Catherine made it a point to rarely see each other but, when they did, the tension between them was so strong that she wanted him banned from her wedding to his half-brother.

In August of 2000, Michael and Catherine's first child was born, a son they named Dylan Michael, perhaps a combination of the names of Wales' most memorable poet, Dylan Thomas, and the name of the child's father.

Three months later, in November, a spectacular $1.5 million wedding would be staged at the Plaza Hotel in Manhattan.

At the wedding, Cameron, Michael's son, was best man, and Catherine's friend, Bonnie Tyler, sang for the elite of New York and Hollywood.

Collectively, they formed a sea of glittering, glamorous faces. They included one of Michael's best friends, Danny DeVito, along with Christopher Reeve (Superman), confined to a wheelchair. Gladys Knight was there, along with Steven Spielberg, Brad Pitt, Jennifer Aniston, Jack Nicholson, Russell Crowe, hugging close to Meg Ryan, Goldie Hawn, Martha Stewart, Michael Caine, and Art Garfunkel.

Guests remembered a gray-haired Kirk, spending most of the evening chasing after Barbara Walters.

After the wedding, Catherine and Michael greeted fans massed in front of the hotel. She carried her three-month-old son out to face the crowd.

She told the press, "I know my husband thinks I'm sexy. I think he is, too. But I don't go out half-naked with 'sex' written across

A family portrait snapped in Beverly Hills in 1962: Kirk with Anne Buydens, and (lower row), sons Peter and (right) Eric, then aged four or five.

my back."

[A daughter, Carys, would follow in April of 2003, making Kirk a grandfather again.]

***

Eric Douglas, born to Kirk and Anne on June 21, 1958, was the fourth and final son of the veteran actor. On looking back, he said, "My first three boys made me proud, especially *that* Michael, Mr. Super Star, trying to out-shine even me. But Eric…He came from my seed, from Anne's womb, but was so unlike my other boys."

"Eric seemed born under a crossed star, doomed to a life of failure, drugs, arrests—and this dreadful feel of inadequacy when he compared himself not only to me, but to his more accomplished brothers."

"Michael was both a producer and an actor, and my other two boys, Joel and Peter, had the ability to become producers, too. Eric decided to become an actor, like Michael and me. Not only that, but he chose one day to become a stand-up comedian. My God! He seemed delusional in think-ing he might be another Lenny Bruce."

In an interview with the *New York Daily News,* Eric said, "The pressure of being the youngest son of a famous family sometimes got to me. I felt I had to compare myself to them."

Kirk once told a reporter for the *Chicago Tribune,* "My relationship with Eric is very difficult because he's too much like me. He's hyperactive. I sometimes say to him, 'Loving and hating you is like loving and hating myself.'"

"Eric inherited all of my bad qualities, my very worst traits," Kirk claimed.

"My dad and I are both perfectionists," Eric said. "Energetic, passionate, intense, we make things happen. It makes us difficult to be around."

He was only five years old when, during one of his school vacations, he first saw his fa-ther perform on Broadway in the play, *One Flew Over the Cuckoo's Nest.* He was seated in the front row. Kirk had arranged for his two older sons, Michael and Joel, to be cast as or-derlies in a mental hospital. At one point in the drama, his sons had to wheel Kirk out on a gurney.

Eric Douglas—so closely re-sembling his father that some fans defined it as eerie.

When Eric saw that, he thought his father had died and started crying, interrupting the play. An usher was summoned to remove the hysterical boy from the theater, taking him outside to quiet him down.

"It was that night, and in the nights to come, that I came to realize that my son had difficulty at times distinguishing between make-believe and reality," Kirk said. "As he grew older, he made up stories and told them with a certain conviction. He once claimed he met Ava Gardner, who drove him to Disneyland and treated him to a lot of goodies and rides. He'd been missing for about fourteen hours, and that was his excuse. I happen to know that Ava wasn't even in Los Angeles at the time."

Whenever Kirk was shooting on location during school vacations, he enjoyed inviting his sons to visit in such places as Oregon or Arizona. Once, he invited Joel, Eric, and Peter to Honolulu, where he was filming *In Harm's Way* (1965), a World War II drama.

"I didn't invite Michael because I was mad at him, since he seemed to be flunking out of the University of California at Santa Barbara."

***

According to Kirk, "Three of my sons became producers, perhaps the hardest job on any film, since he's the guy who's got to handle financing, coddle the temperamental directors and stars, and bring the damn thing in on budget."

Joel, worked behind the camera on several films throughout the 1970s and '80s, including a role as co-producer of some of his brother's biggest hits like *Jewel of the Nile* and *Romancing the Stone*. *[After three failed marriages, Joel finally got it right, finding the ideal woman in Jo Ann Savitt, the daughter of bandleader Jan Savitt. In 2004, he married her and remained with her until her death in 2013.]*

Peter also became a producer, often working with his father, as he did on the TV remake of *Inherit the Wind* (1988), with Kirk and Jason Robards. *[For that, Peter took home an Emmy for Outstanding Drama or Comedy.]*

Peter was also the producer, through Bryna, of Kirk's film *Amos* (1984), for which he was Emmy-nominated, and pulled together Kirk's sci-fi World War II tale, *The Final Countdown*. Among other works not associated with his father, Peter wrote, directed, and produced *A Tiger's Tale* (1988), starring Ann-Margret.

Eric, however, never managed to fit in as gracefully, presenting a roster of emotions and disciplinary problems that Kirk and Anne had never expected.

When he was enrolled in Los Angeles at an exclusive private school, (the Thomas Dye School), he and his fellow classmate, Ron Reagan, Jr., became intimate friends, almost inseparable.

"Ron and my boy would take turns visiting each other on weekends," Kirk said. "Sometimes, the maid would drive young Eric over to the Reagan household so Eric and Ron, Jr. could be together, often at their ranch."

"When he came home, all that Eric could talk about was Ron, Jr. and how wonderful he was," Kirk said. "I was told that many growing boys form such attachments, and I felt it was just a phase he was going through."

Kirk expressed disappointment when Eric confided that, like Michael, he, too, wanted to be an actor, not in films, but on the stage. "At least that would be a different career path from the one Michael had taken."

To sharpen his skills as an actor, Eric was encouraged to enroll at Pitzer College, the Royal Academy of Dramatic Art, and the London Academy of Dramatic Art. After that, Kirk became instrumental in launching his son into films, setting it up for him to make his movie debut in *A Gunfight* (1971), in which Kirk starred with Johnny Cash.

In 1982, Kirk got Eric a role in an NBC-TV film, *Remembrance of Love,* in which he played a younger version of Kirk in flashback.

Through the rest of the 1980s and early 90s, Eric appeared in a number of lackluster films, such as *Student Confidential* (1987), *The Golden Child* (1986) with Eddie Murphy, and *Tales from the Crypt* (1991).

But as his film career seemed to be going nowhere, Eric made an attempt to launch himself as a stand-up comedian, beginning at a comedy club in Manhattan, where he bombed. Labeling himself as "The Black Sheep" of the Douglas family, he developed a self-deprecating and occasionally funny *schtick* that included: "I came down to breakfast one morning and found my dad sitting at table in a toga. 'Jesus!' I said. He answered, 'No, Spartacus.'"

Eric as he appeared in *The Golden Child* (1986)

Then, he got a booking at The Comedy Store in London, where he faced the toughest audience of his life. His audience sat stone-faced and defiantly silent. Flustered and on the verge of tears, he shouted at them, "*YOU CAN'T DO THIS TO ME. I'M KIRK DOUGLAS' SON!*"

A mocking member of the audience rose to his feet, "No, "*I'M* Kirk Douglas' son!" referencing the iconic final scene from *Spartacus.* Then, the entire audience rose to its feet, raucously chanting, "*I'M SPARTACUS! I'M*

SPARTACUS!"

Bursting into tears, Eric fled from the club and ran out and onto the busy street, where he was almost run over by a London taxi.

Depressed and traumatized, Eric began a downward spiral that would continue through the 1990s and beyond. He became a drug addict, enduring arrests and a total of twenty separate admissions into drug rehab centers, each of them arranged (and paid for) by Kirk and Anne, practicing "tough love" on their self-destructive youngest son.

Sometimes a furious Eric erupted into violence, as when, in Beverly Hills, he physically attacked a police officer who just happened to be a friend of Kirk's.

"The shithead was trying to give me a parking ticket," Eric said in way of his defense.

On October 30, 1994, he was arrested in Los Angeles for cocaine possession. His increasingly cynical and frustrated father would pay, again and again, whatever money was needed to bail him out.

At the Comedy Store in West Hollywood, a heckler challenged him: "Aren't you Kirk Douglas' faggot son?" Eric had been drinking heavily, and he struck his verbal attacker on the head with a beer bottle before escaping from the club.

He got behind the wheel of his car and accelerated. Within a minute he crashed it into a parked Lincoln. Eric was arrested, charged with DUI, and his license was confiscated.

Eager to escape from the angry glares of his parents, Eric fled to Manhattan, where he rented an apartment in Hell's Kitchen. There, when he refused to pay off a drug dealer's demand for money, someone reported him, anonymously as a drug dealer to the police, who broke down the door of his apartment in May of 1996.

Among other drugs, the cops found eleven vials of crack cocaine and 1,085 Xanax pills *[Xanax is a controlled and addictive sedative, sometimes fatal when combined with alcohol, that's used for the treatment of anxiety and panic attacks]*.

Eric was hauled off to jail, and Kirk was alerted in California. After his father paid some topnotch lawyers to defend him, Eric was placed on probation with a mandate to complete a drug rehab program, which he never did.

Fed up with New York, Eric fled once again, this time back to Los Angeles. Within two months, he was arrested on another DUI, this time for driving (with a suspended license) while under the influence of drugs and alcohol.

He was sent to the Silver Hill Hospital, a treatment center for mental health and addiction issues, in New Canaan, Connecticut. Within a week, he was arrested for disorderly conduct. Apparently, there was some out-of-court settlement.

A patient at the Silver Hill center accused Eric of attempted rape. The charges were eventually dropped. Once again, as had happened before, in February of 1997, he was arrested on another DUI for crashing his Hertz rental car into two parked cars. This was similar to a 1994 arrest in Los Angeles, except that this one occurred in New York.

As Eric would later tell celebrity psychic John Cohan, "Being Kirk Douglas' son, and having access to his pay-out money, comes in handy from time to time. Rather often, as a matter of fact."

***

Experiencing meltdown, and in dire need of some guidance he wasn't getting at home, Eric turned to John Cohan, the noted "Psychic to the Stars."

Eric had heard that Cohan had helped and offered insight, over the course of a career that spanned decades, to clients who included Elvis Presley, Joan Crawford, Merv Griffin, Lana Turner, Rock Hudson, Burt Reynolds, and even Playboy's Hugh Hefner.

Cohan played a special role in the troubled saga of Sandra Dee, who had risen to stardom, only to fall down again. "She was the love of my life, all blonde and blue-eyed, all beauty."

Many of his psychic insights and revelations have been published in his memoir, *Catch a Falling Star*, an overview of his encounters with Elizabeth Taylor, Nicole Brown Simpson, Natalie Wood, and many other celebrities, some of them doomed. Cohan's predictions for each upcoming year are published annually in Cindy Adams widely read column in the *New York Post*.

"My gift is something that's been with me since birth," Cohan said. "Throughout most of my adolescence, I ignored or suppressed my psychic ability because I didn't know what it was that possessed me. Finally, I grasped hold of my gift and actually embraced my talent."

When Eric consulted with Cohan, he was

John Cohan, Psychic to the Stars, offered guidance to Eric Douglas.

He later said, "When a person dies before his time, too young, and under horrific circumstances, leaving matters unsettled, the spirit is earthbound and not able to transition."

warmly welcomed. The psychic encountered a young man in torment and coming unglued.

"Eric was always very kind and respectful of me, yet I saw and knew that he was dangerous with people he didn't like. There was a particular love/hate relationship with his father."

"I was a very lonely kid," Eric told Cohan. "Often, I was home alone with just a housekeeper and a dog for company. I bestowed all my love on that dog. Everybody else in my family was away all the time, Dad making movies. Anne and Peter had plenty going on in their lives, too—business that didn't involve me."

"When Ron Reagan, Jr. came into my life in grade school [the Thomas Dye School in Los Angeles], my world changed," Eric confessed. "For the first time ever, I had someone who really cared about me, and wasn't sucking up to me because of my famous father and half-brother, Michael. I met Ron on an even playing field. His father was a famous movie star, too, but in Reagan's case, he moved on to bigger things: Politics."

"With Ron, Jr., I felt I had a friend I needed, one who needed me and whatever I could offer. We spent weekends together and became very, very close."

The two boys even plotted their future together. Eric described his plans to become a stage actor like John Barrymore, as Ron, Jr. defined his hopes for a career as a ballet dancer.

[When Reagan, Jr., was older, he enrolled in the Stanley Holden Dance Center in Los Angeles. Despite her occasional flaws, Nancy Reagan, Ron's mother, as a staunchly conservative Republican and as First Lady of the United States, supported her son in his (early) career choice, fending off the gay

This photo from the National Archives shows the Reagans, Ronald Sr. with Nancy, flanked by their young children, Ron, Jr., and Patti (aka, Patti Davis), from the era when the Douglas and Reagan families encouraged friendships between their respective children.

Ronald Reagan, Sr., is pictured with his arm around his son, Ron, Jr.

Seated, Nancy is seen with their older child, Patti Davis. The Reagans and the Douglas family were of different political stripes. But the intense friendship between Ron, Jr. and Eric Douglas crossed party lines. Eric seemed devoted to the youngest Reagan.

rumors that surfaced.

Nancy told reporters, *"I think the press was surprised by the way my Ronnie [her husband, the U.S. President] handled our son's career choice. Perhaps they thought we'd be embarrassed and might try to distance ourselves. But that never entered our minds. We were surprised by his choice, but we were proud of his dedication and talent."]*

Despite Kirk's status as a liberal Democrat, Kirk and Anne were friendly with the Reagans, supportive of the time Eric was spending outside the classroom with Ron, Jr.

But their sons' friendship was suspended after Anne received a jolting call from Nancy: "Come and pick up your boy at once!" came Nancy's commanding voice over the phone.

"We couldn't imagine what Eric had done," Kirk said. "Then Nancy explained that when he'd seen the Goldwater bumper sticker on the Reagan family's car, he'd yelled, 'BOO GOLDWATER!'"

***

As Eric matured, he developed artistic interests that other members of his family did not share. One of his acting teachers, Helena Kaut-Howson, said, "He was interested in Polish theater, of all things, a very sophisticated art form. He didn't go to see the commercial stuff. He wanted to see the *avant-garde.* He told me he wanted to play Konstantin—the unhappy son of a mother who is a big star—in Chekhov's *The Seagull.*"

Eric told Cohan that, to his dismay, other actors would go to bed with him, hoping he'd use his influence with Kirk or Michael to cast them in one of their projects.

Eric met porn star Cal Culver *[aka Casey Donovan, the male star of* Boys in the Sand, *released in 1971]* when Kirk had worked with his lover, Tom Tryon, for Otto Preminger. *[Tryon and Culver were lovers.]*

Culver, widely known for hustling Hollywood stars before dying tragically of an AIDS-related pulmonary infection in 1987 at the age of 43, got involved with Eric for one-hundred dollars per session.

In meetings with Cohan, Eric admitted that he sometimes hated himself after having sex. He also claimed that an inner demon would consume him at times. He recalled attending a party celebrating the success of *Basic Instinct* (1992), Michael's film with Sharon Stone, in which the actress had revealed her vagina.

In front of the guests, Eric decided to mock the film and took down his pants and mooned the gathering.

Once, on an American Airlines flight, with his dog, he deliberately let the animal run amok among the passengers. For that, he had to spend a night in jail.

"I can't stop taking drugs," he confessed. "Actually, if I don't take them, I become suicidal. So it's a question of either taking drugs or killing myself. Some choice!"

One night, both Michael and Catherine attended one of Eric's performances as a stand-up comedian. Instead of demeaning himself, as he often did, he chose the occasion to mock his family. "My brother Michael and my sister-in-law are the cheapest couple in Hollywood. He's Jewish and she's Scottish."

Irritated and embarrassed, Catherine rose from her table in the audience and called out, "I'm Welsh." Then, infuriated, she headed toward the exit.

Eric told Cohan how much he disliked his half-brother, Michael. "I'm always being compared to him like he's some God and I'm Mr. Nobody. It's Michael this, Michael that. I have to listen to how much he grossed on his latest picture, while I'm appearing in small roles in one turkey after another. I was told that to play a leading man, I would have to wear lifts since I'm small in stature. What am I good at? Taking drugs, getting arrested, and having to be bailed out of jail. I'm also good at running up thousands of dollars in rehab bills."

"At one point near the end of Eric's sessions with Cohan, he made a confession that was so shocking, it defied belief. Could it really have been true?

Eric claimed that he and Kirk had one of their most violent arguments. "Dad told me what he really thought of me, and it wasn't pretty. It was a really nasty exchange, and I shot back with my many charges against him."

"Later that night, I slipped something into his drink—I'm not saying what—and that led to him having a stroke. I swear that's true, but I don't give a damn if you believe me or not."

As the century came to an end, Eric's dependence on drugs had increased. One morning, after ingesting too much Xanax and during breakfast

Unlike the other sons of Kirk, Eric Douglas was conflicted sexually. The porn star, Cal Culver (aka Casey Donovan), took advantage of Eric's desire, charging him for every private sexual liaison.

with Kirk, he choked on a piece of sausage, cutting off his air supply. The maid attempted the Heimlich Maneuver and he coughed up the sausage—but he'd gone a long time without air.

He was rushed to Cedars-Sinai Medical Center, were he remained in a coma for eight days. He emerged with slurred speech and an altered gait.

When Kirk saw that, he said, "Now you and I have something in common: Impaired speech."

***

Years of drug abuse, arrests, and inner turmoil came crashing down on Eric on July 6, 2004. A maid found him lying dead on the floor of his Manhattan apartment, curled into a fetal position.

An autopsy revealed that his death was caused by "acute intoxication from the combined effects of alcohol, tranquilizers, and painkillers." Although his death was officially defined as accidental, many people close to the Douglas family unofficially interpreted it as a suicide. Eric had once taken pride in his trim physique, but the report noted that he weighed 300 pounds.

Reporters had tried to contact a family member, notably Kirk, but to no avail. A press agent issued a statement: "The family is very shocked and saddened by this event. We hope you will respect our privacy at this time."

His body was interred in Westwood Village Memorial Park Cemetery in Westwood, California.

The wife of Karl Malden sent Kirk a note that included a quotation from J.M. Barrie:

> *"One who died is only a little ahead of the procession, all moving that way. When we round the corner, we'll see him again. We have only lost him for a moment, because we fell behind, stopping to tie a shoe-lace."*

In the months that followed Eric's death, Kirk and Anne, on occasion, visited his gravesite to talk to him. "That helps us," Kirk said. "I would say to him, 'Eric, I hope you've found peace. Someday, I'll be buried beside you.'"

He always kept a deeply cynical poem found in Eric's apartment on the day his body was discovered. Eric's poem read:

> *"I start the day in a happy mood, feeling positive about life.*
> *But I see a hole in front of me.*
> *I know I should avoid it, but I know I will fall into it.*
> *And I do."*

616

***

Kirk's grandson, Cameron, was the son of Michael Douglas and his first wife, Diandra Luker, whom he'd divorced in 1995.

As Cameron was growing up, he did not spend much time with his father, who was always away somewhere shooting a movie. *[That same situation had prevailed with Michael when he was growing up with his own absentee father, Kirk, who was often far away, filming.]*

Cameron drifted into drugs, eventually becoming an addict. Michael, his father, began fearing that he'd follow in the fatal footsteps of Eric, Michael's half-brother.

During Michael's filming of *The American President* (1995), Cameron was enrolled in a rehab center for an addiction to cocaine.

Michael tried to take an interest in his son. When he heard of his fascination with music, he invested in the Third Stone, a record label, perhaps with the intention of creating a niche for his son within its ranks.

In 2007, Cameron, then twenty-eight, was arrested in Manhattan. A police officer had noticed a syringe lying on the front seat of his car following a routine traffic violation. It turned out to be filled with liquid cocaine. In court, Cameron admitted to a misdemeanor and was ordered into rehab.

Two years later, on July 28, 2009, when he was thirty, Cameron was arrested by the Drug Enforcement Agency as part of a three-year undercover sting operation. He entered a plea of guilty after being charged with the intent to distribute half a pound of methamphetamine.

Michael came to the rescue,

Two views of Cameron Douglas, Kirk's grandson, in scenes from *It Runs in the Family* (2003). In the lower photo, he's with Michelle Monaghan.

617

putting up bail money. His son was released but put under house arrest to await sentencing in April of 2010.

However, in January of 2011, he was arrested once again. The charge was bizarre. His girlfriend, Kelly Soot, was arrested and charged with trying to smuggle heroine into Cameron's apartment in an electric toothbrush. For that, she was sentenced to seven months in prison.

The dreaded day of Cameron's sentencing finally arrived. In a courtroom, with Michael present, he faced Richard Berman, a Federal judge of the U.S. District Court. The charges against him mandated a minimum ten-year prison sentence.

The judge had received several dozen character references, notably one from his grandfather, Kirk himself. At the age of ninety-three, he pleaded with Berman to spare his grandson. "I want to see him a free man before I die. He will rebound from this trouble and start life anew if given a chance. I love him."

Cameron's mother also weighed in. "Being the son and grandson of two famous movie stars is an incredible cross to bear. Cameron felt defeated before he was out the gate because he knew he could never achieve the stature of those two."

Perhaps because of these entreaties, Cameron received a lighter-than-expected sentence of five years in prison, plus $300,000 of his net worth, estimated at a half-million dollars. It was understood that at the end of his time in prison, he'd complete 450 hours of community service, and that in the years that followed, he'd be under close supervision.

A few months later, Kirk's attention focused not on Cameron, but on his own son. Michael, who came to him with tragic medical news: His doctors had diagnosed him with stage four of throat cancer, which was nearly always fatal. Michael vowed to fight it with chemo and radiation therapies. And he did.

As for Cameron, on December 21, 2011, his five-year prison sentence was extended for an additional four and a half years. He'd been caught trying to smuggle drugs into his cell.

In August of 2016, it was announced in the press that Cameron had been released from prison after serving nearly seven years in a halfway house. Buff and very fit, and "accessorized" with a startling and extensive set

Cameron Douglas (left photo), the grandson of Kirk, had a remarkable resemblance to the fabled star. But their lifestyles were very, very different.

of tattoos, he was ready to start a new life at the age of thirty-seven. He told a reporter that he planned to write a tell-all book about his experiences.

According to Cameron, "In these difficult times, Michael and I have grown closer, and I also see my grandfather, Kirk Douglas, who is still holding on into another century. Michael and I have an amazing relationship. I love spending time with my father."

***

As he moved into the second century of his life, Kirk claimed that every morning, he looked at his wrinkled and ravaged face in a mirror, and remembered the lines: *Grow old along with me! The best is yet to come.*

Then, with wry humor and in his weak, fading voice, he'd say, "Well, I'm waiting…I'm still waiting…"

***

Late in Kirk's life, he mused, "I know I'm living on borrowed time. I hope I've obtained immortality as an actor. I've been more adventurous in my choice of roles that most stars of my generation. That's strength. I've come close to being typed as macho. That's a shame, because in my best roles, I expressed weakness and vulnerability, too."

"When film historians look at my career, I hope they showcase my accomplishments by viewing my best movies: *Champion, Ace in the Hole, The Bad and the Beautiful, 20,000 Leagues Under the Sea, The Indian Fighter, Lust for Life, Paths of Glory, Spartacus, Lonely Are the Brave,* and *Seven Days in May.*"

"About that other kind of immortality, I have grave doubts. When a dog dies, does he go to heaven? Why should we think we're so special that we cannot just die? No, you go around only once, and just hope you get the brass ring. The rest is ego."

"Everyone else gets older…Death is up there ahead, the end of the road. Nobody likes the idea, but you get used to it. You get used to the idea that in nature, there is no justice. That God doesn't run a clean shop."

"My beloved mother, Bryna, told me that one day she looked out the window and discovered me in a gold box with silver strings tied to heaven," Kirk said.

"Every day when I look out the window, I expect to see that gold box come to take me back."

619

Kirk Douglas, a *Champion* by anyone's definition

The Ragman's Son, Kirk Douglas *(center)*; Kirk's son (Michael Douglas, *left*); and Kirk's grandson (Cameron Douglas, *right*); as they presented themselves as a family trio in this publicity shot from *It Runs in the Family*.

DARWIN PORTER

As an intense nine-year-old, **Darwin Porter** began meeting movie stars, TV personalities, politicians, and singers through his vivacious and attractive mother, Hazel, an eccentric but charismatic Southern girl who had lost her husband in World War II. Migrating from the Depression-ravaged valleys of western North Carolina to Miami Beach during its most ebullient heyday, Hazel became a stylist, wardrobe mistress, and personal assistant to the vaudeville *comedienne* **Sophie Tucker**, the bawdy and irrepressible "Last of the Red Hot Mamas."

Virtually every show-biz celebrity who visited Miami Beach paid a call on "Miss Sophie," and Darwin, as a pre-teen loosely and indulgently supervised by his mother, was regularly dazzled by the likes of **Judy Garland, Dinah Shore,** and **Frank Sinatra.**

It was at Miss Sophie's that he met his first political figure, who was actually an actor at the time. Between marriages, **Ronald Reagan** came to call on Ms. Sophie, who was his favorite singer. He was accompanied by a young blonde starlet, **Marilyn Monroe**.

At the University of Miami, Darwin edited the school newspaper. He first met and interviewed **Eleanor Roosevelt** at the Fontainebleau Hotel on Miami Beach and invited her to spend a day at the university. She accepted, much to his delight.

After graduation, he became the Bureau Chief of *The Miami Herald* in Key West, Florida, where he got to take early morning walks with the former U.S. president **Harry S Truman**, discussing his presidency and the events that had shaped it.

Through Truman, Darwin was introduced and later joined the staff of **Senator George Smathers** of Florida. His best friend was a young senator, **John F. Kennedy**. Through "Gorgeous George," as Smathers was known in the Senate, Darwin got to meet Jack and Jacqueline in Palm Beach. He later wrote two books about them—*The Kennedys, All the Gossip Unfit to Print*, and one of his all-time bestsellers, *Jacqueline Kennedy Onassis—A Life Beyond Her Wildest Dreams*.

For about a decade in New York, Darwin worked in television journalism and advertising with his long-time partner, the journalist, art director, and arts-industry socialite **Stanley Mills Haggart**.

Stanley (as an art director) and Darwin (as a writer and assistant), worked as freelance agents in television. Jointly, they helped produce TV commercials that included testimonials from **Joan Crawford** (then feverishly promoting Pepsi-Cola); **Ronald Reagan** (General Electric); and **Debbie Reynolds** (Singer sewing machines). Other personalities appearing and delivering televised sales pitches included **Louis Armstrong, Lena Horne,** and **Arlene Dahl,** each of them hawking a commercial product.

Beginning in the early 1960s, Darwin joined forces with the then-fledgling **Arthur Frommer** organization, playing a key role in researching and writing more than 50 titles and defining the style and values that later emerged as the world's leading travel guidebooks, *The Frommer Guides,* with particular emphasis on Europe, New England, and the Caribbean. Between the creation and updating of hundreds of editions of detailed travel guides to England, France, Italy, Spain, Portugal, Austria, Hungary, Germany, Switzerland, the Caribbean, and California, he continued to interview and discuss the triumphs, feuds, and frustrations of celebrities, many by then reclusive, whom he either sought out or encountered randomly as part of his extensive travels. **Ava Gardner, Debbie Reynolds,** and **Lana Turner** were particularly insightful.

It was while living in New York that Darwin became fascinated by the career of a rising real estate mogul changing the skyline of Manhattan. He later, of course, became the "gambling czar" of Atlantic City and a star of reality TV.

Darwin began collecting an astonishing amount of data on Donald Trump, squirreling it away in boxes, hoping one day to write a biography of this charismatic, controversial figure.

Before doing that, he penned more than thirty-five uncensored, unvarnished, and unauthorized biographies on subjects that included **Playboy's Hugh Hefner, Debbie Reynolds and Carrie Fisher, Bill and Hillary Clinton, Ronald Reagan and Nancy Davis, Jane Wyman, Jacqueline Kennedy, Jack Kennedy, Lana Turner, Peter O'Toole, James Dean, Marlon Brando, Merv Griffin, Katharine Hepburn, Howard Hughes, Humphrey Bogart, Michael Jackson, Paul Newman, Steve McQueen, Marilyn Monroe, Elizabeth Taylor, Rock Hudson, Frank Sinatra, Vivien Leigh, Laurence Olivier, the notorious porn star Linda Lovelace, Zsa Zsa Gabor and her sisters, Tennessee Williams, Gore Vidal,** and **Truman Capote.**

As a departure from his usual repertoire, Darwin also wrote the controversial *J. Edgar Hoover & Clyde Tolson: Investigating the Sexual Secrets of America's Most Famous Men and Women,* a book about celebrity, voyeurism, political and sexual repression, and blackmail within the highest circles of the U.S. government.

Porter's biographies, over the years, have won thirty first prize or "runner-up to first prize" awards at literary festivals in cities or states which include New England, New York, Los Angeles, Hollywood, San Francisco, Florida, California, and Paris.

Darwin can be heard at regular intervals as a radio and television commentator, "dishing" celebrities, pop culture, politics, and scandal.

A resident of New York City, Darwin is currently at work on a startling new biography of **Burt Reynolds,** *Put the Pedal to the Metal: How a Nude Centerfold Sex Symbol Seduced Hollywood.*

DANFORTH PRINCE

The co-author of this book, **Danforth Prince** is president and founder of Blood Moon Productions, a publishing venture that's devoted to salvaging, compiling, and marketing the oral histories of America's entertainment industry.

Prince launched his career in journalism in the 1970s at the Paris Bureau of *The New York Times*. In the early '80s, he joined Darwin Porter in developing first editions of many of the titles within *The Frommer Guides*. Together, they reviewed and articulated the travel scenes of more than 50 nations, most of them within Europe and the Caribbean. Authoritative and comprehensive, they became best-selling "travel bibles" for millions of readers.

Prince, in collaboration with Porter, is also the co-author of several award-winning celebrity biographies, each configured as a title within **Blood Moon's Babylon series.** These have included *Hollywood Babylon—It's Back!; Hollywood Babylon Strikes Again; The Kennedys: All the Gossip Unfit to Print; Frank Sinatra, The Boudoir Singer, Elizabeth Taylor: There Is Nothing Like a Dame; Pink Triangle: The Feuds and Private Lives of Tennessee Williams, Gore Vidal, Truman Capote, and Members of their Entourages;* and *Jacqueline Kennedy Onassis: A Life Beyond Her Wildest Dreams.* More recent efforts include *Lana Turner, Hearts and Diamonds Take All; Peter O'-Toole—Hellraiser, Sexual Outlaw, Irish Rebel; Bill & Hillary—So This Is That Thing Called Love; James Dean, Tomorrow Never Comes; Rock Hudson Erotic Fire; Carrie Fisher and Debbie Reynolds, Princess Leia & Unsinkable Tammy in Hell,* and *Playboy's Hugh Hefner, Empire of Skin.*

One of his recent projects, co-authored with Darwin Porter, is *Donald Trump, The Man Who Would Be King.* Released directly into the frenzy of the 2016 presidential elections, it won three literary awards at book festivals in New York, California, and Florida. It's a celebrity exposé of the decades of pre-presidential scandals—personal, political, and dynastic—associated with **Donald Trump** during the rambunctious decades when no one ever thought he'd actually get elected.

Prince is also the co-author of four books on film criticism, three of which won honors at regional bookfests in Los Angeles and San Francisco.

A graduate of Hamilton College and a native of Easton and Bethlehem, Pennsylvania, he is the president and founder of the Georgia Literary Association (1996), and of the Porter and Prince Corporation (1983) which has produced dozens of titles for Simon & Schuster, Prentice Hall, and John Wiley & Sons. In 2011, he was named "Publisher of the Year" by a consortium of literary critics and marketers spearheaded by the J.M. Northern Media Group.

He has electronically documented some of the controversies associated with his stewardship of Blood Moon in at least 50 documentaries, book trailers, public

623

speeches, and TV or radio interviews. Most of these are available on **YouTube.com** and **Facebook** *(keyword: "Danforth Prince")*; on **Twitter** *(#BloodyandLunar)*; or by clicking on **BloodMoonProductions.com**.

He is currently at work researching and writing an upcoming biography on **Burt Reynolds,** a Hollywood hellraiser, and laying the foundations for a new publishing imprint, MAGNOLIA HOUSE, whose launch title, *Celebrity and the Ironies of Fame,* is described in the pages that follow.

Do you want to meet him, up close and personal? Prince is also an innkeeper, running a historic bed & breakfast in New York City, **Magnolia House (www.Mag-noliaHouseSaintGeorge.com)**. Affiliated with AirBnb, and increasingly sought out by filmmakers as an evocative locale for moviemaking, it lies in St. George, at the northern tip of Staten Island, a district that's historically associated with Henry James, Theodore Dreiser, the Vanderbilts, and key moments in America's colonial history.

Set in a large, elaborately terraced garden, and boasting a history of visits from literary and show-biz stars who have included Tennessee Williams, Gloria Swanson, Jolie Gabor, Ruth Warrick, Greta Keller, Lucille Lortel, and many of the luminaries of Broadway, the inn is within a ten-minute walk to the ferries sailing at 20- to 30-minute intervals to Lower Manhattan.

Publicized as "a reasonably priced celebrity-centric retreat with links to the book trades," and the beneficiary of rave ("superhost") reviews from hundreds of previous clients, **Magnolia House** is loaded with furniture and memorabilia that Prince collected during his decades as a travel journalist for the Frommer Guides.

*Stay with Us! Learn more about "Celebrity-Centric Sleepovers" at Blood Moon's **Magnolia House,** a historic and moderately priced "Airbnb" in New York City.*

For more information about the hospitality that's waiting for you in NYC at the Bed and Breakfast affiliate of Blood Moon Productions, click on
MagnoliaHouseSaintGeorge.com

Now, There's a GUIDEBOOK to accompany your visit to one of Staten Island's Most Intriguing Landmarks:

Blood Moon Productions proudly announces the release of an illustrated history of **Magnolia House**, a historic home that's internationally famous for its associations with celebrities.

Its authors, media gurus **Darwin Porter and Danforth Prince**, describe it as a 230-page "pamphlet," the first in their new series about how travel writing for **THE FROMMER GUIDES** evolved into a celebrity adventure.

As stated by **Danforth Prince**, Blood Moon's President and Director of Development, "Whereas a conventional autobiography would have been too boring and too embarrassing, we opted intead to filter this memoir through the lens of the historic monument that witnessed—up close and intimately—some of the most widely celebrated characters of "The American Century."

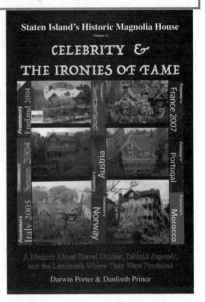

Staten Island's Historic Magnolia House
(Volume 1)

CELEBRITY &
THE IRONIES OF FAME

A Memoir About Travel Guides, Tabloid *Exposés*, and the Landmark Where They Were Produced

Darwin Porter & Danforth Prince

STATEN ISLAND'S HISTORIC MAGNOLIA HOUSE, VOLUME ONE

CELEBRITY & THE IRONIES OF FAME:

A Memoir About Travel Guides, Tabloid Exposés, & the Landmark Where They Were Produced.

Softcover, 6" x 9", with 230 pages, at least a hundred photos, and scads of gossip about who did what to whom during the course of 50 years as the world's pre-eminent travel journalists. Available everywhere online through Amazon.com, BarnesandNoble.com, or as a free giveaway to overnight guests. ISBN 978-1-936003-65-5.

WHAT IS MAGNOLIA HOUSE? The name it bears has been on record with Staten Island's Borough Hall for at least a century, as it's a byproduct of owners who, in the immediate aftermath of the Civil War, gave it a name that evoked their native Virginia. Dating from the 1830s, it's a *Grande Dame* with a knack for nourishing high-functioning eccentrics. Many of them have lived or been entertained here since New York's State Senator Howard Bayne, a transplanted Southerner, moved in with his wife, the daughter of the Surgeon General of the Confederate States of America, in the aftermath of that bloodiest of wars on North American soil, the War between the American States. Since then, many dozens of celebrities—some of them notorious—have whispered their secrets and rehearsed their ambitions within its walls.

This is the story of how this "Wise Victorian Lady"—in its role as the editorial headquarters for many of THE FROMMER GUIDES and later for BLOOD MOON PRODUCTIONS—adapted to America's radically changing tastes, times, circumstances, and values.

CARRIE FISHER & DEBBIE REYNOLDS
PRINCESS LEIA & UNSINKABLE TAMMY IN HELL

It's history's first comprehensive, unauthorized overview of the greatest mother-daughter act in showbiz history, **Debbie Reynolds** ("hard as nails and with more balls than any five guys I've ever known") and her talented, often traumatized daughter, **Carrie Fisher** ("one of the smartest, hippest chicks in Hollywood"). Evolving for decades under the unrelenting glare of public scrutiny, each became a world-class symbol of the social and cinematic tastes that prevailed during their heydays as celebrity icons in Hollywood.

It's a scandalous saga of the ferociously loyal relationship of the *"boop-boop-a-doop"* girl with her intergalactic STAR WARS daughter, and their iron-willed, "true grit" battles to out-race changing tastes in Hollywood.

Loaded with revelations about "who was doing what to whom" during the final gasps of Golden Age Hollywood, it's an All-American story about the price of glamour, career-related pain, family anguish, romantic betrayals, lingering guilt, and the volcanic shifts that affected a scrappy, mother-daughter team—and everyone else who ever loved the movies.

CARRIE FISHER & DEBBIE REYNOLDS
Princess Leia & Unsinkable Tammy in Hell

ANOTHER OUTRAGEOUS TITLE IN BLOOD MOON'S BABYLON SERIES
DARWIN PORTER & DANFORTH PRINCE

"Feeling misunderstood by the younger (female) members of your gene pool? This is the Hollywood exposé every grandmother should give to her granddaughter, a roadmap like Debbie Reynolds might have offered to Billie Lourd." —**Marnie O'Toole**

"Hold onto your hats, the "bad boys" of Blood Moon Productions are back. This time, they have an exhaustively researched and highly readable account of the greatest mother-daughter act in the history of show business: Debbie Reynolds and Carrie (Princess Leia) Fisher. If celebrity gossip and inside dirt is your secret desire, check it out. This is a fabulous book that we heartily recommend. It will not disappoint. We rate it worthy of four stars."
—**MAJ Glenn MacDonald, U.S. Army Reserve (Retired),** © MilitaryCorruption.com

"How is a 1950s-era movie star, (TAMMY) supposed to cope with her postmodern, substance-abusing daughter (PRINCESS LEIA), the rebellious, high-octane byproduct of Rock 'n Roll, Free Love, and postwar Hollywood's most scandal-soaked marriage? Read about it here, in Blood Moon's unauthorized double exposé about how Hollywood's toughest (and savviest) mother-daughter team maneuvered their way through shifting definitions of fame, reconciliation, and fortune."

—**Donna McSorley**

Another compelling title from Blood Moon's Babylon Series
Winner of the coveted "Best Biography" Award from the 2018 New York Book Festival

CARRIE FISHER & DEBBIE REYNOLDS,
UNSINKABLE TAMMY & PRINCESS LEIA IN HELL
Darwin Porter & Danforth Prince

630 pages Softcover with photos. Now online and in bookstores everywhere
ISBN 978-1-936003-57-0

LANA TURNER

The Sweater Girl, Celluloid Venus, Sex Nymph to the G.I.s who won World War II, and Hollywood's OTHER Most Notorious Blonde

Beautiful and Bad, Her Full Story Has Never Been Told.
UNTIL NOW!

Lana Turner was the most scandalous, most copied, and most gossiped-about actress in Hollywood. When her abusive Mafia lover was murdered in her house, every newspaper in the Free World described the murky dramas with something approaching hysteria.

Blood Moon's salacious but empathetic new biography exposes the public and private dramas of the girl who changed the American definition of what it REALLY means to be a blonde.

Here's how **CALIFORNIA BOOKWATCH** and **THE MID-WEST BOOK REVIEW** described the mega-celebrity as revealed in this book:

"Lana Turner: Hearts and Diamonds Take All belongs on the shelves of any collection strong in movie star biographies in general and Hollywood evolution in particular, and represents no lightweight production, appearing on the 20th anniversary of Lana Turner's death to provide a weighty survey packed with new information about her life.

"One would think that just about everything to be known about The Sweater Girl would have already appeared in print, but it should be noted that Lana Turner: Hearts and Diamonds Take All offers many new revelations not just about Turner, but about the movie industry in the aftermath of World War II.

"From Lana's introduction of a new brand of covert sexuality in women's movies to her scandalous romances among the stars, her extreme promiscuity, her search for love, and her notorious flings - even her involvement in murder - are all probed in a revealing account of glamour and movie industry relationships that bring Turner and her times to life.

"Some of the greatest scandals in Hollywood history are intricately detailed on these pages, making this much more than another survey of her life and times, and a 'must have' pick for any collection strong in Hollywood history in general, gossip and scandals and the real stories behind them, and Lana Turner's tumultuous career, in particular."

Lana Turner, Hearts & Diamonds Take All
Winner of the coveted "Best Biography" Award from the San Francisco Book Festival
By Darwin Porter and Danforth Prince
Softcover, 622 pages, with photos. ISBN 978-1-936003-53-2
Available everywhere, online and in stores.

LINDA LOVELACE

INSIDE LINDA LOVELACE'S DEEP THROAT
DEGRADATION, PORNO CHIC, AND THE RISE OF FEMINISM

THE MOST COMPREHENSIVE BIOGRAPHY EVER WRITTEN OF AN ADULT ENTERTAINMENT STAR, HER TORMENTED RELATIONSHIP WITH HOLLYWOOD'S UNDERBELLY, AND HOW SHE CHANGED FOREVER THE WORLD'S PERCEPTIONS ABOUT CENSORSHIP, SEXUAL BEHAVIOR PATTERNS, AND PORNOGRAPHY.

Darwin Porter, author of some twenty critically acclaimed celebrity exposés of behind-the-scenes intrigue in the entertainment industry, was deeply involved in the Linda Lovelace saga as it unfolded in the 70s, interviewing many of the players, and raising money for the legal defense of the film's co-star, Harry Reems.

In this book, emphasizing her role as an unlikely celebrity interacting with other celebrities, he brings inside information and a never-before-published revelation to almost every page.

"This book drew me in..How could it not?"
Coco Papy, *Bookslut.*

THE BEACH BOOK FESTIVALS GRAND PRIZE WINNER FOR "BEST SUMMER READING OF 2013"

RUNNER-UP TO "BEST BIOGRAPHY OF 2013" *THE LOS ANGELES BOOK FESTIVAL*

Another hot and insightful commentary about major and sometimes violently controversial conflicts of the American Century, from Blood Moon Productions.

Inside Linda Lovelace's Deep Throat, by Darwin Porter
Softcover, 640 pages, 6"x9" with photos.
ISBN 978-1-936003-33-4

LOVE TRIANGLE:
RONALD REAGAN
JANE WYMAN, & NANCY DAVIS

HOW MUCH DO YOU REALLY KNOW ABOUT THE REAGANS? THIS BOOKS TELLS EVERYTHING ABOUT THE SHOW-BIZ SCANDALS THEY DESPERATELY WANTED TO FORGET.

Unique in the history of publishing, this scandalous triple biography focuses on the Hollywood indiscretions of former U.S. president Ronald Reagan and his two wives. A proud and Presidential addition to Blood Moon's Babylon series, it digs deep into what these three young and attractive movie stars were doing decades before two of them took over the Free World.

As reviewed by Diane Donovan, Senior Reviewer at the California Bookwatch section of the Midwest Book Review: *"Love Triangle: Ronald Reagan, Jane Wyman & Nancy Davis may find its way onto many a Republican Reagan fan's reading shelf; but those who expect another Reagan celebration will be surprised: this is lurid Hollywood exposé writing at its best, and outlines the truths surrounding one of the most provocative industry scandals in the world.*

"There are already so many biographies of the Reagans on the market that one might expect similar mile-markers from this: be prepared for shock and awe; because Love Triangle doesn't take your ordinary approach to biography and describes a love triangle that eventually bumped a major Hollywood movie star from the possibility of being First Lady and replaced her with a lesser-known Grade B actress (Nancy Davis).

"From politics and betrayal to romance, infidelity, and sordid affairs, Love Triangle is a steamy, eye-opening story that blows the lid off of the Reagan illusion to raise eyebrows on both sides of the big screen.

"Black and white photos liberally pepper an account of the careers of all three and the lasting shock of their stormy relationships in a delightful pursuit especially recommended for any who relish Hollywood gossip."

In 2015, LOVE TRIANGLE, Blood Moon Productions' overview of the early dramas associated with Ronald Reagan's scandal-soaked career in Hollywood, was designated by the Awards Committee of the **HOLLYWOOD BOOK FESTIVAL** as Runner-Up to Best Biography of the Year.

LOVE TRIANGLE: Ronald Reagan, Jane Wyman, & Nancy Davis
Darwin Porter & Danforth Prince
Softcover, 6" x 9", with hundreds of photos.   ISBN 978-1-936003-41-9

THOSE GLAMOROUS GABORS
BOMBSHELLS FROM BUDAPEST

Zsa Zsa, Eva, and Magda Gabor transferred their glittery dreams and gold-digging ambitions from the twilight of the Austro-Hungarian Empire to Hollywood. There, more effectively than any army, these Bombshells from Budapest broke hearts, amassed fortunes, lovers, and A-list husbands, and amused millions of *voyeurs* through the medium of television, movies, and the social registers. In this astonishing "triple-play" biography, designated "Best Biography of the Year" by the Hollywood Book Festival, Blood Moon lifts the "mink-and-diamond" curtain on this amazing trio of blood-related sisters, whose complicated intrigues have never been fully explored before.

"You will never be Ga-bored...this book gives new meaning to the term compelling. Be warned, *Those Glamorous Gabors* is both an epic and a pip. Not since *Gone With the Wind* have so many characters on the printed page been forced to run for their lives for one reason or another. And Scarlett making a dress out of the curtains is nothing compared to what a Gabor will do when she needs to scrap together an outfit for a movie premiere or late-night outing.

"For those not up to speed, Jolie Tilleman came from a family of jewelers and therefore came by her love for the shiny stones honestly, perhaps genetically. She married Vilmos Gabor somewhere around World War 1 (exact dates, especially birth dates, are always somewhat vague in order to establish plausible deniability later on) and they were soon blessed with three daughters: **Magda**, the oldest, whose hair, sadly, was naturally brown, although it would turn quite red in America; **Zsa Zsa** (born 'Sari') a natural blond who at a very young age exhibited the desire for fame with none of the talents usually associated with achievement, excepting beauty and a natural wit; and **Eva**, the youngest and blondest of the girls, who after seeing Grace Moore perform at the National Theater, decided that she wanted to be an actress and that she would one day move to Hollywood to become a star.

"Given that the Gabor family at that time lived in Budapest, Hungary, at the period of time between the World Wars, that Hollywood dream seemed a distant one indeed. The story—the riches to rags to riches to rags to riches again myth of survival against all odds as the four women, because of their Jewish heritage, flee Europe with only the minks on their backs and what jewels they could smuggle along with them in their *decolletage*, only to have to battle afresh for their places in the vicious Hollywood pecking order—gives new meaning to the term 'compelling.' The reader, as if he were witnessing a particularly gore-drenched traffic accident, is incapable of looking away."

—New York Review of Books

Those Glamorous Gabors, Bombshells from Budapest, by Darwin Porter & Danforth Prince
Softcover, 730 pages, with hundreds of photos   ISBN 978-1-936003-35-8

PETER O'TOOLE

HELLRAISER, SEXUAL OUTLAW, IRISH REBEL

At the time of its publication early in 2015, this book was widely publicized in the *Daily Mail,* the *New York Daily News,* the *New York Post,* the *Midwest Book Review, The Express (London), The Globe,* the *National Enquirer,* and in equivalent publications worldwide

One of the world's most admired (and brilliant) actors, Peter O'Toole wined and wenched his way through a labyrinth of sexual and interpersonal betrayals, sometimes with disastrous results. Away from the stage and screen, where such films as *Becket* and *Lawrence of Arabia,* made film history, his life was filled with drunken, debauched nights and edgy sexual experimentations, most of which were never openly examined in the press. A hellraiser, he shared wild times with his "best blokes" Richard Burton and Richard Harris. Peter Finch, also his close friend, once invited him to join him in sharing the pleasures of his mistress, Vivien Leigh.

"My father, a bookie, moved us to the Mick community of Leeds," O'Toole once told a reporter. "We were very poor, but I was born an Irishman, which accounts for my gift of gab, my unruly behavior, my passionate devotion to women and the bottle, and my loathing of any authority figure."

Author Robert Sellers described O'Toole's boyhood neighborhood. "Three of his playmates went on to be hanged for murder; one strangled a girl in a lovers' quarrel; one killed a man during a robbery; another cut up a warden in South Africa with a pair of shears. It was a heavy bunch."

Peter O'Toole's hell-raising life story has never been told, until now. Hot and uncensored, from a writing team which, even prior to O'Toole's death in 2013, had been collecting under-the-radar info about him for years, this book has everything you ever wanted to know about how THE LION navigated his way through the boudoirs of the Entertainment Industry IN WINTER, Spring, Summer, and a dissipated Autumn as well.

Blood Moon has ripped away the imperial robe, scepter, and crown usually associated with this quixotic problem child of the British Midlands. Provocatively uncensored, this illusion-shattering overview of Peter O'Toole's hellraising (or at least very naughty) and demented life is unique in the history of publishing.

PETER O'TOOLE: *HELLRAISER, SEXUAL OUTLAW, IRISH REBEL*
DARWIN PORTER & DANFORTH PRINCE
Softcover, with photos. ISBN 978-1-936003-45-7

JAMES DEAN

TOMORROW NEVER COMES

HONORING THE 60TH ANNIVERSARY OF HIS VIOLENT AND EARLY DEATH

America's most enduring and legendary symbol of young, enraged rebellion, James Dean continues into the 21st Century to capture the imagination of the world.

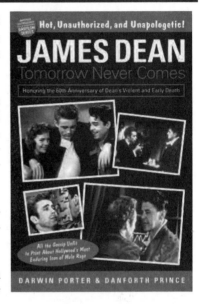

After one of his many flirtations with Death, which caught up with him when he was a celebrity-soaked 24-year-old, he said, "If a man can live after he dies, then maybe he's a great man." Today, bars from Nigeria to Patagonia are named in honor of this international, spectacularly self-destructive movie star icon.

Migrating from the dusty backroads of Indiana to center stage in the most formidable boudoirs of Hollywood, his saga is electrifying.

A strikingly handsome heart-throb, Dean is a study in contrasts: Tough but tender, brutal but remarkably sensitive; he was a reckless hellraiser badass who could revert to a little boy in bed.

A rampant bisexual, he claimed that he didn't want to go through life "with one hand tied behind my back." He demonstrated that during bedroom trysts with Marilyn Monroe, Rock Hudson, Elizabeth Taylor, Paul Newman, Natalie Wood, Shelley Winters, Marlon Brando, Steve McQueen, Ursula Andress, Montgomery Clift, Pier Angeli, Tennessee Williams, Susan Strasberg, Tallulah Bankhead, and FBI director J. Edgar Hoover.

Woolworth heiress Barbara Hutton, one of the richest and most dissipated women of her era, wanted to make him her toy boy.

Tomorrow Never Comes is the most penetrating look at James Dean to have emerged from the wreckage of his Porsche Spyder in 1955.

Before setting out on his last ride, he said, "I feel life too intensely to bear living it."

Tomorrow Never Comes presents a damaged but beautiful soul.

JAMES DEAN—TOMORROW NEVER COMES
DARWIN PORTER & DANFORTH PRINCE
Softcover, with photos. ISBN 978-1-936003-49-5

BURT REYNOLDS

PUT THE PEDAL TO THE METAL

How a Nude Centerfold Sex Symbol Seduced Hollywood

In the 1970s and '80s, Burt Reynolds represented a new breed of movie star: Charming and relentlessly macho, he was a good old Southern boy who made hearts throb and audiences laugh. He was Burt Reynolds, a football hero and a guy you might have shared some jokes with in a redneck bar. After an impressive but tormented career, rivers of negative publicity, a self-admitted history of bad choices, and a spectacular fall from Hollywood grace, he died in Jupiter, Florida, at the age of 82 in September of 2018.

For five years, both in terms of earnings and popularity, he was the number one box office star in the world. *Smokey and the Bandit* (1977) became the biggest-grossing car-chase film of all time. As he put it, perhaps as a means of bolstering his image, "I like nothing better than making love to some of the most beautiful women in the world." Perhaps he was referring to his romantic and sexual involvements with dozens of celebrities from New Hollywood. More unusual dalliances occurred with Marilyn Monroe, whom he once picked up on his way to the Actors Studio in New York City. Love with another VIP came in the form of that "Sweetheart of the G.I.s," Dinah Shore, sparking chatter. "I appreciate older women," he once said in a moment of self-revelation. According to Sally Field, "Burt still lives in my heart." But then she expressed relief that, because of his recent death, he never read what she'd said about him in her memoir.

Men liked him too: He played poker with Frank Sinatra; shared boozy nights with John Wayne; intercepted a "pass" from closeted Spencer Tracy; talked "penis size" with Mark Wahlberg; went "wench-hunting" with Johnny Carson; and threatened to kill Marlon Brando, to whom his appearance was often compared. He also hung out with Bette Davis. ("I always had a thing for her.")

His least happy (some said "most poisonous") marriage—to Loni Anderson—was rife with dramas played out more in the tabloids than in the boudoir. According to Reynolds, "She's vain, she's a rotten mother, she sleeps around, and she spent all my money."

This biography—the first comprehensive overview of the "redneck icon" ever published—reveals the joys and sorrows of a movie star who thrived in, but who was then almost buried by the pressures and insecurities of the New Hollywood. A tribute to "truck stop" America, it's about the accelerated life of a courageous spirit who "Put His Pedal to the Metal" with humor, high jinx, and pizzazz. He predicted his own death: "Soon, I'll be racing a hotrod in Valhalla in my cowboy hat and a pair of aviators." On his tombstone, he wanted it writ: "He was not the best actor in the world, but he was the best Burt Reynolds in the world."

BURT REYNOLDS: PUT THE PEDAL TO THE METAL

Darwin Porter & Danforth Prince; ISBN 978-1-936003-63-1;   450 pages with photos.
Coming Soon from Blood Moon Productions